BLACKSTONE'S GUIDE TO

The Human Rights Act 1998

EIGHTH EDITION

BLACKSTONE'S GUIDE TO

The Human Rights Act 1998

EIGHTH EDITION

John Wadham, Helen Mountfield KC,
Raj Desai, Sarah Hannett KC, Jessica Jones,
Eleanor Mitchell, and Aidan Wills

OXFORD
UNIVERSITY PRESS

OXFORD
UNIVERSITY PRESS

Great Clarendon Street, Oxford, OX2 6DP,
United Kingdom

Oxford University Press is a department of the University of Oxford.
It furthers the University's objective of excellence in research, scholarship,
and education by publishing worldwide. Oxford is a registered trade mark of
Oxford University Press in the UK and in certain other countries

First Edition published in 1999
Seventh Edition published in 2015

Published in the United States of America by Oxford University Press
198 Madison Avenue, New York, NY 10016, United States of America

British Library Cataloguing in Publication Data
Data available

Library of Congress Control Number: 2023951138

ISBN 978–0–19–288505–0

DOI: 10.1093/oso/9780192885050.001.0001

Printed in the UK by
Ashford Colour Press Ltd, Gosport, Hampshire

MIX
Paper from
responsible sources
FSC
www.fsc.org
FSC® C011748

Preface to the Eighth Edition

The Human Rights Act received Royal Assent twenty-five years ago, on 9 November 1998. The first edition of this book was published just two months later. The Act came into force on 2 October 2000, after an extensive programme of education and awareness building for judges, government officials, local authorities, the police and other public authorities.

The messaging around the introduction of the legislation included frequent reminders that British Conservative politicians, Winston Churchill and David Maxwell-Fyfe had been architects of the European Convention on Human Rights, and that it had been signed in the immediate aftermath of the Second World War, to underpin the enduring values of a democratic society.

The Act was intended to 'bring rights home' by making the Convention enforceable in domestic courts, and at first enjoyed overwhelming all-party support. It was a moment when there was a re-evaluation of the relationship between citizen and state. Jack Straw, the then-Home Secretary, wrote in the foreword to the first edition of this book that:

The Human Rights Act 1998 is the most significant statement of human rights in domestic law since the 1689 Bill of Rights. It will strengthen representative and democratic government. It will do so by enabling people to challenge more easily actions of the state if they fail to match the standards set by the European Convention on Human Rights.

Nothing in the Act will take away the freedoms that people already enjoy. But those freedoms alone are not enough: they need to be complemented by positive rights that people can assert when they believe that they have been treated unfairly by the state, or that the state and its institutions have failed properly to protect them. The Act will guarantee to every-one the means to enforce a set of basic civil and political rights, establishing a floor below which standards will not be allowed to fall.

The Act was an act of constitutional realism. Its object was to raise awareness of Convention rights and to bring rights 'home' by making them enforceable in domestic courts. But because, in our dualist legal system, international instruments are not directly incorporated into domestic law unless Parliament says so, the mechanism which it used was to set out a schedule of 'Convention rights' which were given 'further effect' in domestic law, through two principal mechanisms. First, by imposing a statutory duty on public authorities to act compatibly with the Convention unless a statute required them to act differently; and secondly, by requiring all laws to be interpreted, where possible, compatibly with Convention rights. This latter requirement meant that the Human Rights Act had some effect in the interpretation of rights as between individuals, ie 'horizontally'.

But the Act maintained the fundamental principle of Parliamentary sovereignty, by providing that if a law could not be applied or interpreted compatibly with Convention rights, then the courts must apply it as it stood. In those circumstances, the court's remedial power was limited to making a declaration of the incompatibility between domestic law and internationally enforceable rights, which the executive could then amend if it chose to do so, through a remedial order which both Houses of Parliament approved.

In its early years, the Human Rights Act was successfully used to protect people where 'the state and its institutions had failed to protect them', in a wide range of contexts—for example preventing the discriminatory indefinite detention of foreign terrorist suspects,[1] broadening the ambit of procedural justice,[2] recognising the rights of trans people to marry someone of their birth gender (before civil partnership and same-sex marriage existed),[3] protecting free speech even where it offends,[4] and ensuring that the state does not retain the DNA of innocent people.[5]. This means of securing domestic enforcement of the Convention was intended to be an enduring part of our constitutional settlement.

In the Preface to the (2015) seventh edition of this book, we said that 'if it was ever a matter of doubt, it [was] now plain that the Human Rights Act can no longer be regarded as just another statute. Rather it places on an ever-speaking statutory basis an assumption that certain legal norms are fundamental and underpin all other statutory interpretation. Lord Justice Laws placed it in a category of "constitutional statutes" which included the Magna Carta and the European Communities Act 1972'.[6]

However, this assumption that—whatever the controversies surrounding individual cases—the legitimacy of the statutory mechanism was secure—proved optimistic. Indeed, the uncertainty as to the future of the Act is the explanation for the fact there were seven editions of this book between the first (in 1999) and the seventh (in 2015), but that this eight edition is being published almost nine years later.

It is worth considering how an Act passed with all-party support, to give effect to a Convention which had been part of our international law for almost fifty years before it was passed, has come to be so controversial and contested.

Firm support for a law passed to hold government to account was tested early. Less than a year after the Act had come into force, the 9/11 bombings took place in New York, and the 'War on Terror' followed, with various extraordinary measures introduced. There was much controversy after the House of Lords that declared anti-terrorism measures which allowed for the 'preventative detention' of foreign national terrorist suspects (but not British terrorist suspects) without trial, were

---

[1] *A v Secretary of State for the Home Department* [2004] UKHL 56, [2005] 2 AC 68.
[2] For example, for Iraqi families of those killed in detention by British troops (*R (Al-Skeini) v Secretary of State for Defence* [2007] UKHL 26, [2008] 1 AC 153.
[3] *Bellinger v Bellinger* [2003] UKH 21, [2003] 2 AC 467.
[4] *Livingston v Adjudication Panel for England* [2006] EWHC 2533 (Admin) [2006] LGR 799.
[5] *R (GC & C) v Commissioner of the Police for the Metropolis* [2011] UKSC 21, [2011] 1 WLR 1230.
[6] *Thoburn v Sunderland City Council* [2002] EWHC 195 (Admin), [2002] 3 WLR 247.

incompatible with the Convention[7]. So even those who had introduced the Act with a view to creating positive and enforceable rights where the state had treated someone unfairly did not take kindly to those rights being enforced. In 2006, the then-Prime Minister Tony Blair criticised a judgment (later upheld on appeal) about the rights of a group of Afghans who had hijacked a plane as an 'abuse of common sense'. Application of Convention rights in controversial policy areas, like social security, asylum, counter-terrorism and immigration helped fuel damaging media narratives about the Act.

The interpretative obligation upon the courts of Convention rights led to greater scrutiny of the judicial role and criticisms of judges for being 'activist'; and the whole debate became tied up with attacks on 'European' judges, often confusing the courts of the European Union and the Council of Europe, but suffused with a rhetoric that foreign values had been 'imposed' on the UK by 'foreign courts'. Finally, the interpretative obligation in section 3 of the Human Rights Act was criticised by some as an attack on the sovereignty of Parliament.

So instead of being merely a domestic articulation and application of internationally binding Convention rights which the UK had co-created and which it had been one of the first states to ratify in 1951, the Human Rights Act became a problematic policy football.

Although in evidence to the Joint Parliamentary Committee on Human Rights in 2007,[8] the then-Labour government described the Act as a 'received part of our constitutional arrangements', it nonetheless held a consultation on whether to amend the Act to include a Bill of Rights containing specific civic 'duties' and 'responsibilities'. The (then) Conservative opposition went further and called for a 'British Bill of Rights' to replace the Human Rights Act, with a greater ability for national courts to depart from Convention.

In 2010, the call to repeal 'Labour's' Human Rights Act was a prominent pillar of the Conservative Party manifesto. This commitment was dropped as part of the deal to create a Coalition Government that year, and the Coalition instead established a Commission on a Bill of Rights, whose terms of reference required it to 'investigate' a UK Bill of Rights *that incorporates and builds on all our obligations under the European Convention on Human Rights*, ensures that these rights continue to be enshrined in UK law, and protects and extend our liberties'. Ultimately, after the resignation of one of its members and an inability of the Commission to reach a unanimous conclusion, the matter was parked for the remainder of the 2010–2015 Parliament.

After 2015, however, calls to repeal or replace the Human Rights Act, or even to withdraw from the European Convention on Human Rights altogether, have become more frequent and more shrill—albeit (to date) ultimately eclipsed by the drama and turmoil caused by Britain's departure from the European Union.

---

[7] *A and others v Secretary of State for the Home Department* [2004] UKHL 56; [2005] 2 AC 68 (the 'Belmarsh' case).

[8] A Bill of Rights for the UK? 29th Report (2007–2008) HL 165-I HC 150-I, vol II Jack Straw Ev 78.

David Cameron's Conservative Party had gone into the May 2015 General Election on a manifesto commitment to 'scrap the Human Rights Act and curtail the role of the European Court of Human Rights'. It also pledged to renegotiate the European Union treaties and then to hold a referendum on the United Kingdom's future membership of the EU. After the referendum, delivering Brexit became the more pressing political issue for the ruling Conservative party. In December 2016, it was announced that repeal of the Human Rights Act would not take place until after Brexit.

The Conservative party's manifesto for the 2017 General Election (which it narrowly won, led by Theresa May) ruled out repealing or replacing the Human Rights Act 'while Brexit was underway', but promised to review the 'human rights legislative framework' once Britain had left the EU.

However, the party's turmoil around Brexit led to a new leader and a new election in 2019. The Conservative manifesto for the December 2019 general election (into which it was led by Boris Johnson) was rather more opaque. It promised (on page 48) to 'update' the 1998 HRA 'after Brexit' to 'ensure that there is a proper balance between the rights of individuals, our vital national security and effective government'.

Following Johnson's landslide victory, the government established an Independent Human Rights Act Review (IHRAR) chaired by Sir Peter Gross, a retired judge of the Court of Appeal. This Review made a call for evidence to which there was a very wide and very well informed response. Most of the 150+ responses were published on the Review's website[9] which means that the website contains 'an exceptional store of knowledge and learning on the HRA'. The IHRAR report, on 14 December 2021[10] found that the Act was generally working well overall, but made some small but significant specific suggestions for amendment.

The government did not respond directly to the IHRAR report. Instead, on the day it was published, the Ministry of Justice immediately put out a fresh consultation document entitled *Human Rights Act Reform, a modern Bill of Rights*,[11] which was in effect a consultation on repealing the Act altogether and replacing it with a significantly weaker instrument.

Had that 'Bill of Rights' been passed, it would have retained UK membership of the Council of Europe and the obligation of public authorities to comply with Convention rights. But it would have changed or removed a large number of provisions of the Human Rights Act which, as the Law Society observed, would have 'requir[ed] claimants to prove they have (or would) suffer significant disadvantage as a result of a breach of their rights before they [could] take their claim to court' and led to very significant departures, in practice, from our international law obligations under the Convention.[12] Between 80% and 90% of the responses

---

[9] <https://www.gov.uk/guidance/independent-human-rights-act-review>

[10] The Report of the Independent Human Rights Act Review, 14 December 2021, CP 587.

[11] <https://consult.justice.gov.uk/human-rights/human-rights-act-reform/supporting_documents/humanrightsreformconsultation.pdf>, CP 588.

[12] For example, the Bill of Rights Bill would have required courts to refrain from any reading of Convention rights—even if it was the meaning ascribed to the right by the Strasbourg court—which would have imposed a positive obligation on a public authority.

to the four-month consultation which followed, including from the Bar Council and the Law Society, opposed the proposals. As the Law Society put it, these proposals would have damaged the rule of law, prevented access to justice, reduced or removed rights, led to more cases being taken to the ECtHR, had an adverse impact on devolution, have damaged the UK's international reputation, and created legal uncertainty.

Notwithstanding the overwhelming opposition to the proposal from consultees, the Bill of Rights Bill was introduced into Parliament in June 2022, and would—but for the replacement of Boris Johnson as Prime Minister and the death of Queen Elizabeth II—have received its second reading on 14 September 2022. However, the Bill was halted when Liz Truss became Prime Minister and removed Dominic Raab from office as Secretary of State for Justice.

Dominic Raab was reinstated to this post when Liz Truss in turn was replaced as Prime Minister by Rishi Sunak on 25 October 2022, but was forced to resign again after allegations of bullying of officials were upheld in the independent report of Adam Tolley KC commissioned by the Prime Minister. On 27 June 2023, the current Minister for Justice and Lord Chancellor Alex Chalk announced to Parliament that there were no plans to reintroduce the Bill of Rights in the current Parliament.[13]

So, for now, the Human Rights Act remains in force, but its future is far from assured. The populist calls to repeal the Act have not gone away; indeed, many front bench politicians (and at least one senior former judge) go further and suggest that the UK should depart from the European Convention on Human Rights altogether.

At the time of writing, the debate has been re-ignited following the unanimous decision of the United Kingdom Supreme Court finding that the current Government's Rwanda asylum policy[14] violates Article 3 of the ECHR (among other international human rights obligations), and in view of the on-going prospect of human rights challenges before the domestic courts or the European Court of Human Rights even after the passage of primary legislation purporting to reverse the Supreme Court's judgment.[15] There are reports that the Prime Minister is considering fighting the general election in 2024 on a manifesto pledge to leave the European Convention on Human Rights, although it is also clear that many MPs in the Conservative Party are strongly opposed to this.

Understanding and engaging with the Act has never been more important. What this points to is the importance of civil society engagement, and in robust and informed education and discussion of human rights and the protection of human rights; something which takes it beyond the current weaponization of our existing legislation and applications of it in culture wars.

---

[13] <https://hansard.parliament.uk/commons/2023-06-27/debates/FE807865-51C0-4E01-AE13-42E21 9714C99/TopicalQuestions#>
[14] [2023] UKSC 42.
[15] Currently before Parliament in the form of the Safety of Rwanda (Asylum and Immigration) Bill.

When writing this Preface, I was struck by an important section of the Executive Summary of the Independent Human Rights Act Review:

Perceptions and the HRA

The vast majority of submissions in response to the Call for Evidence spoke strongly in support of the HRA, emphasising that it was not to be viewed through the prism of a few high-profile cases; what happened outside the courtroom was every bit as important, a telling example being the impact of the development of a human rights culture on the provision of care in care homes. Conversely, the fact and persistence of hostility to the HRA in other quarters was noteworthy, suggesting much needs to be done to dispel this negative perception of the HRA and increase a sense of public ownership. Two strands of thought stood out. First, that human rights belong to everybody; human rights abuses can affect anyone. Developing the necessary level of settled acceptance requires majority ownership of the HRA and its concepts. Secondly, a markedly stronger and more positive public perception of the HRA was noted in Northern Ireland, Scotland and Wales than was apparent in England.

Public ownership of rights

Public or Civic education: The need for greater public or civic education concerning the HRA and rights more generally was repeatedly and cogently emphasised to the Panel....

In the light of these observations, the Review strongly recommended to Government, for its consideration, a focus on civic, constitutional education on the HRA and rights more generally including the difficult balances human rights questions often require, and on individual responsibilities. Finally, it observed that:

Addressing concerns as to public ownership of the HRA and related civic education is a shared endeavour calling for the active involvement of all three branches of the State; it is not a matter for the Judiciary alone. [The Review Panel] does not underestimate the challenges with regard to civic education and a sense of increased public ownership of the HRA but is of the clear view, in the interests of civil society, that these are issues which cannot sensibly be overlooked.

These are important and wise observations, which I hope will inform the next government, of whatever political persuasion. And I hope that this book can inform the conversation.

Helen Mountfield KC
Mansfield College, Oxford
15 December 2023

Acknowledgements

Since the first edition of this Guide, we have been lucky to receive the help and assistance of many colleagues and friends. We remain enormously grateful to everyone with whom we have discussed the Human Rights Act and the European Convention on Human Rights, and to all those whose work in legal practice and academia has shaped and developed the law of human rights as reflected in this book. The thanks which we have recorded in all of the previous editions still stand. We also record our thanks to Elizabeth Prochaska who helped to write the last edition, and to Daniel Rudd and Rebecca Khan from the Legal Support Service at Matrix Chambers for their invaluable assistance in finalizing this edition.

At Oxford University Press we wish to thank Matthew Williams and Fay Gibbons who stuck with us despite the delays in delivering the manuscript.

The law is stated at 1 July 2023 but, where possible, more recent significant developments have been included.

Contents

Table of Cases

Table of International Instruments

Table of European Legislation

Table of Statutes

Table of Statutory Instruments

Table of Other Legislation

1

INTRODUCTION

A. INTRODUCTION

The Human Rights Act 1998 has been in force for over 20 years, but the notion 1.01
of rights has a long historic pedigree. Legal philosophers have grappled with the
complex implications of the concept ever since rights first emerged in the Magna
Carta.[1] Despite different perspectives on the debate, however, common threads are
discernible in the theorists' writings. It is generally accepted that rights contain
both a positive ('claim-right') and a negative ('liberty-right') aspect:

[S]tatus of a right entails that a person is both entitled to stand on his own right *and* to require
others to be duty bound to respect it. It means, for example, that when a person asserts his right

---

[1] Detailed discussions can be found in HLA Hart, *The Concept of Law* (Clarendon Press 1961); Ronald
Dworkin, *Taking Rights Seriously* (Duckworth 1978); Richard Tuck, *Natural Rights Theories: Their Origins
and Development* (CUP 1979); John Finnis, *National Law and Natural Rights* (Clarendon Press 1979);
Joseph Raz, *The Morality of Freedom* (Clarendon Press 1986).

Blackstone's Guide to The Human Rights Act 1998. Eighth Edition. John Wadham, Helen Mountfield KC, Raj Desai, Sarah Hannett KC,
Jessica Jones, Eleanor Mitchell, and Aidan Wills, Oxford University Press. © John Wadham, Helen Mountfield KC, Raj Desai,
Sarah Hannett KC, Jessica Jones, Eleanor Mitchell, and Aidan Wills 2024. DOI: 10.1093/oso/9780192885050.003.0001

to privacy, he has a claim right which others are duty bound to respect; and also that he has a liberty right to privacy which entitles him to insist on an entitlement to be let alone.[2]

1.02　Equally, it is accepted that rights and responsibilities are inextricably linked. In *Rights of Man*, Thomas Paine asserted that 'a Declaration of Rights is, by reciprocity, a Declaration of Duties also ... whatever is my right as a man, is also the right of another; and it becomes my duty to guarantee, as well as to possess'.[3] For Paine, rights were not purely the preserve of the 'selfish' individual but were vital to a healthy civil society. As we discuss later, the relationship between rights and responsibilities has become a central feature of the debate over the future of the Human Rights Act.

1.03　English lawyers were traditionally sceptical of the idea of human rights as a positive concept. They preferred instead to focus on the negative conception of liberties in which 'freedom' consisted of the residual leftovers after the law had been obeyed.[4] While there was no recognized right of free expression, for example, everyone was free to write or say what they liked provided it was not libellous or slanderous, or in breach of confidence, or contrary to the Official Secrets Act, or in contempt of court, or in breach of statute. However, without positive guarantees of rights enshrined in a written constitution or a human rights instrument, this negative liberty offered little protection against the acts or omissions of public bodies that harmed fundamental rights. When the former Prime Minister John Major proclaimed 'we have no need of a Bill of Rights because we have freedom',[5] he failed to appreciate that government may show 'a more mundane but still corrupting insensitivity to liberty, a failure to grasp its force and place in democratic ideals'.[6]

1.04　English lawyers' perspective on the legal protection of liberty began to change during the rapid development of international human rights in the second half of the twentieth century. After the horrors of the Second World War and the Holocaust, the international community framed new covenants explicitly enshrining universal human rights to try to ensure that such atrocities would never occur again. The then Prime Minister, Winston Churchill, said:

> We must never cease to proclaim in fearless tones the great principles of freedom and the rights of man which through Magna Carta, the Bill of Rights, the Habeas Corpus, trial by jury, and the English common law find their most famous expression in the American Declaration of Independence.[7]

1.05　The first major convention that dealt with human rights, the Universal Declaration on Human Rights (UDHR, 1948), recognized civil and political rights as well as economic, social, and cultural rights. In 1966, the UN International Covenant on Civil and Political Rights (ICCPR) was opened for signature. In the same year, the International Covenant on Economic, Social and Cultural Rights (ICESCR) was drawn up, but,

---

[2] Richard Clayton and Hugh Tomlinson, *The Law of Human Rights* (2nd edn, OUP 2009) 22, citing Ronald Dworkin, *Taking Rights Seriously* (Duckworth 1977) ch 7.

[3] Thomas Paine, *The Rights of Man, 1791* (OUP 1995) 165.

[4] See eg *Malone v Metropolitan Police Commissioner* [1979] Ch 344.

[5] Quoted by Lord Irvine, 'The Development of Human Rights in Britain under an Incorporated Convention on Human Rights', Tom Sargant Memorial Lecture, London, 16 December 1997.

[6] Ronald Dworkin, 'Devaluing Liberty' (1988) *17*(8) Index on Censorship 7.

[7] 5th March 1946, speech in Fulton Missouri in the United States.

unlike the ICCPR, the rights contained within it are subject to the availability of resources and the obligations are to be 'progressively realized'. Doubts about the universality and practicability of economic and social rights have been expressed and the nature of the ICESCR accommodates these concerns.[8] A range of other legal instruments aimed at securing key human rights for specified groups of people (including women, ethnic groups, children, people with disabilities, and refugees) and at protecting particular thematic rights (eg the UN Convention against Torture) have since become an integral part of international law. These treaties and conventions articulate a range of different rights that combine the twin concepts of 'positive' and 'negative' rights, and strive to achieve a balance between individuals' rights and their responsibilities.

The development with the most profound impact on English law and, indeed, on international human rights jurisprudence more broadly, has been the European Convention for the Protection of Human Rights and Fundamental Freedoms (described variously as the European Convention on Human Rights, the Convention or the ECHR). Although British lawyers were responsible for much of the drafting of the Convention[9] and the United Kingdom (also UK) was among the first signatories in 1950, it was nearly half a century before the UK government was willing to 'bring rights home' by incorporating Convention rights into domestic law in the Human Rights Act 1998. The explanation for this reticence lies in part in the constitutional and common law traditions that, many judges and politicians believed, already accorded human rights adequate protection. 1.06

B. HUMAN RIGHTS IN THE UNITED KINGDOM BEFORE THE HUMAN RIGHTS ACT

1. Rights in English common law before the Human Rights Act

Prior to the enactment of the Human Rights Act, Britain was almost alone amongst western democracies in not having a positive guarantee of rights. However, various historic constitutional texts offered the English limited guarantees of particular rights. The Magna Carta, drafted in 1215, introduced the concepts of habeas corpus and trial by jury. The Bill of Rights of 1689 contained some provisions that later appeared in other human rights covenants, including a prohibition on cruel and unusual punishment, but it was principally a part of a political settlement limiting the power of the monarch and did not purport to protect the basic rights of the citizen. 1.07

In the eighteenth and early nineteenth centuries, many ideas that we regard as central to the rule of law—such as a philosophy of liberty and the notion of the freedom of the press—were developed by English thinkers such as Tom Paine, John Locke, and JS Mill. But despite their political writings and contemporary events 1.08

---

[8] See Philip Alston and Ryan Goodman, *International Human Rights* (OUP 2012).
[9] See AW Brian Simpson, *Human Rights and the End of Empire: Britain and the Genesis of the European Convention* (OUP 2004).

such as the French Revolution and the American Declaration of Independence, Britain did not adopt a comparable 'Declaration of the Rights of Man'.

1.09   Instead, the English relied upon 'negative' liberty, the most influential exposition of which is contained in Dicey's nineteenth-century theory of residual rights.[10] Dicey's theory holds that individuals may say or do whatever they please provided they do not transgress the substantive law or infringe the legal rights of others. In other words, 'we are free to do everything except that which we are forbidden to do by law'. Further, the Crown and other public authorities may not do anything unless they are so authorized by a rule of common law (including the royal prerogative) or statute, and thus may not interfere with individuals' liberties.

1.10   As well as these residual freedoms, Dicey and others (including Blackstone in his *Commentaries on the Laws of England*)[11] identified a separate body of fundamental rights in English common law including personal security and liberty, private property, freedom of discussion, and assembly. These were protected by the presumption of legality, which holds that rights cannot be removed by Parliament except by express words. These rights were recognized by the courts as part of the compact between monarch and Parliament and the birthright of the people. Dicey argued that this system worked well, as Parliament, elected by the people, was the only body which could legislate rights out of existence. Dicey's confidence in residual rights has not been borne out by experience.

1.11   The enormous growth in the power of public and quasi-public bodies over the lives of individuals during the twentieth century has diluted the ability of Parliament to scrutinize legislation—if, indeed, it ever had such omnipotence. Since Dicey was writing, the way in which power is distributed in modern society has altered fundamentally. It is no longer accurate to talk of constitutional power being shared between the legislature, executive, and judiciary alone. The imposition of strict parliamentary party-political discipline has meant that the executive's power within the legislature is often unchallenged, and the growth of quasi-public bodies performing privatized functions of government has led to a reallocation of public power among a variety of different constitutional actors.

1.12   In any case, as JS Mill observed in *On Liberty*,[12] democracy is not in itself a guarantee against the tyranny of the majority over unpopular minorities. In the notorious *East African Asians Case*[13] the European Commission of Human Rights (ECmHR) found that the Commonwealth Immigrants Act 1968, passed to stop British passport holders in East Africa who were fleeing persecution in their home countries coming to the UK, was motivated by racism. Parliament is also prone to legislating to remove fundamental rights as, for example, in the Criminal Justice and Public Order Act 1994, when the newly created offence of 'trespassory assembly'

---

[10] AV Dicey, *Law of the Constitution*, 1885 (9th edn, Macmillan 1950).
[11] (1765–1769).
[12] JS Mill, *On Liberty* (OUP 1869).
[13] *East African Asians v UK* (1981) 3 EHRR 76.

limited individuals' common law right to assemble or the more recent Police, Crime, Sentencing and Courts Act which came into force in 2022[14] (impacting directly on one of the fundamental rights identified by Dicey). In a fast-changing society, relying on the incremental development of the common law to protect rights proved unsatisfactory.

2. European Convention rights in the United Kingdom before the Human Rights Act

The Convention was drafted with significant input from English lawyers.[15] The UK ratified the Convention in 1951 and recognized the individual right of petition in 1966. Ironically, in light of the UK's contribution to the Convention, the positive guarantees of fundamental rights contained in the international Convention were found wanting by the European Court of Human Rights (ECtHR). However, now the UK has lowest number of adverse findings per year.[16] Under the dualist principles of English law, international treaties ratified by the UK government, such as the Convention, do not have direct legal effect in domestic courts until they are incorporated into domestic law by an Act of Parliament. One reason for this was the judiciary's inability to develop English law consistently with the Convention.

1.13

However, before the Human Rights Act came into force—indeed, even before the Bill was drafted—it was possible for Convention principles to have an impact on domestic law either indirectly (through judgments against the UK in Strasbourg that were then implemented by changes in the law), or directly (by developing the common law through legal arguments based on the Convention).

1.14

Over the five decades preceding the enactment of the Human Rights Act, the Convention indirectly had an increasing impact on the development of the English law. Findings of violations against the UK led to several changes being made to primary legislation. The Strasbourg Court's judgment in *Sunday Times v UK (No 1)*[17] was an important factor leading to the reform of the law of contempt by the Contempt of Court Act 1981. The violation of the right to respect for private life in Article 8 found by the ECtHR in the telephone-tapping case of *Malone v UK*[18] led to the enactment of the Interception of Communications Act 1985 (provisions and principles now contained in the Regulation of Investigatory Powers Act 2000 and the Investigatory Powers Act 2016).

1.15

---

[14] 'The Act makes wide-ranging changes across the criminal justice system in areas including police powers, judicial procedures and offender rehabilitation. It will also have a serious impact on human rights, particularly the right to protest.' *Liberty* <https://www.libertyhumanrights.org.uk/advice_information/pcsc-policing-act-protest-rights/>.

[15] See n 9.

[16] See the partial list of (pre-incorporation) violations in Murray Hunt, *Using Human Rights Law in English Courts* (Hart Publishing 1997) app 1. See Chapter 8 for the latest figures.

[17] *Sunday Times v UK (No 1)* (1979) 2 EHRR 245.

[18] *Malone v UK* (1984) 7 EHRR 14.

1.16   The judiciary was also able to directly consider the provisions of the Convention in cases before the domestic courts. Some of the most important pre-Act uses of the Convention were as follows:

(a) as an aid to the construction of legislation in cases of ambiguity, for example in *R v Secretary of State for the Home Department, ex p Brind*.[19] There is a presumption that Parliament does not intend to act in breach of international law (and the specific treaty obligations the UK government has committed to on behalf of the Crown), so where there is ambiguity in a statute the courts will construe the law consistently with these international treaty obligations;

(b) to establish the scope of the common law where it is developing and uncertain, or where it is certain but incomplete. For example, in *Derbyshire County Council v Times Newspapers Ltd*[20] Article 10 informed the House of Lords' decision that a local authority could not bring an action for libel as it would offend against the freedom of expression protections in the Convention;

(c) to inform the exercise of judicial (as opposed to administrative) discretion. For example, in *R v Khan*[21] the House of Lords held that a trial judge may have regard to the Convention as a material consideration in exercising the discretion conferred by section 78 of the Police and Criminal Evidence Act 1984 as to whether to exclude evidence; and

(d) to inform decisions on European Union (EU) law taken by the domestic courts. For example, in *Johnston v Chief Constable of the Royal Ulster Constabulary*[22] the European Court of Justice (ECJ) took Articles 6 and 13 into account in determining that the applicant did not have an effective remedy in her sex discrimination case. The ECJ has declared that the general principles of EU law include the protection of fundamental rights. However, 'Brexit', the UK's exit from the European Union, complicates the extent to which ECJ judgments can be considered in cases against the UK.

1.17   These techniques continue to be important, and are still used in relation to other international treaties that have not been incorporated into English law.[23]

C. THE INCORPORATION OF THE CONVENTION

1.18   The initial justifications advanced by Parliament for not giving full effect to the provisions of the Convention included concerns that the constitutional doctrines of parliamentary sovereignty and separation of powers would be irreparably harmed.

---

[19] *R v Secretary of State for the Home Department, ex p Brind* [1991] 1 AC 696.
[20] *Derbyshire County Council v Times Newspapers Ltd* [1992] QB 770.
[21] *R v Khan* [1996] 3 WLR 162.
[22] *Johnston v Chief Constable of the Royal Ulster Constabulary* [1987] QB 129.
[23] For a more detailed analysis, see Murray Hunt, *Using Human Rights Law in English Courts* (Hart Publishing 1997); Shaheed Fatima, *Using International Law in Domestic Courts* (Hart Publishing 2005).

In particular, commentators were worried that judges would wield too much power and that difficult societal questions and conflicts of interests would be resolved by judges rather than through political debate by elected MPs. Opponents also argued that it was an unnecessary step given that rights were already adequately protected by the common law, and indeed the incorporation of the 'vague' general principles of the Convention would be a retrograde step for the protection of rights in the UK as the 'flexibility' of the unwritten constitution would be constrained.

Over the past 70 years, those views on the incorporation of the Convention into domestic law slowly changed, culminating in the Human Rights Act. Supporters of a Bill of Rights had long argued that the common law safeguards for rights were inadequate and open to attack by politicians in the grip of party politics. They pointed out that the strict party discipline imposed on the parliamentary political parties did not allow for a fully independent legislature, and so a Bill of Rights was needed to deal with what Lord Hailsham called an 'elective dictatorship'. Supporters relied, too, on the unavoidable facts that the UK was one of a handful of western democracies that did not have a written Bill of Rights and that British citizens were forced to undertake a lengthy and expensive route to enforcing their Convention rights in Strasbourg. The debate on a Bill of Rights during this period was not the preserve of one political party or political philosophy. In the late 1940s, the main British protagonists of what became the Convention were Conservatives such as Winston Churchill and Harold Macmillan. Equally, it was the Labour Attlee government that ratified the Convention in 1951, the Churchill government that ratified the First Protocol in 1953, and the Labour government under Wilson that accepted the right of individual petition to the ECtHR in 1966.

1.19

In 1968, the publication of the pamphlet *Democracy and Individual Rights* by Anthony Lester (later the Liberal Democrat peer Lord Lester QC) marked the beginning of the debate that led eventually to the Human Rights Act. Lester suggested that incorporating the Convention was only a first step for enshrining human rights guarantees but would be no more than an interim measure. In subsequent years, the issue of incorporating the Convention was debated a number of times from a variety of political perspectives. An important step forward was made in 1974, when Sir Leslie Scarman (later the cross-bench peer Lord Scarman) wrote of the need for an instrument to challenge the sovereignty of Parliament and to protect basic human rights which could not be adequately protected by the legislature alone. Scarman was in favour of entrenchment. He believed that only by making a Bill of Rights superior to the machinations of Parliament could such fundamental rights be protected.[24]

1.20

The Labour Party National Executive Committee unveiled a Charter of Human Rights in 1975. This document advocated an unentrenched Human Rights Act. This proposal was regarded as insufficient by many who considered that such an Act would offer inadequate protection to individual interests against the growing power of the state. In particular, many Conservatives (including Sir Geoffrey Howe (later Lord Howe), Lord Brittan, and Roy Jenkins (later Lord Jenkins)) preferred

1.21

---

[24] Lord Scarman, *English Law—The New Dimension*, Hamlyn Lectures, 26th Series (Stevens 1974).

the concept of a Bill of Rights with entrenched clauses that would prevent even Parliament from granting the executive excessive power over the lives of individuals.

1.22 Lord Wade as a Liberal in 1976 moved a Bill in the House of Lords which proposed to entrench the Convention as a part of all existing legislation and to make it an entrenched part of all subsequent enactments unless Parliament specifically legislated otherwise. Lord Wade and Lord Harris continued to be the chief advocates for a Bill of Rights in the Lords. In 1978, a House of Lords Select Committee examined the arguments for and against legislation to incorporate the Convention and create a Bill of Rights. However, traditional constitutional views prevailed, particularly a concern about the idea of judges deciding 'human rights' cases. The fear was that this would remove the judiciary from its traditionally impartial role, supposedly beyond politics, and embroil it in (party) political questions.

1.23 After John Smith became leader of the Labour Party in 1992, there was a clear shift in Labour Party policy. The Labour Party Conference in October 1993 adopted a two-stage policy supporting the incorporation of the European Convention of Human Rights (ECHR) to be followed by the enactment of a domestic Bill of Rights. The Labour Party planned to entrench Convention rights by the use of a 'notwithstanding clause' procedure. This was similar to the Canadian Charter of Rights and Freedoms, and would have led to the Convention overriding domestic law unless Parliament expressly provided for it to apply notwithstanding that it would violate the Bill of Rights. The conference also advocated the establishment of a human rights commission to monitor and promote human rights. Tony Blair MP (shortly before he became leader of the Labour Party) set out his views in the *Guardian* and reaffirmed the need for strengthened incorporation and the idea of a 'notwithstanding clause'.[25]

1.24 Lord Lester of Herne Hill continued his human rights work in the Lords by introducing a Bill in November 1994. The Bill did not receive support from the Conservative government. Particular aspects of the proposed Bill were criticized by the Law Lords, but significantly they supported incorporation insofar as it allowed UK judges to interpret human rights domestically.

1.25 In December 1996, Jack Straw MP and Paul Boateng MP published a Consultation Paper, *Bringing Rights Home*, setting out the Labour Party's plans to incorporate the Convention if it won the election due in 1997. Whereas the 1993 policy had advocated incorporation to be followed by a second stage in the form of a home-grown Bill of Rights, the Consultation Paper deferred the second stage, and the five key issues posed by the paper concerned only the incorporation of the Convention. In May 1997, Labour won a landslide victory on a manifesto which included a commitment to incorporate the Convention into domestic law. The debate then turned to how the Convention should be incorporated, and in particular to whether it should be permitted to override statutes, subject to a 'notwithstanding clause'. The unique solution adopted in the Human Rights Act is the subject of Chapters 3 to 4 of this book.

---

[25] 16 July 1994.

The incorporation of the Convention is not the end of the story. The Convention 1.26
is by no means a perfect human rights treaty and there remain gaps in the protection of human rights in the UK. The Convention was drafted in the aftermath
of the Second World War. If the Convention were to be drafted today, a number of rights might be included that are not currently found within its scope. For
example, the Convention does not contain a right to freedom of information;[26]
the anti-discrimination provision is 'parasitic' in that it applies only where another
Convention right has been violated;[27] there is little specific recognition of children's rights or environmental rights; and it does not contain an absolute prohibition against self-incrimination for criminal defendants.[28] In addition, the types of
Convention rights are limited in range compared with the nature of rights more
broadly, and offer little protection to social and economic rights. In contrast, the
Charter of Fundamental Rights of the European Union contains more wide-ranging
rights, including employment, equality, and children's rights. The Convention's
deficiencies are replicated in the Human Rights Act, which simply incorporated
the Convention in English law. However, the UK government could easily increase
the protections that the Convention provides by ratifying and then adding to the
Schedule to Human Rights Act, the rights contained in Protocols 4, 7, and 12.

D. THE HUMAN RIGHTS ACT AS A CONSTITUTIONAL INSTRUMENT

In the lead-up to the enactment of the Human Rights Act, some commentators 1.27
expressed concern about the relationship between the new statute and the existing constitutional arrangements. The flashpoint for many was the perceived tension between the English tradition of regarding the sovereignty of the democratic
Parliament as being the cornerstone of its (unwritten) constitution and the fact that
the Convention was to be enforceable in the courts.[29] Similar concerns have resurfaced in recent attacks on the Human Rights Act, with detractors claiming that
it gives the judiciary the power to override the will of the democratically elected
Parliament and draws judges into societal debates in a manner that is alien to the
UK's constitutional settlement. To gauge the strength of these criticisms, each of
the claims is examined below.

---

[26] See Chapter 7, para 7.366.

[27] See discussion of art 14 and Protocol 12 in Chapter 8, para 8.159.

[28] For further discussion, see John Wadham, 'Why Incorporation of the European Convention on
Human Rights is Not Enough' in Richard Gordon and Richard Wilmot-Smith (eds), *Human Rights in
the United Kingdom* (OUP 1996) 25; John Wadham and Rachel Taylor, 'Bringing More Rights Home'
[2002] European Human Rights Law Review 713; John Wadham and Fiona K Byrne, 'More Human
Rights: Protocols 4, 7, and 12 of the European Convention on Human Rights; and the Human Rights Act
1998' [2023], European Human Rights Law Review 528,.

[29] See eg KD Ewing, 'The Human Rights Act and Parliamentary Democracy' [1999] Modern Law
Review 79.

1. Parliamentary sovereignty and entrenchment

1.28   The idea that Parliament is the supreme legal power has been a consistent theme in English law as reflected in the writings of Coke, Blackstone, and Dicey. The doctrine has several elements. According to the theory, the sovereign legislature (the Queen, the House of Lords, and the House of Commons) can make and repeal any legislation whatsoever, so that no Parliament can bind its successors. As a result, it is impossible to 'entrench' particular legislation (eg a Bill of Rights) by specifying that it would be repealable only under some specially safeguarded process. A corollary is that no act of the sovereign legislature can be invalid in the eyes of a court, because Parliament alone has the legal and political power to make laws. The potency of the parliamentary sovereignty theory was only diluted temporally by the changes to the domestic legal system effected by the European Communities Act 1972 until Brexit, albeit only to the extent provided for by the 1972 Act. A strict adherence to the doctrine would be problematic. It would limit the ability of courts to uphold human rights and could mean that a future Parliament could legislate such rights out of existence merely by passing ordinary legislation inconsistent with rights. To protect fundamental rights, some form of 'entrenchment' is necessary.

1.29   The solution adopted in the Human Rights Act is a nuanced one, reflecting a delicate political compromise between 'incorporating' Convention rights and retaining parliamentary sovereignty. The rule of construction in section 3 of the Human Rights Act places courts under a strong interpretative obligation to read and give effect to all legislation, whether primary or secondary, old or recent, in a way which is compatible with Convention rights 'so far as it is possible to do so'. Section 4 makes it clear that if a conflict between the provisions of a piece of legislation and Convention rights cannot be overcome, higher courts will have to make a declaration of incompatibility. The court cannot 'strike down' the offending Act, and so it remains operative after such a declaration. The scheme of the Human Rights Act means that the only legal effect of a declaration of incompatibility is to permit (but not oblige) a minister to amend the impugned legislation by a 'remedial order' under section 10. If the declaration of incompatibility is not accepted by the government, and there is no overwhelming parliamentary pressure to change the law, there is no domestic legal obligation to change the law. Further, section 6(3) excludes Parliament from the definition of 'public authority' so that it is not bound by the provisions of the Human Rights Act.

1.30   This form of legislation for human rights is not as strong as the Canadian model, which gives courts the power to strike down primary legislation but allows the legislature to enact measures for a limited period 'notwithstanding' its contravention of provisions in the Charter of Fundamental Rights and Freedoms. It is, however, stronger than the New Zealand model, which imposes only a weak obligation upon courts to 'prefer' an interpretation of legislation that is consistent with the Bill of Rights Act over an inconsistent one if possible.[30]

---

[30] See Kris Gledhill, *Human Rights Acts: The Mechanisms Compared* (Bloomsbury 2015).

Ultimately, the Human Rights Act protects the principle of parliamentary sovereignty because it does not permit the Convention to be used so as to override primary legislation: if a statute is clear in its terms, and clearly incompatible with the Convention, courts must give effect to it. Equally, if the terms of the primary legislation require subordinate legislation made under it (which will usually be in a statutory instrument) to be interpreted in a way that means that the subordinate legislation is incompatible with the Convention, it must still be given effect even though this may result in a breach of a Convention right.[31] **1.31**

2. Politicizing the judiciary?

Before the Human Rights Act came into force, some legal and academic commentators[32] warned that it would infringe the basic constitutional tenet that 'Parliament makes the laws, the judiciary interpret them'.[33] The strong approach to statutory construction required by section 3 would lead to a politicization of the judiciary and an encroachment on Parliament's constitutional sphere. However, English courts reviewing controversial issues is not a new phenomenon. The Human Rights Act may have brought about a more intense degree of judicial scrutiny of executive and parliamentary action, but not scrutiny of a different kind. Indeed, one of the important effects of the Human Rights Act has been to focus public attention and debate on the proper nature and scope of the judicial function. **1.32**

In response to criticisms of judicial activism, the former Lord Chief Justice Lord Woolf has pointed out that: **1.33**

judges are only doing what they have to swear to do on appointment and that is to give a judgement according to law. The law now includes the HRA. By upholding the HRA the courts are not interfering with the will of Parliament. On the contrary, when they interfere, the judges are protecting the public by ensuring that the Government complies with the laws made by Parliament. The courts are therefore acting in support of Parliament and not otherwise.[34]

The Human Rights Act itself provides a mechanism for balancing the role of the executive, Parliament, and the courts in the form of section 19. It presumes that new legislation is to be (and can be) read compatibly with the Convention. When legislation is introduced into Parliament for a second reading, the introducing minister must make a statement that, in his or her view, the legislation is compatible with the Convention, or make a statement that, although the legislation is not compatible with the Convention, the government still wishes to proceed. It is unlikely that governments will often wish to state publicly that they are acting incompatibly with an internationally binding human rights instrument, though they have been prepared to do so on occasion. Where a 'section 19' statement is made, Parliament **1.34**

---

[31] For more details, see Nicholas Bamforth, 'Parliamentary Sovereignty and the Human Rights Act 1998' [1998] Public Law 572.

[32] See n 29. See also John Griffith, *The Politics of the Judiciary* (5th edn, Fontana Press 1997).

[33] Lord Diplock in *Duport Steels Ltd v Sirs* [1980] 1 WLR 142.

[34] 'The Impact of Human Rights', speech at Oxford Lyceum, 6 March 2003.

has the opportunity to thoroughly examine the minister's assertion before the Bill is passed. Reports of the Joint Parliamentary Committee on Human Rights (see para 1.42) demonstrate that section 19 statements have the potential to be powerful democratic tools for scrutinizing Bills, when Parliamentarians press for detailed reasoning behind statements of compatibility from the government, rather than accepting generalized, uninformative statements that Bills are Convention compliant. A section 19 statement of compatibility also gives a strong indication to the judiciary that the government intended its new legislation to be human rights compliant and that the judges are able to proceed with their judicial scrutiny with that intention in mind.

1.35   Despite some commentators' claims, since the Human Rights Act came into force judges have erred on the side of caution rather than judicial activism.[35] They have developed the concept of a 'discretionary area of judgment' (sometimes called 'deference') which considers when it is appropriate (and when it is not) for courts to defer to decisions made by other constitutional bodies such as the legislative, executive, or administrative branches. The appropriateness and breadth of the discretionary area of judgment that should be applied have been hotly debated by Law Lords (now Supreme Court Justices), practitioners, and academics alike and are considered in more detail in Chapter 4.[36]

1.36   The notion of 'democratic dialogue' is the most helpful for evaluating the interaction between Parliament, the executive, and the judiciary under the new constitutional arrangement ushered in by the Human Rights Act.[37] This 'dialogue' takes place when a court, in reviewing legislative and executive action, scrutinizes the justification for laws or actions which limit fundamental human rights within the framework of the Convention, and seeks to make the law compatible with the Convention, by interpretation, if possible, or to declare the fact of incompatibility, if not. The final word on the content of law, however, still rests with Parliament. In the leading Canadian Supreme Court case of *Vriend v Alberta*[38] Iacobucci J concluded that:

a great value of judicial review and this dialogue among the branches is that each of the branches is made somewhat accountable to the other. The work of the legislature is reviewed by the courts and the work of the court in its decisions can be reacted to by the legislature in the passing of new legislation ... This dialogue between and accountability of each of the branches has the effect of enhancing the democratic process, not denying it.

1.37   Despite the ongoing concerns about parliamentary sovereignty and judicial activism, both the judiciary and government have acknowledged the place of the Human Rights Act in the UK constitution. Lord Bingham called the Human Rights Act

---

[35] See Ian Leigh and Rodger Masterman, *Making Rights Real: The Human Rights Act in Its First Decade* (Hart Publishing 2009) and Brice Dickson, *Human Rights and the United Kingdom Supreme Court* (OUP 2013).

[36] See eg the *Elan-Cane* case [2021] UKSC 56, and see Chapter 4, paras 4.119–4.130.

[37] See eg Richard Clayton, 'Judicial Deference and "Democratic Dialogue": The Legitimacy of Judicial Intervention under the Human Rights Act 1998' [2004] Public Law 33; Tom R Hickman, 'Constitutional Dialogue, Constitutional Theories and the Human Rights Act 1998' [2005] Public Law 306.

[38] *Vriend v Alberta* [1998] 1 SCR 495.

'an important constitutional instrument'.[39] As Lord Justice Laws explained, this is so because the Act conditions the legal relationship between citizen and state and determines the scope of what we now regard as fundamental constitutional rights.[40] However, some commentators are concerned that the Supreme Court has been, more recently, taking a more 'hands off' approach with human rights arguments becoming less effective.[41]

E. THE INSTITUTIONAL FRAMEWORK—CREATING A CULTURE OF RESPECT FOR HUMAN RIGHTS

Many commentators, including the authors, hoped that as well as transforming the legal landscape, the 1998 Act would have a broad impact on our political and social culture. There are two dimensions to this new culture—ethical and institutional. The ethical dimension involves individual members of society developing an understanding that they enjoy certain rights by virtue of being human (not merely as a contingent gift of the state); *and* that with these rights comes the responsibility to respect the human rights of other individual citizens. Developing an institutional human rights culture involves mainstreaming fundamental principles into the design and delivery of policy, legislation, and public services so that decisions taken by public authorities such as schools and hospitals are proportionate, rational, and respectful of fundamental rights. The obligation on public authorities imposed by the Human Rights Act goes beyond non-interference with rights and requires such bodies to take active steps to protect people's rights against interference by others.[42] 1.38

The Act's aim of creating an institutional human rights culture has not been completely successful. Research undertaken on the effect of the Human Rights Act has demonstrated that public bodies have not always taken advantage of the benefits a human rights culture could offer for improved decision-making by using the framework of the Act to inform best practice. Instead, public bodies have too often confined human rights to their legal compliance departments, adopting a minimalist approach to protecting people's fundamental rights by 'Strasbourg-proofing' their policies and procedures to avoid litigation.[43] 1.39

The Human Rights Act is also widely misunderstood and mistrusted by the public, caricatured by the popular press as a 'charter for criminals and terrorists'. As we discuss later, the future of the Act is uncertain. The failure to set up a body at the Human Rights Act's inception to promote understanding and awareness of the benefits of human rights left it vulnerable to these attacks because it was without 1.40

---

[39] *Brown v Stott* [2003] 1 AC 681, para 703.
[40] See Laws LJ in *Thoburn v Sunderland City Council* [2002] 3 WLR 247.
[41] See eg Professor Conor Gearty, 'In the Shallow End', London Review of Books, 27 January 2022.
[42] See Chapter 2, para 2.39.
[43] See the excellent and continuing work by the British Institute of Human Rights, including 'Something for Everyone: The Impact of the Human Rights Act and the Need for a Human Rights Commission' (2002); Audit Commission, 'Human Rights: Improving Service Delivery' (2003); EHRC, 'Human Rights Inquiry' (2009).

a powerful, institutional champion to defend the benefits of human rights. This failure was belatedly and inadequately remedied by the creation of the Equality and Human Rights Commission.[44]

1. A human rights culture in Parliament?

1.41　Both the Labour Party Consultation Paper, *Bringing Rights Home*, and the White Paper, *Rights Brought Home*, stated that 'Parliament itself should play a leading role in protecting the rights which are at the heart of parliamentary democracy'.[45] A Human Rights Committee has proved to be a fundamental part of this. The idea of a Human Rights Committee in Parliament originated in Francesca Klug's *A People's Charter: Liberty's Bill of Rights*.[46] Klug's suggestion was that the new Committee could conduct inquiries on a range of human rights issues, produce reports to assist the government and Parliament in deciding what action to take, and range more widely, examining issues relating to the other international obligations of the UK.

1.42　The Joint Committee on Human Rights (JCHR) (a Select Committee consisting of members of both Houses of Parliament) was appointed in January 2001. Its terms of reference are to consider:

(a) matters relating to human rights in the UK (excluding consideration of individual cases);

(b) proposals for remedial orders, draft remedial orders, and remedial orders made under section 10 of, and laid under Schedule 2 to, the Human Rights Act; and

(c) in respect of draft remedial orders and remedial orders, whether the special attention of the House should be drawn to them on any of the grounds specified in Standing Order 73 (Joint Committee on Statutory Instruments).

1.43　The JCHR carries out important work, including prolific scrutiny of important bills, pre-legislative scrutiny work (to draw the attention of Parliament and the government to any potential pitfalls in relation to a proposed policy course) and post-legislative scrutiny (to assess whether the implementation of new laws has produced unwelcome human rights implications).

2. Human rights commissions

1.44　The first human rights commission to be set up in the UK was the Northern Ireland Human Rights Commission.[47] This was a requirement of the peace process and the

---

[44] See paras 1.44–1.51.

[45] Jack Straw and Paul Boateng, 'Bringing Rights Home: Labour's Plans to Incorporate the ECHR into UK Law: A Consultation Paper' (1997); White Paper, 'Rights Brought Home: The Human Rights Bill' (Cm 3782, 1997).

[46] National Council for Civil Liberties, 1991.

[47] Northern Ireland's troubled history resulted in the first official human rights body in the UK—The Standing Advisory Commission on Human Rights—but this did not have the independence and powers

Belfast Good Friday Agreement (in parallel with the creation of a similar body in the Republic of Ireland).[48] However, one of the initial tasks the JCHR undertook was an inquiry into whether a human rights commission was needed for the UK as a whole (or for separate commissions for each country). It concluded that the case for setting up a Commission for Human Rights was compelling.[49] Without it, the development of a 'culture of understanding of rights and responsibilities' envisaged by the original proposals was stalled.

After a series of consultation papers between 2002 and 2004, the government   1.45
confirmed that it would set up a new, single Commission for Equality and Human Rights for England and Wales and brought forward legislation to establish that body.[50] There were good reasons for establishing an integrated body. Not only have other countries demonstrated the practical benefits of linking human rights and equality work (eg in the Australian Human Rights and Equal Opportunity Commission), but, conceptually, human rights and equality are inextricably linked. Equality is treated as a fundamental human right in the core international human rights treaties, and human rights and equality derive from the same fundamental principle: equal respect for the inherent dignity of all.

The Equality and Human Rights Commission[51] started work in October 2007.   1.46
The Equality Act 2006 set out specific legal duties for the Commission, including a duty to promote understanding of the importance of human rights and to encourage compliance with the Human Rights Act.[52]

In order to carry out its duties the Equality Act provided the Commission with   1.47
a range of legal powers. In particular, it can conduct formal inquiries into any matters relating to its duties,[53] intervene in litigation,[54] bring judicial review in its own name,[55] and provide legal assistance to individuals in proceedings concerning the equality enactments.[56] In June 2009 the Commission published the results of its Inquiry to assess the effectiveness and enjoyment of a culture of respect for human rights in Great Britain.[57] The Inquiry found that while the vast majority of people want to see human rights embedded in national law, there were significant misunderstandings and misconceptions about human rights. Where a human rights approach has been adopted, the Inquiry found that it led to speedy positive resolution of problems and systemic changes in service delivery by public authorities.

---

necessary to comply with the 'Paris Principles' and, therefore, to be properly accredited by the United Nations (UN) as a 'National Human Rights Institution'.

   [48] 'Rights, Safeguards and Equality of Opportunity', para 5, April 1998.
   [49] JCHR, *The Case for a Human Rights Commission*, 6th Report (2002–2003), HL 67-I, HC 489-I.
   [50] Equality Act 2006 (EA 2006).
   [51] EA 2006, s 1 establishes the 'Commission for Equality and Human Rights' but the body has adopted the name 'Equality and Human Rights Commission'.
   [52] EA 2006, ss 3, 8, 9, 10, and 11.
   [53] EA 2006, s 16.
   [54] EA 2006, s 30. See eg *R (JL) v Secretary of State for Justice* [2008] UKHL 68, [2009] 1 AC 588.
   [55] EA 2006, s 30(1).
   [56] EA 2006, s 28.
   [57] Equality and Human Rights Commission, 'Our Human Rights Inquiry' (June 2009) <https://www.equalityhumanrights.com/sites/default/files/hri_report.pdf>.

1.48   The Scottish Parliament also set up the Scottish Human Rights Commission, which set out its first strategic plan in December 2008.[58] This Commission has its own powers and duties but these are restricted to devolved matters—matters within the competence of the Scottish Parliament.[59]

1.49   The creation of these commissions represented an important opportunity to improve understanding of the Human Rights Act as well as the ECHR, and to promote human rights. The Equality and Human Rights Commission took some time to come to terms with its role and remit, and to resolve the issues arising from the merger of the three equality commissions.

1.50   The Equality and Human Rights Commission was criticized by the Parliamentary Joint Human Rights Committee, in 2010:

> We have sometimes been frustrated at the EHRC's lack of engagement in major human rights debates. We heard nothing from the Commission on policing and protest, for example, an issue with which we were engaged for a calendar year from June 2008 and which was the subject of considerable public debate, particularly after the G20 protests in April 2009. We were also critical of the evidence we received from the EHRC during our business and human rights inquiry, because it was limited to equality matters, indicating a broader failure to integrate effectively equality and human rights work.[60]

1.51   The substance of the Equality and Human Rights Commission's work on human rights has improved, notably through the publication of a review of the UK's compliance with the ECHR.[61] This was followed up in August 2014 by a major review of the UK's progress against the recommendations from the second cycle of the UN Universal Periodic Review.[62] The Commission has also exercised its power to intervene in several human rights cases.[63]

F. THE FUTURE OF HUMAN RIGHTS PROTECTION IN THE UNITED KINGDOM

1.52   Since the Human Rights Act came into force it has been the focus of intense political debate. The Act is widely blamed for administrative and judicial decisions that have been caricatured as privileging the rights of criminals, migrants, and terrorists over their 'victims'. In particular, the Convention prohibition on deporting individuals to countries where there is a real risk that they will be tortured has attracted significant press criticism. More recently, decisions by the courts which have prevented the deportation of non-British citizens who have committed serious

---

[58] EA 2006, s 7; and see <http://www.scottishhumanrights.com>.

[59] Scottish Human Rights Commission Act 2006.

[60] The Equality and Human Rights Commission, 2 March 2010.

[61] The Human Rights Review (EHRC 2012) <https://www.equalityhumanrights.com/sites/default/files/human-rights-review-2012-executive-summary.pdf>.

[62] *Mid-Term Universal Periodic Review Report*, EHRC, August 2014 and see <https://www.equalityhumanrights.com/sites/default/files/upr_mid-term_report_ehrcfinal210814_web.pdf>

[63] See <https://www.equalityhumanrights.com/en/legal-casework/human-rights-legal-cases>.

criminal offences—based on the fact that they (or their children) have established family ties in the UK and deporting them would breach their right to family life (or that of their children) have been subject to sustained criticism by some politicians and sections of the media.

The Act also received criticism from media organizations for enabling the judiciary to create a law of privacy unsanctioned by Parliament, but this criticism lost some of its fervour in the wake of the evidence of newspapers hacking into mobile telephones of celebrities and others and the Leveson Report.[64] Amongst human rights advocates, there is a consensus that the government 'failed to explain the basic philosophy of the Human Rights Act to the people'.[65] As the Equality and Human Rights Commission found in its Human Rights Inquiry, there is a general lack of public awareness of the positive role that human rights can play in individual lives.

1.53

Reform of the Human Rights Act has also been under consideration since its inception. It was as far back as 2007 that then Prime Minister Gordon Brown published a Green Paper[66] and a statement[67] exploring the possibility of a British Bill of Rights to replace the Human Rights Act but to include all of its key provisions. The JCHR[68] raised concerns that the proposed Bill could be a vehicle for diluting the protections of the Human Rights Act. In March 2009, the Labour government published a Green Paper, *Rights and Responsibilities: Developing our Constitutional Framework*.[69] A summary of responses was produced in March 2010 but the Labour Party then lost the general election and the Coalition government took over instead.[70]

1.54

1. Proposals for reform or repeal 2010 to 2015

In 2010 the Coalition government set up a Commission on a Bill of Rights after a particular political concern over prisoners' voting rights. Parliament refused to legislate to give even a small minority of prisoners the right to vote as required by the judgment of the European Court judgment in *Hirst v UK*.[71] The Commission reported at the end of 2012. There was, however, no consensus on what, if anything, needed to change.[72]

1.55

Nevertheless the Conservative Party went on in 2014 to propose the repeal of the Human Rights Act and its replacement by a 'British Bill of Rights and

1.56

---

[64] This report, by the Rt Hon Lord Justice Leveson, was sparked by the hacking of the mobile phone of a murdered teenager and expanded to cover the culture, practices, and ethics of the press in its relations with the public, the police, and politicians, published November 2012.

[65] JCHR, *A Bill of Rights for the UK?* 29th Report (2007–2008), HL 165-I, HC 150-I, vol II, Klug Ev 1.

[66] *The Governance of Britain* (Cm 7170, 2007).

[67] Prime Minister's statement on constitutional reform, HC, col 819 (3 July 2007).

[68] JCHR, *A Bill of Rights for the UK?* 29th Report (2007–2008), HL 165-I, HC 150-I.

[69] Cm 7577, 2009.

[70] Rights and Responsibilities: Developing Our Constitutional Framework Summary of Responses, March 2010.

[71] *Hirst v UK (No 2)* (2006) 42 EHRR 41.

[72] The Commission on a Bill of Rights' report Ministry of Justice, 'A UK Bill of Rights?—The Choice Before Us', 18 December 2012.

Responsibilities'. The proposal was condemned as unworkable by many lawyers in the UK, human rights NGOs, and others, including Dominic Grieve QC MP (Conservative Attorney General from May 2010 to July 2014),[73] Kenneth Clarke QC MP (Conservative Secretary of State for Justice from May 2010 to September 2012),[74] Tim Owen QC and Alex Bailin QC, and Professor Conor Gearty.[75] The Council of Europe itself criticized the proposals.

2. Proposals for reform or repeal 2015 to 2023

1.57 The Conservative Party's 2015 manifesto included a commitment to repeal the Human Rights Act, promising to 'scrap the Human Rights Act and curtail the role of the European Court of Human Rights, so that foreign criminals can be more easily deported from Britain'. Theresa May, the then Home Secretary, also called for the UK to withdraw from the ECHR, arguing that it can:

bind the hands of Parliament, adds nothing to our prosperity, makes us less secure by preventing the deportation of dangerous foreign nationals—and does nothing to change the attitudes of governments like Russia's when it comes to human rights.[76]

1.58 The Joint Human Rights Committee subsequently published its report 'Twenty Years of the Human Rights Act: Extracts from the Evidence' in November 2018, giving a very different perspective. Its Chair, the Rt Hon Harriett Harman MP, stated:

Today marks twenty years since the Human Rights Act was passed. It is worth reflecting on the difference the Act has made. Now public service providers, such as the police, prisons or health service, all think about human rights. And before the Human Rights Act, if your human rights were abused, you had to go to the European Court of Human Rights in Strasbourg, which took a further five years and an extra £30,000 after you had been through the courts in the UK. Most people could not enforce their rights. Now you can go to court in the UK and get your rights enforced and protected.[77]

1.59 The Conservative Party's election manifesto adopted a potentially more moderate position in respect of human rights law reform in 2019 promising in place of outright repeal to:

update the Human Rights Act and administrative law to ensure that there is a proper balance between the rights of individuals, our vital national security and effective government.

1.60 The new Conservative government then established an Independent Human Rights Act Review (IHRAR) in December 2020 with a remit to consider how the Human Rights Act was working in practice and whether any change was needed. Its report was published in December 2021, along with all the responses to the

---

[73] *Independent*, 4 October 2014.
[74] *The Guardian*, 3 October 2014.
[75] <http://www.theguardian.com/commentisfree/2014/oct/03/tories-proposal-british-bill-of-rights-incoherent-human-rights-act-strasbourg>.
[76] 25 April 2016.
[77] 9 November 2018.

Review's call for evidence and the notes from a number of its Roundtables.[78] The Report concluded that:

overall, the HRA has been a success, there is clear room for a coherent package of reforms carrying both domestic and international benefits.

...

[T]he vast majority of submissions ... spoke strongly in support of the HRA [and] did not find that extensive reform of the HRA was necessary.[79]

In relation to reform of the Act the report suggested that: 1.61

- there should be more work to educate the public on the Human Rights Act and rights more generally;
- section 2 of the Act should be amended to clarify the priority of rights protection by making UK legislation, common law, and other case law the first port of call, before ECtHR case law is taken into account;
- that the tension between the need to avoid 'an ECtHR straightjacket'—an unnecessary and rigid compliance with every ECtHR judgment—on the one hand or a gap between rights protection by the UK courts and ECtHR needed to be resolved;
- section 3 should be amended to clarify the order of priority of interpretation although the HRAR found little evidence of a problem in the way it operated;
- there should be a database of section 3 judgments and an enhanced role for Parliament (and in particular the JCHR) to improve understanding of the operation of section 3;
- where secondary legislation has been found to be incompatible, there should be a power to suspend, or only make an order for the prospective quashing of that legislation (rather than the judgment itself having the effect of quashing the secondary legislation);[80]
- the Human Rights Act's extraterritorial application is unsatisfactory and this should be addressed by discussions in the Council of Europe and a dialogue between the UK courts and the ECtHR; (see ch? para? for more details of the extraterritorial application of the Convention); and
- section 10 should be amended so that remedial orders cannot be used to amend the Human Rights Act itself (see ch? Para? for how section 10 works).

The Joint Human Rights Committee held its own inquiry at the same time, feeding its evidence into the IHRAR, and concluding that there was no compelling case for the reform of the Human Rights Act.[81] 1.62

---

[78] <https://www.gov.uk/guidance/independent-human-rights-act-review>.
[79] Executive Summary, para 9.
[80] Now provided for in the Judicial Review and Courts Act 2022.
[81] 8 July 2021.

1.63   On the same day that the IHRAR report was published, the government published a consultation on reform of the Human Rights Act—'Human Rights Act Reform: A Modern Bill of Rights'.[82] This appeared to ignore both the evidence submitted to the IHRAR and the IHRAR's conclusions. The vast number of responses to this consultation disagreed with the proposals set out by the government, but these responses also appear to have been largely ignored and the government's subsequently published the Bill of Rights Bill essentially reflected the government's original intentions.[83]

1.64   According to the government the Bill would have 'continue[d] to give effect to the same rights and freedoms—the Convention rights—drawn from the European Convention on Human Rights ("the Convention")'. The government's stated intentions were to ensure that human rights are not interpreted 'over-expansively', to increase 'democratic oversight of human rights issues', to add a new hurdle for claimants to overcome (a permission stage for human rights claims), limit the Bill's extraterritorial application, give greater weight to 'public protection' in the interpretation of rights, and, of the greatest political importance for the government, to ensure that rights cannot prevent the deportation of foreign criminals.[84]

1.65   However, others, including former Supreme Court Justices, the Law Society, and the authors of this book, are more critical of both the detailed content of the Bill and the overall intention of the government, taking the view that overall the Bill of Rights Bill failed to provide a workable 'basic scheme for converting the Convention rights into rights in UK law' and would have unjustifiably eroded the level of protection of fundamental rights, significantly weakened the ability to enforce these rights through the courts, placed the UK in breach of its international law obligations under the Convention, and heralded both a decline in the influence of UK courts on the case law of the ECtHR and a significant increase in adverse rulings against the UK.[85]

1.66   The Bill of Rights Bill never received a Second Reading in Parliament. Its main proponent, the Secretary of State for Justice, the Rt Hon Dominic Raab, resigned for unrelated reasons and the government subsequently announced that the Bill would not be taken forward. However, it is possible that, should the Conservative Party be re-elected to government, some of the proposals in the Bill of Rights Bill may be revived. As such, a brief description of its key provisions is provided below,

---

[82] <https://www.gov.uk/government/consultations/human-rights-act-reform-a-modern-bill-of-rights>.

[83] <https://bills.parliament.uk/bills/3227>.

[84] Bill of Rights Bill: Explanatory Notes <https://publications.parliament.uk/pa/bills/cbill/58-03/0117/en/220117en.pdf>.

[85] Annual Human Rights Lecture 2022, by Lady Hale, previous President of the Supreme Court, Northern Ireland Human Rights Commission <https://nihrc.org/news/detail/annual-human-rights-lecture-2022-lady-hales-keynote-address-in-full>; the Law Society of England and Wales, 8 November 2022 <https://www.lawsociety.org.uk/topics/human-rights/human-rights-act-reforms>. See also the critical assessment by Lord Mance: 'Its provisions mix the polemical or political with the substantive. Substantively, it was designed, first, to open up potential water or space between Strasbourg and UK jurisprudence and, secondly, to mould the approach of UK courts and the resulting jurisprudence in a manner viewed by more acceptable to those proposing the bill ... ' <https://www.scribd.com/document/603723617/The-Protection-of-Rights-this-way-that-way-forwards-backwards#>.

accompanied by reference to the incisive assessment of the JCHR regarding the effect of these provisions, with which we concur:[86]

- The Bill would have required the domestic courts to focus on the original text of the Convention rather than on the subsequent case law of the ECtHR. The JCHR warned that this would mean ignoring 'the many social changes that have taken place over the past 70 years. It would encourage divergence between UK courts and the ECtHR, putting at risk the positive judicial dialogue between them and the respect that the Strasbourg court pays to UK decisions ... '

- The Bill would have prohibited the domestic courts from applying any new positive obligations adopted by the ECtHR following enactment of the Bill (post-commencement interpretations) and would moreover have required the courts, in deciding whether to apply an *existing* positive obligation (pre-commencement interpretations), to give 'great weight to the need to avoid adopting an interpretation of Convention rights that would result in certain consequences for local authorities that the Government sees as too onerous.' The JCHR described the suggestion that positive obligations can be severed from negative obligations and either ignored or applied in a restricted manner as 'simply untenable' given that they are core to the protection of Convention rights' and advised that this would almost certainly result in more adverse ECtHR judgments against the UK.

- The Bill proposed to remove the obligation in section 3 of the Human Rights Act to read legislation compatibly with Convention rights. As the JCHR pointed out, this 'risk[ed] undermining years of settled case law by restoring incompatible legislation'. While there was provision in the Bill giving the Secretary of State a secondary legislative power to preserve judgments made in reliance on section 3 by making regulations within two years, the JCHR did not regard it as 'possible to identify all such judgments' and assessed such a wide regulation-making power as constitutionally inappropriate.

- The Bill would have created additional hurdles before a human rights claim could proceed in the courts including a requirement for Court permission and for a claimant to demonstrate that they have suffered 'significant disadvantage'. The JCHR was of the view that these proposals would 'prevent meritorious claims being heard' and were 'inconsistent with the UK's obligations under the ECHR and undermine the primary role that domestic courts play in enforcing Convention rights'.

- The Bill would have created a statutory a duty on the courts to assume that Parliament, in making laws, had carried out the proportionality balancing exercise required under qualified Convention rights. As the JCHR explained, this would have meant that the courts must accept that Parliament had, in every case, 'struck the right balance between competing rights or policy aims—even if those haven't been considered, and then to give "the greatest possible weight" to the principle that it is for Parliament (not the courts) to strike that balance'.

---

[86] Legislative Scrutiny: Bill of Rights Bill, 17 January 2023.

This risked 'inhibiting the Courts' ability to protect rights in accordance with the ECHR' and again increased the likelihood of adverse ECtHR judgments against the UK.

1.67 The Bill contained various additional reforms to current human rights protections. The Bill omitted the current requirement for a minister to make a statement on the compatibility of all government Bills with Convention Rights,[87] which the JCHR advised would have hindered Parliament's ability to make a proper human rights assessment; it would have restricted entitlement to compensation following a finding of a violation of a Convention right in manner likely to undermine victims' right to an effective remedy; it would have paved the way for future legislation to limit the extraterritorial application of the Convention which, absent amendment to the Convention itself, would have undermined the responsibility of the UK state to protect people from violations of the Convention and led to an increase in adverse ECtHR judgments; and it would have prevented the domestic courts from taking into account interim measures from the ECtHR thereby potentially further putting the UK in breach of its international obligations.

3. Piecemeal erosion of the Human Rights Act?

1.68 Members of the current Conservative government have not ruled out going further in eroding rights and have recently resurrected the proposal that the UK should withdraw from the ECHR itself, in particular if the Supreme Court or ECtHR were to rule against the government's proposals to remove asylum seekers to Rwanda.[88]

1.69 In the meantime, entitlements previously provided by the Human Rights Act are being disapplied by new legislation in particular legislative contexts.

1.70 In July 2023, the Illegal Migration Act obtained Royal Assent.[89] The purpose of the Act is stated to be 'to prevent and deter unlawful migration, and in particular migration by unsafe and illegal routes, by requiring the removal from the United Kingdom of certain persons who enter or arrive in the United Kingdom in breach of immigration control'.[90]

1.71 The Act creates a new legal duty for the Secretary of State to make arrangements for the removal of people who enter the UK illegally. The Act also renders the asylum claims of those to whom its central regime applies, as well as human rights claims challenging the lawfulness of return to their country of origin, automatically and mandatorily inadmissible; expands the powers of the Secretary of State to

---

[87] Section 19.

[88] See the evidence to the Joint Human Rights Committee by the Secretary of State for Justice, 14 December 2022 and comments by the Home Secretary—see the *Guardian* <https://www.theguardian.com/commentisfree/2022/dec/08/suella-braverman-human-rights-undermines-rishi-sunak>.

[89] One of the Prime Minister's five pledges for his government included the following 'We will pass new laws to stop small boats, making sure that if you come to this country illegally, you are detained and swiftly removed', 4 January 2023.

[90] Section 1(1).

remove them to a third country; and dramatically limits their ability to challenge this type of removal, including in reliance on the Human Rights Act.

The Bill's explanatory notes state that the government is satisfied that the Bill's provisions are capable of being applied compatibly with Convention rights.[91] However, before the Second Reading of the Bill the Home Secretary made a statement under section 19(1)(b) of the Human Rights Act confirming that she was unable to say that in her view its provisions were compatible with the Convention rights, but that the government nevertheless wished to proceed with the Bill. The government's ECHR memorandum subsequently acknowledged that the approach taken in relation to modern slavery in particular was 'radical' and 'new and ambitious'.[92] **1.72**

This introductory chapter is not the place to analyse the provisions of the Illegal Migration Act in detail, but the issues which particularly impinge on the universal application of the Human Rights Act include: **1.73**

- Section 1(5) of the Act, which states that section 3 of the Human Rights Act (the interpretation provision) does not apply to provision made by or by virtue of the Act.

- Section 13, which seeks to oust the supervisory jurisdiction of the courts in respect of the lawfulness of a person's immigration detention for the first 28 days.

- Sections 22–25, which disapply existing protections for victims of modern slavery for many of those to whom the Act's central regime applies.

- Sections 5 and 38–54, which dramatically limit the ability of those to whom the central regime applies to prevent or suspend their removal to a third country on the basis that this would breach their Convention rights. In particular, these provisions limit automatically suspensive claims to those which fall within a new and narrow statutory regime; defer determination of a conventional human rights claim until after removal; and seek to prevent courts and tribunals from granting any interim remedy which prevents or delays removal (even, implicitly, on the basis that it would be unlawful under s 6 of the Human Rights Act).

- Section 55, which provides that where the ECtHR has indicated interim measures in relation to a person's removal, a minister may decide to disapply the duty to make removal arrangements; but, if they decline to do so, the Secretary of State, immigration officers, and the courts and tribunals must disregard the existence of those measures (see paras xx Insert cross-reference to passages covering interim measures).

The UN High Commissioner for Human Rights, Volker Türk and UN High Commissioner for Refugees, Filippo Grandi have commented that: **1.74**

The Illegal Migration Bill, which has now been passed by Parliament in the United Kingdom, is at variance with the country's obligations under international human rights and refugee law and will have profound consequences for people in need of international protection.

---

[91] Illegal Migration Bill Explanatory Notes, 7 March 2023, 39.
[92] Illegal Migration Bill European Convention on Human Rights Memorandum, 7 March 2023 and Supplementary Memorandum, 23 April 2023.

The Bill extinguishes access to asylum in the UK for anyone who arrives irregularly, having passed through a country—however briefly—where they did not face persecution. It bars them from presenting refugee protection or other human rights claims, no matter how compelling their circumstances. In addition, it requires their removal to another country, with no guarantee that they will necessarily be able to access protection there. It creates sweeping new detention powers, with limited judicial oversight.[93]

1.75   At the time of writing the Victims and Prisoners Bill also threatens to erode the universal approach of the Human Rights Act. Clauses 42, 43, and 44 would disapply section 3 of the Human Rights Act in relation to release, licences, supervision, and recall of indeterminate and determinate sentenced offenders. According to the government's Explanatory Notes on the clauses in the Bill:

By removing this duty in respect of the release legislation, it ensures that, should the courts—or others—find these provisions incompatible, they will apply the section as it is intended to be applied, and not use section 3 to alter the interpretation. In such cases, declarations of incompatibility under section 4 HRA will be available ...

When considering such a challenge the court must give the greatest possible weight to the importance of reducing the risk to the public from those persons who have been convicted of a criminal offence. Requiring the courts to give the greatest possible weight to this factor reinforces the precautionary approach and means that public protection will be given appropriate consideration in any balancing exercise.[94]

G. CONCLUSION

1.76   The journey to ensure the protection of human rights in the UK has been a long one. For most, it would start in England in the thirteenth century with the Magna Carta, through the 1669 Bill of Rights, habeas corpus in 1679, the creation of the United Nations and the 1948 Universal Declaration of Human Rights—the beginning of the modern age. The European Convention on Human Rights and ratification by the UK in 1953 was, largely, seen as merely symbolic by politicians (except for the outrageous treatment of people in the 'Colonies').[95]

1.77   The key steps towards realizing meaningful rights protection were the UK's acceptance of the right of individual petition to the European Court of Human Rights in 1966 and then the policy of 'Bringing Rights Home' in 1997, followed by the enactment of the Human Rights Act in 1998 in an elegant and delicate constitutional settlement where the role of protecting rights is shared between the arms of the state, whilst maintaining the UK's traditional commitment to parliamentary sovereignty. Unfortunately, despite this, it has since been a continuing struggle not to move backwards with a series of political critiques, commitments,

---

[93] 18 July 2023.
[94] At 44.
[95] See the definitive and fascinating account by AW Brian Simpson, *Human Rights and the End of Empire: Britain and the Genesis of the European Convention* (OUP 2001).

reviews, and legislative initiatives threatening to weaken or altogether remove international and domestic rights protections. The course charted domestically by recent legislation—apparently enacted in the knowledge that it contravenes the UK's international law obligations under the Convention—sets the UK on a collision course with the European Court and the Council of Europe Committee of Ministers, absent withdrawal from the Convention itself. How this will be resolved politically and legally remains to be seen, though it bears noting that resolutions to past conflicts and standoffs have been found. We therefore remain hopeful. As Martin Luther King, Jr reminded us, 'the arc of the moral universe is long, but it bends toward justice'.

2

THE FRAMEWORK OF THE
EUROPEAN CONVENTION
ON HUMAN RIGHTS

A. INTRODUCTION

The European Convention for the Protection of Human Rights and Fundamental **2.01**
Freedoms (Convention) is an international human rights treaty agreed by states
that are members of the Council of Europe. The Council of Europe was established
in 1949 as part of the Allies' programme to 'reconstruct durable civilization on the
mainland of Europe'.[1] Today it has 46 members with a wide variety of political

---

[1] *Rights Brought Home: The Human Rights Bill* (Cm 3782, 1997) para 1.1.

Blackstone's Guide to The Human Rights Act 1998. Eighth Edition. John Wadham, Helen Mountfield KC, Raj Desai, Sarah Hannett KC,
Jessica Jones, Eleanor Mitchell, and Aidan Wills, Oxford University Press. © John Wadham, Helen Mountfield KC, Raj Desai,
Sarah Hannett KC, Jessica Jones, Eleanor Mitchell, and Aidan Wills 2024. DOI: 10.1093/oso/9780192885050.003.0002

traditions, including many former Communist states from Eastern Europe.[2] The Convention came into force on 3 September 1953.

2.02   The rights guaranteed by the Convention are modelled on those contained in the United Nations (UN) Universal Declaration of Human Rights (UDHR, 1948), but the content of the rights and qualifications to them are more specific, reflecting the states' intention that the rights be legally enforceable. The Convention was then followed by the UN's International Covenant on Civil and Political Rights (ICCPR) although some of the rights in the latter are more extensive and were subsequently picked up by the Council of Europe in Protocols 4, 7, and 12 to the Convention, none of which have been ratified by the United Kingdom (UK). The Convention's provisions are mostly civil and political in nature (with the notable exceptions of the right to property and the right to education in Protocol 1). However, the interpretation of Convention rights may extend into the sphere of social and economic rights[3] in order to 'safeguard the individual in a real and practical way'.[4] As well as allowing states to bring proceedings against one another, individuals are able to enforce their Convention rights against states that have accepted the right of 'individual petition'.

2.03   The UK ratified the Convention in 1951 but, unlike many of the other signatories, did not set about incorporating the Convention rights into domestic law. Incorporation was thought to be unnecessary, as it was believed that the rights safeguarded by the Convention already flowed from English common law.

2.04   In 1966, the UK accepted the right of individual petition. This has meant that, even before its incorporation into domestic law, the Convention offered individual litigants in Britain the possibility of redress in international law where their civil liberties had been infringed by the state, and where no adequate remedy could be provided by the domestic courts. (It is important to appreciate that, as a matter of international law, the Convention creates rights against states, not against private individuals.)

2.05   The Convention originally established three bodies to monitor human rights within the countries that had ratified it: the European Commission of Human Rights (ECmHR),[5] the European Court of Human Rights (ECtHR),[6] and the Committee of Ministers. All three were based in Strasbourg. Until November 1998, the ECmHR and the ECtHR heard complaints from individuals about violations of their rights. The ECmHR exercised a 'screening' function, and could refer cases to the ECtHR for a final determination. From November 1998 a one-tier system was introduced in which all cases are dealt with by different chambers of the ECtHR itself. Decisions of the ECtHR are binding on the country concerned.[7]

---

[2] Following the invasion of Ukraine by Russia the Council of Europe expelled Russia on 15 March 2022.
[3] See eg *Sidabras v Lithuania* App No 55480/00, 1 July 2003; *R (Limbuela) v Secretary of State for the Home Department* [2005] UKHL 66, [2006] 1 AC 396.
[4] *Airey v Ireland* (1979) 2 EHRR 305, para 26.
[5] Established in 1954.
[6] Established in 1959.
[7] Note that Protocol 14 to the Convention empowers the Committee of Ministers to ask the ECtHR to interpret a final judgment if it encounters difficulties in doing so when supervising its execution. In order to further the aim of rapid execution of judgments, Protocol 14 also allows the Committee of Ministers

The Convention is unlike a UK statute. Its broad provisions cannot be interpreted   2.06
according to the traditional English 'black-letter' approach that closely defines the
scope and content of a power. The ECtHR, and latterly the UK courts under the
Human Rights Act 1998, have developed a sophisticated jurisprudence built upon
underlying principles and interpretative techniques which 'flesh out' the scope of
the rights to give them meaning in the context of individual cases. The domestic
approach to the principles discussed below is considered in Chapter 4.

B. INTERPRETING THE CONVENTION

The interpretative principles set out below should not be treated in isolation, with   2.07
one given more importance than another—they are part of a single, complex juris-
prudential exercise to ensure that the 'object and purpose' of the Convention are
fulfilled.

1. 'Object and purpose'

The Convention is an international treaty and as such should be interpreted in   2.08
accordance with Articles 31–33 of the Vienna Convention on the Law of Treaties
1969 (Vienna Convention). Article 31(1) states:

A treaty shall be interpreted in good faith in accordance with the ordinary meaning to be given
to the terms of the treaty in their context and in light of its object and purpose.[8]

The Convention is intended to be interpreted purposively, that is, to give effect   2.09
to its central purposes. The text, Preamble, annexes, and related agreements and
instruments of the contracting states are relevant to determining what these are.[9]
The ECtHR has held that the 'objects and purpose' of the Convention include:

(a) the 'maintenance and further realization of human rights and fundamental
    freedoms'[10] and the 'protection of individual human rights'.[11] The effective pro-
    tection of the rights of the individual has been described by the ECtHR as the
    'overriding function of this Convention';[12]

(b) the promotion of the ideals and values of a democratic society,[13] which supposes
    'pluralism, tolerance and broadmindedness'[14] so as to achieve a balance between

---

to decide, in exceptional circumstances and with a two-thirds majority, to initiate proceedings of non-
compliance in the Grand Chamber of the ECtHR in order to make the state concerned execute the Court's
initial judgment.

[8] See also Vienna Convention, art 33(4).
[9] Vienna Convention, art 31(2).
[10] Preamble to the Convention.
[11] *Soering v UK* (1989) 11 EHRR 439.
[12] *Austria v Italy* (1961) 4 YB 116, para 138.
[13] *Kjeldsen, Busk Madsen and Pedersen v Denmark* (1979) 1 EHRR 711.
[14] *Handyside v UK* (1976) 1 EHRR 737.

individual and group interests which 'ensures the fair and proper treatment of minorities and avoids any abuse of a dominant position';[15]

(c) the rule of law.[16]

2.10   As the essence of the Convention is to protect the fundamental rights of persons from violation by contracting parties, limitations or qualifications of the rights set out in the Convention are to be narrowly construed.[17] The ECtHR will try to:

seek the interpretation that is most appropriate in order to realize the aim and achieve the object of the treaty; not that which would restrict to the greatest possible degree the obligations undertaken by the parties.[18]

2. Effectiveness principle

2.11   The Convention is intended to guarantee rights that are not merely 'theoretical and illusory' but 'practical and effective'.[19] The ECtHR is concerned with the reality of the individual's position and will 'look behind appearances and examine the realities of the procedure in question'.[20]

2.12   In order for some rights to provide 'effective' protection in accordance with the 'object and purpose' of the Convention, it may be necessary to read an element into a right that is not expressly provided for. An example of reading in these 'implied rights' can be found in the ECtHR's interpretation of Article 6 in *Golder v UK*.[21] In that case a prisoner complained that he could not get to court at all—a right not expressly contained in the text of Article 6. The ECtHR considered that to interpret Article 6 as merely providing procedural guarantees in the course of existing proceedings would enable contracting parties to remove the jurisdiction of the courts in relation to certain claims and thus undermine the protection of the right. To correct this, the ECtHR held that the right of access to the courts constituted 'an element which is inherent in the right stated by Article 6(1)'.[22]

2.13   The ECtHR has also recognized that in order to secure truly effective protection, certain rights must be read as imposing obligations on the state to take action to ensure that they are protected. This doctrine of positive obligations is considered more fully at paragraphs 2.33 to 2.38.

---

[15] *Young, James and Webster v UK* (1982) 4 EHRR 38.

[16] Preamble to the Convention; *Golder v UK* (1979) 1 EHRR 524, para 35; *Klass v Germany* (1978) 2 EHRR 379, para 55; *Salabiaku v France* (1988) 13 EHRR 379, para 28; *Gorraiz Lizarraga v Spain* App No 62543/00, 10 November 2004, para 64.

[17] *Sunday Times v UK (No 1)* (1979) 2 EHRR 245, para 65.

[18] *Wemhoff v Germany* (1968) 1 EHRR 55, para 8.

[19] *Marckx v Belgium* (1979) 2 EHRR 330, para 31; *Artico v Italy* (1981) 3 EHRR 1, para 33.

[20] *Deweer v Belgium* (1980) 2 EHRR 439.

[21] *Golder v UK* (1979) 1 EHRR 524.

[22] ibid para 35.

3. Autonomous concepts

Some specific Convention terms are 'autonomous', in the sense of having a particu- 2.14
lar meaning defined by the ECtHR, and the concepts they contain may go beyond
their ordinary or domestic meaning. This is necessary both so that there is uniformity of meaning and understanding across the different national legal systems of
the parties to the Convention, and to protect human rights from the possibility of
being undermined by manipulation of terms by contracting states.

Examples of these autonomous concepts include the free-standing definitions of 2.15
'criminal charge' and 'civil rights and obligations' under Article 6. The ECtHR has
created its own classification criteria for these concepts. These criteria are not solely
dependent on the classification determined by the domestic law of the respondent country. Without this 'autonomous concepts' doctrine a state could, without
breaching Article 6, exercise arbitrary power and act in a manner repugnant to
the rule of law: it could 'do away with its courts, or take away their jurisdiction
to determine certain classes of civil actions and entrust to it organs dependent
on the Government'.[23] Other concepts, such as 'private life' and 'family life', have
developed incrementally since 1950 to ensure that the protection offered by the
Convention is 'effective'. Further consideration of these terms is found in Chapter 5.

The 'autonomous concepts' doctrine has become important in English law, some- 2.16
times ensuring that UK domestic courts avoid an artificial approach to the interpretation of a Convention article.[24] However, the 'autonomous concepts' doctrine
has also been used to prevent the Human Rights Act from becoming a mechanism
for a more expansive interpretation of the scope of Convention rights than that
afforded by the Strasbourg organs.[25]

4. Dynamic interpretation

The Convention is not to be interpreted as it would have been by those who drafted 2.17
it 60 years ago. It is a 'living instrument which must be interpreted in the light of
present-day conditions'.[26] As such its meaning will develop over time and new case
law will develop in an organic way without old case law being specifically overruled.
Thus, when an English court is considering the meaning and effect of a judgment
by the ECtHR, it must nevertheless interpret the Convention by the standards of
society today, and not those when the Convention was drafted or even when older
cases were decided.

---

[23] ibid; cited by Lord Hoffmann in *Runa Begum v Tower Hamlets* [2003] UKHL 5, [2003] 2 AC 430, para 29.
[24] See eg *Han v Commissioners of Customs and Excise; Martins v Commissioners of Customs and Excise* [2001] EWCA Civ 1040, [2001] 4 All ER 687.
[25] *Secretary of State for Work and Pensions v M* [2006] UKHL 11, [2006] 2 AC 91 (though note that the ECtHR subsequently disagreed with the House of Lords on what the ambit of art 1 of Protocol 1 and art 8 were in *JM v UK* App No 37060/06, 28 September 2010); *R v Briggs-Price* [2009] UKHL 19, [2009] 1 WLR 1101. See, to the same effect, *R (A) v London Borough of Croydon* [2009] UKSC 8, [2009] 1 WLR 2557, para 64.
[26] *Tyrer v UK* (1978) 2 EHRR 1, para 31; *Johnson v Ireland* (1986) 9 EHRR 203, para 53.

2.18   The case law surrounding the Article 8 rights of trans people provides a good example of the 'growth' of the Convention to accommodate changing social attitudes. In *Rees v UK*[27] the ECtHR considered that the rule that a trans person could not alter their birth certificate to reflect their gender reassignment did not, by the standards of the mid-1980s, contravene Article 8. But it was conscious of the seriousness of the problems and distress faced by people in that situation and stated:

> The Convention has always to be interpreted and applied in the light of the current circumstances. The need for appropriate legal measures should therefore be kept under review having regard particularly to the scientific and societal developments.[28]

2.19   Having followed its decision in *Rees* in a number of cases,[29] the ECtHR changed tack in *Goodwin v UK*[30] and held that in present conditions, the lack of legal recognition of the applicant's new gender did result in a violation of Article 8. The ECtHR stated that:

> It is of crucial importance that the Convention is interpreted and applied in a manner which renders its rights practical and effective, not theoretical and illusory. A failure by the Court to maintain a dynamic and evolutive approach would indeed risk rendering it a bar to reform or improvement.[31]

There are, however, limits to the extent to which the ECtHR is willing to interpret the Convention in the light of changing social attitudes. In *Schalk and Kopf v Austria*,[32] for instance, the ECtHR refused to accept that Article 12 protected the right to same-sex marriage, however the right to have the relationship recognized officially has been accepted.[33]

5. Recourse to other human rights instruments

2.20   In interpreting the Convention, the ECtHR is required by the Vienna Convention on the Interpretation of Treaties to take account of 'any relevant rules of international law applicable in the relations between the parties'.[34] The ECtHR has regularly cited the Vienna Convention, holding that the Convention 'cannot be interpreted in a vacuum' and 'should, so far as possible be interpreted in harmony with other rules of international law of which it forms part'.[35] Council of Europe instruments such as Conventions and Resolutions of the Parliamentary Assembly, the European Social Charter, and separate European Union (EU) materials may be relevant (including the Charter of Fundamental Rights of the European Union). In

---

[27] *Rees v UK* (1987) 9 EHRR 56.
[28] ibid para 47.
[29] See eg *Cossey v UK* (1990) 13 EHRR 622; *Sheffield and Horsham v UK* (1999) 27 EHRR 163.
[30] *Goodwin v UK* (2002) 35 EHRR 18.
[31] ibid para 74.
[32] *Schalk and Kopf v Austria* App No 30141/04, 24 June 2010.
[33] *Oliari and others v Italy* App No 18766/11, 21 July 2015
[34] Vienna Convention, art 31(3)(c).
[35] *Al-Adsani v UK* (2001) 34 EHRR 273, para 55; *Al-Saadoon and Mufdhi v UK* App No 61498/08, 2 March 2010, para 126.

addition, UN human rights instruments such as the ICCPR, the Convention on the Elimination of all Forms of Racial Discrimination (CERD), the Convention on the Rights of the Child (UNCRC), and other standards and 'general comments' from the human rights bodies of the UN have been used to help determine the scope of fundamental human rights.[36]

Indeed, the ECtHR now regards recourse to other international law as a manda- 2.21
tory interpretative tool for the proper construction of the ECHR—in particular when considering the definition and scope of discrimination. In *Demir & Baykara v Turkey*[37] the Grand Chamber held that:

in defining the meaning of terms and notions in the text of the Convention, [it] *can and must* take into account elements of international law other than the Convention, the interpretation of such elements by competent organs, and the practice of European States reflecting their common values.

Likewise, in *Opuz v Turkey*,[38] the Court concluded that 'when considering the definition and scope of discrimination against women, in addition to the more general meaning of discrimination as determined in its case-law ... the Court *has to have regard to* the provisions of more specialised legal instruments and the decisions of international legal bodies on the question of violence against women' (emphasis added).

Thus, there are now many examples of use by the ECtHR of relevant interna- 2.22
tional law rules when interpreting the Convention. For example, in *Demir*, the Court took into account the jurisprudence arising under International Labour Organization (ILO) Conventions and the European Social Charter to determine the scope of freedom of association under Article 11 of the Convention, overruling its previous holdings that the right to bargain collectively and to enter into collective agreements did not constitute an inherent element of Article 11. In *Opuz*, it cited the UN Convention on the Elimination of Discrimination Against Women (CEDAW), among other instruments, to create a positive obligation to protect women against foreseeable violence. Similarly on race the Court has used the International Convention on the Elimination of All Forms of Racial Discrimination for interpretation purposes.[39]

In *T and V v UK*,[40] the ECtHR relied in part on the UNCRC and the Standard 2.23
Minimum Rules for the Administration of Juvenile Justice ('Beijing Rules') to find that the UK's procedures for trying children charged with serious crimes did not enable the defendants to participate fully and effectively in the trial process and so violated their Article 6 rights to a fair trial. Similarly, in *S and Marper v UK*, the ECtHR drew on the UNCRC in condemning the indefinite retention of

---

[36] See eg *Sejdic and Finci v Bosnia and Herzegovina* 28 BHRC 201 [GC], paras 19 and 43.
[37] *Demir & Baykara v Turkey* (2009) 48 EHRR 54, para 85.
[38] *Opuz v Turkey* (2010) 50 EHRR 28, para 185. See too *Eremia v Moldova* [2014] 58 EHRR 2.
[39] *Timishev v Russia* App No 55762/00, 13 December 2005; *Sejdic and Finci v Bosnia and Herzegovina* 28 BHRC 201 [GC].
[40] *T and V UK* (2000) 30 EHRR 121.

children's DNA on the UK police database.[41] The ECtHR also regularly cites the EU Charter of Fundamental Rights.[42] The Court has also taken into account the UN Convention on the Rights of Persons with Disabilities (CRPD) into account when considering local authority social care provision in *Macdonald v UK*.[43] The CPRD was also referred to in other cases, for instance, in the cases of *Glor v Switzerland*,[44] *Gl v Italy*,[45] *Arnar Helgi Larusson v Iceland*,[46] and *Cam v Turkey*.[47]

6. Jurisdiction

2.24   The basis for the jurisdictional scope of the Convention is found in Article 1, which provides that states 'shall secure to everyone within their jurisdiction the rights and freedoms defined in Section 1 of this Convention'. The meaning of the phrase 'within their jurisdiction' has been considered by the Grand Chamber of the ECtHR in the leading cases of *Bankovic v Belgium and others*,[48] and *Al-Skeini v UK*.[49] The Court considered that jurisdiction should be interpreted in accordance with the principles of public international law, which holds that states are ordinarily only responsible for acts and omissions in their national territory. However, it accepted that there were certain, limited situations in which a state may be responsible for acts or omissions occurring outside its territory. For instance, where a contracting state, through its agents, exercises control and authority over an individual.[50] Secondly, where one contracting state is occupied by the armed forces of another: the occupying state should be held accountable for breaches of human rights within the occupied territory, for otherwise there would be a 'vacuum' of protection within the 'Convention legal space'. The third situation, confirmed to exist in *Al-Skeini*, concerns acts carried out in the territory of a non-contracting state which is under the 'effective control' of a contracting state as a consequence of military action. In *Al-Skeini*, the Court held that the Convention was engaged in relation to the killing of Iraqi citizens by UK army personnel in security operations near Basra, which was part of Iraq over which the UK had assumed responsibility for the maintenance of security following the removal from power of the Ba'ath regime.[51]

---

[41] *S and Marper v UK* (2008) 25 BHRC 557, para 124. For an example of the domestic courts referring to the UNCRC, see *R (Williamson) v Secretary of State for Education and Employment* [2005] UKHL 15, [2005] 2 AC 246, para 80 per Baroness Hale.

[42] See eg *Schalk and Kopf v Austria* App No 30141/04, 24 June 2010.

[43] *Macdonald v UK* App No 4241/12, 20 May 2014. See also use of the CRDP in *Kiyutin v Russia* [2011] 53 EHRR 26; *Seal v UK* [2012] 54 EHRR 6; and *Kiss v Hungary* [2013] 56 EHRR 38.

[44] *Glor v Switzerland* App No 13444/04, 30 April 2004, para 53.

[45] (2009) App No 13444, para 62.

[46] *Arnar Helgi Larusson v Iceland* App No 20377/19, 31 May 2022, para 59.

[47] *Cam v Turkey* App No 51500/08, 23 February 2016, para 67.

[48] *Bankovic v Belgium and others* (2007) 44 EHRR SE5.

[49] *Al-Skeini v UK* (2011) 30 BHRC 561.

[50] See eg *Soering v UK* (1989) 11 EHRR 439.

[51] *Al-Skeini v UK* (2011) 30 BHRC 561, para 149.

Notably, Article 1 is not incorporated into English law under the Human Rights Act, though the approach to the extra-territorial application of the Human Rights Act is informed by the principles which arise under Article 1. This is considered further in Chapter 4[52] and Chapter 5.[53]

2.25

C. THE SCOPE OF CONVENTION RIGHTS

1. Absolute, limited, and qualified rights

In broad terms, Convention rights may be placed into three categories: 'absolute' rights capable of no derogation; rights which are expressly or impliedly limited; and rights which are expressly qualified. This is not a precise taxonomy but a way of understanding the nature and structure of the Convention rights.

2.26

(a) *Absolute rights*

Absolute rights under the Convention include the right to life under Article 2 (except in respect of deaths resulting from lawful acts of war), the prohibition on torture under Article 3, the prohibition on slavery and servitude under Article 4(1), and the right not to be subjected to retrospective criminal offences under Article 7(1).[54] No derogations from these articles are permitted under Article 15 and there are no circumstances in which infringements of these rights can be justified in the public interest.

2.27

The power of absolute rights was illustrated in *Chahal v UK* in which the ECtHR was asked to consider the UK's attempt to expel a suspected Sikh terrorist despite the real risk of his being subjected to torture in the receiving country.[55] The ECtHR held that, despite the national security threat allegedly posed by the applicant, 'the Convention prohibits in absolute terms torture or inhuman or degrading treatment or punishment irrespective of the victim's conduct'.[56] If a claimant can prove on the balance of probabilities that the state has acted in violation of an absolute right, the state is not entitled to mount a justification of its conduct. This principle has come under sustained attack from the British government (and the tabloid press). The government intervened in *Saadi v Italy* to attempt to change the ECtHR's view of absolute rights, but the ECtHR reiterated the traditional principles in forceful terms.[57]

2.28

---

[52] See Chapter 4, para 4.105.
[53] See Chapter 5, para 5.05.
[54] The right to hold a religion or belief under art 9(1) is sometimes considered absolute, but art 9 can be derogated from under art 15. See Chapter 7, para 7.547.
[55] *Chahal v UK* (1997) 23 EHRR 413.
[56] ibid para 78.
[57] *Saadi v Italy* (2008) 24 BHRC 123.

(b) *Limited rights*

2.29 Limited rights include Article 5 (right to liberty and security of the person), Article 6 (fair trial rights), Article 12 (right to marry and found a family), Protocol 1, Article 2 (right to an education), and Protocol 1, Article 3 (right to free elections). These rights can be restricted in explicit and finite circumstances as set out in the article itself, or may be subject to restrictions implied by the ECtHR.[58]

2.30 Restrictions have been implied into the right to education under Article 2 of Protocol 1[59] and into fair trial rights (in addition to the express limitations set out in art 6).[60] However, any limitations are to be construed narrowly, as a wide interpretation 'would entail consequences incompatible with the notion of the rule of law from which the whole Convention draws its inspiration'.[61] In *Ashingdane v UK* the ECtHR held that the right of access to the Court may be subject to restrictions, but that any limitation 'will not be compatible with Article 6(1) if it does not pursue a legitimate aim and if there is not a reasonable relationship of proportionality between the means employed and the aim sought to be achieved'.[62] Thus, implied restrictions will be subject to the general principles applicable to the qualified rights (discussed at para 2.41).

(c) *Qualified rights*

2.31 The 'qualified rights' are largely those that include a general qualification provision in the second paragraph of the article. They are the rights that most obviously raise conflicts with the overall interests of society or the rights of others—for example, the right to respect for private life (art 8), freedom of thought, conscience, and religion (art 9), freedom of expression (art 10), freedom of assembly and association (art 11), and the right to the enjoyment of possessions (Protocol 1, art 1).

2.32 'Qualified rights' are usually set out in two parts in the text of the Convention. The first paragraph of the article sets out the substantive right, which is then qualified in the second paragraph. The precise terms of the limitations vary (contrast, eg, art 10(2) with art 8(2)), but a restriction will be compatible with the Convention only if it meets the general principles applicable to all restrictions on rights, namely it is 'in accordance with the law'; the interference is directed towards an identified legitimate aim; and the aim is 'necessary in a democratic society' (which encompasses the test of 'pressing social need' and proportionality). These general principles are considered in detail at paragraphs 2.40–2.68.

2. Positive obligations

2.33 The principal purpose of the Convention is to protect individual rights from infringement by states, and this is achieved by the imposition of so-called 'negative'

---

[58] See the discussion of the controversial 'inherent limitations' doctrine in Richard Clayton and Hugh Tomlinson, *The Law of Human Rights* (2nd edn, OUP 2009) 377–81.
[59] See eg *Sahin v Turkey* (2007) 44 EHRR 5, para 154.
[60] See eg *Golder v UK* (1975) 1 EHRR 524.
[61] *Engel v Netherlands* (1976) 1 EHRR 647, para 69.
[62] *Ashingdane v UK* (1985) 7 EHRR 528.

obligations on the states, which require them to refrain from interference with the rights in question. However, the wording of certain articles also imposes positive duties on the state, such as the obligation under Protocol 1, Article 3 to hold free elections. In addition to these express positive obligations, the ECtHR has recognized that, when combined with the general Article 1 duty, there is a broader need for positive steps to be taken by the state to provide the legal or institutional structures or resources to protect human rights—for example, to provide laws which prevent private parties from infringing individual rights, to provide proper institutional protection from domestic violence, or to provide free legal assistance in criminal cases under Article 6(3)(c), or to enable access to institutions to provide education under Protocol 1, Article 2.

2.34   The ECtHR has expressly declined to develop any 'general theory' of positive obligations, and thus attempts to extract key principles from the jurisprudence of the ECtHR in order to locate positive obligations in a coherent legal framework have been subject to some controversy.[63] It is, however, accepted that the legal basis for reading the Convention in a way which imposes positive obligations is found in a combination of: the overarching duty on states in Article 1 'to secure to everyone within their jurisdiction' the rights and freedoms set out in the Convention; express wording in some articles (eg the right to life 'shall' be protected by law); the principle set out in Convention case law that protection of rights is intended to be 'practical and effective' not merely theoretical; and the right to an adequate remedy for arguable breaches of Convention rights under Article 13.

2.35   There are five main positive duties under the Convention:

(a) a duty to have in place a legal framework which provides effective protection for Convention rights;

(b) a duty to prevent breaches of Convention rights;

(c) a duty to provide information and advice relevant to a breach of Convention rights;

(d) a duty to respond to breaches of Convention rights; and

(e) a duty to provide resources to individuals to prevent breaches of their Convention rights.

2.36   The types of legal and administrative measures that the ECtHR has held are necessary to fulfil these duties vary according to the article in issue. For example, Article 2 provides that the right to life 'shall be protected by law', and this has been interpreted as an obligation on the state to:

secure the right to life by putting in place effective criminal law provisions to deter the commission of offences against the person, backed up by law enforcement machinery for the prevention, suppression and sanctioning of breaches of such provisions.[64]

---

[63] See Alastair R Mowbray, *The Development of Positive Obligations under the European Convention on Human Rights by the European Court of Human Rights* (Hart Publishing 2004) and Laurens Lavrysen, *Human Rights in a Positive State: Rethinking the Relationship between Positive and Negative Obligations under the European Convention on Human Rights* (Intersentia 2016).

[64] *Osman v UK* (2000) 29 EHRR 245.

Although the ECtHR varies in the extent of the measures it will hold necessary to comply with its positive protective obligations, it is still accurate to say that not only is the state required to adopt an adequate system of law to deter and punish individuals guilty of violating the Convention rights of others, but it is also recognized that the police[65] and other relevant public bodies[66] can be under a positive obligation to take reasonable operational measures to prevent a violation of individuals' rights under Articles 2 and 3. The Court will hold that states are under a duty to protect vulnerable individuals from foreseeable third-party mistreatment. For example, in *CN v United Kingdom*,[67] the Court held that Article 4 required a positive obligation to have in place and enforce an adequate criminal law and investigative framework to protect people from being subjected to forced labour; and in *Eremia v Moldova*,[68] it held that failure properly to investigate or to support a complainant of domestic violence amounted to condoning the discriminatory attitudes which underlay it, contrary to Articles 3 and 14. In *KU v Finland*,[69] it reached a similar conclusion under Article 8 and, in *S v Sweden*,[70] the Court emphasized the need for a state to have a criminal law framework in place to protect individuals from violations of Convention standards by third parties.[71]

2.37   In cases under Article 8, the ECtHR recognizes that access to relevant information can help individuals to protect their Convention rights. In *Guerra v Italy*[72] the ECtHR established that, on the specific facts of the case, the respondent state was under a positive obligation to provide information to the applicants who lived near a 'high risk' chemical factory and were very likely to be adversely affected by environmental pollution. In *McGinley and Egan v UK*[73] the ECtHR held that when a government engages in hazardous activities, such as nuclear testing, which might have hidden adverse effects on the health of those involved, 'Article 8 requires that an effective and accessible procedure be established which enables persons to seek all relevant and appropriate information'.[74]

2.38   When determining whether or not a positive obligation exists, the ECtHR will have regard to 'the fair balance that has to be struck between the general interest of the community and the interests of the individual, the search for which balance is inherent in the whole of the Convention'.[75]

---

[65] ibid.
[66] See eg local authorities in *Z v UK* (2002) 34 EHRR 3.
[67] *CN v United Kingdom* [2013] 56 EHRR 24.
[68] *Eremia v Moldova* [2013] ECHR 3564/11.
[69] *KU v Finland* [2009] 48 EHRR 52.
[70] *S v Sweden* [2014] 58 EHRR 36.
[71] In relation to protecting women from domestic violence, see eg *Branko Tomašić and others v Croatia* App No 46598/06, 15 January 2009; *Opuz v Turkey* (2010) 50 EHRR 28; *Tkhelidze v Georgia* App No 72475/10, 2 September 2021; *A and B v Georgia* App No 73975/16, 10 February 2022.
[72] *Guerra v Italy* (1998) 26 EHRR 357.
[73] *McGinley and Egan v UK* (1999) 27 EHRR 1.
[74] ibid para 101. See also *Taskin v Turkey* (2006) 42 EHRR 50; *Fadeyeva v Russia* (2007) 45 EHRR 10; *Öneryildiz v Turkey* (2004) 18 BHRC 145.
[75] *Goodwin v UK* (2002) 35 EHRR 18.

A number of factors may have a bearing on the extent of any positive obli- 2.39
gation, including whether the right in question is broadly or narrowly defined;
whether essential aspects of a right are at issue; the extent of any burden that may
be imposed on the state; and the uniformity of views or practices in other contracting states.[76] However, one of the most important factors taken into consideration
by the ECtHR is the severity of the effect of the omission on the applicants' rights
(particularly their fundamental rights such as those protected by arts 2 and 3, or
their intimate rights such as those of 'private and family life' protected under art
8).[77] The more serious the effect, the more likely it is that the state will be obliged
to prevent or remedy it.

D. RESTRICTING CONVENTION RIGHTS

The Convention seeks to balance the rights of the individual against other public 2.40
interests, but the object of human rights jurisprudence in democratic systems is not
simple majoritarian rule. The rule of law is also required to ensure that democracy
does not mean that the tyranny of the majority causes disproportionate interference with the rights of minorities. Once a complaint has been shown to infringe
a limited or qualified right, the Strasbourg institutions consider the justification
advanced by the state in order to determine whether there has been a violation.

The Convention seeks to ensure that the limitations placed upon an individual's 2.41
protected rights, in the name of the common or competing interests, are imposed
only if they are:

(a) prescribed by law;

(b) intended to achieve a legitimate objective; and

(c) 'necessary in a democratic society' (which incorporates the vital requirement of
    proportionality).

These general principles apply specifically to qualified rights but are likely to govern
any restrictions on any right under the Convention.

1. Legality

The rule of law is at the heart of the Convention. It is described in the Preamble as 2.42
part of the 'common heritage' that the signatories share, and is one of the 'fundamental principles of a democratic society'.[78] No interference with a right protected
under the Convention is permissible unless the citizen is able to ascertain the legal

---

[76] See the discussion in Richard Clayton and Hugh Tomlinson, *The Law of Human Rights* (2nd edn,
OUP 2009) 364–69.

[77] *Mosley v United Kingdom* (2011) 53 EHRR 30; see also *Swift v Secretary of State for Justice* [2012]
EWHC 2000 (QB), para 27.

[78] *Iatridis v Greece* App No 31107/96, 25 March 1999, para 62. See also *R (Gillan) v Commissioner of the
Police for the Metropolis* [2006] UKHL 12, [2006] 2 AC 307, para 34.

basis for the interference. In the absence of such detailed authorization by the law, any interference, however justified, will violate the Convention. In Strasbourg jurisprudence, a derogation must also have an ascertainable legal basis.

2.43 The legal basis for a measure naturally includes statute law, but the ECtHR has ruled that secondary legislation,[79] applicable rules of EU law,[80] the common law,[81] and even rules of a professional body[82] may be sufficient if validly made and available to those bound by them.

2.44 In addition to being formally prescribed by law, the law itself must fulfil the substantive requirement that it have the appropriate 'qualities' to make it compatible with the rule of law.[83] The ECtHR explained this concept in *Sunday Times v UK (No 1)*:

> Firstly, the law must be adequately accessible: the citizens must be able to have an indication that is adequate in the circumstances of the legal rules applicable to a given case. Secondly, a norm cannot be regarded as a 'law' unless it is formulated with sufficient precision to enable the citizen to regulate his conduct.[84]

2.45 The accessibility rule is intended to counter arbitrary power by providing that a restriction cannot be justified, even if it is authorized in domestic law, unless the applicable law is published in a form accessible to those likely to be affected by it. Internal guidelines from government departments or agencies probably do not fulfil the accessibility requirement unless they are published or their content made known.[85]

2.46 The certainty rule is intended to enable individuals likely to be affected by a restriction on their rights to understand the circumstances in which any such restriction may be imposed, and to enable such individuals to foresee with a reasonable degree of accuracy the consequences of their actions.[86] Where the state covertly monitors its citizens it is still required to adhere to minimum safeguards to ensure that it does not wield its power arbitrarily.[87]

2.47 For instance, in *Liberty v UK and Big Brother Watch and others v UK* the Court found that the law regulating the system of interception of telephone calls, including 'bulk' surveillance did not 'indicate with reasonable clarity the scope and manner of exercise of the relevant discretion conferred on the public authorities'.[88] And in *Gillan and Quinton v UK*, the Court found that the 'stop and search' powers under the Terrorism Act 2000, which gave the police extremely broad discretion

---

[79] *Barthold v Germany* (1985) 7 EHRR 383.
[80] See *Groppera Radio AG v Switzerland* (1990) 12 EHRR 321.
[81] *Sunday Times v UK (No 1)* (1979) 2 EHRR 245.
[82] *Barthold v Germany* (1985) 7 EHRR 383.
[83] See *Kopp v Sweden* (1999) 27 EHRR 91, paras 55 and 64.
[84] *Sunday Times v UK (No 1)* (1979) 2 EHRR 245, para 49.
[85] *Govell v UK* [1999] EHRLR 121.
[86] *Silver v UK* (1983) 5 EHRR 347.
[87] *Weber and Saravia v Germany* (2008) 46 EHRR SE5.
[88] *Liberty v UK and Big Brother Watch and others v UK* (2009) 48 EHRR 1, para 69; and *Big Brother Watch & others v UK* App No 58170/13, 13 September 2018. See also *Kennedy v UK* (2010) 52 EHRR 207, paras 155–70.

both to authorize searches and to decide to carry them out, were neither sufficiently circumscribed nor subject to adequate legal safeguards against abuse; they were therefore not 'in accordance with the law'.[89]

The degree of certainty required will depend on the facts of the case, but it is clear that the ECtHR does not require absolute certainty. In *Sunday Times v UK (No 1)* the ECtHR said that: **2.48**

> Whilst certainty is highly desirable, it may bring in its train excessive rigidity and the law must be able to keep pace with changing circumstances. Accordingly, many laws are inevitably couched in terms which, to a greater or lesser extent, are vague and whose interpretation and application are questions of practice.[90]

Applying this principle, the ECtHR accepted that the common law relating to contempt of court was formulated with sufficient precision to satisfy the requirements of the Convention.[91]

In *Wingrove v UK*[92] and *Müller v Switzerland*,[93] cases involving freedom of expression, the ECtHR accepted that the concepts of blasphemy and obscenity were not capable of precise definition, emphasizing 'the impossibility of attaining absolute precision in the framing of laws … in fields in which the situation changes according to the prevailing views of society'.[94] The requirement of legal certainty is thus more flexible in relation to laws whose subject matter touches 'areas of sensitive judgment where public opinion may shift'.[95] **2.49**

2. Legitimate aim

Any interference by a public authority with a Convention right capable of limitation must be directed towards an identified legitimate aim. Without such a legitimate aim there can be no justification for the interference. **2.50**

To establish that an aim exists, the state must show that it was genuinely seeking to advance one or more of the objectives identified in the qualifying paragraphs to the qualified articles, or, in relation to other limited rights, that it was pursuing an acceptable policy goal with regard to the context of the case. In general, the ECtHR and domestic courts accept the aim put forward by the state without a great deal of scrutiny, and it has been suggested that the question of whether there is a 'legitimate aim' for an interference with rights has been dealt with too cursorily.[96] **2.51**

---

[89] *Gillan and Quinton v UK* (2010) 28 BHRC 420.
[90] *Sunday Times v UK (No 1)* (1979) 2 EHRR 245, para 49.
[91] See also *Steel v UK* (1998) 26 EHRR 603. cf *Hashman and Harrup v UK* (2000) 30 EHRR 241.
[92] *Wingrove v UK* (1997) 24 EHRR 1.
[93] *Müller v Switzerland* (1991) 13 EHRR 212.
[94] ibid para 29.
[95] Per Laws LJ in *R (ProLife Alliance) v BBC* [2002] EWCA Civ 297, [2002] 3 WLR 1080, para 24 (the Court of Appeal's decision was reversed by the House of Lords, their Lordships finding that art 10(1) was not engaged and therefore expressing no opinion on the Court of Appeal's approach to art 10(2): [2003] UKHL 23, [2004] 1 AC 185).
[96] Richard Gordon, 'Legitimate Aim: A Dimly Lit Road' [2002] European Human Rights Law Review 421.

2.52   In Articles 8, 9, 10, and 11 the legitimate aims are set out in the second part of each article. Examples of aims which are considered 'legitimate' under the Convention are the interests of public safety, national security, the protection of health and morals, and the economic well-being of the country, or the protection of the rights and freedoms of others. The notion of the 'rights and freedoms of others' (in arts 8, 9, and 11) and the 'reputation and rights of others' (art 10) is not limited to the rights contained under the Convention. These phrases are capable of including other 'rights' and 'freedoms', including rights enshrined only in national law and rights which are not even known to national law.[97] However, the nature of the right that the state is aiming to protect may go to the separate question of the proportionality of the interference.

2.53   The legitimate aims set out under the qualified rights should be read with Article 18 of the Convention, which provides that 'The restrictions permitted under this Convention to the said rights and freedoms shall not be applied for any purpose other than those for which they have been prescribed'.[98] This is effectively a good faith provision. It is very difficult for applicants to establish that an interference was not in reality pursued for the reason claimed by the state. Expert authors have suggested:

> The list is large enough to cover most government activity, whether it is oppressive or benign. The Court has tended to espouse a rather broad and liberal application of the terms, often finding that more than one of the purposes applies to a specific form of interference.[99]

3. 'Necessary in a democratic society'

2.54   Where the Convention allows restrictions on rights it not only requires them to be in accordance with law and justified by a legitimate aim, it also requires the interference to be 'necessary in a democratic society'. This phrase incorporates the proportionality standard that determines all permissible restrictions on rights.

2.55   The ECtHR has made clear that the term 'necessary' is not synonymous with 'indispensable', and it is certainly a less stringent test than those that appear elsewhere in the Convention: in Article 2(2) ('absolutely necessary'); Article 6(1) ('strictly necessary'); and Article 15(1) ('to the extent strictly required by the exigencies of the situation').[100]

2.56   Nevertheless, 'necessary in a democratic society' is a rigorous test. In *Handyside v UK* and *Sunday Times v UK (No 1)* the ECtHR established that the term 'necessary' does not have the 'flexibility of such expressions as "admissible", "ordinary", "useful", "reasonable" or "desirable" [and] it implies the existence of a "pressing social need"'.[101]

---

[97] *VgT Verein Gegen Tierfabriken v Switzerland* (2001) 34 EHRR 159, paras 59–62; *Chapman v UK* (2001) 33 EHRR 399, paras 80–82; see also *R (Craven) v Secretary of State for the Home Department* [2001] 2 Cr App R 181.

[98] See eg *Refah Partisi (The Welfare Party) v Turkey* (2003) 37 EHRR 1.

[99] William A Schabas, *The European Convention on Human Rights: A Commentary* (OUP 2015) 404.

[100] *Handyside v UK* (1976) 1 EHRR 737, para 48.

[101] ibid; *Sunday Times v UK* (1979) 2 EHRR 245, para 59.

The ECtHR has not developed a consistent set of principles that it uses to assess   2.57
necessity in every case. However, it set out a three-fold test in *Sunday Times v UK*
(No 1) that is now generally applied in relation to the qualified rights:

(a) whether the interference complained of corresponded to a 'pressing social need'; and
(b) whether it was 'proportionate to the legitimate aim pursued'; and
(c) whether the reasons given by the national authority to justify it were 'relevant and sufficient'.[102]

When addressing limited rights, the Court may apply this test in full or simply ask
whether the measures taken by the state were proportionate. Each aspect of the
Sunday Times test is considered in turn below.

(a) *Pressing social need*

A 'pressing social need' must accord with the requirements of a democratic society,   2.58
which supposes 'pluralism, tolerance and broadmindedness'.[103] In assessing whether
there is a 'pressing social need' in play, the ECtHR pays close regard to the importance
of the relevant right. A very powerful need will be required if there is an interference
with a right—or an aspect of a right—the ECtHR considers to be particularly important. The 'pressing social need' that the state must show in order to justify an interference with an intimate aspect of private life, for example, will be particularly strong.[104]

A 'pressing social need' is distinct from a legitimate aim. Thus, in *Dudgeon v UK*   2.59
the ECtHR recognized that one of the purposes of the legislation criminalizing
homosexual behaviour was 'to afford safeguards for vulnerable members of society,
such as the young, against the consequences of homosexual practices' and accepted
that this was then a legitimate aim. However, it went on to say that:

> It cannot be maintained in these circumstances that there is a 'pressing social need' to make
> such acts criminal offences, there being no sufficient justification provided by the risk of harm
> to vulnerable sections of society requiring protection or by the effects on the public.[105]

In contrast, the ECtHR will generally accept the existence of a pressing social   2.60
need where the state asserts national security considerations[106] or threats to the
stability of its democratic institutions.[107]

(b) *Proportionality*

Proportionality is at the heart of the necessity test. As the ECtHR put it in   2.61
Soering v UK:

> Inherent in the whole of the Convention is a search for the fair balance between the demands of
> the general interest of the community and the requirements of the protection of the individual's
> human rights.[108]

---

[102] *Sunday Times v UK* (1979) 2 EHRR 245, para 59.
[103] *Handyside v UK* (1976) 1 EHRR 737.
[104] *Dudgeon v UK* (1981) 4 EHRR 149.
[105] ibid para 60.
[106] See eg *Leander v Sweden* (1987) 9 EHRR 433.
[107] See eg *Refah Partisi (The Welfare Party) v Turkey* (2003) 37 EHRR 1.
[108] *Soering v UK* (1989) 11 EHRR 439, para 89.

2.62   Proportionality is a principle that helps strike that 'fair balance'. It requires a reasonable relationship between the goal pursued and the means the state has chosen to achieve that goal.[109] This means that even if a policy which interferes with a Convention right might be aimed at securing a legitimate aim of social policy, for example the prevention of crime, this will not in itself justify the violation if the means adopted to secure the aim are excessive in the circumstances. In other words, at the very least, the state must not 'use a sledgehammer to crack a nut'.

2.63   Proportionality arises in a number of different contexts. It is most commonly associated with the balancing exercise the ECtHR adopts in determining claims under Articles 8, 9, 10, and 11—as one element of the 'necessary in a democratic society' test. However, it also arises in other discrete ways in the Convention. It is the yardstick by which the scope of restrictions on implied rights are measured;[110] it is used when determining whether a positive obligation should be imposed on a contracting state;[111] it is the central mechanism for determining whether interferences with property are justified under Protocol 1, Article 1;[112] and it is relevant to the prohibition of discrimination under Article 14.[113]

2.64   The general factors relevant to the ECtHR's proportionality exercise include:

(a) the extent to which the interference impairs the 'very essence' of a right, which effectively means a very serious interference.[114] The ECtHR will distinguish between different types of rights arising under the same Convention article. For example, the state will need to adduce particularly weighty reasons to justify an interference with political speech. In contrast, the ECtHR gives greater latitude to the state when assessing interference with commercial speech;[115]

(b) whether the state has adopted a blanket policy that does not permit examination of the merits of individual cases. Thus, in *S and Marper* the ECtHR was particularly concerned by the 'blanket and indiscriminate nature of the power of retention' of the DNA of all those arrested for criminal offences, no matter how minor and regardless of whether the individual was ever charged.[116] A policy that only permits assessment of individual circumstances in 'exceptional' cases may also prove disproportionate;[117]

---

[109] *Fayed v UK* (1994) 18 EHRR 393, para 71.
[110] See para 2.30.
[111] See para 2.33.
[112] See Chapter 7, para 7.02.
[113] See Chapter 6, para 6.604.
[114] See eg *Dudgeon v UK* (1981) 4 EHRR 149.
[115] See Chapter 6, para 6.438.
[116] *S and Marper* App Nos 30562/04 and others, 4 December 2008. See also *O'Donoghue and others v UK* (2010) 30 BHRC 85 (successful challenge to the scheme designed to prevent 'sham' marriages).
[117] *Dickson v UK* (2008) 24 BHRC 19.

(c) whether a less restrictive, yet equally effective, alternative measure is available to the state to achieve the legitimate aim pursued. For example, in *Campbell v UK* the ECtHR held that the blanket opening of all prisoners' mail was disproportionate because the less intrusive measure of opening only those letters reasonably considered to contain prohibited material would have achieved the same aim;[118]

(d) whether there are any effective safeguards or legal controls over the measures in question. This includes the adequacy of compensation or legal remedies for those affected by the measures.[119] In Article 10 cases, the ECtHR will also examine the opposite question: whether an award of damages for defamation is excessive taking into account all of the circumstances.[120]

The intensity of the proportionality inquiry will vary according to the right at stake. For example, where property rights are in issue the ECtHR will apply less exacting scrutiny than where there is an interference with the right to privacy or freedom of expression (especially if compensation for loss of the property is provided).[121]   2.65

Proportionality also incorporates a concept of procedural fairness. An infringement of a qualified right is less likely to be a proportionate response to a legitimate aim if the person affected by the action was not consulted, or not given the right to a hearing, than if he or she was given such opportunities. The ECtHR has stated that, 'whilst Article 8 contains no explicit procedural requirements, the decision-making process leading to measures of interference must be fair and such as to afford due respect to the interests safeguarded by Article 8'.[122] However, in some cases this guarantee may be redundant as the stronger procedural protections of Article 6 will apply. Unfortunately, although the Article 8 procedural rights are often very important in an immigration context, immigration proceedings are not subject to Article 6 as the Court has decided they do not constitute a determination of civil rights.[123]   2.66

(c) *Relevant and sufficient reasons*

The final element of the 'necessary in a democratic society' test involves the ECtHR's assessment of whether the state's reasons for interfering with the right are 'relevant and sufficient'.[124] This is an objective test. It is not enough that the respondent state has acted 'reasonably, carefully and in good faith'.[125] The ECtHR will examine the reasons for the state's actions and determine whether they are adequate. In   2.67

---

[118] *Campbell v UK* (1992) 15 EHRR 137. See also *Hirst v UK (No 2)* 19 BHRC 546.
[119] See eg *Motais de Narbonne v France* App No 48161/99, 2 July 2002; *Akkus v Turkey* (2000) 30 EHRR 365.
[120] *Steel and Morris v UK* (2005) 41 EHRR 22.
[121] See eg *Pye v UK* (2008) 46 EHRR 34.
[122] *McMichael v UK* (1995) 20 EHRR 205, para 87.
[123] *Maaouia v France* App No 39652/98, 5 October 2000 [GC].
[124] *Jersild v Denmark* (1995) 19 EHRR 1.
[125] *Olsson (No 1)* (1988) 11 EHRR 259, para 58; *Vogt v Germany* (1995) 21 EHRR 205, para 52.

Smith and Grady v UK[126] and *Lustig-Prean and Beckett v UK*,[127] for example—cases involving a ban on homosexuals serving in the army—it was not enough for the respondent state simply to assert that the reason for the ban was 'operational effectiveness' or 'threat to morale'. Cogent evidence was needed, and the state could not provide it. Where no evidence is adduced in support of the reasons given for a restriction, a breach of the Convention is almost inevitable.[128]

2.68   The ECtHR adopted a particularly strong approach to reason-giving in *Hirst v UK*, in which it held that the state's reasons for banning convicted prisoners from voting were inadequate.[129] This was despite the lack of consensus in other Member States on this issue, and the fact that Parliament had voted for an express ban in a piece of primary legislation. The Grand Chamber stated:

> There is no evidence that Parliament has ever sought to weigh the competing interests or to assess the proportionality of a blanket ban on the right of a convicted prisoner to vote ... [It] cannot be said that there was any substantive debate by members of the legislature on the continued justification in light of modern day penal policy and of current human rights standards for maintaining such a general restriction on the right of prisoners to vote.[130]

By contrast in *Animal Defenders International v UK*,[131] the Grand Chamber relied upon the extensive degree of parliamentary and judicial scrutiny to hold that a complete ban on political television advertising fell within the state's margin of appreciation and so did not violate Article 10, notwithstanding that this apparently contradicted a recent Grand Chamber judgment on a similar issue.[132]

4. Restrictions specifically provided for by reservations and derogations

(a) *Reservations*

2.69   Article 57 entitles states to make reservations in respect of rights contained in the Convention. A reservation to an international treaty is a device used by a signatory state to reserve particular policies or law in order to exempt them from challenge under the instrument. They are often used as a temporary measure, which gives states time to bring their laws into line with the requirements of the Convention. Reservations can be made only at the time of signing or ratification and must comply with Article 31(1) of the Vienna Convention on the Law of Treaties, which states:

> A treaty shall be interpreted in good faith in accordance with the ordinary meaning to be given to the terms of the treaty in their context and in the light of its objects and purpose.

---

[126] *Smith and Grady v UK* (1999) 29 EHRR 493, paras 71–112.
[127] *Lustig-Prean and Beckett v UK* (1999) 29 EHRR 548, paras 64–105.
[128] *Autronic AG v Switzerland* (1990) 12 EHRR 485.
[129] *Hirst v UK* (2006) 42 EHRR 41.
[130] ibid para 79.
[131] *Animal Defenders International v UK* [2013] 57 EHRR 21 [GC].
[132] *Verein gegen Tierfabriken Schweiz v Switzerland* [2011] 52 EHRR 8.

A reservation is likely to be invalid if it seeks to circumvent key terms or underlying principles contained within the treaty in question. 2.70

There is only one reservation by the UK to the Convention, which pertains to the second sentence of Protocol 1, Article 2 (which requires education to be provided in conformity with parents' religious and philosophical convictions). The UK has accepted this provision only so far as it is compatible with the provision of efficient instruction and training and the avoidance of unreasonable public expenditure.[133] 2.71

Any reservation must meet the requirements of Article 57(2) of the Convention and not be couched in terms that are too vague or broad for it to be possible to determine their exact scope and meaning.[134] 2.72

(b) Derogations
Article 15(1) of the Convention states: 2.73

In time of war or other public emergency threatening the life of the nation any High Contracting Party may take measures derogating from its obligations under this Convention to the extent strictly required by the exigencies of the situation, provided that such measures are not inconsistent with its obligations under international law.

This enables states to restrict the exercise of some of the rights and freedoms without violating the Convention. Any derogation must be proportionate to the threat and must be necessary to deal with the emergency. As a matter of international law, a state, by lodging a derogation in Strasbourg, can, to the extent that the derogation is lawful under Article 15, avoid a particular obligation in particular circumstances. Article 15 does not allow derogations from Article 2 (the right to life), Article 3 (freedom from torture), Article 4(1) (slavery and servitude), and Article 7 (retrospective criminal penalties). 2.74

At the time of writing the UK has no derogations in place.[135] 2.75

5. Restrictions under Articles 16, 17, and 18

The rights contained in the Convention are subject to express restrictions in three specific areas: 2.76

(a) Article 16 (restrictions on the political activities of aliens);

(b) Article 17 (restrictions on activities aimed at the destruction of Convention rights); and

(c) Article 18 (prohibition on using Convention restrictions for an improper purpose).

The exact scope of these articles is considered in detail in Chapter 6.

---

[133] The full text of the reservation is set out in Part II of Sch 3 to the Human Rights Act 1998; see App 1.
[134] *Belilos v Switzerland* (1988) 10 EHRR 466.
[135] See the discussion of previous derogations in Chapter 7, paras 7.567–7.578.

E. THE MARGIN OF APPRECIATION

2.77 The meaning of the term 'margin of appreciation' is not immediately apparent, originating as it does from French administrative law. In essence, it refers to the freedom that a state is permitted in the manner in which it observes Convention rights.

2.78 As Clayton and Tomlinson point out, it fulfils two functions in Convention jurisprudence.[136] First, it establishes 'an interpretative obligation' to respect the varying cultural traditions of the contracting states. As the Convention is an international human rights instrument, policed by an international court, the Strasbourg institutions have to be sensitive to the need for 'subsidiarity', that is, to ensuring that the Member States' own political and cultural traditions are respected. For example, actions that may offend religious sensitivities in one country may be a recognized act of free speech in another. Secondly, the margin of appreciation functions as a standard of review that enables the ECtHR to take a 'hands-off' approach to certain issues where national authorities are better placed to make an assessment of proportionality.

2.79 The doctrine was developed by the ECtHR in *Handyside v UK*, which concerned the publication in England in 1971 of the *Little Red School Book*, which was intended for children and included a section on sex.[137] The police seized the books and a forfeiture order was obtained on the grounds that the books contravened the Obscene Publications Act 1959. The applicant claimed a violation of the right to freedom of expression and the government argued that the restriction was necessary for the purpose of the 'protection of morals'. The Court accepted that the limitation was 'prescribed by law' and thus had to decide whether the limitation in question was proportionate and 'necessary in a democratic society'. The Court stated:

By reason of their direct and continuous contact with the vital forces of their countries, state authorities are in principle in a better position than the international judge to give an opinion on the extent of these requirements as well as on the 'necessity' of a 'restriction' or 'penalty' intended to meet them.

2.80 The doctrine has now been incorporated into the convention itself. Article 1 of Protocol 15 to the Convention introduced an additional paragraph at the end of the Preamble to the Convention itself:

Affirming that the High Contracting Parties, in accordance with the principle of subsidiarity, have the primary responsibility to secure the rights and freedoms defined in this Convention

---

[136] Richard Clayton and Hugh Tomlinson, *The Law of Human Rights* (2nd edn, OUP 2009) 315.
[137] *Handyside v UK* (1976) 1 EHRR 737 (following the ECmHR in *Lawless v Ireland (No 3)* (1979–1980) 1 EHRR 15).

and the Protocols thereto, and that in doing so they enjoy a margin of appreciation, subject to the supervisory jurisdiction of the European Court of Human Rights established by this Convention,

This power of 'appreciation' is not unlimited, however, and over the years, the Court has developed its case law in this area such that it can be said that the margin of appreciation has become a central element of the ECtHR's method of reasoning even before Protocol 15 was adopted. The case law was summarized in *S and Marper v UK*[138] as follows:

A margin of appreciation must be left to the competent national authorities ... The breadth of this margin varies and depends on a number of factors including the nature of the Convention right in issue, its importance for the individual, the nature of the interference and the object pursued by the interference. The margin will tend to be narrower where the right at stake is crucial to the individual's effective enjoyment of intimate or key rights ... Where a particularly important facet of an individual's existence or identity is at stake, the margin allowed to the State will be restricted ... Where, however, there is no consensus within the Member States of the Council of Europe, either as to the relative importance of the interest at stake or as to how best to protect it, the margin will be wider.

In *Hirst v UK* the ECtHR made clear that the lack of a common European approach to the problem was not in itself determinative of the issue[139] and indicated that certain forms of blanket interference with rights could fall outside the margin of appreciation altogether:

2.81

[S]uch a general, automatic and indiscriminate restriction on a vitally important Convention right must be seen as falling outside any acceptable margin of appreciation, however wide that margin might be ... While the Court reiterates that the margin of appreciation is wide, it is not all-embracing.[140]

It is certainly true that the Court often uses the 'margin of appreciation' concept to avoid ruling on acutely sensitive issues which involve an element of political controversy. In *Lautsi v Italy*, for instance, the Grand Chamber (overturning an earlier Chamber decision) held that the decision whether crucifixes should be present in state-school classrooms was, in principle, a matter falling within the margin of appreciation of the respondent state, and that in light of this, the decision did not lead to a form of indoctrination such as to violate Article 2 of Protocol 1 to the Convention.[141] And in *Mosley v UK*, the Court found that whether or not a pre-notification requirement should be

2.82

---

[138] *S and Marper v UK* (2008) 25 BHRC 557, para 102; for a fuller exposition, see *Mosley v UK* App No 48009/08, 10 May 2011, paras 108–11.

[139] *Hirst v UK (No 2)* (2005) 19 BHRC 546, para 81.

[140] ibid para 82. See also *Dickson v UK* (2008) 24 BHRC 19.

[141] *Lautsi v Italy* (2011) 54 EHRR 60.

imposed on the press to protect a person's privacy fell within the state's margin of appreciation.[142]

2.83   In its use as a standard of review, the margin of appreciation is controversial.[143]

2.84   As discussed in more detail in Chapter 4, the margin of appreciation is a principle reflecting the relationship between the ECtHR and Member States, and so should not be employed directly by the domestic courts.[144]

---

[142] *Mosley v UK* (2011) 31 BHRC 409. See also *Animal Defenders International v UK* [2013] 57 EHRR 21.

[143] For a more detailed analysis see Pieter van Dijk and others, *Theory and Practice of the European Convention on Human Rights* (5th edn, Intersentia 2018) 327; William A Schabas, *The European Convention on Human Rights: A Commentary* (OUP 2015); and David Harris and others, *Law of the European Convention on Human Rights* (5th edn, OUP 2023) 14.

[144] See Chapter 4, paras 4.119–4.130.

3

THE FRAMEWORK OF THE HUMAN RIGHTS ACT

Blackstone's Guide to The Human Rights Act 1998. Eighth Edition. John Wadham, Helen Mountfield KC, Raj Desai, Sarah Hannett KC, Jessica Jones, Eleanor Mitchell, and Aidan Wills, Oxford University Press. © John Wadham, Helen Mountfield KC, Raj Desai, Sarah Hannett KC, Jessica Jones, Eleanor Mitchell, and Aidan Wills 2024. DOI: 10.1093/oso/9780192885050.003.0003

A. INTRODUCTION

3.01 The Human Rights Act is a special statute imbued with constitutional significance. It is described in its long title as an Act to give 'further effect' to the rights and freedoms guaranteed under the European Convention for the Protection of Human Rights and Fundamental Freedoms (Convention). The special status of the Human Rights Act has been recognized judicially,[1] academically,[2] and by parliamentarians.[3]

3.02 The overriding objective of the Act is to weave the Convention into the existing legal system, so that all courts will consider Convention arguments, and rights which previously could only be vindicated in Strasbourg can be secured in national courts, while minimizing disruption to the existing legal system. The method adopted, however, is a complex one, reflecting a delicate constitutional balance between 'incorporating' Convention rights and retaining parliamentary sovereignty.

3.03 The Human Rights Act created a general statutory requirement that all legislation, primary or secondary, whenever enacted, must be read and given effect in a way which is compatible with Convention rights *whenever possible.* This principle of construction, contained in section 3 of the Human Rights Act, requires a generous and progressive approach to interpretation to give effect to the purpose of this constitutional statute. If it is not possible to interpret legislation in a Convention compliant way then the higher courts may declare the legislation to be incompatible with the Convention.

3.04 This principle of construction applies to all litigation, whether or not a public authority is involved. It can, therefore, affect the rights of private persons between themselves. But the Human Rights Act does not directly create a new cause of action for 'breach of the Convention' against private bodies.

3.05 Pursuant to section 6, the Human Rights Act requires public authorities—including courts—to act compatibly with the Convention unless they are prevented from doing so by statute. This means that the courts have their own primary statutory duty to give effect to the Convention unless positively prevented from doing so. Section 7 gives the 'victim' of any act or proposed act of a public authority which is incompatible with the Convention power to rely on the Convention to bring proceedings against the authority or to found a defence in any legal proceedings.

3.06 This chapter explains the mechanisms of the Human Rights Act, and the effect they have in proceedings involving public authorities and private parties. It begins with a very brief summary of the effect of the Human Rights Act, followed by an overview of the key provisions of the Act and the relationship of the Act with the common law. The next part contains a more detailed analysis of the main operative

---

[1] See eg *R v Offen* [2001] 1 WLR 253, para 275 per Lord Woolf; *Thoburn v Sunderland City Council* [2002] EWHC 195 (Admin), [2002] 3 WLR, para 247 per Laws LJ.

[2] See eg Jeffrey Jowell and Jonathan Cooper (eds), *Delivering Rights: How the Human Rights Act is Working* (Hart Publishing 2003) 2.

[3] Constitution Committee, Sixth Report, Session 2006–2007, para 8.

provisions of the Act and how they interact, including discussion of what the Act means by the terms 'public authority' and 'functions of a public nature'. The chapter then examines some of the ways in which the Act has been applied in litigation involving private parties. The final section concerns certain 'special cases' identified under the Act. Procedural issues concerning bringing a claim under the Human Rights Act, key Convention concepts in domestic law, and the remedies available under the Act are discussed in Chapter 4.

B. SUMMARY OF THE EFFECTS OF THE HUMAN RIGHTS ACT

In summary, the wide-reaching effects of the Human Rights Act are as follows.   3.07

(a) In *all* cases in which Convention rights are in question, the Human Rights Act gives 'further effect' to the Convention, whether the litigants are private persons or public authorities. It does this in three ways:

   (i) by obliging courts to decide all cases before them (whether brought under statute or the common law) compatibly with Convention rights unless prevented from doing so either by primary legislation or by provisions made under primary legislation which cannot be read compatibly with the Convention;[4]

   (ii) by placing an obligation upon courts to interpret existing and future legislation in conformity with the Convention wherever possible;[5]

   (iii) by requiring courts to take Strasbourg case law into account in determining any question in connection with a Convention right, insofar as they consider it is relevant to proceedings before them.[6]

(b) The Human Rights Act does not make Convention rights *directly* enforceable against a private litigant, nor against a functional public authority (ie a body which is not obviously public in form but which has some functions of a public nature) if it is acting in a private capacity.[7] But in cases against a private litigant, or functional public authority acting in exercise of its private law functions, the Human Rights Act may still have an effect on the outcome, because the court:

   (i) is obliged to interpret legislation in conformity with the Convention wherever possible;

   (ii) must exercise any judicial discretions compatibly with the Convention; and

   (iii) must ensure that its application of common law or equitable rules is compatible with the Convention.

---

[4] Section 6(1)–(3).
[5] Section 3.
[6] Section 2(1).
[7] See paras 3.58–3.73.

(c) Section 7 of the Human Rights Act creates directly enforceable rights against public bodies. First, it has introduced a new ground of illegality into proceedings brought by way of judicial review, namely, a failure to comply with the Convention rights protected by the Human Rights Act, subject to a defence that there is a clear statutory obligation to act incompatibly with the Convention. Secondly, it has created a stand-alone private law cause of action against public bodies that fail to act compatibly with the Convention. Thirdly, Convention rights are available via the Human Rights Act as a ground of defence or appeal in cases brought by public bodies against private persons (in both criminal and civil cases). However, the scope and meaning of 'public authority' remains uncertain and open to argument following the leading decision of the House of Lords in *YL v Birmingham City Council*[8] and subsequent case law.

(d) Section 7 can be used only by 'victims' of violations of the Convention, the term 'victim' being defined in section 7(7). However, even a litigant who is not defined as a 'victim', and so cannot challenge a public authority's decision directly using the provisions of the Human Rights Act, is able to rely on the courts' obligation under section 3 of the Human Rights Act to interpret legislation compatibly with the Convention where possible, and to use Convention arguments in the circumstances in which this was possible before the Human Rights Act was brought into force.[9]

(e) The Human Rights Act does not permit the Convention to be used so as to override primary legislation: if it is not possible to interpret a statute compatibly with Convention rights, courts must give effect to it. Equally, if the terms of the primary legislation require subordinate legislation made under it (which will usually be in a statutory instrument) to be interpreted in a way which means that the subordinate legislation is incompatible with the Convention, it must still be given effect even though this may result in a breach of a Convention right. Thus parliamentary sovereignty is preserved.[10] But if legislation cannot be read so as to comply with the Convention, the higher courts have the power to issue 'declarations of incompatibility', and a fast-track procedure exists whereby the government can legislate to remedy such incompatibility.[11]

C. OVERVIEW OF THE KEY PROVISIONS OF THE HUMAN RIGHTS ACT

3.08   The Human Rights Act is a short and elegantly drafted piece of legislation. It is nonetheless helpful to approach it schematically rather than simply reading the sections in the order in which they appear.

---

[8] *YL v Birmingham City Council* [2007] UKHL 27, [2008] 1 AC 95.
[9] Section 11.
[10] Section 3(2)(b) and (c).
[11] Sections 4, 10, and Sch 2.

1. Section 1 and Schedule 1—definition of Convention rights

After the long title, which states that the Act gives 'further effect' to the rights and freedoms guaranteed under the Convention, section 1 and Schedule 1 define the 'Convention rights', which have been incorporated, subject to any designated derogations or reservations.[12] Article 1 (the obligation on contracting states to the Convention to 'secure' Convention rights to 'everyone within their jurisdiction') and Article 13 (the right to an effective remedy in a national court) are not specifically designated as 'Convention rights' within this definition.   3.09

'The Convention' in this context means 'the Convention ... as it has effect for the time being in relation to the United Kingdom'.[13] The House of Lords has held that this means that the Convention does not have effect if it is limited or extinguished by some other, overriding provision of international law, such as a United Nations (UN) Security Council Resolution.[14] The effect of the Convention is usually, but not always, territorially limited. The Supreme Court has held, following the decision of the European Court of Human Rights (ECtHR) in *Al-Skeini v UK*, that it covers British armed forces serving outsider the territory of the UK.[15]   3.10

2. Section 2—interpretation of Convention rights

Section 2 requires any court or tribunal determining a question that has arisen in connection with a Convention right to 'take into account' the jurisprudence of the Strasbourg organs (the ECtHR, the European Commission of Human Rights (ECmHR), and the Committee of Ministers). This jurisprudence must be considered 'so far as, in the opinion of the court or tribunal, it is relevant to the proceedings in which that question has arisen', whenever the judgment, decision, or opinion to be taken into account was handed down.[16] Section 2 is considered in detail at paragraph 3.50.   3.11

3. Section 3—interpretation of legislation

Section 3 is the lynchpin of the Act, 'pivotal to [its] operation'.[17] It requires primary and subordinate legislation to be read and given effect in a way which is compatible with Convention rights, 'so far as it is possible to do so', whether the legislation in question was enacted before or after the Human Rights Act. Section 3 is a general requirement, addressed to any person reading the legislation, not just to the courts.   3.12

---

[12] Section 1(2).

[13] Section 21(1).

[14] *R (Al-Jedda) v Secretary of State for Defence* [2007] UKHL 58, [2008] 1 AC 332 (although see subsequently *Al-Jedda v UK* (2011) 30 BHRC 637 finding no overriding provision of international law to exist). See also *R (Quark Fishing Ltd) v Foreign Secretary* [2005] UKHL 57, [2006] 1 AC 529, paras 25, 32, 87, and 97; and *Al-Skeini v UK* (2011) 53 EHRR 589.

[15] *R (Smith) v Ministry of Defence* [2013] UKSC 41, [2014] 1 AC 52.

[16] Section 2(1).

[17] Anthony Bradley, 'The Sovereignty of Parliament—Form or Substance?' in Jeffrey Jowell and Colm Oliver (eds), *The Changing Constitution* (9th edn, OUP 2007) 37.

This strong interpretative obligation is one of the key provisions in the Human Rights Act. Section 3 is dealt with in more detail at paragraph 3.33.

4. Section 19—statements of compatibility

3.13   Section 19 requires the minister with conduct of any Bill,[18] before its second reading, to either make and publish a 'statement of compatibility',[19] or make a statement that although he or she is unable to state that the legislation is compatible with the Convention rights, the government nevertheless wishes to proceed with the Bill.[20] Section 19 is dealt with in more detail at paragraph 3.45.

5. Sections 4, 5, 10, and Schedule 2—incompatibility of legislation

3.14   If it is *not* possible to read legislation so as to give effect to the Convention, then that legislation remains in force. The courts cannot, as in some constitutional structures, 'strike it down' as being incompatible with Convention principles. Section 3(2)(b) and (c) of the Act expressly provide that if legislation cannot be read compatibly, this does not affect its validity, continuing operation, or enforcement. Instead, in such circumstances, section 4 empowers the higher courts to express their view that the legislation is not compatible with the Convention by making a 'declaration of incompatibility'. If such a declaration is to be sought, the Crown has a right to be notified, and to intervene, under section 5 of the Act. In circumstances where a court has made a declaration of incompatibility, the Act provides a 'fast track' legislative procedure, by which the executive can act to cure the incompatibility, which is contained in section 10 of, and Schedule 2 to, the Act. These provisions are described in more detail in Chapter 4, paragraph 4.90. However, it is important to note that a declaration of incompatibility—as with any declaration—is a discretionary remedy, and the Supreme Court has indicated, for example, that it will not be institutionally appropriate for it to grant a declaration of incompatibility if a similar declaration has already been made on a particular issue.[21] The ultimate decision as to whether or not to comply with international law obligations under the Convention remains a matter for the Crown and Parliament, and not the courts.

6. Section 6—acts of public authorities

3.15   Section 6 makes it unlawful in most circumstances for a public authority to act in a way which is incompatible with a Convention right. A public authority may only do so if it is required to by primary legislation, or by secondary legislation made under primary legislation, which cannot be interpreted compatibly with the Convention. 'Act' in section 6 includes failure to act.[22] This general obligation is very wide, and

---

[18] There is no such requirement for Private Members' Bills.
[19] Section 19(1)(a).
[20] Section 19(1)(b).
[21] *R (Chester) v Secretary of State for Justice* [2013] UKSC 63, [2014] AC 271.
[22] Section 6(6).

means that in the exercise of any power or duty, any public body must act in such a way as to give effect to the Convention.

'Giving effect to the Convention' means more than simply requiring the public   3.16
authority to avoid violating negative Convention prohibitions. Where a public authority has positive obligations under the Convention, that is, a duty to act in such a way as
to protect people from having their Convention rights violated by third parties, then
section 6 will also require the public authority to discharge these.[23] For example, a public authority could violate the right to freedom of association under Article 11 of the
Convention, not only by prohibiting a demonstration, but also by failing to police it so
as to ensure that demonstrators are not assaulted by violent counter-demonstrators.[24]

Section 6(1) is limited only insofar as is necessary to preserve the concept of parlia-   3.17
mentary sovereignty. First, section 6(2)(a) provides that the duty under section 6(1) to
give effect to Convention rights does not apply if the public authority *could not* have
acted differently as a result of one or more provisions of primary legislation. Section
6(2)(b) provides that section 6(1) does not apply if the authority was acting to give
effect to or to enforce one or more provisions made under primary legislation which
cannot be read or given effect in a way which is compatible with the Convention
rights. Plainly there is some overlap between section 6(2)(a) and (2)(b), both in effect
amounting to a 'primary legislation defence', and the House of Lords has recognized
this.[25] In practice, section 6(2) is rarely applied.[26] Most powers or duties *can* be read in
a way which is compatible with the Convention: and if public authorities do not themselves comply with section 6(1) by reading their powers and duties in a Convention-
compliant way, the courts (as public authorities themselves) are under their own duty
to find a reading of the legislation which permits the public authority to comply with
the Convention if at all possible. A provision of secondary legislation that is incompatible with Convention rights, which does not fall within the limited exception in section 6(2)(b) of the Act, is to be disregarded by a public authority, tribunal, or court.[27]

The second limit on the effect of section 6(1) is that Parliament in its legislative   3.18
capacity is not a 'public authority'[28] and so is not bound by section 6(1).[29] Thus,
even if Parliament has failed to enact legislation which is arguably required in order
to give effect to Convention principles, that is not a matter which can be challenged
in domestic courts. Though the 'act' of a public authority which can be challenged
includes an omission, it does not include a failure to legislate.[30]

---

[23] See Chapter 2, para 2.33.

[24] *Plattform Artze für das Leben v Austria* (1988) 13 EHRR 204.

[25] *R (Hooper) v Secretary of State for Work and Pensions* [2005] UKHL 29, [2005] 1 WLR 1681, where Lord Hoffmann and Lord Hope held that the appropriate defence was s 6(2)(b) and Lord Scott and Lord Brown held that it was s 6(2)(a).

[26] As to the extent and effect of s 6(2), see *Ghaidan v Godin-Mendoza* [2004] UKHL 30, [2004] 2 AC 557; see also *R (GC and C) v Commissioner of Police of the Metropolis* [2011] UKSC 21, [2011] 1 WLR 1230, paras 19–44; *R (Chester) v Secretary of State for Justice* [2013] UKSC 63, [2014] AC 271.

[27] *R v Secretary of State for Work and Pensions* [2019] UKSC 52, [2019] 1 WLR 6430, paras 18–32.

[28] Section 6(3).

[29] ibid.

[30] Section 6(6)(a).

3.19   Section 6(3)(a) makes courts and tribunals (including previously the House of Lords in its judicial capacity)[31] public authorities, and so subject to their own primary duty to act compatibly with the Convention. This is important when considering the effect of the Convention in private law litigation, because the courts are themselves subject to a duty to 'give effect' to the Convention in reaching their decisions, if they can.

3.20   Public authorities are in a special position under the Human Rights Act, because the Convention rights scheduled to the Act can be directly enforced against them. The Convention has also been relevant in determining some cases between private individuals, as well as those between an individual and the state, because as a 'public authority' a court is obliged to act in a way which is compatible with the Convention. This 'horizontal' impact of the Human Rights Act is considered at paragraphs 3.71-73.

7. Section 7—proceedings against public authorities

3.21   Section 7 deals with proceedings under the Human Rights Act, both free-standing and other proceedings in which the Act is relevant. It may be used only by a person who is or would be a 'victim' of the unlawful act,[32] a term which is analysed in Chapter 4 at para 4.15. A 'victim' may rely on Convention rights in two ways in legal proceedings. First, under section 7(1)(a) he or she may bring free-standing proceedings against a public authority which infringes a Convention right 'in the appropriate court or tribunal'. The appropriate forum is determined by the subject matter of the claim and rules made by the Secretary of State concerned or the Lord Chancellor (which also deal with other jurisdictional matters, such as remedies).[33] Section 7(5) imposes a limitation period for bringing free-standing proceedings. Secondly, section 7(1)(b) permits a person to rely on the Convention right or rights concerned in 'any legal proceedings'. Section 22(4) provides that section 7(1)(b) can be used as a defence whenever the act in question took place, but proceedings may be instigated under section 7(1)(a) only in relation to acts committed after the Human Rights Act came into force on 2 October 2000.

3.22   The Human Rights Act creates three ways in which Convention rights can be directly enforced against public authorities:

(a)   as a statutory cause of action for breach of human rights where a public authority has not acted compatibly with the Convention. For example, Scottish prisoners were awarded damages after enduring the practice of slopping out in prison;[34]

---

[31] Section 6(4).

[32] Section 7(3) and (7).

[33] Section 7(2) and (9)–(14); Civil Procedure (Amendment No 4) Rules 2000, SI 2000/2092, concerning human rights issues in the Administrative Court; Family Procedure Rules 2011, Practice Direction 29B (the Human Rights Act 1998); CPR Pt 33 and Practice Direction 30 concerning transfer between courts; Criminal Procedure Rules 2020, rr 36.12, 50.28; and, in the Supreme Court, Supreme Court Rules 2009, r 40 and Practice Direction 9 (the Human Rights Act 1998); CPR 7.11 says that a direct claim under s 7(1)(a) in respect of a judicial act may only be brought in the High Court: see eg *A v B (Investigatory Powers Tribunal: Jurisdiction)* [2009] UKSC 12, [2010] 2 AC 1.

[34] *Somerville v Scottish Ministers* [2007] UKHL 44, [2007] 1 WLR 2734.

(b) as a head of illegality in judicial review proceedings. For example, it could be argued that a decision to refuse to allow a journalist access to a prisoner was ultra vires because rules contravened Article 10 of the Convention and the primary legislation did not require them to be read or given effect in that form, so founding a claim for judicial review;[35]

(c) as a defence in any proceedings that a public authority might itself bring against an individual which are themselves contrary to the Convention or founded on a breach of the Convention. For example, a defendant in criminal proceedings might raise a violation of the Convention by the prosecution in his or her defence.[36]

8. Section 8—judicial remedies

Section 8(1) gives a court a wide power to grant such relief, remedies, or orders as it considers just and appropriate, provided they are within its existing powers.[37] The different remedies that may be granted by courts are discussed in Chapter 4 at para 4.58. Briefly, damages may be awarded, but only if necessary to afford 'just satisfaction' to the claimant.[38] If another remedy or exercise of the court's power could achieve this effect, damages should not be awarded.

3.23

9. Section 9—judicial acts

Section 9 focuses on how the 'public body' provisions operate against courts which have allegedly acted contrary to the Convention. Although courts are public authorities, proceedings may not be brought directly against them for failure to comply with section 6(1) during the course of their determinations. Proceedings in respect of judicial acts under section 7(1)(a) may be brought only by exercising a right of appeal or as prescribed by rules. However, awards of damages may be made against the Crown if they are necessary to compensate a person as required by Article 5(5) of the Convention or a judicial act that is incompatible with Article 6 of the Convention and results in detention.

3.24

10. Section 11—safeguard for existing human rights

Section 11 of the Act provides, for the avoidance of doubt, that reliance on Convention rights does not restrict reliance on other legal rights, or procedural methods of enforcing them. This has two important effects. First, it cannot be argued that any pre-existing right (eg under an existing discrimination statute) is

3.25

---

[35] *R v Secretary of State for the Home Department, ex p Simms* [2000] 2 AC 115.
[36] *R (Kebilene) v DPP* [2002] 2 AC 326 and see recently eg *DPP v Ziegler* [2021] UKSC 23, [2022] AC 408 and *In re Abortion Services (Safe Access Zones) Northern Ireland) Bill* [2022] UKSC 32, [2023] AC 505. See also, in a civil law context, *Manchester City Council v Pinnock* [2010] UKSC 45, [2011] 2 AC 104.
[37] The powers of existing courts or tribunals may be enlarged by order: s 7(11).
[38] Section 8(3).

impliedly limited by reference to Strasbourg jurisprudence: the Convention rights are a floor, not a ceiling. Secondly, litigants are not required to pursue alternative remedies before relying on the Convention. A Human Rights Act argument can be run at the same time as any other arguments a litigant may have, without any requirement first to exhaust alternative remedies.

11. Sections 12 and 13—respect for freedoms

3.26 Sections 12 and 13 provide specific assurances as to the respect that will be afforded to freedom of expression and freedom of thought, conscience, and religion: these are 'comfort clauses' for sections of the press and certain religious organizations.[39]

12. Designated derogations and reservations

3.27 The Human Rights Act provides for limited 'designated derogations and reservations' from the effect of the Convention under sections 1(2), 14–17, and Schedules 2 and 3. The provisions in the Convention which allow the protection of human rights to be limited are considered in Chapter 2, paragraphs 2.40–2.76.

13. Relationship with the common law

3.28 Although the common law previously recognized some fundamental rights and the Convention could be used in some circumstances to give clarity to English law, there were clear lacunae in the protection offered to human rights in the UK. The protection of privacy, for example, has been significantly developed and extended by the application of Convention principles.[40] This has led some commentators to argue that the Human Rights Act has 'reinvigorated' the common law.[41]

3.29 However, there has been a growing judicial tendency to emphasize the power of the common law to protect rights. The relationship between the common law and the Human Rights Act was, for example, analysed by the Supreme Court in *Kennedy v Charity Commission*, a case concerning the scope of the right to receive information under Article 10.[42] Lord Mance forcefully asserted the primacy of the common law as a starting point for the protection of human rights:

Since the passing of the Human Rights Act 1998, there has too often been a tendency to see the law in areas touched on by the Convention solely in terms of the Convention rights. But the Convention rights represent a threshold protection; and, especially in view of the contribution which common lawyers made to the Convention's inception, they may be expected, at least generally even if not always, to reflect and to find their homologue in the common or domestic statute law ... In some areas, the common law may go further than the Convention,

---

[39] See the discussion at paras 3.80–3.83.
[40] See Chapter 6, paras 6.309–6.313.
[41] Lord Irvine, 'The Impact of the Human Rights Act' [2003] Public Law 308; and Rosalind English and Philip Havers (eds), *An Introduction to Human Rights and the Common Law* (Hart Publishing 2000).
[42] *Kennedy v Charity Commission* [2014] UKSC 20, [2014] 2 WLR 808.

and in some contexts it may also be inspired by the Convention rights and jurisprudence (the protection of privacy being a notable example). And in time, of course, a synthesis may emerge. But the natural starting point in any dispute is to start with domestic law, and it is certainly not to focus exclusively on the Convention rights, without surveying the wider common law scene ... Greater focus in domestic litigation on the domestic legal position might also have the incidental benefit that less time was taken in domestic courts seeking to interpret and reconcile different judgments (often only given by individual sections of the European Court of Human Rights) in a way which that court itself, not being bound by any doctrine of precedent, would not itself undertake.[43]

This focus on the common law may prefigure the Supreme Court's response should the Human Rights Act ever be repealed. In some areas at least, common law rights could potentially provide similar protection to Convention rights.

D. THE HUMAN RIGHTS ACT MECHANISM IN MORE DETAIL

The key Human Rights Act mechanism is the interplay between sections 6, 3, 4, and 2, which—though they preserve parliamentary sovereignty—have fundamentally altered both the manner in which courts can scrutinize legislation and the ways in which judges must interpret common law.[44]   3.30

1. Section 6

As outlined earlier, section 6(1) provides that it is unlawful for a 'public authority' to act in a way which is incompatible with a Convention right. As courts and tribunals are defined as public authorities they have their own primary duty to act compatibly with the Convention.[45] Parliamentary sovereignty is preserved by section 6(2), which limits the section 6(1) duty in circumstances where the court or tribunal could not have acted differently as a result of a statutory obligation which *cannot* be read to give effect to it in a way which is compatible with the Convention rights, notwithstanding the obligation in section 3 to do so if possible. This clever device places courts and tribunals themselves under a primary obligation to give effect to Convention rights except where they are prevented from doing so by statute.   3.31

The obligation upon courts to give effect to the Convention wherever possible applies to all cases. The consequence is that Convention questions are pivotal in cases where courts or tribunals are deciding the scope of a statutory provision (even one which regulates the behaviour of one private individual to another); where they   3.32

---

[43] ibid para 46. As Lord Toulson stated at para 133: 'it was not the purpose of the Human Rights Act that the common law should become an ossuary'. See also eg *R (UNISON) v Lord Chancellor (Nos 1 and 2)* [2017] UKSC 51, [2020] AC 869. But cf more recently *R (Elgizouli) v Secretary of State for the Home Department* [2020] UKSC, [2021] AC 937 indicating a cautious approach to developing new common law rights 'in line with the Convention, but not beyond' (para 193).

[44] *R (Kebilene) v DPP* [2000] 2 AC 326 per Lord Hope.

[45] Section 6(3)(a).

are determining what the common law is (insofar as this is within their jurisdiction); or when they are exercising a judicial discretion—for example, the exercise of judicial discretion as to whether to grant an injunction to give effect to Articles 8 and 10.[46]

2. Section 3

3.33　The interpretative obligation in section 3(1) of the Human Rights Act[47] is a strong one. The requirement that courts and tribunals *must* read primary and subordinate legislation and give it effect in a way which is compatible with Convention rights 'so far as it is possible to do so' has been held to mean 'unless it is plainly impossible'.[48] The government rejected amendments proposed during the passage of the Human Rights Bill to reduce this to 'so far as it is *reasonable* to do so' precisely because it wished to preserve the strong obligation to find all 'possible' interpretations of a provision which were compatible with the Convention. Section 3 has been characterized as a 'strong interpretative obligation',[49] not an 'optional canon of construction'.[50]

3.34　The interpretative obligation applies to both primary and secondary legislation whenever it was enacted, that is, whether before or after the enactment of the Human Rights Act so 'it is as though legislation which predates [the Human Rights Act] and conflicts with the Convention has to be treated as being subsequently amended to incorporate the language of section 3'.[51]

3.35　The interpretative obligation in section 3(1) is a general one: a claimant seeking a declaration as to the meaning of legislation under section 3(1) need not be a 'victim'—it is sufficient that he or she has an interest and standing.[52]

3.36　The approach to statutory construction under section 3 is similar to that adopted by the Court of Justice of the European Union (CJEU) in giving effect to European Union (EU) law.[53]

3.37　When applying section 3 in practice the courts first, using ordinary principles of statutory construction, decide whether the primary legislation is compatible with a Convention right. If there is an incompatibility they will then go on to consider the application of section 3. In doing this, courts try to isolate and identify the

---

[46] *Re S (a child) (identification: restrictions on publication)* [2004] UKHL 47, [2005] 1 AC 593.

[47] See further Conor Gearty, 'Reconciling Parliamentary Democracy and Human Rights' (2002) 118 Law Quarterly Review 248; Conor Gearty, 'Revisiting s 3(1) of the Human Rights Act' (2003) 119 Law Quarterly Review 551; Philip Sales, 'A Comparison of the Principle of Legality and Section 3 of the Human Rights Act 1998' (2009) 125 Law Quarterly Review 598.

[48] *R v A (No 2)* [2001] UKHL 25, [2002] 1 AC 45.

[49] See Lord Steyn and Lord Cooke in *R (Kebilene) v DPP* [2002] 2 AC 326; see also Lord Bingham in *A-G's Reference (No 4 of 2002)* [2004] UKHL 43, [2005] 1 AC 264 ('the interpretative obligation under section 3 is a very strong and far reaching one').

[50] Lord Nicholls in *Re S (care order: implementation of a care plan)* [2002] UKHL 10, [2002] 2 AC 291, para 37.

[51] Lord Woolf in *Donoghue v Poplar Housing* [2001] EWCA Civ 595, [2002] QB 48.

[52] *R (Rusbridger) v Attorney General* [2003] UKHL 38, [2004] 2 AC 357 per Lord Steyn.

[53] See eg *Litster v Forth Dry Dock and Engineering Co Ltd* [1990] 1 AC 546.

precise word or phrase in the legislation which is incompatible. Claimants must identify 'with precision' the particular statutory provision which is said to contravene Convention rights.[54]

The House of Lords has confirmed that section 3 may require legislation to be given a Convention-compliant meaning even where there is no ambiguity in the statute which would lead to doubt about its alternative 'natural' meaning.[55] Additionally, the obligation under section 3 may sometimes require the courts to adopt a linguistically strained interpretation of legislation.[56] This exercise requires the court to depart from the parliamentary intention behind the Act as expressed in the statutory language.[57]   3.38

Courts may comply with the interpretative obligation by 'reading in' additional words, or by 'reading down' so as to apply a narrow interpretation of the legislation and enable the court to render it compatible with Convention rights. For example, in *R (GC) v Commissioner of Police of the Metropolis*, section 3 was applied so as to read down section 64(1A) of the Police and Criminal Evidence Act 1984 (which provides that fingerprints and DNA samples 'may be retained after they have fulfilled the purposes for which they were taken'); it did not give the police the power to retain such data from all suspects indefinitely.[58] In this way, the domestic provision was consistent with Article 8 of the Convention.[59] Another technique the courts may use involves clarifying what the effect of the provision is without altering the ordinary meaning of the words used.[60]   3.39

In *Ghaidan v Godin-Mendoza*[61] the House of Lords stressed that the strong interpretative obligation in section 3 is crucial to the working of the Human Rights Act, that it should provide the main remedy, and that 'in practical effect there is a strong rebuttable presumption in favour of an interpretation consistent with Convention rights'. A broad approach to interpretation is necessary to fulfil the 'core remedial purpose' of section 3. Arguments based on parliamentary sovereignty, though a significant consideration, should not be used to limit the interpretative obligation in section 3 or the constitutional purpose of the Human Rights Act to protect Convention rights.[62] During the passage of the Human Rights Bill, the Lord Chancellor said that 'in 99% of all cases that will arise, there will be no need for judicial declarations of incompatibility because of the intended impact of s 3'.[63] However, the structure of the Human Rights Act preserves parliamentary sovereignty. If Parliament disagrees   3.40

---

[54] *R v A (No 2)* [2001] UKHL 25, [2001] 1 AC 45, para 110 per Lord Hope; *In re Abortion Services (Safe Access Zones) Northern Ireland) Bill* [2022] UKSC 32, [2023] AC 505, para 23.
[55] Lord Nicholls in *Ghaidan v Godin-Mendoza* [2004] UKHL 30, [2004] 2 AC 557, para 29.
[56] *R v A (No 2)* [2001] UKHL 25, [2001] 1 AC 45, paras 4–45 and 67–68 per Lord Steyn.
[57] Lord Nicholls in *Ghaidan v Godin-Mendoza* [2004] UKHL 30, [2004] 2 AC 557, para 30.
[58] *R (GC) v Commissioner of Police of the Metropolis* [2011] UKSC 21, [2011] 1 WLR 1230.
[59] In this way, the Supreme Court gave effect to the ECtHR judgment in *S and Marper v UK* (2008) 48 EHRR 1169 and departed from its earlier decision in *R (S) v Chief Constable of the South Yorkshire Police* [2004] UKHL 39, [2004] 1 WLR 2196.
[60] Lord Hope in *R v Lambert* [2001] UKHL 37, [2002] 2 AC 545.
[61] *Ghaidan v Godin-Mendoza* [2004] UKHL 30, [2004] 2 AC 557, para 50.
[62] ibid para 106 per Lord Rodger.
[63] *Hansard*, HL, col 840 (5 February 1998).

with the courts' interpretation of a statute in line with the Convention it is free to override their decision by amending the legislation and expressly reinstating the provision that conflicts with fundamental rights.[64]

3.41   Moreover, though stronger than any previous common law rule of interpretation, section 3 is still:

> only a rule of interpretation. It does not entitle the judges to act as legislators ... The compatibility is to be achieved only so far as this is possible. Plainly this will not be possible if the legislation contains provisions which expressly contradict the meaning which the enactment would have to be given to make it compatible.[65]

Similarly, when reading words into legislation, the courts have stressed that these words must be consistent with the scheme and essential principles of the legislation.[66]

3.42   A leading case on the limits of section 3 is *Re S (care order: implementation of care plan)*.[67] The House of Lords held the Court of Appeal's attempt to construe the Children Act 1989 as compatible with the Convention departed too far from the scheme of the legislation and key principles of the Children Act: 'a meaning which departs substantially from a fundamental feature of an Act of Parliament is likely to have crossed the boundary between interpretation and amendment'.[68] Similarly, in *R (Wright) v Secretary of State for Health*, the statute could not properly be read in a compatible manner. Baroness Hale declined to set out how she would 'right' the problem, emphasizing that it was not for their Lordships 'to attempt to rewrite the legislation'.[69]

3.43   Compatible interpretation through section 3(1) is also impossible where the legislation in question has wide-ranging implications and raises policy issues which it would be inappropriate or impossible for courts to determine, or would require the construction of a wide-ranging new extra-statutory scheme.[70]

3.44   When examining the rationale which underlies legislation and determining the policy objective of particular provisions, courts can refer to sources outside the statute such as white papers, *Hansard*, and explanatory notes. However, resort to materials such as *Hansard* should be rare and the court should be careful to use them only as background material to inform ascertain or confirm the purpose of the legislation, not treat the ministerial or other statement as indicative of the objective intention of Parliament, and assess the proportionality of any statutory measure by

---

[64] cf Conor Gearty, 'Reconciling Parliamentary Democracy and Human Rights' (2002) 118 Law Quarterly Review 248.

[65] *R v A (No 2)* [2001] UKHL 25, [2001] 1 AC 45 para 108. See also *R v Lambert* [2001] UKHL 37, [2002] 2 AC 545, para 79 per Lord Hope; *R v Secretary of State for the Home Department, ex p Anderson and Taylor* [2002] UKHL 46, [2003] 1 AC 837.

[66] Lord Bingham in *R v Secretary of State for the Home Department, ex p Anderson and Taylor* [2002] UKHL 46, [2003] 1 AC 837, para 70.

[67] *Re S (care order: implementation of care plan)* [2002] UKHL 10, [2002] 2 AC 291.

[68] ibid para 40.

[69] *R (Wright) v Secretary of State for Health* [2009] UKHL 3, [2009] 1 AC 739, para 39.

[70] *Re S (care order: implementation of a care plan)* [2002] UKHL 10, [2002] 2 AC 291; *Bellinger v Bellinger* [2003] UKHL 11, [2003] 2 AC 467; *R (Wright) v Secretary of State for Health* [2009] UKHL 3, [2009] 1 AC 739, para 39; *AS (Somalia) v Secretary of State for the Home Department* [2009] UKHL 32, [2009] 1 WLR 1385. For a recent example see *Mercer v Alternative Future Gorup Ltd and another* [2022] EWCA Civ 379, [2022] ICR 1034.

reference to the facts of the measure or case before the court alone. However, the extent to which matters relevant to the Court's assessment of proportionality were considered is one of a number of considerations relevant to the degree of respect a court will accord the primary judgment of Parliament.[71]

3. Interplay of sections 3 and 19

Section 19 requires the minister introducing a piece of legislation to express an opinion as to the compatibility of the legislation with the Convention. It is intended to encourage the executive to address the issue of whether proposed legislation is compatible with the Convention at a formative stage. A statement of compatibility under section 19(1)(a) cannot be ascribed to Parliament.[72] Cabinet Office guidance says that if, after further debate or amendment, a minister considered that the provisions of a Bill no longer met the standards required for a section 19(1)(a) statement, 'it would be a breach of the Ministerial Code to proceed towards Royal Assent without either amending the provisions or informing Parliament of the issue'.[73] It is only in very rare circumstances that a minister has made a statement under section 19(1)(b) that, although he or she cannot be sure that legislation may be incompatible with the Convention, the Government wishes to pass it anyway.[74]

3.45

In practice, a statement under section 19 has not had a significant effect upon courts.[75] Lord Hope described it as 'no more than expressions of opinion by the minister ... they are not binding on the court, nor do they have any persuasive authority'.[76] When Whitehall assesses whether a particular provision complies with the Convention, it applies the traditional 'Strasbourg-proofing' test, which existed before the Human Rights Act—that is, whether, on the balance of probabilities, the provisions of the Bill would be found compatible with Convention rights if challenged in court.[77] In addition, ministers seem to assume that all those public authorities that have to implement the provision will act in compliance with the Convention if they have the power to do so. So, for instance, a Bill that gave wide

3.46

---

[71] See Lord Nicholls in *Wilson v Secretary of State for Trade and Industry* [2003] UKHL 40, [2004] 1 AC 816, paras 61–67; *R (SC and others) v Secretary of State for Work and Pensions* [2012] UKSC 26, [2022] AC 223, paras 166–185.

[72] *R (SC and others) v Secretary of State for Work and Pensions* [2012] UKSC 26, [2022] AC 223, para 170.

[73] Cabinet Office, *Guide to Making Legislation 2022*, para 11.24 <Guide to making legislation - GOV. UK (www.gov.uk)>.

[74] See the s 19(1)(b) statement made in respect of the ban on the broadcasting of political advertising in the Communications Act 2003, ss 319 and 321, made in the light of *Vgt Verein gegen Tierfabriken v Switzerland* (2001) 34 EHRR 159. The House of Lords—and later the Grand Chamber of the ECtHR—in fact held the ban to be compatible with art 10 in *R (Animal Defenders International) v Secretary of State for Culture, Media and Sport* [2008] UKHL 15, [2008] 1 AC 1312 and *Animal Defenders International v United Kingdom* [2013] 57 EHRR 21.

[75] Though see Lord Bingham in *Animal Defenders* at para 33 explaining why the s 19(1)(b) statement in fact gave Parliament's judgment on the importance of the legislation particular weight.

[76] *R v A (No 2)* [2001] UKHL 25, [2002] 1 AC 45, para 69 per Lord Hope and see now *R(SC and others) v Secretary of State for Work and Pensions* [2012] UKSC 26, [2022] AC 223, para 170.

[77] Home Office evidence to the Joint Committee on Human Rights (as set out in para 15 of JCHR Report 2000–2001, HL 66, HC 332).

discretion to the police to act in ways which would clearly violate the Convention would still be assessed as complying with the Convention because the discretion would be constrained by the Human Rights Act.[78]

4. Interplay of sections 3 and 4

3.47   The dividing line between interpreting and legislating under section 3 of the Human Rights Act has an important impact upon the power conferred on higher courts to make 'statements of incompatibility' under section 4.[79] Section 4 states that, where legislation cannot be read compatibly with the Convention, courts are empowered to make a declaration of incompatibility. Logically, if courts find it impossible to construe primary legislation compatibly with the Convention under section 3 then, as 'a measure of last resort',[80] they should declare it incompatible under section 4 unless there is a good reason to exercise their discretion not to do so.[81]

3.48   In *Secretary of State for the Home Department v MB*[82] the Court of Appeal applied section 3 to achieve a Human Rights Act-compatible construction of the 'control order' provisions in the Prevention of Terrorism Act 2005, and reversed the declaration of incompatibility made by the High Court.[83] However, in *R (Hooper) v Secretary of State for Work and Pensions*[84] the provisions of the Social Security (Contributions and Benefits) Act 1992 relating to 'widows' could not be read under section 3 to include 'widowers'. As a result, the court held that the discriminatory provisions (on the grounds of sex within art 14 read with art 8) were incompatible with the Convention, and the court made a declaration of incompatibility under section 4 of the Human Rights Act.

3.49   When the whole scheme of the legislation is inconsistent with Convention rights (or where it contains several incompatibilities) it is unlikely that section 3 can be used to remedy the defect in the statute. Therefore, the courts will need to turn to section 4 and consider making a declaration of incompatibility. For example, in *R (Wright and others) v Secretary of State for Health* the House of Lords considered it impossible to use section 3 to interpret the 'provisional blacklisting' provisions for care workers in the Care Standards Act 2000 in a Human Rights Act-compliant manner, and therefore declared the relevant provisions incompatible.[85] And in *R (F) v Secretary of State for the Home Department* the Supreme Court likewise held that the indefinite requirements imposed on those convicted of sexual offences to

---

[78] *R v A (No 2)* [2001] UKHL 25, [2002] 1 AC 45.

[79] See Philip Sales, 'Rights—Consistent Interpretation and the Human Rights Act 1998' (2011) 127 Law Quarterly Review 217.

[80] Lord Steyn in *Ghaidan v Godon-Mendoza* [2004] UKHL 30, [2004] 2 AC 557.

[81] For discussion of such circumstances see eg *R (Nicklinson and another) v Ministry of Justice* [2014] UKSC 38, [2015] AC 657.

[82] *Secretary of State for the Home Department v MB* [2006] EWCA Civ 1140, [2007] QB 415.

[83] See also the appeal to the House of Lords: [2007] UKHL 46, [2008] 1 AC 440.

[84] *R (Hooper) v Secretary of State for Work and Pensions* [2003] EWCA Civ 813; and upheld by the House of Lords at [2005] UKHL 29, [2005] 1 WLR 1681.

[85] *R (Wright and others) v Secretary of State for Health* [2009] UKHL 3, [2009] 1 AC 739.

notify the authorities of their travel plans by virtue of the Sexual Offences Act 2003 were incompatible with Article 8 of the Convention; a declaration of incompatibility was therefore made.[86]

5. Section 2

Section 2[87] is the provision by which Convention rights have been 'brought much more fully into the jurisprudence of the courts throughout the United Kingdom and their interpretation ... far more subtly and powerfully woven into our law'.[88] It provides that a court or tribunal determining a question which has arisen under any statute in connection with a Convention right *must* take account of any judgment, decision, declaration, or advisory opinion of the ECtHR, opinion or decision of the Commission, or decision of the Committee of Ministers, whenever made or given, so far as, in the opinion of the court or tribunal, it is relevant to the proceedings in which that question has arisen. The decisions of the different Strasbourg organs carry different weights, and decisions of the Court sitting as a Grand Chamber take precedence.[89]

3.50

Section 2 of the Human Rights Act requires a court only to take a Strasbourg judgment into account, and not to follow it.[90] However, the domestic courts have adopted the view that the purpose of section 2 is to ensure that the same Convention rights are enforced under the Human Rights Act as would be enforced by the Strasbourg Court and that section 2 does not permit courts to adopt an autonomous domestic meaning of Convention rights.[91] As Lord Bingham said in *R (Ullah) v Special Adjudicator*:[92]

3.51

It is of course open to member states to provide for rights more generous than those guaranteed by the Convention, but such provision should not be the product of interpretation of the Convention by national courts, since the meaning of the Convention should be uniform throughout the states party to it. The duty of national courts is to keep pace with the Strasbourg jurisprudence as it evolves over time: no more, but certainly no less.[93]

The approach adopted is essentially that, absent special circumstances, the domestic courts will follow any clear and consistent case law of the Strasbourg Court, and

---

[86] *R (F) v Secretary of State for the Home Department* [2010] UKSC 17, [2011] 1 AC 331.

[87] Francesca Klug and Helen Wildbore, 'Follow or Lead? The Human Rights Act and the European Court of Human Rights' [2010] European Human Rights Law Review 621.

[88] See *Rights Brought Home: The Human Rights Bill* (Cm 3782, 1997) para 1.14.

[89] See Chapter 8.

[90] *R v Horncastle* [2009] UKSC 14, [2010] 2 AC 373 (a seven-judge court).

[91] *N v Secretary of State for the Home Department* [2005] UKHL 31, [2005] 2 AC 296; *R (Ullah) v Special Adjudicator* [2004] UKHL 26, [2004] 2 AC 323; *R (Al Jedda) v Secretary of State for Defence* [2007] UKHL 58, [2008] 1 AC 332; and more recently *R (Elan-Cane) v Secretary of State for the Home Department* [2021] UKSC 56, [2022] 2 WLR 133, paras 86–89 and 101.

[92] *R (Ullah) v Special Adjudicator* [2004] UKHL 26, [2004] 2 AC 323.

[93] See also Lord Hope in *N v Secretary of State for the Home Department* [2005] UKHL 31, [2005] 2 AC 296, para 25. This case has been consistently followed on numerous occasions by the House of Lords and Supreme Court.

especially a considered judgment of the Court sitting as a Grand Chamber.[94] While occasionally the Supreme Court appeared to go further than strictly required by Strasbourg, typically when ECtHR jurisprudence was not well developed,[95] in general *Ullah* was interpreted to require a strict adherence to Strasbourg decisions. As Lord Rodger famously stated in *AF (No 3)*: 'Strasbourg has spoken, the case is closed'.[96]

3.52   Over recent years, the willingness of the domestic courts to depart from Strasbourg case law has increased. It was established early in the life of the Human Rights Act that one circumstance in which domestic courts may decline to follow Strasbourg case law is when the decision is based on a clear misunderstanding of domestic law or procedure.[97] The principle was stretched in *R v Horncastle* in which the Supreme Court actively entered into a dialogue with the Strasbourg Court over the admission of hearsay evidence in criminal trials.[98] The Supreme Court declined to follow the decision in *Al-Khawaja and Tahery v UK* and effectively invited the UK to appeal to the Grand Chambers to reconsider its decision in *Al-Khawaja*.[99] The Grand Chamber accepted the Supreme Court's analysis of the hearsay rules and found that hearsay could be admitted in certain circumstances without violating Article 6.[100]

3.53   Some senior judges have questioned the wisdom of the *Ullah* principle. Baroness Hale argued in 2011 that the 'mirror principle ... can suggest a position of deference [to the Strasbourg Court] from which it is difficult to have an effective dialogue'.[101] In *Ambrose v Harris*, Lord Kerr attacked the '*Ullah*-type reticence' under which 'it is ... considered wrong to attempt to anticipate developments at the supra-national level of the Strasbourg court' and which dictates that domestic courts 'should not go where Strasbourg has not yet gone'.[102] However, the Supreme Court has more recently endorsed a restrictive approach (overruling dicta in a number of House of Lords and Supreme Court cases[103]) holding that where the Strasbourg Court has

---

[94] *R (Alconbury Development Ltd) v Secretary of State for Environment Transport and the Regions* [2001] UKHL 23, [2003] 2 AC 295, para 26 and *R. (Anderson) v Secretary of State for the Home Department* [2002] UKHL 46, [2003] 1 AC 837, para 18.

[95] See eg *Re G* [2008] UKHL 38, [2009] 1 AC 173; *EM (Lebanon) v Secretary of State for the Home Department* [2008] UKHL 64, [2009] 1 AC 1198.

[96] *Secretary of State for the Home Department v AF (No 3)* [2009] UKHL 28, [2010] 2 AC 269, para 98. See also *Manchester City Council v Pinnock* [2010] UKSC 45, [2011] 2 AC 104, para 48.

[97] *R v Spear* [2002] UKHL 31, [2003] 1 AC 734, paras 12–13, declining to follow *Morris v UK* (2002) 34 EHRR 1253; see *R v Horncastle* [2009] UKSC 14, [2010] 2 AC 373, declining to follow *Al Khawaja and Tahery v UK* (2009) 49 EHRR 1 (with the Grand Chamber thereafter following the approach of the Supreme Court: (2012) 54 EHRR 24), and *Tomlinson and others v Birmingham City Council* [2010] UKSC 8, [2010] 2 WLR 471.

[98] *R v Horncastle* [2009] UKSC 14, [2010] 2 AC 373.

[99] *Al Khawaja and Tahery v UK* (2009) 49 EHRR 1.

[100] *Al Khawaja and Tahery v UK* (2012) 54 EHRR 24.

[101] 'Argentoratum Locutum: Is the Supreme Court Supreme?', Nottingham Human Rights Lecture, 2011.

[102] *Ambrose v Harris* [2011] UKSC 43, [2011] 1 WLR 2435, para 126. See also *Children's Rights Alliance for England (CRAE) v Secretary of State for Justice and others* [2013] EWCA Civ 34, [2013] 1 WLR 3667, para 64 per Lord Justice Laws. See also Lord Justice Laws, 'The Common Law and Europe', The Hamlyn Lectures, 27 November 2013. He described *Ullah* as a 'wrong turning in our law', para 26.

[103] See eg *In re G (Adoption: Unmarried Couple)* [2009] 1 AC 173 and *R (Nicklinson) v Ministry of Justice* [2014] UKSC 38, [2015] AC 657.

found the Convention not to be breached because an issue falls within the state's margin of appreciation, it will not be open to the domestic courts to find a breach in the same situation.[104] This approach reflects the prevailing understanding of the current composition of the Supreme Court as to the proper constitutional relationship between Parliament and the courts. However, in our view it is ultimately inconsistent with the parliamentary intention behind the Human Rights Act to 'bring rights home', the associated constitutional role assigned to the domestic courts to adjudicate on compliance with these domestic rights, and the fact that in so doing the domestic courts are not subject to the same institutional disadvantages of physical and cultural distance, which underpin the international law concept of the margin of appreciation, as is the Strasbourg Court.[105] The domestic courts nevertheless still can and must aim to anticipate how the Strasbourg Court might be expected to decide the case applying established principles to circumstances not yet addressed in its case law.[106]

Section 2 does not displace the doctrine of precedent in English law. In *Kay v Lambeth London Borough Council*, the House of Lords held that lower courts remained bound to follow higher domestic authority in preference to Strasbourg case law, save in wholly exceptional cases where the previous domestic decision was reached without reference to the Convention, before the Human Rights Act was in force and led to a finding against the United Kingdom in the European Court of Human Rights.[107]

    3.54

E. PUBLIC AUTHORITIES AND THE HUMAN RIGHTS ACT: MEANING OF 'PUBLIC AUTHORITY' AND 'FUNCTIONS OF A PUBLIC NATURE'

Section 6 of the Human Rights Act imposed a new statutory duty upon all public authorities to act compatibly with the Convention, and section 7 created new causes of action through which these 'vertically effective' obligations can be enforced. In other words, if a body is a public authority, then individuals have *direct* statutory remedies against them for breach of section 6(1), either by way of judicial review or for breach of statutory duty. A defendant can also rely on their rights against a public authority in any legal proceedings. As a result, the question of which types of bodies come within the definition of a 'public authority' for the purposes of the

    3.55

---

[104] *R (Elan-Cane) v Secretary of State for the Home Department* [2021] UKSC 56, [2022] 2 WLR 133, paras 68–108.

[105] See eg *Re Recovery of Medical Costs for Asbestos Diseases (Wales) Bill* [2015] UKSC 3, [2015] AC 1016, para 54 per Lord Mance.

[106] *R (AB) v Secretary of State for Justice* [2021] UKSC 28, [2021] 3 WLR 494, paras 54–59; *R (Elan-Cane) v Secretary of State for the Home Department* [2021] UKSC 56, [2022] 2 WLR 133, para 101.

[107] *Kay v Lambeth London Borough Council* [2006] UKHL 10, [2006] 2 AC 465. Where a Court of Appeal decision is inconsistent with a later decision of the ECtHR, the Court of Appeal may, but is not obliged to, depart from its previous decision: *R (RJM)(FC) v Secretary of State for Work and Pensions* [2008] UKHL 63, [2008] 3 WLR 1023.

Act is a very important one, not only for individual litigants seeking to ascertain whether they have a cause of action (or defence), but for the overall ambit of the Act.

3.56　'Public authorities' that are subject to the direct 'vertical' effect of the Human Rights Act include core public authorities, which are 'obviously' public in nature, in respect of all their functions, whether the nature of those functions is public or private.[108] However, section 6(3)(b) and (5) also deem to be a public authority any person certain of whose functions are functions of a public nature *in respect of the performance of those public functions*, but not in respect of acts *the nature of which is private*. The concepts of 'functions of a public nature' and acts 'the nature of which is private' are therefore critical to understanding the ambit of the Act. The case law on this subject is complex and controversial.

1. 'Core' public authorities

3.57　'Core' public authorities include all bodies that are obviously public in nature, such as government departments and ministers, local authorities, NHS Trusts, coroners, police, prisons, bodies such as the Parole Board, Legal Aid Agency, and the General Medical Council. The House of Lords has favoured a relatively narrow test for core public authority status.[109] Core public authorities must act in conformity with the Convention whether exercising functions governed by public law (eg assessment to tax) or private law (eg employment). Core public authorities do not enjoy the protection of Convention rights; in contrast, functional public authorities are not absolutely excluded from the protection of Convention rights.[110]

2. 'Functional' public authorities

3.58　'Functional' or 'hybrid' public authorities in section 6(3)(b) include any person 'certain of whose functions are functions of a public nature', but only in relation to public functions. Section 6(5) provides that 'In relation to a particular act, a person is not a public authority by virtue only of subsection (3)(b) if the nature of the act is private'.

3.59　The Human Rights Act was intended to apply to 'a wide rather than a narrow range of public authorities'[111] and to encompass:

a realistic and modern definition of the state so as to provide a correspondingly wide protection against the abuse of human rights.[112]

3.60　The Lord Chancellor said that:

[Section 6(3)(b)] is there to include bodies which are not manifestly public authorities, but some of whose functions are only of a public nature ... Railtrack would fall into that category because

---

[108] Section 6(3)(a).
[109] *Aston Cantlow and Wilmcote with Billesley Parochial Church Council v Wallbank* [2003] UKHL 37, [2004] 1 AC 546.
[110] ibid para 11.
[111] *Hansard*, HL, col 1232 (3 November 1997).
[112] Jack Straw, *Hansard*, HC, cols 405–08 (17 June 1998).

it exercises public functions in its role as a safety regulator, but it is acting privately as a property developer. A private security company would be exercising public functions in relation to the management of a contracted out prison but would be acting privately when, for example, guarding commercial premises. Doctors in general practice would be public authorities in relation to their National Health Service functions, but not in relation to their private patients.[113]

The intention was to reflect the line of Strasbourg case law which holds that a state cannot escape liability under the Convention by delegating essentially public functions to private bodies.[114] The effect is that a direct cause of action is available against functional public authorities for acting in breach of the Convention, and hence unlawfully, when the act under challenge is of a public nature, including in contexts where its functions would potentially otherwise be amenable to judicial review; but not when they are acting within the scope of their *private* law activities.   3.61

The extent to which private organizations performing delegated public functions should be regarded as functional public authorities has proved controversial.[115] In *Aston Cantlow Parochial Church Council v Wallbank*[116] the determining factor was said to be whether the nature of the function performed was public.[117] It was held that there should be a 'generously wide' interpretation of public function but that there was 'no single test of universal application ... given the diverse nature of governmental functions and the variety of means by which these functions are discharged today'. Relevant factors included the extent to which in carrying out the relevant function the body is publicly funded, or is exercising statutory powers, or is taking the place of central government or local authorities, or is providing a public service.[118]   3.62

However, although the House of Lords in *Aston Cantlow* appeared to lay down a broad functional approach, it did not expressly overrule the decisions in earlier cases in which courts had taken rather narrower approaches to what factors were relevant to deciding whether a body was a 'functional' public authority. Those cases focused more narrowly on the institutional features of the situation, rather than the nature of the functions being performed, and their place in public service provision.[119] Relevant features, in rendering a function which would otherwise be private, public, had been held to include, for example, whether the body was exercising   3.63

---

[113] *Hansard*, HL, vol 583, col 811 (24 November 1997).

[114] *Costello-Roberts v United Kingdom* (1995) 19 EHRR 112.

[115] See JCHR Report, 'The Meaning of Public Authority under the Human Rights Act', 7th Report (2003–04), HL 39, HC 382, February 2004; Maurice Sunkin, 'Pushing Forward the Frontiers of Human Rights Protection: The Meaning of Public Authority under the Human Rights Act' [2004] Public Law 643; Dawn Oliver, 'Functions of a Public Nature under the Human Rights Act' [2004] Public Law 329; Paul Craig, 'Contracting Out, the Human Rights Act, and the Scope of Judicial Review' (2002) 118 Law Quarterly Review 551.

[116] *Aston Cantlow Parochial Church Council v Wallbank* [2003] UKHL 37, [2004] 1 AC 546.

[117] ibid para 41 per Lord Hope.

[118] ibid paras 11–12 per Lord Nicholls.

[119] See eg *Donoghue v Poplar Housing Association* [2001] EWCA Civ 595, [2002] QB 48, para 58; *R (Heather) v Leonard Cheshire Foundation* [2002] EWCA Civ 366, [2002] 2 All ER 936.

statutory authority not available to private persons,[120] and the proximity of the relationship between the private body and the delegating public authority.

3.64   The Joint Committee on Human Rights (JCHR) expressed concern about the 'deficit' in protection resulting from the *Leonard Cheshire* decision[121] for those who received public services on a contracted-out basis.[122]

3.65   Since then, a number of cases in the lower courts have examined the issue of which bodies are 'functional public authorities' for the purposes of the Human Rights Act.[123] They sometimes appeared to focus closely on the legal nature of the *body* in question, and inadequately on the reality of the functions that particular bodies are performing, notwithstanding that Jack Straw (then Home Secretary) had said, when introducing the Bill:

[A]s we are dealing with public functions and with an evolving situation, we believe that the test must relate to the substance and nature of the act, not to the form and legal personality.[124]

3.66   The law therefore took a serious, and, in our view, wrong turn when, in 2007, the House of Lords considered the point of principle in *Leonard Cheshire* and, by a bare majority of 3–2, endorsed it in what remains the leading case on the meaning of 'functions of a public nature', *YL v Birmingham City Council*.[125] In that case, the House of Lords held that a privately owned care home which provided accommodation and care for an elderly and vulnerable resident which was both arranged and paid for by the local authority nonetheless did not perform a 'function of a public nature' in doing so. Although the House of Lords endorsed the list of factors it had earlier set out in *Aston Cantlow*, the judges in the majority and the minority afforded significantly different weight to the various factors in that balance.

3.67   The majority of the House of Lords in *YL* (Lord Scott, Lord Mance, and Lord Neuberger) held that there was a distinction between the council's function in arranging and paying for the care and accommodation pursuant to its statutory duty, and that of the private company in providing the care and accommodation under contract, on a commercial basis (albeit paid for by public money), rather than on the basis of a direct subsidy from public funds. They focused heavily on the company's commercial purposes:

---

[120] See eg *R (A) v Partnerships in Care Ltd* [2002] EWHC 529 (Admin), [2002] 1 WLR 2610, where the decision of managers of a private psychiatric hospital to alter the care and treatment of a patient was an act of a public nature, susceptible to judicial review, and the hospital managers were, by virtue of the statutory regime and regulations under the Registered Homes Act 1984 and the Mental Health Act 1983, a public authority for the purposes of the Human Rights Act.

[121] *R (Heather) v Leonard Cheshire Foundation* [2002] EWCA Civ 366, [2002] 2 All ER 936.

[122] JCHR, 'The Meaning of Public Authority under the Human Rights Act', 7th Report (2003–2004), HL 39, HC 382, February 2004.

[123] See eg *Cameron v Network Rail Infrastructure Ltd* [2006] EWHC 1133 (QBD); *R (Mullin) v Jockey Club Appeal Board (No 1)* [2005] EWHC 2197 (Admin), [2006] ACD 2; *R (Beer) v Hampshire County Council* [2003] EWCA Civ 1056, [2004] 1 WLR 233; *R (West) v Lloyds of London* [2004] EWCA Civ 506, [2004] 3 All ER 251, supply of electricity; *James v London Electricity plc* [2004] EWHC 3226 (QB).

[124] *Hansard*, HC, cols 409–10 (17 June 1998).

[125] *YL v Birmingham City Council* [2007] UKHL 27, [2008] 1 AC 95.

It is neither a charity nor a philanthropist ... It receives no public funding, enjoys no special statutory powers, and ... charge[s] whatever fees in its commercial judgment it thinks suitable.[126]

In a strongly worded dissent, Lord Bingham and Baroness Hale disagreed. Lord   3.68
Bingham said:

When the 1998 Act was passed, it was very well known that a number of functions formerly carried out by public authorities were now carried out by private bodies. Section 6(3)(b) of the 1998 Act was clearly drafted with this well-known fact in mind. The performance by private body A by arrangement with public body B, and perhaps at the expense of B, of what would undoubtedly be a public function if carried out by B, is in my opinion, precisely the case which section 6(3)(b) was intended to embrace. It is, in my opinion, this case.[127]

Baroness Hale attached importance to the public interest in the provision of such care, the fact that there was public funding for such care, and the coercive regulatory powers of the state,[128] and concluded:

Taken together, these factors lead inexorably to the conclusion that the company, in providing accommodation, health and social care for [YL], was performing a function of a public nature. This was a function performed for [YL] pursuant to statutory arrangements, at public expense and in the public interest.[129]

With respect, we agree with the minority in that case that the decision of the   3.69
majority does not reflect the clear intention of Parliament in adopting a 'functional' approach to the concept of a 'public authority', but, rather, places an erroneous focus on the nature of the provider and its commercial motivation.[130] The specific outcome in *YL* in respect of the application of the Human Rights Act to care homes was reversed by legislation,[131] but the general approach to the scope of the functional public authority test prevails.

The consequence of *YL* has been considerable uncertainty as to the ambit of   3.70
the Human Rights Act. For example, the Court of Appeal has held that housing management functions performed by a registered social landlord were 'public functions'.[132] It has also led to a serious protection gap for vulnerable individuals in relation to public services procured from the private sector.[133] As the JCHR pointed out following its inquiry into this issue, the consequence is that 'a central provision of the Human Rights Act has been compromised in a way which reduces

---

[126] ibid para 26 per Lord Scott.

[127] ibid para 20.

[128] ibid paras 67–69.

[129] ibid para 73.

[130] See also the criticisms of Baroness Hale (one of the minority) in her speech to the Salford Human Rights Conference, 4 June 2010 <http://Microsoft Word - SALFORD HUMAN RIGHTS CONFERENCE 2010 delivered.doc (supremecourt.uk)>.

[131] See Health and Social Care Act 2008, s 145.

[132] *London Quadrant Housing Trust v Weaver* [2009] EWCA Civ 58, [2010] 1 WLR 363.

[133] See eg recently *R (Boyce) v Teeside and Hartlepool Senior Coroner* [2022] EWHC 107 Admin, [2022] 4 WLR 15, para 40 (delegated care and accommodation provided by a private provider to children subject to a s 31 Care Act 2014 care and supervision order not an exercise of a public function).

the protection it was intended to give to people at some of the most vulnerable moments in their lives'.[134]

F. PRIVATE PARTIES AND THE HUMAN RIGHTS ACT

3.71   The Convention is not 'directly effective' against private litigants. In litigation concerning purely private bodies, or 'functional public authorities' in pursuit of their 'functions of a private nature', there is no stand-alone cause of action for 'breach of the Convention' under section 7 of the Act.[135] It is not therefore possible for one private individual to sue another private legal person for a tort of 'breach of the Convention'.

3.72   The Convention is, however, indirectly enforceable against a private legal person in the following ways:

(a) Where the effect of a statutory provision is in question in a dispute between private individuals, the courts—as 'public authorities' for the purposes of the Act—are under an obligation to interpret the legislation insofar as possible to accord with the Convention (under s 3 in conjunction with s 6(3) of the Human Rights Act). For example, in *Wilson v First County Trust (No 2)*[136] both parties were 'private' individuals. This did not prevent the Court of Appeal deciding that the bar against enforcing a credit agreement breached the pawnbroker's right of access to a court under Article 6 of the Convention and the right to property under Article 1 of Protocol 1.[137]

(b) Similarly, where there is a judicial discretion to be exercised, section 6 requires it to be exercised so as to give effect to a Convention right (eg in civil proceedings between private parties when the court has a discretion regarding the admission of evidence obtained in breach of a Convention right).

(c) Where the rights in question touch upon positive obligations (especially under art 2, 3, 4, 8, 10, 11, or 14) the court is itself under a positive obligation to protect individuals from the violation of their rights by other private individuals. For example, in *Venables and Thompson v Newsgroup Newspapers and Associated Newspapers Ltd*[138] the two children who had been convicted of the murder of James Bulger were granted permanent injunctions preventing publication of further information about them on the basis that the Court of Appeal was

---

[134] JCHR, 'The Meaning of Public Authority under the Human Rights Act', 7th Report (2003–2004), HL 39, HC 382, February 2004.

[135] *Campbell v MGN Ltd* [2004] UKHL 22, [2004] 2 AC 457; and the Court of Appeal in *X v Y* [2004] EWCA Civ 662, para 58. See also the rationale advanced by Murray Hunt in 'The "Horizontal Effect" of the Human Rights Act' [1998] Public Law 423 and Lord Steyn in '2000–2005: Laying the Foundations of Human Rights Law in the United Kingdom' [2005] European Human Rights Law Review 349.

[136] *Wilson v First County Trust (No 2)* [2001] EWCA Civ 633, [2002] QB 74.

[137] See also the House of Lords' decision at [2003] UKHL 40, [2004] 1 AC 816 (reversed on other grounds).

[138] *Venables and Thompson v Newsgroup Newspapers and Associated Newspapers Ltd* [2001] 2 WLR 1038; and *Campbell v MGN Ltd* [2004] UKHL 22, [2004] 2 AC 457.

under a positive obligation to secure their right to life (art 2) and right to respect for private life (art 8). The Strasbourg jurisprudence on such positive obligations is a developing field. See Chapter 2, paragraphs 2.33–2.39.

(d) Where the courts are dealing with cases involving the common law they have developed the common law in harmony with Convention rights and values (including pursuant to the duty in s 6(3)). The 'horizontal' effects of the Human Rights Act in private litigation have been especially marked in this area.

The effects of the Convention on evolving the common law torts have been seen most clearly in a series of cases concerning the privacy of public figures and the misuse of private information, in which the boundaries of common law torts have been transformed, analysed further in Chapter 6. It has now become clear that a litigant, A, who wishes to use a Convention argument in a case brought against a private opponent, B, may be able to do so if A finds an existing private law argument on which to 'hang' the Convention argument (eg breach of confidence in tort in relation to an infringement of the right to respect for private life). A could also focus the action on a public body, C, which has failed to protect A's rights from being violated by B. In this way Convention standards have infiltrated, influenced, and even created new common law rights, and will continue to do so.   3.73

G. EXCEPTIONS AND SPECIAL CASES

The Human Rights Act is principally a constitutional instrument of general application. However, one important omission from the Schedule to the Act (art 13) and two specific provisions (ss 12 and 13) about particular interest groups (the press and religious organizations) require brief explanation.[139]   3.74

1. Article 13

Article 13 imposes a duty on the state to provide the opportunity to test at a national level whether a Convention right has been violated. It guarantees in general terms that there is a suitable national avenue of redress capable of providing a remedy in an appropriate case. However, it does not mean that states have to ensure that a *particular* result is secured. So, for example, the right will be breached where the victim has no right of recourse in the domestic courts[140] or where primary legislation excludes any such challenge. Article 13 is not a free-standing right (ie a claim cannot be founded on the article alone and must be brought in connection with an alleged breach of another Convention right), but it is not necessary to show a breach of another Convention right before the court can consider its application—it is enough to show that the complaint in relation to the other right is 'arguable' but   3.75

---

[139] For a full discussion of the scope and content of arts 8, 9, 10, and 13 of the Convention, see Chapter 6.
[140] *Halford v United Kingdom* (1997) 24 EHRR 523.

cannot be argued because there is no means for this to be done before a national court.[141]

3.76   Although Article 13 is not one of the rights included in the Schedule to the Human Rights Act, it was intended that the Act itself would give effect to Articles 1 and 13 by securing the rights and freedoms of the Convention. In other words, Article 13 is given effect by establishing a scheme under which Convention rights can be raised and remedied before UK courts. In *Re S (FC) and others* Lord Nicholls said:

> Article 13 guarantees the availability at the national level of an effective remedy to enforce the substance of Convention rights. Sections 7 and 8 seek to provide that remedy in this country. The object of these sections is to provide in English law the very remedy article 13 declares is the entitlement of everyone whose rights are violated.[142]

2. Section 12

3.77   The object of section 12 is to emphasize that the courts must pay due regard to Article 10 and the right to freedom of expression contained in that article. It was a response to lobbying by some sections of the press during the passage of the Human Rights Bill which argued that the judiciary might interpret Article 8 of the Convention (right to respect for private and family life) in a way which unacceptably limited the freedom of the press. In practice, those concerns are not justified[143] and section 12 has had little effect.

3.78   Section 12 has a number of components. First, it prevents 'gagging injunctions' being granted *ex parte* except in the rarest of circumstances. It provides that if a court is considering whether to grant any relief that might affect the exercise of the Convention right to freedom of expression *ex parte*, there is a presumption against the grant of such relief.[144] 'No such relief is to be granted' unless the court is satisfied that the person seeking the relief has taken all practicable steps to notify the defendant, or there are compelling reasons why the defendant should not be notified.[145] Secondly, the merits of the claimant's case must be tested before any such restraint is made. Section 12(3) provides that no relief is to be granted so as to restrain publication before trial unless the court is satisfied that the applicant is likely to establish

---

[141] *Boyle and Rice v United Kingdom* (1988) 10 EHRR 425.

[142] *Re S (FC) and others* [2002] UKHL 10, [2002] 2 AC 291, para 61.

[143] See *Re S (A child) (identification) restrictions on publication* [2004] UKHL 47, [2005] 1 AC 593, in which Lord Steyn explained the 'balancing exercise' that needs to take place in order to balance the competing demands of respect for private life and freedom of expression.

[144] For a discussion of the scope of the term 'relief', see *A v British Broadcasting Corporation (Scotland)* [2014] UKSC 25, [2014] 2 All ER 1037.

[145] Section 12(1) and (2). Note that in *X & Y v Persons Unknown* [2007] EMLR 290 Eady J concluded that its ambit covered not only the parties to the proceedings but also non-parties who in practice are likely to have their art 10 right constrained by an injunction. The Report of the Committee on Super-Injunctions, chaired by Lord Neuberger, emphasized that a failure to provide advance notice is only justifiable in exceptional circumstances: para 3.22.

that publication should not be allowed.[146] Thirdly, section 12(4) provides that the court must have 'particular regard' to the right to freedom of expression, and that where the proceedings relate to material which the respondent claims is, or which appears to the court to be, journalistic, literary, or artistic material, the court must have regard to the extent to which the material has been, or is about to become, available to the public, or it is, or would be, in the public interest for the material to be published.[147] It must also have regard to any relevant privacy code.

Perhaps because Article 10 itself requires 'particular regard' to be given to the right to freedom of expression, in practice, domestic courts have made clear that section 12 adds little to existing domestic or Strasbourg jurisprudence[148] and the court will need to form its own view on the balance between Articles 8 and 10 on the facts of a particular case. This topic has been one of acute public controversy (and considerable public misunderstanding), fuelled by the granting of the first 'super-injunction' in the *Trafigura* case[149] and a number of anonymized injunctions.[150] Whilst it is fairly clear that super-injunctions have been applied for only rarely, and have normally been granted (if at all) only for a limited period, it has been stressed that 'such injunctions [should] only be granted following intense scrutiny by the court in the individual case, and only when it is strictly necessary as a means to ensure that justice is done'.[151]

3.79

3. Section 13

During the passage of the Human Rights Bill, fears were expressed on behalf of the Church of England, for example, that the Human Rights Act might lead to questions about whether they could refuse to marry gay couples,[152] or dismiss church schoolteachers who had lost their faith. To address these fears, section 13 provides that if the court's determination of any question under the Act might affect the exercise by a religious organization, whether as an organization or by its members collectively, of the Convention right to freedom of thought, conscience, and

3.80

---

[146] See *Cream Holdings v Banerjee* [2004] UKHL 44, [2005] 1 AC 253 where the House of Lords considered the test under s 12(3) and accorded it a relatively limited effect. See also *Campbell v MGN Limited* [2004] UKHL 22, [2004] 2 AC 457, para 55 per Lord Hoffmann and para 141 per Baroness Hale; and, recently, *ETK v News Group Newspapers* [2011] EWCA Civ 439, para 10(6).

[147] See *Green Corns Ltd v Clavery Group* [2005] EWHC 958 (QB), where the fact that the information in question was available to the public did not justify withholding an injunction under s 12 because the information was not so widely in the public domain, and re-publication could have an effect and was likely to impact on art 8 rights.

[148] For the courts' general approach, see *Ashdown v Telegraph Group* [2001] EWCA Civ 1142, [2001] 3 WLR 1368; *Clayton v Clayton* [2006] EWCA Civ 878; and *Re Ward; BBC v CAFCASS Legal* [2007] EWHC 616 (Fam).

[149] *RJW & SJW v The Guardian News and Media Ltd*, Order of Maddison J of 11 September 2009.

[150] See, in particular, *CTB v News Group Newspapers and Imogen Thomas* [2011] EWHC 1232 (QB) (injunction granted); *Terry v Persons Unknown* [2010] EWHC 119 (QB) (injunction refused).

[151] Report of the Committee on Super-Injunctions, para 2.37; see also para 2.28.

[152] The Marriage (Same Sex Couples) Act 2013 provides that no person can be compelled to perform a marriage of same-sex couples, thus enabling the church to opt out of solemnizing same-sex unions.

religion, it must have particular regard to the importance of that right. This is something that is inherent in the structure of Article 9 of the Convention, which is where that guarantee is to be found. Since the whole scheme of the Convention is to give particular regard to a prima facie right, permitting derogations from it only if they are necessary, proportionate, and so on, the effect of this section is really to add political comfort to religious interests rather than to add anything in terms of practical effect.[153] In many cases where a dispute about the meaning of section 13 might arise, the question is now one governed by the provisions protecting people from discrimination on the grounds of religion or belief,[154] or on the grounds of sexual orientation.[155]

---

[153] See per Richards J (as he then was) in *R (Amicus) v Secretary of State for Trade and Industry* [2004] EWHC 860 (Admin), [2004] ELR 31, para 41: 'section 13 of the 1998 Act does not give greater weight to [art 9] rights than they would otherwise enjoy under the Convention'; see too *R (Williamson) v Secretary of State for Education and Employment* [2002] EWCA Civ 1926 (for s 13 discussion, not overruled by House of Lords); and *R (Surayanda) v Welsh Ministers* [2007] EWCA Civ 893. Ordinarily, the courts do not refer to s 13 when applying art 9 of the Convention: see eg *Ladele v London Borough of Islington* [2009] ICR 387 (EAT) and *Ladele v Islington LBC* [2009] EWCA Civ 1357, [2010] 1 WLR 955.

[154] Equality Act 2010, s 10.

[155] Equality Act 2010, s 12.

4

ENFORCING THE HUMAN RIGHTS ACT

Blackstone's Guide to The Human Rights Act 1998. Eighth Edition. John Wadham, Helen Mountfield KC, Raj Desai, Sarah Hannett KC, Jessica Jones, Eleanor Mitchell, and Aidan Wills, Oxford University Press. © John Wadham, Helen Mountfield KC, Raj Desai, Sarah Hannett KC, Jessica Jones, Eleanor Mitchell, and Aidan Wills 2024. DOI: 10.1093/oso/9780192885050.003.0004

A. INTRODUCTION

4.01 The Human Rights Act was intended to 'bring rights home', so that any remedy which can be secured in Strasbourg is available in national courts and tribunals. This chapter deals with the practicalities of how the Human Rights Act seeks to achieve this objective and addresses the domestic application of the concepts discussed in Chapter 2. All section references in the footnotes are to the Human Rights Act, unless indicated otherwise.

4.02 In recognition of the espoused aim of the Act, section 7 is constructed so that litigants can raise Convention arguments in existing causes of action, claims, and proceedings; or, if no such domestic law causes of action are available, to bring stand-alone proceedings to allege breach of a Convention right against a public authority as a statutory tort.

4.03 Section 7 provides that a person who claims that a 'public authority'[1] has acted, or proposes to act, in a way that is incompatible with Convention rights[2] can either bring proceedings against the authority in an appropriate court or tribunal or can raise the Convention arguments concerned in any legal proceedings, but only if they can show that they are, or would be, a 'victim' of the unlawful act.[3]

4.04 To 'bring rights home' effectively, the Human Rights Act was drafted to ensure that victims of violations of Convention rights could seek remedies in domestic courts which would afford them 'just satisfaction' for any breaches of Convention rights they had suffered. Reflecting this intention, the Act creates both a cause of action, including a right to damages, under section 8, *and* gives higher courts the power to grant 'declarations of incompatibility' under section 4. The courts also retain existing remedies that fall within the jurisdiction of the relevant court, so other remedies which can be and are awarded under section 8(1) are familiar, such as (in a civil law context): damages; declarations; injunctions; and a mandatory quashing or prohibiting order in judicial review proceedings governed by Part 54 of the Civil Procedure Rules (CPR). In criminal proceedings, the remedies available to a defendant who establishes a violation of his or her Convention rights include: an order withdrawing the issue of a summons; a motion to quash an indictment; a stay of the criminal proceedings as abuse of process; the dismissal of the prosecution; the exclusion of evidence (or an order requiring the inclusion of evidence); or even (to reflect the breach) a reduction in sentence. The Court of Appeal has the power to quash a conviction where there has been a breach of Article 6 in the course of the trial.

4.05 However, the case law on damages for violations of the Act is increasing but remains relatively underdeveloped, and despite the broad phrasing of section 8 permitting courts to grant any relief or remedy within their powers as they consider 'just and appropriate', imaginative remedies remain relatively rare.

---

[1] The definition of this term is discussed in Chapter 3.
[2] Section 6(1).
[3] Section 7(1).

B. THE APPROPRIATE FORUM FOR AN ARGUMENT UNDER THE HUMAN RIGHTS ACT

The Human Rights Act was designed to ensure that the Convention becomes an   4.06
intrinsic part of all aspects of the UK legal system and that all courts and tribunals
are able to consider arguments brought under the Convention. Convention arguments are available in every public forum in which legal rights are determined,
from the magistrates' court to the Supreme Court (even though only the higher
courts have the power to make a declaration of incompatibility and the power to
award damages is restricted—see Chapter 3). Section 7 refers to bringing proceedings against a public authority 'in the appropriate court or tribunal'[4] and to relying
on Convention rights 'in any legal proceedings'.[5] 'Legal proceedings' is defined as
including 'proceedings brought by or at the instigation of a public authority' and
'an appeal against the decision of a court or Tribunal'.[6]

The 'appropriate court or tribunal' is determined by rules issued under the   4.07
Human Rights Act[7] but, broadly, claims go to the court or tribunal most accus-
tomed to dealing with claims analogous to the subject matter in question. For example, the Civil Procedure (Amendment No 4) Rules 2000[8] set out the procedure to
be adopted in the Administrative Court; and Part 29 of the Family Procedure Rules
2010[9] give details of the treatment of human rights issues in the family courts.[10]
Practice Direction 9 of the Supreme Court Rules 2009[11] makes provision for the
treatment of human rights points in the Supreme Court.

Some illustrative examples of an appropriate forum are as follows. In a false   4.08
imprisonment claim, a person who wishes to claim damages for breach of Article 3
(freedom from torture or inhuman or degrading treatment) or Article 5 (the right to
liberty and security of the person) could bring a damages claim for breach of statutory duty under section 6(1) of the Human Rights Act in the King's Bench Division
of the High Court or the county court. Alternatively, the breach could be the basis
for a habeas corpus or judicial review application in the Administrative Court.
A demonstrator who is prosecuted for obstruction of the highway or obstruction of
a police officer may be able to invoke the right to peaceful assembly in Article 11 as
a defence in the Crown Court or magistrates' court.

The lower courts and tribunals do not, however, have the power under section   4.09
4(5) of the Human Rights Act to issue a declaration of incompatibility. Where

---

[4] Section 7(1)(a).
[5] Section 7(1)(b).
[6] Section 7(6).
[7] Section 7(2) and (9).
[8] SI 2000/2092.
[9] SI 2010/2995. Practice Direction 29B (the Human Rights Act 1998).
[10] Applications for substantive relief (declarations and/or damages) under the Human Rights Act should
be issued as civil proceedings by way of a CPR Part 8 claim, not by using family proceeding forms, even if
within existing Children Act 1989 proceedings: *In re W (Children) (Convention Rights Claim: Procedure)*
[2017] EWHC 450 (Fam), [2017] 1 WLR 3451.
[11] SI 2009/1603.

proceedings are brought in the county court and a question of making a declaration of incompatibility has arisen, Part 30 of the CPR requires the court to consider transferring the proceedings to the High Court. However, it is not necessary to transfer the proceedings to the High Court merely because a breach of a Convention right is alleged, if resolving that breach does not involve a declaration of incompatibility.[12]

4.10   In civil proceedings generally, where a party is seeking to rely on any provision of, or right arising under, the Human Rights Act, or seeks a remedy available under the Act, he or she must, in the statement of case:

(a) give details of the Convention right which it is alleged has been infringed and details of the alleged infringement;

(b) specify the relief sought;

(c) state whether the relief sought includes a declaration of incompatibility pursuant to section 4 of the Human Rights Act and, if so, give precise details of the legislative provision which is alleged to be incompatible and details of the alleged incompatibility;

(d) state whether the relief sought includes damages in respect of a judicial act (to which s 9(3) applies) and, if so, the judicial act complained of and the court or tribunal which is alleged to have made it; and

(e) give details of any finding of unlawfulness by another court or tribunal upon which the claim is based.[13]

4.11   Where a declaration of incompatibility is sought, the Court may at any time consider whether notice should be given to the Crown so that it can be joined as a party to the proceedings.[14] Unless the Crown has been given 21 days' formal notice (or other such period as the court directs) the court may not make a declaration of incompatibility.[15]

4.12   This is a complex area and reference to the detailed procedures to be followed should be sought out from comprehensive practitioner works such as the *White Book*[16] and *Blackstone's Criminal Practice*.[17]

C. STANDING: WHO MAY BRING PROCEEDINGS UNDER THE HUMAN RIGHTS ACT?

4.13   Any private, natural, or legal person can use the Human Rights Act. This includes companies, since to restrict the benefit of the Act to natural persons would probably

---

[12] See *V (a child) (care proceedings: human rights claims)* [2004] EWCA Civ 54, [2014] 1 WLR 1433, para 8.
[13] CPR Practice Direction 16, para 14.
[14] See CPR, Pt 19 and the accompanying Practice Direction.
[15] CPR, r 19.1, and Human Rights Act, s 5.
[16] Sweet & Maxwell 2023.
[17] OUP 2023.

infringe the provisions of Articles 6 and 14 (right to a fair trial in respect of civil rights and obligations, and right not to be discriminated against in application of the Convention rights).[18] By virtue of section 7(1) and (3), however, the Act cannot be used to bring proceedings by a person who is not, or would not be, a 'victim' of the violation (under art 34 of the Convention), even if he or she would otherwise have standing to be a party to judicial review proceedings on the broader test of 'standing' employed under Part 54 of the CPR.

The 'victim' provision means that it is necessary to determine whether a claimant is a 'victim' in order to decide whether they have standing to bring a claim under the Human Rights Act.   4.14

1. Victims

The concept of a victim in section 7(7) of the Human Rights Act is taken from Article 34 of the Convention as amended by Protocol 11.[19] This provides that the Court 'may receive applications from any person, non-governmental organization or group of individuals claiming to be the victim of a violation'. Pursuant to section 7(7), only an applicant who would have standing as a victim to bring proceedings in the European Court of Human Rights (ECtHR) is a victim for the purposes of section 7. According to the ECtHR, a person has standing as a victim only if directly affected by the act or the omission that is the subject of the complaint. For example, in *R (Devonhurst Investments Limited) v Luton Borough Council* the Article 8 rights of the commercial landlord served with a planning enforcement notice requiring the cessation of the use of land as residential accommodation were not breached. The occupiers whose Article 8 rights were said to have been breached could speak for themselves, and in any event, the landlord did not represent them.[20]   4.15

In *JM v UK* the Court held that an applicant is not required to show that he or she has suffered (financial) prejudice: that is relevant only in the context of just satisfaction.[21]   4.16

There is, however, no role for individual 'public defenders' of human rights to be recognized.[22] For example, in *R (Reprieve and others) v Prime Minister*[23] the Court of Appeal held that the claimants (an NGO and two members of Parliament) did not have victim status under section 7 and therefore did not have standing to bring a judicial review challenge based on the Article 3 investigative duty to the Prime Minister's decision not to hold an inquiry into allegations of UK involvement in torture of detainees in the aftermath of 11 September 2001. As this case illustrates,   4.17

---

[18] For the position of public bodies, see para 4.22.

[19] Before the amendment the provision was in art 25, to which the earlier case law refers.

[20] *R (Devonhurst Investments Limited) v Luton Borough Council* [2023] EWHC 978 (Admin), paras 82–88.

[21] *JM v UK* (2010) 30 BHRC 60, para 27.

[22] See *Klass v Germany* (1979–80) 2 EHRR 214. See, similarly, *JR1, Re Judicial Review* [2011] NIQB 5 (finding that an eight-year-old child did not have standing to challenge on art 2 grounds the decision by police to introduce tasers in Northern Ireland).

[23] *R (Reprieve and others) v Prime Minister* [2021] EWCA Civ 972, [2022] QB 447.

the victim requirement has tended to prevent public interest groups from bringing claims under the Human Rights Act.[24]

4.18   Similarly, there is limited scope for claimants to bring their claim on behalf of others. For example, in *R (Broadway Care Centre Limited) v Caerphilly County Borough Council* the court held that a care home operator served with a termination notice by the local authority could not bring proceedings under Article 8 on behalf of the residents.[25]

4.19   If a person is not at risk of a breach of a Convention right unless and until a particular decision is taken, the person cannot claim to be a victim unless and until such a decision is made.[26] But in the Strasbourg case law it is not always necessary for standing that the applicant has actually suffered the alleged breach. An applicant may bring a claim if there is a risk of their being directly affected by it in the future.[27] It will suffice if a person is required either to modify his conduct or risk being prosecuted.[28] For example, a gay man living in Northern Ireland was allowed to complain (successfully) about the criminalization of all homosexual conduct in private between consenting males, even though he had not yet been prosecuted under the law.[29] The risk of being affected must be a real threat, not a theoretical possibility.[30] Examples include cases in which challenges were made to legislation discriminating against children born out of wedlock, who were held to be victims of that legislation,[31] and a case where a litigant successfully persuaded the Court that she was a victim of the ban on divorce in Ireland because of the consequences for certain family relationships.[32] The ECtHR approach has been reflected in English decisions such as *R (Hooper) v Secretary of State for Work and Pensions* where the House of Lords considered that the applicants were 'victims' for the purposes of the Article 34 test because they could establish that they would have claimed the benefits alleged to have breached Article 14 had it been open to them to do so.[33]

---

[24] This can be contrasted with the traditionally more generous approach taken in judicial review proceedings more generally under the CPR, r 54 test (although arguably the Courts have adopted a more restrictive stance in recent years: see eg *R (Good Law Project) v Prime Minister* [2022] EWHC 298 (Admin)).

[25] *R (Broadway Care Centre Limited) v Caerphilly County Borough Council* [2012] EWHC 37 (Admin), para 74; and see *R (Devonhurst Investments) v Luton Borough Council* [2023] EWHC 978 (Admin).

[26] *AXA General Insurance Ltd v HM Advocate* [2011] UKSC 46, [2012] 1 AC 868, para 111 per Lord Reed, citing *Vijayanathan and Pusparajah v France* (1992) 15 EHRR 62, para 46.

[27] *Klass v Germany* (1979–80) 2 EHRR 214, and *Marckx v Belgium* (1979) 2 EHRR 330 (where the applicants were found to be directly affected by legislation which would limit the child's right to inherit property from her mother upon her mother's eventual death); cf *Willis v UK* (2002) 35 EHRR 547 where the risk of the applicant being refused a widow's pension on the grounds of sex at a future date was found to be hypothetical since it was not certain that she would otherwise fulfil the statutory conditions for the payment of the benefit on the relevant date.

[28] *Burden v UK* (2008) 47 EHRR 857, para 34.

[29] *Dudgeon v UK* (1981) 4 EHRR 149; and *Norris v Ireland* (1988) 13 EHRR 186.

[30] *Campbell and Cosans v UK* (1982) 4 EHRR 293. In *AXA General Insurance Ltd v HM Advocate* [2011] UKSC 46, [2012] 1 AC 868 Lord Hope said that the question was whether the consequences for the applicants of the measure in question 'are too remote or tenuous for them to be directly affected by it' (at para 27).

[31] *Marckx v Belgium* (1979) 2 EHRR 330.

[32] *Johnston v Ireland* (1986) 9 EHRR 203.

[33] *R (Hooper) v Secretary of State for Work and Pensions* [2005] UKHL 29, [2005] 1 WLR 1681, para 59 per Lord Hoffmann *obiter*.

In *R (Reprieve) v Prime Minister* the Court identified two broad groups of cases   4.20
in which the Strasbourg Court has decided that a person who does not allege, or
cannot show, that he himself has suffered a breach of a Convention right he nevertheless falls within the scope of Article 34.[34]

The first group of cases concerns secret surveillance. For example, in *Zakharov v*   4.21
Russia[35] the ECtHR stated:

[A]n applicant could claim to be the victim of a violation occasioned by the mere existence of secret
surveillance measures, or legislation permitting secret surveillance measures, if the following conditions were met. First, the court would take into account the scope of the legislation permitting
secret surveillance measures by examining whether the applicant could possibly be affected by it,
either because he belonged to a group of persons targeted by the contested legislation or because the
legislation directly affected all users of communication services by instituting a system where any
person could have his communications intercepted. Second, the court would take into account the
availability of remedies at the national level and would adjust the degree of scrutiny depending on
the effectiveness of such remedies. Where the domestic system did not afford an effective remedy
to the person who suspected that he was subjected to secret surveillance, widespread suspicion and
concern among the general public that secret surveillance powers were being abused could not
be said to be unjustified. In such circumstances, the menace of surveillance could be claimed in
itself to restrict free communication through the postal and telecommunication services, thereby
constituting for all users or potential users a direct interference with the right guaranteed by art.8.

The *Zakharov* exception has been narrowly construed by the domestic courts. In   4.22
Privacy International v Secretary of State for Foreign and Commonwealth Affairs, for
example, the Court of Appeal held that the NGO claimants did not have standing
to claim that a policy document issued by the Security Service which gave guidance explaining the circumstances in which it might use agents who participated in
criminality breached the Convention.[36] The claims were not brought by individuals, and were not confined to issues of secret surveillance.

The second group of cases identified by the Court of Appeal in *R (Reprieve) v*   4.23
Prime Minister includes three broad types: (a) where direct victims have died in
circumstances which engage Article 2, others such as the close relatives, can bring
a claim and be treated as 'victims';[37] (b) applicants who die in the course of their
claim for a breach of a Convention right; and (c) claims brought by a representative
organization on behalf of actual or likely victims.

Examples of the third category of cases are rare and generally turn on their spe-   4.24
cific facts. For example, in *Lizarraga v Spain*,[38] a claim was brought under Article

---

[34] *R (Reprieve) v Prime Minister* [2021] EWCA Civ 972, [2022] QB 447, paras 40–47.

[35] *Zakharov v Russia* (2016) 63 EHRR 17. See also *Big Brother Watch v UK* (2022) 74 EHRR 17, paras 467–72.

[36] *Privacy International v Secretary of State for Foreign and Commonwealth Affairs* [2021] EWCA Civ 330, [2021] QB 1087, paras 122–29.

[37] *Rabone v Pennine Care NHS Trust* [2012] 2 AC 72, paras 44–58. See also *R (Holub) v Secretary of State for the Home Department* [2001] 1 WLR 1359 in which the Court of Appeal at para 14 considered *obiter* that the parents of a minor whose Convention rights have been breached have standing to complain under s 7.

[38] *Lizarraga v Spain* (2007) 45 EHRR 45. See also *Câmpeanu v Romania* (2014) 37 BHRC 423, discussed in *Reprieve*, para 44.

6 by five individuals and an association set up to coordinate opposition to the construction of a dam. The association was held to satisfy the victim requirement as it had been a party to domestic proceedings (on behalf of its members) in respect of which the Article 6 complaint arose.

4.25 Finally, organs of government are not victims for the purposes of Article 34. Thus in *Aston Cantlow and Wilmcote with Billesley Parochial Church Council v Wallbank* the House of Lords confirmed that local authorities are not able to use the Human Rights Act.[39]

2. Standing of the Equality and Human Rights Commission

4.26 The Equality Act 2006 provides that the Commission may either institute or intervene in litigation 'if it appears to the Commission that the proceedings are relevant to a matter in connection with which the Commission has a function'.[40] To facilitate this power section 30(3) provides:

The Commission may, in the course of legal proceedings for judicial review which it institutes (or in which it intervenes), rely on section 7(1)(b) of the Human Rights Act 1998 (breach of Convention rights); and for that purpose—

(a) the Commission need not be a victim or potential victim of the unlawful act to which the proceedings relate,

(b) the Commission may act only if there is or would be one or more victims of the unlawful act,

(c) section 7(3) and (4) of that Act shall not apply ...

Section 30(2) is of similar effect in relation to Scottish proceedings.

4.27 This gives the Commission the power to take cases directly in its own name, and intervene in cases brought by others (interventions are dealt with separately at para 4.47). The Commission's most recent Strategic Plan says that the Commission will intervene in legal cases or take its own legal action if they 'think it is the most effective way to enforce the law, to make the law clearer, or to bring about broader change'.[41]

4.28 In practice, the Commission's exercise of its litigation powers in relation to the Human Rights Act to date has largely been through interventions; the Commission's use of its power to bring proceedings in its own name has been rarely used.[42]

---

[39] *Aston Cantlow and Wilmcote with Billesley Parochial Church Council v Wallbank* [2003] UKHL 37, [2004] 1 AC 546. See in particular Lord Hope at paras 43–47. See also *R (Westminster City Council) v Mayor of London* [2002] EWHC (Admin) 2440 where the High Court held that a local authority could not be considered a 'non-governmental organization' for the purposes of art 34 and so could not bring proceedings under the Act. See also Howard Davis, 'Public Authorities as "Victims" under the Human Rights Act' (2005) 64(2) Cambridge Law Journal 315.

[40] Section 30(1).

[41] EHRC, Strategic plan: 2022–25 (29 March 2022) 14 <https://www.equalityhumanrights.com/sites/default/files/about-us-strategic-plan-2022-2025.pdf> accessed 29 December 2023.

[42] See eg *R (Equality and Human Rights Commission) v the Prime Minister and others* [2011] EWHC 2401 (Admin), [2012] 1 WLR 1389. The Commission has also occasionally exercised its power to bring proceedings in relation to equality matters: see eg *R (Equality and Human Rights Commission) v Secretary of State for Justice* [2010] EWHC 147 (Admin) and *Commission for Equality and Human Rights v Griffin and others*

D. LIMITATION PERIODS: ARE THERE TIME LIMITS FOR BRINGING A CLAIM UNDER THE HUMAN RIGHTS ACT?

Section 7(5) of the Human Rights Act creates a primary limitation period of one **4.29** year for cases against public bodies alleging a breach of a Convention right, beginning with the date on which the act complained of took place. This can be extended where the court considers it 'equitable having regard to all the circumstances'.

Under section 7(5)(b) the usual one-year limitation period is also subject to any **4.30** more restrictive rule which imposes a stricter time limit in relation to the proceeding in question (eg the three-month time limit for bringing proceedings by way of judicial review contained in Part 54 of the CPR). The one-year time limit applies only to claims that directly allege breach of the Convention by a public authority, that is, only where there is a cause of action created by section 7(1)(a). There is no time limit to the interpretative obligation in section 7(1)(b).

Section 7A, introduced by the Overseas Operations (Service Personnel and **4.31** Veterans) Act 2021 with effect from 30 June 2021, imposes specific obligations on a court when considering extending time under section 7(5)(b) in proceedings relating to the actions of armed forces overseas. Time may not be extended beyond the later of (a) the end of the period of six years beginning with the date on which the act complained of took place; and (b) the end of the period of 12 months beginning with the date of knowledge (s 7A(4)). The date of knowledge includes the date that the person bringing the proceedings *ought* to have known of the act complained of and that it was an act of the Ministry of Defence or Secretary of State for Defence: section 7A(5). If a court is considering extending time for a period within the outer limits set by section 7A(4), it is required to have particular regard to the matters specified in section 7A(2), which includes the effect of the delay on the cogency of evidence and the likely impact of the proceedings on the mental health of any witness who is or was a member of His Majesty's Forces.

Since the Human Rights Act came into force, the time limits imposed on personal **4.32** injury claims have been challenged unsuccessfully by claimants who argued that the Limitation Act 1980 should be interpreted in line with Convention rights and asked the courts to apply section 3 of the Human Rights Act retrospectively.[43] In *Dunn v Parole Board* the claimant prisoner had been recalled to prison while on licence four years before instituting proceedings.[44] He argued unsuccessfully that an extension of time should be granted as he had brought his claim within one year of the House of

---

[2010] EWHC 3343 (Admin) (the latter proceedings brought in relation to discriminatory provisions in the British National Party's constitution).

[43] *Rowe v Kingston upon Hull City Council* [2003] EWCA Civ 1281, [2003] ELR 771 on whether a dyslexic's claim for negligence against his former school was within the time limit for bringing a personal injury claim under the Limitation Act, s 14; and *A v Hoare* [2008] UKHL 6, [2008] 1 AC 844 in which a victim of an intentional sexual assault argued that the cut-off imposed by the Limitation Act, s 2 should be extended in light of the Human Rights Act.

[44] *Dunn v Parole Board* [2008] EWCA Civ 374, [2009] 1 WLR 728.

Lords' decision in *R (Smith) v Parole Board*, which established that Article 5(4) was engaged when a prisoner was recalled.[45] The Court of Appeal rejected this argument, but importantly noted that, on the evidence, the decision in *Smith* had played no part in the prisoner's delay; if it could have been shown that he had been waiting for this decision, the court's exercise of discretion may have differed.

4.33   In *O'Connor v Bar Standards Board*[46] the Supreme Court held that the phrase 'the date on which the act complained of took place' in section 7(5)(a) of the Human Rights Act was apt to cover a single continuous course of conduct (here the bringing and pursuing of disciplinary proceedings by the BSB).[47] Whether conduct amounts to a single act or a continuing course of conduct is a question of fact to be resolved by the court.[48]

4.34   Relatedly, the courts have given consideration to the question of when time begins to run in the case of a continuing act (eg unlawful segregation or detention). Section 7(5)(a) of the Human Rights Act refers to 'the date on which the act complained of took place'; the question in such cases is whether time runs from the date the act ceased, or when it began. In *A v Essex County Council* Baroness Hale expressed the view (*obiter*) that time begins to run from the date the breach ended.[49] The High Court in *R (G) v Secretary of State for Justice*[50] noted that 'there is no doubt about the principle, particularly in European law but obviously extendable to Human Rights legislation, in many authorities, that where there is a continuing obligation, a continuing state of affairs, which continue not to be put right by the Defendant, time does not run against a claimant at least until that state of affairs has come to an end'.

4.35   A court has a 'wide discretion' in determining whether it is equitable to extend time under section 7(5)(b).[51] In *Rafiq v Thurrock Borough Council*[52] Collins Rice J summarized the principles articulated in previous cases. The judge noted first that it may be appropriate for a court to have regard to the factors set out in section 33(3) of the Limitation Act 1980 if it considers it appropriate in the circumstances of a particular case, but they must not be treated as a fetter.[53] Rather, the 'court is to examine all the relevant factors in a case and consider whether it is equitable to

---

[45] *R (Smith) v Parole Board* [2005] UKHL 1, [2005] 1 WLR 350.

[46] *O'Connor v Bar Standards Board* [2017] UKSC 78, [2017] 1 WLR 4813.

[47] ibid para 23.

[48] See eg *Kulumbegov v Home Office* [2023] EWHC 377 (KB) where the judge held that decisions to refuse leave to remain, and the conduct of the Home Office in the defence of an appeal against those decisions, were not a single continuous course of conduct: paras 81–90.

[49] *A v Essex County Council* [2010] UKSC 33, [2011] 1 AC 280, para 113, referring to *Somerville v Scottish Ministers* [2007] UKHL 44, [2007] 1 WLR 2734.

[50] *R (G) v Secretary of State for Justice* [2010] EWHC 3407 (Admin).

[51] *Rabone v Pennine Care NHS Trust* [2012] UKSC 2, [2012] 2 AC 72, para 75.

[52] *Rafiq v Thurrock Borough Council* [2022] EWHC 584 (KB) cited in *CJ and others v Chief Constable of Wiltshire Police* [2022] EWHC 1661 (KB), [2023] PIQR P2, paras 47–50. See also *Newell v Ministry of Justice* [2021] EWHC 810 (KB), paras 89–94.

[53] See eg *R (Rafiq) v Thurrock Borough Council* [2022] EWHC 584 (KB), paras 14–15, referring to the decision of the Supreme Court in *Rabone v Pennine Care NHS Trust* [2012] UKSC 2, [2012] 2 AC 72, para 75. See also the review of the authorities in *Solaria Energy UK Limited v Department for Business, Energy and Industrial Strategy* [2020] EWCA Civ 1625, [2021] 1 WLR 2349, paras 42–53. The courts have repeatedly

allow a period of longer than one year. There is no predetermined list of relevant factors, although proportionality will generally be taken into account. The weight to be given to any particular factor is a matter for the court'.[54] The judge added that *P v Tameside MBC* is also authority:[55]

that a court must have regard to the policy reasons for Parliament adopting a much tighter limitation period in HRA claims than usual, and that these may be similar to those for the tight 3-month limit in judicial review proceedings. It is clearly the policy of the legislature that HRA claims should be dealt with both swiftly and economically. All such claims are by definition brought against public authorities, and there is no public interest in these being burdened by expensive, time consuming and tardy claims brought years after the event. The court must look critically at the explanations given for the delay, set against these policy considerations. Delay is always a relevant consideration whether or not there is actual trial prejudice to a defendant. However the 'burden of persuasion' on a claimant is not necessarily a heavy one and there is no burden to establish lack of prejudice to the defendant.

In *Alseran v Ministry of Defence* the court emphasized the importance of the merits of the claim as militating in favour of granting an extension.[56] The court added, however, that 'evidential prejudice' to a defendant (where delay means that witnesses cannot be traced or memories have faded) may point the other way.[57] There is now a body of case law that provides examples of when the court has extended time under section 7(5)(b)[58] and when it has declined to do so.[59]

    4.36

E. RETROSPECTIVITY

The Human Rights Act does not in general apply retrospectively to the acts of public authorities completed prior to its entry into force on 2 October 2000.[60] As such, generally, acts of public authorities (including acts of courts and tribunals) taken before this critical date cannot be challenged pursuant to sections 6 and 7 of the Human Rights Act by way of civil claim, judicial review, or on appeal.[61]

    4.37

---

warned against adding a gloss to the words of s 7(5): see eg *Dunn v Parole Board* [2008] EWCA Civ 374, [2009] 1 WLR 728, para 30 per Thomas LJ.

[54] *R (Rafiq) v Thurrock Borough Council* [2022] EWHC 584 (KB), para 15, citing *P v Tameside MBC* [2017] EWHC 65 (QB), [2017] 1 WLR 2127, para 67.

[55] *R (Rafiq) v Thurrock Borough Council* [2022] EWHC 584 (KB), para 16.

[56] *Alseran v Ministry of Defence* [2017] EWHC 3289 (KB), [2019] QB 1251, para 869.

[57] ibid para 869.

[58] See eg *Alseran v Ministry of Defence* [2017] EWHC 3144 (KB), [2019] QB 1251; *Newell v Ministry of Justice* [2021] EWHC 810 (KB), paras 84–94; *CJ and others v Chief Constable of Wiltshire Police* [2022] EWHC 1661 (KB), [2023] PIQR P2, paras 48–50.

[59] See eg *Bedford v Bedfordshire County Council* [2013] EWHC 1717 (QB), [2014] LGR 44; *P v Tameside MBC* [2017] EWHC 65 (KB), [2017] 1 WLR 2127; *London College of Business Ltd v Secretary of State for the Home Department* [2017] EWHC 3144; *Rafiq v Thurrock Borough Council* [2022] EWHC 584 (KB), paras 22–66; *Solaria Energy UK Limited v Department for Business, Energy and Industrial Strategy* [2020] EWCA Civ 1625, [2021] 1 WLR 2349.

[60] See s 22(4); and *Re McQuillan* [2021] UKSC 55, [2022] AC 1063, paras 151–53.

[61] *In re McKerr* [2004] UKHL 12, [2004] 1 WLR 807; *Re McQuillan* [2021] UKSC 55, [2022] AC 1063.

This applies to criminal appeals post-dating the coming into force of the Act.[62] It has also been held that the interpretative obligation in section 3 does not, in general, apply to acts, agreements, or transactions made before the Human Rights Act came into force,[63] but the possibility that, in some circumstances, this presumption against retrospectivity might be rebutted where this would not give rise to unfairness has been left open.[64]

4.38   The one exception identified in section 22(4) is where legal proceedings are brought against a person by or at the instigation of a public authority, in which case that person may rely on their Convention rights as a defence 'whenever the act in question took place' as permitted by section 7(1)(b). It has been suggested that the intention is to enable 'Convention rights [to be] used as a shield to defeat proceedings brought against victims by public authorities, but not as a sword'.[65] Thus a prosecution that relies on evidence gathered in violation of the Convention in 1999 could be challenged by a defendant on that basis at a trial taking place after 2 October 2000.[66]

4.39   Inquest proceedings are not proceedings brought against those participating them and thus do not fall within the section 22(4) exception.[67] However, as considered in Chapter 5, in a line of House of Lords and Supreme Court cases concerning, in particular, deaths implicating agents of the state during the Troubles in Northern Ireland, the courts have held that the detachable procedural investigative obligation arising under Articles 2 and 3 can apply to deaths pre-dating the entry into force of the Human Rights Act in defined circumstances. The interpretative exercise undertaken by the courts in identifying these circumstances has been to weigh the specific intention of Parliament against retrospectivity as underlined by section 22(4), against the general intention that the rights protected under the Human Rights Act should mirror the rights applicable against the United Kingdom as a state.[68]

F. INTERVENTIONS IN HUMAN RIGHTS ACT CASES

1. Interventions by public interest groups

4.40   The Human Rights Act does not give an express right to intervene, except to the Crown, and, as referred to above, the Commission also has a statutory power to

---

[62] *R v Kansal (No 2)* [2001] UKHL 62, [2002] 2 AC 69 (in which a majority followed the decision of the House of Lords in *R v Lambert* [2001] UKHL 37, [2002] 2 AC 545 despite considering it to be wrongly decided).

[63] *Wilson v First County Trust* [2003] UKHL 40, [2004] 1 AC 816.

[64] ibid para 21 per Lord Nicholls and paras 101–02 per Lord Hope. For an example of this exception being applied see *PW v Milton Gate Investments* [2004] Ch 142.

[65] *R (Hurst) v London Northern District* Coroner [2007] UKHL 13, [2007] 2 AC 189, para 62.

[66] For an example of reliance on s 22(4) in a non-criminal context, see *Aston Cantlow and Wilmcote with Billesley Parochial Church Council v Wallbank and another* [2003] UKHL 37, [2004] 1 AC 546 (defence to enforcement of chancel repair liability).

[67] *R (Hurst) v London Northern District Coroner* [2007] UKHL 13, [2007] 2 AC 189, para 62.

[68] *Re McQuillan* [2021] UKSC 55, [2022] AC 1063, para 158. See further Chapter 5, para 5.54.

intervene. However, the courts have been willing to allow third-party interventions under the normal rules of court.[69]

Prior to the implementation of the Human Rights Act interventions by third parties was relatively unusual. There was an exponential growth in interventions by public interest bodies in approximately the first 15 years of the Human Rights Act.[70] The reasons why the courts welcomed interventions over this period is clear: they can provide considerable benefits to courts and litigants, particularly in the context of the Human Rights Act where experience from other countries and details of other international human rights standards may be of great use. They can draw to the court's attention the wider significance of a point in a way that an individual litigant may be unable to do. They may provide supporting statistical or other evidence. They can help the court to determine whether an interference with a Convention right is 'necessary in a democratic society' or 'proportionate' by drawing to the court's attention the wider social significance or effects of a particular outcome.[71] For example, in *YL v Birmingham City Council* detailed witness statements and submissions were presented to the courts by the British Institute of Human Rights, Help the Aged, and the National Council on Ageing, adding important contextual evidence as to the practical ramifications of the narrow definition of 'public authority' under section 6.[72] In *R (Tigere) v Secretary of State for Business, Innovation and Skills*, the youth organization Just for Kids Law intervened to provide evidence on the impact of the impugned statutory regime on young people other than the claimant.[73]

4.41

Indeed in *Re E*[74] the House of Lords recognized the specialist expertise that statutory bodies and NGOs can and have offered in public interest cases, Lord Hoffmann noting that:

4.42

In recent years the House has frequently been assisted by the submissions of statutory bodies and non-governmental organisations on questions of general public importance. Leave is given

---

[69] In judicial review proceedings the court has an express power to receive evidence and submissions from persons who are not parties: see CPR, r 54.17. There is guidance in the Practice Direction to CPR, r 54 as to the process by which applications to intervene must be made: paras 12.1–12.7. There is no specific procedure in the Court of Appeal, but an application to intervene may be made by application notice. The Supreme Court Rules make provision for intervention: see rules 15 and 26, and Practice Direction 6. For a useful guide on preparing interventions, see Justice, *To assist the court: third party interventions in the public interest* (2016) <https://files.justice.org.uk/wp-content/uploads/2016/06/06170721/To-Assist-the-Court-Web.pdf> accessed 29 December 2023.

[70] In 2000, there were five petitions for leave to intervene in House of Lords' cases (with one granted leave to make full written and oral submissions, and four written submissions alone), rising to 14 petitions only two years later in 2002 (with eight being granted full oral and written submissions, and four written submissions alone). See Sarah Hannett, 'Third Party Intervention: In the Public Interest?' [2003] Public Law 128.

[71] See Mona Arshi and Colm O'Cinneide, 'Third-party Interventions: The Public Interest Reaffirmed' [2004] Public Law 69. See, for the contrary view, Policy Exchange, 'How and why To Constrain Interveners and Depoliticise Our Courts' (7 December 2022) <https://policyexchange.org.uk/publication/how-and-why-to-constrain-interveners-and-depoliticise-our-courts/> accessed 23 December 2023.

[72] *YL v Birmingham City Council* [2007] UKHL 27, [2008] 1 AC 95. The case is analysed in Chapter 3.

[73] *R (Tigere) v Secretary of State for Business, Innovation and Skills* [2015] UKSC 57, [2015] 1 WLR 3820, para 9.

[74] *Re E* [2008] UKHL 66, [2008] 3 WLR 1208, paras 2, 6, 69.

to such bodies to intervene and make submissions, usually in writing but sometimes orally from the bar, in the expectation that their fund of knowledge or particular point of view will enable them to provide the House with a more rounded picture than it would otherwise obtain. The House is grateful to such bodies for their help.[75]

4.43   The Independent Review of Administrative Law chaired by Lord Edward Faulks KC noted the increase in the use of intervention since 2000.[76] The Panel expressed concern that the development was the 'product of unfettered judicial discretion', that the courts had 'effectively adopted a policy of drift', and that '[i]ntervention as a lobbying tactic also raises concerns for the integrity of the adjudicative process and separate identity of the courts'.[77] The Review recommended that criteria for permitting intervention should be developed and published.

4.44   Those concerns appear to be reflected in a more recent cooling of judicial enthusiasm for interventions. Lord Reed's comments in *R (SC) v Secretary of State for Work and Pensions* deprecating 'campaigning organisations' who lobby unsuccessfully against legislation in Parliament and subsequently litigate the same legislation, were not aimed at third-party interveners, but the sentiment may apply equally.[78] In a Practice Note amending Practice Direction 6 issued by the President of the Supreme Court, Lord Reed, on 21 April 2023 guidance was given both as to the test the Supreme Court will apply when determining an application to intervene and the procedure by which such applications should be made.[79] The revised Practice Direction provides that '[p]ermission will only be given for interventions which will provide the court with significant assistance over and above the assistance it can expect to receive from the parties, and only where any cost to the parties or any delay consequent on the intervention is not disproportionate to the assistance that is expected'.[80] That reflects the further comments of Lord Hoffmann in *Re E* that an 'intervention is … of no assistance if it merely repeats points which the appellant or respondent has already made'.[81] Perhaps most significantly, the amended Practice Direction provides that, in considering applications for permission to intervene, 'the Court will be mindful of the need to maintain a balance between the arguments before it, and the importance of the appearance, as well as the reality, of an equality of arms'.[82]

4.45   In the Supreme Court interventions will be allowed in writing only 'unless compelling reasons are shown for the allowance of oral intervention'.[83] Submissions

---

[75] ibid para 2.
[76] Independent Review of Administrative Law Review (March 2021) <https://assets.publishing.service. gov.uk/media/6053383dd3bf7f0454647fc4/IRAL-report.pdf> accessed 23 December 2023 para 4.107.
[77] ibid para 4.108.
[78] *R (SC) v Secretary of State for Work and Pensions* [2021] UKSC 26, [2022] AC 223, para 162.
[79] <https://www.supremecourt.uk/news/practice-note-april-2023.html>. The amendments made to the Supreme Court Practice Direction 6 are similar to the contents of a Notice issued to the legal profession by the Supreme Court of Canada in November 2021: <https://www.scc-csc.ca/ar-lr/notices-avis/21-11-eng.aspx>.
[80] Supreme Court Practice Direction 6, para 6.9.5.
[81] *Re E* [2008] UKHL 66, [2008] 3 WLR 1208, para 3.
[82] Supreme Court Practice Direction 6, para 6.9.6.
[83] ibid.

should focus on advancing the intervener's argument on a legal issue before the court, and interveners should not ordinarily seek to introduce new evidence 'especially where that would cause procedural unfairness to a party or undermine the basis on which the legal issues were considered by the courts below'.[84] The latter suggests that permission for the types of interventions in *YL v Birmingham City Council* and *R (Tigere) v Secretary of State for Business, Innovation and Skills* described above will be less likely in the future.

In judicial review proceedings provision has been made for the costs of interventions in section 87 of the Criminal Justice and Courts Act 2015. A claimant or a defendant in judicial review proceedings cannot be ordered to pay an intervener's costs unless there are exceptional circumstances that make such a costs order appropriate.[85] Where certain conditions apply, the High Court or the Court of Appeal must order the intervener to pay costs incurred by a party unless there are exceptional circumstances.[86] In the Supreme Court the starting point is that interveners bear their own costs, and any additional costs to the appellant or the respondent resulting from an intervention are costs in the appeal.[87]   4.46

2. Interventions by the Equality and Human Rights Commission

The Commission, with the permission of the court, can intervene in cases, including judicial review, where the Commission is not a party.[88] The Commission's role in an intervention is not to support one side or the other; it is to provide independent arguments to the court to promote the objectives set out for it in the Equality Act 2006.[89]   4.47

The Commission has intervened in a number of cases concerning human rights, and at a range of levels. Examples include: 4.48

- *R (G) v The Governors of X School* (Supreme Court): extent to which legal representation is required under Article 6 in employment tribunal proceedings (where the consequences go beyond the employment context);[90]

---

[84] ibid para 6.9.8.

[85] Criminal Justice and Courts Act 2015, s 87.

[86] See s 87(5), (6), and (7). The conditions are: (a) the intervener has acted, in substance, as the sole or principal applicant, defendant, appellant or respondent; (b) the intervener's evidence and representations, taken as a whole, have not been of significant assistance to the court; (c) a significant part of the intervener's evidence and representations relates to matters that it is not necessary for the court to consider in order to resolve the issues that are the subject of the stage in the proceedings; or (d) the intervener has behaved unreasonably.

[87] Supreme Court Rules 2009, r 46(3) provides: 'Orders for costs will not normally be made either in favour of or against interveners but such orders may be made if the Court considers it just to do so (in particular if an intervener has in substance acted as the sole or principal appellant or respondent).' See also Supreme Court Practice Direction 6.

[88] Equality Act 2006, s 30.

[89] See Equality Act 2006, ss 3, 8–11.

[90] *R (G) v The Governors of X School* [2011] UKSC 30, [2012] 1 AC 167.

- *JM v United Kingdom* (ECtHR): whether same-sex couples are a 'family' for the purposes of Article 8;[91]
- *In the matter of an application by the Northern Ireland Human Rights Commission for Judicial Review*: whether the criminalization of abortion in Northern Ireland violates Article 3 or 8;[92]
- *R (TP & AR) v Secretary of State for Work and Pensions*: whether the regulations for moving severely disabled benefit claimants onto Universal Credit violate Article 14 read with Article 8 and/or Article 1 of Protocol 1;[93]
- *R (AB) v Secretary of State for Justice*: whether solitary confinement of children in Young Offenders' Institutions violates Article 3.[94]

G. OTHER MEANS OF ENFORCEMENT BY THE EQUALITY AND HUMAN RIGHTS COMMISSION

4.49   Alongside the power to take judicial review proceedings in its own name to prevent breaches of the Human Rights Act, and the power to intervene in proceedings taken by others which raise human rights issues, the Commission also has a range of other enforcement tools at its disposal, including the power to conduct formal inquiries and to fund organizations providing legal assistance in human rights. This allows the Commission to enforce the Human Rights Act without necessarily engaging in litigation. The Commission also undertakes legal policy work, including briefing ministers and parliamentarians on human rights issues in draft legislation, and contributing to international treaty monitoring bodies.

1. The duties of the Commission

4.50   The Equality Act 2006 sets out the Commission's legal duties. Section 3 contains a general duty:

The Commission shall exercise its functions under this Part with a view to encouraging and supporting the development of a society in which—

(a) people's ability to achieve their potential is not limited by prejudice or discrimination,
(b) there is respect for and protection of each individual's human rights,
(c) there is respect for the dignity and worth of each individual,
(d) each individual has an equal opportunity to participate in society, and
(e) there is mutual respect between groups based on understanding and valuing of diversity and on shared respect for equality and human rights.

---

[91] *JM v UK* (2010) 30 BHRC 60.
[92] *In the matter of an application by the Northern Ireland Human Rights Commission for Judicial Review* [2018] UKSC 27, [2019] 1 All ER 173.
[93] *R (TP & AR) v Secretary of State for Work and Pensions* [2020] EWCA Civ 37, [2020] PTSR 1785.
[94] *R (AB) v Secretary of State for Justice* [2021] UKSC 28, [2022] AC 487.

The Commission's specific legal duties concerning human rights are set out in   4.51
section 9. 'Human rights' in this context includes the Convention rights, but also
'other human rights' not set out in the Convention.[95] Section 9(1) provides that:

The Commission shall, by exercising the powers conferred by this Part—

(a) promote understanding of the importance of human rights,
(b) encourage good practice in relation to human rights,
(c) promote awareness, understanding and protection of human rights, and
(d) encourage public authorities to comply with section 6 of the Human Rights Act 1998 (compliance with Convention rights).

Section 11(1) requires the Commission to 'monitor the effectiveness of the equal-   4.52
ity and human rights enactments' and provides that it may advise central government on its findings, make recommendations to it regarding whether to amend,
repeal, or consolidate any of the equality and human rights enactments, and advise
central or devolved government (in Scotland, Wales, or Northern Ireland) about the
effect of an enactment, or the likely effect of a proposed change of law.[96] This 'pre-
emptive' role—preventing breaches of the Human Rights Act before they occur—
is not unfamiliar: the Parliamentary Joint Committee on Human Rights (JCHR)
scrutinizes all government Bills and picks out those with significant human rights
implications for further examination.

The Commission's powers in relation to human rights issues with no equal-   4.53
ity dimension are limited. Unless there is an equality dimension to the case, the
Commission does not have the power to give legal assistance to individuals on
human rights grounds alone.

2. Inquiries, investigations, and assessments

The Commission has a range of investigation and assessment powers. It may con-   4.54
duct an inquiry, or undertake an investigation or assessment (ss 16, 20, and 31).
It has power to require any person to provide written or oral evidence or relevant
documents, which gives teeth to its inquiry powers.

(a) Inquiries

The Commission may conduct 'an inquiry into a matter' relating to any of its duties   4.55
under sections 8 (equality), 9 (human rights), or 10 (groups).[97] Schedule 2 to the
Equality Act deals with the logistics of such inquiries: terms of reference, representations, evidence, reports, recommendations, and the effects of reports. Inquiries can
be general or specific; they could be thematic (eg related to one particular Convention
right), sectoral (looking at, eg, the treatment of children in custodial establishments
that are managed by private companies), or relate to one or more named parties.

---

[95] Equality Act 2006, s 9(2)(b). The Commission must, however, have particular regard to the importance of exercising its powers in relation to the Convention rights: s 9(3).
[96] Equality Act 2006, s 11(2).
[97] Equality Act 2006, s 16(1).

4.56   Inquiries have included examinations into the use of restraint by schools, home care of older people, non-natural deaths in detention of adults with mental health conditions, disability related harassment, and human trafficking in Scotland.[98]

(b) *Investigations and assessments*

4.57   An investigation is a tool that enables the Commission to investigate whether or not a particular person (natural or legal) has committed an unlawful act, or failed to comply with a notice given to that person by the Commission, or an agreement that person has made with the Commission following an earlier finding that the person has behaved unlawfully.[99] The Commission may also conduct an assessment of a public authority's compliance with the public sector duties regarding gender, race, and disability. The power to initiate investigations and assessments is restricted to the Commission's equality remit.

H. REMEDIES

1. Damages

(a) *Jurisdiction and procedure*

4.58   Section 8(1) of the Human Rights Act authorizes a court which has found that an act or proposed act of a public authority is unlawful, to grant 'such relief or remedy, or make such order, within its powers as it considers just and appropriate'. This can be used to found a claim for relief, including damages, against a public authority. Courts and tribunals of limited jurisdiction cannot award a remedy if it is outside their statutory power to do so. For example, an employment tribunal is not able to order an injunction to prevent a discriminatory dismissal going ahead (because it has no statutory power to do so), even if it were to consider this necessary to afford just satisfaction of a Convention right.

4.59   Section 8(2) permits a court to make an award of damages under the Act where it has the power to award compensation (even if it is not otherwise called 'damages'). This, in principle, includes statutory tribunals such as employment tribunals. Criminal courts cannot award damages under section 8(2).[100]

4.60   The Court of Appeal laid down procedural guidelines for courts considering claims for damages in respect of maladministration leading to a breach of Convention rights in *Anufrijeva v Southwark London Borough Council*.[101] The guidelines, which are of general importance, included the following:

---

[98] For a full list, see <https://www.equalityhumanrights.com/our-work/inquiries-and-investigations > accessed 29 December 2023.

[99] Equality Act 2006, s 20(1).

[100] *R v Galfetti* [2002] EWCA Civ 1916, [2002] MHLR 418.

[101] *Anufrijeva v Southwark London Borough Council* [2003] EWCA Civ 1406, [2004] QB 1124. For a more detailed discussion of the practical ramifications of the guidelines laid down in *Anufrijeva*, see Richard Clayton, 'Damage Limitation: The Courts and the Human Rights Act Damages' [2005] Public Law 429.

(a) A claim for damages alone cannot be brought by judicial review but it should still be brought in the Administrative Court by an ordinary claim. Courts should look critically at any attempt to recover damages under the Human Rights Act for maladministration by any procedure other than judicial review.

(b) Claimants should first exhaust (or explain why it would not be more appropriate to use) any available internal complaint procedure, or proceed by making a claim to the parliamentary or local government ombudsman.

(c) If there is a legitimate claim for other relief, permission should, if appropriate, be limited to that relief, and consideration given to deferring permission for the damages claim, adjourning or staying that claim until use has been made of alternative dispute resolution procedures.

(d) In determining quantum of damages, citations should in general be limited to three authorities, and, except in exceptional circumstances, the hearing should be limited to half a day.

In *R (Fayad) v Secretary of State for the Home Department* the Court of Appeal emphasized that claims for judicial review which include a claim for damages for breach of the Human Rights Act should be 'properly pleaded and particularised'.[102] They should set out 'at least in brief' the principles applied by the ECtHR under Article 41 of the Convention which are said to be relevant.

(b) *Principles of assessment*

There is no automatic entitlement to damages under the Human Rights Act—courts may exercise their power to award damages to victims whose Convention rights have been breached but they are not bound to do so in all cases. Section 8(3) provides that damages are to be awarded only where they are necessary to afford 'just satisfaction' to the victim. When courts are deciding whether a monetary award is necessary they will take account of all the circumstances of the case, including any other remedy granted by the court or any other court, and the consequences of any decision (of that or any other court) in respect of the breach.[103]

Section 8(4) provides that a court or tribunal deciding whether to award damages and how much to award must take into account the principles applied by the ECtHR in relation to the award of compensation under Article 41 of the Convention.

The President of the ECtHR has issued a Practice Direction on Just Satisfaction Claims which summarizes the principles that the ECtHR will apply when considering such applications ('the Practice Direction').[104] It remains, however, difficult to identify a concrete set of principles from the ECtHR case law on Article 41 to

4.61

4.62

4.63

4.64

---

[102] *R (Fayad) v Secretary of State for the Home Department* [2018] EWCA Civ 54, para 54.

[103] See eg *Dobson v Thames Water Utilities* [2009] EWCA Civ 28, [2009] 3 All ER 319 (where damages were available in nuisance against a sewerage undertaker, such damages themselves constituted just satisfaction and no further damages were awarded).

[104] Issued on 28 March 2007 and amended on 9 June 2022 <https://www.echr.coe.int/documents/pd_satisfaction_claims_eng.pdf>.

which domestic courts can refer when considering awarding damages under the Human Rights Act. As the Law Commission put it, the 'most striking feature' of the Strasbourg case law on damages is 'the lack of clear principles as to when damages should be awarded and how they should be measured'.[105]

4.65   Despite this practical problem, it is possible to identify the following broad themes used by the ECtHR:[106]

(a) Compensation is discretionary and is not an automatic consequence of a finding that there has been a breach of a Convention right. It will only be awarded 'where necessary'. The ECtHR may decline to award compensation on the basis that the finding of a violation constitutes in itself just satisfaction for the violation.[107]

(b) There must be a 'causal link' between the breach of the applicant's Convention rights, any alleged resulting harm, and the compensation sought.[108]

(c) Where it is shown that the violation has caused pecuniary damage (ie financial loss) to the applicant, the ECtHR will normally award the full amount of the loss as just satisfaction. The ECtHR will apply the principle of 'restitutio in integrum', that is, that the applicant is, so far as possible, put back into the situation in which he or she would have been but for the violation of his or her Convention rights.[109]

(d) The ECtHR has awarded non-pecuniary damages in respect of pain, suffering, and physical or psychological injury,[110] including distress and anxiety[111] where the existence of such damage is established.[112]

---

[105] Law Commission, *Damages under the Human Rights Act* (Law Com No 266, 2000)(Cm 4853) para 3.4.

[106] See eg *Alseran v Ministry of Defence* [2017] EWHC 3289 (KB), [2019] QB 1251, paras 908–16 per Leggatt J. Leggatt J drew the guidance from the Practice Direction, and from decisions of the ECtHR and the domestic courts. See also the analysis of Lord Woolf in *Anufrijeva v Southwark London Borough Council* [2003] EWCA Civ 1406, [2004] QB 1124, *D v Commissioner of Police of the Metropolis* [2014] EWHC 2493 (KB), [2015] 1 WLR 1833, paras 16–41 per Green J, and the Law Commission Report at section III.

[107] *Alseran v Ministry of Defence* [2017] EWHC 3289 (KB), [2019] QB 1251, para 909, and see the Practice Direction, para 2. In *R (SXC) v Secretary of State for Work and Pensions* [2019] EWHC 2774 (Admin) Swift J, para 12 drew a distinction between claims under the Human Rights Act brought as a vehicle to vindicate rights equivalent to those recognized in private law, and those where the Human Rights Act is relied on in a purely public law challenge. He stated that in the 'overwhelming majority' of cases, the award of a public law remedy will suffice for just satisfaction. It remains to be seen whether this distinction will be adopted in subsequent cases.

[108] *Alseran v Ministry of Defence* [2017] EWHC 3289 (KB), [2019] QB 1251, para 910; see also the Practice Direction, para 9; and *Kingsley v UK* (2002) 35 EHRR 10, para 40.

[109] *Alseran v Ministry of Defence* [2017] EWHC 3289 (KB), [2019] QB 1251, para 911; and see the Practice Direction, para 8.

[110] See eg *Aydin v Turkey* (1998) 25 EHRR 251.

[111] *Doustaly v France*, 70 Rep Judg & Dec 1998 II 850.

[112] See eg *Alseran v Ministry of Defence* [2017] EWHC 3289 (KB), [2019] QB 1251, para 912; and the Practice Direction, paras 10–14. Leggatt J in *Alseran* noted at para 912: 'The case law of the European court shows that awards for mental suffering are by no means confined to cases where there is medical evidence that the applicant has suffered psychological harm and that compensation may be awarded for injury to feelings variously described as distress, anxiety, frustration, feelings of injustice or humiliation, prolonged uncertainty, disruption to life or powerlessness. The case law also shows that the court will often be ready to infer from the nature of the violation that such injury to feelings has been suffered.'

(e) The purpose of an award under Article 41 is to compensate the applicant and not to punish the state responsible for the violation. As such, the ECtHR does not award punitive or exemplary damages.[113]

(f) In deciding what, if any, award is necessary to afford just satisfaction, the ECtHR does not consider only the loss or damage sustained by the applicant but also the 'overall context' in which the breach of the Convention occurred when deciding what is just and equitable.[114]

(g) As part of the overall context the ECtHR may have regard to the conduct of the state.[115]

(h) The ECtHR may also take account of the applicant's conduct and find reason in equity to award less than the full amount of the actual damage sustained or not to make any award at all.[116]

Finally, the ECtHR may order the reimbursement to the applicant of costs and expenses which he or she has necessarily incurred (at the domestic level and in proceedings before the ECtHR itself) in trying to prevent the violation happening or in trying to obtain redress.[117]   4.66

The approach of the English courts to damages under the Human Rights Act to date has reflected, and attempted to develop, the broad themes discernible in the ECtHR jurisprudence.[118] In *R (Greenfield) v Secretary of State for the Home Department* the House of Lords considered how English courts should take Strasbourg judgments into account when determining 'just satisfaction'. Lord Bingham stated:[119]   4.67

The court routinely describes its awards as equitable, which I take to mean that they are not precisely calculated but are judged by the court to be fair in the individual case. Judges in England and Wales must also make a similar judgment in the case before them. They are not inflexibly bound by Strasbourg awards in what may be different cases. But they should not aim to be significantly more or less generous than the court might be expected to be, in a case where it was willing to make an award at all.

---

[113] *Alseran v Ministry of Defence* [2017] EWHC 3289 (KB), [2019] QB 1251, para 913; and see the Practice Direction, para 2.

[114] *Alseran v Ministry of Defence* [2017] EWHC 3289 (KB), [2019] QB 1251, para 914, noting that this may require account to be taken of 'moral injury': See eg *Varnava v Turkey* (2010) 50 EHRR 21 [GC], para 224 and *Al-Jedda v UK* (2011) 53 EHRR 23 [GC], para 114.

[115] *Alseran v Ministry of Defence* [2017] EWHC 3289 (KB), [2019] QB 1251, para 915, citing *Anufrijeva v Southwark London Borough Council* [2003] EWCA Civ 1406, [2004] QB 1124, para 68.

[116] *Alseran v Ministry of Defence* [2017] EWHC 3289 (KB), [2019] QB 1251, para 916, citing the 'striking example' of *McCann v United Kingdom* (1995) 21 EHRR 97 in which the ECtHR held that the killing of IRA gunmen in Gibraltar by British soldiers breached art 2 but did not make an award under art 41 'having regard to the fact that the three terrorist suspects who were killed had been intending to plant a bomb in Gibraltar' (para 219).

[117] Practice Direction, paras 15–19. These will typically include the cost of legal assistance, court registration and translation fees, postal expenses, etc. They may also include travel and subsistence expenses.

[118] See eg *Anufrijeva v Southwark London Borough Council* [2003] EWCA Civ 1406, [2004] QB 1124; and *R (Greenfield) v Secretary of State for the Home Department* [2005] UKHL 14, [2005] 1 WLR 673.

[119] *R (Greenfield) v Secretary of State for the Home Department* [2005] UKHL 14, [2005] 1 WLR 673, para 19.

4.68   In *R (Faulkner) v Secretary of State for Justice* Lord Reed drew three conclusions that will guide lower courts when they determine the quantum of damages to award in a human rights claim:[120]

> First, at the present stage of the development of the remedy of damages under section 8 of the 1998 Act, courts should be guided, following *Greenfield*, primarily by any clear and consistent practice of the European court. Secondly, it should be borne in mind that awards by the European court reflect the real value of money in the country in question. The most reliable guidance as to the quantum of awards under section 8 will therefore be awards made by the European court in comparable cases brought by applicants from the UK or other countries with a similar cost of living. Thirdly, courts should resolve disputed issues of fact in the usual way even if the European court, in similar circumstances, would not do so.[121]

4.69   The High Court applied *Faulkner* in a claim for damages for the failure by the police to effectively investigate rapes and sexual assaults committed by serial rapist, John Worboys.[122] The Court examined awards made by the Strasbourg Court for claims from other signatory states and made adjustments for higher cost of living in the UK and for inflation since the date of the awards.

4.70   Finally, it should be noted that the level of awards under section 8 of the Human Rights Act should not affect the proper level of damages an applicant is entitled to receive for breach of any other tort, such as false imprisonment. Section 11 of the Act provides that a person may rely on a Convention right without prejudice to any other right or freedom conferred on him or her by or under any (other) law having effect in the United Kingdom.

(c) Quantum

4.71   As well as the difficulties in trying to gain guidance from the ECtHR authorities on quantum identified by Lord Reed in *Faulkner* at paragraph XX, Leggatt J in *Alseran v Ministry of Defence* noted that, with one exception, the ECtHR has not established scales of awards for particular types of case. Thus 'the court hardly ever refers to amounts which is has awarded previously in other cases and when awarding compensation for non-pecuniary damage, the court generally gives little or no explanation of how it has arrived at a particular figure'.[123] What can be observed is that the quantum of awards granted by the Strasbourg Court is generally cautious, particularly for 'non-pecuniary' damage such as in cases of unlawful detention. For example, in *Johnson v United Kingdom* the Strasbourg Court awarded damages of £10,000 for a wrongful detention in a maximum security psychiatric hospital lasting three-and-a-half years.[124]

---

[120] *R (Faulkner) v Secretary of State for Justice* [2013] UKSC 23, [2013] 2 AC 254, para 3.

[121] ibid para 39.

[122] *DSD and NBV v Commissioner of the Police for the Metropolis* [2014] EWHC 2493 (Admin), [2015] 1 WLR 1833.

[123] *Alseran v Ministry of Defence* [2017] EWHC 3289 (KB), [2019] QB 1251, para 920. The exception concerns cases involving excessive delays in proceedings, in breach of art 6, where the ECtHR has established scales: see *Scordino v Italy* (2006) 45 EHRR 7, para 176.

[124] *Johnson v United Kingdom* (1999) 27 EHRR 296.

At the time the Human Rights Act came into force there was considerable debate   4.72
as to whether damages for tort were the most relevant domestic analogy to damages
under section 8 of the Human Rights Act, and whether the quantum rules in tort
should be treated as the prima facie measure to be applied—unless the results were
inconsistent with Strasbourg case law under Article 41.[125] Some of the early case law
supported this approach.[126]

However, in *R (Greenfield) v Secretary of State for the Home Department*,[127] Lord   4.73
Bingham rejected the submissions that damages under the Human Rights Act should
not be on the low side compared to tortious awards; that English courts should be free
to depart from the scale of damages awarded by the ECtHR; and that English awards
(whether tortious or public law remedies) should provide the appropriate comparator. He pointed out that: the objectives of the Human Rights Act were different and
broader than those of a tort statute; a finding of a violation is an important part of a
claimant's remedy and an important vindication of the right asserted; and the purpose
of incorporating the Convention was to give claimants the same remedies they would
recover in Strasbourg. He also pointed out that section 8(4) requires the courts to take
into account the principles of the ECtHR in determining the amount of damages. He
suggested that the courts under the Human Rights Act 'should not aim to be significantly more or less generous than the ECtHR might be expected to be, in a case where
it was willing to make an award at all'.

The approach taken by the English courts to date has been disappointing, and the   4.74
general principles formulated by the House of Lords in *Greenfield* and *Faulkner* are
more restrictive than the terms of the Human Rights Act itself would mandate. The
effect of their Lordships' approach has been that damages for breaches of Convention
rights are considered and awarded rarely, with successful claimants often receiving
no damages.[128] Even where they are available, they are generally much lower than the
comparable awards for discrimination under the Equality Act 2010. There is a powerful argument that this approach not only has the effect of downgrading human rights
but also frustrates the intention of the Human Rights Act, which envisaged domestic
courts being able to provide an effective remedy for breaches of Convention rights. This
restrictive approach also causes difficulty in obtaining public funding for cases because
of the relatively low monetary value assigned to human rights cases—although many
should still pass the criteria for funding under the 'public interest' test.[129]

---

[125] Law Commission, *Damages under the Human Rights Act* (Law Com No 266, 2000) (Cm 4853) para
4.20; Lord Lester and David Pannick, 'Law Com No 266 (2000): The Impact of the Human Rights Act
on Private Law: The Knight's Move' (2000) 116 Law Quarterly Review 380 (referring to the creation of a
'constitutional tort' of infringing Convention rights); Richard Clayton and Hugh Tomlinson, *The Law of
Human Rights* (OUP 2000) para 21.21 (referring to the creation of a public law remedy).

[126] See eg *R (Bernard) v London Borough of Enfield* [2001] EWCA Civ 1831, [2002] HLR 860 in support
of this approach; likewise *Anufrijeva v Southwark London Borough Council* [2003] EWCA Civ 1406, [2004]
QB 1124.

[127] *R (Greenfield) v Secretary of State for the Home Department* [2005] UKHL 14, [2005] 1 WLR 673,
para 19.

[128] See eg *R (SL) v Commissioner of Police for the Metropolis* [2008] EWHC 1442 (Admin).

[129] This is a particular problem in art 5 'false imprisonment' cases taken in the county courts.

4.75   That said, the courts have made sizeable damages awards in some cases. In *Wilson v Commissioner of the Police of the Metropolis* the Investigatory Powers Tribunal (IPT) awarded the claimant £182,945 and £35,000 in pecuniary and non-pecuniary losses for breaches of Articles 3, 8, 10, 11, and 14.[130] In *DSD and NBV v Commissioner of the Police for the Metropolis* the High Court awarded £22,250 and £19,000 to the claimants respectively for the failure by the police to investigate and apprehend a serial rapist which led to assaults on the claimants.[131] In *Alseran v Ministry of Defence* the court made orders of between £12,700 and £28,040 for breaches of Articles 3 and 5 caused by the treatment of Iraqi civilians in the detention of UK Armed Forces.[132]

4.76   It should be borne in mind that, in judicial review proceedings in particular, where separate damages hearings are ordered after the substantive hearing, settlement on quantum will often be reached. This means that the reported case law does not necessarily reflect the reality of Human Rights Act awards.

(d) Claims against judicial bodies and Parliament

4.77   In general, it is not possible to make a claim for damages against a court which has breached the Convention, even though it is a public authority. Where a first instance court acts unlawfully, section 9 of the Human Rights Act requires proceedings in respect of its decision to be brought on appeal from the decision, by way of judicial review[133] or in such other forum as may be prescribed by rules.[134] However, there is provision in section 9(3) and (4) for awards of damages against the Crown where any judicial body has been guilty of a breach of Article 5 in, for example, cases of false imprisonment following a bail application. To claim this remedy, the 'appropriate person', if not already a party to the proceedings, must be joined.[135] The appropriate person (defined in s 9(5)) is the minister responsible for the court concerned, or a person or government department nominated by him or her. In *R (KB) v Mental Health Review Tribunal* the claimants were awarded 'modest' damages after they had established breaches of Article 5(4) rights arising from the failure of the Mental Health Review Tribunal to deal speedily with their applications for a review of their detention.[136]

---

[130] *Wilson v Commissioner of the Police of the Metropolis* IPT/11/167/H (24 January 2022). For the IPT's judgment on the breaches of the Convention, see [2021] UKTrib IPT_11_167_H.

[131] *DSD and NBV v Commissioner of the Police for the Metropolis* [2014] EWHC 2493 (Admin), [2015] 1 WLR 1833.

[132] *Alseran v Ministry of Defence* [2017] EWHC 3289 (KB), [2019] QB 1251, paras 949–82.

[133] In *Mazhar v Lord Chancellor* [2019] EWCA Civ 1558, [2021] Fam 103 the Court of Appeal held that this provision preserved the existing rules of law which govern the circumstances in which a court may be the subject of judicial review (para 45).

[134] In *Mazhar v Lord Chancellor* [2019] EWCA Civ 1558, [2021] Fam 103 the Court of Appeal held that the way in which a judicial act is usually to be the subject of proceedings under the Human Rights Act is by way of an appeal or (where it is otherwise available) by judicial review. The only circumstances in which a claim is permissible under s 9(1)(c) ('in such forum as may be prescribed by rules') is where that is necessary to enable a claim to be brought for damages for unlawful detention in breach of art 5, in accordance with Human Rights Act, s 9(3): see para 54.

[135] See also CPR, r 19.4A. There can be no question of the Lord Chancellor being vicariously liable for the judicial acts of a judge: see *Mazhar v Lord Chancellor* [2019] EWCA Civ 1558, [2021] Fam 103, para 15.

[136] *R (KB) v Mental Health Review Tribunal* [2003] EWHC 193 (Admin), [2004] QB 936.

There is *no* right in damages where the breach of the Convention is caused by an Act of Parliament. It is still not clear how the Human Rights Act intends 'just satisfaction' to be afforded in cases where the breach of the Convention is a consequence of a statutory provision, and where a court has made a declaration of incompatibility under section 4, given the failure to incorporate Article 13. It is possible that *ex gratia* payments of compensation under section 10 are intended to be the appropriate remedy.[137]

4.78

This is an area of law which changes rapidly, and reference should be made to up-to-date discussions and analysis in practitioner texts, such as the *White Book*, the European Human Rights Law Review, and the UK Human Rights Reports.

4.79

2. Section 4—declarations of incompatibility

One of the remedies provided by the Human Rights Act that has been used relatively regularly is the 'declaration of incompatibility'. Under section 4(2), higher courts have the option of declaring that primary legislation is incompatible with the Convention if it is impossible for them to interpret the legislation in such a way as to render it compatible. However, the making of a declaration of incompatibility does not result in the proceedings being resolved in favour of the litigant whose rights were violated. As the courts must give primacy to the statute, this declaration does not affect the validity, continuing operation, or enforcement of the legislation, and 'is not binding on the parties to the proceedings in which it is made'.[138]

4.80

Section 4 is a central part of the carefully crafted mechanism in the Human Rights Act which allows for a balance between the constitutional principles of parliamentary sovereignty and judicial protection of human rights (see Chapter 1). A declaration of incompatibility does not 'strike down' legislation but brings any tension between Convention rights and a particular statutory scheme to the attention of Parliament. It also triggers the power to take remedial action in response under section 10, which provides a 'fast-track' procedure for the amendment of legislation to bring it into line with human rights principles. However, unlike for judgments of the ECtHR, there is no legal obligation on the government to take remedial action following a declaration of incompatibility, nor upon Parliament to accept any remedial measures the government may propose.

4.81

A declaration of incompatibility is intended to be 'a measure of last resort ... [which] ... must be avoided unless it is plainly impossible to do so'.[139] The courts try to avoid making such declarations by striving to find meanings for statutory provisions that conform with the Convention under the strong interpretative obligation in section 3 of the Human Rights Act, which allows the courts to construe legislation compatibly with Convention rights.

4.82

---

[137] See eg *R (H) v Mental Health Review Tribunal* [2001] EWCA Civ 415, [2001] 3 WLR 512 and the payment scheme established by the government following a declaration of incompatibility.

[138] Section 4(6)(b). It is understood that this provision is designed to allow the government to take a different position from that of the court should the case be argued in the ECtHR.

[139] See Lord Steyn in *R v A (No 2)* [2001] UKHL 25, [2002] 1 AC 45, para 44.

4.83   The Supreme Court has declined to make a declaration of incompatibility where it was possible for guidance to be disapplied and legislation interpreted in a Convention-compatible manner.[140]

4.84   Even where it is not possible to interpret a provision compatibly with Convention rights, courts retain their discretion whether to grant a declaration (which is exercised according to the normal principles governing the grant of declarations). Whether a court will exercise its discretion or not will depend on all the circumstances of the case.[141] That the executive proposes to introduce compliant legislation into Parliament will not necessarily mean the court will decline to grant a declaration of incompatibility.[142]

4.85   Finally, where a complaint relates to the absence of legislation it is important to note that any lacuna in a statutory scheme cannot result in a declaration of incompatibility under the Human Rights Act.[143]

(a) Jurisdiction, procedure, and notice provisions

4.86   The power to make declarations of incompatibility is available only in the higher courts. These include the High Court, the Court of Appeal, and the Supreme Court, but not the various tribunals that sit in place of the High Court and from which appeals lie to the Court of Appeal (eg the Employment Appeal Tribunal and the Immigration Appeal Tribunal).[144]

4.87   There is no strict requirement that a person who seeks a declaration of incompatibility is a 'victim' within the definition of section 7, provided he or she has sufficient interest and standing.[145] However, the court will normally only grant a declaration of incompatibility to a person who is a victim of an actual or proposed breach of a Convention right, and in any event a person cannot apply for a declaration of incompatibility on the basis of a hypothetical argument, or if he or she is not adversely affected by the measure in question.[146] In the *Northern Ireland Abortion Case*[147] the Supreme Court considered that sections 58–59 of the Offences Against the Person Act 1861 which criminalized abortion were incompatible with Article 8 but, having found that the Northern Ireland Human Rights Commission did not have standing to bring the claim, did not have jurisdiction to make a declaration of incompatibility.

---

[140] *R (GC and C) v Commissioner of Police of the Metropolis* [2011] UKSC 21, [2011] 1 WLR 1230.

[141] cf *R (Nicklinson) v Ministry of Justice* [2014] UKSC 38, [2015] AC 657 (declaration not granted) and *R (Steinfeld) v Secretary of State for International Development* [2018] UKSC 32, [2020] AC 1 (declaration granted). See also *Wilson v First County Trust Ltd (No 2)* [2001] EWCA Civ 633, [2002] QB 74, para 46; overruled on other grounds by the House of Lords at [2003] UKHL 40, [2003] 3 WLR 568.

[142] *Bellinger v Bellinger* [2003] UKHL 21, [2003] 2 AC 467, paras 55, 79.

[143] See *Re S (minors) (care order: implementation of care plan)* [2002] 2 UKHL 10, [2002] 2 AC 291.

[144] See Chapter 3 for further detail as to the duties of the lower courts when confronted with compatibility arguments.

[145] *R (Rusbridger) v Attorney General* [2003] UKHL 38, [2003] 3 WLR 232, para 21per Lord Steyn.

[146] *Taylor v Lancashire County Council and Secretary of State for the Environment, Food and Rural Affairs* [2005] EWCA Civ 284, [2005] HRLR 17.

[147] *Northern Ireland Abortion Case* [2018] UKSC 27, [2019] 1 All ER 173.

(b) Examples of declarations of incompatibility in specific cases

Although there have been many challenges to legislation since the Human Rights   4.88
Act came into force, declarations of incompatibility have been made and upheld by
the courts in a relatively small number of cases.[148]

In most instances the government has responded to the declarations issued by the   4.89
courts by amending, repealing, or introducing new legislation. Examples include
the following:

(a) *R v Secretary of State for the Home Department, ex p Anderson* involved a challenge
to the Home Secretary's power under the Crime (Sentences) Act 1997 to set the
minimum period that must be served by a mandatory life sentence prisoner
before he was considered for release on licence.[149] Following the Strasbourg ruling in *Stafford v United Kingdom*[150] the House of Lords found that the involvement of the Home Secretary, as a member of the executive, in fixing the tariff
term of imprisonment for those convicted of murder was incompatible with
Article 6(1). The impugned law was repealed by the Criminal Justice Act 2003
and new sentencing provisions were introduced in Chapter 7 of, and Schedules
21 and 22 to, that Act.

(b) In *Bellinger v Bellinger* a post-operative trans woman appealed against a decision
that she was not validly married to her husband because the law still regarded
her as a man.[151] The House of Lords held that section 11(c) of the Matrimonial
Causes Act 1973 was incompatible with Articles 8 and 12 of the Convention.
The declaration of incompatibility was made following the Strasbourg Court's
decision in *Goodwin v United Kingdom*[152] and Parliament enacted the Gender
Recognition Act 2004 to remedy the breach.

(c) *R (Clift) v Secretary of State for the Home Department; Secretary of State for the
Home Department v Hindawi*[153] was a conjoined appeal in which the appellants were all former or serving prisoners. The issue on appeal was whether
the early release provisions, to which each of the appellants was subject, were
discriminatory. Sections 46(1) and 50(2) of the Criminal Justice Act 1991
were declared incompatible with Article 14 taken together with Article 5 on
the basis that they discriminated on grounds of national origin. The provisions

---

[148] The government database that listed declarations of incompatibility is no longer available. The
Ministry of Justice's paper 'Responding to Human Rights judgments: Report to the Joint Committee on
Human Rights on the Government's Response to human rights judgments 2021–2022' reports that, as of
December 2022, there had been 46 declarations of incompatibility made since the Human Rights Act came
into force on 2 October 2000. The report records that 10 declarations of incompatibility were overturned
on appeal, 30 have been fully addressed by changes in law, and 6 are ongoing (4 of which are subject to
proposed Remedial order, and 2 subject to appeal). See <https://www.gov.uk/government/publications/res
ponding-to-human-rights-judgments-2021-to-2022> accessed 29 December 2023.
[149] *R v Secretary of State for the Home Department, ex p Anderson* [2002] UKHL 46, [2003] 1 AC 837.
[150] *Stafford v United Kingdom* (2002) 35 EHRR 32.
[151] *Bellinger v Bellinger* [2003] UKHL 21, [2003] 2 AC 467.
[152] *Goodwin v United Kingdom* (2002) 35 EHRR 18.
[153] *R (Clift) v Secretary of State for the Home Department; Secretary of State for the Home Department v
Hindawi* [2006] UKHL 54, [2007] 1 AC 484.

had already been repealed and replaced by the Criminal Justice Act 2003, but continued to apply on a transitional basis to offences committed before 4 April 2005. Section 27 of the Criminal Justice and Immigration Act 2008 therefore amended the Criminal Justice Act 1991 to remove the incompatibility in the transitional cases.

(d) In *R (Wright and others) v Secretary of State for Health* the House of Lords found the 'provisional blacklisting' provisions for care workers in the Care Standards Act 2000 incompatible with Articles 6 and 8.[154] By the date of the House of Lords' judgment, the transition to a new scheme under the Safeguarding Vulnerable Groups Act 2006 was already underway. The new scheme did not include the feature of provisional listing which was the subject of challenge in the *Wright* case.

(e) *R (F and Thompson) v Secretary of State for the Home Department* concerned the indefinite requirements imposed on those convicted of sexual offences to notify the authorities of their travel plans by virtue of the Sexual Offences Act 2003. The Supreme Court held that these requirements were incompatible with Article 8 of the Convention; a declaration of incompatibility was therefore made.[155] In June 2011 the government published the draft Sexual Offences Act 2003 (Remedial) Order 2011 in response to the judgment.[156]

(f) *R (T) v Chief Constable of Greater Manchester and others* concerned the blanket disclosure of convictions and cautions under the provisions of the Police Act 1997 and Rehabilitation of Offenders Act 1974 (Exceptions) Order 1975. The claimants argued that they were incompatible with the Article 8 right to private life. The Court of Appeal found the provisions incompatible with Article 8 and made a declaration of incompatibility. Parliament amended the legislation to reflect the judgment.[157] A declaration of incompatibility was also made in respect of the revised scheme's compatibility with Article 8: *P, G & W v Chief Constable of Surrey Police & others*.[158] Further amendments to the statutory scheme were made in light of this judgment.

(g) *R (Steinfeld & Keidan) v Secretary of State for International Development*[159] concerned the exclusion of different-sex couples from civil partnerships under the Civil Partnership Act 2004, which were available only to same-sex couples.

---

[154] *R (Wright and others) v Secretary of State for Health* [2009] UKHL 3, [2009] 2 WLR 267.

[155] *R (F and Thompson) v Secretary of State for the Home Department* [2010] UKSC 17, [2011] 1 AC 331. For details of other cases, see *R (H) v Mental Health Review Tribunal* [2001] EWCA Civ 415, [2001] 3 WLR 512; *R (Wilkinson) v Inland Revenue Commissioners* [2003] EWCA Civ 814, [2003] 1 WLR 2683; and *International Transport Roth GmbH v Secretary of State for the Home Department* [2002] EWCA Civ 158, [2002] 3 WLR 344.

[156] See <http://www.homeoffice.gov.uk/publications/about-us/legislation/sexual-offences-remedial-order> accessed 29 December 2023.

[157] The government appealed the Court of Appeal decision to the Supreme Court after amending the legislation. The Supreme Court upheld the Court of Appeal decision: *R (T) v Chief Constable of Greater Manchester* [2014] UKSC 35.

[158] *P, G & W v Chief Constable of Surrey Police & others* [2019] UKSC 3, [2020] AC 185.

[159] *R (Steinfeld & Keidan) v Secretary of State for International Development* [2018] UKSC 32, [2020] AC 1.

Same-sex couples were also entitled to marry but, when the Marriage (Same Sex Couples) Act 2013 was introduced, the government did not repeal the Civil Partnerships Act. By the time of the Supreme Court hearing, the government accepted that this caused an inequality of treatment between same-sex and different-sex couples, engaging Article 14 and Article 8 of the Convention. The question was whether this was justified. The Supreme Court held that it was not, and made a declaration of incompatibility in respect of sections 1 and 3 of the Civil Partnerships Act (which limited their scope to same-sex couples). The government responded by extending eligibility to enter civil partnerships to different-sex couples.

(c) Difficulties with the declaration of incompatibility procedure

Unfortunately the declaration of incompatibility procedure does not tend to have speedy results. For example, the amendments to the Criminal Justice Act 1991 made as a result of *Clift* (Section 4.89 c) only came into force in July 2008, although the judgment was handed down in December 2006—and this has been one of the quickest responses.[160] In one case, the High Court made a declaration of incompatibility in November 2006,[161] the Court of Appeal overturned it in October 2007,[162] and the House of Lords then reinstated the declaration on 21 January 2009.[163] The legislation was repealed with effect from 12 October 2009.   **4.90**

Even when attempts are made to rectify the incompatibility identified in a declaration, they may not succeed in doing so. The repeated litigation and declarations of incompatibility in respect of the statutory scheme for disclosure of criminal convictions is one example where the government's attempts to remove an identified incompatibility have been insufficient to ensure that the overall scheme is compatible with the Convention.   **4.91**

In our view, while the government may never have refused to respond as such, periods of years (or even months when dealing with urgent issues or vulnerable groups) throughout which it claims to be 'considering how to remedy the incompatibility' are unacceptable, and undermine the government's claim that the regime is compliant with Article 13 (the right to an effective remedy). It might be noted that the ECtHR has held that the declaration of incompatibility is not (yet) an effective remedy for breach of a Convention right, given the various other restrictions on its availability (the facts that it does not assist the individual litigant, that it is not binding, and that ministers can exercise the power to amend under s 10 only where there are 'compelling reasons' for doing so—see Section 4.98),[164] although   **4.92**

---

[160] See JCHR, *Monitoring the Government's Response to Human Rights Judgments: Annual Report 2008*, 31st Report (2007–2008), HL 173, HC 1078, para 107.

[161] *R (Wright and others) v Secretary of State for Health and Secretary of State for Education and Skills* [2006] EWHC 2886 (Admin).

[162] *R (on the application of Wright) v Secretary of State for Health* [2007] EWCA Civ 999, [2008] 2 WLR 536.

[163] *R (on the application of Wright) v Secretary of State for Health* [2009] UKHL 3, [2009] 2 WLR 267.

[164] Second Monitoring Report, paras 110–21. See *Burden and Burden v UK* (2008) 24 BHRC 709.

it has indicated that, in time, the United Kingdom could potentially persuade the court otherwise:

> It is possible that at some future date evidence of a long-standing and established practice of ministers giving effect to the courts' declarations of incompatibility might be sufficient to persuade the Court of the effectiveness of the procedure.[165]

Regrettably, the government appears to have taken this judgment as 'an endorsement of its current approach',[166] rather than a heavy hint from Strasbourg to adopt a clear and consistent policy. As matters stand, the declaration of incompatibility is not an effective remedy for Convention purposes, which means that a litigant need not, at present, pursue such a remedy before going to Strasbourg if it is the only one realistically available in order to exhaust domestic remedies.

4.93   A further worrying lacuna in the Act relates to the position where the government ignores a judgment of the ECtHR condemning the United Kingdom for violating Convention rights. The domestic courts have thus far taken the general view that once a declaration of incompatibility has been made, no further relief will be granted. This issue was particularly acute following the refusal of successive governments to implement the judgment of the ECtHR in *Hirst v UK (No 2)*[167] in relation to the prohibition on serving prisoners being able to vote.[168] It took until 2017, 11 years after the ECtHR's judgment, for the UK to propose limited measures to address the breach (permitting prisoners released on temporary licence to vote), which the Council of Europe agreed as an acceptable resolution.

4.94   Given the continued existence of legislation which cannot be read compatibly with Convention rights, there can be no question of a statutory tort being committed under section 6 of the Human Rights Act. Consequently, there is no right to damages under section 8 of the Act or any other remedy for the ongoing violation of Convention rights. One can therefore readily appreciate why the ECtHR has held that the declaration of incompatibility mechanism does not amount to an effective remedy for the purposes of Article 13 of the Convention.

4.95   It is worth noting that the position is different in respect of secondary legislation which has been deemed to be incompatible with the Convention (but which the government has not yet repealed or amended). The Supreme Court in *RR v Secretary of State for Work and Pensions*[169] held that public authorities, courts, and tribunals are required to disapply or disregard offending secondary legislation if it is possible to do so without affecting the statutory scheme. That reflects the difference in the constitutional status of primary and secondary legislation and the balance struck by the Human Rights Act not to impinge on the validity of primary legislation.

---

[165] *Burden and Burden v UK* (2007) 44 EHRR 709.

[166] Ministry of Justice, *Responding to Human Rights Judgments: Government Response to the Joint Committee on Human Rights' Thirty-first Report of Session 2008* (Cm 7524), 39.

[167] *Hirst v UK (No 2)* (2006) 42 EHRR 41.

[168] See *R (Chester) v Secretary of State for Justice* [2013] UKSC 63, [2014] AC 271. The ECtHR has recently ruled that prisoners are not entitled to compensation for unlawful disenfranchisement: *Firth and others v UK*, App No 47784/09, 12 August 2014.

[169] *RR v Secretary of State for Work and Pensions* [2019] UKSC 52, [2019] 1 WLR 6430.

3. Section 10—'fast-track' procedure

A declaration of incompatibility under section 4 should prompt legislative change— either directly by amendment of primary legislation, or under the Human Rights Act's fast-track procedure. Indeed, in practice declarations of incompatibility do usually prompt such change, although this change may be slow to come about. As of December 2022, 34 declarations of incompatibility have become final.[170] Of these:

- sixteen have been remedied by primary or secondary legislation;
- eight have been remedied by a remedial order under section 10 of the Human Rights Act;
- five relate to provisions that had already been remedied by primary legislation at the time of the declaration;
- one has been addressed by various measures;
- four have not yet been remedied.

As these statistics show, such changes are usually made through amendments to primary legislation or the introduction of new legislation, and the fast-track procedure is rarely used. The JCHR, which has been highly critical of the government's failure to speedily and effectively respond to both declarations of incompatibility in the domestic courts and adverse judgments from Strasbourg, has recommended that greater use should be made of remedial orders.[171]

The fast-track procedure is contained in section 10 of, and Schedule 2 to, the Human Rights Act. It is a power to take remedial action (in respect of both declarations of incompatibility and ECtHR judgments) through the making of a remedial order in certain circumstances. Under section 10 this power can be triggered:

(a) following a declaration of incompatibility made under section 4 where all parties have exercised or abandoned any rights of appeal or the time limit for appealing has expired;

(b) where the government decides, following a decision of the ECtHR, that a provision of legislation is incompatible with a Convention right. It is not necessary that the judgment of the court is in favour of the applicant; or

(c) in relation to incompatible subordinate legislation, where a minister considers that it is necessary to amend the parent legislation.

If there are 'compelling reasons' for doing so, section 10 empowers a minister to make a 'remedial order' embodied in a statutory instrument that amends legislation so far as necessary to remove its incompatibility with the Convention. The Human

4.96

4.97

4.98

---

[170] See the Ministry of Justice's paper 'Responding to Human Rights judgments: Report to the Joint Committee on Human Rights on the Government's Response to human rights judgments 2021–2022'; <https://www.gov.uk/government/publications/responding-to-human-rights-judgments-2021-to-2022>

[171] JCHR, *Monitoring the Government's Response to Human Rights Judgments: Annual Report 2008*, 31st Report (2007–2008), HL 173, HC 1078, para 6.

Rights Act provides two procedures for making a remedial order: a standard procedure in Schedule 2, paragraph 2(a), and an emergency procedure in Schedule 2, paragraph 2(b).

4.99 A remedial order can be fairly wide in scope, have retrospective effect, and can 'make different provision for different cases'. This retrospective effect is limited by Schedule 2, paragraph 1(3), which states that, 'no person is to be guilty of an offence solely as a result of the retrospective effect of a remedial order'. The power to change the law retrospectively could be used to backdate a change to the date of the domestic court's decision on incompatibility or the judgment of the ECtHR.

4.100 The standard procedure[172] is a 'positive resolution procedure'. The minister must first[173] lay before Parliament a document containing a draft of the proposed order together with what is called the 'required information', which is:

(a) an explanation of the incompatibility that the proposed order seeks to remove, including particulars of the court declaration, finding, or order that caused the minister to propose a remedial order; and

(b) a statement of the reasons for proceeding under section 10 and for making an order in the terms proposed.[174]

4.101 This document must be before Parliament for at least 60 days, during which time representations about the draft order may be made to the minister, either by Parliament in the form of a report or resolution, or by any other person. The minister can amend the draft in the light of these representations. Whether or not the draft is amended it must be laid before Parliament again, this time accompanied by a summary of any representations that have been made and details of any changes made as a result. The order does not come into effect unless it is approved by a resolution of each House within 60 days after it is laid for the second time.

4.102 Under the emergency procedure[175] the minister may make the order before laying it before Parliament, but must state in the order that it appears to him or her that, because of the urgency of the matter, it is necessary to make it without prior parliamentary approval. However, after making an order under this emergency procedure the minister must[176] lay the order before Parliament, with the required information, for 60 days, during which time representations may be made, as under the standard procedure. The minister can amend the order in the light of the representations, but, whether or not it is amended, the order must be laid before Parliament again, with a summary of representations and details of amendments, and it will cease to have effect 120 days after it was made unless it is approved by a resolution of each House. This procedure was adopted following the Court of Appeal's decision in *R (H) v Mental Health Review Tribunal*,[177] when the Secretary of State introduced the

---

[172] Schedule 2, para 2(a).
[173] Schedule 2, para 3.
[174] Schedule 2, para 5.
[175] Schedule 2, para 2(b).
[176] Schedule 2, para 4.
[177] *R (H) v Mental Health Review Tribunal* [2001] EWCA Civ 415, [2001] 3 WLR 512.

Mental Health Act 1983 (Remedial) Order 2001[178] using this urgent procedure. This route was probably used because the problem involved fundamental rights to personal liberty and, if not rectified quickly, would have created confusion as the tribunal system would have been unsure what burden of proof it should be applying.

The power given by section 10 to amend legislation applies to both primary and **4.103** secondary legislation. This provision allows campaigners, lobbyists, and lawyers to make representations to government to amend primary legislation following any case in the ECtHR that raises questions about legislation. The government is not, of course, bound to act by way of either primary or secondary legislation, even following a declaration of incompatibility. However, if it does not do so, the victim could then seek just satisfaction in the ECtHR. This would then impose an obligation on the government as a matter of international law to remedy its violation. However, the Strasbourg Court has held on a number of occasions that the discretionary nature of the power under section 10, and the statutory limitations on the circumstances in which it can be used, prevent it from constituting an 'effective remedy' in Convention terms.[179]

I. KEY CONVENTION CONCEPTS IN THE DOMESTIC COURTS

As discussed in Chapter 2, there are particular interpretative concepts that the **4.104** ECtHR has developed in order to give meaning and effect to the Convention. The domestic courts have adopted these concepts when interpreting Convention rights under the Human Rights Act. As revealed by the number of successful applications to Strasbourg made after the Human Rights Act came into force, the domestic courts do not always apply Convention principles in the same manner as the ECtHR. The following discussion of some of the key concepts highlights points of similarity and divergence.

1. Territoriality

We discuss the approach of the ECtHR to extra-territoriality of the Convention **4.105** in Chapter 2, paragraphs 2.24–2.25.[180] The UK courts have struggled with extra-territoriality in a number of cases which we discuss in greater detail in Chapter 5.[181] After some to and fro between the UK courts and the ECtHR, the approach of the domestic and European courts is now consistent and it is agreed that the Convention will apply extra-territorially in exceptional circumstances. These circumstances include the important category of 'state agent authority and

---

[178] SI 2001/3712.
[179] See, for example, *Benkharbouche v United Kingdom* (2023) 76 EHRR 1 at para 58.
[180] See Chapter 2, paras 2.24–2.25.
[181] See Chapter 5, paras 5.04–5.11.

control'. Whenever the state through its agents exercises control and authority over an individual, the state will be under an obligation to secure to that individual the rights and freedoms under the Convention that were relevant to the situation of that individual. The Supreme Court has also accepted that the UK has jurisdiction over its armed forces abroad and is obliged to respect the rights of its soldiers when they serve abroad.[182]

2. Positive obligations

4.106   As discussed in Chapter 2,[183] positive obligations provide a critical interpretative tool for the ECtHR to expand the protection of the Convention beyond the bare minimum authorized by the text of the articles. Domestic courts have proved cautious in imposing positive obligations on public authorities, aware that political and economic considerations are often at stake. The nature of positive obligations was considered by the House of Lords in *R (Pretty) v DPP*, a case questioning whether the applicant, who suffered from terminal motor neurone disease, could claim a right to die under Articles 2 and 8 of the Convention.[184] Following Strasbourg authority, Lord Bingham emphasized that the question of whether a positive obligation exists depends on striking a fair balance between the general interests of the community and the interests of the individual. Diane Pretty's application was not upheld by either the House of Lords or the Strasbourg Court.[185]

4.107   Domestic cases on the scope of positive obligations have largely concerned Article 2, Article 3, and Article 8.[186] The first two sets of cases have met with the most success in domestic courts. In a trio of cases—*Amin*,[187] *Middleton*,[188] and *JL*[189]—the House of Lords found violations of the positive obligation under Article 2 to conduct an investigation into deaths or near-deaths in custody. In *Savage v South Essex Partnership NHS Foundation Trust* the House of Lords found that the obligation to protect life extends to providing a proper system for the supervision of mental patients,[190] a position confirmed by the Supreme Court in *Rabone v Pennine Care NHS Trust*.[191] In *R (B) v Director of Public Prosecutions*[192] and *OOO v Commissioner of Police of the Metropolis*,[193] the High Court found breaches of the state's positive obligations under Article 3. So too were there breaches of the state's positive obligations under Article 3 in *DSD & NBV v Commissioner of the Police of*

---

[182] *R (Smith) v Ministry of Defence* [2013] UKSC 41, [2014] AC 52.
[183] See Chapter 2, paras 2.33–2.39.
[184] *R (Pretty) v DPP* [2001] UKHL 61, [2002] 1 AC 800.
[185] *Pretty v UK* (2002) 35 EHRR 1.
[186] For further detail, see Chapters 5 and 6.
[187] *R (Amin) v Secretary of State for the Home Department* [2003] UKHL 51, [2004] 1 AC 653.
[188] *R v Coroner for Western District of Somerset, ex p Middleton* [2004] UKHL 10, [2004] 2 AC 182.
[189] *R (JL) v Secretary of State for Justice* [2008] UKHL 68, [2008] 3 WLR 1325.
[190] *Savage v South Essex Partnership NHS Foundation Trust* [2008] UKHL 74, [2009] 2 WLR 115.
[191] *Rabone v Pennine Care NHS Trust* [2012] UKSC 2, [2012] 2 AC 72.
[192] *R (B) v Director of Public Prosecutions* [2009] EWHC 106 (Admin), [2009] 1 WLR 2072.
[193] *OOO v Commissioner of Police of the Metropolis* [2011] EWHC 1246 (QB), [2011] HRLR 29.

the Metropolis[194] arising from the police's failure properly to investigate allegations of rape and sexual assault.

Positive obligations under Article 8 are harder to establish. In *Re S (a care plan)* the House of Lords rejected the Court of Appeal's development of a positive obligation to secure a child in care with 'a family for life'.[195] In *Secretary of State for Work and Pensions v M* the House of Lords said that Strasbourg was 'well aware' of the dangers of any 'unrestrained and unprincipled' extension of Article 8, and stated that many social welfare measures with only an indirect effect on private or family life were not even within the ambit of the duty to respect it.[196] In *R (Mcdonald) v Royal Borough of Kensington and Chelsea*, the Supreme Court held that while in principle there could be a positive obligation on local authorities to provide social care support, there was no such obligation to the claimant to provide nursing staff overnight to avoid the indignity of having to wear incontinence pads.[197] In *R (Elan-Cane) v Secretary of State for the Home Department* the Supreme Court held that there was no positive obligation under Article 8 requiring the state to permit a non-gendered individual to specify 'X' (rather than 'M' or 'F') in respect of their gender on their passport.[198] The Supreme Court confirmed that there is a wide margin of appreciation in respect of positive obligations because 'the imposition of such obligations requires contracting states to modify their laws and practices, and possibly (as in the present case) to incur public expenditure, in order to advance social policies which they may not wholly support, or which they may not regard as priorities, without the imposition of the obligation being supported by any democratic mandate or accountability. While not a conclusive objection, those characteristics of positive obligations include the importance of exercising caution before they are imposed.'[199] That said, the courts have occasionally recognized the potential role for positive obligations under Article 8: in *Bryant and others v Commissioner of Police for the Metropolis* the High Court held that it is arguable that the police are under a positive obligation to inform citizens of information that indicates that respect for their private life is potentially threatened.[200]

4.108

Where an omission by a public authority can be said to amount to inhuman or degrading treatment, the court may be more willing to impose a positive obligation. In *R (Limbuela) v Secretary of State for the Home Department*, for example, the House of Lords held that Article 3 required basic subsistence to be given to asylum-seekers.[201] In *DSD and NBV v Commissioner of Police for the Metropolis*, the High

4.109

---

[194] *DSD & NBV v Commissioner of the Police of the Metropolis* [2018] UKSC 11, [2019] AC 196.

[195] See *W and B (children: care plan)* [2001] EWCA Civ 757, [2001] 2 FLR 582.

[196] *Secretary of State for Work and Pensions v M* [2006] UKHL 11, [2006] 2 AC 91.

[197] *R (Mcdonald) v Royal Borough of Kensington and Chelsea* [2011] UKSC 33, [2011] 4 All ER 881. The ECtHR held that the case did not need to be analysed in terms of positive obligations but by reference to the negative obligation, as the claimant had experienced a reduction in care support: *Mcdonald v UK* (2015) 60 EHRR 1.

[198] *R (Elan-Cane) v Secretary of State for the Home Department* [2021] UKSC 56, [2023] AC 559.

[199] [2021] UKSC 56, [2023] AC 559, para 54.

[200] *Bryant and others v Commissioner of Police for the Metropolis* [2011] EWHC 1314 (Admin), [2011] HRLR 27, para 54.

[201] *R (Limbuela) v Secretary of State for the Home Department* [2005] UKHL 66, [2006] 1 AC 396.

Court (upheld by the Court of Appeal and Supreme Court) found that there was a positive duty imposed upon the police to conduct investigations into particularly severe violent acts perpetrated by private parties in a timely and efficient manner.[202] The police failure to investigate serious claims of sexual assault violated the claimants' Article 3 rights.

3. Legality

4.110   As discussed in Chapter 2,[203] the requirement of legality is a critical first step to determining whether any limitation on rights can be justified. It has been considered in the domestic context on a number of occasions since the Human Rights Act came into force. The House of Lords adopted the approach of the ECtHR in *R v Shayler*.[204] Lord Hope explained that the court had to address itself to three questions: whether there was a legal basis in domestic law for the restriction; whether the law was sufficiently accessible and precise; and, finally, whether the law had been arbitrarily applied.[205]

4.111   The Lords strayed from this strict approach in *R (Gillan) v Commissioner of Police for the Metropolis*, a case concerning the use by the Metropolitan Police of random stop-and-search powers under the Terrorism Act 2000.[206] The basis on which the police decided to stop and search individuals had never been published; nor had members of the public been informed that random stop-and-search powers were being deployed in the London area. However, their Lordships found that the bare fact that the Act authorized the powers was sufficient guarantee of legality. Lord Bingham accepted that powers were broadly drawn, but stated that 'a measure of vagueness was inevitable if excessive rigidity was to be avoided' and, in any event, there were 'strong reasons' for not publishing details of the authorizations and confirmations.[207] This approach was not in keeping with the Strasbourg jurisprudence, as the ECtHR subsequently found.[208]

4.112   Other domestic decisions have more satisfactorily upheld the principle of legality. In *R (Laporte) v Chief Constable of Gloucestershire* the House of Lords found that action taken to prevent demonstrators from reaching a demonstration was not prescribed by domestic law as there had been no imminent breach of the peace to justify intercepting the demonstrators.[209] Likewise, in the case of *R (Moos and McClure) v Commissioner of Police of the Metropolis*[210] the Divisional Court held

---

[202] *DSD v Commissioner of Police of the Metropolis* [2014] EWHC 436 (QB); *DSD and NBV v Commissioner of Police for the Metropolis* [2015] EWCA Civ 646, [2019] Q.B. 285; *Commissioner of Police of the Metropolis v DSD* [2018] UKSC 11, [2019] AC 196

[203] See Chapter 2, paras 2.42–2.49.

[204] *R v Shayler* [2002] UKHL 11, [2003] 1 AC 247.

[205] ibid para 56.

[206] *R (Gillan) v Commissioner of Police for the Metropolis* [2006] UKHL 12, [2006] 2 WLR 537.

[207] Ibid para 33.

[208] *Gillan and Quinton v UK* App No 4158/05, 12 January 2010.

[209] *R (Laporte) v Chief Constable of Gloucestershire* [2006] UKHL 55, [2007] 2 AC 105.

[210] *R (Moos and McClure) v Commissioner of Police of the Metropolis* [2011] EWHC 957 (Admin), [2011] HRLR 24.

that there had been no imminent breach of the peace such as to justify 'kettling' members of the public on the facts of the case. In *R (Bridges) v South Wales Police*, the Court of Appeal found that the use of live facial recognition technology on members of the public was not subject to a sufficient legal framework to comply with the principle of legality.[211] In *R (T) v Secretary of State for the Home Department* the Supreme Court found that the statutory procedure for disclosure of convictions and cautions fell foul of the principle of legality.[212] Lord Wilson disagreed, arguing that it was necessary to preserve a distinction between legality and necessity, and that the legislation was disproportionate but not inadequately precise.[213]

4. Proportionality

(a) *Introduction and overview*

As discussed in Chapter 2,[214] proportionality is the standard of review applied by the ECtHR in its assessment of justifications for infringing limited and qualified Convention rights. This is the standard now adopted under the Human Rights Act, which has heralded a far closer level of scrutiny of public decision-making than was previously the case in ordinary domestic judicial review proceedings. In relation to all qualified rights, the question is whether any intrusion into the right is lawful, in the sense of having a lawful basis, being intended to meet a legitimate aim, and being a means of achieving that aim which is 'necessary in a democratic society'. The standard of scrutiny, in judicial review proceedings raising Human Rights Act grounds, is therefore now that of 'proportionality' rather than the common law standard which permits judicial interference only in cases of 'irrationality'. However, there has been some debate on whether, why, and to what extent, courts ought to 'defer' to the decisions reached by other arms of government or expert decision-makers. This section considers the current law on the test for determining whether there is a departure from or exception to a Convention principle. The next section addresses the concepts of deference and the 'discretionary area of judgment'.

4.113

(b) *The development and application of the proportionality principle in domestic law*

Before the Human Rights Act came into force, the test for challenging the actions of public authorities by way of judicial review was that they must be unlawful or 'irrational'; in Lord Diplock's oft-quoted explanation of *Wednesbury*[215] unreasonableness, 'a decision which is so outrageous in its defiance of logic or accepted moral standards that no sensible person who had applied his mind to the question to be decided could have arrived at it'.[216] It is very hard to challenge a decision on this basis; and although in later cases, where fundamental rights were at stake, the test was redefined so that the greater the interference with fundamental rights, the greater the

4.114

---

[211] *R (Bridges) v South Wales Police* [2020] EWCA Civ 1058, [2020] 1 WLR 5037.
[212] *R (T) v Secretary of State for the Home Department* [2014] UKSC 35, [2015] AC 49.
[213] ibid para 38.
[214] See Chapter 2, paras 2.61–2.66.
[215] *Associated Provincial Picture Houses Ltd v Wednesbury Corp* [1948] 1 KB 223.
[216] *Council of Civil Service Unions v Minister for the Civil Service* [1985] AC 375, para 410.

level of scrutiny required,[217] the ECtHR held that even this reformulated level of scrutiny was insufficient to meet the requirements of Article 13 of the Convention.[218]

4.115   The four-stage approach to proportionality now followed by the courts in Human Rights Act cases was first set out by the House of Lords in *Huang v Secretary of State for the Home Department*,[219] and re-stated by the Supreme Court in an oft-cited paragraph of *Bank Mellat v Her Majesty's Treasury*:

> [T]he question depends on an exacting analysis of the factual case advanced in defence of the measure, in order to determine (i) whether its objective is sufficiently important to justify the limitation of a fundamental right; (ii) whether it is rationally connected to the objective; (iii) whether a less intrusive measure could have been used; and (iv) whether, having regard to these matters and to the severity of the consequences, a fair balance has been struck between the rights of the individual and the interests of the community. These four requirements are logically separate, but in practice they inevitably overlap.[220]

(c) *Deference and the 'discretionary area of judgment'*

4.116   The role of courts, in the Convention system of rights protections, is to scrutinize the 'necessity' of infringements to human rights. However, the ECtHR is conscious of the limits of the social judgments it can make as a supranational court, lacking sensitivity to nuances of the particular societies of the Council of Europe states. Thus, as explained in Chapter 2,[221] the ECtHR frequently invokes what it calls the 'margin of appreciation' to afford Member States a reasonable sphere within which it will not interfere with their power to evaluate their public policy decisions, though they are subject to review.

4.117   This doctrine is an international one, based on the limitations of the international court. It has no place in domestic arrangements for protecting human rights and should not be used when the Convention is applied by national courts. It was created to allow national judicial bodies a degree of flexibility; to enable an international judicial review system to give due weight to local political and cultural traditions; and to take into account the geographical, cultural, philosophical, historical, and intellectual distance between the judges in Strasbourg and local institutions. The domestic courts do not need the doctrine because this gap does not exist. As the Grand Chamber stated in *A v UK*:

> The doctrine of the margin of appreciation has always been meant as a tool to define relations between the domestic authorities and the Court. It cannot have the same application to the

---

[217] See the formulation in *R v Ministry of Defence, ex p Smith* [1996] QB 517.

[218] See *Smith and Grady v UK* (1999) 29 EHRR 493; *Hatton v UK* (2003) 37 EHRR 28.

[219] *Huang v Secretary of State for the Home Department* [2007] UKHL 11, [2007] 2 AC 167. For a different set of questions to be asked, at least in an art 8 context, see *R (F) v Secretary of State for Justice* [2010] UKSC 17, [2010] 2 WLR 992, para 41 per Lord Phillips: '(i) What is the extent of the interference with article 8 rights? (ii) How valuable are the notification requirements [regarding a sex offender's foreign travel plans] in achieving the legitimate aims [of the legislation in question]? and (iii) to what extent would that value be eroded if the notification requirements were made subject to review?'

[220] *Bank Mellat v Her Majesty's Treasury* [2013] UKSC 39, [2014] AC 700, para 20.

[221] See Chapter 2, paras 2.77–2.84.

relations between the organs of State at the domestic level ... the question of proportionality is ultimately a judicial decision ... [222]

In the first case on the Human Rights Act to reach the House of Lords, *R* **4.118** *(Kebilene) v DPP*, this position was confirmed.[223] Lord Hope stated that the doctrine of margin of appreciation:

is an integral part of the supervisory jurisdiction which is exercised over state conduct by the international court. By conceding a margin of appreciation to each national system, the court has recognised that the Convention, as a living system, does not need to be applied uniformly by all states but may vary in its application according to local needs and conditions. This technique is not available to the national courts when they are considering Convention issues arising within their own countries. But in the hands of the national courts also the Convention should be seen as an expression of fundamental principles rather than as a set of mere rules. The questions which the courts will have to decide in the application of these principles will involve questions of balance between competing interests and issues of proportionality.[224]

However, the concept of 'deference' or a 'discretionary area of judgment' has **4.119** been embraced by domestic courts as a means of respecting democratic decision-making and avoiding judicial determination of sensitive matters of social policy. In early Human Rights Act jurisprudence, a concept of 'deference' to the legislature was developed, which, in essence, involved the domestic courts attempting to translate the international law concept of 'margin of appreciation' into domestic law.

One aspect of the debate arose in the context of human rights challenges to social **4.120** welfare benefit decisions, where the concept of deference was interpreted for a time as displacing the ordinary proportionality assessment where the compatibility with Convention rights of an economic or social measure in the field of welfare benefits was in issue, and instead imposing a singular test of whether the measure was 'manifestly without reasonable foundation'. In *R (SC) v Secretary of State for Work and Pensions*,[225] the Supreme Court confirmed that the ordinary proportionality analysis should apply in all cases and that the 'manifestly without reasonable foundation' formulation did not 'express a test' but 'indicates the width of the margin of appreciation, and hence the intensity of review, which is in principle appropriate in the field of welfare benefits, other things being equal'. However, 'it is more useful to think of there being a range of factors which tend to heighten, or lower, the intensity of review. In any given case, a number of these factors may be present, possibly pulling in different directions, and the court has to take them all into account to make an overall assessment.' Thus, where the ground of difference in treatment under Article 14 is one of the 'suspect' grounds of discrimination (such as sex or gender, race, or sexual orientation), a strict standard of proportionality review will ordinarily be adopted and 'very weighty reasons' will be required to justify the interference. On the other hand, a wide margin is usually allowed to a state when

---

[222] *A v UK* (2009) 26 BHRC 1.
[223] *R (Kebilene) v DPP* [2000] 2 AC 326.
[224] ibid para 380.
[225] *R (SC) v Secretary of State for Work and Pensions* [2021] UKSC 26, [2022] AC 223.

it comes to general measures of social or economic strategy, and so a less intensive proportionality review may be appropriate in such cases.

4.121 The concept of 'deference' is not one that appears on the face of the Human Rights Act. However, two possible theoretical bases have been advanced by commentators: (i) constitutional legitimacy, and (ii) institutional competence.

4.122 (i) *Constitutional legitimacy* This is the suggestion that, as a matter of constitutional law and constitutional principle, the courts are less democratically accountable, and therefore less legitimate, than the elected branches of government, in particular when dealing with issues of acute social sensitivity, such as terrorism.[226]

4.123 This approach was powerfully advanced by Lord Hoffmann in *R (Prolife Alliance) v BBC*.[227] He held that a social judgement as to the 'offensiveness' or otherwise of material contained in a proposed party election broadcast was one which Parliament had decided was apt to be reached by the broadcasters themselves, and that it would be contrary to the principle of the separation of powers for the courts to abrogate that role. Similarly, in *R (Nicklinson) v Ministry of Justice* the Supreme Court held that decisions about whether to decriminalize assisted suicide raised controversial questions of social policy that should be decided by Parliament.[228]

4.124 (ii) *Institutional competence* Another, more nuanced argument for a form of deference is based on 'institutional competence'—the idea that the courts and the legislature have differing expertise, and also differing access to the relevant information.

4.125 This approach has been proposed by, among others, Lord Steyn. He wrote an influential article in Public Law which was highly critical of Lord Hoffmann's approach in the *ProLife Alliance* case, instead commending the 'balanced approach' to deference based on institutional competence. 'At the risk of over-simplification', he said:

> The rule of law requires that courts do not surrender their responsibilities. So far as the courts desist from making decisions in a particular case it should not be on grounds of separation of powers, or other constitutional principle. Deference may lead the courts not to make their own decisions on an issue. The degree of deference which the courts should show will, of course, depend on and vary with the context. The true justification for a court exceptionally declining to decide an issue, which is within its jurisdiction, is the relative institutional competence or capacity of the branches of government.[229]

4.126 This approach to deference, based on relative institutional competence, has been applied in a number of cases, the courts indicating that there is an area of judgment within which the judiciary will defer, on democratic grounds, to the considered opinion of the legislature or the executive.[230] The Lord Chancellor summarized this approach in 2006:

---

[226] See eg *(RB) Algeria v Secretary of State for the Home Department* [2009] UKHL 10, [2009] 2 WLR 512.

[227] *R (Prolife Alliance) v BBC* [2003] UKHL 23, [2004] 1 AC 185.

[228] *R (Nicklinson) v Ministry of Justice* [2014] UKSC 38, [2015] AC 657.

[229] Lord Steyn, 'Deference: A Tangled Story' [2005] Public Law 346, 352.

[230] See eg *R (Lord Carlile) v Secretary of State for the Home Department* [2014] UKSC 60, [2015] AC 945, paras 22, 32; and, in respect of the executive, *R (MM (Lebanon)) v Secretary of State for the Home Department* [2017] UKSC 10, [2017] 1 WLR 771, para 75.

Whether and to what extent the courts will recognise a 'discretionary area of judgment' depends upon the subject matter of the decision being challenged, but policy decisions made by Parliament on matters of national security, criminal justice and economic policy are accorded particular respect.[231]

Indeed, in *Begum v Special Immigration Appeals Commission*,[232] the Supreme Court confirmed that significant deference must be shown to the Secretary of State's assessments in a national security context, 'for reasons both of institutional capacity (notwithstanding the experience of members of SIAC) and democratic accountability'.   4.127

J. ENFORCEMENT OF THE HUMAN RIGHTS ACT IN SUMMARY

Regardless of the rhetoric as to the constitutional significance of the Human Rights Act, its key purpose was to give citizens a practical right to use the Convention in our national courts—to 'bring rights home'. The Human Rights Act seeks to achieve this through the various mechanisms described in this chapter, bolstered by the Equality and Human Rights Commission's powers to bring cases in its own right and to inquire into human rights issues. Human rights arguments can be made and relied upon in any court or tribunal in the United Kingdom. There remain, however, a number of logistical and conceptual difficulties with the Human Rights Act which undermine its ability to ensure that rights are 'practical and effective' rather than 'theoretical and illusory'. In particular, the courts' restrictive approach to Human Rights Act remedies has been disappointing, especially given the broad statutory leeway in section 8; and the repeated and lengthy delays by government in responding to declarations of incompatibility from the courts frustrate the Act's central purpose.   4.128

Pre-emptive measures to protect and promote human rights are, of course, preferable to 'after-the-fact' remedies. Ideally, there should be less litigation under the Human Rights Act, not because of restrictions on access to justice, but because fewer statutes, rules, or practices that violate human rights remain in force. The importance of pre-emptive measures has long been recognized by many jurisdictions throughout Europe, which have processes of 'abstract review' whereby the judiciary is able to evaluate the general compliance of Bills or recently enacted statutes for their compatibility with Convention rights.[233] While no such process exists under the Human Rights Act (apart from the limited and exceptional approach adopted in *R (Rusbridger) v Attorney General*),[234] there are now a number of forms of pre-legislative scrutiny, including the Commission's power to advise government   4.129

---

[231] *Review of the Implementation of the Human Rights Act*, Executive Summary (25 July 2006).

[232] *Begum v Special Immigration Appeals Commission* [2021] UKSC 7, [2021] AC 765.

[233] See also the discussion of the Select Committee on the Constitution on 'advisory declarations' (in which the courts would be called upon to give guidance to the Government on Convention rights): Sixth Report (2006–2007), HL 151, para 11.

[234] *R (Rusbridger) v Attorney General* [2003] UKHL 38, [2004] 1 AC 357.

on the likely effect of a proposed change of law or existing enactment.[235] The Joint Committee on Human Rights also plays a crucial role, highlighting concerns at an early stage. Indeed, this is recognized by the Cabinet Office guidance to ministers, which reminds them that, in preparing a compatibility statement for a Bill pursuant to section 19 of the Human Rights Act, they should bear in mind that the Joint Committee 'will report on the ECHR issues raised by a Bill and is likely to examine closely the arguments put forward by the department justifying interference with a Convention right'.[236]

---

[235] Equality Act 2006, s 11(2).

[236] Cabinet Office, *Guide to Making Legislation: ECHR*, 15 August 2022 <https://www.gov.uk/governm ent/publications/guide-to-making-legislation> 23 December 2023.

5

THE CONVENTION RIGHTS: ABSOLUTE RIGHTS

A. INTRODUCTION

This chapter summarizes the content of Articles 1–4 of the European Convention 5.01
for the Protection of Human Rights and Fundamental Freedoms (Convention).
These rights are generally considered absolute, in the sense that no restriction may
be placed upon them and no derogation from them may be made under Article
15. Further discussion of the nature of absolute rights can be found in Chapter 2.[1]

For each article, an overview is given of the jurisprudence of the European Court 5.02
of Human Rights (ECtHR) and any remaining important cases from the European

---

[1] See Chapter 2, paras 2.25–2.27.

Blackstone's Guide to The Human Rights Act 1998. Eighth Edition. John Wadham, Helen Mountfield KC, Raj Desai, Sarah Hannett KC,
Jessica Jones, Eleanor Mitchell, and Aidan Wills, Oxford University Press. © John Wadham, Helen Mountfield KC, Raj Desai,
Sarah Hannett KC, Jessica Jones, Eleanor Mitchell, and Aidan Wills 2024. DOI: 10.1093/oso/9780192885050.003.0005

Commission on Human Rights (ECmHR). Where the domestic courts have considered an article in claims brought under the Human Rights Act, their approach is discussed alongside the European case law, and any divergences are noted.

5.03   When inviting a court to consider Convention jurisprudence under section 2 of the Human Rights Act it is important to be aware that the decisions are context-specific and often fact-sensitive. The Strasbourg organs confine themselves to an examination of the particular case before them. They are not required to review an entire system or practice, but only to determine whether the manner in which this system or practice was applied to, or affected, the individual applicants gave rise to any violations of the Convention. Nevertheless, the Court often sets out new principles in cases (more often in Grand Chamber cases), and those principles will then be regularly repeated in all subsequent judgments.

B. ARTICLE 1: JURISDICTION

5.04   Article 1 binds contracting parties to the Convention to secure the other Convention rights to everyone, regardless of their nationality, who is 'within their jurisdiction'. This effectively establishes a jurisdictional limitation on the application of the Convention. The primary basis on which jurisdiction arises is territorial. Contracting parties are responsible under the Convention for their actions within their own territory, even if the effects of their actions are felt abroad, as in cases of deportation to countries where there is a real risk of torture.[2]

5.05   A more complex question arises as to when 'jurisdiction' covers extra-territorial acts. The key ECtHR authority on extra-territorial jurisdiction is *Al-Skeini v UK*,[3] where the Grand Chamber held that claims under Article 2 resulting from the death of five Iraqi citizens who had been killed during the course of military operations conducted by British forces in Iraq fell within the jurisdiction of the Convention. Building on the approach the Court had taken in *Bankovic v Belgium and others*,[4] the Court found that, while jurisdiction under Article 1 is 'essentially territorial', extra-territorial jurisdiction under the Convention will arise in certain circumstances. The Court identified two bases of extra-territorial jurisdiction: where there is an 'exercise of physical power and control over the person' by agents of the state and where a contracting party 'through the consent, invitation or acquiescence of the government of [another] territory' 'exercises all or some of the public powers normally to be exercised by that government'. In *Georgia v Russia (II)*, the Court recognized that this includes the case where a contracting party, following lawful or unlawful military action, exercises effective control of a territory outside its national territory.[5] These have become known as the 'state agent authority and control' and 'public powers' or 'effective control of an area' bases of jurisdiction.

---

[2] See eg *Chahal v UK* (1997) 23 EHRR 413 [GC].
[3] *Al-Skeini v UK* (2011) 53 EHRR 18 [GC].
[4] *Bankovic v Belgium and others* (2001) 11 BHRC 435 [GC].
[5] *Georgia v Russia (II)* (2021) 73 EHRR 6 [GC].

In *R (Al Saadoon) v Secretary of State for Defence*,[6] a series of claims brought   5.06
in respect of the actions of British forces in Iraq (and decided after the Grand
Chamber judgment in *Al-Skeini*), the Court of Appeal examined the 'power and
control' basis for extra-territorial jurisdiction and held that a person is within the
jurisdiction of the United Kingdom (UK) for the purposes of Article 1 where there
is 'an element of control prior to the use of lethal force'. On the 'public powers'
basis for extra-territorial jurisdiction, the Court of Appeal also found that Article
1 jurisdiction arose in occupied Iraq, as British armed forces 'remained in Iraq at
the request of the Iraqi government in order to perform security functions. They
were, "through the consent, invitation or acquiescence" of the government of Iraq
exercising some of the public powers normally to be exercised by that government.'

In *HF v France*,[7] the Grand Chamber considered a claim for breach of Article 3   5.07
of the Convention arising from France's refusal to repatriate French women who
had left France to join Daesh in Syria, and who were then detained by Kurdish
authorities in terrible conditions in north-east Syria. The Grand Chamber (finding that France did not have authority and control such as to ground jurisdiction)
confirmed that the exercise of authority and control over an individual gives rise
to 'an obligation under Article 1 to secure to that individual the rights and freedoms under Section 1 of the Convention that are relevant to his or her situation.
In this sense, therefore, the Convention rights can be "divided and tailored"'—
meaning that jurisdiction may arise in respect of some substantive rights and not
others, depending on the nature of the authority and control which is exercised, or
any other jurisdictional link which the circumstances create. The Supreme Court
reached a similar conclusion in *R (Smith) v Ministry of Defence*,[8] where the issue was
whether the UK had jurisdiction for the purposes of Article 2 of the Convention in
respect of its soldiers deployed abroad. The Supreme Court found, on an application of *Al Skeini*, that the UK did have jurisdiction, and that the package of rights
in the Convention could be divided and tailored to the particular circumstances of
the extra-territorial act in question.

Article 1 jurisdiction was an issue in the interstate case of *Georgia v Russia*, aris-   5.08
ing from Russia's invasion of Abkhazia and South Ossetia in 2008. In *Georgia v
Russia (II)*,[9] the Grand Chamber found that Russia had jurisdiction for the purposes of Article 1 (applying the control over territory basis for jurisdiction) once
it was in occupation of those states,[10] but not during active hostilities. In what
some commentators have considered to be a retrograde step for the jurisprudence of
Article 1,[11] the Grand Chamber considered that Russia did not have jurisdiction in

---

[6] *R (Al Saadoon) v Secretary of State for Defence* [2016] EWCA Civ 811, [2017] QB 1015.

[7] *HF v France* (2022) 75 EHRR 31 [GC].

[8] *R (Smith) v Ministry of Defence* [2013] UKSC 41, [2014] 1 AC 52.

[9] *Georgia v Russia (II)* (2021) 73 EHRR 6 [GC].

[10] A similar decision was reached on admissibility in *Ukraine v Russia*, arising from Russia's invasion of
Crimea: *Ukraine v Russia* App Nos 20958/14 & another, 16 December 2020 [GC].

[11] Marko Milanovic, 'Georgia v. Russia No. 2: The European Court's Resurrection of Bankovic in the
Contexts of Chaos' (EJIL: Talk!, 25 January 2021) <https://www.ejiltalk.org/georgia-v-russia-no-2-the-
european-courts-resurrection-of-bankovic-in-the-contexts-of-chaos/> accessed 10 January 2024.

relation to the allegations of substantive breach of Article 2 during active hostilities but, in a further example of jurisdiction being 'divided and tailored' for different rights, that did not prevent a finding that Russia did have jurisdiction in respect of allegations arising from the detention of individuals during that same period.[12]

5.09   A further basis for extra-territorial jurisdiction has been recognized by the ECtHR in respect of the Article 2 investigative duty, in *Güzelyurtlu v Cyprus & Turkey*,[13] *Hanan v Germany*,[14] and *Georgia v Russia (II)*. In *Güzelyurtlu*, the suspects of a murder committed in Cyprus had fled to Turkish-occupied northern Cyprus. Turkish authorities had commenced an investigation (as had the Cypriot authorities). The Grand Chamber held that if the investigative or judicial authorities of a contracting state institute their own criminal investigation or proceedings concerning a death outside the jurisdiction of the state, the institution of those proceedings is sufficient to provide a jurisdictional link for the purposes of Article 1, and therefore require the investigation to comply with the procedural limb of Article 2. Further, where a contracting state has not initiated an investigation, there may nevertheless be 'special features' which cause the Court to consider that jurisdiction under Article 1 arises. In that case, relevant 'special features' included Turkey's occupation of northern Cyprus (a territory over which Turkey has effective control), and the fact that the suspects' flight to occupied northern Cyprus prevented the Cypriot authorities from conducting an Article 2-compliant investigation.

5.10   In *Hanan v Germany*, the Grand Chamber reached the same conclusion as in *Güzelyurtlu* on very different facts. *Hanan* was a case about Germany's liability under the procedural limb of Article 2 in respect of deaths arising from an airstrike in Afghanistan. Germany had initiated a criminal investigation into the deaths of civilians during the airstrike but the Court found that (unlike in *Güzelyurtlu*) that was not enough to ground Article 1 jurisdiction. One concern contributing to the slight departure from *Güzelyurtlu* was the Grand Chamber's desire not to dissuade states from commencing investigations for fear that to do so would engage Article 1 and therefore impose requirements for Convention compliance.[15] There were, however, other special features in *Hanan* giving rise to jurisdiction—including the duty on Germany under customary international humanitarian law to investigate the airstrike, the obligation under German domestic law that an investigation be commenced, and the exclusive right of Germany under the relevant agreements with Afghanistan to bring criminal proceedings against German troops for acts committed in Afghanistan, meaning that Afghan authorities were prevented from investigating.

---

[12] The basis on which the Grand Chamber makes this finding is not clear. While it would make sense as an application of 'state agent authority and control' over the individual, the Grand Chamber does not specify that as the reason it finds jurisdiction in respect of the detention complaints and instead seems to suggest it is because most of the detentions occurred after active hostilities ceased: see *Georgia v Russia (II)*, paras 239 and 269.

[13] *Güzelyurtlu v Cyprus & Turkey* (2019) 69 EHRR 12 [GC].

[14] *Hanan v Germany* (2021) 73 EHRR 24 [GC].

[15] ibid para 135.

While extra-territorial jurisdiction on the basis of the existence of 'special features' 5.11
has predominantly arisen in the context of the Article 2 investigative obligation, the
Grand Chamber in *HF v France* found that there was 'special features' jurisdiction
in respect of Article 3(2) of Protocol 4 ('no-one shall be deprived of the right to enter
the territory of the State of which he is national'—a provision not ratified by the
UK), but not in respect of the Article 3 claims which the applicants also brought.

C. ARTICLE 2: RIGHT TO LIFE

Article 2 has, not surprisingly, been described by the ECtHR as 'one of the most 5.12
fundamental provisions in the Convention'.[16] With very limited exceptions, it cannot be subject to derogation under Article 15, and those exceptions are now irrelevant given the ratification and incorporation by the UK of Protocol 13. Article 2
is comprehensive, imposing a substantive obligation to protect the right to life, a
substantive prohibition on the taking of life, and a graduated procedural obligation
to investigate and to call state authorities to account for potential breaches of the
substantive Article 2 obligations. The ECtHR and the domestic courts must, when
called upon to make their assessment in an Article 2 case, apply 'most anxious' or
'particularly thorough' scrutiny.[17]

Although Article 2 does not explicitly prohibit the use of a death penalty that has 5.13
been properly authorized, this sentence is now 'redundant' in light of Protocols 6
(which abolishes the death penalty in peacetime) and 13 (which extends the abolition to wartime).[18] Further, the ECtHR confirmed in *Al-Saadoon and Mufdhi v UK*
that the scope of Article 2 of the Convention has evolved as a result of state practice
so as to prohibit the death penalty in all circumstances and that its use will also
violate Article 3.[19]

1. 'Everyone'

The precise starting point of the right to life under Article 2 is controversial. Early 5.14
case law suggested it applied post-natally only.[20] However, more recent ECtHR
cases have indicated that this is not a hard-and-fast line. In *Boso v Italy*, the ECtHR
accepted, without deciding the issue, that a foetus could potentially be a 'victim'
under Article 34.[21] In *Vo v France* the Grand Chamber specifically noted that:

---

[16] *McCann v UK* (1996) 21 EHRR 97, para 197.

[17] *Sergey Shevchenko v Ukraine* App No 32478/02, 4 April 2006, para 42; *Aktaş v Turkey* App No
24351/94, 23 October 2003, para 271; *McCann v UK* (1996) 21 EHRR 97, para 150.

[18] Per Hammarberg, Commissioner for Human Rights, *Viewpoint* (Strasbourg: Office of the
Commissioner for Human Rights, 21 August 2006). At the time of writing, all 46 members of the Council
of Europe have signed and ratified Protocol 6. Forty-five members have signed Protocol 13, of which only
Armenia has not ratified it. Azerbaijan has not signed Protocol 13.

[19] *Al-Saadoon and Mufdhi v UK* App No 61498/08, 2 March 2010.

[20] *Paton v UK* (1980) 19 DR 244.

[21] *Boso v Italy* App No 50490/99, 5 September 2002. The case was held inadmissible on other grounds.

The Court has yet to determine the issue of the 'beginning' of 'everyone's right to life' within the meaning of this provision and whether the unborn child has such a right.[22]

5.15   In *Evans v UK* the Grand Chamber of the ECtHR stated that in the absence of any European consensus on the scientific and legal definition of the beginning of life, 'the issue of when the right to life begins comes within the margin of appreciation which the Court generally considers that States should enjoy in this sphere'.[23]

5.16   In *Vo v France* the Grand Chamber sidestepped the issue of whether Article 2 applies to the foetus, taking a 'decision not to decide', which has been criticized.[24] The applicant suffered a miscarriage after she was mistakenly given a procedure for removal of a coil while five months' pregnant, and brought a criminal complaint of unintentional homicide against the doctor. The French courts held that the foetus was not a human person for the purposes of the French Criminal Code.[25]

5.17   The Grand Chamber did not decide whether Article 2 applied to the foetus, instead holding that, even if it did apply, France had not violated its provisions because its administrative remedies were sufficient. The majority considered it 'neither desirable, nor even possible ... to answer in the abstract' the question of whether a foetus is a person.[26]

5.18   However, a minority of three judges did examine the word 'everyone' and considered that Article 2 was applicable in light of scientific advances that enable a foetus to reach viability earlier.[27] In their view, this would not necessarily render abortion illegal under the Convention; a non-absolute right to life for the foetus could be recognized, thus balancing the interests of the foetus and the mother.[28]

5.19   In *Tysiac v Poland* the ECtHR did not engage directly with the question of foetal rights under Article 2 in the case of a woman denied a therapeutic abortion despite significant risks to her eyesight as a consequence of her pregnancy.[29] Determining the case under Article 8, the ECtHR held that the failure of the Polish authorities to provide effective mechanisms for determining whether she met the conditions for obtaining a lawful abortion violated her right to a private life. In an emotive dissent, Judge Borrego Borrego held that the majority favoured 'abortion on demand' and their reasoning implied that the child's 'right to be born' contradicted the Convention.[30]

5.20   In *A, B and C v Ireland* the Court again declined to determine whether the foetus had a right to life under Article 2, reiterating that the question of when the right to life begins falls within the state's margin of appreciation.[31] And in *Senturk v Turkey*,

---

[22] *Vo v France* [2004] 2 FCR 577, para 82.
[23] *Evans v UK* [2007] 1 FLR 1990, para 46.
[24] See also Goldberg, 'Vo v France and Fetal Rights: The Decision Not to Decide' [2005] 18 Harvard Human Rights Journal.
[25] *Vo v France* [2004] 2 FCR 577, para 19.
[26] ibid para 85.
[27] ibid, concurring opinion of Judge Costa; see also the dissenting opinion of Judges Rees and Mularoni.
[28] ibid, annex (b), para 12.
[29] *Tysiac v Poland* (2007) 45 EHRR 42.
[30] ibid paras 13–15, dissenting judgment of Judge Borrego Borrego.
[31] *A, B and C v Ireland* App No 25579/05, 4 December 2014, para 237.

the ECtHR considered a complaint of breach of Article 2 arising out of the death of a mother and her unborn child following grossly negligent medical treatment. The Court found that the life of the foetus was intimately connected with that of the mother such that the Article 2 complaint in respect of the foetus did not require separate examination. In these circumstances, it found no reason to depart from the approach in *Vo* and *A, B and C.*[32] The Court's reluctance to determine this issue is understandable in light of the divergence of European opinion on abortion, but it is legally unsatisfactory. To apply a margin of appreciation to the scope of a concept, rather than the extent of obligation to protect a particular right, sits oddly with the 'autonomous concepts' doctrine used elsewhere in the Convention.

The position as it stands for the purposes of the domestic law of the UK, absent   5.21
any further development in the Strasbourg case law, is that the unborn do not have Convention rights.[33]

2. Obligation to protect the right to life

The first sentence of Article 2 imposes a positive obligation on states to protect the   5.22
right to life. This obliges states to 'take appropriate steps to safeguard the lives of those within [their] jurisdiction'.[34] The principal specific duty arising from this positive obligation is to provide effective criminal legislation supported by law enforcement machinery.[35]

However, this also imposes on the state a general 'systems duty' to have in place   5.23
a legislative and administrative framework to effectively deter threats to life and safeguard life more broadly.[36] For example, in the healthcare context, this entails having effective administrative and regulatory systems in place designed to protect patients from professional incompetence resulting in death.[37] A similar duty also arises where a public body is responsible for the welfare of individuals within its care and under its exclusive control, particularly young children who are especially vulnerable.[38] And, in the context of dangerous activities, it may require state regulation to ensure the effective protection of citizens whose lives might be endangered by the inherent risks of the activities in question.[39]

---

[32] *Senturk v Turkey* (2015) 60 EHRR 4, paras 107–09.

[33] *Evans v Amicus Healthcare Ltd* [2004] EWCA Civ 727, [2005] Fam 1; *Re Northern Ireland Human Rights Commission's Application for Judicial Review* [2018] UKSC 27, [2019] 1 All ER 173, para 21; *R (Crowter and another) v the Secretary of State for Health and Social Care* [2022] EWCA Civ 1559, [2023] 1 WLR 989, para 41.

[34] *Osman v UK* (2000) 29 EHRR 245, para 115.

[35] *Keenan v UK* (2001) 3 EHRR 38, para 88.

[36] *Öneryildiz v Turkey* (2005) 41 EHRR 20; *R(Maguire) v HM Senior Coroner for Blackpool and Fylde* [2023] UKSC 20, [2023] 3 WLR 103, para 10.

[37] *Powell v UK* (2000) 30 EHRR CD362; *Rabone v Pennine Care NHS Trust* [2012] UKSC 2, [2012] 2 AC 72, paras 19 and 93.

[38] *Kemaloğlu v Turkey* (2015) 61 EHRR 36, para 35.

[39] *Öneryildiz v Turkey* (2005) 41 EHRR 20, para 90. For a recent summary of the various contexts in which administrative measures have been required by the framework duty see: *R (MG) v Secretary of State for the Home Department* [2022] EWHC 1849 Admin, [2023] 1 WLR 284, para 6(6)–(7).

5.24   In addition to the general positive duty, the ECtHR has affirmed that, in certain circumstances, the state is subject to an 'operational duty' 'to take reasonable preventive operational measures to protect a specific person or persons whose life is at risk from a real and immediate risk to life actually or constructively known to the State,[40] such as from the criminal acts of another individual'[41] or from suicide.[42]

5.25   As the Supreme Court explained in *Rabone v Pennine Care NHS Trust*, the ECtHR has proceeded on a case-by-case basis in identifying the situations in which an operational duty to take protective steps will arise in response to a real and immediate risk to life. Relevant factors include whether there is an assumption of responsibility by the state for the individual's welfare and safety (including by exercise of control over them), with the paradigm example being situations where the state detains an individual in prison, in a psychiatric hospital, in immigration detention, or otherwise. The ECtHR has also emphasized the vulnerability of the victim as a relevant consideration and has been prepared to find a duty to arise even in the absence of an assumption of responsibility where there is sufficient vulnerability. Finally, the nature of the risk is relevant with a general distinction drawn between ordinary risks which individuals in the relevant category can be expected to take and exceptional risks or dangerous situations posed by violent, unlawful acts of others or man-made or natural hazards.[43]

5.26   One paradigm situation in which the operational duty arises concerns the duty of the police to protect members of the public from the risk of violent criminal acts. In the famous case of *Osman v UK*, the applicant argued that the police had violated Article 2 by failing to protect him and his father from a schoolteacher known to have been obsessed with the applicant. The teacher shot and wounded the applicant and killed his father. The ECtHR held that in order for the positive obligation to be engaged, the state authorities must have known or ought to have known that there was a real and immediate risk to life yet failed to take measures within the scope of their power which, judged reasonably, might have been expected to avoid that risk.[44] However, on the facts of the case, the ECtHR found that the applicant was unable to point to any decisive stage in the sequence of events leading to the tragic shooting when it could be said that the police knew or ought to have known that the lives of the Osman family were at real and immediate risk, such that there was no violation of Article 2.[45] Subsequent cases have confirmed that the real and immediate risk to life need not be to an identified or identifiable person or persons for an operational duty to arise.[46]

5.27   The broad scope of the Article 2 positive obligation is demonstrated by the case of *Öneryildiz v Turkey*.[47] The Grand Chamber unanimously held that the state

---

[40] *R (Maguire) v HM Senior Coroner for Blackpool and Fylde* [2023] UKSC 20, [2023] 3 WLR 103, paras 10–11 and 240–41.
[41] *Osman v UK* (2000) 29 EHRR 245.
[42] *Keenan v UK* (2001) 3 EHRR 38.
[43] *Rabone v Pennine Care NHS Trust* [2012] UKSC 2, [2012] 2 AC 72, paras 22–25.
[44] *Osman v UK* (2000) 29 EHRR 245, para 116.
[45] *Re Officer L* [2007] UKHL 36, [2007] 1 WLR 2135, paras 22 et seq.
[46] *Sarjantson and another v Chief Constable of Humberside Police* [2014] QB 411.
[47] *Öneryildiz v Turkey* (2005) 41 EHRR 20.

had violated Article 2 by failing to take appropriate steps to prevent the accidental death of the applicant's relatives, who were slum dwellers living at a rubbish tip, in response to a real and immediate threat to their lives known (or which ought to have been known) to the Turkish authorities. The reasonable steps included either implementing appropriate measures for waste storage or providing information to people living on slum land regarding the dangers they faced.

The ECtHR has also applied the operational obligation to situations of failure 5.28 by the state to take action to prevent domestic violence. In *Opuz v Turkey* the state failed to prosecute a husband who had repeatedly attacked his wife and daughter, eventually killing his wife.[48] The ECtHR held that prosecutions and other appropriate preventative measures should have been pursued despite the withdrawal of the victim's complaints. Subsequent case law has further highlighted the requirement to assess the existence of a real and immediate risk to life taking due account of the particular context of domestic violence and the requirement for an immediate response, proper risk assessment by properly trained officers, and special diligence in dealing with any such risk.[49]

Although Article 2 has the potential to touch a broad range of state activities, 5.29 the requirement of a 'real and immediate' risk to life has been said to set a high threshold for engagement of the operational duty.[50] In *Van Colle v Chief Constable of Hertfordshire Police*, a man intending to give evidence in a Crown Court trial for theft was murdered by the defendant.[51] The House of Lords held that the high threshold for state liability imposed by the *Osman* test had not been met on the facts. The fact that the victim had been an intended witness for the prosecution (the state) did not increase the nature of the duty on the police. The ECtHR unanimously reached the same conclusion holding that, while the relevant officer ought to have been aware of an escalating situation of intimidation of a number of prosecution witnesses (including Mr Van Colle), there was no decisive stage when the officer knew or ought to have known of a real and immediate risk to the life of Mr Van Colle.[52] Two judges appended concurring opinions expressing concern at the restrictive nature of the *Osman* test.[53]

Similarly, in *Mitchell v Glasgow City Council* the defendant did not violate Article 5.30 2 by its failure to protect a council tenant from a neighbour the defendant knew to have been abusive. No sufficient basis had been identified as to why it could be said that the defendant housing authority knew or ought to have known of a real and immediate risk of a violent attack. Additionally, preventing criminal violence was the responsibility of the police not the local housing authority.[54]

---

[48] *Opuz v Turkey* (2010) 50 EHRR 28.
[49] *Kurt v Austria* (2022) 74 EHRR 6; *Tkhelidze v Georgia* App No 33056/17, 8 July 2021; *A and B v Georgia* App No 73975/16, 10 February 2022.
[50] See eg *Younger v UK* (2003) 33 EHRR CD252; *Mastromatteo v Italy* App No 37703/97, 24 October 2002.
[51] *Van Colle v Chief Constable of Hertfordshire Police* [2008] UKHL 50, [2009] 1 AC 225.
[52] *Van Colle v UK* App No 7678/09, 13 November 2012.
[53] Judges Garlicki and Vucinic.
[54] *Mitchell v Glasgow City Council* [2009] UKHL 11, [2009] AC 874.

5.31   The positive protective obligations also mean that states must provide appropriate medical treatment to those detained.[55] However, it does not extend to cases of mere medical negligence in public hospitals outside the context of detention by the state.[56] In such settings, the state generally has only regulatory obligations pursuant to a general duty, and only in 'very exceptional circumstances' will its obligations extend beyond this. These very exceptional circumstances are two-fold. First, where an individual patient's life is knowingly put in danger by denial of access to life-saving emergency treatment, as opposed to merely receiving deficient, incorrect, or delayed treatment. And, secondly, where a systemic or structural dysfunction in hospital services results in a patient being deprived of access to life-saving emergency treatment and the authorities knew about or ought to have known about the risk caused by the systemic dysfunction and failed to undertake the necessary measures to prevent that risk from materializing, thus putting the patients' lives, including the life of the particular patient concerned, in danger.[57]

5.32   In *Savage v South Essex Partnership NHS Foundation Trust*, the House of Lords considered the case of a psychiatric patient who escaped from detention in a hospital and committed suicide.[58] Their Lordships held that Article 2 would be engaged in such circumstances where members of staff knew or ought to have known that the detained patient presented a real and immediate risk of suicide and would require the hospital authorities to do all that they could reasonably be expected to do to prevent the patient committing suicide.

5.33   In *Rabone v Penine Care NHS Trust*,[59] the Supreme Court considered the case of a seriously mentally unwell young woman admitted to hospital as an informal (non-detained) patient after a serious suicide attempt; she subsequently committed suicide after being released by the hospital on home leave. It held that an operational duty to take reasonable steps to prevent the suicide could arise because the hospital had assumed responsibility for the patient's safety, she was under the hospital's control, and the hospital had the statutory means to prevent her leaving. The duty was breached because, at the time that she went on home leave, there was a real and immediate risk of suicide and no reasonable psychiatrist would have allowed her to leave.

5.34   In *R (Maguire) v HM Senior Coroner for Blackpool and Fylde*,[60] the Supreme Court considered whether alleged individual failings in securing healthcare for a person in a care home, who lacked capacity so as to be subject to a deprivation of liberty for the purposes of Article 5 ECHR, could breach the Article 2 operational duty. A core question (relevant both to alleged breaches of the systems and

---

[55] *Tarariyeva v Russia* App No 4353/03, 13 December 2006; *Renolde v France* App No 5608/05, 16 October 2008.

[56] *Powell v UK* (2000) 30 EHRR CD362; *Dodov v Bulgaria* App No 59548/00, 17 January 2008; *Savage v South Essex Partnership NHS Foundation Trust* [2008] UKHL 74, [2009] 1 AC 681; *R (Humberstone) v Legal Services Commission* [2010] EWCA 1479, [2011] 1 WLR 1460.

[57] *Lopes de Sousa Fernandes v Portugal* (2018) 66 EHRR 28 [GC].

[58] *Savage v South Essex Partnership NHS Foundation Trust* [2008] UKHL 74, [2009] 2 WLR 115.

[59] *Rabone v Penine Care NHS Trust* [2012] UKSC 2, [2012] 2 AC 72.

[60] *R (Maguire) v HM Senior Coroner for Blackpool and Fylde* [2023] UKSC 20, [2023] 3 WLR 103.

operational duties) was whether care settings could be distinguished from hospital and other healthcare settings where - as considered above - the state's duties are not engaged by individual instances of negligent treatment. The Supreme Court essentially held that care settings could not be distinguished. Moreover, for the purposes of the operational duty, placement in a care home did not entail an assumption of responsibility for every aspect of physical needs. Staff in care homes were not medically trained and their responsibility was to look after the person on behalf of the state in substitution for their family, which entailed no more than a duty to enable them to have access to the healthcare available to the population generally in the same way that a family could secure such access for a vulnerable member. On the facts of the case, there was no arguable case that the care staff had failed to do so.[61]

Assisted suicide was considered by the House of Lords in *R (Pretty) v Director of Public Prosecutions*[62] and the ECtHR in *Pretty v UK*.[63] It was argued that Article 2 extends beyond the right to life and protects the more comprehensive right to self-determination in relation to issues of life and death. However, both the House of Lords and the ECtHR rejected this, holding that Article 2 does not confer a right to die.[64]   5.35

Despite this approach to assisted suicide, Article 2 does not impose a continuing obligation to provide treatment to patients in a permanent vegetative state.[65] In *Lambert v France*,[66] concerning a decision to discontinue nutrition and hydration which was keeping a patient alive artificially, the Court noted the margin of appreciation accorded to states on issues of complex scientific, legal, and ethical issues such as whether to permit withdrawal of life support and the detailed arrangements governing such arrangements to balance protection of a patients' right to life and the protection of their right to respect for their private life and personal autonomy. The Court underlined, however, that this margin of appreciation is not unlimited and that it reserves the power to review whether or not the state has complied with its obligations under Article 2.   5.36

In the context of armed conflict, the House of Lords held in *R (Gentle) v Prime Minister* that Article 2 does not apply to the process of deciding on the legality of sending British troops into combat overseas.[67] In that case, the mothers of two British soldiers who died in the Iraq conflict argued that the failure to take proper steps to ascertain whether the participation in the invasion of Iraq would comply with international law violated Article 2. The Lords held unanimously that it was   5.37

---

[61] ibid paras 147–57 and 185–204.

[62] *R (Pretty) v Director of Public Prosecutions* [2001] UKHL 61, [2002] 1 AC 800. See also *R (Purdy) v Director of Public Prosecutions* [2009] UKHL 45, [2010] 1 AC 345.

[63] *Pretty v UK* (2002) 35 EHRR 1.

[64] cf *Savage v South Essex Partnership NHS Foundation Trust* [2008] UKHL 74, [2009] 1 AC 681, para 11 per Lord Scott.

[65] *NHS Trust v M* [2001] Fam 348. cf *R (Burke) v General Medical Council* [2005] EWCA Civ 1003, [2006] QB 273.

[66] *Lambert v France* (2016) 62 EHRR 2, paras 144–48 and 181–82.

[67] *R (Gentle) v Prime Minister* [2008] UKHL 20, [2008] 1 AC 1356.

impossible to infer a duty to comply with international law from the government's positive obligation to protect life within its jurisdiction. In *R (Smith) v Secretary of State for Defence* it was accepted by the government that the failure to protect a soldier from heatstroke could violate Article 2 where the soldier died within the UK's extra-territorial jurisdiction, as understood under the Convention.[68]

5.38   The Supreme Court returned to the question of the applicability of Article 2 in combat situations in *R (Smith) and another v Ministry of Defence*,[69] concerning Article 2 claims brought by widows of British soldiers killed in Iraq on the basis of alleged shortcomings in the provision of vehicles and equipment. The Court was again divided on the correct approach. The majority held that decisions were likely to fall beyond the reach of Article 2 where they concerned either, on the one hand, (a) training, procurement, or the conduct of operations taken at a high level of command and closely linked to the exercise of political judgment or policy, or, on the other, (b) decisions closely linked to avoiding death or injury of persons actively engaged in direct contact with the enemy. But it was not prepared to exclude the possibility of a breach of Article 2 in respect of decisions falling in between and declined to strike out the claims on the facts as they stood.[70] The minority considered this approach to be unclear and unprincipled and would have held that Article 2 had no application to this type of decision at all.[71]

5.39   In *Hassan v United Kingdom*,[72] the Grand Chamber confirmed its previous case law that, even in situations of international armed conflict, the requirements of Article 2 apply, but that these requirements are to be interpreted against the background of international humanitarian law. In *Georgia v Russia No 2*,[73] the Grand Chamber held that during the active phase of the hostilities in Georgia, Russia lacked jurisdiction for the purposes of Article 2, such that the requirements of Article 2 did not apply; however, that during the phase of Russian occupation Article 2 did apply.[74]

5.40   The ECtHR has held that the positive Article 2 duties apply to environmental disasters. For example, in *Budayeva and others v Russia* the ECtHR ruled that the Russian authorities had not taken all possible steps to mitigate the impact of mudslides on the applicants' lives.[75] A number of cases are currently before the Grand Chamber of the ECtHR regarding the novel and important issue of the nature and extent of states' obligations (including under the art 2 protective duties) in respect of the climate emergency.[76]

---

[68] *R (Smith) v Secretary of State for Defence* [2010] UKSC 29, [2011] AC 1.

[69] *R (Smith) and another v Ministry of Defence* [2013] UKSC 41, [2014] AC 52.

[70] ibid para 76 per Lord Hope

[71] ibid paras 148–51 per Lord Mance.

[72] *Hassan v United Kingdom* App No 29750/09, 16 September 2014 [GC].

[73] *Georgia v Russia No 2* (2021) 73 EHRR 6.

[74] ibid paras 144 and 175.

[75] *Budayeva and others v Russia* App Nos 15339/02 & others, 20 March 2008.

[76] *Verein Klimaseniorinnen Schweiz and others v Switzerland* App No 53600/20, 17 March 2021; *Carême v France* App No 7189/21, 7 June 2022; and *Duarte Agostinho and others v Portugal and 32 others* App No 39371/20, 13 November 2020.

3. Prohibition on taking life

In addition to the protective obligation, Article 2 expressly prohibits the state from intentionally taking life. Unintentional taking of life is implicitly prohibited in a situation where the use of force is permitted under Article 2(2), but the force used is more than absolutely necessary and results in death.[77] **5.41**

It has been held by the domestic courts that an operation to separate conjoined twins, which would inevitably result in the death of one of them, would not violate the prohibition on intentional killing since the intention of the doctors performing the operation was to save the life of one twin rather than take the life of the other.[78] **5.42**

Killing arising through state negligence may amount to a violation of Article 2, for example if a warning shot kills someone.[79] Additionally, failures in the planning of an operation in which fatal force is used may violate Article 2.[80] In exceptional circumstances, and depending on a number of factors, Article 2 may apply to force used by the state even in the absence of death. However, usually such situations will be considered under Article 3.[81] **5.43**

Intentional and unintentional killing through the use of force which exceeds the Article 2(2) exceptions must be subject to criminal sanctions.[82] In *Da Silva v United Kingdom*, the Grand Chamber found the English domestic criminal law test of self-defence to be compatible with the requirements of Article 2.[83] **5.44**

The negative duty under Article 2 extends to a prohibition on deportation or removal of a person to another jurisdiction in circumstances where there are substantial grounds for believing that that person will face a real risk of being subjected to treatment contrary to Article 2 in the receiving state (such as the death penalty).[84] However, the Supreme Court has held that—as yet—Article 2 does not establish a principle prohibiting the sharing of information relevant to a criminal prosecution in a foreign country merely because it carries a risk of leading to the death penalty.[85] **5.45**

4. Procedural obligation

Article 2 imposes a positive procedural obligation relating to the investigation of and the opportunity to call state authorities to account for potential breaches of the substantive Article 2 obligations discussed above. As the Supreme Court has explained, 'the precise content of the procedural obligation ... varies according to the context in which an issue regarding the application of Article 2 arises. There **5.46**

---

[77] *McShane v UK* (2002) 35 EHRR 23, para 93.

[78] *Re A (children) (conjoined twins: surgical separation)* [2001] Fam 147, [2001] 2 WLR 480.

[79] *Ogur v Turkey* (2001) 31 EHRR 40, para 83. See also *McShane v UK* (2002) 35 EHRR 23, para 102.

[80] *McCann v UK* (1996) 21 EHRR 97.

[81] *Makaratzis v Greece* (2005) 41 EHRR 49 [GC], para 51.

[82] *Osman v UK* (2000) 29 EHRR 245 (intentional killing); *McShane v UK* (2002) 35 EHRR 23, para 93 (unintentional killing resulting from the use of force).

[83] *Da Silva v UK* (2016) 63 EHRR 12, paras 249–56.

[84] *Soering v UK* (1989) 11 EHRR 439; *Al-Saadoon and Mufdhi v UK* App No 61498/08, 2 March 2010.

[85] *R (Elgizouli) v Secretary of State for the Home Department* [2020] UKSC, [2021] AC 937 (Lord Kerr dissenting). But it was a breach of the Data Protection Act 2018 at least on the facts of the case.

is no simple monolithic form of procedural obligation which applies in every such case. Rather, the procedural obligation applies in a graduated way depending on the circumstances of the case and the way in which in a particular context the state may be called upon to provide due accountability in relation to the steps taken to protect the right to life under Article 2.'[86]

5.47 Three levels of the graduated procedural obligation have been identified by the Supreme Court from the ECtHR and domestic case law.[87] First, there is a 'basic procedural obligation' applicable in the case of all deaths to ascertain whether there might be any question of a potential breach of a person's right to life under Article 2 which, for example, requires steps to establish whether the cause of death is from natural causes rather than criminal violence or other foul play. Secondly, an 'enhanced procedural obligation' will arise in particular contexts, requiring the state on its own initiative to take further steps to investigate possible breaches of the Article 2 substantive obligations with a view to ensuring appropriate accountability and redress and, as appropriate, with a view to punishing persons responsible for the death. This enhanced procedural is considered further below (para 5.48+). This duty will be triggered automatically in certain cases because of the importance attached to the need to provide full accountability in relation to the death, such as in the case of a suspicious death in custody. Finally, there is a more limited 'redress procedural obligation' to provide means by which a person complaining of possible breaches may ventilate that complaint, have it investigated and obtain redress. For example, in the context of provision of medical services, where it is alleged that there has been negligence by medical practitioners, the ECtHR has consistently held that a civil or disciplinary remedy may suffice to discharge the state's procedural duties and that the enhanced procedural duty does not apply.

5.48 The ECtHR and domestic case law has long made clear that protection of the substantive rights under Article 2 requires that there should be an effective official investigation into deaths wherever there is an arguable breach of the state's Article 2 substantive duties (whether a negative duty or positive duty).[88] This investigative obligation has in the past been described as the 'procedural aspect' of Article 2, but following the Supreme Court decision in *Maguire*, discussed above, it is helpful to distinguish the 'enhanced procedural obligation' from other aspects of the procedural duty arising under Article 2. The case law on the enhanced procedural obligation under Article 2 is equally applicable to this aspect of the procedural obligation arising under Article 3.[89]

5.49 As the ECtHR has held, the rationale for inferring an obligation to investigate is based on the positive obligation to protect life: the state is required to maintain a

---

[86] *R (Maguire) v HM Senior Coroner for Blackpool and Fylde* [2023] UKSC 20, [2023] 3 WLR 1, para 12.

[87] ibid paras 14–21.

[88] *R v Coroner for Western District of Somerset, ex p Middleton* [2004] UKHL 10, [2004] 2 AC 182; *Tanase v Romania* App No 41720/13, 25 June 2019 [GC], para 161.

[89] See eg *Opuz v Turkey* (2010) 50 EHRR 28, para 168 and para 5.114+.

system of law that values and protects life.[90] The obligation is engaged both where death has resulted from state use of force, and where death has resulted from a state's failure to protect the right to life.[91] It is not necessary that a state agent is directly involved in the death.[92] In *Opuz v Turkey* the ECtHR considered that a case of prolonged domestic abuse of a mother and daughter, which had led to the mother's death, engaged the procedural obligation under Article 2.[93]

The essential purpose of the investigation has been described by the Grand Chamber of the ECtHR, as follows: 5.50

> to secure the effective implementation of the domestic laws safeguarding the right to life and, in those cases involving state agents or bodies, to ensure their accountability for deaths occurring under their responsibility ... However, the investigation should also be broad enough to permit the investigating authorities to take into consideration not only the actions of the state agents who directly used lethal force but also all the surrounding circumstances, including such matters as the planning and control of the operations in question, where this is necessary in order to determine whether the state complied with its obligation under art 2 to protect life.[94]

The procedural obligation is 'separate and autonomous'. As such, it has been held that it can arise in respect of deaths which have occurred prior to the date of the state's ratification of the Convention (meaning that no breach of the state's substantive obligations could arise) where steps in the investigation have occurred, or should have occurred, post-ratification. In *Silih v Solvenia* the majority of the Grand Chamber stated: 5.51

> The procedural obligation to carry out an effective investigation under Article 2 has evolved into a separate and autonomous duty [which] ... can be considered to be a detachable obligation arising out of Article 2 capable of binding the state even when the death took place before the critical date [the date of the entry into force of the Convention with respect to that state party].[95]

The Supreme Court applied *Silih* in *Re McCaughey*.[96] Revisiting (in part) the earlier House of Lords' decision in *Re McKerr*,[97] the Court was at pains to stress that there was no continuing obligation to investigate deaths that occurred before the introduction of the Human Rights Act, but where the state had decided to hold an inquest into such a death, it had to be Article 2-compliant. The Supreme Court, however, regarded aspects of the ECtHR's reasoning in *Silih* as 'far from clear'.[98]   5.52

---

[90] See eg *Gül v Turkey* (2002) 34 EHRR 28, para 88; *Brecknell v UK* (2008) 46 EHRR 42, para 65. See also *R (Sacker) v West Yorkshire Coroner* [2004] UKHL 11, [2004] 1 WLR 796, para 11.

[91] *R (Smith) v Secretary of State for Defence* [2010] UKSC 29, [2011] AC 1, para 87 per Lord Phillips.

[92] *Menson v UK* App No 47916, 6 May 2003; *R (JL) v Secretary of State for Justice* [2008] UKHL 68, [2009] 1 AC 588, para 26.

[93] *Opuz v Turkey* (2010) 50 EHRR 28.

[94] *Al Skeini v UK* (2011) 53 EHRR 18, para 163.

[95] *Silih v Solvenia* (2009) 49 EHRR 37, para 69.

[96] *Re McCaughey* [2011] UKSC 20, [2012] 1 AC 725.

[97] *Re McKerr* [2004] UKHL 12, [2004] 1 WLR 807.

[98] *Re McCaughey* [2011] UKSC 20, [2012] 1 AC 725, para 49 per Lord Philip. Lord Rodger, dissenting, would have declined to re-visit *Re McKerr* and to apply *Silah* in domestic law.

5.53   In *Janowiec v Russia*,[99] the Grand Chamber sought to clarify the applicable principles. It confirmed that a renewed procedural duty could be triggered by credible new material emerging after the coming into force of the Convention concerning events pre-dating this otherwise critical date. However, in all but certain exceptional cases, a procedural duty would only be triggered where the period of time between the underlying events and the critical date was reasonably short and a major part of the investigation had, or should have been, carried out after the entry into force of the Convention.

5.54   In *Re McQuillan*,[100] concerning requests for fresh investigations into inconclusive investigations in Northern Ireland into the fatal shooting of a woman in 1972 and use of interrogation techniques on detainees in 1971, the Supreme Court confirmed that it was established law that the Article 2 and 3 investigative duties can be revived if sufficiently weighty and compelling new evidence comes to light.[101] However, it held that, where a triggering event preceded the coming into force of the Human Rights Act 1998, one of two additional conditions must also be satisfied. Either there must additionally be a 'genuine connection' between the triggering event and the date of the Act coming into force (including both a sufficiently close temporal connection of generally no more than 10 years, and that a major part of the investigation must have or ought to have been carried out after entry into force of the Act). Or, alternatively, there must be exceptional circumstances satisfying the so-called 'Convention values' test, that is, a need to ensure protection of the guarantees and the underlying values of the Convention.[102] The Supreme Court held that neither test was satisfied on the facts of the case.

5.55   The precise form of the Article 2 investigation is flexible, but, in all cases, the authorities must engage the investigative mechanism on their own initiative.[103] In order to guarantee its effectiveness, the investigation must be independent,[104] prompt,[105] open to an element of public scrutiny,[106] and with involvement of the next of kin to the extent required to safeguard their legitimate interests.[107] The ECtHR has confirmed that the procedural obligation continues to apply even in difficult security conditions, including in a context of armed conflict, and that all reasonable steps must be taken to ensure that an effective, independent investigation is conducted into alleged breaches of the right to life.[108]

5.56   The requirement of independence means that it is necessary for the persons responsible for carrying out the investigation to be independent from those

---

[99] *Janowiec v Russia* App Nos 55508/07 and 29520/09, 21 October 2013 [GC].
[100] *Re McQuillan* [2021] UKSC 55, [2022] AC 1063.
[101] ibid paras 116–19.
[102] ibid paras 133–45 and 167–68.
[103] *Nachova and others v Bulgaria* (2006) 42 EHRR 43, para 111.
[104] *Brecknell v UK* (2008) 46 EHRR 42.
[105] See eg *Angelova v Bulgaria* (2008) 47 EHRR 7; *Brecknell v UK* (2008) 46 EHRR 42.
[106] *Edwards v UK* | (2002) 35 EHRR 19, paras 69–73; *Ramsahai and others v Netherlands* App No 52391/99, 15 May 2007, para 353. See also *R (D) v Secretary of State for the Home Department* [2006] EWCA Civ 143, [2006] 3 All ER 946.
[107] *Al-Skeini and others v the United Kingdom* (2011) 53 EHRR 18, para 167.
[108] See eg *Al Skeini v UK* (2011) 53 EHRR 18, para 164.

implicated in the events. This requires a lack of hierarchical or institutional connection, such as where the investigator belongs to the same police force as those under investigation.[109] The ECtHR has held that an investigation into the actions of British soldiers in Iraq by the Special Investigation Branch was not sufficiently independent from the military chain of command because Special Branch was not free to decide for itself when to start and cease an investigation, and the commanding officer had the final say on whether the matter should be referred for prosecution.[110] The procedural duty also requires practical independence. For example, where the issue to be investigated is whether national policy is adequate to meet the state's positive Article 2 obligations, the fact that the investigator had spent his working life applying that policy may deprive him of the practical independence necessary to perform his work effectively.[111]

In *McShane v UK*, the applicant's husband was killed when a security forces' 5.57 vehicle struck a hoarding under which he had fallen during a disturbance in Belfast.[112] The applicant complained that there was no effective investigation into her husband's death. Although there was a police investigation and inquest proceedings were scheduled to commence, the ECtHR held that a number of deficiencies rendered both inconsistent with the investigative obligation. In particular, the involvement of police officers indirectly connected with the security operation in the police investigation was held to cast doubts on its independence. A series of delays in both the investigation and inquest proceedings, including a delay of over five months in questioning the driver of the vehicle, demonstrated a lack of the requisite promptness.

Although the required degree of public scrutiny may vary from case to case, 5.58 it is necessary in all cases for the victim's next of kin to be involved to the extent required to safeguard their legitimate interests.[113] However, in *Hackett v UK*, concerning a sectarian murder in Northern Ireland, the ECtHR said that in the early stages of an investigation, particularly when there is an indeterminate possibility of other persons being criminally charged, Article 2 may require fairly minimal family involvement.[114] As the investigation progresses, the public and family should be informed of its findings and recommendations. The family does not have an automatic right to be given access to police reports or investigative materials.[115]

In *Ramsahai v Netherlands*, the Grand Chamber emphasized that the primary 5.59 characteristic of an effective investigation is that it is 'adequate', and adequacy may be compromised by the possibility of collusion between police officers involved in the incident.[116] Adequacy requires that the investigation is capable of leading to the

---

[109] See eg *Shanaghan v UK* App No 37715/97, 4 May 2001, para 104.
[110] *Al Skeini v UK* (2011) 53 EHRR 18.
[111] *SP v Secretary of State for Justice* [2009] EWHC 13 (Admin), para 81.
[112] *McShane v UK* (2002) 35 EHRR 23.
[113] *Edwards v UK* (2002) 12 BHRC 190, para 73.
[114] *Hackett v UK* (2005) 5 EHRR 543.
[115] *R (Green) v Police Complaints Authority* [2004] UKHL 6, [2004] 1 WLR 725.
[116] *Ramsahai v Netherlands* App No 52391/99, 15 March 2007. See also *R (Saunders) v Independent Police Complaints Commission* [2008] EWHC 2372 (Admin).

identification and punishment of those responsible. Accordingly, civil proceedings will not constitute an effective investigation.[117]

5.60   The domestic courts have closely followed the ECtHR's approach to the procedural duty under Article 2. In the cases of *R (Amin) v Secretary of State for the Home Department*,[118] *R v Coroner for Western District of Somerset, ex p Middleton*,[119] and *R (JL) v Secretary of State for Justice*,[120] the House of Lords found violations of the investigative obligation in the context of deaths or near-deaths in custody. *Amin* concerned a death in a young offenders' institution. The deceased, an Asian man, was battered to death with a wooden table leg by his white cellmate who had a history of violent and racist behaviour. A number of investigations were commenced, but the Secretary of State refused the family's request for a public inquiry into the death on the grounds that such an inquiry would add nothing of substance and would not be in the public interest.

5.61   The House of Lords held that the investigations conducted were neither singly nor cumulatively adequate for the purposes of discharging the Article 2 enhanced investigative duty. While the ECtHR had not prescribed a particular model of investigation suitable for all cases, it had laid down minimum standards that had to be adhered to whatever the form of the investigation. A properly conducted inquest could have discharged the state's obligation under Article 2 but, in its absence, it was necessary for the death to be publicly investigated before an independent judicial tribunal with an opportunity for the relatives to participate.

5.62   In *Middleton* an inquest had taken place in relation to a prisoner who hanged himself in his prison cell. The coroner directed the jury by reference to section 11(5) of the Coroners Act 1988, and the Coroners Rules, that their findings were confined to the identity of the deceased and to 'how', when, and where he came by his death, and that they could express no opinion on any other matter. 'How' was narrowly interpreted in section 11(5) and the Rules to connote 'by what means', and they could not return a verdict of neglect, since this might appear to determine criminal or civil liability.

5.63   The House of Lords, however, held that the inquest was the means by which the state sought to discharge the obligation under Article 2 to investigate the accountability of state agents for deaths which occurred when the deceased was their responsibility, and it should culminate in 'an expression of the jury's conclusion on the central, factual issues in the case'.[121] The narrow interpretation of 'how' the deceased came by his death, coupled with the jury's inability to refer to neglect previously accepted by the domestic courts, meant that in many cases the central issue could not be determined and, accordingly, the current coronial regime did not meet the requirements of Article 2.[122] The Court held that the word 'how' in

---

[117] *McShane v UK* App No 43290/98, 28 March 2002, para 125. See generally Thomas and others, *Inquests: A Practitioner's Guide* (Legal Action Group 2014).

[118] *R (Amin) v Secretary of State for the Home Department* [2003] UKHL 51, [2004] 1 AC 653.

[119] *R v Coroner for Western District of Somerset, ex p Middleton* [2004] UKHL 10, [2004] 2 AC 182.

[120] *R (JL) v Secretary of State for Justice* [2008] UKHL 68, [2008] 3 WLR 1325.

[121] *R v Coroner for Western District of Somerset, ex p Middleton* [2004] UKHL 10, [2004] 2 AC 182, paras 13, 16–20.

[122] ibid paras 30–32.

section 11(5) should be interpreted to connote 'by what means and in what circumstances'.[123] The *Middleton* case led to those inquests that were held to discharge the state's Article 2 obligations becoming known as *Middleton* inquests.

The scope of the investigative duty was clarified again in *R (JL) v Secretary of State for Justice* in which the House of Lords considered the requirements of Article 2 in the context of near-suicides in prison.[124] Lord Phillips stated that 'death requires a spectrum of different types of investigation, depending upon the circumstances of the particular case'.[125] In some cases where death has resulted, a coroner's inquest will satisfy Article 2, while in others it may be necessary to hold a full-blown public inquiry (referred to as a 'D-type' inquiry).[126] In the case of a near-suicide in custody that leaves the prisoner with the possibility of a serious long-term injury, it would automatically be necessary to hold an 'enhanced investigation'. Their Lordships considered that a D-type inquiry might be required in a variety of circumstances that it was not appropriate to prescribe.[127]   5.64

Compliance with the procedural obligation is closely related to the Article 13 right to an effective remedy. The very purpose of an investigation is to secure the effective implementation of domestic laws which protect the right to life and, in those cases involving state agents or bodies, to ensure their accountability for deaths occurring under their responsibility. However, violation of Article 2 stemming from non-compliance with the procedural obligation will not necessarily constitute a violation of Article 13.[128]   5.65

5. Use of force

Article 2(2) details the circumstances in which it is permissible to use lethal force. All these situations involve curbing violence or the control of prisoners or criminals—generally, maintaining law and order. The crucial test for these exceptions is that 'no more force than is absolutely necessary' is used. The ECmHR examined this phrase in *Stewart v UK*, and held that force is 'absolutely necessary' if, having regard to the nature of the aim pursued, the dangers and risks inherent in the situation, and all relevant circumstances, it is 'strictly proportionate to the achievement of the permitted purpose'.[129] In this way, it is a stricter test than that found under paragraphs 2 of Articles 8–11. The ECmHR found that the exceptions included in Article 2(2) indicate that this provision extends to, but is not concerned exclusively with, intentional killing.   5.66

The leading case on the use of lethal force is still *McCann v UK*, in which three Provisional IRA members were shot and killed by British soldiers in Gibraltar in   5.67

---

[123] This is now enshrined in the Coroners and Justice Act 2009, s 5(2).

[124] See n 105.

[125] *R (JL) v Secretary of State for Justice* [2008] UKHL 68, [2008] 3 WLR 1325, para 31.

[126] See eg *R (D) v Secretary of State for the Home Department* [2006] EWCA Civ 143, [2006] 3 All ER 946.

[127] cf Lord Brown ibid, para 104.

[128] *McShane v UK* (2002) 35 EHRR 23.

[129] *Stewart v UK* (1985) 7 EHRR CD 453.

1988. The ECtHR held, by a slim 10–9 vote, that there had been a violation of Article 2.[130] In making its decision, the ECtHR took into consideration 'not only the actions of the organs of the state who actually administer the force but also the surrounding circumstances including such matters as the planning and control of the actions under examination'. The concept of 'planning and control' is critical and failures can result in a violation of Article 2 as they did in *McCann*. The ECtHR held that the state must give appropriate training, instructions, and briefing to its agents who are faced with a situation where the use of lethal force is possible.[131] The state must also exercise 'strict control' over any operations that may involve use of lethal force.

5.68   The test articulated by the ECtHR to assess the Article 2 compatibility of the actual fatal force used—since confirmed and explained by the Grand Chambers in *Da Silva v United Kingdom*[132] (concerning the fatal shooting of Jean Charles de Menezes at Stockwell Tube station)—is whether the force was based on an honest belief, which was perceived, for good reason, to be valid at the time, even if the belief turns out subsequently to be mistaken. In *Da Silva*, the Grand Chamber clarified that reasonableness is a factor in the assessment of the required honest belief (rather than a separate element, as many had understood it to be) and is assessed subjectively having full regard to the circumstances pertaining at the relevant time.[133] In *Andronicou v Cyprus*, for example, police shot a gunman and his hostage, mistakenly believing that the gunman had more ammunition and weapons than he actually possessed.[134] The ECtHR held that, even though the police were mistaken about the gunman's weapons, they had good reason to believe as they did, and were pursuing the legitimate aims of Article 2(2). It also held that the police actions were adequately designed and controlled to minimize the risk to the lives of the gunman and his hostage.

5.69   Similarly, in *Bubbins v UK*, the ECtHR found no violation of Article 2 where an individual was mistakenly shot dead by a police officer after he pulled a replica gun which the officer believed to be real.[135] The ECtHR held that it could not substitute its own assessment for that of the officer in the situation and that his actions were proportionate.

5.70   In *Giuliani and Gaggio v Italy*, the Grand Chamber found no breach in respect of the fatal shooting of a violent demonstrator by an Italian police officer during the G8 summit in Genoa, finding no failings in the organization and planning of the event insofar as they could be linked directly to the death.[136]

5.71   Article 2 also requires an appropriate administrative and legal framework to be put in place defining the limited circumstances in which officers can use arms and

---

[130] *McCann v UK* (1995) 21 EHRR 97.
[131] See also *Gül v Turkey* (2002) 34 EHRR 28.
[132] *Da Silva v UK* (2016) 63 EHRR 12, paras 249–56.
[133] *McCann v United Kingdom* (1996) 21 EHRR 97, para 200; *Da Silva v United Kingdom* (2016) 63 EHRR 12, paras 244–48.
[134] *Andronicou v Cyprus* (1997) 25 EHRR 491.
[135] *Bubbins v UK* App No 50916/99, 17 March 2005.
[136] *Giuliani and Gaggio v Italy* App No 23458/02, 24 March 2011.

force in line with international standards, and with regard to the fundamental value of life.[137] Applying these principles, the Court has, for example, found to be deficient the legal framework in Bulgaria which permitted the police to fire on any fugitive member of the armed forces who did not immediately surrender following an oral warning and the firing of a warning shot in the air, and did not contain clear safeguards to prevent the arbitrary deprivation of life.[138]

6. Standing

Relatives of the deceased are considered 'victims' of breaches of Article 2, within the meaning of Article 34.[139] In *Savage v South Essex Partnership NHS Foundation Trust*, Lord Scott suggested in *obiter* observations that complaints concerning breaches of the substantive obligations under Article 2 could not be brought by victims' relatives on the grounds that private causes of action were open to the relatives to pursue.[140] This was inconsistent with the case law of the ECtHR, which domestic courts are obliged to apply under section 2 of the Human Rights Act.[141] In *Rabone v Pennine Care NHS Trust*,[142] the Supreme Court firmly disapproved these *obiter* comments and confirmed that family members can be 'victims' of both a substantive and a procedural breach of Article 2 arising out of the death of their family member.[143]   5.72

It is not necessary for a person to have died in order for a claim under Article 2 to be brought. A living applicant may bring a claim for state conduct that put his or her life at grave risk.[144]   5.73

D. ARTICLE 3: PROHIBITION OF TORTURE

Article 3 concerns freedom from torture and inhuman and degrading treatment. Like Article 2, it is one of the most fundamental provisions of the Convention.[145] Its importance is reflected in its absolute and non-derogable status.[146] The Grand Chamber of the ECtHR has described the prohibition of torture and inhuman or degrading treatment of punishment as 'a value of civilization closely bound up with respect for human dignity'.[147]   5.74

---

[137] ibid para 97.
[138] ibid paras 99–102.
[139] *Brecknell v UK* (2008) 46 EHRR 42; *Yasa v Turkey* (1999) 28 EHRR 408; *McShane v UK* (2002) 35 EHRR 23, para 93.
[140] *Savage v South Essex Partnership NHS Foundation Trust* [2008] UKHL 74, [2009] 1 AC 681, paras 2–3.
[141] See Chapter 4.
[142] *Rabone v Pennine Care NHS Trust* [2012] UKSC 2, [2012] 2 AC 72.
[143] ibid paras 44–48 per Lord Dyson, and see also Lady Hale at para 92.
[144] See eg *Acar v Turkey* App No 36088/97, 24 May 2005, para 79; *R (JL) v Secretary of State for Justice* [2008] UKHL 68, [2009] 1 AC 588.
[145] *Pretty v UK* (2002) 35 EHRR 1.
[146] *Saadi v UK* (2008) 24 BHRC 123.
[147] *Bouyid v Belgium* (2016) 62 EHRR 32, para 81.

5.75   Article 3 places a negative duty on the state not to inflict the proscribed suffering on persons within their jurisdiction, as well as a positive duty to ensure that these forms of suffering are not endured. In common with Article 2, it also includes a procedural obligation to conduct an effective investigation in certain circumstances.[148]

5.76   Article 3 applies irrespective of the conduct of an applicant.[149]

1. Scope of Article 3

5.77   In *Ireland v UK* the ECtHR considered the types of treatment that are prohibited by Article 3.[150] It characterized the prohibited activities as follows:

(a) *torture*: deliberate inhuman treatment that causes very serious and cruel suffering;

(b) *inhuman treatment*: treatment that causes intense physical and mental suffering; and

(c) *degrading treatment*: treatment that arouses in the victim a feeling of fear, anguish, and inferiority capable of humiliating and debasing the victim and possibly breaking his or her physical or moral resistance.

5.78   The prohibition under Article 3 does not relate to all instances of ill-treatment.[151] Such treatment must attain 'a minimum level of severity' to fall within Article 3.[152] The ECtHR describes the determination of this minimum level as 'relative' and has set out criteria, such as the duration of the treatment, its physical or mental effects, and, in some circumstances, the sex, age, and state of health of the victim.[153] The ECtHR will also take other factors into consideration, in particular: (a) the purpose for which the ill-treatment was inflicted, together with the intention or motivation behind it (although the absence of an intention to humiliate or debase the victim cannot conclusively rule out its characterization as 'degrading' and prohibited by art 3); (b) the context in which the ill-treatment was inflicted, such as an atmosphere of heightened tension and emotions; and (c) whether the victim is in a vulnerable situation, which is normally the case for persons deprived of their liberty.[154] These factors are relevant in two contexts: when determining whether the suffering caused is sufficient to amount to inhuman or degrading treatment or punishment; and when distinguishing between these lesser kinds of ill-treatment and torture.

5.79   In *R (AB) v Secretary of State for Justice* the Supreme Court rejected the argument that the solitary confinement of a child in a Young Offenders Institution was always a breach of Article 3 and did not require consideration of the particular circumstances.[155]

---

[148] See eg *Assenov v Bulgaria* (1998) 28 EHRR 652; *Šečić v Croatia* (2007) 23 BHRC 24; and *R (Green) v Police Complaints Authority* [2004] UKHL 6, [2004] 1 WLR 725.

[149] See *Chahal v UK* (1997) 23 EHRR 413; *Gäfgen v Germany* (2011) 52 EHRR 1; and *Hassan-Daniel v HMRC* [2010] EWCA Civ 1443, [2011] QB 866.

[150] *Ireland v UK* (1978) 2 EHRR 25.

[151] *Savran v Denmark* (2021) 53 BHRC 201, para 122.

[152] *Ireland v UK* (1978) 2 EHRR 25, para 162.

[153] *Ireland v UK* (1978) 2 EHRR 25, para 162; *Ahmad v UK* (2013) 56 EHRR 1, para 178; *Bouyid v Belgium* (2016) 62 EHRR 32, para 86; *Muršic v Croatia* (2017) 65 EHRR 1, para 97; *Savran v Denmark* (2021) 53 BHRC 201, para 123.

[154] *Khlaifia and others v Italy* App No 16483/12, 15 December 2016 [GC], para 160.

[155] *R (AB) v Secretary of State for Justice* [2021] UKSC 28, [2022] AC 487, paras 50–67.

As the Convention is a living instrument, acts that have previously been classed **5.80** as inhuman treatment, for example, could well be classed differently in the future.[156] In keeping with the Strasbourg approach, the domestic courts accept that the concept of 'torture' is not immutable and may shift over time. Lord Bingham indicated in *A and others v Secretary of State for the Home Department (No 2)* that the conduct complained of in *Ireland v UK* may well be considered to now fall within the definition of 'torture'.[157] In *Re McQuillan* the Supreme Court stated that it was 'likely' that the treatment in *Ireland v UK* would be characterized today 'applying the standards of 2021' as torture.[158]

Further, treatment which does not violate Article 3 may nevertheless violate the **5.81** right to autonomy and dignity now recognized under the rubric of Article 8.[159] Conversely, treatment may constitute such a gross breach of another article of the Convention as to amount to inhuman or degrading treatment under Article 3.[160]

(a) *Torture*

The prohibition of torture has achieved the state of *jus cogens* or a peremptory norm **5.82** in international law.[161] Torture is an aggravated form of inhuman or degrading treatment or punishment. Classification of treatment as torture implies suffering of a particular intensity and cruelty.[162] Such treatment will usually have a purpose such as obtaining information or a confession, or inflicting punishment.[163] The ECtHR has found that the distinction between 'torture' and 'inhuman or degrading treatment' was intended to 'attach a special stigma to deliberate inhuman treatment causing very serious and cruel suffering'.[164] The Court attaches significant importance to drawing the distinction between the different forms of ill-treatment, and will do so even where the state has accepted that its conduct broadly violated Article 3.[165]

---

[156] *Selmouni v France* (2000) 29 EHRR 403.

[157] *A and others v Secretary of State for the Home Department (No 2)* [2005] UKHL 71, [2006] 2 AC 221, para 53.

[158] *Re McQuillan* [2021] UKSC 55, [2022] AC 1063, para 186. In *Ireland v UK* (2018) 67 EHRR SE1, however, the ECtHR declined to revise its judgment in the earlier case.

[159] See eg *Wainwright v UK* (2007) 44 EHRR 40 where the ECtHR found that strip searches on visitors to prisoners did not breach art 3 but did constitute a breach of art 8; and *Re Northern Ireland Human Rights Commission's Application for Judicial Review* [2018] UKSC 27, [2018] HRLR 14 where a majority of the Supreme Court held that the criminalization of abortion in Northern Ireland was not, in the abstract, incompatible with art 3. A majority of the Court held that insofar as the law prohibits abortion in cases of (a) fatal foetal abnormality, (b) pregnancy as a result of rape, and (c) pregnancy as a result of incest, it was disproportionate and incompatible with art 8. The Court decided, however, that the claimant, the Northern Ireland Human Rights Commission, did not have standing and therefore dismissed the appeal.

[160] See eg *East African Asians v UK* (1981) 3 EHRR 76.

[161] *Advisory opinion on the applicability of statutes of limitation to prosecution, conviction and punishment in respect of an offence constituting, in substance, an act of torture* (Request no P16-2021-001, 26 April 2022), para 59.

[162] *Ireland v UK* (1978) 2 EHRR 25.

[163] *Greek Case* App No 3321/67 & others, 5 November 1969.

[164] See eg *Ciorap v Moldova* [2007] ECHR App No 12066/02, 19 June 2007, para 62.

[165] *Gäfgen v Germany* (2011) 52 EHRR 1.

5.83   In *Aydin v Turkey* the complainant had been raped, blindfolded, beaten, stripped, and sprayed with high-pressure water while in the custody of the Turkish security forces. This treatment was held to amount to torture. The ECtHR commented that a finding of torture would have been made even in the absence of rape.[166] The accumulation of similarly violent and humiliating treatment was classified as torture in *Selmouni v France*, where the complainant had been urinated on, threatened with a blowtorch, and severely beaten by the police.[167] In *Husayn (Abu Zubaydah) v Poland* the Court had no difficulty in concluding that the techniques deployed by the CIA in interrogating terrorist suspects on Polish territory, including water boarding and placing in stress positions, constituted torture.[168]

5.84   Mental anguish alone may constitute torture if it reaches a certain level of severity.[169] The ECtHR has found that the threat of torture can violate the prohibition on inhuman and degrading treatment provided it is sufficiently real and immediate.[170]

5.85   The Strasbourg Court has developed a strong principle that a state may not extradite an individual to a country where there are substantial grounds for believing that there is a real risk that he or she would be subjected to torture or ill-treatment.[171] This principle has been the subject of extensive case law before both the ECtHR and domestic courts.

5.86   The House of Lords considered its duties relating to the prohibition of torture under international law in *Jones v Saudi Arabia*.[172] The Court upheld the principle of sovereign state immunity and unanimously denied jurisdiction in a claim brought by four UK citizens to seek redress against acts of torture committed against them by a foreign state and its officials. The ECtHR agreed with the House of Lords.[173] Although not of direct relevance to Article 3, the decision is indicative of a cautious approach to torture-related issues in the absence of a settled consensus at international level.

(b) *Inhuman and degrading treatment or punishment*

5.87   The terms 'inhuman' and 'degrading' bear different meanings under the Convention, though one is rarely found to exist without the other.

5.88   Treatment or punishment is considered 'inhuman' where it is premeditated, applied over a period of hours at a stretch, and causes either actual bodily injury or intense physical or mental suffering.[174] Whether treatment or punishment is degrading depends on all the circumstances: the nature and context of the treatment or punishment, and the method and manner of its execution.[175]

---

[166] *Aydin v Turkey* (1997) 25 EHRR 251.
[167] *Selmouni v France* (2000) 29 EHRR 403.
[168] *Husayn (Abu Zubaydah) v Poland* (2015) 60 EHRR 16.
[169] *Denmark v Greece* App No 3321/67 & others, 31 May 1968
[170] *Campbell and Cosans v UK* (1982) 4 EHRR 293, para 26; *Gäfgen v Germany* (2011) 52 EHRR 1.
[171] *Soering v UK* (1989) 11 EHRR 439.
[172] *Jones v Saudi Arabia* [2006] UKHL 26, [2007] 1 AC 270.
[173] *Jones and others v UK* (2014) 59 EHRR 1.
[174] See eg *Kudla v Poland* (2002) 35 EHRR 11, para 92.
[175] *Tyrer v UK* (1978) 2 EHRR 1.

In *Pretty v United Kingdom* the Court explained 'degrading' as follows: 'Where   5.89
treatment humiliates or debases an individual showing a lack of respect for, or
diminishing, his or her human dignity or arouses feelings of fear, anguish or inferiority capable of breaking an individual's moral and physical resistance, it may be
characterised as degrading.'[176] As judicial punishment inevitably entails a degree of
humiliation, degrading punishment must involve a degree of humiliation or debase-
ment that exceeds that which is usual in punishment.[177] Unlike torture, it is not
necessary that there be any specific intention or purpose such as intent to debase,
although an aim to humiliate or debase will be highly relevant.[178] The ECtHR has
noted a 'particularly strong link' between the concepts of 'degrading treatment or
punishment' and respect for 'dignity'.[179]

In *Ireland v UK* the ECtHR examined five techniques used by the British gov-   5.90
ernment to interrogate prisoners allegedly involved in terrorism, which included
forcing them to stand against a wall in an uncomfortable position, hooding,
subjecting them to loud, continuous noise, and depriving them of food, drink,
and sleep. Although not rising to the level of torture, the ECtHR determined
that these practices constituted degrading treatment and, therefore, violated
Article 3.[180]

Race discrimination may constitute degrading treatment. In *East African Asians*   5.91
v UK the applicants were British passport holders but had been refused permission
to take up residence in the UK. The ECmHR considered that the discriminatory
immigration legislation constituted an interference with their human dignity which
amounted to degrading treatment in the sense of Article 3 of the Convention.[181]

In *Soering v UK* the ECtHR concluded that 'death row phenomenon' experi-   5.92
enced by many prisoners awaiting execution in the United States (US) constituted
inhuman and degrading treatment.[182] States cannot extradite suspected criminals
to countries where there is a real risk of exposure to such treatment.

2. State responsibility

The state is responsible for the actions of its agents under Article 3. The ECtHR   5.93
has held that where the behaviour of a state agent is unlawful, the question of
whether the impugned acts can be imputed to the state requires an assessment of
the totality of the circumstances. Whether a person is an agent of the state will be
assessed on the basis of a number of actors, none of which is determinative on its
own. The key criteria for determining whether the state is responsible for the acts of
a person (whether formally a public official or not) are: (a) manner of appointment,

---

[176] *Pretty v UK* (2002) 35 EHRR 1, para 52.
[177] *Tyrer v UK* (1978) 2 EHRR 1.
[178] *Peers v Greece* (2001) 33 EHRR 51.
[179] *Bouyid v Belgium* (2016) 62 EHRR 32, para 90.
[180] *Ireland v UK* (1978) 2 EHRR 25. See, however, the subsequent comments from the domestic courts
as to how that conduct would be viewed today: para 5.80 above.
[181] *East African Asians v UK* (1981) 3 EHRR 76.
[182] *Soering v UK* (1989) 11 EHRR 439; *Al-Saadoon and Mufdhi v UK* (2010) 51 EHRR 9.

(b) supervision and accountability, and (c) the objectives, powers, and functions of the person in question.[183] The acquiescence or connivance of the authorities of a state in the acts of private individuals which violate the Convention rights of other individuals within its jurisdiction may engage the state's responsibility.[184]

5.94   In *Cyprus v Turkey* the ECmHR found the state responsible for rapes committed by its soldiers as satisfactory action had not been taken to prevent these attacks and disciplinary measures after the conduct were insufficient.[185] The ECtHR held in *Ireland v UK* that the higher authorities of a state are 'under a duty to impose their will on subordinates and cannot shelter behind their inability to ensure that it is respected'.[186]

3. Negative obligation

5.95   Article 3 is generally characterized as containing both a negative obligation to refrain from inflicting harm and a positive obligation to protect people from a real and immediate risk of harm. The utility of this analysis has been questioned by Lord Brown, who suggested that 'the real issue in all these cases is whether the state is properly to be regarded as responsible for the harm inflicted (or threatened) upon the victim'.[187] The ECtHR has itself blurred the boundaries between the positive and negative duties on occasion.[188] Nevertheless, there is a critical distinction to be drawn between the two: the obligation not to do harm is absolute, while the positive obligation requires the state to do all that it reasonably can to prevent harm from occurring.[189]

(a) Counter-terrorism

5.96   The House of Lords considered the negative obligation in the leading counter-terrorism decision *A v Secretary of State for the Home Department (No 2)*,[190] the second key case concerning the government's legislative response to the terrorist attacks in the US on 11 September 2001. The applicants were detained under Part IV of the Anti-Terrorism, Crime and Security Act 2001 on the Home Secretary's suspicion of involvement in or links to international terrorism. They appealed against their detention to the Special Immigration Appeals Commission (SIAC). The SIAC was entitled to receive evidence that would not be admissible in court. At issue before the House of Lords was whether evidence which may have been obtained through torture abroad could be admissible in UK proceedings.

---

[183] *VK v Russia* (2018) 66 EHRR 7, paras 174–75.
[184] *Chernega v Ukraine* (2020) 70 EHRR 9, para 127.
[185] *Cyprus v Turkey* (1976) 4 EHRR 482.
[186] *Ireland v UK* (1978) 2 EHRR 25, para 159.
[187] *R (Limbuela) v Secretary of State for the Home Department* [2005] UKHL 66, [2006] 1 AC 396, para 92.
[188] *Mubilanzila Mayeka v Belgium* (2008) 46 EHRR 23.
[189] See eg *Re E* [2008] UKHL 66, [2008] 3 WLR 1208, para 10 per Baroness Hale.
[190] *A v Secretary of State for the Home Department (No 2)* [2005] UKHL 71, [2006] 2 AC 221.

Their Lordships held unanimously that evidence of a suspect or witness which   5.97
had been obtained through torture had long been regarded as inherently unreliable,
unfair, offensive to ordinary standards of humanity and decency, and incompatible
with the principles on which courts should administer justice. The opinions drew
not only on Article 3 jurisprudence and international law, but also on the common
law, Lord Bingham referring to the unacceptability of torture as a 'constitutional
principle',[191] Lord Nicholls as 'a bedrock moral principle in this country'.[192]

Although unanimous on the central issue, the House was divided in relation   5.98
to the application of the exclusionary rule. A majority determined that the SIAC
should admit evidence unless it was established on the balance of probabilities that
it had been obtained by torture.

In *Ahmed and another v R* the Court of Appeal applied *A (No 2)* in considering   5.99
whether a prosecution should be stayed because the defendant claimed that UK
authorities had been complicit in his torture in Pakistan after he was alleged to have
committed the offences.[193] The Court of Appeal dismissed the appeal on the basis
that the torture must have had an impact on the trial, which in this case it had not.

In joined cases *RB (Algeria) v Secretary of State for the Home Department* the   5.100
House of Lords adopted a different approach to the admission of torture evidence
in a foreign trial.[194] RB and OO were terrorist suspects whom the government
wished to deport to states with a reputation for ill-treatment. They claimed that if
they were deported, they would face trials at which evidence obtained by torture
would be admitted. The House of Lords held that the use of evidence obtained by
torture in a foreign trial would not necessarily amount to a 'flagrant denial of justice' sufficient to prevent the deportation of the suspect.[195] The ECtHR considered
the applications of RB and OO in *Othman v UK*.[196] It disagreed with the House of
Lords and found that there was a real risk that evidence obtained by the torture of
third parties would be used in the trial and would therefore violate Article 6.

In *Shagang Shipping Company Ltd v HNA Group Company Ltd* the Supreme   5.101
Court held that the Court of Appeal was wrong to find that, if the use of torture
has not been proved on the balance of probabilities, a serious possibility that a statement was obtained by torture must be ignored by a court in estimating the weight
to be given to the statement. Rather, the true position was that where there are
reasonable grounds for suspecting that a statement was obtained by torture, this is
a matter which the judge could and should take into account, along with all other
relevant circumstances, in assessing the reliability of the statement as evidence of
the facts stated.[197]

---

[191] ibid para 51.
[192] ibid para 64.
[193] *R v Ahmed (Rangzieb)* [2011] EWCA Crim 184, [2011] Crim LR 734.
[194] *RB (Algeria) v Secretary of State for the Home Department* [2009] UKHL 10, [2009] 2 WLR 512.
[195] See Chapter 6, para 6.99.
[196] *Othman Abu Qatada v UK* (2012) 55 EHRR 1.
[197] *Shagang Shipping Co Ltd v HNA Group Co Ltd* [2020] UKSC 34, [2020] 1 WLR 3549, para 112.

(b) *Sentencing*

5.102   Criminal sentences have been an active field of Article 3 complaints. In *Kafkaris v Cyprus* the applicant was found guilty of premeditated murder which carried a mandatory sentence of life imprisonment without any possibility for a judicial body to consider the applicant's detention thereafter.[198] The majority of the Grand Chamber suggested that a sentence of life imprisonment, if irreducible, might raise an issue under Article 3. However, the provisions of the Cypriot Constitution which conferred on the President a discretion to remit, suspend, or commute a life sentence were sufficient to render the sentence reducible despite the fact that they had been exercised very infrequently.

5.103   The question of whole life tariffs led to a stand-off between the ECtHR and the UK government. While the Court of Appeal accepted in 2001 that the imposition of an automatic life sentence could constitute inhuman and degrading treatment,[199] the question whether whole life tariffs imposed at the discretion of the judge are compatible with the Convention has proved more controversial.[200] The Grand Chamber considered the question in *Vinter and others v UK*. It held that in order for whole life sentences under section 269 of the Criminal Justice Act 2003 to remain compatible with Article 3, there had to be a possibility of review and release.[201] It found that the operation of the provision in section 30 of the Crime (Sentences) Act 1997 that allows the Secretary of State to release a prisoner on licence where there are exceptional circumstances amounting to compassionate grounds was not sufficiently clear to constitute an adequate review mechanism. The decision inflamed the British popular press and the government announced that it would refuse to implement the judgment.

5.104   In *R v McLoughlin*,[202] a specially constituted five-judge panel of the Court of Appeal held that the Grand Chamber had not outlawed whole life tariffs per se and that it had been wrong to conclude that UK law did not provide for release. Section 30 provided for possible exceptional release and the Secretary of State was bound to exercise the power in compliance with principles of public law and Article 3.

5.105   In *Hutchinson v UK* the ECtHR reversed course, finding that the Court of Appeal in *McLoughlin* had resolved the lack of clarity as regards the scope and grounds of the review by the Secretary of State, the manner in which it should be conducted, as well as the duty of the Secretary of State to release a whole life prisoner where continued detention can no longer be justified on legitimate penological grounds. As such, whole life sentences can now be regarded as reducible, in keeping with Article 3.[203]

---

[198] *Kafkaris v Cyprus* (2009) 49 EHRR 35, para 98. See also the separate opinion of Sir Nicholas Bratza who considered that whole life sentences were intrinsically inhuman. See also *De Boucherville v Mauritius* [2008] UKPC 37, (2008) 25 BHRC 433, para 8.

[199] *R v Offen (Matthew Barry) (No 2)* [2001] 1 WLR 253, para 95. See also *R (Wellington) v Secretary of State for the Home Department* [2008] UKHL 72, [2009] 2 WLR 48, discussed at para 5.133.

[200] *R v Lichniak and Pyrah* [2002] UKHL 47, [2003] 1 AC 903. See also *R v Bieber* [2008] EWCA Crim 1601, [2009] 1 WLR 223.

[201] *Vinter and others v UK* (2013) 34 BHRC 605.

[202] *R v McLoughlin* [2014] EWCA Crim 188, [2014] 3 All ER 73.

[203] *Hutchinson v UK* (2017) 43 BHRC 667, paras 70–72.

(c) *Detention*

Prison conditions have been held to constitute degrading treatment.[204] For exam- 5.106
ple, in *Price v UK* the ECtHR held that the detention of a severely disabled person
in conditions where she was dangerously cold, risked developing sores because her
bed was too hard, and was unable to go to the toilet or keep clean without the greatest of difficulty, constituted degrading treatment contrary to Article 3, despite the
absence of any intention to subject her to degrading treatment.[205]

In *Muršic v Croatia* the ECtHR identified a minimum standard of floor surface 5.107
per detainee in multi occupancy accommodation. When the personal space available to a detainee falls below this minimum, a strong presumption of a violation
of Article 3 arises. The burden of proof moves to the respondent state to rebut the
presumption by demonstrating that there were factors capable of adequately com-
pensating for the scare allocation of personal space.[206]

There have been a number of domestic cases in which the court has consid- 5.108
ered whether segregation of a prisoner infringed Article 3. The Supreme Court in
Shahid v Scottish Ministers considered the following factors in concluding that the
segregation in that case did not violate Article 3: (a) the regime did not involve the
prisoner's total isolation from other prisoners or from other human contacts; (b) the
segregation did not result in any severe or permanent injury to his health; and (c) the
segregation was for a legitimate objective, namely the protection of the prisoner
from attack by other prisoners.[207] The duration of the segregation, 56 months, was
'undesirable' but did not entail a violation of Article 3.[208] Similarly, in *R (Dennehy)
v Secretary of State for Justice* segregation of the claimant for 32 months did not
amount to a breach of Article 3.[209] Both cases emphasize, however, that segregation
cannot be imposed on a prisoner indefinitely.

There have also been a series of challenges to the lack of in-cell sanitation and to 5.109
the practice of 'slopping out'. In almost all of these cases the Court has found no
breach of Article 3.[210]

---

[204] See eg *Kalashnikov v Russia* (2002) 36 EHRR 34; *Peers v Greece* (2001) 33 EHRR 51; *Napier v Scottish Ministers* [2002] UKHRR 308; *R v Governor of Frankland Prison, ex p Russell* [2000] 1 WLR 2027.

[205] *Price v UK* (2002) 34 EHRR 53.

[206] *Muršic v Croatia* (2017) 65 EHRR 1, paras 136–41.

[207] *Shahid v Scottish Ministers* [2015] UKSC 58, [2016] AC 429, paras 32–36.

[208] ibid para 37.

[209] *R (Dennehy) v Secretary of State for Justice* [2016] EWHC 1219 (Admin). Singh J held (at paras 121–28) that the following factors were relevant: (a) there was no suggestion that the claimant had been kept in segregation with the intention of debasing or humiliating her; (b) the segregation regime had not amounted to total solitary confinement; (c) the impact of segregation on the claimant's health had been closely moni-tored and it had been certified that she could continue to remain in that environment; (d) the claimant's segregation had at all material times had a legitimate aim; (e) the need for continued segregation had been kept under review on a regular basis; and (f) the claimant had access to an independent judicial authority, namely the court, which was able to assess the continuing need for segregation.

[210] See eg *Grant and Gleaves v Ministry of Justice* [2011] EWHC 3379 (QB) (and the Scottish cases cited in para 225); and *Kelly v Ministry of Justice* [2014] EWHC 3440 (QB). The one exception is *Napier v Scottish Ministers* (2005) SLT 379. In *Grant* (para 225), Hickinbottom J distinguished *Napier* from the subsequent claims as: (a) in *Napier* the complainant shared a cell and had to perform toilet functions in front of his cellmate; (b) the complainant had no access to a flushing toilet overnight; and (c) the conditions of deten-tion caused him to suffer eczema.

5.110   The effect of prison conditions on relatives can also lead to a violation of Article 3. In *Salakhov and Islyamova v Ukraine* the ECtHR held that a mother's mental suffering caused by the failure to treat her dying son while he was imprisoned constituted inhuman and degrading treatment.[211]

5.111   Detention for the purposes of immigration control may also violate Article 3. In *Popov v France* the detention for 15 days of two young children and their parents in a holding centre for illegal immigration violated Article 3.[212] In *R (Detention Action) v Secretary of State for the Home Department*[213] the Divisional Court held that the increased risk of Covid-19 infection in the context of immigration detention did not give rise to a seriously arguable claim under Article 3 given the steps the defendant was taking to ensure the arrangements in detention centres were safe.

5.112   Detention in the mental health context could give rise to a breach of Article 3. In *R (Munjaz) v Mersey Care NHS Trust* the House of Lords found by a majority that a hospital's policy on seclusion of mentally ill patients contained sufficient safeguards to prevent ill-treatment.[214] The ECtHR agreed with the House of Lords.[215]

(d) Mental health

5.113   In the context of compulsory treatment for mental health disorders, the ECtHR has held that 'as a general rule, a measure which is a therapeutic necessity cannot be regarded as inhuman or degrading'.[216] The court must satisfy itself that the medical necessity has convincingly been shown to exist, and that procedural guarantees exist and are complied with.[217]

4. Positive obligations

(a) Investigative duty

5.114   The ECtHR has held that the combined effect of Articles 1 and 3 is to require an effective official investigation into credible allegations of serious ill-treatment, whether by state agents or private actors.[218] The ECtHR has held that the 'essential purpose' of an investigation is to 'secure the effective implementation of the domestic laws prohibiting torture and inhuman or degrading treatment or punishment in cases involving State agents or bodies, and to ensure their accountability for ill-treatment occurring under their responsibility'.[219] In *Bouyid v Belgium* the ECtHR set out a number of further requirements: (a) for an investigation

---

[211] *Salakhov and Islyamova v Ukraine* App No 28005/08, 14 March 2013.
[212] *Popov v France* (2016) 63 EHRR 8.
[213] In *R (Detention Action) v Secretary of State for the Home Department* [2020] EWHC 732 (Admin), [2020] ACD 70.
[214] *R (Munjaz) v Mersey Care NHS Trust* [2005] UKHL 58, [2006] 2 AC 148.
[215] *Munjaz v UK* App No 2913/06, 17 July 2012.
[216] *Herczegfalvy v Austria* (1992) 15 EHRR 437, para 82.
[217] ibid. See eg *Jalloh v Germany* (2007) 44 EHRR 32, para 69; *R (B) v Ashworth Hospital Authority* [2005] UKHL 20, [2005] 2 AC 278.
[218] *Assenov v Bulgaria* (1998) 28 EHRR 652; *Šečić v Croatia* (2007) 23 BHRC 24; *Opuz v Turkey* (2009) 27 BHRC 159.
[219] *Bouyid v Belgium* (2016) 62 EHRR 32, para 117.

to be effective, the institutions and persons responsible for carrying it out must be independent from those targeted by it, which requires not only a lack of any hierarchical or institutional connection but also practical independence;[220] (b) the authorities must act of their own motion; (c) to be effective, the investigation must be capable of leading to the identification and punishment of those responsible; (d) although not an obligation of results to be achieved but of means to be employed, any deficiency in the investigation which undermines its ability to establish the cause of injuries or the identity of the persons response will risk falling foul of the required standard of effectiveness; (e) there is an implicit requirement of promptness and reasonable expedition; (f) the victim should be able to participate effectively in the investigation; and (g) the investigation must be thorough, which means that the authorities must always make a serious attempt to find out what happened and should not rely on hasty or ill-founded conclusions to close their investigation.[221]

In *Husayn (Abu Zubaydah) v Poland* the Court considered that the Polish government had failed to conduct an appropriate investigation into '*prima facie* credible allegations' that terrorist suspects were detained and tortured on its territory.[222] The Polish parliamentary inquiry that took place was clearly inadequate as it was conducted in private and produced no findings.   5.115

In *R (AM) v Secretary of State for the Home Department* a majority of the Court of Appeal held that the government had failed to satisfy its obligation to investigate ill-treatment during a disturbance at an immigration detention centre where detainees were kept confined while water leaked into their cells and then ordered into the exercise yard while still wet.[223] The Court of Appeal rejected the proposition that because the victim in an Article 3 claim was still alive and therefore had recourse to law, the investigation was not governed by the same principles as those under Article 2. The Court held that the primary question was whether the victim could secure adequate investigation without an ad hoc inquiry instituted by the state. The purpose of the investigation was, as under Article 2, to maximize future compliance with Article 3.[224] The case law on the obligation under Article 2 should therefore be considered equally applicable to Article 3.   5.116

As a result of allegations of ill-treatment of Iraqi detainees by UK forces, the government has been forced to establish two public inquiries. The Baha Mousa Inquiry reported its findings in 2011. The report concluded British soldiers had subjected detainees to 'serious, gratuitous violence' and made 73 recommendations to improve the treatment of detainees in British custody. The Al Sweady Inquiry   5.117

---

[220] In *Re McQuillan's Application for Judicial Review* [2021] UKSC 55, [2022] AC 1063 the Supreme Court stated that it did not understand the ECtHR as dictating that there should be complete hierarchical or institutional disconnection as 'there are ways in which a state can inject independence into the structure of hierarchies and institutions' (para 111).

[221] *Bouyid v Belgium* (2016) 62 EHRR 32, paras 118–23. See also *In re McQuillan's Application for Judicial Review* [2021] UKSC 55, [2022] AC 106, para 109.

[222] *Husayn (Abu Zubaydah) v Poland* (2015) 60 EHRR 16.

[223] *R (AM) v Secretary of State for the Home Department* [2009] EWCA Civ 219, [2009] UKHRR 973.

[224] ibid para 57.

into the abuse and unlawful killing of Iraqi detainees at a British military camp reported on 17 December 2014, concluding that certain aspects of the way in which the detainees were treated by the British military, during the time they were in British custody during 2004, amounted to actual or possible ill-treatment and making a number or recommendations. The Ministry of Defence established the Iraq Historic Allegations Team (IHAT) in 2010 to investigate further claims of mistreatment. The IHAT was closed in June 2017 and the remaining investigations were reintegrated into the service police system. The High Court found that the IHAT was sufficiently independent to satisfy the procedural requirements of Article 3 but ordered the Secretary of State to provide additional safeguards, including the appointment of a judge to oversee the investigations.[225]

5.118   Following applications for judicial review by relatives of Afghan civilians alleged to have been shot dead by UK forces in night raids (*Saifullah v Secretary of State for Defence*[226] and *Noorzai v Secretary of State for Defence*), the Ministry of Defence on 15 December 2022 established an independent statutory inquiry, to be led by a senior judge, to investigate and report on allegations of wrongdoing by the British Armed Forces in relation to their conduct of deliberate detention operations in Afghanistan between 2010 and 2013.

5.119   Finally, the investigative duty extends to Article 3 ill-treatment inflicted by third parties.[227]

(b) Prevention

5.120   As well as refraining from inflicting treatment violating Article 3, states also have a positive obligation to prevent it. This obligation means that states must take certain steps to ensure that individuals within their jurisdiction are not subjected to torture or other forms of ill-treatment, including that administered by private individuals or agents of other states.[228] Furthermore, the positive obligation to prevent harm must be interpreted in a way which is not incompatible with other Convention rights. For example, social workers cannot take such extreme steps to protect a child from the potential risk of harm in a family that they disproportionately infringe the child's right to respect for his family life under Article 8.[229]

5.121   For a positive operational obligation to arise it must be established that the authorities knew or ought to have known at the time of the existence of a real and immediate risk of ill-treatment of an identified individual from the criminal acts of a third party and that they failed to take measures within the scope of their powers which, judged reasonably, might have been expected to avoid that risk.[230] Further, it is not necessary to show 'but for' the state omission the ill-treatment would not have happened. A failure to take reasonably available measures which could have

---

[225] *R (Mousa) v Secretary of State for Defence (No 2)* [2013] EWHC 1412 (Admin), [2013] HRLR 32.
[226] *Saifullah v Secretary of State for Defence* [2022] EWHC 3328 (Admin).
[227] *Commissioner for Police of the Metropolis v DSD* [2018] UKSC 11, [2019] AC 196.
[228] *Mahmut Kaya v Turkey* (1999) 28 EHRR 1; *Z and others v UK* (2002) 34 EHRR 3; *Husayn (Abu Zubaydah) v Poland* (2015) 60 EHRR 16.
[229] *Re B* [2008] UKHL 35, [2009] 1 AC 11.
[230] *X and others v Bulgaria* (2021) 50 BHRC 344, para 183.

had a real prospect of altering the outcome or mitigating the harm is sufficient to engage the responsibility of the state.[231]

In *A v UK* the child applicant had been hit by his stepfather with a stick.[232] The stepfather was charged with assault occasioning actual bodily harm. The stepfather contended that the assault amounted to reasonable punishment, which was a defence to a charge of assault of a child by a parent, and he was acquitted. The ECtHR decided that there was a violation of Article 3 because the law failed adequately to protect the child by insufficiently defining what constituted 'reasonable punishment'.[233]

As a result of the decision, Parliament introduced section 58 of the Children Act 2004 to remove the defence of reasonable punishment to charges of assault occasioning actual bodily harm. However, it is still possible to raise the defence in cases of common assault. Section 58 has yet to be considered by the ECtHR.[234]

In both *Z v UK*[235] and *E v UK*[236] the ECtHR found that the UK had breached Article 3 in failing to protect children from prolonged abuse and neglect which the authorities knew about. In *E*, they had failed to monitor the family after a stepfather had been convicted of sexual abuse. The ECtHR held that 'a failure to take reasonably available measures which could have had a real prospect of altering the outcome or mitigating the harm is sufficient to engage the responsibility of the state'.[237] In *O'Keeffe v Ireland* the Grand Chamber held that the Irish authorities had failed to protect primary school children from sexual abuse.[238]

The ECtHR has considered state obligations in relation to domestic violence. It held in *Eremia v Moldova*[239] that failure properly to investigate or to support a complainant of domestic violence amounted to condoning the discriminatory attitudes which underlay it, contrary to Articles 3 and 14.

The House of Lords considered the extent of the obligation to prevent harm in *Re E*.[240] Catholic schoolgirls on their way to school in Northern Ireland were subjected to a barrage of abuse over a number of months by protestors lining their route to school. The House was in no doubt that the children had been subjected

5.122

5.123

5.124

5.125

5.126

---

[231] *O'Keeffe v Ireland* [2014] 35 BHRC 601, para 149.

[232] *A v UK* (1998) 5 BHRC 137.

[233] *A v UK* (1999) 27 EHRR 611. See also *Tyrer v UK* (1978) 2 EHRR 1; *Campbell v UK* (1982) 4 EHRR 293; and *Costello-Roberts v UK* (1993) 19 EHRR 112.

[234] In *Northern Ireland Commissioner for Children and Young Peoples' Application* [2007] NIQB 115, the Northern Ireland High Court considered that the law satisfied art 3. The Court of Appeal held that the Commissioner was not a victim under the Human Rights Act and did not consider the substantive issue: [2009] NICA 10.

[235] *Z v UK* (2002) 34 EHRR 97.

[236] *E v UK* (2003) 36 EHRR 519.

[237] ibid para 99.

[238] *O'Keeffe v Ireland* [2014] 35 BHRC 601. See, by contrast, the decision of the Grand Chamber in *X and others v Bulgaria* (2021) 50 BHRC 344 [GC], paras 197–99, where the ECtHR found no breach of the positive duty in art 3 to take preventative operational measures where children in an orphanage had been subject to sexual abuse.

[239] *Eremia v Moldova* (2014) 58 EHRR 2. See also *Volodina v Russia* App No 41261/17, 9 July 2019, paras 78, 85, and 91.

[240] *Re E* [2008] UKHL 66, [2008] 3 WLR 1208.

to inhuman and degrading treatment, but found that the police had done all they reasonably could to protect the children from harm.[241]

5.127 In *Commissioner of Police for the Metropolis v DSD* the Supreme Court held that Article 3 applied to operational failures as well as to systemic failures, but only 'conspicuous or substantial errors' in investigation would qualify.[242] The Court found that the catalogue of failures by the police, which were systemic as well as operational, amounted to a breach of Article 3.[243]

5.128 As the ECtHR made clear in the case of *Pretty v UK*, the positive obligation to prevent ill-treatment does not extend to the provision of a lawful opportunity for assisted suicide in circumstances of significant physical and mental suffering.[244]

(c) Deportation and removal

5.129 The positive obligation also manifests itself in the principle established in the *Soering* case that a state may not extradite an individual to a country where there are substantial grounds for believing that there is a real risk that he or she would be subjected to torture or ill-treatment.[245]

5.130 In *Chahal v UK* the ECtHR made it plain that the question of whether Article 3 prevented deportation was not influenced by the fact that the individual under threat of deportation posed a threat to national security.[246]

5.131 This issue was revisited in *Saadi v Italy*, in which the UK intervened to argue that the *Chahal* principle should be modified to allow a degree of risk of torture to be balanced against the threat posed to the public or the state.[247] The Grand Chamber unanimously rejected these arguments and robustly reasserted the absolute character of Article 3. It was not possible to distinguish between torture by a Convention state and torture by another state to which the Convention state has removed the victim.[248]

5.132 Domestic courts have grappled with the implications of these decisions on a number of occasions. *R (Bagdanavicius) v Secretary of State for the Home Department* concerned a Lithuanian family who claimed that they were at risk, due to their Roma origins, of inhuman or degrading treatment from non-state actors if returned to Lithuania.[249] The House of Lords held that on any claim against removal on Article 3 grounds the court had to make an assessment of conditions in the receiving country so that it could determine whether there was a real risk of ill-treatment when returned, which would violate Article 3. As any harm inflicted by non-state agents would not violate Article 3 unless the state had failed to provide reasonable

---

[241] The claim failed in the ECtHR, see *PF and EF v UK* App No 28326/09, 23 November 2010.
[242] *Commissioner of Police for the Metropolis v DSD* [2018] UKSC 11, [2019] AC 196, paras 29–30 per Lord Kerr; paras 85, 93 per Lord Neuberger.
[243] *Commissioner of Police for the Metropolis v DSD* [2018] UKSC 11, [2019] AC 196.
[244] *Pretty v UK* (2002) 35 EHRR 1. See also *R (Nicklinson) v Ministry of Justice* [2014] UKSC 38, [2015] AC 657.
[245] *Soering v UK* (1989) 11 EHRR 439.
[246] *Chahal v UK* (1997) 23 EHRR 413.
[247] *Saadi v Italy* (2008) 24 BHRC 123.
[248] ibid para 138.
[249] *R (Bagdanavicius) v Secretary of State for the Home Department* [2005] UKHL 38, [2005] 2 AC 668.

protection, to avoid expulsion on Article 3 grounds an individual must establish, first, a real risk of suffering serious harm from non-state agents, and secondly, that the receiving country did not provide a reasonable level of protection against such harm for those within its territory. The test was not satisfied in this case.

In *R (Wellington) v Secretary of State for the Home Department* the House of Lords   5.133
considered the application of Article 3 to the extradition of a murder suspect to Missouri.[250] If found guilty, the appellant would automatically receive a sentence of life imprisonment without parole. The sentence could only be reduced by the governor, who had almost never exercised his right to commute such sentences. Relying on a passage in the ECtHR's decision in *Soering*, Lord Hoffmann held that 'the desirability of extradition is a factor to be taken into account in deciding whether the punishment likely to be imposed in the receiving state attains the "minimum level of severity" which would make it inhuman and degrading'.[251] As he accepted, this creates a 'relativist' approach to the scope of inhuman and degrading treatment.[252] Applying this reasoning, the majority of the House held that an irreducible sentence might breach Article 3 domestically, but if imposed by a foreign country it would only contravene Article 3 if it were disproportionate to the crime committed.[253] The ECtHR gave detailed consideration to the reasoning of the House of Lords in *Harkins and Edwards v UK*.[254] It disapproved of Lord Hoffman's view, stating that an assessment of the minimum level of severity under Article 3 should not be informed by the reasons for extradition.[255]

The House of Lords considered the adequacy of diplomatic assurances to prevent   5.134
a violation of Article 3 in *RB (Algeria) v Secretary of State for the Home Department*.[256] Their Lordships held that the two terrorist suspects could be deported because the government could properly rely on the assurances made by Algeria and Jordan that they would not be mistreated. This was so despite the fact that the assurances did not entirely eliminate the risk of mistreatment.[257] In *Othman v UK* the ECtHR considered the Jordanian assurances and accepted that they were adequate.[258] In *Khasanov and Rakhmanov v Russia* the Grand Chamber held that assurances are not in themselves sufficient to ensure adequate protection against the risk of ill-treatment. The weight to be given to assurances from the receiving state depends, in each case, on the circumstances prevailing at the material time.[259] The Supreme

---

[250] *R (Wellington) v Secretary of State for the Home Department* [2008] UKHL 72, [2009] 2 WLR 48.
[251] ibid para 24.
[252] ibid para 27.
[253] Baroness Hale and Lord Carswell agreed with Lord Hoffmann. Lord Brown and Lord Scott preferred to interpret art 3 as imposing an absolute standard.
[254] *Harkins and Edwards v UK* (2018) 66 EHRR SE5.
[255] ibid para 124.
[256] *RB (Algeria) v Secretary of State for the Home Department* [2009] UKHL 10, [2009] 2 WLR 512, applied in *Inzunza v USA* [2011] EWHC 920 (Admin).
[257] *RB (Algeria) v Secretary of State for the Home Department* [2009] UKHL 10, [2009] 2 WLR 512, para 114 per Lord Phillips.
[258] *Othman (Abu Qatada) v UK* (2012) 55 EHRR 1.
[259] *Khasanov and Rakhmanov v Russia* (2022) 75 EHRR 19, para 101.

Court has accepted assurances given by a receiving state were sufficient to remove any real risk of ill-treatment contrary to Article 3 in *Lord Advocate v Dean*[260] and in *Zabolotnyi v Hungary*.[261] Most recently in *R (AAA (Syria)) v Secretary of State for the Home Department* the Supreme Court held that the policy of removing asylum-seekers to Rwanda, where their asylum claims would be considered, breached Article 3 as there were substantial grounds for believing that there is a real risk that persons sent to Rwanda will be returned to their home countries where they faced persecution or other inhumane treatment when, in fact, they have a good claim for asylum.[262]

5.135   In a dramatic extension of the *Soering* principle, the ECtHR held in *D v UK* that deportation of the applicant who suffered from HIV/AIDS to his home country where he would not receive adequate medical treatment would violate Article 3.[263] The applicant was near death and the ECtHR referred to the 'very exceptional circumstances' of the case and the 'compelling humanitarian considerations at stake'.[264] Since the decision in *D* there has been some back and forth as to the applicable test in such cases.

5.136   In *N v Secretary of State for the Home Department* the House of Lords unanimously held that returning a seriously ill, HIV-positive woman to Uganda would not constitute inhuman or degrading treatment.[265] It was accepted that her condition had stabilized after lengthy medical treatment in the UK, and that she would remain well for 'decades' if this continued; in Uganda, this treatment would not be accessible to her and the inevitable outcome of this would be an early death 'after a period of acute physical and mental suffering'.[266] Their Lordships distinguished *D v UK* as *N*'s present medical condition was not critical and she remained fit to travel.

5.137   *N* confirmed that the domestic courts regarded the *D* case to be wholly exceptional, and that the obligation not to remove on health grounds will be triggered only in very extreme factual circumstances. The ECtHR affirmed the correctness of the House of Lords' approach, emphasizing that expulsion of an alien who is suffering from a serious mental or physical illness to a country where the facilities for the treatment of that illness are inferior to those available in the deporting state will only raise an issue under Article 3 in a very exceptional case.[267]

5.138   In *Paposhvili v Belgium* the Grand Chamber revisited its decisions in *D* and in *N*.[268] The ECtHR held that the applicant's deportation to Georgia would (amongst

---

[260] *Lord Advocate v Dean* [2017] UKSC 44, [2017] 1 WLR 2721.
[261] *Zabolotnyi v Hungary* [2021] UKSC 14, [2021] 1 WLR 2569.
[262] *R (AAA (Syria)) v Secretary of State for the Home Department* [2023] UKHL 42; [2023] 1 WLR 4433 at paras 101–105.
[263] *D v UK* (1997) 24 EHRR 423. cf *Bensaid v UK* (2001) 33 EHRR 205.
[264] *D v UK* (1997) 24 EHRR 423, para 54.
[265] *N v Secretary of State for the Home Department* [2005] UKHL 31, [2005] 2 AC 296.
[266] ibid para 20, per Lord Hope.
[267] *N v UK* (2008) 47 EHRR 39. See also *Yoh-Ekale Mwanje v Belgium* (2013) 56 EHRR 35 where the ECtHR held that the return of the HIV-positive applicant to Cameroon, where she would be unable to receive antiretroviral therapy, would not violate her rights under art 3, observing that the case was indistinguishable from the Grand Chamber's decision in *N* (at para 80).
[268] *Paposhvili v Belgium* [2017] Imm AR 867.

other things) breach his rights under Article 3 in light of his grave hill-health. The applicant had suffered from chronic lymphocytic leukaemia for 10 years. He was receiving treatment (without which he would be likely to die within six months) and if he remained in Belgium there was the possibility of a transplant which would provide a cure. Neither the treatment nor the transplant was available in Georgia.

The Grand Chamber stated that the views expressed previously should be 'clarified'.[269] It stated that the 'other very exceptional cases' referred to in *N* which may raise an issue under Article 3 should be understood to refer to situations involving the removal of a seriously ill person in which substantial grounds have been shown for believing that he or she, 'although not at imminent risk of dying, would face a real risk, on account of the absence of appropriate treatment in the receiving country or the lack of access to such treatment, of being exposed to a serious, rapid and irreversible decline in his or her state of health resulting in intense suffering or to a significant reduction in life expectancy'.[270] Where the applicant adduces such evidence, the state must subject the risk to close scrutiny, and consider the foreseeable consequences of removal for the individual concerned in the receiving state.[271]   5.139

The Supreme Court considered the effect of the judgment in *Paposhvili* in *AM (Zimbabwe) v Secretary of State for the Home Department*.[272] The Court noted that the application of the new test to the *N* case would suggest a violation of Article 3.[273] The Court held that the Court of Appeal had been wrong to conclude that 'a significant reduction in life expectancy' meant 'the imminence of death'; rather 'significant' here means 'substantial', and only a substantial reduction in life expectancy would reach the level of severity required by Article 3.[274] The Court noted that Grand Chamber in *Paposhvili* held that it was for the applicant to adduce evidence 'capable of demonstrating that there are substantial grounds for believing' that if removed, he or she would be exposed to a real risk of being subjected to treatment contrary to Article 3.[275] The Court noted that this was a demanding threshold for an applicant to cross.[276] The Court held that in the light of the judgment in *Paposhvili,* the Court should now depart from the decision of the House of Lords in *N*.[277]   5.140

Finally in *Savran v Denmark* the Grand Chamber considered the removal of a Turkish national with paranoid schizophrenia from Denmark. The Grand Chamber confirmed that the standard set out in *Paposhvili* applies to mental illness.[278] The Chamber had found there to be a breach of Article 3.[279] The Grand Chamber held   5.141

---

[269] *Paposhvili v Belgium* [2017] Imm AR 867 [GC], para 182.
[270] ibid para 183.
[271] ibid paras 187–91.
[272] *AM (Zimbabwe) v Secretary of State for the Home Department* [2020] UKSC 17, [2021] AC 633.
[273] ibid paras 22, 27.
[274] ibid paras 30–31.
[275] ibid para 23.
[276] ibid para 32.
[277] ibid para 34.
[278] *Savran v Denmark* (2021) 53 BHRC 201 [GC], paras 137–39.
[279] *Savran v Denmark* [2019] ECHR 651.

that in reaching that conclusion, the Chamber had not assessed the case from the standpoint of the threshold test established in *Paposhvili*.[280] It was only after the threshold had been met that the returning state's obligation to dispel any doubts comes into play.[281]

5.142   In *A v France* the Divisional Court held that the *Paposhvili* and *Savran* line of Strasbourg cases did not apply to extradition cases. The Court identified a fundamental difference between immigration and extradition cases: that Member States owe a duty of care to prisoners, but no such duty is owed in relation to healthcare provision generally.[282]

5.143   The courts have shown some willingness to consider health claims under Article 8, which does not impose the high threshold of Article 3.[283]

(d) State support

5.144   The application of Article 3 to welfare provision has not frequently been considered by the ECtHR. In *O'Rourke v UK* the applicant was evicted from temporary accommodation provided for him when he came out of prison.[284] He lived on the streets, to the detriment of his various medical conditions. In an admissibility decision, the Strasbourg Court held that this experience did not attain the requisite level of severity to engage Article 3.

5.145   The Court of Appeal and House of Lords have found that denying state support to individuals lacking other means of subsistence or shelter may amount to inhuman or degrading treatment.[285] Distinguishing the decision in *O'Rourke*, the House of Lords held in *R (Limbuela) v Secretary of State for the Home Department* that a decision to withdraw support to an asylum-seeker under section 55 of the Nationality, Immigration and Asylum Act 2002 violated Article 3.[286] In determining whether treatment in a particular case had reached the minimum level of severity required by Article 3, the court was not to apply a more exacting test where the treatment or punishment which would otherwise be found to be inhuman or degrading was the result of legitimate government policy. The correct test was for the court to look at the context and facts of the particular case, including factors such as the age, sex, and health of the claimant, and the length of time spent or likely to be spent without the required means of support, and ask whether the 'entire package' of work restrictions and deprivations that surrounded the claimant was so severe that it could properly be described as inhuman or degrading treatment. The threshold of severity will be crossed where a person deprived of support under section 55 is obliged to sleep in the street, or is seriously hungry or unable to satisfy the most basic requirements of hygiene.

---

[280] *Savran v Denmark* (2021) 53 BHRC 201, para 140.

[281] ibid paras 135, 140.

[282] *A v France* [2022] EWHC 841 (Admin), para 54.

[283] See eg *R (SQ) v Upper Tribunal Immigration and Asylum Chamber* [2013] EWCA Civ 1251.

[284] *O'Rourke v UK* App No 39022/97, 26 June 2001.

[285] *R (Limbuela) v Secretary of State for the Home Department* [2005] UKHL 66, [2006] 1 AC 396. See also *R (Q and others) v Secretary of State for the Home Department* [2003] EWCA Civ 364, [2004] QB 36.

[286] *R (Limbuela) v Secretary of State for the Home Department* [2005] UKHL 66, [2006] 1 AC 396.

Subsequently in *MSS v Belgium and Greece* the Grand Chamber held that Greece 5.146
had breached Article 3 by failing to provide for the most basic needs for food,
hygiene, and shelter for an asylum-seeker who had spent many months living on
the streets in extreme poverty.[287] More recently, in *R (NB) v Secretary of State for
the Home Department* the Court held that the accommodation of asylum-seekers in
former military barracks did not breach Article 3.[288]

(e) *Self-inflicted conditions*

In cases concerning political prisoners the ECtHR has been faced with the ques- 5.147
tion of whether the fact that harm is self-inflicted negates or dilutes a state's positive obligation under Article 3.[289] Following periods on hunger strike a number
of Turkish prisoners suffered physical and mental effects of malnutrition, which
in some cases took an extreme form (irreversible brain damage). The ECtHR held
that, while the Convention could not be interpreted as laying down a 'general obligation' to release a detainee on health grounds, the prisoner's clinical picture was
now one of the factors which a state must take into account under Article 3 in
assessing a person's fitness for detention.

The ECtHR found that their imprisonment violated Article 3, and that the 5.148
self-inflicted nature of their conditions did not release Turkey from its Article 3
obligations.[290]

In *Hassan-Daniel v HMRC* the Court of Appeal, considering the state's obliga- 5.149
tions to a drug smuggler who died from ingestion of drugs while in detention,
found that the criminality defence, which holds that it is offensive to public notions
of fairness to compensate someone for their own criminal conduct in civil claims,
did not apply to claims brought under the Human Rights Act 1998.[291]

E. ARTICLE 4: PROHIBITION OF SLAVERY AND FORCED LABOUR

Article 4 concerns the twin issues of slavery or servitude (art 4(1)) and forced or 5.150
compulsory labour (art 4(2)). Article 4(1) is another of the absolute rights from
which no derogation is allowed under Article 15. The Article 4(2) prohibition—
while absolute (in the sense that interferences cannot be justified)—is derogable
under Article 15.

Jurisprudence on Article 4—both international and domestic—has seen signifi- 5.151
cant development over a relatively short period, particularly in relation to human
trafficking.

---

[287] *MSS v Belgium and Greece* (2011) 53 EHRR 2, paras 249–64.
[288] *R (NB) v Secretary of State for the Home Department* [2021] EWHC 1489 (Admin), [2021] 4 WLR 92,
paras 265–67. The Court found, however, that the standard of failed to comply with the Immigration and
Asylum Act 1999, s 96, read with Council Directive 2003/9/EC.
[289] See eg *Tekin Yildiz v Turkey* App No 22913/04, 10 November 2005.
[290] ibid.
[291] *Hassan-Daniel v HMRC* [2010] EWCA Civ 1443, [2011] QB 866.

1. Slavery and servitude

5.152 'Slavery' was defined by the ECtHR in 2005. In *Siliadin v France* the ECtHR drew on historical notions, citing the Slavery Convention of 1926: 'slavery is the status or condition of a person over whom any or all of the powers attaching to the right of ownership are exercised'.[292] For four years the applicant, a minor at the time, whose passport was confiscated and who had no immigration status, worked for private individuals against her will and without pay, although no physical force was used. The ECtHR held that this constituted servitude and forced labour, but not slavery.

5.153 'Servitude' differs from slavery in that no ownership of the person is claimed. It includes, 'in addition to the obligation to perform certain services for others ... the obligation of the "serf" to live on another person's property and the impossibility of altering his condition'.[293]

5.154 In *CN and V v France* the ECtHR clarified the distinction between servitude and forced labour, stating that servitude is an aggravated form of forced labour that depends on the victim's belief, based on objective evidence, that their situation is immutable.[294] It found that one of the applicants—a national of Burundi—had been 'effectively kept in a state of servitude' by relatives in France, where as a minor and then an adult she was responsible for all household chores, seven days a week, with 'no time for leisure activities'; 'could not free herself from their hold without placing herself in an illegal situation'; and 'had the feeling that her condition ... was permanent and could not change'.[295]

2. Forced or compulsory labour

5.155 The Strasbourg approach to the concept of 'labour' is a generous one. It is not limited to physical labour and encompasses all forms of work,[296] including (eg) sex work.[297]

5.156 In order for labour to be forced or compulsory, the work or service must be 'extracted from the person under the menace of any penalty' and the person must not have offered or consented to perform it voluntarily.[298] Both concepts have been interpreted widely. Thus, the 'menace of any penalty' extends beyond threats of physical violence and encompasses threats of (eg) denouncing a person without status or work rights to the police or immigration authorities.[299] The concepts of voluntariness and consent take account of potential abuse of power or

---

[292] *Siliadin v France* (2005) BHRC 654, para 122.

[293] ibid para 123.

[294] *CN and V v France* App No 67724/09, 11 October 2012; see also *Chowdury v Greece* App No 21884/15, 30 March 2017, para 99.

[295] *CN and V v France* App No 67724/09, 11 October 2012, paras 74, 88–92.

[296] *Van der Mussele v Belgium* (1983) 6 EHRR 163.

[297] See eg *SM v Croatia* (2021) 72 EHRR 1, paras 300, 303(iii).

[298] *Siliadin v France* (2005) 20 BHRC 654, clarifying earlier case law of the ECmHR; *X v Germany* (1974) 17 YB 148, drawing on the International Labour Organization Convention of 1930.

[299] See eg *CN and V v France* App No 67724/09, 11 October 2012, paras 77–78; *SM v Croatia* (2021) 72 EHRR 1, para 284.

vulnerability.[300] Whether work has been undertaken voluntarily, particularly where there has been prior consent, falls to be determined in light of all relevant circumstances.[301]

The scope of the prohibition is delimited by Article 4(3), which provides that   5.157
forced or compulsory labour 'shall not include' the following.[302] First, 'any work required to be done in the ordinary course of detention imposed according to the provisions of Article 5 of [the] Convention or during conditional release from such detention'. This means that complaints about the level of pay for working prisoners or their exclusion from the state's social security system are generally inadmissible under, or at least cannot give rise to breaches of, Article 4.[303] Secondly, 'any service of a military character or, in case of conscientious objectors in countries where they are recognised, service exacted instead of compulsory military service'. In *Chitos v Greece* the ECtHR held that this carve-out related only to 'compulsory military service in States where such a system is in place', and hence that the applicant's conditions of compulsory service as an army medic in exchange for free tertiary study were capable of constituting forced labour.[304] Thirdly, 'any service exacted in case of an emergency or calamity threatening the life or well-being of the community'. This carve-out appears seldom to have been relied on, but the ECmHR has found that it included an obligation on holders of shooting rights to participate in the gassing of foxholes to protect against rabies.[305] Fourthly, 'any work or service which forms part of normal civic obligations'. One example is compulsory jury service.[306]

Outside the context of human trafficking and modern slavery (as to which see paras   5.158
5.160–5.165), the complaints deemed admissible under Article 4(2) have included complaints concerning the treatment of prisoners (often resulting in consideration of the first carve-out discussed above); professionals compelled to provide their services free to the community; and people engaged in domestic labour. As to professional services, in *Van der Mussele v Belgium* a barrister tried to extend the boundaries of Article 4 when he claimed that being made to do *pro bono* legal work for indigent defendants violated the prohibition on forced labour.[307] The ECtHR asked whether the labour

---

[300] See eg *Chowdury v Greece* [2017] ECHR 300, para 96; *SM v Croatia* (2021) 72 EHRR 1, para 285.

[301] *Chowdury v Greece* App No 21884/15, 30 March 2017, paras 90, 96; *SM v Croatia* (2021) 72 EHRR 1, para 285. Thus, eg, the fact that a person initially offers themselves for work voluntarily and believes in good faith that they will be paid does not exclude the possibility of forced labour if the situation later changes as a result of the employer's conduct: *Zoletic v Azerbaijan* (2022) 75 EHRR 10, para 167. For an interesting example see *Mentes v Turkey* (2018) 67 EHRR 13.

[302] The ECtHR has stressed that the purpose of art 4(3) is not to 'limit' the right protected by art 4(3) but to 'delimit' its content: *Stummer v Austria* (2012) 54 EHRR 11, para 120. It therefore 'forms a whole with paragraph 2 and indicates what is not considered forced or compulsory labour': *Chitos v Greece* App No 51637/12, 4 June 2015, para 80. These carve-outs do not apply to situations properly characterized as slavery or servitude: see the decision of the ECmHR in *X, Y and Z v United Kingdom* App No 3435/67 and others, 19 July 1968.

[303] See eg *Stummer v Austria* (2012) 54 EHRR 11. See also *Meier v Switzerland* App No 10109/14, 9 February 2016 (concerning compulsory prison work after retirement age).

[304] *Chitos v Greece* App No 51637/12, 4 June 2015.

[305] *S v Germany* App No 9686/82, 4 October 1984.

[306] *Adami v Malta* App No 17209/02, 20 June 2006.

[307] *Van der Mussele v Belgium* (1983) 6 EHRR 163. See also *Steindel v Germany* App No 29878/07, 14 September 2010.

imposed 'a burden which was so excessive or disproportionate to the advantages attached to the future exercise of the profession that the service could not be treated as having been voluntarily accepted'.[308] Ruling against the barrister, the ECtHR relied on the fact that he had entered the profession of his own will, knowing that *pro bono* work was expected of him.[309] In the context of domestic labour, in *CN v France* the ECtHR considered work undertaken for family members; it used the notion of a 'disproportionate burden' to assess whether the applicants had been subjected to forced or compulsory labour, finding for one and not the other on the facts.[310]

5.159   Article 4 has rarely—again, outside the context of human trafficking—been raised in the domestic courts.[311] The House of Lords in *Sepet v Secretary of State for the Home Department* rejected an argument that Article 4 recognized a fundamental right to refuse to undertake military service on grounds of conscience.[312] The Supreme Court applied *Van de Mussele* in *R (Reilly) v Secretary of State for Work and Pensions*.[313] It found that the requirement that a person undertake unpaid work as a condition of receiving jobseeker's allowance did not amount to forced labour.

3. Human trafficking

5.160   In the seminal case of *Rantsev v Cyprus and Russia* the ECtHR held that, '[i]n view of its obligation to interpret the Convention in light of present-day conditions', human trafficking (as defined in art 3(a) of the Palermo Protocol and art 4(a) of the European Convention Against Trafficking (ECAT)) 'falls within the scope of Article 4'.[314] The UK domestic courts have consistently endorsed this approach.

5.161   Human trafficking is defined in Article 4 of ECAT as: 'the recruitment, transportation, transfer, harbouring or receipt of persons, by means of the threat or use of force or other forms of coercion, of abduction, of fraud, of deception, of the abuse of power or of a position of vulnerability or of the giving or receiving of payments or benefits to achieve the consent of a person having control over another person, for the purpose of exploitation'.

5.162   The definition is often (and helpfully) broken down into three elements.[315] The first is an *act*—a person must be recruited, transported, transferred, harboured,

---

[308] *Van der Mussele v Belgium* (1983) 6 EHRR 163, para 37. The same approach was applied in *Chitos v Greece* App No 51637/12, 4 June 2015: see the reference at para 96 to a 'disproportionate burden'.

[309] cf *Zarb Adami v Malta* (2006) 20 BHRC 703. A similar conclusion was reached more recently in *Danoiu v Romania* App No 54780/15, 25 January 2022.

[310] *CN v France* App No 67724/09, 11 October 2012.

[311] In addition to the two House of Lords' decisions discussed here, art 4 was raised in the planning context in *MacLeod v Secretary of State for Communities and Local Government* [2008] EWHC 384 (Admin). The challenge was rejected as plainly unarguable.

[312] *Sepet v Secretary of State for the Home Department* [2003] UKHL 15, [2003] 3 All ER 304.

[313] *R (Reilly) v Secretary of State for Work and Pensions* [2013] UKSC 68, [2014] AC 453.

[314] *Rantsev v Cyprus* 28 BHRC 313, paras 272–82. The Grand Chamber did not consider it necessary to decide whether human trafficking—generally or as suffered in the case before it—fell under art 4(1) or art 4(2).

[315] This breakdown was referred to with apparent approval by the Grand Chamber in *SM v Croatia* (2021) 72 EHRR 1, paras 302 and 303(ii).

or received. The second is the use of a specified *means*—the person must be (eg) recruited 'by means of' force (violence); the threat of force; other forms of coercion; abduction; fraud; deception; the abuse of power; or the abuse of a position of vulnerability. Where any of these means have been used, the fact that the victim consented to the intended exploitation is irrelevant to whether they were trafficked.[316] Where the victim is a child, the 'means' element does not need to be present for the definition to be met.[317] The third element is the *purpose*, which must be exploitation.[318] The definition of trafficking specifies that exploitation 'shall include, at a minimum, the exploitation of the prostitution of others or other forms of sexual exploitation, forced labour or services, slavery or practices similar to slavery, servitude or the removal of organs'. The list (as appears on its face) is not exhaustive: for example, the UK courts have held that forced marriage is 'necessarily' a form of exploitation for the purposes of the trafficking definition.[319] Detailed discussion of each element of the definition is beyond the scope of this text.

The Grand Chamber in *SM v Croatia*—reaffirming the conclusion reached in *Rantsev v Cyprus*[320]—stressed that that all three elements must be present for a case of trafficking to fall within Article 4.[321]   5.163

For completeness, 'modern slavery' is an umbrella term often used to encompass slavery, servitude, forced or compulsory labour, and human trafficking.   5.164

The UK has sought to give effect to its obligations under ECAT, and to combat modern slavery more broadly, via the establishment of the 'National Referral Mechanism' (NRM) for victims of modern slavery; the promulgation of associated guidance;[322] and the enactment of the Modern Slavery Act 2015. The identification of victims under the NRM is a three-stage process: a person is referred by a 'first responder'; receives a 'reasonable grounds' decision from one of the 'competent authorities',[323] which determines whether there are 'reasonable grounds to believe that an individual is a victim of slavery or human trafficking'; and finally receives a 'conclusive grounds' decision, which determines this status on the balance of probabilities.[324] These decisions, and associated matters such as the level and duration of the support received by potential or confirmed victims of trafficking, have   5.165

---

[316] ECAT, art 4(b).

[317] ECAT, art 4(c)–(d).

[318] For a discussion of the closeness of connection required to establish 'purpose', see *R (MN) v Secretary of State for the Home Department* [2020] EWCA Civ 1746, [2021] 1 WLR 1956, paras 333–43.

[319] ibid para 335 (noting that this was the conclusion of the Court below and that it had not been challenged on appeal).

[320] *Rantsev v Cyprus* (2010) 51 EHRR 1, paras 292–93, 303(i).

[321] *SM v Croatia* (2021) 72 EHRR 1, paras 290, 303(ii).

[322] At the time of writing the current guidance, promulgated under the Modern Slavery Act 2015, s 49, is *Modern Slavery: Statutory Guidance for England and Wales and Non-Statutory Guidance for Scotland and Northern Ireland*, v 3.1, January 2023.

[323] Currently there are two: the 'Single Competent Authority' and the 'Immigration Enforcement Competent Authority'.

[324] This standard was affirmed as lawful in *R (MN) v Secretary of State for the Home Department* [2020] EWCA Civ 1746, [2021] 1 WLR 1956.

generated a considerable body of domestic jurisprudence drawing on relevant provisions of ECAT[325] and on Article 14 ECHR taken with Article 4.

4. Negative obligations

5.166 In addition to the obvious obligation not to subject those within their jurisdiction to treatment contrary to Article 4, states are obliged to refrain from expelling anyone to a real risk of such treatment.[326] This is the analogue of the duty established in *Soering v United Kingdom* in the context of Article 3.[327] The UK Supreme Court has confirmed that, where a person appeals to the First-tier Tribunal on the basis that their removal would breach Article 4, the Tribunal is not bound—in deciding whether they have been a victim of trafficking in the past—by the outcome of any 'conclusive grounds' decision, but must determine the issue for itself based on the evidence before it.[328] It has also confirmed that it will be contrary to Article 4 to expel a person in circumstances where this would render the UK unable to fulfil the investigative duty described below.[329]

5. Positive obligations

5.167 It is now well established that Article 4 imposes three main types of positive obligation: the 'systems' or 'systemic' duty, the 'operational' or 'protection' duty, and the 'investigative' duty.[330] These are broadly the same types of obligation which arise under Articles 2 and 3; the Grand Chamber confirmed in *SM v Croatia* that the understanding and development of the positive duties under Article 4 should continue to be 'informed' by the case law under Articles 2 and 3.[331] The duties derive from Article 1, which requires states to 'secure' for 'everyone' within their jurisdiction the rights and freedoms of the Convention in a genuine and effective way.[332] In the specific context of Article 4, the ECtHR has confirmed that these duties 'must

---

[325] The domestic courts have held that, where the express intention of a policy is to comply with the UK's obligations under ECAT, the question of whether they do so is justiciable: see eg *R (PK (Ghana) v Secretary of State for the Home Department* [2018] EWCA Civ 98, [2018] 1 WLR 3955.

[326] While the issue does not appear to have arisen before the ECtHR, the domestic courts and tribunals have had no difficulty accepting this proposition in light of the other parallels between art 4 and arts 2 and 3. This was, eg, uncontroversial in the proceedings in *MS (Pakistan) v Secretary of State for the Home Department* [2020] UKSC 9, [2020] 1 WLR 1373; see also (in the extradition context) *Vilionis v Vilnius County Court Lithuania* [2017] EWHC 336 (Admin), para 13.

[327] *Soering v UK* (1989) 11 EHRR 439.

[328] *MS (Pakistan) v Secretary of State for the Home Department* [2020] UKSC 9, [2020] 1 WLR 1373, paras 11–15 (endorsing as correct a late concession by the Secretary of State).

[329] ibid paras 34–36. The extent to which this reasoning might be applied to a potential breach of the operational duty, even in the absence of a real risk of treatment contrary to art 4 on return, has yet to be considered by the higher courts.

[330] See eg *SM v Croatia* (2021) 72 EHRR 1, para 306. This categorization has been adopted by the UK courts: see eg *R (TDT (Vietnam) v Secretary of State for the Home Department* [2018] EWCA Civ 1395, [2018] 1 WLR 4922, para 17; *R (MN) v Secretary of State for the Home Department* [2020] EWCA Civ 1746, [2021] 1 WLR 1956, para 46.

[331] *SM v Croatia* (2021) 72 EHRR 1, para 309.

[332] *Siliadin v France* (2005) BHRC 654, paras 77, 89.

be construed in light of [ECAT]'[333] and that it is 'guided' by ECAT and the manner in which it has been interpreted.[334]

(a) Systems duty

The ECtHR established in *Siliadin v France* that Article 4 entails a specific positive obligation on Member States to penalize and prosecute effectively any act aimed at maintaining a person in a situation of slavery, servitude, or forced or compulsory labour.[335] The Court held that, in order to comply with this obligation, states are required to put in place a legislative and administrative framework, capable of realistic enforcement, to prohibit and punish conduct by individuals which violates Article 4. The scope of the obligation is identical to that under Article 3.[336]

5.168

Until the Coroners and Justice Act was passed in 2009, there was no offence in English law of subjecting another to servitude.[337] That failure was challenged in *CN v United Kingdom*.[338] The Court held that there had been an ineffective investigation into complaints of domestic servitude as a result of the absence of legislation. The Coroners and Justice Act 2009, and later the Modern Slavery Act 2015, filled the lacuna.

5.169

Since *Siliadin v France* the systems duty has been formulated in ways which go beyond the sphere of criminal law. In *Rantsev v Cyprus* the Grand Chamber noted that 'the spectrum of safeguards set out in national legislation must be adequate to ensure the practical and effective protection of the rights of victims or potential victims of trafficking',[339] and found that Cyprus had breached the systems duty as a result of 'a number of weaknesses' in the legal and administrative framework governing the 'artiste visa' regime under which Ms Rantseva had entered the country.[340] In *Chowdury v Greece* the Court reiterated that states are required 'to put in place, in addition to the measures aimed at punishing the traffickers, measures to prevent trafficking and to protect the victims'.[341]

5.170

(b) Operational duty

The 'operational' or 'protection' duty is to 'take operational measures to protect victims of potential victims' of breaches of Article 4.[342] As most of the key cases on the operational and investigative duties have concerned human trafficking, most

5.171

---

[333] ibid para 112.

[334] *Chowdury v Greece* App No 21884/15, 30 March 2017, para 104.

[335] *Siliadin v France* (2005) 20 BHRC 654.

[336] ibid para 89.

[337] Section 71. See general discussion in Joint Committee on Human Rights, Twenty-Sixth Report, October 2006.

[338] *CN v UK* (2013) 56 EHRR 24.

[339] *Rantsev v Cyprus* (2010) 28 BHRC 313, para 284. See also *VCL and AN v United Kingdom* (2021) 73 EHRR 9, para 151.

[340] *Rantsev v Cyprus* (2010) 28 BHRC 313, paras 290–93.

[341] *Chowdury v Greece* App No 21884/15, 30 March 2017, para 87.

[342] *Rantsev v Cyprus* (2010) 28 BHRC 313, para 286; *Chowdury v Greece* [2017] ECHR 300, para 88; *R (TDT (Vietnam) v Secretary of State for the Home Department* [2018] EWCA Civ 1395, [2018] 1 WLR 4922, para 17.

observations on the scope of the duty are couched in this language; the same principles will of course apply to cases of slavery, servitude, or forced or compulsory labour.

5.172 The operational duty is triggered where the authorities are or ought to be aware of circumstances giving rise to a 'credible suspicion' that an individual is at 'real and immediate risk' of trafficking or re-trafficking.[343] A 'real' risk is one which is more than fanciful.[344] An 'immediate' risk—drawing on the Article 2 jurisprudence— is one which is present and continuing; it does not need to be imminent.[345] The threshold for a 'credible suspicion' is a low one: the ECtHR has equated it with a claim which is not 'inherently implausible',[346] and the UK Court of Appeal with a case where there are 'reasonable grounds for suspecting' that a person is a victim.[347] It does not depend on an express complaint or allegation of trafficking being made by the person concerned,[348] as many victims of trafficking do not know to recognize themselves as such. As a result, the threshold may (depending on the facts) be crossed even before a 'reasonable grounds' decision has been made by a competent authority.[349] Indeed, the UK courts have held that it will be crossed in 'most cases' where a potential or confirmed victim has escaped their traffickers only relatively recently; a person with a history of being trafficked is 'the paradigm case of someone who is likely to be at real and immediate risk'.[350]

5.173 Once triggered, the operational duty requires states to take 'appropriate measures within the scope of their powers to remove the individual from that situation or risk'.[351] The measures required are of course context-specific; they may (eg) include taking steps to prevent the individual falling back into the hands of their traffickers[352] and/or providing material support and assistance such as accommodation.[353]

---

[343] *Rantsev v Cyprus* (2010) 28 BHRC 313, para 286.

[344] See the discussion in *R (TDT (Vietnam) v Secretary of State for the Home Department* [2018] EWCA Civ 1395, [2018] 1 WLR 4922, paras 44–46. This is consistent with the approach to 'real risk' in the expulsion context.

[345] *R (TDT (Vietnam)) v Secretary of State for the Home Department* [2018] EWCA Civ 1395, [2018] 1 WLR 4922, paras 44–45; *Batayav v SSHD* [2003] EWCA Civ 1489, paras 37–38.

[346] *CN v United Kingdom* (2013) 56 EHRR 24, para 72. For example, in *VCL and AN v United Kingdom* (2021) 73 EHRR 9 it was enough that the applicants were Vietnamese boys or young men discovered on or near cannabis factories, in circumstances where the authorities were well aware that the cultivation of cannabis was an activity likely to be carried out by child victims of trafficking: paras 117–21.

[347] *R (TDT (Vietnam) v Secretary of State for the Home Department* [2018] EWCA Civ 1395, [2018] 1 WLR 4922, para 38.

[348] This is implicit in the ECtHR's approach to the operational duty in, eg, *VCL and AN v United Kingdom* (2021) 73 EHRR 9.

[349] *R (TDT (Vietnam) v Secretary of State for the Home Department* [2018] EWCA Civ 1395, [2018] 1 WLR 4922, para 35.

[350] ibid paras 40–42.

[351] *Rantsev v Cyprus* (2010) 28 BHRC 313, para 286; *Chowdury v Greece* App No 21884/15, 30 March 2017, para 88.

[352] See eg the facts found to lead to a breach of the operational duty in *Rantsev v Cyprus* (2010) 28 BHRC 313 and *R (TDT (Vietnam) v Secretary of State for the Home Department* [2018] EWCA Civ 1395, [2018] 1 WLR 4922 (where the authorities had failed to release the claimant from detention only into safe accommodation).

[353] *J v Austria* App No 58216/12, 17 January 2017, para 109.

Accurately identifying victims is often crucial to discharging the operational duty,[354] given the likelihood that appropriate protective measures will not be taken where a person's history—and hence the risks they face—is not properly appreciated. Indeed, in *J v Austria* the ECtHR went so far as to refer to the Austrian authorities' 'positive obligation to identify and support the applicants as (potential) victims of human trafficking';[355] and in *R (DS) v Secretary of State for the Home Department* it was common ground between the parties that the UK was 'under a duty'—arising under both ECAT and Article 4 ECHR—to 'identify victims of human trafficking'.[356] The measures required may also extend to refraining from prosecuting a potential victim of trafficking, or from pursuing the prosecution of a confirmed victim.[357] The duty must not be interpreted in a manner which places an 'impossible or disproportionate' burden on the state.[358]

There is an open question regarding the extent to which the content of the operational duty should be informed by, and therefore overlap with, the provisions of ECAT dealing with support and assistance to potential victims of trafficking.[359] As noted above, the ECtHR has confirmed the relevance of ECAT to the interpretation of the positive duties under Article 4 generally. It has also described one of the 'two principal aims' of the operational duty (the first being 'to protect the victim of trafficking from further harm') as being 'to facilitate his or her recovery'.[360] However, the Court has yet to hold expressly that any failure to comply with relevant ECAT obligations will or is likely to give rise to a breach of the operational duty. In the UK, the Court of Appeal has cautioned that 'despite their inter-relationship' there is 'no automatic read-across' between Article 4 and ECAT;[361] the Supreme Court in *MS (Pakistan) v Secretary of State for the Home Department* left open the exact extent of the overlap.[362]

5.174

The operational duty (and the investigative duty) can be invoked against a state even where the individual concerned is no longer within its territorial jurisdiction. Thus, for example, in *Rantsev* it was said that the applicant had been trafficked from Russia to Cyprus, where she was ultimately killed. Russia argued that because 'the events forming the basis of the application' had 'taken place outside its territory', the application was inadmissible.[363] The ECtHR disagreed, noting that the applicant's

5.175

---

[354] See eg ibid para 109; *VCL and AN v United Kingdom* (2021) 73 EHRR 9, para 160.

[355] Ibid, paras 109 and 111.

[356] *R (DS) v Secretary of State for the Home Department* [2019] EWHC 3046 (Admin), para 50.

[357] *VCL and AN v United Kingdom* (2021) 73 EHRR 9, paras 159–83. The Court stressed that this is by no means an absolute prohibition; its assessment was dependent on the authorities' repeated failures to engage properly with the evidence of trafficking. cf the application declared inadmissible in *GS v United Kingdom* App No 7604/19, 23 November 2021.

[358] *Rantsev v Cyprus* (2010) 28 BHRC 313, para 287.

[359] In particular ECAT, arts 10–13, which require that particular forms of support be provided to potential victims of trafficking until the identification process is complete and during a 'recovery and reflection' period lasting at least 30 days.

[360] *VCL and AN v United Kingdom* (2021) 73 EHRR 9, para 159.

[361] *R (TDT (Vietnam) v Secretary of State for the Home Department* [2018] EWCA Civ 1395, [2018] 1 WLR 4922, para 31.

[362] *MS (Pakistan) v Secretary of State for the Home Department* [2020] UKSC 9, [2020] 1 WLR 1373, para 27.

[363] *Rantsev v Cyprus* (2010) 28 BHRC 313, para 203.

complaints about Russia concerned its 'failure to take the necessary measures to protect [the applicant] from the risk of trafficking and exploitation' and to investigate her potential trafficking and suspicious death and that the alleged trafficking 'commenced in Russia'; and concluding that 'in view of the obligations undertaken by Russia to combat trafficking' the Court could consider whether it had complied with those duties 'within the limits of its own jurisdiction and powers'.[364]

(c) Investigative duty

5.176   The investigative duty is triggered where there is a 'credible suspicion' that an individual has been trafficked (or otherwise subjected to a breach of art 4): see paras 5.171–5.172.[365] As with the operational duty, the threshold may be crossed even without an express complaint being made by the potential victim (or their family).[366]

5.177   Once triggered, the duty requires the state to conduct an 'effective' investigation. This means, inter alia, that the investigation must: (a) be independent from those implicated in the events; (b) be capable of leading to the identification and punishment of the individuals responsible;[367] (c) be undertaken promptly and with reasonable expedition in all cases, and urgently where there is a possibility of removing the individual concerned from a harmful situation;[368] and (d) involve the victim or next of kin 'to the extent necessary to safeguard their legitimate interests'.[369] For further detail see paras 5.48–5.65 (in the context of art 2) and 5.114–5.119 (in the context of art 3). These are not exhaustive criteria: it is 'not possible to reduce the variety of situations' where a deficiency in the investigative process might lead it to 'fall foul' of the requirement of effectiveness.[370] In cases of cross-border trafficking, the authorities must also cooperate effectively with the relevant authorities of other states concerned.[371] The court should apply 'particularly thorough scrutiny' in determining whether these requirements have been met,[372] though only 'significant

---

[364] ibid paras 206–07. As a result the Court considered only the operational measures which could have been taken on Russian territory: para 304. cf *J v Austria* App No 58216/12, 17 January 2017, where the applicants' exploitation had taken place entirely prior to their arrival in Austria (in the Philippines and the UAE); the ECtHR held that the Austrian authorities, which did recognize them as victims of trafficking, were not required to investigate the potential offences committed against them abroad: paras 113–14.

[365] See eg *CN v United Kingdom* (2013) 56 EHRR 24, paras 71–72. Later cases have instead referred to the existence of an 'arguable claim' and 'prima facie evidence', but with no indication that this was intended as suggesting a different threshold: see eg *SM v Croatia* (2021) 72 EHRR 1, para 324.

[366] See eg *Rantsev v Cyprus* (2010) 28 BHRC 313, para 288; and (in the domestic context) *OOO v Commissioner of Police for the Metropolis* [2011] EWHC 1246 (QB), para 163.

[367] ibid. This is an obligation of means, not of result. An investigation may fail to meet this criterion where, eg, the authorities fail to follow an obvious and significant line of inquiry: *SM v Croatia* (2021) 72 EHRR 1, paras 336–46.

[368] See further the discussion at *OOO v Commissioner of Police for the Metropolis* [2011] EWHC 1246 (QB), para 153.

[369] *Rantsev v Cyprus* (2010) 28 BHRC 313, para 288; *Chowdury v Greece* App No 21884/15, 30 March 2017, para 89.

[370] *SM v Croatia* (2021) 72 EHRR 1, para 318.

[371] See eg *Rantsev v Cyprus* (2010) 28 BHRC 313, para 289.

[372] *SM v Croatia* (2021) 72 EHRR 1, para 317.

shortcomings' are likely to be capable of rendering an investigation ineffective.[373] However, as with the operational duty, the investigative duty must not be interpreted in such a way as to impose an 'impossible or disproportionate' burden on the authorities.[374]

Again, the investigative duty may arise even where the applicant is not (or is no longer) in the territory of the relevant state: see para 5.175. Thus, in *Rantsev* the Grand Chamber found that the Russian authorities were obliged to 'investigate the possibility that individual agents or networks operating in Russia [had been] involved in trafficking Ms Rantseva to Cyprus'.[375]

5.178

---

[373] ibid paras 320, 334.
[374] ibid para 315.
[375] *Rantsev v Cyprus* (2010) 28 BHRC 313, para 307. This does not extend to a requirement to provide for universal jurisdiction over trafficking (etc) offences committed abroad: *J v Austria* App No 58216/12, 17 January 2017, para 114.

6

THE CONVENTION RIGHTS: LIMITED AND QUALIFIED RIGHTS

Blackstone's Guide to The Human Rights Act 1998. Eighth Edition. John Wadham, Helen Mountfield KC, Raj Desai, Sarah Hannett KC, Jessica Jones, Eleanor Mitchell, and Aidan Wills, Oxford University Press. © John Wadham, Helen Mountfield KC, Raj Desai, Sarah Hannett KC, Jessica Jones, Eleanor Mitchell, and Aidan Wills 2024. DOI: 10.1093/oso/9780192885050.003.0006

A. INTRODUCTION

6.01   This chapter summarizes the content of the limited and qualified rights under Articles 5–14 of the European Convention for the Protection of Human Rights and Fundamental Freedoms (Convention) and the general restrictions on rights found in Articles 15–18. Discussion of the nature of limited and qualified rights can be found in Chapter 2.[1]

---

[1] See Chapter 2, paras 2.29–2.32.

As in Chapter 5, an overview is given of the jurisprudence of the European Court   6.02
of Human Rights (ECtHR) and any remaining important cases from the European
Commission on Human Rights (ECmHR). Where the domestic courts have considered an article in claims brought under the Human Rights Act, their approach is
discussed alongside the European case law and any divergences are noted.

B. ARTICLE 5: RIGHT TO LIBERTY AND SECURITY

Article 5 protects the 'right to liberty and security of person' and has been described   6.03
by the Grand Chamber as, together with Articles 2, 3, and 4, 'in the first rank of
the fundamental rights that protect the physical security of an individual'.[2] It is a
combined right, so the phrase 'right to liberty and security of person' should be
read as a whole and not as two distinct rights. 'Security of the person' must be
understood as physical liberty, not personal safety.[3] Article 5 ensures protection
from deprivations of liberty of any kind, but not from other interferences with the
physical liberty of the person, such as the prevention of attack or the inadequacy of
welfare benefits.[4]

The key purpose of the right is to prevent arbitrary or unjustified deprivations   6.04
of liberty.[5] As considered below, deprivations of liberty must fall within one of
the exceptions outlined in sub-paragraphs (1)(a)—(f) of Article 5(1). The Grand
Chamber has repeatedly asserted that in peacetime[6] this list is exhaustive and
cannot be enlarged by the interests of the state against those of the detainee.[7]
Deprivations of liberty must also be 'lawful', which entails more than just compliance with the requirements of domestic law and is intended to ensure conformity
with general principles implied by the Convention. These principles include the
rule of law, the related requirement of legal certainty, and the principle of proportionality. However, subject to compliance with these requirements, the Court's task
under Article 5 stops short of assessing the appropriateness of the methods chosen
by the state.[8] As such, Article 5 does not specifically apply to the conditions in
which a person is detained.[9] However, if the place and conditions of detention do
not 'genuinely conform' to, or rationally link, with the reason for a deprivation of

---

[2] *McKay v UK* (2007) 44 EHRR 41, para 30; *Denis and Irvine v Belgium* App Nos 62819/17 & others,
1 June 2021 [GC], para 123.

[3] *East African Asians v UK* (1981) 3 EHRR 76.

[4] *Bozano v France* (1986) 9 EHRR 297.

[5] *Engel v Netherlands* (1976) 1 EHRR 647; *Brogan v UK* (1988) 11 EHRR 117; *Kurt v Turkey* (1998) 27
EHRR 373; *Denis and Irvine v Belgium* App Nos 62819/17 & others, 1 June 2021 [GC], para 123.

[6] See paras 6.07–6.09 regarding the position in armed conflicts.

[7] See eg *Merabishvili v Georgia* App No 72508/13, 28 November 2017 [GC], para 298 (and cases cited
therein).

[8] *Saadi v UK* (2008) 47 EHRR 17, paras 67–69; *Denis and Irvine v Belgium* App Nos 62819/17 & others,
1 June 2021 [GC], paras 125–33.

[9] *Ashingdane v UK* (1985) 7 EHRR 528; *S v Airedale NHS Trust* [2003] EWCA Civ 1036, [2004] QB
395; *Munjaz v UK* App No 2913/06, 17 July 2012, paras 67–72 (seclusion in high security hospital not a
further deprivation of liberty).

liberty advanced by the state under Article 5(1)(a)–(f), that will breach the implied requirement that detention must not be 'arbitrary' and Article 5 will be violated. As returned to below, the requirement of arbitrariness in the context of certain of the sub-paragraphs of Article 5(1) also includes an assessment of whether detention is necessary to achieve the stated aim.[10]

6.05   In addition to protecting the basic right to liberty, Article 5 provides persons who are deprived of their liberty with a number of procedural rights, detailed in paragraphs (2)–(5) and considered further below.

6.06   Article 5 also applies to deprivations of liberty by a contracting state acting outside its territory.[11] In *R (Al-Jedda) v Secretary of State for Defence* the House of Lords considered the plight of an individual detained in Iraq for over three years without charge by UK forces acting under United Nations (UN) authority.[12] A majority of the Lords concluded that the UK might lawfully, where it was necessary for imperative reasons of security, exercise the power to detain individuals as authorized by the Security Council, but it had to ensure that the detainee's rights under Article 5 were not infringed to a greater extent than was inherent in such detention. However, the Grand Chamber of the ECtHR disagreed, finding that the relevant Security Council resolution did not unambiguously indicate an intention to displace Article 5. Since none of the grounds in Articles 5(1)(a)–(f) authorized preventative detention, the applicant's detention violated Article 5(1).[13]

6.07   The Grand Chamber returned to the question of the extra-territorial application of Article 5 during armed interventions in *Hassan v UK*.[14] It was faced with a situation of apparent 'norm conflict' between the provision permitting preventative detention under international humanitarian law (IHL) and the exhaustive grounds for detention in Article 5(1), which do not include preventative detention. In a pragmatic decision, the Grand Chamber by a majority 'read down' Article 5 to allow preventative detention where this is permitted under IHL. It stipulated, however, that detention must also remain in keeping with the fundamental purpose of Article 5(1) to protect the individual from arbitrariness.[15] Detention must also be subject to review pursuant to Article 5(4). The decision recognizes that the full guarantees of review of the lawfulness of detention by a court may not be practicable within the course of an international armed conflict but requires that the reviewing body must provide 'sufficient guarantees of impartiality and fair procedure' to protect against arbitrariness.[16]

6.08   The minority pointed to the wider ramifications of the majority's decision, which permits states to intern prisoners of war, as well as civilians considered to pose a threat to security, for the duration of hostilities without the strict limitations that

---

[10] *Mayeka v Belgium* App No 13178/03, 12 October 2006, para 102; *Saadi v UK* (2009) 47 EHRR 17 [GC], paras 69–71.
[11] *Cyprus v Turkey* (1976) 4 EHRR 482; *Freda v Italy* (1980) 21 DR 250.
[12] *R (Al-Jedda) v Secretary of State for Defence* [2007] UKHL 58, [2008] 1 AC 332.
[13] *Al-Jedda v UK* App No 27021/08, 7 July 2011 [GC], paras 100–10.
[14] *Hassan v UK* App No 29750/09, 18 September 2014 [GC].
[15] ibid para 104.
[16] ibid para 106.

would be imposed by a requirement to derogate from Article 5 pursuant to Article 15.[17] It considered that the majority's novel reading of Article 5(1) did not 'conform with the text, object or purpose of Article 5(1) of the Convention, as this provision has been consistently interpreted by [the] Court for decades, and the structural mechanism of derogation in times of war provided by Article 15'.[18]

In *Al-Waheed v Ministry of Defence*, a majority of the Supreme Court rejected an argument that the approach in *Hassan* was inapplicable to detentions under the authority of a Security Council resolution during the *non-international* armed conflict stage of the Iraq war. While there were material differences between international and non-international armed conflicts, the majority concluded that these did not render the reasoning of the Grand Chamber in *Hassan* inapplicable, which it interpreted as drawing a distinction between peacetime and non-peacetime norms. A minority (Lords Reed and Kerr) interpreted *Hassan* more strictly and considered it to be restricted to international armed conflicts.   6.09

Article 5 rights are not absolute in the sense that they can be derogated from under Article 15. However, as these guarantees are of such fundamental importance in a democratic society and 'executive detention is the antithesis of the right to liberty and security of person',[19] any UK government attempt to derogate from Article 5 will be closely scrutinized by the courts.[20] The UK lodged a derogation from Article 5(1)(f) with the Council of Europe following the terrorist attacks in the United States on 11 September 2001, the purpose of which was to enable the detention without trial of foreign nationals suspected of links to international terrorism under the provisions of the Anti-Terrorism, Crime and Security Act 2001. In the famous case of *A and others*, the House of Lords held that the derogation was incompatible with Articles 5 and 14 of the Convention and therefore unlawful.[21] The Grand Chamber followed the reasoning of the House of Lords.[22]   6.10

1. Deprivation of liberty

Article 5 is concerned with deprivation of liberty rather than mere restrictions on freedom of movement.[23] As the ECtHR noted in *HM v Switzerland*, restrictions on freedom of movement are the concern of Article 2 of Protocol 4 (which is not a Convention right for the purposes of the Human Rights Act).[24] However, it is not always easy to distinguish between a 'deprivation of' and a 'restriction on' liberty,   6.11

---

[17] See further in Chapter 7.

[18] ibid, dissenting opinion of Judge Spano, joined by Judges Nicolaou, Bianku, and Kalaydjieva, paras 5–6.

[19] *A and others v Secretary of State for the Home Department* [2004] UKHL 56, [2005] 2 AC 68, para 222 per Baroness Hale.

[20] See eg ibid.

[21] ibid.

[22] *A and others v UK* (2009) 26 BHRC 1.

[23] *Engel v Netherlands* (1976) 1 EHRR 647, para 58.

[24] *HM v Switzerland* (2004) 38 EHRR 17. See also *Austin v Commissioner of Police for the Metropolis* [2009] UKHL 5, [2009] 2 WLR 372, para 42.

since the difference is one of degree rather than substance.[25] In *Guzzardi v Italy* (concerning compulsory residence of the applicant on an isolated island, albeit in the company of his wife and child) the ECtHR made clear that in determining whether there has been a deprivation:

the starting point must be the concrete situation of the individual concerned and account must be taken of a whole range of factors arising in a particular case such as the type, duration, effects and manner of implementation of the measure in question.[26]

6.12 This guidance has been repeatedly cited by the ECtHR in later cases.[27] On the facts of the case, the ECtHR held by a majority that there was a deprivation of liberty drawing an analogy with the situation in an open prison. Examples of circumstances which the Strasbourg organs have held to amount to deprivations of liberty include long-term measures such as house arrest;[28] short-term measures such as detention in order to carry out a compulsory blood test;[29] detention of foreign nationals for an hour prior to their being put on a chartered aircraft in order to be expelled from the country;[30] involuntary presence in airport transit zones for a prolonged period;[31] holding vulnerable migrants (including children) in a land transit zone for nearly four months;[32] detention of a five-year-old in an immigration detention centre without her parents;[33] and holding migrants arriving by sea in reception facilities and on ships for a number of days in order to process their applications without the ability to leave.[34] An 'informal' patient in a mental hospital has also been held to be deprived of liberty,[35] as has the involuntary placement of a person lacking capacity in a care home.[36] However, the ECtHR has held that a change in a prisoner's security categorization does not engage Article 5, even though it has an effect on their likely release date,[37] and some curfews may not constitute deprivations of liberty.[38]

---

[25] *Ashingdane v UK* (1985) 7 EHRR 528, para 41.

[26] *Guzzardi v Italy* (1980) 3 EHRR 333, para 92.

[27] See eg *HL v UK* (2004) 40 EHRR 761, para 89; *Austin and others v United Kingdom* (2012) 55 EHRR 14, para 57; *Stanev v Bulgaria* App No 36760/06, 17 January 2012 [GC], para 11; *Khlaifa and others v Italy* App No 16483/12, 15 December 2016 [GC], para 64.

[28] *Greek Case* (1969) 12 YB 1; *Buzadji v Moldova* App No 23/755/07, 5 July 2016 [GC], paras 104–05.

[29] *X v Austria* (1979) 18 DR 154.

[30] *X and Y v Sweden* (1977–1978) 7 DR 123.

[31] *Amuur v France* App No 19776/92, 25 June 1996; *ZA and others v Russia* App Nos 61411/15 & others, 21 November 2019 [GC], para 156.

[32] *RR and others v Hungary* App No 3603717, 2 March 2021; cf *Ilias and Ahmed v Hungary* App No 47287/15, 21 November 2019 [GC], concerning the same transit zone—no deprivation of liberty was found due to the ability of asylum-seekers in a Hungarian land transit zone to return to Serbia, a county which offered relevant guarantees of non-refoulement to their countries of origin. In *Ilias* the Grand Chamber set out the factors to be considered when determining whether measures applied to foreigners in transit zones constitute restrictions on movement or deprivations of liberty (see paras 217–18). These were applied in *RR*.

[33] *Mubilanzila Mayeka v Belgium* (2008) 46 EHRR 23.

[34] *Khlaifa and others v Italy* App No 16483/12, 15 December 2016 [GC], para 72.

[35] *HL v UK* (*Bournewood*) (2004) 40 EHRR 761.

[36] *Stanev v Bulgaria* App No 36760/06, 17 January 2012 [GC].

[37] *Ashingdane v UK* (1985) 7 EHRR 528.

[38] *Cyprus v Turkey* (1976) 4 EHRR 482, para 235; *Raimondo v Italy* (1994) 18 EHRR 237, para 39.

In *Terheş v Romania*,[39] the ECtHR held that a blanket lockdown measure in Romania during the Covid-19 pandemic lasting for 52 days, pursuant to which everyone was required to remain at home other than in certain circumstances laid down by law but without provision for monitoring of individuals by the state, did not amount to a deprivation of liberty.[40] The ECtHR placed weight on the important public health purpose of the measure.[41] The decision is an example of how the Court's assessment of the existence of a deprivation of liberty can encompass considerations of justification which might methodologically be more appropriately addressed under the exhaustive exceptions outlined in Article 5(1)(a)–(f).[42] The decision does not amount to a finding that no 'lockdown' measures will engage Article 5(1). The Court remarked, for example, on the absence of evidence from the particular applicant as to the impact on him and the absence of any suggestion that he was not able to avail himself of the exceptions so as to be able to leave his home.[43] In *R (Dolan) v Secretary of State for Health and Social Care*[44] the Court of Appeal held that it was unarguable that the effect of the UK Covid regulations—containing numerous express exceptions permitting persons to leave their homes which were non-exhaustive and subject to an overriding exception of having a reasonable excuse—amounted to a deprivation of liberty.[45]

6.13

A person is not deprived of their liberty if they have validly consented to the confinement in question.[46] However, giving oneself up to be taken into detention does constitute a deprivation of liberty, especially when it is not disputed that a person is legally incapable of consenting to, or disagreeing with, their proposed detention.[47] In *Birmingham City Council v D*,[48] the Supreme Court considered the limits of the ability of a parent to consent to a deprivation of liberty on behalf of their child. In that case a 15-year-old child without capacity was placed in an educational setting under a regime which entailed constant supervision with the consent of his parents. By a majority, the Supreme Court held that this constituted a deprivation of liberty. Parental consent could not substitute for the required subjective consent to what was objectively a confinement attributable to the state. The result was that approval of the detention by the Court of Protection was required.

6.14

In domestic law, the notion of a deprivation of liberty has on occasion been restrictively interpreted. The House of Lords considered its meaning in relation to the government's anti-terrorism measures on a number of occasions. In the case of *R (Gillan) v Commissioner of Police for the Metropolis*, concerning suspicionless stop-and-search powers under the Terrorism Act 2000, the House of Lords adopted a narrow

6.15

---

[39] *Terheş v Romania* App No 49933/20, 13 April 2021.
[40] ibid paras 38–47.
[41] ibid para 39.
[42] For a further examples see the discussion of *Austin v UK* (2012) 55 EHRR 14, paras 7.20–23 and *S, V and A v Denmark* App Nos 35553/12 & others, 22 October 2018 [GC], see para 6.40.
[43] *Terheş v Romania* App No 49933/20, 13 April 2021, para 44.
[44] *R (Dolan) v Secretary of State for Health and Social Care* [2020] EWCA Civ 1605, [2021] 1 WLR 2326.
[45] ibid paras 93–94.
[46] *Storck v Germany* (2005) 43 EHRR 6, para 74; *Stanev v Bulgaria* (2012) 55 EHRR 22 [GC], para 117.
[47] *Stanev v Bulgaria* (2012) 55 EHRR 22 [GC], paras 117–19.
[48] *Birmingham City Council v D* [2019] UKSC 42, [2019] 1 WLR 5403.

approach to the issue of 'deprivation', holding that Article 5(1) did not apply.[49] This was despite the fact that an individual who has been stopped has no choice but to comply with the search as there is a statutory power to detain, reasonable force may be used to enforce compliance, and non-compliance is a criminal offence. When the case reached Strasbourg, the ECtHR did not determine the application of Article 5, but noted that the coercive element of stop-and-search procedures were indicative of a deprivation of liberty.[50] The judgment suggests that the House of Lords may have adopted too limited an approach. Nevertheless, in *Roberts v Commissioner of Police of the Metropolis*, the Court of Appeal did not consider that the ECtHR's reasoning in *Gillan v UK* required a departure from the House of Lords' approach in *Gillan* and found that a stop and search under the analogous power in section 60 of the Criminal Justice and Public Order Act 1994 did not result in a deprivation of liberty.[51]

6.16   The fact-sensitive approach to assessing the existence of a deprivation of liberty under Article 5 is also illustrated by the House of Lords' determination of three cases concerning the lawfulness of 'control orders' under the Prevention of Terrorism Act 2005. Control orders were imposed on suspected terrorists in place of indefinite detention, which the House of Lords had ruled unlawful in *A and others* (para 6.86). In *Secretary of State for the Home Department v JJ* the House of Lords considered the terms of a control order which confined the suspected terrorist to a one-bedroom flat for 18 hours every day, required visitors to be approved in advance, and prevented him from leaving a defined urban area.[52] By a majority of three to two it was held that the control orders constituted a deprivation of liberty. The majority emphasized that the factual scenarios in such cases may differ and it was therefore inappropriate to specify a formula by which the legality of a control order could be tested. In dissent, Lord Hoffmann stated that:

In order to preserve the key distinction between the unqualified right to liberty and the qualified rights of freedom of movement, communication, association and so forth, it is essential not to give an over-expansive interpretation to the concept of deprivation of liberty.[53]

6.17   In the cases of *E* and *MB*, the House of Lords unanimously held that various lesser restrictions did not amount to deprivations of liberty.[54] The control order cases are considered further in relation to Article 6 below.[55] The Terrorism Prevention and Investigation Measures Act 2011 abolished control orders and established a system for imposing less restrictive terrorism investigation and prevention measures

---

[49] *R (Gillan) v Commissioner of Police for the Metropolis* [2006] UKHL 12, [2006] 2 AC 307.

[50] *Gillan & Quinton v UK* (2010) 28 BHRC 420, para 57.

[51] *R (Roberts) v Chief Constable for the Metropolis* [2014] EWCA Civ 69, [2014] 1 WLR 3299, paras 12–13. There was no appeal against this finding: *R(Roberts) v Commissioner of Police of the Metropolis* [2015] UKSC 79, [2016] 1 WLR 210, para 14.

[52] *Secretary of State for the Home Department v JJ* [2007] UKHL 45, [2008] 1 AC 385.

[53] ibid para 44.

[54] *Secretary of State for the Home Department v E and another* [2007] UKHL 47, [2008] 1 AC 499; *Secretary of State for the Home Department v MB* [2007] UKHL 46, [2008] 1 AC 440. See also *Secretary of State for the Home Department v AH* [2008] EWHC 1018 (Admin).

[55] See para 6.176.

(so-called TPIMs) on terrorist suspects. TPIMs were introduced in part in order to avert the legal difficulties that had arisen with ensuring the compatibility of control orders with Article 5. Whether the measures imposed under a TPIM constitute a deprivation of liberty will depend on application of the *Guzzardi v Italy* test as explained and applied in the subsequent case law.[56]

In *Austin v Metropolitan Police Commissioner* the House of Lords adopted a restrictive approach to Article 5, finding that the detention of thousands of protestors for several hours inside a police cordon (or 'kettle') did not constitute a deprivation of liberty.[57] Noting that detention for public safety or public order was not a permissible ground for detention under Article 5(1), the Lords held that a pragmatic approach to the substance of the right needed to be adopted which took account of the purpose of the detention. Where, as here, the police had a legitimate purpose and had not acted disproportionately in their pursuit of it, the court would not consider that a deprivation of liberty had occurred.   6.18

The ECtHR agreed with the conclusion of the House of Lords regarding the engagement of Article 5. The majority expressed a concern not to interpret Article 5 in a manner that would make it impracticable for the police to fulfil their duties, provided that compliance with the underlying principle of Article 5 to protect the individual from arbitrariness was ensured. The majority was at pains to underline that this conclusion turned on the 'specific and exceptional' facts of the case where the police had had no alternative but to impose the cordon to avert a real risk of serious injury or damage. It asserted that the underlying public interest motive has no bearing on whether a person is deprived of their liberty, which only becomes relevant at the second stage of considering whether the deprivation was justified by one of the sub-paragraphs of Article 5(1). However, drawing a somewhat subtle distinction, the ECtHR held that the requirement to take account of the 'type' and 'manner of implementation' allowed regard to the exceptional public order context.[58]   6.19

The minority questioned how exceptional the facts of the case truly were and suggested that the majority's reasoning could be interpreted as establishing a novel and dangerous proposition that, where it is necessary to impose a coercive and restrictive measure for a legitimate public-interest purpose, the measure does not amount to a deprivation of liberty. In their view, this would undermine the unqualified nature of the right and give '*carte blanche*' to the police.[59]   6.20

The domestic courts were called on to analyse the meaning of deprivation of liberty in a context not previously considered by the ECtHR in *P and another v Cheshire West and Chester Council*.[60] The courts were asked to determine whether   6.21

---

[56] For example, in *Secretary of State for the Home Department v JM and LF* [2021] EWHC 266 (Admin) it was held that reporting and appointments measures requiring (in combination with obligations associated with the conditions of a suspended sentence) required LF to be in a particular place between 13 and 15 occasions per week over a period of 10 months did not amount to a deprivation of liberty: see ibid paras 221–25.

[57] *Austin v Metropolitan Police Commissioner* [2009] UKHL 5, [2009] 2 WLR 372.

[58] *Austin and others v United Kingdom* (2012) 55 EHRR 14, paras 52–69.

[59] ibid paras 3 and 8 per Judges Tulkens, Spielmann, and Garlicki.

[60] *P and another v Cheshire West and Chester Council* [2014] UKSC 19, [2014] AC 896.

living arrangements made for mentally incapacitated persons by local authorities in an ordinary domestic setting, in their best interests, constituted a deprivation of liberty. In finding that the claimants had not been deprived of their liberty, the Court of Appeal took account of the 'relative normality' of the arrangements for disabled persons in the claimants' position. However, the majority of the Supreme Court found that this approach ran contrary to the fundamental principle that disabled persons have the same rights as non-disabled persons, and rejected relative normality, compliance, or lack of objection, and the reason or purpose behind the placement as irrelevant factors.[61] The Court instead identified a universal 'acid test' for the deprivation of liberty in this context from the ECtHR's case law founded on the dual elements that a person is (a) 'under continuous supervision and control'; and (b) 'not free to leave'.[62]

6.22   In *R (Jalloh) v Secretary of State for the Home Department*[63] the Supreme Court declined to align the concept of imprisonment at common law (which is, eg, relevant to establishing the common law tort of false imprisonment) with the Article 5 concept of deprivation of liberty. Having reviewed the two concepts as considered in the case law, the Court emphasized that there could be an imprisonment at common law without there being a deprivation of liberty, but doubted (without deciding) whether it was right to say that there could ever be a deprivation of liberty without there also being an imprisonment.

6.23   A real risk of a 'flagrant breach' of Article 5 can be relied on to resist expulsion to another state. This would arise, for example, where there was a real risk of the receiving state arbitrarily detaining the individual for many years without the intention of bringing them to trial, imprisoning them for a substantial period on the basis of a previous conviction following a flagrantly unfair trial, or subjecting them to 'extraordinary rendition' which entails detention 'outside the normal legal system' and which, 'by its deliberate circumvention of due process, is anathema to the rule of law and the values protected by the Convention'.[64]

2. Exceptions to the right to liberty

6.24   Article 5(1) sets out an exhaustive list of circumstances in which the state may deprive a person of their liberty in peacetime[65] in paragraphs (a)–(f). These grounds are to be given a narrow interpretation, and the excepted forms of detention must be both lawful and in accordance with a procedure prescribed by law.[66]

---

[61] ibid paras 45–47 and 50 per Lady Hale, giving the leading judgment.
[62] ibid para 49.
[63] *R (Jalloh) v Secretary of State for the Home Department* [2020] UKSC 4, [2020] 2 WLR 418.
[64] *Othman Abu Qatada* (2012) 55 EHRR 1; *El Masri v former Yugoslav Republic of Macedonia* (2013) 57 EHRR 25 [GC], para 239.
[65] For the situation during armed conflicts see paras 6.07–6.09.
[66] *Winterwerp v Netherlands* (1979) 2 EHRR 387; *Amuur v France* (1996) 22 EHRR 533; *A and others* (2009) 26 BHRC 1; *Medvedyev v France* App No 3394/03, 29 March 2010.

(a) *Lawfulness of deprivation of liberty*

The Convention requirement of 'lawfulness' encompasses, in addition to compli-   6.25
ance with domestic law, the 'quality of law' requirement found in other Convention
rights. The Grand Chamber summarized the position in respect of Article 5(1) as
follows in *Del Rio Prada v Spain*:

> Where the 'lawfulness' of detention is in issue, including the question whether 'a procedure
> prescribed by law' has been followed, the Convention refers essentially to national law and lays
> down the obligation to conform to the substantive and procedural rules of national law. This pri-
> marily requires any arrest or detention to have a legal basis in domestic law but also relates to the
> quality of the law, requiring it to be compatible with the rule of law, a concept inherent in all the
> articles of the Convention. The 'quality of the law' implies that where a national law authorises
> deprivation of liberty it must be sufficiently accessible, precise and foreseeable in its application
> to avoid all risk of arbitrariness. The standard of 'lawfulness' set by the Convention requires that
> all law be sufficiently precise to allow the person—if need be, with appropriate advice—to fore-
> see, to a degree that is reasonable in the circumstances, the consequences which a given action
> may entail. Where deprivation of liberty is concerned, it is essential that the domestic law define
> clearly the conditions for detention.[67]

The ECtHR has at times adopted a generous approach to the application of these   6.26
requirements. For example, in *Steel and others v UK*, it was prepared to accept
that—despite their vague and general terms—the English law concepts of breach
of the peace and the power to bind over were sufficiently foreseeable, with the assistance of legal advice, due to their having been clarified by the English courts over
two decades.[68]

In contrast, the UK fell foul of the lawfulness requirement in *HL v UK*. The   6.27
ECtHR found that the system for detaining mental patients without capacity
pursuant to the common law doctrine of necessity breached Article 5 essentially
because there were no fixed procedural rules governing the admission and continued detention of the patients.[69]

In *Morgan v Ministry of Justice*, the Supreme Court held that a retrospective   6.28
change enacted by the Counter-Terrorism and Sentencing Act 2021 to the timing
of automatic early release on licence for prisoners convicted of certain terrorism
offences from the half-way point to the two-thirds point in their sentence complied
with the requirement of 'lawfulness' under Article 5(1). This was, in particular,
because the term of the sentences imposed was calculated without regard to early
release provisions and the changes to the early release provisions themselves were
sufficiently foreseeable.[70]

---

[67] *Del Rio Prada v Spain* (2014) 58 EHRR 37, para 125. See also *Mooren v Germany* (2009) 50 EHRR
23 [GC], paras 72–76; *Khlaifia & others v Italy* App No 16483/12, 16 December 2016 [GC], paras 91–92.
[68] *Steel and others v UK* (1999) 28 EHRR 603, paras 55 and 75–78.
[69] *HL v UK* (2004) 40 EHRR 761. See the discussion in *G v E* [2010] EWCA Civ 822, [2011] 1 FLR 239.
[70] *Morgan v Ministry of Justice* [2023] UKSC 14, [2023] 2 WLR 905, paras 119–28. See also *R (Khan) v
Secretary of State* [2020] EWHC 2084 Admin, [2020] 1 WLR 3932.

(b) *Article 5(1)(a)*

6.29   Article 5(1)(a) permits 'the lawful detention of a person after conviction[71] by a competent court'. A competent court under this article is one with jurisdiction to try the case.[72] It is not necessary that the proceedings before the court have fully complied with all the requirements of Article 6. Only if a conviction occurs as a result of proceedings which were a 'flagrant denial of justice' will Article 5(1)(a) be violated by the failure to conform with Article 6 standards.[73]

6.30   In order for a detention to be 'lawful' there must be a court judgment that justifies the confinement, as well as lawful procedures followed to effect the detention. The ECtHR has held that Article 5(1)(a) does not permit the ECtHR to review convictions or sentences imposed by a domestic court, though any such decision would have to comply with Articles 3 and 6.[74] For example, the Grand Chamber held in *Vinter and others v UK* that whole life sentences without a possibility of review and release would violate Article 3.[75]

6.31   The ECtHR considered the relationship between detention and conviction under Article 5(1)(a) in *Weeks v UK*.[76] A prisoner who had received an indeterminate life sentence was recalled to prison after his release. The ECtHR held that it was necessary for there to be a causal connection between the original conviction and detention. In this case the causal connection had not been broken because the prisoner remained a danger to the public. The Court reached a different conclusion in *Stafford v UK*.[77] The continued detention of a prisoner after he had served a prison sentence for forgery on the basis of an earlier mandatory life sentence from which he had been released on licence was not sufficiently causally connected to his original conviction to satisfy the requirements of Article 5(1)(a).

6.32   The House of Lords addressed the application of Article 5(1)(a) in *R (James) v Secretary of State for Justice*.[78] The claimants were convicted of specified violent and sexual offences, which deemed them to pose a significant risk of serious harm to members of the public, and sentenced to an indeterminate sentence of imprisonment for public protection (IPP). Their only hope for release was to persuade the Parole Board that they no longer proved a threat to the public. However, the Secretary of State had systemically failed to provide sufficient places on the offending behaviour courses that the claimants needed to undertake to demonstrate that their risk had diminished to the extent necessary. As a result, the Parole Board was unable to recommend their release. The Court found that the failure to provide access to these courses did not itself breach Article 5(1)(a). It was only when a matter of years had passed without the Parole Board being able to conduct an effective

---

[71] This includes a finding of civil contempt, see eg *Hammerton v UK* (2016) 63 EHRR 23.
[72] *X v Austria* (1987) 11 EHRR 112.
[73] *Stoichkov v Bulgaria* (2007) 44 EHRR 14.
[74] *Krzycki v Germany* (1978) 13 DR 57; *Weeks v UK* (1987) 10 EHRR 293.
[75] *Vinter and others v UK* (2013) 34 BHRC 605 and see discussion in Chapter 5, para 5-103.
[76] *Weeks v UK* (1987) 10 EHRR 293. See also *Van Droogenbroeck v Belgium* (1982) 4 EHRR 443, para 40.
[77] *Stafford v UK* (2002) 35 EHRR 32. cf *Waite v UK* (2003) 36 EHRR 54; *R (Hirst) v Secretary of State for the Home Department* [2006] EWCA Civ 945, [2006] 1 WLR 3083.
[78] *R (James) v Secretary of State for Justice* [2009] UKHL 22, [2010] 1 AC 553.

review of the case that the causal connection between the conviction and detention may be broken.

When the case was considered by the ECtHR,[79] it disagreed with the House of Lords, finding a breach of Article 5(1). The ECtHR accepted that a causal link between the original sentence and the detention remained but held that the absence of an opportunity to embark on rehabilitative courses, the successful completion of which was indispensable to establishing suitability for release, rendered continued detention arbitrary and contrary to Article 5(1). The ECtHR recognized that it would be unrealistic to expect rehabilitative work to be immediately available to prisoners and founded the breach on the substantial periods of delay in the applicants' cases.[80]   6.33

The domestic courts initially struggled with the implications of the Article 5 requirement identified by the ECtHR in *James* for prisoners who have completed the tariff element of a life or indeterminate sentence to be given a real opportunity for rehabilitation. In *R (Kaiyam) v Secretary of State for Justice*,[81] the Supreme Court accepted the ECtHR's conclusion that such an obligation arose, but declined to accept that it was imposed under Article 5(1) and instead characterized it as a freestanding 'ancillary obligation'. The Court's concern was to avoid any implication that IPP and life prisoners detained without access to rehabilitation courses were entitled to immediate release, and with it the prospect of having to declare the statutory scheme providing for release by the Parole Board incompatible with Convention rights pursuant to section 4 of the Human Rights Act. The Supreme Court found the ancillary obligation to be breached in the case of each of the claimants. When the claimants applied to the ECtHR in *Kaiyam v United Kingdom*, asserting breaches of Article 5(1), their applications were each declared to be manifestly ill-founded and inadmissible. However, the ECtHR declined to adopt the Supreme Court's ancillary duty analysis and adhered to its reasoning in *James*.[82] In doing so, the Court made clear that the threshold for a breach of Article 5(1) due to detention having become arbitrary as a result of a failure to provide access to rehabilitative courses is a high one. That threshold was not even, for example, crossed by an 18-month post-tariff delay in one of the cases before it. The approach adopted in the *James* case was subsequently cited with approval by the Grand Chamber.[83]   6.34

In *Brown v Parole Board for Scotland*,[84] the Supreme Court departed from its analysis in *Kaiyam* and followed what it now recognized to be a clear and consistent line of ECtHR case law. It noted that this was an unusual situation where the approach of the Supreme Court had in fact become more demanding than the approach of the ECtHR. The Court was reassured that the threshold for a breach of Article 5(1)(a) was high, but—more fundamentally—it now recognized that the ECtHR had concluded in *James* that the requirement under Article 5(4)   6.35

---

[79] *Lee, James and Wells v United Kingdom* App Nos 25119/09 & others, 18 September 2012.
[80] ibid paras 194 and 220.
[81] *R (Kaiyam) v Secretary of State for Justice* [2014] UKSC 66, [2015] AC 1344.
[82] *Kaiyam v United Kingdom* (2016) 62 EHRR SE13, paras 71–72.
[83] *Murray v the Netherlands* (2016) 64 EHRR 3, para 102.
[84] *Brown v Parole Board for Scotland* [2017] UKSC 69, [2018] AC 1.

was satisfied by the availability of judicial review in order to secure access to the required means to demonstrate rehabilitation.[85]

(c) Article 5(1)(b)

6.36 Article 5(1)(b) sanctions the detention of a person who has failed to observe a court order or failed to fulfil a legal obligation. Article 5(1)(b) presumes that the person arrested or detained has had an opportunity to comply with the court order and has failed to do so, which obviously entails their having been notified of the order.[86] The reference to a failure to fulfil a legal obligation concerns cases where the law permits the detention of a person to compel them to fulfil a specific legal obligation[87] which already applies to them and which they have until then failed to satisfy. Detention must be aimed at or directly contribute to securing the fulfilment of that obligation and must not be punitive in character. The nature of the obligation must itself be compatible with the Convention and a balance must be struck between the importance in a democratic society of securing the immediate fulfilment of the legal obligation and the importance of the right to liberty.[88]

6.37 'Court orders' can include failure to: pay a fine imposed by a court;[89] submit to a court-ordered medical examination;[90] comply with a court order to relinquish custody of children;[91] and a breach of a bind-over to keep the peace.[92] 'Legal obligations' found to justify detention have included the obligation to undertake military service,[93] to keep an identity card,[94] and to comply with a police officer's instruction under public order legislation not to engage in violence at a football match.[95] Failure by a bankrupt to cooperate with a trustee in bankruptcy has also been found to fall within Article 5(1)(b).[96]

6.38 A period of detention will in principle be lawful if carried out pursuant to a court order. A subsequent finding that the court erred under domestic law in making the order will not necessarily retrospectively affect the validity of the period of detention. The ECtHR has therefore generally refused to uphold applications from persons convicted of criminal offences who complain that their convictions or sentences were found by the appellate courts to have been based on errors of fact or law.[97]

---

[85] ibid paras 14–16 and 25, and paras 42–45.
[86] *Beiere v Latvia* App No 30954/05, 29 November 2011, paras 49–50.
[87] Thus a general obligation to comply with the criminal law will not suffice: see eg *R (Hicks) v Commissioner of Police of the Metropolis* [2017] UKSC 9, [2017] AC 256, paras 27 and 40.
[88] *S, V & A v Denmark* App Nos 35553/12 & others, 22 October 2018 [GC], paras 80–83.
[89] *Airey v Ireland* (1977) 8 DR 42 (ECommHR).
[90] *X v Germany* (1975) 3 DR 92.
[91] *Paradis v Germany* App No 4065/04, 4 September 2007.
[92] *Steel v UK* (1998) 28 EHRR 603.
[93] *Johansen v Norway* (1985) 44 DR 155.
[94] *Freda v Italy* (1980) 21 DR 250.
[95] *Ostendorf v Germany* App No 15598/08, 17 March 2013.
[96] *Hickling v Baker* [2007] EWCA 287, [2007] 1 WLR 2386.
[97] *Benham v UK* (1996) 22 EHRR 293, para 42.

In *Beghal v Director of Public Prosecutions*, concerning the power under Schedule   6.39
7 of the Terrorism Act 2000 to detain a person for questioning and search at a port
of entry which does not require reasonable grounds of suspicion, the Supreme Court
held that while this fell within Article 5(1)(b) it was not the case that a detention was
'automatically justified'. The level of intrusion occasioned by detention for up to the
maximum permitted six hours, or removal to a police station, was of a different order
to that occasioned by routine compulsory questioning and search. Detention which
went beyond what was necessary to complete the routine questioning process would
thus require an objectively demonstrated suspicion in order to be proportionate.[98]

The ECtHR has had to grapple with the compatibility with Article 5(1)(b) of   6.40
preventative measures to avoid apprehended football hooliganism. In *S, V & A v
Denmark* the Grand Chamber considered the requirement under the Article 5(1)
(b) case law that the legal obligation relied on must be sufficiently 'specific and
concrete'. The Court reiterated that Article 5(1)(b) does not permit administrative
internment to compel a person to discharge their general duty of obedience to the
law. In the context in issue, an obligation would only be sufficiently specific and
concrete if the place and time of the imminent commission of the offence and its
potential victim(s) have been sufficiently specified; if the person concerned was
made aware of the specific act which they were to refrain from committing; and if
that person showed themselves not to be willing to refrain from committing that
act.[99] Whether or not a specific police order not to engage in particular conduct,
with a warning as to the consequences, was issued has been a significant factor in
whether detention has been found to be compatible with Article 5(1)(b) or not.[100]

(d) *Article 5(1)(c)*

Article 5(1)(c) concerns the arrest or detention of suspects in the course of the   6.41
administration of criminal justice. In essence, it contemplates arrest and detention
on remand. Arrest or detention is lawful only if it is based on a reasonable suspicion
that a person has committed a crime, or when it is reasonably considered necessary
to prevent a person from committing a crime or from fleeing after committing one.
Detention must be a proportionate measure in the circumstances.[101]

The test of reasonable suspicion is an objective one; an honestly held suspicion   6.42
is insufficient. The applicants in *Fox v UK* had been arrested under the Northern
Ireland (Emergency Provisions) Act 1978, which required only that the arresting
official 'genuinely and honestly' suspected the person arrested to be a terrorist.[102]
The ECtHR found a violation of Article 5(1)(c) on the basis that this was a lower
standard than reasonable suspicion, as 'reasonable suspicion supposes the existence

---

[98] *Beghal v Director of Public Prosecutions* [2015] UKSC 49, [2016] AC 88, paras 52–56.
[99] *S, V & A v Denmark* App Nos 35553/12 & others, 22 October 2018 [GC], paras 79–87.
[100] Compare *Schwabe and M.G. v Germany* App nos 8080/08 & others, 1 December 2011, with *Ostendorf
v Germany* App No 15598/08, 7 March 2013; and see *S, V and A v Denmark* App Nos 35553/12 & others,
22 October 2018 [GC], para 83.
[101] *Ladent v Poland* App No 11036/03, 18 March 2008.
[102] *Fox v UK* (1990) 13 EHRR 157.

of facts or information which would satisfy an objective observer that the person concerned may have committed the offence'. Facts which raise a suspicion need not be of the same level as is required to justify a conviction or even the bringing of a charge, which comes at the next stage of the process of criminal investigation, but sufficient facts must be available at the time of the arrest and cannot be retrospectively supplied.[103] If detention continues after a point at which the investigating authorities cease to have a reasonable suspicion that an offence has been committed that will breach Article 5(1)(c).[104]

6.43   There has been a debate in the case law as to the extent to which—if at all— Article 5(1)(c) permits preventive detention. In *Lawless v Ireland (No 3)* the state argued that the second limb of Article 5(1)(c), permitting detention where it is reasonably necessary to prevent a crime, allowed preventive detention of terrorist suspects.[105] The ECtHR held that this would 'lead to conclusions repugnant to the fundamental principles of the Convention'.[106] An arrest is lawful under Article 5(1) (c) only if the purpose is to bring the detainee before a competent legal authority. However, the fact that the suspect may not ultimately be brought before a court or charged with a crime does not undermine the arrest since 'the existence of such a purpose must be considered independently of its achievement'.[107]

6.44   In *Ostendorf v Germany*[108] the applicant was arrested, detained, and then released after one hour under a power authorizing detention to prevent the imminent commission of a criminal offence. The majority of the ECtHR held that the authorization was not permissible under Article 5(1)(c).[109] Applying post-*Lawless* developments in its case law, the reference in Article 5(1)(c) to 'when it is reasonably considered necessary to prevent his committing an offence' was held to cover only pre-trial detention, and not custody for preventive purposes without the person concerned being suspected of having *already* committed an offence. Moreover, the majority held that the purpose of bringing the person before a court must be for the purpose of trial, and not just for the purpose of determining the legality of preventive detention. The minority considered that the analysis in *Lawless* was correct: Article 5(1)(c) was capable of applying in a case of detention for preventive purposes followed by early release (ie before the person could practicably be brought before a court) and it was sufficient that the lawfulness of the detention could subsequently be challenged and decided by a court.

6.45   In *R (Hicks) v Commissioner of Police of the Metropolis*, the Supreme Court considered the same issue in the context of the arrest and detention of a number of anti-monarchist protestors prior to the royal wedding on the basis of apprehended breaches of the peace, who were then released without charge after the wedding

---

[103] ibid para 32; *O'Hara v UK* (2002) 34 EHRR 32; *Selahattin Demirtas v Turkey (No 2)* App No 14305/17, 22 December 2020 [GC], paras 314–21.
[104] *Zenati v Commissioner of Police of the Metropolis and another* [2015] EWCA Civ 80, [2015] QB 758.
[105] *Lawless v Ireland (No 3)* (1979–1980) 1 EHRR 15.
[106] ibid para 14. See also *M v Germany* (2009) 28 BHRC 521.
[107] *Brogan v UK* (1988) 11 EHRR 117.
[108] *Ostendorf v Germany* App No 15598/08, 7 March 2013.
[109] Though on the facts the majority considered it to fall under art 5(1)(b).

on the basis that the risk that they were thought to pose had passed. The Court reiterated the fundamental purpose of Article 5 to protect the individual from arbitrary detention and that an essential part of that is timely judicial control, but it considered that (applying the approach to construction adopted in *Austin v UK*[110]) Article 5 must not be interpreted in a way that would make it impracticable for the police to perform their duties. It considered that this would be the position if the police could not lawfully arrest and detain a person for a relatively short time (too short for it to be practical to take the person before a court) in circumstances where this is reasonably considered to be necessary for the purpose of preventing imminent violence. The Court held that the qualification on the power of arrest or detention under Article 5(1)(c) ('for the purpose of bringing him before the competent legal authority') had to be read as being implicitly dependent on the cause for detention continuing long enough for the person to be brought before the court.[111] In so doing, the Court effectively preferred the view of the minority in *Ostendorf v Germany*.[112]

In *S, V and A v Denmark*,[113] the Grand Chamber endorsed the approach of the   6.46
Supreme Court in *Hicks*. It considered that there were good reasons to prefer the construction of the ECtHR in *Lawless* and the minority in *Ostendorf v Germany*. As such, it confirmed that the lawful detention of a person outside the context of criminal proceedings is, as a matter of principle, permissible under Article 5(1)(c). The purpose requirement of Article 5(1)(c) was to be interpreted with a 'a certain flexibility' and did not exclude short-term preventive detention where the purpose was not to bring the detainees before a judge but rather to release them after a short period, as soon as the risk had passed and before the person could as a matter of practicality be brought before a court. However, the Grand Chamber stressed that this flexibility was constrained by the safeguards under Article 5(1) and 5(3) and (5). The deprivation of liberty must be lawful and in keeping with the purpose of protecting the individual from arbitrariness, the offence must be concrete and specific as regards to, in particular, the place and time of its commission and its victims, and the authorities must furnish some facts or information which would satisfy an objective observer that the person concerned would in all likelihood have been involved in the concrete and specific offence had its commission not been prevented by the detention. The flexibility is further circumscribed by the requirement that the arrest and detention be 'reasonably considered necessary'.[114]

In *Archer v Commissioner of Police of the Metropolis*,[115] the Court of Appeal   6.47
held that it was not inherently incompatible with Article 5(1)(c) for a person to be detained for their own protection in the period between their initial arrest on

---

[110] See para 6.18.

[111] *S, V and A v Denmark* App Nos 35553/12 & others, 22 October 2018 [GC].

[112] In *Renyard and others v UK* App No 57884/17, 5 March 2019, an application by the claimants in the *Hicks* case was dismissed as inadmissible in light of the Grand Chamber decision in *S, V and A v Denmark* App Nos 35553/12 & others, 22 October 2018 [GC], considered immediately below.

[113] *S, V and A v Denmark* App Nos 35553/12 & others, 22 October 2018 [GC].

[114] *S, V and A v Denmark* App Nos 35553/12 & others, 22 October 2018 [GC], paras 98–127 and 137.

[115] *Archer v Commissioner of Police of the Metropolis* [2021] EWCA Civ 1662, [2022] QB 401.

reasonable suspicion of having committed an offence and their production before a court, provided that such detention was on the basis of circumstances relating to nature of the offences concerned. In the case of detention of a juvenile, as was at issue in *Archer*, all pre-trial detention will be subject to rigorous scrutiny by the court and such detention will only be compatible with Article 5(1) if it is a measure of last resort, it is for as short a period as possible, and if the juvenile detainee is kept separate from adult detainees.[116]

(e) *Article 5(1)(d)*

6.48　Article 5(1)(d) covers the detention of minors for the purposes of educational supervision or for the purpose of bringing a minor before a competent legal authority. The accepted European classification of a 'minor' is a person under the age of 18. This exception is designed primarily to cover the detention of children for purposes such as placement in care or secure accommodation. The words 'educational supervision' are not equated rigidly with notions of classroom teaching, and in the context of a young person in local authority care, educational supervision can embrace wider aspects of the exercise of parental rights for the benefit and protection of the person concerned.[117] However, in *P and another v Poland*,[118] the ECtHR unsurprisingly held that detention of a 14-year-old, who had been the victim of rape and was seeking an abortion, with the purpose of separating her from her parents (who supported her obtaining an abortion) and in order to prevent the abortion taking place could under 'no stretch of the imagination' be considered to have been ordered for educational supervision within the meaning of Article 5(1)(d).

(f) *Article 5(1)(e)*

6.49　Article 5(1)(e) is drafted in language which now appears very dated. It permits the detention of those with infectious diseases, persons of unsound mind, alcoholics, drug addicts, and vagrants. According to early Strasbourg authorities, these people are specified because 'they have to be considered as occasionally dangerous for public safety' and 'their own interests may necessitate their detention'.[119] The ECtHR has emphasized that in applying Article 5(1)(e), detention must be 'necessary' in the circumstances and in accordance with the principle of proportionality.[120]

6.50　The detention of persons of unsound mind is the most commonly invoked of the Article 5(1)(e) grounds.[121] This term has an autonomous meaning in Convention case law and the ECtHR has emphasized that it is a term whose meaning evolves as psychiatry progresses.[122] Three minimum requirements must

---

[116] ibid paras 118–26.

[117] *Koniarska v United Kingdom* App No 33670/96, 12 October 2000.

[118] *P and another v Poland* [2013] 1 FCR 476.

[119] *Guzzardi v Italy* (1980) 3 EHRR 333.

[120] *Enhorn v Sweden* App No 56529/00, 25 January 2005, para 36.

[121] In the UK, this element of art 5(1)(e) is primarily of relevance in the context of, and compliance with it is primarily secured through, the Mental Health Act 1983.

[122] *Ilnseher v Germany* App Nos 10211/12 & another, 4 December 2018 [GC], para 127.

be satisfied to justify the detention of persons of unsound mind, these are known as the '*Winterwerp* criteria':

(a) the individual must be reliably shown to be of unsound mind;

(b) the mental disorder must be of a kind or degree warranting compulsory confinement; and

(c) the validity of continued confinement depends upon the persistence of such a disorder.[123]

In respect of the first of these requirements, a competent authority (generally a court) must be satisfied that the person in question has a recognized mental disorder, which must be sufficiently serious so as to necessitate treatment in an institution for mental health patients. That requires objective medical expertise which must be sufficiently recent;[124] the competent authority must subject that evidence to strict scrutiny and reach its own decision. Absent the opinion of a medical expert, the deprivation of liberty on this basis is likely to be regarded as arbitrary.[125] As to the second requirement, a mental disorder will be of a degree warranting compulsory confinement if this 'is necessary because the person needs therapy, medication or other clinical treatment to cure or alleviate his condition, but also where the person needs control and supervision to prevent him from, for example, causing harm to himself or other persons'.[126] There is no requirement that the detained person has committed any offence.[127]   6.51

The *Winterwerp* criteria apply regardless of whether the relevant mental disorder is curable and/or whether the person is amenable to treatment.[128] These criteria also apply to recall decisions where, for example, a person has been recalled to a secure hospital following a breach of conditions attached to a conditional discharge from detention.[129] The authorities bear the burden of proof of establishing that these criteria are satisfied when detaining and continuing to detain mental health patients.[130] A measure taken without the prior consultation of the interested person will attract especially careful scrutiny.[131]   6.52

Finally, detention of a person as a mental health patient will only be lawful under Article 5(1)(e) if it takes place in a hospital, clinic, or other appropriate institution.[132] By   6.53

---

[123] *Winterwerp v Netherlands* (1979) 2 EHRR 387; *Stanev v Bulgaria* App No 36760/06, 17 January 2012 [GC], para 145; *Ilnseher v Germany* App Nos 10211/12 & another, 4 December 2018 [GC], paras 127–34.

[124] The ECtHR has found art 5(1)(e) to have been breached in cases where the domestic authorities have relied on medical opinions which were not sufficiently recent, see eg *Miklić v Croatia* App No 41023/19, 7 April 2022.

[125] See the discussion of the relevant principles in *PW v Austria* App No 10425/19, 21 June 2022, para 31.

[126] *Ilnseher v Germany* App Nos 10211/12 & another, 4 December 2018 [GC], para 129.

[127] *Denis and Irvine v Belgium* App Nos 62819/17 & another, 1 June 2021 [GC], para 168.

[128] *Rooman v Belgium* App No 18052/11, 31 January 2019 [GC], para 190.

[129] *M v Secretary of State for Justice* [2018] UKSC 60, [2019] AC 712, para 11.

[130] See eg *Hutchison Reid v UK* App No 50272/99, 20 February 2003, paras 69–74.

[131] *Stanev v Bulgaria* App No 36760/06, 17 January 2012 [GC], para 157.

[132] *Ilnseher v Germany* App Nos 10211/12 & another, 4 December 2018 [GC], para 138. In the UK the Mental Health Act does not permit the First-tier Tribunal or Secretary of State to impose conditions which would amount to a deprivation of liberty on a person who is conditionally discharged from a hospital (*M v Secretary of State for Justice* [2018] UKSC 60, [2019] AC 712).

way of example, the ECtHR found Switzerland to be in breach of Article 5(1)(e) where authorities held a person with a serious personality disorder and psychopathy (who posed a very high risk of committing further violent offences) in an ordinary prison.[133]

6.54   There is limited case law on the deprivation of liberty to prevent the spreading of infectious diseases. In *Enhorn v Sweden*, the ECtHR emphasized the 'last resort' nature of detention for this reason.[134] In assessing the lawfulness of deprivation of liberty on this basis, the 'essential criteria' are that the spreading of the disease would be dangerous for public health and safety; detention of the person is necessary in order to prevent this; and less severe measures have been considered and found to be insufficient to safeguard the public interest. The ECtHR has held that 'when these criteria are no longer fulfilled, the basis for the deprivation of liberty will cease to exist'.[135] However, deprivation of liberty on this basis is not limited to situations where the detained individual has already been found to be infectious or where there has been an individualized assessment of risk—it can be purely preventative.[136] The UK's requirement for travellers arriving from certain countries during the Covid-19 pandemic to quarantine in hotel accommodation for 10 days was held to fall within Article 5(1)(e) and was upheld as lawful.[137]

6.55   So far as the detention of alcoholics and drug addicts is concerned, the ECtHR has held that this is not limited to persons who are in a clinical state of addiction: 'persons who are not medically diagnosed as "alcoholics", but whose conduct and behaviour under the influence of alcohol pose a threat to public order or themselves, can be taken into custody for the protection of the public or their own interests, such as their health or personal safety'.[138] Article 5(1)(e) does not, however, permit the detention of a person merely because they have consumed alcohol.[139] Again, detention is a last resort and the authorities would need to show that less severe measures have been considered and deemed to be insufficient to meet the relevant threat; whether or not a person was released as soon as they had ceased to be under the influence of alcohol is likely to be an important consideration in determining whether their detention was necessary.[140]

(g) Article 5(1)(f)

6.56   Article 5(1)(f) provides that a person can be deprived of their liberty to (i) prevent them from effecting an unauthorized entry into the country; or (ii) where the state is

---

[133] *WA v Switzerland* App No 38958/16, 2 November 2021, para 46.

[134] *Enhorn v Sweden* (2005) 41 EHRR 633.

[135] ibid para 44.

[136] *R (Hotta) v Secretary of State for Health and Social Care* [2021] EWHC 3359 (Admin), [2022] 4 WLR 31, para 18.

[137] *R (Hotta) v Secretary of State for Health and Social Care* [2021] EWHC 3359 (Admin), [2022] 4 WLR 31; *R (Khalid) v Secretary of State for Health and Social Care* [2021] EWHC 2156 (Admin).

[138] *Kharin v Russia* App No 37345/03, 3 February 2011, para 34. This same reasoning is likely to apply to the taking of drugs; however, where the drugs are controlled/proscribed drugs there may be an alternative basis under art 5(1) for depriving a person of their liberty.

[139] ibid.

[140] ibid paras 40 and 45.

taking action against them with a view to their deportation or extradition. In some circumstances both grounds for deprivation of liberty will apply. This provision is concerned with controlling the 'liberty of aliens in an immigration context'.[141]

Detention is for the purpose of preventing unauthorized entry where a person enters a country unlawfully in a manner that evades border controls, for example by a small boat,[142] as well as where they arrive by lawful means but have not (yet) been authorized to enter to the country.[143] As the Grand Chamber has explained: 6.57

> States have the right, as a matter of well-established international law and subject to their treaty obligations including the Convention, to control the entry, residence and expulsion of aliens ... It is a necessary adjunct to this right that States are permitted to detain would-be immigrants who have applied for permission to enter, whether by way of asylum or not. Deprivation of liberty of asylum-seekers to prevent their unauthorised entry into a State's territory is not in itself in contravention with the Convention.[144]

In a judgment on the application of Article 5(1)(f) to asylum-seekers who had surrendered to immigration authorities and then been detained in 'reception centres', a majority of the Grand Chamber in *Saadi v UK* agreed with the domestic courts[145] and found that: 6.58

> until a state has 'authorised' entry to the country, any entry is 'unauthorised' and the detention of a person who wishes to effect entry and who needs but does not yet have authorisation to do so, can be, without any distortion of language, to 'prevent his effecting an unauthorised entry'.[146]

The Grand Chamber has stressed that in this context: 'the place and conditions of detention should be appropriate, bearing in mind that "the measure is applicable not to those who have committed criminal offences but to aliens who, often fearing for their lives, have fled from their own country"'.[147] 6.59

In contrast to a number of the other exceptions under Article 5(1), there is no requirement, as a matter of Convention law, that detention be necessary for or proportionate to the aim of preventing a person from effecting unauthorized entry into and/or deporting them from the country.[148] In respect of detention with a view to deportation or extradition, for the purposes of Article 5(1)(f) it is 'immaterial whether the underlying decision to expel can be justified under national or Convention law'.[149] 6.60

---

[141] *Khlaifia & others v Italy* App No 16483/12, 16 December 2016 [GC], para 89.

[142] ibid para 96.

[143] *ZA and others v Russia* App Nos 61411/15 and others, 21 November 2019 [GC] (concerning persons arriving by air who did not have visas to enter the country but claimed asylum at the airport).

[144] ibid para 160.

[145] See *R (Saadi and others) v Secretary of State for the Home Department* [2002] UKHL 41, [2002] 1 WLR 3131.

[146] *Saadi v UK* (2008) 24 BHRC 123 [GC], para 65; *Khlaifia & others v Italy* App No 16483/12, 16 December 2016 [GC], para 90. cf *Riad and Idiab v Belgium* App Nos 29787/03 and 29810/03, 24 January 2008.

[147] *Saadi v UK* (2008) 24 BHRC 123 [GC], para 74 (citing *Amuur v France* (1996) 22 EHRR 533).

[148] *Saadi v UK* (2008) 24 BHRC 123 [GC], para 73; cf the position in respect of art 5(1)(b), (d), and (e), see *Denis and Irvine v Belgium* App Nos 62819/17 & others 1 June 2021 [GC], para 130.

[149] *AB and others v France* App No 11593/12, 12 July 2016, para 120. The position in respect of children is different—a test of necessity applies, and where the would-be detainee is a vulnerable person,

6.61   Detention on either (or both) of the grounds contained in Article 5(1)(f) must comply with the following principles: (a) detention must not exceed the period reasonably required for that purpose;[150] (b) accordingly, detention will remain justified only as long as deportation proceedings are 'in progress' and are being prosecuted with 'due diligence'[151] (but Convention case law does not lay down any maximum time period for detention for these purposes);[152] and (c) that, in consequence, where there is no realistic prospect of a person being deported for a particular period, and/or where the state is taking no concrete steps towards deportation (even where it is keeping the situation under 'active review'),[153] continued deprivation of liberty will be 'arbitrary' (and thus unlawful).[154]

6.62   The ECtHR will not, under Article 5, examine the necessity or proportionality of the decision to detain and/or deport/extradite a person.[155] The scope of its review is limited to examining whether there is a legal basis for the detention and whether the domestic courts have properly considered and applied the principles set out above. However, the ECtHR has held that the above principles used to determine whether detention has become arbitrary for the purposes of Article 5(1)(f) are almost identical to those applied by the UK courts (at common law, see para 6.63), which are generally regarded as providing a significant safeguard in respect of detention in this context and ensuring a high intensity of review of detention.[156]

6.63   Domestic decisions on the lawfulness of immigration detention are based on the following principles enshrined in English law prior to the Human Rights Act 1998, known as the *Hardial Singh* principles[157] (which, as noted above, are broadly equivalent to the principles applied by the ECtHR under art 5(1)(f)):

(i) the Secretary of State must intend to deport the person and can only use the power to detain for that purpose; (ii) the deportee may only be detained for a period that is reasonable in all the circumstances; (iii) if, before the expiry of the reasonable period, it becomes apparent that the Secretary of State will not be able to effect deportation within a reasonable period, he should not seek to exercise the power of detention; (iv) the Secretary of State should act with reasonable diligence and expedition to effect removal.[158]

---

national authorities must consider using less severe measures, ie those short of detention (*VM v UK* App No 49734/12, 1 September 2016, para 94).

[150] *A & others v UK* (2009) 26 BHRC 1 [GC], para 164.

[151] ibid; *Khlaifia & others v Italy* App No 16483/12, 16 December 2016 [GC], para 90; *Chahal v UK* (1997) 23 EHRR 413, para 113; *VM v UK* App No 49734/12, 1 September 2016, paras 86–87.

[152] *JN v UK* App No 37289/12, 19 May 2016, paras 83 and 90.

[153] This consideration is of particular relevance where a person is stateless or there are difficulties with obtaining a travel document to enable them to be removed to, eg, their country of origin.

[154] *A & others v UK* (2009) 26 BHRC 1 [GC], para 167.

[155] *Saadi v UK* (2008) 47 EHRR 427; *R (Kambadzi) v Secretary of State for the Home Department* [2011] UKSC 23, [2011] 1 WLR 1299, para 76.

[156] *JN v UK* App No 37289/12, 19 May 2016, para 97.

[157] *R v Governor of Durham Prison, ex p Hardial Singh* [1984] 1 WLR 704, approved by the Supreme Court in *R (Lumba) v Secretary of State for the Home Department* [2011] UKSC 12, [2012] 1 AC 245.

[158] *R (Lumba) v Secretary of State for the Home Department* [2011] UKSC 12, [2012] 1 AC 245, para 22.

The courts have to consider these matters for themselves when determining   **6.64**
whether detention is lawful. When it is brought into force, section 12 of the Illegal
Migration Act 2023 will limit the role of the courts in reviewing detention on the
basis of the *Hardial Singh* principles. Article 5(1)(f) may then assume a greater role
in the courts' review of detention in this context.

3. Procedural safeguards

(a) *Article 5(2)*
Under Article 5(2), everyone arrested has the right to be informed promptly in a   **6.65**
language he or she understands of the reasons for the arrest and of any charge. The
Grand Chamber has described this as 'an elementary safeguard' and an 'integral
part of the scheme of protection afforded by Article 5'.[159] The purpose of this obligation is to enable the arrested person to challenge the lawfulness of their detention.[160]

The ECtHR has held that the terms 'arrest' and 'charge' under Article 5(2) are not   **6.66**
intended to limit the duty to give reasons to the criminal context.[161] The duty applies
equally to all detention, including that of mental health patients. It also extends to
situations in which a person who has been released from custody is recalled.[162]

What is required may however depend on the context and the specific circum-   **6.67**
stances.[163] The reasons that must be given to a person deprived of their liberty
should disclose the 'essential legal[164] and factual grounds' for depriving them of
their liberty.[165] Reasons need not, however, be in writing and they can be provided
in the context of interrogation or questioning.[166] In some cases the ECtHR has
accepted that reasons may be implied from the attendant circumstances because
they were obvious. The Court has, for example, held that to be the case where a
person was detained in the context of a search (undertaken in the immediate aftermath of a high-profile series of explosions) during which explosives were found,[167]
where a person was necessarily aware that he had entered a country illegally and
was detained for that reason,[168] and where a person was aware from the nature of
the process conducted by the authorities that he was being detained due to his
immigration status.[169] However, it will generally be insufficient for arresting officers
only to make reference to the relevant statutory provisions authorizing the arrest.[170]

---

[159] *Khlaifia & others v Italy* App No 16483/12, 16 December 2016 [GC], para 115.
[160] *X v UK* (1982) 4 EHRR 188.
[161] *Van der Leer v Netherlands* (1990) 12 EHRR 567, para 27.
[162] See eg *R (Lee-Hirons) v Secretary of State for Justice* [2016] UKSC 46, [2017] AC 52.
[163] *Khlaifia & others v Italy* App No 16483/12, 16 December 2016 [GC], para 115.
[164] For an example of a case where the insufficient information was provided about the legal basis for
detention see *Khlaifia & others v Italy* App No 16483/12, 16 December 2016 [GC].
[165] ibid para 115.
[166] *MA v Cyprus* App No 41872/10, 23 July 2013, para 229; *MS v Slovakia and Ukraine* App No 17189/11,
11 June 2020, para 102.
[167] *Grubnyk v Ukraine* App No 58444/15, 17 September 2020.
[168] *MS v Slovakia and Ukraine* App No 17189/11, 11 June 2020, para 100.
[169] *MA v Cyprus* App No 41872/10, 23 July 2013, para 234.
[170] *Ireland v UK* (1978) 2 EHRR 25.

6.68   What 'promptness' requires is also context specific and depends on all the circumstances of a person's arrest/detention.[171] This requirement does not mean that in all cases the full reasons must be provided by the arresting officer at the time a person is detained; the ECtHR has accepted that reasons can be provided later.[172] However, longer delays have been held to violate Article 5(2). By way of example, in *Saadi v UK* the ECtHR found that the UK had violated Article 5(2).[173] The applicant was arrested and detained in an immigration reception centre without explanation until his representative was informed of the basis for his detention some 76 hours after his arrest. The Grand Chamber held that reasons had not been supplied promptly.

6.69   A breach of Article 5(2) will not generally (and without more) render a person's detention unlawful.[174]

(b) *Article 5(3)*

6.70   Article 5(3) lays down procedural safeguards which must accompany deprivation of liberty for the purpose of bringing a person before a competent legal authority on reasonable suspicion of having committed an offence. There are two limbs to the provision. The first requires that anyone arrested be brought promptly before a judge or other officer authorized by law to exercise judicial power. The aim of this requirement is to impose a limit on the length of detention authorized by Article 5(1)(c) and thereby to ensure that provisional detention is not unreasonably prolonged.[175] The second limb requires that a person should be tried within a reasonable time and be released on bail pending a trial unless there are sufficient reasons not to release the detainee.[176]

6.71   The first limb encompasses both procedural and substantive elements. There is a procedural requirement that a detained person shall be brought before a judicial officer and have an opportunity to be heard (this must be automatic and cannot depend on an application being made by a detained person).[177] There is a substantive obligation for the judicial officer to consider the merits of the person's detention, that is, to consider whether their detention falls within the permitted exception to liberty under Article 5(1)(c).[178] Inherent in the first limb is a requirement that the judicial officer who performs this exercise must have the 'requisite guarantees of independence from the executive and the parties' and they must be empowered to order the detainee's release.[179] The ECtHR adopts a strict approach to the requirement of promptness in the first limb—there is a very little scope for

---

[171] *Khlaifia & others v Italy* App No 16483/12, 16 December 2016 [GC], para 115.
[172] See eg *Fox v UK* (1990) 13 EHRR 157, para 40; *MA v Cyprus* App No 41872/10, 23 July 2013, para 228. See also, in the context of recalls to secure hospitals, *X v United Kingdom* (1981) 4 EHRR, para 107.
[173] *Saadi v UK* (2008) 24 BHRC 123.
[174] *R (Lee-Hirons) v Secretary of State for Justice* [2016] UKSC 46, [2017] AC 52, paras 38–39.
[175] *Wemhoff v Germany* (1979–80) 1 EHRR 55; *Neumeister v Austria* (1968) 1 EHRR 91.
[176] *De Wilde, Ooms and Versyp v Belgium* (1971) 1 EHRR 373.
[177] *McKay v UK* (2007) 44 EHRR 41 [GC], para 34.
[178] *Buzadji v Moldova* (2016) 42 BHRC 398 [GC], paras 98–99.
[179] ibid; *McKay v UK* (2007) 44 EHRR 41 [GC], para 35; *Klamecki v Poland* (2003) 39 EHRR 7.

flexibility.[180] The court has held that, for the purposes of Article 5(3), a detained person must be brought before a judicial officer no later than four days after they were first detained.[181] Promptness may, however, require that this first review takes place sooner where, for example, the detainee is vulnerable,[182] a minor,[183] and/or there is no proper justification for not bringing them before a judge earlier because there are no 'special difficulties' or 'particular circumstances'.[184]

The protection of the second limb of Article 5(3) is triggered as soon as a person   6.72
is deprived of their liberty on grounds falling within Article 5(1)(c).[185] The Grand Chamber has stressed that there is a presumption in favour of release from detention pending trial and the authorities are required to consider whether alternative means, short of detention, could be used to secure a person's attendance at trial.[186] It is only if there are 'relevant and sufficient reasons' to justify detention on remand that the state may refuse to release a person pending trial. The ECtHR has accepted that the following justifications are acceptable reasons for refusing bail: the danger of absconding; the risk of pressure being brought to bear on witnesses or of evidence being tampered with, or a detainee otherwise seeking to interfere with the course of justice; the risk of collusion; the risk of reoffending; the risk of causing public disorder; and the need to protect the detainee.[187] Any such risks must be substantiated and the justifications relied on by the authorities should not be 'abstract, general or stereotyped'.[188]

In 2016 the Grand Chamber went further than previous ECtHR case law and   6.73
held that when the judicial officer referred to under the first limb of Article 5(3) must review promptly after a person's arrest determine not only whether there is a reasonable suspicion a person has committed a crime (meaning that their defendant may be justified under art 5(1)(c)) but *additionally* whether there are relevant and sufficient reasons for their being detained pending trial.[189] The Court decided to 'synchronize' the second limb with the first on the basis that this would bring clarity and greater to certainty to Convention case law, while also providing enhanced protection against detention beyond a reasonable time.[190]

The ECtHR has emphasized repeatedly that continued pre-trial detention of an   6.74
accused person can be justified 'only if there are specific indications of a genuine

---

[180] *McKay v UK* (2007) 44 EHRR 41 [GC], para 33.

[181] ibid para 47. In wholly exceptional circumstances, the ECtHR has held a longer period to be compatible with art 5(3), including where a person was detained on a Spanish customs ship 5500km from Spanish territory (*Rigopolous v Spain* App No 37388/97, 12 January 1999).

[182] *Gutsanovi v Bulgaria* App No 34529/10, 15 October 2013 (three days and five hours).

[183] *Ipek v Turkey* App No 17019/02, 3 February 2009 (three days and nine hours).

[184] ibid para 37.

[185] *Buzadji v Moldova* (2016) 42 BHRC 398 [GC], para 97.

[186] ibid paras 88–89.

[187] ibid para 88; see further *Merabishvili v Georgia* App No 72508/13, 28 November 2017 [GC], paras 223–24; and *Wemhoff v Germany* (1979–80) 1 EHRR 55.

[188] *Merabishvili v Georgia* App No 72508/13, 28 November 2017 [GC], para 222.

[189] *Buzadji v Moldova* (2016) 42 BHRC 398 [GC], paras 100–02; see also *Merabishvili v Georgia* App No 72508/13, 28 November 2017 [GC], para 222.

[190] *Buzadji v Moldova* (2016) 42 BHRC 398 [GC], paras 101–02.

requirement of public interest which, notwithstanding the presumption of innocence, outweighs the rule of respect for individual liberty laid down in Article 5 of the Convention'.[191] The Court has stressed that 'the persistence of a reasonable suspicion is a condition sine qua non for the validity of the continued detention' of a person under Article 5(1)(c).[192] Accordingly, even if it is established that such suspicion existed when a person was first arrested, it is for the authorities to show that such suspicion persisted throughout the period of detention.[193]

6.75　　Where, during the period of pre-trial detention, investigating authorities cease to have a reasonable suspicion that the detained person committed the offence in question, it is implicit in Article 5(3) (and art 5(1)(c)) that they are 'required to bring the relevant facts to the attention of the court as soon as possible,'[194] and a failure to do so may give rise to a breach of these parts of Article 5 from the date on which a detainee would have been released had this information been placed before the court.[195] Further, it is not only the reasonable suspicion that must be shown to endure throughout a period of pre-trial detention—the authorities must also show that the additional 'relevant and sufficient' reasons for which a person should not be at liberty while awaiting trial continue to exist.[196] In this context there is an important link with Article 5(4) (see paras 6.79–6.84) because one of the mechanisms through the courts review these matters during a period of pre-trial detention is through a detainee exercising their right to have their detention reviewed.[197]

6.76　　In *Gault v UK* the ECtHR held that the fact that the applicant's third retrial would be held promptly was not sufficient reason to deny bail.[198] As the Court emphasized, Article 5(3) does not permit a choice for the authorities between a speedy trial and granting bail. It is, however, legitimate for the courts to adjust the recognizance required by way of bail to reflect the gravity of the offence or the extent of financial liability.[199] It is not permissible to place decisive reliance on the gravity of the charges to justify lengthy periods of pre-trial detention.[200] In *Caballero v UK* the automatic denial of bail under section 25 of the Criminal Justice and Public Order Act 1994 in the case of persons charged with or convicted of homicide or rape after a previous conviction of such an offence was held to be a

---

[191] See eg *Labita v Italy* (2008) 46 EHRR 50 [GC], para 152.

[192] Albeit for the reasons given above, this alone is not sufficient to justify detention on remand.

[193] See eg *Selahattin Demirtaş v Turkey (No. 2)* App No 14305/17, 22 December 2020, para 320; *Merabishvili v Georgia* App No 72508/13, 28 November 2017 [GC], para 234.

[194] *Zenati v Commissioner of Police for the Metropolis & Director of Public Prosecutions* [2015] EWCA Civ 80, [2015] QB 758, para 20.

[195] *AAA v Chief Constable of Kent* [2017] EWHC 3600 (QB), para 36.

[196] *Merabishvili v Georgia* App No 72508/13, 28 November 2017 [GC] is an example of a case in which the ECtHR accepted that there was a sufficient basis when the applicant was first detained but not four months later (see ibid paras 231–35).

[197] See eg *Dimov & another v Bulgaria* App No 30044/10, 7 July 2020 (available only in French), para 70. In that case the court considered the application of art 5(4) with reference to the requirements of art 5(3).

[198] *Gault v UK* (2008) 46 EHRR 1202; *Allen v UK* [2011] Crim LR 147.

[199] *Mangouras v Spain* App No 12050/04, 28 September 2010.

[200] *Kislitsa v Russia* App No 29985/05, 19 June 2012 [GC], para 36.

breach of Article 5(3).[201] Parliament amended this section in order to comply with the judgment making provision for the grant of bail in exceptional circumstances.

What constitutes a trial 'within a reasonable time' and thus a reasonable period 6.77 of pre-trial detention is context and fact specific. It will depend on, among other things, the scope and complexity of the investigation and judicial proceedings which follow.[202] The authorities are expected to act with 'special diligence' in investigating offences and bringing them to trial.[203] However, the ECtHR has stressed that:

while an accused person in detention is entitled to have his case given priority and conducted with particular expedition, this must not stand in the way of the efforts of the judges to clarify fully the facts in issue, to give both the defence and the prosecution all facilities for putting forward their evidence and stating their cases and to pronounce judgment only after careful reflection on whether the offences were in fact committed and on the sentence.[204]

The obligation to act with special diligence falls on the courts (and not directly on 6.78 police or prosecutors), and it is for the courts to ensure that the cases of persons in detention are given priority and conducted with particular expedition.[205] However, in *Zenati v Commissioner of Police for the Metropolis* the Master of the Rolls explained that the conduct of investigative and prosecutorial authorities is relevant to Article 5(3) in two ways:

[First] lack of diligence on the part of those who are responsible for investigating the case and preparing for trial will always be relevant to the question of whether the court has conducted the proceedings with 'special diligence' and whether a detention has been for an unreasonably long period. It is the duty of the court to grant bail where a detention has been for an unreasonably long time…. If delay on the part of the investigating/prosecuting authorities causes the court to fail to conduct the proceedings with special diligence, then those who are responsible for the delay will be responsible for the breach of article 5.3.

[Second] if the investigating authorities fail to bring to the attention of the court material information of which the court should be made aware when reviewing a detention, this may have the effect of causing a decision by the court to refuse bail to be in breach of article 5.3. The investigating authorities must not prevent the court from discharging its duty of reviewing the lawfulness of the detention fairly and with a proper appreciation of all the relevant facts of which the authorities should make the court aware. Unless this is done, there is a risk that the court will make decisions which lead to arbitrary detention in breach of article 5.3.[206]

---

[201] *Caballero v UK* (2000) 30 EHRR 643.

[202] *Ilnseher v Germany* App Nos 10211/12 & another, 4 December 2018 [GC], para 252; *Wemhoff v Germany* (1979–80) 1 EHRR 55, para 17.

[203] *Buzadji v Moldova* (2016) 42 BHRC 398 [GC], para 87.

[204] *Wemhoff v Germany* (1979–80) 1 EHRR 55, para 17; *Tomasi v France* (1993) 15 EHRR 1, para 102.

[205] *Zenati v Commissioner of Police for the Metropolis & Director of Public Prosecutions* [2015] EWCA Civ 80, [2015] QB 758, paras 35, 42–43.

[206] *Zenati v Commissioner of Police for the Metropolis & Director of Public Prosecutions* [2015] EWCA Civ 80, [2015] QB 758, paras 43–44, 64. In *Zenati* the Court of Appeal accepted (on an appeal against the striking out of a claim) that it was arguable that the actions of the police and the Crown Prosecution Service caused the claimant's detention to be considerably longer than was necessary or justified and may have breached art 5. Subsequent authorities suggest that it would take an exceptional case (probably requiring a 'game changing' factor or information not to have been put before the court) for the police to be held to have breached art 5 on this basis (see eg *AAA v Chief Constable of Kent* [2017] EWHC 3600 (QB), paras 40–41; *Andrews v Chief Constable of Suffolk* [2022] EWHC 3162 (KB)).

(c) *Article 5(4)*

6.79　Article 5(4) gives persons deprived of their liberty the right to challenge the lawfulness of their detention before a court. Following the institution of proceedings by a detained person, Article 5(4) also encompasses the rights to a speedy judicial determination of whether their detention is lawful and to release if a court determines it not to be so.[207] While this right is primarily designed to provide a safeguard to persons who *are* in detention, the ECtHR has confirmed that persons who are no longer detained but who wish to challenge their erstwhile detention can still rely on Article 5(4), save that the speediness requirement falls away.[208]

6.80　The 'court' does not necessarily have to be a court of law in the formal sense of the term. However, the body must 'exhibit the necessary judicial procedures and safeguards appropriate to the kind of deprivation of liberty in question, including most importantly independence of the executive and of the parties'.[209] In addition, the body must have the ability to decide the lawfulness of the detention and to order release if detention is found to be unlawful.[210] For example, in *Weeks v UK* the ECtHR found that the Parole Board could be considered a court for the purposes of Article 5(4).[211]

6.81　What constitutes a 'speedy' review of the lawfulness of a person's detention depends on the circumstances (including the complexity of the case, the status of detainee and what is at stake).[212] As with the second limb of Article 5(3) (see para 6.77), the ECtHR has refrained from laying down timeframes that will or will not be considered speedy in the abstract. However, the Court has held that Article 5(4)'s expedition requirement is more exacting than that of Article 6(1):[213] 'while one year per instance may be a rough rule of thumb in Article 6(1) cases, Article 5(4), concerning issues of liberty, requires particular expedition'.[214] Accordingly, the approach of the ECtHR is to examine the particular facts of the case before it and to consider whether, in those specific circumstances, there was a failure to proceed with reasonable speed. Domestic law will not be determinative of this issue.[215]

6.82　In cases of prolonged detention, this right is of ongoing application and requires the availability of a process to enable the lawfulness of the detention to be reviewed at reasonable intervals.[216] What constitutes reasonable intervals depends on the purpose and context of a person's detention (including the applicable exception under art 5(1)). Pre-trial detention under Article 5(1)(c) is generally recognized

---

[207] *Ilnseher v Germany* App Nos 10211/12 & another, 4 December 2018 [GC], para 251; *Khlaifia & others v Italy* App No 16483/12, 16 December 2016 [GC], paras 128–31.

[208] See eg *Osmanović v Croatia* App No 67604/10, 6 November 2012, paras 48–49.

[209] *Benjamin and Wilson v UK* (2003) 36 EHRR 1, para 33; see also *Chahal v UK* (1997) 23 EHRR 413.

[210] ibid.

[211] *Weeks v UK* (1987) 10 EHRR 293. But the ECtHR held that its procedures were inadequate at the time.

[212] See eg *Ilnseher v Germany* App Nos 10211/12 & another, 4 December 2018 [GC], paras 252–53; *GB & another v Turkey* App No 4633/15, 17 October 2019, paras 166–67.

[213] See paras 6.169–6.174.

[214] *Hutchison Reid v UK* App No 50272/99, 20 February 2003, para 79.

[215] See eg *Yaman v Turkey* App No 32446/96, 2 November 2004.

[216] *Bezicheri v Italy* (1989) 12 EHRR 210.

necessitating frequent reviews because there is a presumption that detention on this basis should be strictly limited in duration.[217] Detention pending deportation or extradition (under art 5(1)(f)) also demands shorter intervals between reviews because, the ECtHR has held, the factors affecting the lawfulness of detention are likely to evolve faster in other contexts.[218] Regular reviews are also of particular importance in the context of persons detained on the basis that they are of unsound mind (art 5(1)(e)) to ensure that the *Winterwerp* criteria continue to be satisfied, which, as noted above, involves ensuring that conclusions (and thus detention) are founded on up-to-date medical opinions.[219]

The requirement for reviews of detention at regular intervals does not extend to imprisonment during a determinate sentence of imprisonment imposed by a court.[220] That is because, for the duration of that period, the lawfulness of the person's detention has been decided through judicial proceedings (including any appeal procedures) and that process fulfils the requirements of Article 5(4).[221] In *Whiston* a majority of the Supreme Court held that Article 5(4) does not apply where a person who has been released on licence[222] is recalled to prison during the licence period (which forms part of the sentence imposed by the trial court). Indeed, it does not apply to any fixed-term sentence prisoner (including extended sentence prisoners), regardless of whether or not they are released on licence.[223]   6.83

The position is different in respect of indeterminate sentence prisoners whose detention must be reviewed at regular intervals after the expiry of any tariff period determined by the trial court. The Grand Chamber has explained the reasons for this as follows: 6.84

[C]ontinued detention depends on elements of dangerousness and risk associated with the objectives of the original sentence … These elements may change with the course of time, and thus new issues of lawfulness arise requiring determination by a body satisfying the requirements of Article 5 § 4. It can no longer be maintained that the original trial and appeal proceedings satisfied, once and for all, issues of compatibility of subsequent detention of mandatory life prisoners with the provisions of Article 5 § 1 of the Convention.[224]

---

[217] *Abdulkhakov v Russia* App No 14743/11, 2 October 2012, para 213.

[218] ibid para 214.

[219] The ECtHR has on occasions held art 5(4) to be breached because the authorities have refused to undertake fresh assessments of a detainee's mental health, see eg *Ruiz Rivera v Switzerland* App No 8300/06, 18 February 2014, paras 59–66.

[220] *R (Whiston) v Secretary of State for Justice* [2014] UKSC 39, [2015] AC 176, paras 21–24, 27–28, 38–39; *De Wilde, Ooms and Versyp v Belgium (No 1)* (1970) 1 EHRR 373, para 76.

[221] ibid.

[222] In that case the claimant was actually discretionarily released on home detention curfew prior to the compulsory release after serving 50% of the sentence. He was recalled when it became apparent that his whereabouts could no longer be electronically monitored.

[223] See the observations of the Court of Appeal in *R (Youngsam) v Parole Board* [2019] EWCA Civ 229, [2019] 3 WLR 33, considering the effect of *Whiston*. See also *Brown v Parole Board for Scotland* [2017] UKSC 69, [2018] AC 1, paras 46 and 58.

[224] *Stafford v UK* (2002) 35 EHRR 32, para 87; see also *R (Giles) v Parole Board* [2003] UKHL 32, [2004] 1 AC 1, para 51, where Lord Hope observed that 'The cases where the basic rule has been departed from are cases where decisions as to the length of the detention have passed from the court to the executive and there is a risk that the factors which informed the original decision will change with the passage of time'.

6.85   While Article 5(4) does not require that that the court reviewing a person's detention be permitted to carry out a full merits review (with the possibility of substituting its own assessment for that of the decision maker) the judicial review must be 'wide enough to bear on those conditions which are essential for the "lawful" detention of a person according to Article 5(1)'.[225] For the purposes of Article 5(4), the judicial proceedings need not always be attended by the same guarantees as those required by Article 6(1) for civil or criminal litigation.[226] That is because Articles 5(4) and 6 serve different purposes (the former is concerned with preventing arbitrary detention by ensuring the lawfulness of detention is reviewed, whereas the latter is concerned with ensuring the fairness of the substantive trial) and this 'difference of aims explains why Article 5(4) contains more flexible procedural requirements than Article 6 while being much more stringent as regards speediness'.[227] An oral hearing is not always necessarily in order to comply with Article 5(4), this depends on, inter alia, what the court needs to examine to review the detention, whether there is a need for the examination of witnesses and whether there is a need to clarify particular matters.[228] There are nevertheless procedural requirements that do apply for the purposes of Article 5(4) including adversarial proceedings (which may involve calling and questioning witnesses), the exchange of evidence, and ensuring that there is an equality of arms (including disclosure of documents relevant to the lawfulness of ongoing detention).[229]

6.86   In *A and others v UK*, concerning the indefinite detention of foreign terrorist suspects under the Anti-Terrorism, Crime and Security Act 2001, the Grand Chamber considered the extent of disclosure required by the guarantee of procedural fairness in Article 5(4).[230] In the proceedings before the Special Immigration Appeals Commission, the applicants had been denied access to 'closed material', deemed too sensitive to reveal on the grounds of national security. The 'special advocate' procedure designed by the government was intended to remedy any unfairness in the lack of disclosure by permitting the special advocate to see the closed material and make submissions on the detainee's behalf. The Grand Chamber concluded that there was no difficulty in principle with such a procedure so long as the allegations in the open material were 'sufficiently specific' for the detainee to provide information to his representatives with which to refute them.

---

[225] *A & others v UK* (2009) 26 BHRC 1 [GC], para 202.

[226] *Winterwerp v Netherlands* (1979) 2 EHRR 387; *A & others v UK* (2009) 26 BHRC 1 [GC], paras 203–04.

[227] *Reinprecht v Austria* App No 67175/01, 15 November 2005, paras 39–40.

[228] *Derungs v Switzerland* App No 52089/09, 10 May 2016, paras 72 and 75; *Reinprecht v Austria* App No 67175/01, 15 November 2005, para 41. The effect of art 5(4) is that the Parole Board will generally need hold an oral hearing when considering whether post-tariff indeterminate sentence prisoners need to remain in detention due to the risk they pose (*R (Osborn) v Parole Board* [2013] UKSC 61, [2020] 1 WLR 3932, paras 102–12).

[229] *A & others v UK* (2009) 26 BHRC 1 [GC]; *Reinprecht v Austria* App No 67175/01, 15 November 2005; *Zarakolu v Turkey* App No 15064/12, 15 September 2020 (available only in French); *Sanchez-Reisse v Switzerland* (1986) 9 EHRR 71; *Weeks v UK* (1987) 10 EHRR 293; *Klamecki v Poland* (2003) 39 EHRR 7.

[230] *A and others v UK* (2009) 26 BHRC 1.

Domestically, Article 5(4) arises most frequently in the context of challenges   6.87
to decisions of the Parole Board. This has often been in the context of delays in
the Board considering whether to direct the release of a post-tariff indeterminate
sentence prisoner. In *R (Noorkoiv) v Home Secretary and Parole Board*, the Court
of Appeal considered the delay between the expiry of the tariff period of the appellant's automatic life sentence and the decision of the Parole Board to release him.[231]
The Court held that the delay of two months was incompatible with Article 5(4).
The fact that the delay occurred as a result of resource constraints was no justification in light of the 'imperative need to release from prison any post-tariff prisoner
who no longer remains a danger'.[232] The Supreme Court subsequently confirmed
that a failure to review such a prisoner's detention speedily (if the delay is of at least
three months) should normally result in award of modest damages (as compensation for mental suffering) for a breach of Article 5(4), even if it is not possible to
establish they would have been released earlier were it not for the delay (although
damages are likely to be greater where that is the case).[233]

4. Positive obligations

Article 5 imposes positive obligations to protect vulnerable individuals from dep-   6.88
rivation of liberty by private actors, not to acquiesce in such deprivations,[234] and
effectively to investigate unlawful deprivations of liberty by third parties.[235]

In *Storck v Germany* the applicant alleged a violation of Article 5 because of her   6.89
forced confinement in a private psychiatric institution.[236] The ECtHR held that the
authorities were obliged 'to take measures providing effective protection of vulnerable persons, including reasonable steps to prevent a deprivation of liberty of which
the authorities have or ought to have knowledge'.[237] In *Re A and C* the High Court
considered the extent of local authority obligations where the authority is aware of
restrictions on the liberty of vulnerable individuals.[238] The Court set out in detail
the measures that should be taken in such circumstances, including investigation,
monitoring, and taking reasonable steps to bring the situation to an end.[239]

In *El-Masri v the Former Yugoslav Republic of Macedonia*,[240] the Grand Chamber   6.90
considered a case where the Macedonian authorities had unlawfully detained the

---

[231] *R (Noorkoiv) v Home Secretary and Parole Board* [2002] EWCA Civ 770, [2002] 1 WLR 3284.

[232] ibid para 58.

[233] *R (Faulkner) v Secretary of State for Justice* [2013] UKSC 23, [2013] 2 WLR 1157, paras 54–55, 62, 66, 75.

[234] See eg *Rantsev v Cyprus & Russia* App No 25965/04, 7 January 2010 (which concerned Cypriot the authorities handing a person over to a person who subsequently unlawfully confined her in his apartment; see ibid paras 319–21).

[235] See paras 2.33-2.39 and 4.106-4.109.

[236] *Storck v Germany* (2006) 43 EHRR 6.

[237] ibid para 102.

[238] *Re A and C* [2010] EWHC 978 (Fam), [2010] 2 FLR 1363.

[239] ibid paras 80–96.

[240] *El-Masri v the Former Yugoslav Republic of Macedonia* (2013) 57 EHRR 25 [GC].

applicant in a hotel and then handed him over to the US authorities in the knowledge that he would be subject to extraordinary rendition. It held that Article 5 lays down an obligation not only to refrain from unlawfully depriving people of their right to liberty, but also to take appropriate steps to provide protection against an unlawful interference of Article 5 to everyone within its jurisdiction. This included a procedural obligation to conduct a prompt effective investigation into an arguable claim that a person has been taken into custody and has not been seen since. The Court found that Macedonia had inter alia breached the procedural aspect of Article 5 by failing to undertake any meaningful investigation into the applicant's credible allegations that he was detained arbitrarily.[241] Since the applicant had been handed over to the US authorities in circumstances where it was clear that there would be a 'flagrant breach' of his Article 5 rights, the Macedonian authorities were also held responsible for his subsequent detention by US authorities.

5. Right to compensation

6.91 Article 5(5) guarantees a direct and enforceable right to compensation if a person has been detained in violation of Article 5.[242] This right is reflected in section 9(3)–(5) of the Human Rights Act. This includes the possibility of seeking damages against the Lord Chancellor in respect of a breach of Article 5 arising from a judicial act.[243] This right does not, of course, mean that there is an entitlement to compensation any time a person successfully appeals against a conviction or custodial sentence—they are likely to have been deprived of their liberty on the basis of a conviction by a competent court (per art 5(1)(a)).[244]

6.92 Compensation may cover both non-pecuniary damage (such as injury to feelings or distress) as well as pecuniary loss they have suffered.[245] However, only compensatory—not exemplary—damages can be awarded.[246] In determining damages under Article 5, regard must be had to the ECtHR's case law on the award of damages under Article 41 of the Convention and to the fact that a finding of a breach may constitute just satisfaction.[247]

---

[241] ibid paras 230–43.

[242] See eg *Brogan v UK* (1988) 11 EHRR 117; *Fox v UK* (1990) 13 EHRR 157; *Caballero v UK* (2000) 30 EHRR 643; *Curley v UK* (2001) 31 EHRR 14.

[243] See the discussion in *Mazhar v Lord Chancellor* [2019] EWCA Civ 1558, [2021] Fam 103, paras 42–44, 49, 64, 67.

[244] *LL v Lord Chancellor* [2017] EWCA Civ 237, [2017] 4 WLR 162, para 65.

[245] See eg *R (Faulkner) v Secretary of State for Justice* [2013] UKSC 23, [2013] 2 WLR 1157. See paras 4.58–4.79.

[246] Human Rights Act, s 9; *R (KB) v Mental Health Review Tribunal (Damages)* [2003] EWHC 193 (Admin), [2004] QB 936.

[247] For a detailed overview see *R (Faulkner) v Secretary of State for Justice* [2013] UKSC 23, [2013] 2 WLR 1157; see also *R (Greenfield) v Secretary of State for the Home Department* [2005] 1 WLR 673.

C. ARTICLE 6: RIGHT TO A FAIR TRIAL

The right to a fair trial is a paradigm human right. It is central to the existence of   6.93
the rule of law, because the guarantee of all other rights depends upon the proper
administration of justice.[248] As the House of Lords held in *Secretary of State for the
Home Department v AF (No 3)* the right to a genuinely fair trial is a 'core principle'
which cannot give way to competing concerns.[249] It is explicitly referred to in the
Preamble. Given the importance of the rule of law to a democratic society, the
courts have repeatedly emphasized that Article 6 should be given a broad and pur-
posive interpretation, and its exceptions narrowly construed. In *Delcourt v Belgium*,
for example, the ECtHR stated that:

> In a democratic society within the meaning of the Convention, the right to a fair administration
> of justice holds such a prominent place that a restrictive interpretation of Article 6 (1) would not
> correspond to the aim and the purpose of that provision.[250]

In keeping with this broad interpretive approach, Article 6 offers protection   6.94
which goes beyond the trial itself, extending to any part of the criminal or civil
process which may impact on the outcome of a case. For example, considering
whether or not a trial is fair can include making sure that proper procedures have
been followed by the police at the investigation and charging stages.

Article 6 does not apply to all proceedings which one might consider to be 'legal',   6.95
and the nature of proceedings must therefore be carefully considered together with a
number of other significant limitations set out in Article 6. Article 6(1) applies to determinative legal proceedings generally, whether criminal or civil. Although the specific
guarantees in Article 6(2) and (3) relate to criminal cases only, the overarching requirements of Article 6(1) may under certain circumstances require similar guarantees even
in civil proceedings. Criminal practitioners should also bear in mind that the Article
6(1) case law may be of relevance to them, even when it concerns civil matters.

The courts have repeatedly held that the right to a fair trial protected by Article   6.96
6(1) is absolute in the sense that a conviction obtained in breach of it cannot stand,
but the constituent elements of Article 6 are not unlimited. 'The only balancing
permitted is in respect of what the concept of a fair trial entails.'[251] The central
consideration in any limitation of the constituent rights is whether the essence of
the overarching right to a fair hearing is preserved.[252] In determining whether this
is the case, the ECtHR will have regard to the proceedings as a whole, including

---

[248] *Golder v UK* (1975) 1 EHRR 524, para 35.

[249] *Secretary of State for the Home Department v AF (No 3)* [2009] UKHL 28, [2009] 3 WLR 74.

[250] *Delcourt v Belgium* (1970) 1 EHRR 335, para 25. See also *Moreira de Azevedo v Portugal* (1990) 13
EHRR 721, para 66; *R (Morgan Grenfell and Co Ltd) v Special Commissioner of Income Tax* [2002] UKHL
21, [2003] 1 AC 563; *Multiplex v Croatia* App No 58112/00, 10 July 2003, para 44.

[251] See eg *Heaney and McGuinness v Ireland* (2001) 33 EHRR 12; *R v A (No 2)* [2001] UKHL 25, [20002]
1 AC 45, para 38 per Lord Steyn who confirmed *Brown v Stott* [2003] 1 AC 681.

[252] See eg *Heaney and McGuinness v Ireland* (2001) 33 EHRR 12; *R v Sellick (Santino)* [2005] EWCA
Crim 651, [2005] 1 WLR 3257.

appellate proceedings, and may consider whether or not the appellate proceedings have rectified any defect which arose at the first instance hearing.[253] For example, in *Gäfgen v Germany*, a case concerning Article 3, the ECtHR held that in the context of the use of evidence obtained by inhuman and degrading treatment, the fairness of a criminal trial was only compromised where breach had been shown to have had a bearing on the outcome of the proceedings against the defendant.[254] The judgment of fairness is fact-sensitive.[255] Further, fairness is an evolving concept so procedures once deemed to be fair may occasionally merit reassessment.[256]

6.97   Although derogation from Article 6 is permitted in theory, any such derogation would be extremely difficult to justify.

1. Scope of Article 6

6.98   The ECtHR has repeatedly confirmed that the definitions of the core elements of Article 6(1)—'determination', 'civil rights and obligations', and 'criminal charge'—are to be given an *autonomous* (or independent) Convention meaning.[257] This ensures that the application of the fair trial guarantee is consistently and fairly applied, and is not dependent on the varying meanings of such terms in the national laws of Member States.[258] The ECtHR concerns itself with what fairness demands in particular circumstances.[259] Thus, although an examination of the claimant's rights as a matter of domestic law is the proper starting point, it is also necessary to look behind appearances and investigate the realities of the procedure.[260]

6.99   As with Article 2 or 3, a Member State may be responsible for violation of Article 6 by exposing an individual within its jurisdiction to an unfair trial by deporting or extraditing him or her to a third country.[261] However, there is no breach of Article 6 unless there is a real risk of a 'flagrant violation' of the fundamental rights protected by Article 6, meaning a breach so fundamental as to amount to a nullification or destruction of the very essence, of the guaranteed rights.[262] Examples include use of torture evidence; conviction *in absentia* with no possibility subsequently to obtain a fresh determination of the merits of the charge; a trial which is summary in nature and conducted with a total disregard for the rights of the defence; detention without any access to an independent and impartial tribunal to have the legality of the detention reviewed; and deliberate and systematic refusal of access to a

---

[253] *Edwards v UK* (1993) 15 EHRR 417.
[254] *Gäfgen v Germany* (2011) 52 EHRR 1, para 178.
[255] *R v S* [2010] EWCA Crim 1579, [2011] Crim LR 671.
[256] *R v H* [2004] UKHL 3, [2004] 2 AC 134.
[257] See eg *Naït-Liman v Switzerland* (2018) 45 BHRC 639 [GC], para 106; *Grzęda v Poland* (2022) 53 BHRC 631 [GC], para 287.
[258] *Engel v Netherlands* (1976) 1 EHRR 647; *Adolf v Austria* (1982) 4 EHRR 313.
[259] *König v Federal Republic of Germany* (1978) 2 EHRR 170.
[260] *Crosbie v Secretary of State for Defence* [2011] EWHC 879 (Admin), para 80.
[261] *Soering v UK* (1989) 11 EHRR 439.
[262] *R (Ullah) v Secretary of State for the Home Department* [2004] UKHL 26, [2004] AC 323; *Othman Abu Qatada* (2012) 55 EHRR 1.

lawyer, especially for an individual detained in a foreign country.[263] The principle was found to be breached by the ECtHR for the first time in the *Abu Qatada* case on the basis of a real risk of use of torture evidence by the Jordanian authorities.[264]

The evidential threshold for a 'flagrant denial of justice' was considered by the House of Lords in *RB (Algeria) and others v Secretary of State for the Home Department* (part of the *Abu Qatada* litigation). It held that a high degree of assurance that evidence obtained from torture of third parties would be relied on was required to engage the principle.[265] However, when the case reached the ECtHR, it held that the familiar 'real risk' test from the Article 2 and 3 expulsion cases was applicable and found this to be satisfied on the evidence before it, distinguishing this case from the general and unspecific alleged breach found to be insufficient by the Grand Chamber in the *Mamatkulov and Askarov* case.[266]   6.100

That is not to say, however, that a more pervasive defect in a receiving state's judicial system cannot be relied upon: thus in *Kapri v Lord Advocate*,[267] a case concerning alleged systemic judicial corruption in Albania, the Supreme Court found that it was not obvious that the only way the 'flagrant denial of justice' test could be met was by pointing to particular facts or circumstances affecting the case of the particular individual. It considered that the allegations made in the case before it were sufficiently serious to require that the case be remitted.   6.101

(a) Determination

Article 6 applies only to the 'determination' of civil rights or obligations, or criminal charges. 'Determination' essentially requires that there be a dispute or 'contestation',[268] and a resolution procedure. It encompasses all proceedings (including those between private parties), the result of which is 'decisive' for civil rights and obligations[269] or which involves the individual being 'substantially affected' in relation to a criminal charge.[270] The Grand Chamber in *Grzęda v Poland* recently summarized the principles applicable to claims under the civil limb of Article 6:[271]   6.102

(a) there must be a 'dispute' ('contestation' in French) over a right which can be said, at least on arguable grounds, to be recognized under domestic law, irrespective of whether that right is protected under the Convention;

---

[263] *Othman Abu Qatada* (2012) 55 EHRR 1, paras 259 and 267.

[264] ibid. This decision was applied domestically by the Special Immigration Appeals Commission, and upheld by the Court of Appeal in *Othman v Secretary of State for the Home Department* [2013] EWCA Civ 277.

[265] *RB (Algeria) and others v Secretary of State for the Home Department* [2009] UKHL 10, [2010] 2 AC 110.

[266] *Othman Abu Qatada* (2012) 55 EHRR 1, paras 259–61 citing *Mamatkulov and Askarov v Turkey* (2005) 41 EHRR 25.

[267] *Kapri v Lord Advocate* [2013] UKSC 48, [2013] 1 WLR 2324.

[268] See eg *König v Germany* (1978) 2 EHRR 170, para 87.

[269] *Ringeisen v Austria* (1971) 1 EHRR 466, para 94.

[270] *Deweer v Belgium* (1980) 2 EHRR 439, para 46; *Heaney and McGuinness v Ireland* (2001) 33 EHRR 12; *Quinn v Ireland* (2000) 29 EHRR CD234.

[271] *Grzęda v Poland* (2022) 53 BHRC 631 [GC], para 257.

(b) the dispute must be genuine and serious; it may relate not only to the actual existence of a right but also to its scope and the manner of its exercise;[272]

(c) the outcome of the proceedings must be directly decisive for these rights and obligations (this requires something more than a 'tenuous connection or remote consequences'); and

(d) the right must be a 'civil' right in the autonomous sense of the Convention.

6.103   The Strasbourg and domestic case law contain many examples of quasi-legal proceedings that were held to fall outside the scope of Article 6 because there was no 'determination'—most notably, inquiries or investigations. For example, in *Fayed v UK* the ECtHR held that Article 6 was not engaged in relation to a Department of Trade and Industry inspector's highly critical report on a takeover by the applicant that was essentially investigative, and did not itself determine any dispute.[273] Similarly, in *R (Reprieve) v Prime Minister* the Court of Appeal held that Prime Minister's decision not to hold a public inquiry into the alleged complicity of agents of the British state in the unlawful rendition, detention, and mistreatment of individuals by other states following the 9/11 attack did not engage Article 6.[274] The Court held that the claim was 'a pure public law claim. It does not affect, let alone is it decisive of, any civil right of the claimants. They do not have a civil right to require the Prime Minister to make a lawful decision whether to hold an inquiry into alleged complicity in unlawful rendition, detention and mistreatment.'[275]

6.104   The courts usually consider only final decisions to be 'determinations'. In *De Tommaso v Italy*, the ECtHR referred to a dispute being 'conclusively settled'.[276] In certain circumstances, however, pre-trial proceedings and interim decisions will also fall within the remit of Article 6. In *Micallef v Malta*,[277] departing from its historic approach, the Grand Chamber held that where interim proceedings (such as an injunction application) can be regarded as determining the issue in the proceedings, they would fall within the scope of Article 6.[278]

6.105   The House of Lords in *R (Wright and others) v Secretary of State for Health and Secretary of State for Education and Skills* held that the interim 'listing' of care workers, which prevented them from working with vulnerable adults, had so great an effect on the rights of the persons affected as to amount to a determination, even though in theory the measures were only provisional.[279]

---

[272] See eg *Naït-Liman v Switzerland* (2018) 45 BHRC 639 [GC] the Court found that there was a 'genuine and serious dispute' where the Member State did not contest the existence of a right of a victim of torture to obtain compensation, but did contest its extra-territorial application: see ibid para 107.

[273] *Fayed v UK* (1994) 18 EHRR 393.

[274] *R (Reprieve) v Prime Minister* [2021] EWCA Civ 972, [2022] QB 447, paras 50–52.

[275] *R (Reprieve) v Prime Minister* [2021] EWCA Civ 972, [2022] QB 447, para 50.

[276] *De Tommaso v Italy* (2017) 65 EHRR 19 [GC], para 153.

[277] *Micallef v Malta* App No 17056/06, 15 October 2009 [GC].

[278] ibid paras 83–86.

[279] *R (Wright and others) v Secretary of State for Health and Secretary of State for Education and Skills* [2009] UKHL 3, [2009] 1 AC 739, para 21 per Baroness Hale. Similarly, the ECtHR has found that disciplinary proceedings that do not directly interfere with a person's ability to continue to practice a profession fall outside of art 6: see *Marušic v Croatia* App No 79821/12 (23 May 2017), paras 74–75.

In *R (G) v Governing Body of X School*,[280] the Supreme Court considered whether   6.106
disciplinary proceedings against a teacher by a school attracted the protection of
Article 6 due to their potential impact on the subsequent determination by the
Independent Safeguarding Authority (ISA) as to whether the teacher would be
barred from teaching. The Supreme Court approved a pragmatic and context-
sensitive test, derived by the Court of Appeal from the ECtHR case law, namely
whether the initial proceedings would have a 'substantial influence or effect' on the
latter proceedings. It found that this test was not satisfied due to the fact that the
ISA was required to form its own independent view on a different question to that
considered by the school's disciplinary panel.[281]

Costs proceedings have usually been regarded as part of a 'determination' of civil   6.107
rights and obligations.[282]

(b) Civil rights and obligations

The autonomous Convention meaning of 'civil rights and obligations'[283] requires   6.108
the arguable existence of a legal right recognized under domestic law.[284] In order
to amount to a 'right' it must be more than a mere expectation or hope, or a mere
privilege.[285] In *Boulois v Luxembourg* the ECtHR stated:

> The court may not create by way of interpretation of article 6.1 a substantive right which has
> no legal basis in the state concerned. The starting-point must be the provisions of the relevant
> domestic law and their interpretation by the domestic courts. This court would need strong rea-
> sons to differ from the conclusions reached by the superior national courts by finding, contrary
> to their view, that there was arguably a right recognised by domestic law.[286]

The autonomous meaning of a 'civil' right or obligation was explained by the   6.109
ECtHR in *König v Germany* as follows:

> Whether or not a right is to be regarded as civil within the meaning of this expression in the
> Convention must be determined by reference to the substantive content and effects of the
> right—and not its legal classification—under the domestic law of the state concerned ... Only
> the character of the right (at issue) is relevant.[287]

The ECtHR's case law makes clear that in many respects, 'civil rights and obli-   6.110
gations' is a wide phrase, whatever may have been the original intention of the

---

[280] *R (G) v Governing Body of X School* [2011] UKSC 30, [2012] 1 AC 167.
[281] ibid. In particular, see paras 69–84 per Lord Dyson.
[282] See eg *Robins v UK* (1998) 26 EHRR 527; *Ziegler v Switzerland* App No 33499/96, 21 February 2002.
[283] See eg *Benthem v Netherlands* (1986) 8 EHRR 1, para 34; *Ferrazzini v Italy* (2002) 34 EHRR 1068.
[284] *Roche v UK* (2006) 42 EHRR 30; See also *Acquaviva v France* App No 19248/91, 21 November 1995, para 46; *Le Compte, Van Leuven and De Meyere v Belgium* (1981) 4 EHRR 1, para 47; *Powell & Rayner v UK* (1990) 12 EHRR 355.
[285] *Bolois v Luxembourg* (2012) 55 EHRR 32 [GC], paras 96–99.
[286] ibid para 91. See also *Károly Nagy v Hungary* App No 56665/09 (14 September 2017) [GC], paras 60–62; *Denisov v Ukraine* App No 76639/11 (25 September 2018) [GC], para 45 and *Naït-Liman v Switzerland* (2018) 45 BHRC 639 [GC], paras 106 and 108.
[287] *König v Germany* (1978) 2 EHRR 170, paras 89, 90. See eg *Pudas v Sweden* (1988) 10 EHRR 380 where the ECtHR held that grant of a taxi licence entailed certain consequential civil rights under Swedish law to continue the business under the licence, which was found to fall within the scope of art 6.

drafters of the Convention. It has been held to cover areas as diverse as property rights,[288] family rights,[289] the right to engage in commercial activities, the right to compensation, the right to practise a profession,[290] and certain welfare benefits. The House of Lords indicated that a 'without notice' local authority application to close a care home on health and safety grounds would constitute a determination of civil rights and obligations.[291] So do the imposition of antisocial behaviour orders,[292] control orders,[293] a domestic terrorist asset freezing order,[294] financial restrictions on banks,[295] the extradition of UK citizens,[296] the failure to comply with a policy concerning the protection, relocation, and compensation of covert human intelligence sources in Afghanistan,[297] temporary exclusion orders under the Counter-Terrorism and Security Act 2015,[298] and confiscation proceedings following conviction.[299] Further, the domestic courts have accepted that a breach of a Convention right protected by the Human Rights Act 1998 is a breach of a civil right in the form of a statutory tort.[300]

6.111   However, matters of pure administrative discretion are not covered. These include decisions as to tax obligations,[301] categorization of prisoners,[302] the right to stand for public office,[303] immigration decisions relating to the entry, stay, and

---

[288] *Sporrong & Lonnroth v Sweden* (1983) 5 EHRR 35.

[289] See eg *W v UK* (1987) 10 EHRR 29.

[290] See eg *König v Germany* (1978) 2 EHRR 170; *Wickramsinghe v UK* App No 31503/96, 9 December 1997 (ECmHR), analysed in [1998] EHRLR 338; *R (G) v Governing Body of X School* [2011] UKSC 30, [2012] 1 AC 167; and *Mattu v University Hospitals of Coventry and Warwickshire NHS Trust* [2021] EWCA Civ 641, [2012] 4 All ER 359.

[291] *Jain v Trent Strategic Health Authority* [2009] UKHL 4, [2009] 1 AC 853.

[292] *R (McCann) v Crown Court at Manchester* [2002] UKHL 39, [2003] 1 AC 787.

[293] *Secretary of State v F (No 3)* [2009] UKHL 28, [2010] 2 AC 269.

[294] *Mastafa v HM Treasury* [2012] EWHC 3578, [2013] 1 WLR 1621, per Collins J, finding such designation to be indistinguishable from the imposition of a control order, and distinguishing the Court of Appeal's judgment in *Secretary of State for the Foreign Office and Commonwealth Affairs v Maftah* [2011] EWCA Civ 350, [2012] QB 477 on the basis of the international context and focus of the challenge to designation on a UN asset freezing list in that case.

[295] *Bank Mellat v HM Treasury (No 4)* [2015] EWCA Civ 1052, [2016] 1 WLR 1187, paras, 14, 23.

[296] *Pomiechowski v District Court of Legnica, Poland* [2012] UKSC 20, [2012] 1 WLR 1604, paras 30–32. In contrast, decisions regarding the entry, stay, and deportation of aliens do not concern the determination of an applicant's civil rights within the meaning of art 6(1): *Maaouia v France* (2001) 33 EHRR 42; *Mammatkulov and Asharov v Turkey* (2005) 41 EHRR 494.

[297] *R (K and others) v Secretary of State for Defence* [2016] EWCA Civ 1149, [2017] 1 WLR 1671, paras 17–22.

[298] *QX v Secretary of State for the Home Department* [2022] EWCA Civ 1541 (though at the time of writing the Secretary of State had been granted permission to appeal to the Supreme Court on this issue among others).

[299] *R v Briggs-Price* [2009] UKHL 19, [2009] 2 WLR 1101; see also *Serious Organised Crime Agency v Gale* [2011] UKSC 49, [2011] 1 WLR 2760.

[300] See eg *In Re S (Minors) (Care Order: Implementation of Care Plan)* [2002] UKHL 10, [2002] 2 AC 291, para 72; *Secretary of State for the Home Department v BC* [2009] EWHC 2927 (Admin), [2010] 1 WLR 1542, para 29; *QX v Secretary of State for the Home Department* [2022] EWCA Civ 1541, paras 118–19.

[301] *Vegotex International v Belgium* (2023) 76 EHRR 15 [GC], para 66; *Ferrazzini v Italy* (2002) 34 EHRR 1068 [GC], para 29; and *King v UK* [2004] STC 911.

[302] *Brady v UK* (1979) 3 EHRR 297.

[303] *Pierre-Bloch v France* (1998) 26 EHRR 202.

removal or extradition of foreign nationals,[304] actions and inactions in the international sphere regarding the listing of persons for asset freezing,[305] a decision to permanently exclude a child from school,[306] segregation decisions in prisons,[307] and the right to freedom of movement within the European Union (EU).[308]

The distinction between 'civil' or 'private' rights, and 'pure public rights' does   6.112
not exactly chime with the distinction between these concepts in domestic law. In *Ringeisen v Austria* the ECtHR noted that Article 6 may be triggered in situations where the public law decisions of public authorities have clear consequences for the private law rights of individuals, but is not engaged unless the intrinsic nature of the right or obligation determined is 'private'.[309] In general terms, the ECtHR considers the substance of the right and balances the public law features against the private law features. If private law features are predominant, Article 6 will apply.[310] For example, in *Tommaso v Italy* the ECtHR stated that Article 6 would apply where a decision had 'direct and significant repercussions on a private right'.[311]

The balance struck by the ECtHR does not necessarily follow traditional domes-   6.113
tic characterization. For example, in *R (Alconbury Developments Ltd) v Secretary of State for Environment, Transport and the Regions*,[312] the House of Lords followed ECtHR case law in finding that planning determinations involved the determination of civil rights within the meaning of Article 6, notwithstanding that such determinations might traditionally be considered by English lawyers to involve 'public law rights' only. Lord Hoffmann was driven to observe:

> Apart from authority, I would have said that a decision as to what the public interest requires is not a 'determination' of civil rights and obligations. It may affect civil rights and obligations but it is not, and ought not to be, a judicial act such as article 6 has in contemplation.[313]

As a result of the ECtHR's dynamic interpretation, the notion of civil rights   6.114
continued to expand.[314] The concept of 'pure public rights' has been significantly reduced in recent years, with the ECtHR increasingly willing to find a 'civil right' within, or alongside, a public law right.

---

[304] *Maaouia v France* (2001) 33 EHRR 42; *R (BB) v SIAC* [2012] EWCA Civ 1499, [2013] 1 WLR 1568; *Lukaszewski v District Court in Torun* [2012] UKSC 20, [2012] 1 WLR 1604.

[305] *Secretary of State for the Foreign Office and Commonwealth Affairs v Maftah* [2011] EWCA Civ 350, [2012] QB 477, as interpreted in *Mastafa v HM Treasury* [2012] EWHC 3578 (Admin), [2013] 1 WLR 1621.

[306] *R (V) v Independent Appeal Panel for Tom Hood School* [2010] EWCA Civ 142, [2010] PTSR 1462, paras. 11-20.

[307] *R (Bourgass) v Secreatyr of State for Justice* [2015] UKSC 54, [2016] AC 384.

[308] *Adams and Benn v UK* (1997) 23 EHRR CD 160.

[309] See eg *Pudas v Sweden* (1988) 10 EHRR 380.

[310] *Feldbrugge v Netherlands* (1986) 8 EHRR 425; *Deumeland v Germany* (1986) 8 EHRR 448 (Series A-100); *Ali v Birmingham City Council* [2010] UKSC 8, [2010] 2 AC 39.

[311] *De Tommaso v Italy* (2017) 65 EHRR 19 [GC], para 151.

[312] *R (Alconbury Developments Ltd) v Secretary of State for Environment, Transport and the Regions* [2001] UKHL 23, [2003] 2 AC 295.

[313] ibid para 74 per Lord Hoffmann. See also *Secretary of State for the Foreign Office and Commonwealth Affairs v Maftah* [2011] EWCA Civ 350, [2012] QB 477.

[314] *Salesi v Italy* (1998) 26 EHRR 187.

6.115   For example, the ECtHR originally held that only claims regarding welfare benefits which formed part of contributory schemes could constitute the subject matter of disputes for 'the determination of civil rights'. This was on the basis of their similarity to private insurance schemes.[315] However, Article 6 was subsequently held also to apply to disputes over entitlements to certain non-contributory welfare benefits, where it could be said that the applicant had an assertable right of an individual and economic nature.[316] This would ordinarily be where the individual had an entitlement to an amount of benefit that was not in the discretion of the public authority. In *Stec v UK* the Grand Chamber confirmed this development and further held that it was in the interests of the coherence of the Convention as a whole that the autonomous concept of 'possessions' in Article 1 of Protocol 1 should be interpreted in a way which is consistent with the concept of pecuniary rights[317] under Article 6.[318]

6.116   The application of Article 6 to social security benefit entitlements has raised a concern regarding the judicialization of public decision-making, with the associated cost and delay to decision-making. As the ECtHR observed in *Feldbrugge v The Netherlands*:

The judicialisation of dispute procedures, as guaranteed by article 6(1), is eminently appropriate in the realm of relations between individuals but not necessarily so in the administrative sphere, where organisational, social and economic considerations may legitimately warrant dispute procedures of a less judicial and formal kind.[319]

6.117   Due to the fast-developing character of the ECtHR's case law, the domestic courts for a number of years declined to rule on the limits of the application of Article 6 in the administrative sphere where it considered it unnecessary to do so. Thus, for example, in *Begum (Runa) v Tower Hamlets*, the House of Lords considered the adequacy of the procedure in respect of the provision of housing under the Housing Act 1996 on the assumption that this involved a 'civil right' without deciding the question.[320] However, in *Ali v Birmingham City Council*, the Supreme Court held that the time had come to seek to bring greater clarity to this area and held that the duties imposed on local authorities under Part VII of the Housing Act 1996 (homelessness) did not fall within the scope of Article 6.[321] Lord Hope drew a fundamental distinction based on the extent of the evaluative judgment involved in determining entitlement:

[C]ases where the award of services or benefits in kind is not an individual right of which the applicant can consider himself the holder, but is dependent upon a series of evaluative judgments

---

[315] *Feldbrugge v the Netherlands* (1986) 8 EHRR 425.
[316] *Salesi v Italy* App No 13023/87, 26 February 1993.
[317] See Chapter 7.
[318] See the decision on admissibility in *Stec v UK* (2005) 41 EHRR SE18, para 48.
[319] *Feldbrugge v The Netherlands* (1986) 8 EHRR 425, 443, para 15.
[320] *Begum (Runa) v Tower Hamlets* [2003] UKHL 5, [2003] 2 AC 430. See also *R (A) v Croydon London Borough Council; R (M) v Lambeth London Borough Council* [2009] UKSC 8, [2009] 1 WLR 2557; 'age assessments' of asylum-seekers, regarding whether or not they are 'children' and so are protected under the Children Act 1989.
[321] *Ali v Birmingham City Council* [2010] UKSC 8, [2010] 2 AC 39.

by the provider as to whether the statutory criteria are satisfied and how the need for it ought to be met, do not engage article 6(1). In my opinion they do not give rise to 'civil rights' within the autonomous meaning that is given to that expression for the purposes of that article.[322]

The Court expressed concern about the 'judicialisation' of welfare services and the implications that this would have for local authority resources.[323] Further, the Court noted that 'no clearly defined stopping point' to the process of the expansion of Article 6 into public law rights had been identified by the ECtHR.[324]   6.118

The claimant in *Ali* applied to the ECtHR. In *Ali v UK* the ECtHR held that Article 6 applied, but accepted that the procedure adopted under the Housing Act 1996 conformed to its requirements.[325] As to the application of Article 6, the ECtHR acknowledged the difference between the instant case and previous cases concerning welfare assistance, as the assistance to be provided under section 193 of the Housing Act 1996 was 'not only conditional but could not be precisely defined' and that the applicant's entitlement to it 'were subject to an exercise of discretion'.[326] These factors did not, in the ECtHR's view, necessarily mitigate against recognition of entitlement as a 'civil right'. The 'discretion' under the Housing Act 1996 had some 'clearly defined limits' in that once the qualifying conditions were met, the local authority was required to secure that accommodation was provided.[327]   6.119

In *Poshteh v Kensington and Chelsea Royal London Borough Council* the Supreme Court considered whether the approach of the ECtHR in *Ali v UK* should be followed domestically.[328] The Court noted that the ECtHR had failed to address in any detail the Supreme Court's reasoning in *Ali v Birmingham City Council*, and in particular the concerns it expressed over the expansion of Article 6 into this area.[329] The Court noted that the duty under section 2 of the Human Rights Act 1998 was to 'take account of' the decision of the court. There was no relevant Grand Chamber decision, but the Court would normally follow a 'clear and constant line' of chamber decisions.[330] It was apparent from the ECtHR's reasoning that it was 'consciously going beyond the scope of previous cases'.[331] The Court doubted that the Chamber judgment in *Ali v UK* would be the last word on the issue, the judgment was not a sufficient reason to depart from the fully considered and unanimous conclusion of the court in *Ali v Birmingham City Council*, and it was appropriate for the Court to await a full consideration by the Grand Chamber before considering whether (and if so how) to modify their position.[332]   6.120

---

[322] ibid para 49.
[323] ibid para 55.
[324] ibid para 6.
[325] *Ali v UK* (2016) 63 EHRR 20.
[326] ibid paras 58–59.
[327] ibid para 59.
[328] *Poshteh v Kensington and Chelsea Royal London Borough Council* [2017] UKSC 36, [2017] AC 624.
[329] ibid para 33.
[330] ibid para 36, citing *Manchester City Council v Pinnock* [2010] UKSC 45, [2011] 2 AC 104, para 48.
[331] ibid, para 36, referring to para 58 of the ECtHR's judgment in *Ali v UK* (2016) 63 EHRR 20.
[332] ibid para 37.

6.121 One area where the distinction between public and 'civil' rights has historically caused particular difficulties is in relation to employment issues. The traditional view was that matters concerning employment in the public sector did not concern 'civil rights' as defined by the ECtHR.[333] However, in *Pellegrin v France* the Grand Chamber held that only decisions concerning functions relating to the 'specific activities' of the public service and direct or indirect participation in the exercise of powers conferred by public law would be outside the protection provided by Article 6.[334] In *Eskelinen v Finland*[335] the Grand Chamber repeated that Article 6 is not excluded from determinations of employment disputes on the basis of the special relationship between the civil servant and the state. It is presumed to apply, unless domestic law contains an express or implied exclusion from access to the court, and the dispute in issue clearly related to the exercise of state power.[336]

6.122 An important area in which the concept of a pure public right remains relatively untouched is the state's power to control its borders by determining the conditions of entry, stay, and removal of foreign nationals.[337] However, as considered elsewhere in this text, these matters are subject to the protections of other Convention rights, in particular Articles 2 and 3 (concerning the prohibition on removal where there is a real risk of art 2 or 3 treatment), and Article 8 (concerning the negative and positive aspects of the right to respect for family and private life).[338]

(c) Criminal charge

6.123 Article 6 protects an individual who is 'charged with a criminal offence' when he or she is subject to a procedure for the 'determination' of that criminal charge. The term 'charge' should be given a substantive rather than a formal meaning, in the sense that the court should consider the scope of what is at stake and not the mere classification in domestic law.[339]

6.124 (i) *What is 'criminal'?* When deciding whether proceedings are 'criminal' for the purposes of the Convention, the courts are not bound by the label given by the state. In *Engel v Netherlands*[340] the Court held that a determination that an individual is subject of a criminal charge rests on three criteria:[341]

---

[333] See eg *Kosieck v Germany* (1987) 9 EHRR 328; *Neigel v France* (2000) 30 EHRR 310; *Balfour v UK* (1997) EHRLR 665; *Huber v France* (1998) 26 EHRR 457.

[334] *Pellegrin v France* (2001) 31 EHRR 651, para 66.

[335] *Eskelinen v Finland* (2007) 45 EHRR 43.

[336] ibid para 62, as clarified by the Grand Chamber in *Grzęda v Poland* (2022) 53 BHRC 631 [GC], paras 291–92. *Eskelinen* was also applied in *R (MK (Iran)) v Secretary of State for the Home Department* [2009] EWHC 3452 (Admin).

[337] *Maaouia v France* (2001) 33 EHRR 42; *R (BB) v SIAC* [2012] EWCA Civ 1499, [2013] 1 WLR 1568.

[338] See Chapter 5 (arts 2 and 3) and paras 6.259–6.381 (art 8).

[339] *Deweer v Belgium* (1979–80) 2 EHRR 439, paras 42, 44, and 46. See also *Ramos Nunes de Carvalho e Sa v Portugal* App Nos 55391/13 & others (6 November 2018) [GC], para 122.

[340] *Engel v Netherlands* (1976) 1 EHRR 647.

[341] Although in *Serious Organised Crime Agency v Gale* [2011] UKSC 49, [2011] 1 WLR 2760 Lord Phillips (giving the majority decision) stated (at para 16) that the three considerations 'tend to blend into each other', citing Kerr LCJ in *Walsh v Director of the Assets Recovery Agency* [2005] NI 383.

(a) the classification of the offence under the domestic legal system which should be the starting point;

(b) the nature of the offence; and/or

(c) the nature and degree of severity of the penalty 'liable to be imposed'.

In practice the last two criteria have carried the greatest significance. The *Engel* criteria have been regularly applied by the Strasbourg and domestic courts.[342] The courts have emphasized that the first criterion—the domestic classification—must be seen as 'no more than a starting point'.[343] If domestic law classifies an offence as criminal, then this will be decisive and the criminal limb of Article 6 will apply; otherwise the Court will look behind the national classification and examine the substantive reality of the procedure in question.[344] One important consideration is whether the intention of a provision is punitive or preventative: preventative measures are generally not considered to be 'criminal'.[345] For example, in *De Tommaso v Italy* the Grand Chamber noted that special supervision of a Mafia suspect did not engage the criminal limb of Article 6(1) as 'special supervision is not comparable to a criminal sanction'.[346] Similarly, in *Birmingham City Council v Jones* the Court of Appeal held an application for an injunction prohibiting gang-related violence and drug-dealing activity, made under section 34 of the Policing and Crime Act 2009 and section 1 of the Anti-social Behaviour, Crime and Policy Act 2014, did not involve the determination of a criminal charge for the purposes of Article 6.[347]   6.125

The second and third of the *Engel* criteria are usually considered as alternatives.[348] For the criminal protections of Article 6 to apply it is enough either that the offence in question is of a 'criminal' nature, or that the offence makes the person liable to what amounts to a 'criminal' sanction given its nature or degree of severity.[349] However, a cumulative approach may be adopted where separate analysis of each individual criterion does not make it possible to reach a clear conclusion as to the existence of a criminal charge.[350]   6.126

---

[342] See eg *Campbell and Fell v UK* (1985) 7 EHRR 165; *Ezeh and Connors v UK* (2004) 39 EHRR 1 [GC]. See also eg *Tangney v Governor of Elmley Prison and Secretary of State for the Home Department* [2005] EWCA Civ 1009, [2005] HRLR 36; *MB v Secretary of State for the Home Department* [2007] UKHL 46, [2008] 1 AC 440.

[343] *Engel v Netherlands* (1976) 1 EHRR 647, para 82; *R (V) v Independent Appeal Panel for Tom Hood School* [2010] EWCA Civ 142, [2010] PTSR 1462.

[344] *Gestur Jónsson and Ragnar Halldór Hall v Iceland* App No 68273/14, 22 December 2020 [GC].

[345] *MB v Secretary of State for the Home Department* [2007] UKHL 46, [2008] 1 AC 440; *R (McCann) v Crown Court at Manchester* [2002] UKHL 39, [2003] 1 AC 787; *R (G) v Governing Body of X School* [2010] EWCA Civ 1, [2010] 1 WLR 2218 (this issue was not subject to appeal to the Supreme Court).

[346] *De Tommaso v Italy* (2017) 65 EHRR 19, para 143.

[347] *Birmingham City Council v Jones* [2018] EWCA Civ 1189, [2019] QB 521, paras 33–39.

[348] *Özturk v Germany* (1984) 6 EHRR 409; *Lutz v Germany* (1988) 10 EHRR 182.

[349] See eg *Öztürk v Germany* (1984) 6 EHRR 409, para 54; *Lutz v Germany* (1988) 10 EHRR 182, para 55.

[350] See eg *Bendenoun v France* (1994) 18 EHRR 54, para 47; *Benham v UK* (1996) 22 EHRR 293, para 56; *Garyfallou AEBE v Greece* (1999) 28 EHRR 344, para 33; *Lauko v Slovakia* (2001) 33 EHRR 40, para 57; *Ezeh and Connors v UK* (2004) 39 EHRR 1 [GC], para 86; *Tangney v Governor of Elmley Prison and Secretary of State for the Home Department* [2005] EWCA Civ 1009, [2005] HRLR 36, para 24.

6.127   In relation to the second criterion, the criminal limb of Article 6 may be engaged by the nature of the matter determined, notwithstanding its relatively minor nature. That an offence is not punishable by imprisonment is not by itself decisive as to the applicability of Article 6.[351] For example, tax and surcharge proceedings have been held to constitute criminal charges where they have a deterrent and punitive purpose despite having a relatively light penalty;[352] and the domestic courts consider committal proceedings for contempt to be criminal given that liberty is at stake and that the acts in question must be proved to the criminal standard of proof.[353]

6.128   The third *Engel* criterion is often the key issue. The Court held in *Engel* that 'in a society subscribing to the rule of law, there belong to the "criminal" sphere deprivation of liberty liable to be imposed as a punishment, except those which by their nature, duration or manner of execution cannot be appreciably detrimental' so the courts must take into account 'the seriousness of what is at stake, the traditions of the Contracting States and the importance attached by the Convention to respect for the physical liberty of the person'.[354] It is the nature and severity of the penalty 'liable to be imposed' which is determinative, rather than the penalty actually incurred.[355] The ECtHR has also held that 'where deprivation of liberty is at stake, the interests of justice in principle call for legal representation'.[356]

6.129   Thus, although classification of prisoners, for example, falls outside the criminal sphere,[357] prison discipline may engage the criminal limb of Article 6,[358] even in respect of proceedings which are not classified as 'criminal' in domestic law.[359]

6.130   However, since a prisoner serving a life sentence is not vulnerable to a punishment imposing additional days of imprisonment, the Court of Appeal has held that internal disciplinary charges against such a prisoner do not amount to 'criminal charges'.[360] Parole Board decisions are not criminal because the decisions to release depend upon an assessment of risk to the public rather than punishment.[361]

---

[351] See eg *Vegotex International v Belgium* (2023) 76 EHRR 15 [GC], para 67; and *Ramos Nunes de Carvalho e Sa v Portugal* App Nos 55391/13 & others 6 November 2018 [GC], para 122.

[352] See eg *Jussila v Finland* (2007) 45 EHRR 39 [GC]; *Vegotex International v Belgium* (2023) 76 EHRR 15 [GC], paras 60–70. In contrast, condemnation proceedings under the Customs and Excise Management Act 1979, s 139 are civil proceedings, see *R (Mudie) v Dover Magistrates Court* [2003] EWCA Civ 237, [2003] QB 1238; and *R (Amos) v Maidstone Crown Court* [2013] EWCA Civ 1643.

[353] *Daltel Europe Ltd (in liquidation) and 5 others v Hassan Ali Makki and others* [2006] EWCA Civ 94, [2006] 1 WLR 2704; *Raja v Van Hoogstraten* [2004] EWCA Civ 968, [2004] 4 All ER 793; *Hammerton v Hammerton* [2007] EWCA Civ 248, [2007] 2 FLR 1133. The ECtHR has treated contempt of court as being either criminal or civil, depending on the facts. The Grand Chamber reviewed its relevant case law in *Gestur Jónsson and Ragnar Halldór Hall v Iceland* (2021) 72 EHRR 30, paras 79–83.

[354] *Engel v Netherlands* (1976) 1 EHRR 647, para 82.

[355] See eg *Campbell and Fell v UK* (1985) 7 EHRR 165, para 72; *Weber v Switzerland* (1990) 12 EHRR 508, para 34; *Demicoli v Malta* App No 13057/87, 27 August 1991, para 34; *Benham v UK* (1996) 22 EHRR 296, para 56; *Garyfallou AEBE v Greece* (1999) 28 EHRR 344, paras 33–34; *Ezeh and Connors v UK* (2004) 39 EHRR 1 [GC], para 120.

[356] *Benham v UK* (1996) 22 EHRR 296, para 61.

[357] *R (Sunder) v Secretary of State for the Home Department* [2001] EWHC Admin 252.

[358] *Campbell and Fell v UK* (1985) 7 EHRR 165, para 69.

[359] *Ezeh and Connors v UK* (2004) 39 EHRR 1 [GC]; *Jussila v Finland* (2007) 45 EHRR 39.

[360] *Tangney v Governor of Elmley Prison* [2005] EWCA Civ 1009, [2005] HRLR 36.

[361] *R (Smith) v Parole Board* [2005] UKHL 1, [2005] 1 WLR 350.

The domestic courts have adopted a narrow definition of 'criminal charge' in **6.131** the context of suspected terrorists, focusing on the intention of the measures rather than their effects. For example, the House of Lords found that non-derogating control orders are not 'criminal' since they are preventive in purpose, even though they impose very severe restrictions on the controlee's private life and freedom of movement.[362] However, the civil limb of Article 6(1) applied and entitled those subject to such orders to 'such measure of procedural protection as was commensurate with the gravity of the potential consequences'.[363] The domestic courts have also held that registration on the Sex Offenders' Register is not a criminal determination as, inter alia, it does not involve a punishment and is not a public announcement of guilt.[364] Nor does exclusion from school involve the determination of a criminal charge.[365]

(ii) *What is a charge?* In addition to satisfying the 'criminal' criteria, the alle- **6.132** gation must also constitute a 'charge'. These two features are often considered coterminously but the ECtHR has confirmed that for a person to be charged, his or her situation must be 'substantially affected'.[366] This may take place at arrest, charge, or when the person becomes aware that 'immediate consideration' is being given to a possible prosecution, depending on the facts of the case.[367] However, car owners being required to identify the driver of a speeding vehicle at the time it was caught on a speed camera or radar-trap are not 'substantially affected' so as to be 'charged' within the autonomous meaning of Article 6(1).[368] The courts have confirmed that giving warnings or cautions to offenders does not amount to the determination of a criminal 'charge',[369] and nor do Article 6 protections apply to those questioned in the context of border control where the statutory power to question did not require any suspicion that the individual had committed an offence.[370] Statements given by French authorities at Guantanamo for the purpose of identifying the detainees and collecting evidence also did not amount to a charge.[371]

2. Rights protected by Article 6(1)

Article 6(1) sets the overall standard of what a fair trial requires, whether the con- **6.133** text is civil or criminal. Article 6(2) and (3) apply only to criminal charges, though equivalent guarantees may be required in civil cases in particular circumstances.

---

[362] *MB v Secretary of State for the Home Department* [2007] UKHL 46, [2008] 1 AC 440.
[363] ibid para 24.
[364] *R (R) v Durham Constabulary* [2005] UKHL 21, [2005] 1 WLR 1184.
[365] *R (V) v Independent Appeal Panel for Tom Hood School* [2010] EWCA Civ 142, [2010] PTSR 1462.
[366] *DeWeer v Belgium* (1980) 2 EHRR 439, para 46.
[367] *X v UK* (1998) 25 EHRR CD88.
[368] *Rieg v Austria* App No 63207/00, 24 March 2005, para 54; *O'Halloran and Francis v UK* (2008) 46 EHRR 21.
[369] *R v UK* (2007) 44 EHRR SE17; *R (R) v Durham Constabulary* [2005] UKHL 21, [2005] 1 WLR 1184.
[370] *Beghal v UK* App No 4755/15, 28 May 2019.
[371] *Sassi and Benchellai v France* App Nos 10917/15 & others, 25 November 2021.

Courts have frequently held that common law and Article 6(1) standards of fairness march 'hand in hand', and that the result ought to be the same whichever is applied.[372]

6.134 The court will imply into Article 6(1) such safeguards as are necessary to guarantee a 'real and effective' fair trial. For example, Article 6 implicitly guarantees the right of access to a court[373]—a requirement discussed in more detail below. It also implicitly precludes the legislature from taking action 'designed to influence the judicial determination of a dispute, save on compelling grounds of general interest', including via the passage of legislation with retrospective effect.[374] This is because retrospective legislation tends to undermine the rule of law and (in particular) legal certainty[375]—a principle 'inherent in all the Articles of the Convention'.[376] As to retrospectivity in the criminal context, see all section D in this chapter.

6.135 Article 6(1) does not compel states to establish appellate courts, but, where they exist, proceedings before them must comply with Article 6 and effective access must therefore be ensured.[377] The existence or otherwise of avenues of appeal or review may also be relevant where a first-instance decision has not fully complied with the requirements of Article 6(1): in some cases, these deficiencies will not result in a breach provided that the decision is subject to supervision on appeal or susceptible to judicial review which is itself compliant.[378] This is because the court assesses the fairness of a trial by reference to the process as a whole: it is the overall process which must reach the required standard. There is not necessarily a need for a 'full judicial rehearing' of all matters of fact and discretion when dealing with unfair administrative decision-making in specialized areas: where the decision-maker has examined the facts, a review of the lawfulness of the decision may suffice.[379] Guidance on when a full merits review would be required was given

---

[372] *R (Smith) v Parole Board* [2005] UKHL 1, [2005] 1 WLR 350; *Kulkarni v Milton Keynes NHS Hospital Trust* [2009] EWCA Civ 789, [2009] IRLR 829; *Secretary of State for the Home Department v AF (No 3)* [2009] UKHL 28, [2010] 2 AC 269, para 96 per Lord Scott.

[373] *Golder v UK* (1975) 1 EHRR 524; *Moldovan and others v Romania* (2007) 44 EHRR 16.

[374] This might include, eg, enacting retrospective legislation which has the effect of making an ongoing case against the state 'unwinnable'. The state's justification for measures of this kind must 'be treated with the greatest possible degree of circumspection': *Vegotex International SA v Belgium* (2023) 76 EHRR 15 [GC], paras 92–94, 102. The state's financial interests alone will not constitute a 'compelling ground of general interest': ibid para 103. By contrast, interpreting or clarifying an older legislative provision in the interests of legal certainty may be a proper justification: ibid para 107. Indeed, a lack of legal certainty on an issue engaging art 6 may itself violate art 6(1) where the case law demonstrates 'profound and long-standing differences' and either domestic law has no mechanism for overcoming these inconsistencies or that mechanism has not been applied: see eg *Lupeni Greek Catholic Parish and others v Romania* App No 76943/1, 29 November 2016 [GC], paras 116–35.

[375] *Vegotex International SA v Belgium* (2023) 76 EHRR 15 [GC], paras 93–94, 115.

[376] ibid para 115.

[377] *Sommerfeld v Germany* (2003) 36 EHRR 33; *Zuvac v Croatia* (2018) 67 EHRR 28 [GC], para 80. The UK Supreme Court has also affirmed that a right of appeal is not an inherent requirement of art 6: *Attorney-General v Crosland* [2021] UKSC 58, [2022] 1 WRL 367, paras 103–04.

[378] See eg *Edwards v UK* (1992) 15 EHRR 417, paras 51–54.

[379] *Bryan v UK* (1995) 21 EHRR 342.

in a Northern Irish case, *Re Brown's Application*.[380] Importantly, not all breaches of Article 6(1) can be 'cured' by appeal.[381]

The elements of the right to a fair trial under Article 6(1) may be limited where the limitation pursues a legitimate aim and is proportionate to that aim.[382] This is despite the fact that, with the exception of the right to a public hearing (paras 6.162–6.168), Article 6(1) is not expressed as a qualified right.[383] In no case may states limit Article 6 rights in such a way or to such an extent that 'the very essence of the right is impaired'.[384] These principles reflect the fact that, as noted above, the overarching right to a fair trial is unqualified—it is the precise requirements of fairness which may vary depending on the circumstances.   6.136

It is possible for an individual to voluntarily waive the protections of Article 6(1).[385] A waiver must be made freely and in an unequivocal manner, and must not run counter to any important public interest.[386] It must also be 'attended by minimum safeguards commensurate with its importance' and must not be 'tainted by constraint'.[387]   6.137

In identifying and describing the many facets of Article 6(1) the ECtHR frequently draws on the principle of 'equality of arms' and the 'adversarial principle', which the Grand Chamber has described as 'fundamental components of the concept of a "fair hearing" within the meaning of Article 6(1)'.[388] Another overarching principle frequently cited in the ECtHR's case law is that, as matters of fact and domestic law are for the national courts and the ECtHR is not 'a court of fourth instance', it will not find a violation of Article 6(1) based on an alleged error in these areas unless it infringes Convention rights—for example, where the courts find against an applicant on a basis which can be described as 'grossly arbitrary'.[389]   6.138

---

[380] *Re Brown's Application* [2003] NIJB 168. See also *Re Brolly (Anne)* [2004] NIQB 69. The court suggested that the 'bare judicial review' approach might be appropriate where the fact-finding process undertaken by the administrative body is tangential or incidental—the implication being that a more robust form of judicial review could be required when the fact-finding is central.

[381] *Findlay v UK* (1997) 24 EHRR 221; *Rowe and Davies v UK* (2000) 30 EHRR 1; *Condron and Condron v UK* (2001) 31 EHRR 1; *De Cubber v Belgium* (1985) 7 EHRR 236, and *R (G) v Governing Body of X School* [2011] UKSC 30, [2011] 1 AC 167.

[382] See eg *Vegotex International SA v Belgium* (2023) 76 EHRR 15 [GC], para 133; *Grzeda v Poland* (2022) 53 BHRC 361 [GC], para 343.

[383] See eg *De Lege v Netherlands* (2023) 76 EHRR 7, para 60.

[384] See eg *Vegotex International SA v Belgium* (2023) 76 EHRR 15 [GC], para 133; *Golder v UK* (1975) 1 EHRR 524; *Belgian Linguistic Case No 2* (1968) 1 EHRR 252; *Secretary of State for the Home Department v AF (No 3)* [2009] UKHL 28, [2010] 2 AC 269, para 106 per Baroness Hale.

[385] See eg *VCL and AN v United Kingdom* (2021) 73 EHRR 9, para 201; *Mutu v Switzerland* App No 40575/10, 2 October 2018, para 96; *Stretford v Football Association* [2007] EWCA Civ 238, [2007] All ER (Comm) 1.

[386] *Håkansson and Sturesson v Sweden* (1991) 13 EHRR 1; *VCL and AN v United Kingdom* (2021) 73 EHRR 9, para 201; *Mutu v Switzerland* App No 40575/10, 2 October 2018, para 96 (and see the application of these principles in the context of submission to an arbitral jurisdiction at paras 103–23). cf *Deweer v Belgium* (1979–80) 2 EHRR 439.

[387] *VCL and AN v United Kingdom* (2021) 73 EHRR 9, para 201 (and see the ensuing application of these principles in the context of plea bargains, on which point see also *Togonidze v Georgia* App No 9043/05, 29 April 2014, paras 88–95).

[388] *Regner v Czech Republic* (2018) 66 EHRR 9 [GC], para 146.

[389] See eg *Bochan v Ukraine (No 2)* (2015) 61 EHRR 14 [GC], paras 61–65.

(a) *General entitlements in criminal and civil proceedings under Article 6(1)*

6.139   A litigant, or potential litigant, has the following rights under Article 6(1)—some of which are implicit and some express:

(i)   real and effective access to a court;

(ii)   a hearing before an independent and impartial tribunal established by law;

(iii)   a hearing in public;

(iv)   a hearing within a reasonable time;

(v)   a real opportunity to present their case;

(vi)   a reasoned decision; and

(vii)   the implementation of the final decision.

These are discussed in turn below.

6.140   (i) *Access to a court* The right of access to a court (or tribunal[390])—that is, the ability to institute proceedings before a court or tribunal in relation to the rights and obligations covered by Article 6[391]—is one of the checks on the danger of arbitrary power.[392] Although it is not explicitly set out under Article 6(1), in the early decision of *Golder v UK* the ECtHR recognized the right as a prerequisite of the exercise of the right to have a claim fairly heard.[393] As with all Convention rights, the right is one of *effective* access.

6.141   In order to guarantee effective access to a court, the state may need to provide publicly funded legal assistance.[394] Whether this is required will depend on the circumstances of each case, having regard to factors such as the complexity of the law, procedure, or claim; the ability of the individual to test the evidence; the potential for fairness to be achieved via other means, such as simplifying existing procedures; and the importance of what is at stake for the applicant.[395] This issue became particularly acute in the UK following the restrictions on the availability of legal aid introduced by the Legal Aid, Sentencing and Punishment of Offenders Act 2012. The state will also need to establish systems and act with the requisite diligence to notify parties or others affected of proceedings or decisions concerning them.[396]

---

[390]   See eg *Mutu v Switzerland* App No 40575/10, 2 October 2018, para 94 ('access to a court is not necessarily to be understood as access to a court of law of the classic kind … the 'tribunal' may be a body set up to determine a limited number of specific issues, provided always that it offers the appropriate guarantees').

[391]   See eg *Naït-Liman v Switzerland* (2018) 45 BHRC 639, para 113.

[392]   *Wilson v First County Trust Ltd (No 2)* [2003] UKHL 40, [2004] 1 AC 816, para 35.

[393]   *Golder v UK* (1975) 1 EHRR 524; see also *Grzeda v Poland* (2022) 53 BHRC 361 [GC], para 342.

[394]   *Airey v Ireland* (1979) 2 EHRR 305.

[395]   ibid; *Steel and Morris v UK* (2005) 41 EHRR 22 (holding also that the entitlement is not absolute, and may depend on the financial situation of the litigant and the prospects of success); *NJDB v UK* [2016] 1 FLR 186. In the domestic context, and for examples of the kinds of cases where legal aid is required, see *R (Gudanaviciene) v Director of Legal Aid Casework* [2014] EWCA Civ 1622, [2015] 1 WLR 2247, applied in *R (Howard League for Penal Reform) v Lord Chancellor* [2017] EWCA Civ 244, [2017] 4 WLR 92, paras 51–147.

[396]   See eg *Schmidt v Latvia* (2018) 66 EHRR 18; *Stichting Landgoed Steenbergen v Netherlands* App No 19732/17, 16 February 2021.

The ECtHR has held that right of access to the court may be subject to limita-   6.142
tions because 'by its very nature, [it] calls for regulation by the state'; that regulation
may vary in time and place according to the needs and resources of the community
and of individuals.[397] The state enjoys 'a certain margin of appreciation' in this
regard.[398] However, any restrictions must not be such that the very essence of the
right is impaired;[399] and must be legally certain,[400] pursue a legitimate aim,[401] and
be proportionate to the aim pursued.[402] For discussion of these requirements in
the context of qualified rights (of which, again, art 6 is not technically one), see
Chapter 2, section D and this chapter, paras 6.365–6.381.

The right of access to a court may be limited by, for example, a substantive provi-   6.143
sion,[403] a procedural rule,[404] or an administrative practice.[405] Complaints about the
right of access must be distinguished from those which really concern the strictures
of the underlying substantive law—which may make a case more difficult to win,
but do not prevent the courts from examining the merits of the case and so do not
constitute a limitation on the right of access.[406]

A procedural hurdle, such as requiring a mental patient to obtain leave of the   6.144
court before issuing a claim, must be properly scrutinized for compatibility with
Article 6. However, it will not necessarily violate it if the requirements at paragraph 6.142 are met.[407] In assessing proportionality, key considerations include the
extent of the applicant's responsibility for any errors which resulted in the procedural requirement not being met; and whether the requirement was applied with
'excessive formalism'.[408]

A common type of procedural hurdle is a financial one, such as court fees. In   6.145
these cases, when assessing proportionality regard is had not only to the applicant's

---

[397] *Golder v UK* (1975) 1 EHRR 524. See eg *Tanase v Romania* App No 41720/13, 25 June 2019 [GC],
para 195; *Zuvac v Croatia* (2018) 67 EHRR 28 [GC], para 78.
[398] *Tanase v Romania* App No 41720/13, 25 June 2019 [GC], para 195; *Zuvac v Croatia* (2018) 67 EHRR
28 [GC], para 78.
[399] See eg *Zuvac v Croatia* (2018) 67 EHRR 28 [GC], para 78.
[400] *Société Levage Prestations v France* (1996) 24 EHRR 351, paras 40–50.
[401] *Ashingdane v UK* (1985) 7 EHRR 528; *Tanase v Romania* App No 41720/13, 25 June 2019 [GC], para
195; *Zuvac v Croatia* (2018) 67 EHRR 28 [GC], para 78.
[402] *Canea Catholic Church v Greece* (1999) 27 EHRR 521, paras 34–42; *Tanase v Romania* App No
41720/13, 25 June 2019 [GC], para 195; *Zuvac v Croatia* (2018) 67 EHRR 28 [GC], para 78. For endorsement of these principles in the domestic context see *Benkharbouche v Secretary of State for Foreign and
Commonwealth Affairs* [2017] UKSC 62, [2019] AC 777, para 14.
[403] *Ashingdane v UK* (1985) 7 EHRR 528, para 57.
[404] *Osman v UK* (2000) 29 EHRR 245.
[405] *Golder v UK* (1975) 1 EHRR 524.
[406] See eg *Lupeni Greek Catholic Parish and others v Romania* App No 76943/1, 29 November 2016 [GC],
paras 99–107; *Wilson v First County Trust Ltd (No 2)* [2003] UKHL 40, [2004] 1 AC 816, para 35.
[407] See eg *Seal v Chief Constable of South Wales* [2007] UKHL 31, [2007] 1 WLR 1910; *Seal v UK* (2012)
54 EHRR 6; *Markovic v Italy* (2007) 44 EHRR 52 [GC]; *Jones v Kingdom of Saudi Arabia* [2006] UKHL
26, [2007] 1 AC 270, following *Al-Adsani v UK* (2001) 34 EHRR 273. See also *Matthews v Ministry of
Defence* [2003] UKHL 4, [2003] 1 AC 1163 (art 6(1) not engaged by legislation preventing an ex-serviceman
from bringing a personal injury claim against the Ministry of Defence); *Fogarty v UK* (2002) 34 EHRR
302; *Tinnelly & Sons Ltd and others and McElduff and others v UK* (1999) 27 EHRR 249.
[408] See eg *Zuvac v Croatia* (2018) 67 EHRR 28 [GC], paras 90–99.

ability to pay but also to the phase of the proceedings and the extent of the financial burden imposed.[409]

6.146   Another is a time limit:[410] in this context the UK Supreme Court has held that, in order to comply with Article 6(1), even limits which appear absolute limits may need to be read as subject to a discretion to grant an extension of time in exceptional circumstances (where to do otherwise would impair the very essence of the right).[411]

6.147   An example of a more substantive hurdle are restrictions on the types of case which can be heard by a domestic supreme court. These have generally been upheld where the role of the supreme court is to deal only with matters of particular significance,[412] and provided of course that the restrictions were otherwise foreseeable and proportionate.[413]

6.148   Rules conferring immunity on particular categories of defendant, or precluding particular types of claim from being brought, have attracted particularly careful scrutiny.[414] In some cases the ECtHR has found that these impair the 'very essence' of the right of access to court—as for example in *Grzeda v Poland*, where the legislation in issue was part of a series of reforms which had weakened judicial independence.[415] The Grand Chamber reached the same conclusion in *Al-Dulimi v Switzerland*, where—despite the absence of a specific rule—the Swiss courts had refused to afford the applicants any opportunity to challenge the inclusion of their names on a UN sanctions list.[416]

---

[409] See the discussion of ECtHR authority in *R (UNISON) v Lord Chancellor* [2017] UKSC 51, [2020] AC 869, paras 110–15. Among many other ECtHR cases see (on court fees) *Stoicescu v Romania* (2011) 31 BHRC 523; *Nalbant v Turkey* App No 59914/16, 3 May 2022; (on security for costs) *Garcia Manibardo v Spain* (2002) 34 EHRR 6; (on costs) *Cernius v Lithuania* App No 73579/17, 18 February 2020; *Zustovic v Croatia* (2022) 74 EHRR 3. Costs regimes may also raise issues under art 6, although not necessarily on the basis of issues with access to court: see eg *Coventry v UK* App No 6016/16, 11 October 2022 [GC] (holding a complaint regarding costs orders arising from success fees and ATE premiums inadmissible insofar as it was based on the right of access to court, but finding a breach of art 6(1) on the basis that the 'very essence of the principle of equality of arms' had been infringed).

[410] See, amongst many other ECtHR cases, *Ivanova and Ivashova v Russia* App Nos 797/14, 67755/14, 26 January 2017.

[411] *Pomiechowski v Poland* [2012] UKSC 20, [2012] 1 WLR 1604 (extradition appeals, invoking HRA, s 3); *R (Adesina and Baines) v NMC* [2013] EWCA Civ 818, [2013] 1 WLR 3156 (professional disciplinary matters); and see the discussion in *Stuewe v Health and Care Professions Council* [2022] EWCA Civ 1605, [2023] 4 WLR 7.

[412] See eg *Zuvac v Croatia* (2018) 67 EHRR 28 [GC], para 83.

[413] ibid paras 85, 87, 90, 104. In assessing proportionality the court will have regard to the extent to which the case was examined by the lower courts: paras 84, 125.

[414] The line between substantive and procedural rules in this area is often difficult to draw: see the discussion in *Benkharbouche v Secretary of State for Foreign and Commonwealth Affairs* [2017] UKSC 62, [2019] AC 777, paras 16 and 18.

[415] *Grzeda v Poland* (2022) 53 BHRC 361 [GC], paras 344–50. In *Gumenyuk v Ukraine* App No 11423/19, 22 July 2021 the ECtHR—taking a slightly different analytical approach—found that legislation preventing judges from challenging their dismissal served a legitimate aim (securing a fair domestic judiciary and speeding up domestic proceedings) but were not proportionate, resulting in an unjustified limitation of the right of access to a court: ibid paras 74–76.

[416] *Al-Dulimi v Switzerland* (2016) 42 BHRC 163 [GC], paras 131–55. The Grand Chamber held that they should at least have been permitted to seek to show that the inclusion was arbitrary.

In the context of immunities founded in international law—such as state 6.149
immunity—the ECtHR's consistent position has been that restricting access to
the domestic courts on this basis is justifiable if the immunity has been properly
invoked as a matter of international law.[417] The UK Supreme Court adopted a similar approach in *Benkharbouche*, concluding that insofar as the State Immunity Act
1978 conferred immunity on the appellants' employers it went beyond the requirements of international law and was therefore incompatible with Article 6(1).[418]
Notably, the ECtHR has to date held that international law has not yet developed
so as to restrict reliance on state immunity to preclude civil claims against another
state or its officials for compensation for acts of torture—though it has left open a
different outcome if customary international law were to develop in future.[419]

The ECtHR has sometimes rejected the UK's approach to immunities within its 6.150
substantive law. For example, in *Osman v UK* it held that what it interpreted as a
blanket ban on bringing a negligence claim against the police for failure to prevent
a crime against a foreseeable target—a ban imposed on public policy grounds—
violated the claimant's right of access to a court. It prevented a court considering
the competing public interests in the case before it and hence was disproportionate.
This decision was criticized academically[420] and judicially.[421] The House of Lords
in *Barrett v Enfield LBC* stated that there was no 'blanket immunity' and that
English law had been misunderstood by the ECtHR.[422] Rather, the test applied was
whether the imposition of a duty of care was 'fair, just and reasonable' in all the
circumstances. The ECtHR in *Z and others v UK* (an art 3 case) accepted the House
of Lords' clarification in *Barrett*.[423] The Court reiterated that any automatic exclusionary rule based on public policy would violate Article 6, but endorsed the more
flexible 'fair, just and reasonable' approach. The House of Lords has since affirmed

---

[417] It has also taken account of what it considered to be developments in customary international law
narrowing the scope of state immunity: see the discussion in *Benkharbouche v Secretary of State for Foreign
and Commonwealth Affairs* [2017] UKSC 62, [2019] AC 777, paras 20–28. Cases include *Sabeh El Leil v
France* App No 34869/05, 29 June 2011 [GC]; *Cudak v Lithuania* App No 15869/02, 23 March 2010 [GC];
Wallishauser v Austria App No 156/04, 19 November 2012; *Radunovic v Montenegro* App Nos 45197/13 and
others, 25 October 2016; and *JC and others v Belgium* App No 11625/17, 12 October 2021.

[418] See likewise *Basfar v Wong* [2022] UKSC 20, [2023] AC 33, paras 23–24 (discussing the earlier decision in *Al-Malik v Reyes* [2019] AC 735, which had held that the restrictions on access to a court arising
from the proper application of international law principles of diplomatic immunity were justifiable under
art 6); and *General Dynamics United Kingdom Ltd v State of Libya* [2021] UKSC 22, [2022] AC 318, para 84
(holding that restrictions on the methods of service on a state which were grounded in international treaties
were thereby justified under art 6). There remains an unresolved difference between the approach of the
ECtHR and that of the domestic courts as to whether, where international law does confer immunity from
jurisdiction, art 6 is engaged at all: see *Benkharbouche*, para 30 and *General Dynamics*, para 83.

[419] See eg *Al-Adsani v UK* (2001) 34 EHRR 273; *Jones v UK* App Nos 34356/06 and 40528/06, 14
January 2014; *Nait-Liman v Switzerland* (2018) BHRC 639; *JC and others v Belgium* App No 11625/17, 12
October 2021.

[420] See eg Conor Gearty, 'Osman Unravels' (2002) 65 Modern Law Review 87, (1998) 29 EHRR 245.

[421] *Barrett v Enfield London Borough Council* [2001] 2 AC 550.

[422] ibid.

[423] *Z and others v UK* (2002) 34 EHRR 97. See also *Al-Adsani v UK* (2001) 34 EHRR 273; *McElhinney
v Ireland* (2002) 34 EHRR 13; *Fogarty v UK* (2002) 34 EHRR 302.

that there is no automatic or 'knock-out' immunity from suit for the police, and instead a flexible, context-specific test applies.[424]

6.151   (ii) *A hearing before an independent and impartial tribunal established by law* Article 6(1) requires an 'independent and impartial tribunal established by law'. The Grand Chamber has emphasized that the elements of this guarantee—the nature of a 'tribunal', the requirements of independence and impartiality, and the 'established by law' requirement—have 'a common thread ... in that they are guided by the aim of upholding the fundamental principles of the rule of law and the separation of powers'.[425]

6.152   A 'tribunal' is a body with a 'judicial function'—that is, the function of 'determining matters within its competence on the basis of legal rules and after proceedings conducted in a prescribed manner'.[426] It must be 'composed of judges selected on the basis of merit', who 'fulfil the requirements of technical competence and moral integrity to perform the judicial functions required of it in a State governed by the rule of law'.[427] Further, if a body is not independent (particularly of the executive) and impartial then it may lose the character of a 'tribunal'.[428]

6.153   To satisfy Article 6(1), the tribunal must have 'jurisdiction to examine all questions of fact and law relevant to the dispute before it' or (at least) have 'sufficient jurisdiction' or provide 'sufficient review'.[429] Article 6 does not necessarily guarantee 'access to a court which can substitute its own assessment or opinion for that of the administrative authorities'.[430] In assessing sufficiency of jurisdiction, relevant factors include (a) the subject matter of the decision appealed against (and in particular whether it concerned a specialized issue requiring professional knowledge or experience, or called for an exercise of administrative discretion); (b) the way the decision was made, and in particular the procedural guarantees available before the administrative body; (c) the content of the dispute, including the actual and desired grounds of appeal; (d) the nature of the rights and obligations at stake; and (e) the nature of the policy objective pursued by the decision-making scheme as a whole.[431]

6.154   The requirement of independence relates to both the 'state of mind' of tribunal members—denoting 'imperviousness to external pressure as a matter of moral integrity'—and 'a set of institutional and operational arrangements' which provide

---

[424] *Brooks v Commissioner for Police for the Metropolis* [2005] UKHL 24, [2005] 1 WLR 1495; *Smith v Chief Constable of Sussex Police* [2008] UKHL 50, [2009] AC 225; and (most significantly) *Robinson v Chief Constable of West Yorkshire Police* [2018] UKSC 4, [2018] AC 736.

[425] *Astraosson v Iceland* App No 26374/18, 1 December 2020 [GC], para 233; *Xhoxhaj v Albania* (2021) 73 EHRR 14, para 290.

[426] *Astraosson v Iceland* App No 26374/18, 1 December 2020 [GC], para 219; *Xhoxhaj v Albania* (2021) 73 EHRR 14, para 282.

[427] ibid paras 220–21.

[428] See eg ibid para 232.

[429] *Ramos Nunes de Carvalho e Sa v Portugal* App No 55391/13 & others (6 November 2018) [GC], paras 176–77.

[430] ibid para 178.

[431] ibid paras 179–83. For examples see *Tsfayo v UK* (2009) 48 EHRR 18, para 47; contrast *Ramos Nunes de Carvalho e Sa v Portugal* App No 55391/13 & others (6 November 2018) [GC]. See also *Begum v Tower Hamlets LBC* [2003] UKHL 5, [2003] 2 AC 430; *R (Wright) v Secretary of State for Health* [2009] UKHL 3, [2009] 1 AC 739.

systemic safeguards against undue influence.[432] When deciding whether a tribunal is independent, the following factors are to be considered:

(a) the way its members are appointed;

(b) their term of office;[433]

(c) the existence of safeguards against outside pressures; and

(d) whether the body appears independent.[434]

This final point is important as Article 6 is concerned not only with actual independence and impartiality, but also with the appearance of these qualities in light of 'the confidence which the courts in a democratic society must inspire in the public'.[435]

6.155 With respect to impartiality, the ECtHR has held that it has both a subjective element—concerned with what a judge's 'personal conviction and behaviour' says about 'whether [they] held any personal prejudice or bias in a given case'—and an objective one, concerned with whether 'the tribunal itself and, among other aspects, its composition, offered sufficient guarantees to exclude any legitimate doubt in respect of its impartiality'.[436] There is no watertight division between the two.[437] The ECtHR applies a presumption that a tribunal is free of personal prejudice or partiality unless the contrary is shown.[438]

6.156 By way of example, the ECtHR found a breach of Article 6(1) in *McGonnell v UK* where the bailiff, who presided over legal proceedings concerning the applicant's planning appeal, had also been sitting as the deputy bailiff when the earlier, detailed development plan had been adopted.[439] It also found a breach of the requirements of independence and impartiality where a judge had faced disciplinary proceedings before a body consisting largely of members appointed by the legislative and executive authorities, who were not employed on a full-time basis;

---

[432] *Astraosson v Iceland* App No 26374/18, 1 December 2020 [GC], para 234; *Xhoxhaj v Albania* (2021) 73 EHRR 14, para 291.

[433] The starting point is that, in order to ensure independence, judges should not be removable from office during their term save where this is a proportionate means of achieving a legitimate aim and 'is not such as to raise reasonable doubt in the minds of individuals as to the imperviousness of the court concerned to external factors and its neutrality with respect to the interests before it': *Astraosson v Iceland* App No 26374/18, 1 December 2020 [GC], para 239. See also *Xhoxhaj v Albania* (2021) 73 EHRR 14, para 298.

[434] *Ringeisen v Austria* (1979–80) 1 EHRR 455; *Campbell and Fell v the United Kingdom* (1985) 7 EHRR 165; *Le Compte, Van Leuven and De Meyere v Belgium* (1981) 4 EHRR 1; *Belilos v Switzerland* (1988) 10 EHRR 466; *Denisov v Ukraine* App No 76639/11, 25 September 2018 [GC], para 60.

[435] See eg *Denisov v Ukraine* App No 76639/11, 25 September 2018 [GC], para 63; *Ramos Nunes de Carvalho e Sa v Portugal* App Nos 55391/13 & others 6 November 2018 [GC], para 149.

[436] See eg *Denisov v Ukraine* App No 76639/11, 25 September 2018 [GC], para 61; *Ramos Nunes de Carvalho e Sa v Portugal* App Nos 55391/13 & others 6 November 2018 [GC], para 145.

[437] See eg *Ramos Nunes de Carvalho e Sa v Portugal* App No 55391/136 November 2018 [GC], para 146.

[438] See eg *Morice v France* (2016) 62 EHRR 1 [GC], para 74 (presumption rebutted—see paras 79–92); *Einarsson v Iceland* (2020) 70 EHRR 3, para 56 (presumption rebutted—see paras 60–92).

[439] *McGonnell v UK* (2000) 30 EHRR 289. See also *Langborger v Sweden* (1989) 12 EHRR 416; *Pabla Ky v Finland* (2006) 42 EHRR 34; *Olujic v Croatia* (2011) 52 EHRR 26; *R (Barclay) v Secretary of State for Justice* [2008] EWCA Civ 1319, [2009] 2 WLR 1205.

and where one of those members had previously been involved in proposing his dismissal.[440] However, there is no absolute requirement for complete separation of powers. For example, in *Kleyn v Netherlands* the Grand Chamber held that a body that both advised on the drafting of planning legislation and determined appeals against planning decisions relating to that legislation did not violate Article 6 as the subject matter was sufficiently distinct that there could be no serious concerns regarding impartiality.[441] In recent cases the Grand Chamber has maintained that complete separation of powers is not required—even where, for example, there is significant executive or legislative involvement in the appointment of judges—notwithstanding that the separation of powers, in particular between the executive and the judiciary, 'has assumed growing importance in its case-law'.[442]

6.157　The ECtHR has found a number of violations of the requirements of independence and impartiality in cases involving military tribunals.[443] For example, it has held that some courts martial (including in the UK) have violated the impartiality requirement and that the trial of a civilian by court martial, in the absence of special circumstances, will be contrary to Article 6.[444] In response the UK amended its procedures, but the ECtHR found in *Morris v UK* that, while these changes went 'a long way' to addressing the problems identified, the court martial procedure still did not comply with Article 6(1).[445] The House of Lords subsequently distinguished the ECtHR's conclusion, finding in *R v Spear* that the 'European Court did not receive all the help that was needed to form a conclusion' as it did not have all the relevant information about safeguards against impartiality or lack of independence.[446]

6.158　A number of ECtHR cases involving the UK, as well as a number of domestic cases, have considered impartiality in the context of criminal proceedings and, more particularly, allegations of jury bias. The specific facts of the cases are important in determining whether evidence of possible bias or preference on the part of a juror will undermine the presumption of impartiality (which applies to jury members as it does to judges).[447] A breach of the requirement of impartiality is more likely to be found where an allegation of bias has been made but not investigated.[448]

---

[440] *Denisov v Ukraine* App No 76639/11, 25 September 2018 [GC], paras 68–72.

[441] *Kleyn v Netherlands* (2004) 38 EHRR [GC].

[442] See eg *Ramos Nunes de Carvalho e Sa v Portugal* App No 55391/13 & others 6 November 2018 [GC], para 144; *Xhoxhaj v Albania* (2021) 73 EHRR 14, para 295.

[443] See eg *Incal v Turkey* (2000) 29 EHRR 449; *Findlay v UK* (1997) 24 EHRR 221; *Hood v UK* (2000) 29 EHRR 365.

[444] *Martin v United Kingdom* (2007) 44 EHRR 31.

[445] *Morris v UK* (2002) 34 EHRR 52. See also *Grieves v UK* (2004) 39 EHRR 2.

[446] *R v Spear* [2002] UKHL 31, [2003] 1 AC 734, para 12 per Lord Bingham.

[447] For examples, see *Pullar v UK* 1996) 22 EHRR 391 (jury included an employee of a key prosecution witness—no breach of art 6(1); *Sander v UK* (2001) 31 EHRR 44 (jury members making racist remarks and jokes—breach of art 6(1) as jury should have been discharged); *Hanif and Khan v UK* App Nos 52999/08 and 61779/08, 20 December 2011 (police officer on jury in case depending on police witnesses—no breach of art 6(1)). In similar vein to *Pullar*, see *R v Thoron (Francois Pierre)* [2001] EWCA Crim 1797. For domestic variants on *Sander*, see *R v Qureshi* [2001] EWCA Crim 1807, [2002] 1 WLR 518; *R v Bajwa* [2007] EWCA Crim 1618; *R v OKZ* [2010] EWCA Crim 2272; and *Skeete v R* [2022] EWCA Crim 1511, paras 26–32.

[448] See eg *Farhi v France* (2009) 48 EHRR 34; *Gregory v United Kingdom* (1998) 25 EHRR 577.

The decisive issue for the domestic courts is whether a fair-minded and informed   6.159
observer would have concluded that there was a real possibility, or real danger, that
the jury was biased.[449] The House of Lords has ruled that evidence emerging *after*
a verdict has been delivered of things said by jurors is inadmissible and cannot be
used as evidence of a breach of Article 6.[450] The importance of jury deliberations
remaining secret has been acknowledged by the ECtHR as a legitimate feature of
English trial law.[451]

In principle a jury trial may be rendered unfair by adverse media publicity par-   6.160
ticularly when 'publicity is unremitting and sensational'.[452] However, the ECtHR
has held that the fact that high-profile criminal cases attract media comment does
not inevitably prejudice a defendant's right to a fair trial. Cogent evidence of concerns about jurors' impartiality will be required to convince the court that the trial
was unfair.[453]

Finally, as to the requirement that the tribunal be 'established by law', this means   6.161
not only that there must be a proper basis in domestic law for the body's existence,
but also that there must be 'compliance by the court or tribunal with the particular
rules that govern it and the composition of the bench in each case'.[454] This includes
the domestic rules for the appointment of judges.[455] In assessing whether a particular irregularity results in non-compliance with the 'established by law' requirement, the ECtHR will consider: (a) whether there has been a 'manifest' breach of
domestic law;[456] (b) whether the irregularity undermines the object and purpose of
the requirement (namely 'to ensure the ability of the judiciary to perform its duties
free of interference'), such that it goes to 'the essence of the right to a tribunal
established by law';[457] and (c) whether and how the domestic courts have considered
the impact of the identified irregularity on the individual's convention rights.[458,459]

(iii) *Public hearing* A public hearing is an essential feature of the right to a fair trial[460]   6.162
and is explicitly protected by Article 6(1). There are two notable components: that

---

[449] See eg *R v Alexander* [2004] EWCA Crim 2341.

[450] *R v Mirza (Shabbir Ali)* [2004] UKHL 2, [2004] 1 AC 1118.

[451] *Gregory v United Kingdom* (1998) 25 EHRR 577.

[452] *Abu-Hamza No 1 v UK* App No 31411/07, 18 January 2011, para 39. This has long been recognized even outside the context of art 6—hence the strict rules on contempt in relation to reports of criminal proceedings set out in the Contempt of Court Act 1981.

[453] ibid.

[454] *Astraosson v Iceland*, App No 26374/18, 1 December 2020 [GC], paras 216, 223.

[455] ibid paras 227, 230.

[456] That is, one 'objectively and genuinely identifiable as such'. The courts will accept domestic courts' view of this issue unless their findings can be regarded as arbitrary or manifestly unreasonable: ibid para 244.

[457] The separate opinion of Judge Pinto de Albuquerque criticizes the majority for having established this test, only to apply a different and more consequentialist one on the facts of the case: see ibid para 5.

[458] The more thoroughly the domestic courts have performed this exercise in compliance with the relevant Convention case law and standards, the less likely the ECtHR is to depart from their conclusions: ibid para 251.

[459] ibid paras 240–45. For a summary of cases where the 'established by law' requirement has been considered, see ibid para 217.

[460] *Axen v Germany* (1984) 6 EHRR 195.

there be a hearing; and that the hearing be held (and judgment pronounced) in public.

6.163　As to the first, this aspect of Article 6(1) usually—but not universally—requires an *oral* hearing attended by the parties (in criminal cases the prosecutor and the accused).[461] This has been characterized as an aspect of the principle of equality of arms.[462] Whether dispensing with an oral hearing is justified (or, otherwise put, whether art 6 requires a one) will depend primarily on the nature of the issues to be determined.[463] An oral hearing is more likely to be required where the court has to assess matters which are difficult to determine on paper, such as an applicant's character, behaviour, or risk level.[464] An oral hearing is not necessarily required at the appellate level;[465] this is more likely where there has been no such hearing at first instance (see further below).[466]

6.164　There is a separate question as to whether Article 6(1) requires that an applicant be permitted to attend the oral hearing of their case (in person or at all). The ECtHR has held that there is no absolute right to be present at one's trial even in criminal proceedings; the critical question is whether the arrangements made are sufficient to guarantee a reasonable opportunity to present one's case without substantial disadvantage vis-à-vis one's opponent (as to which see above).[467] The Covid-19 pandemic also generated domestic jurisprudence on the circumstances in which the right to a fair trial at common law and under Article 6(1) may be satisfied by a remote rather than an in-person hearing.[468]

---

[461] *Fischer v Austria* (1995) 20 EHRR 349; and see in the domestic context *R (Dudson) v Secretary of State for the Home Department* [2005] UKHL 52, [2006] 1 AC 245, paras 25–34 (including a discussion of earlier ECtHR authority).

[462] *Ramos Nunes de Carvalho e Sa v Portugal* App Nos 55391/13 & others 6 November 2018 [GC], para 187.

[463] *De Tommaso v Italy* (2017) 65 EHRR 19, para 163; see also *Xhoxhaj v Albania* (2021) 73 EHRR 14, para 340; and *Altay v Turkey (No 2)* App No 11236/09, 9 April 209, para 74. This chimes with the approach adopted by the House of Lords in *R (Dudson) v Secretary of State for the Home Department* [2005] UKHL 52, [2006] 1 AC 245, paras 35–40.

[464] *De Tommaso v Italy* (2017) 65 EHRR 19, para 167.

[465] *Axen v Germany* (1984) 6 EHRR 195; *Monnell and Morris v UK* (1988) 10 EHRR 205; *Xhoxhaj v Albania* (2021) 73 EHRR 14, para 339. cf a hearing before 'a court of first and only instance', where an oral hearing is required save in exceptional circumstances: *Ramos Nunes de Carvalho e Sa v Portugal* App Nos 55391/13 & others 6 November 2018 [GC], para 188; see also para 190, summarizing circumstances which have been held to be sufficiently exceptional. The 'exceptional circumstances' test was also applied in *Altay v Turkey (No 2)* App No 11236/09, 9 April 209, where there was no provision for an oral hearing either at first instance or on appeal; cf *Mutu v Switzerland* [2019] EHCR 778, para 177, not appearing to impose this test.

[466] See eg *Ramos Nunes de Carvalho e Sa v Portugal* App Nos 55391/13 & others 6 November 2018 [GC]; *Xhoxhaj v Albania* (2021) 73 EHRR 14, para 339. For an application of these principles in the domestic context see *R (Kearney) v Chief Constable of Hampshire Police* [2019] EWCA Civ 1841, [2019] 4 WLR 144 (no breach of art 6 where an application for judicial review had been marked 'totally without merit' on the papers and no right to an oral hearing seeking permission to appeal) and *R (Siddiqui) v Lord Chancellor* [2019] EWCA Civ 1040 (removal of a right to oral renewal on an application for permission to the Court of Appeal not incompatible with art 6).

[467] See the discussion of the ECtHR jurisprudence in *R (Michael) v Governor of HMP Whitemoor* [2020] EWCA Civ 29, [2020] 1 WLR 2524, paras 35–41.

[468] See eg *Re A (Children) (Remote hearing: Care and placement orders)* [2020] EWCA Civ 583, [2020] 1 WLR 4931; *Re C (Children) (Covid 19: Representation)* [2020] EWCA Civ 734.

As to the public nature of the hearing, this serves to protect litigants 'from the 6.165
administration of justice in secret with no public scrutiny'[469] and to maintain public confidence in the judicial system.[470] The right to a public hearing is, however,
the only part of Article 6 which is expressly qualified: the text states that 'the press
and public may be excluded from all or part of the trial in the interest of morals,
public order or national security in a democratic society, where the interests of juveniles or the protection of the private life of the parties so require, or to the extent
strictly necessary in the opinion of the court in special circumstances where publicity would prejudice the interests of justice'. The lawfulness of such restrictions is,
as always, considered on a case-by-case basis. For example, in the criminal context
the Court of Appeal has held that the right to a public hearing will not be violated
where national security concerns or the need to protect witnesses lead to a criminal
trial being held partly or even wholly in private.[471] Any restriction imposed must be
'strictly required' in the particular factual circumstances of the case.[472] The principle was affirmed in *Guardian News and Media v AB and others* where the Court
of Appeal overturned a decision of a trial judge who had ordered that a terrorism
trial be held entirely in private.[473] Most domestic cases in this context are now considered primarily by reference to the common law principle of open justice, rather
than the requirements of Article 6.[474]

On occasion the ECtHR has even accepted general presumptions in favour of 6.166
private hearings as compatible with Article 6(1), for example as in *B v UK* concerning the presumption of privacy in hearings under the Children Act 1989.[475]
However, where a case concerned the transfer of custody of a child to a public
institution rather than a dispute between parents over a child's residence, the
reasons for excluding a case from public scrutiny had to be subjected to careful
examination.[476]

If a public hearing is not held in a lower court, the defect may be cured by 6.167
a public hearing at a higher level but only if the appeal court is able to consider the merits of the case and is competent to deal with the entirety of the
matter.[477]

---

[469] *Pretto v Italy* (1984) 6 EHRR 182, para 21.

[470] *Diennet v France* (1996) 21 EHRR 554, para 33.

[471] *R v Yam* [2008] EWCA Crim 269. See also *Yam v UK* (2020) 71 EHRR 4.

[472] ibid para 34.

[473] *Guardian News and Media v AB and others* [2014] All ER (D) 88 (Jun). See also (in the context of the common law principles of open justice rather than art 6) *Guardian News and Media v Incedal* [2014] EWCA Crim 1861, [2015] 1 Cr App R 4.

[474] See eg *R (Guardian News and Media) v City of Westminster Magistrates* [2012] EWCA Civ 420, [2013] QB 618; *Khuja v Times Newspapers Ltd* [2017] UKSC 49, [2019] AC 161. The common law and art 6 will not inevitably yield an identical response: see *Clifford v Millicom Services UK Ltd* [2023] EWCA Civ 50, paras 29–30.

[475] *B v UK* (2002) 34 EHRR 19.

[476] *Moser v Austria* [2007] 1 FLR 702.

[477] *Diennet v France* (1996) 21 EHRR 554.

6.168 The requirement for a public hearing includes an obligation that judgment be pronounced publicly. This does not necessarily require that the judgment be read in open court, provided that the outcome is publicly available.[478]

6.169 (iv) *Reasonable time* Article 6(1) calls for any hearing to be held 'within a reasonable time'. Unlike Article 5(3), which applies only to individuals under arrest, this provision applies to both civil and criminal cases. The guarantee 'underlines the importance of rendering justice without delays which might jeopardise its effectiveness and credibility'.[479] This issue accounts for many ECtHR judgments and frequently reflects systemic problems.[480]

6.170 The 'time' that must be 'reasonable' is the period between the laying of the 'charge'[481] in criminal matters, or the institution of proceedings in civil matters, and the final determination of the proceedings.[482] This includes, where relevant, the time required for the resolution of appeals and even the resolution of the issue of costs.[483]

6.171 What constitutes a reasonable time will depend on the circumstances. Particularly relevant factors include the complexity of the case (both factually and legally[484]), the applicant's conduct and that of the competent authorities, and the importance of what was at stake for the applicant.[485] The advanced age of the applicant may also be relevant.[486] Another key factor is the length of time since the events occurred, before the institution of proceedings.[487]

6.172 Delay by an applicant weakens a complaint that a dispute has not been resolved within a reasonable time, but a litigant must not be penalized for making use of all available procedures to advance their case.[488] In relation to the conduct of the authorities, the state is under a duty to ensure those who play a role in proceedings avoid unnecessary delay; only delays that are attributable to the state (including the courts) are relevant.[489] A more rigorous standard applies if the

---

[478] *Pretto v Italy* (1984) 6 EHRR 182. Common law principles entail a similar requirement: see *R (Mohamed) v Secretary of State for Foreign and Commonwealth Affairs (No 2)* [2010] EWCA Civ 65, [2011] QB 218.

[479] *Stögmüller v Austria* (1979–80) 1 EHRR 155.

[480] See Steven Greer, *The European Convention on Human Rights: Achievements, Problems and Prospects* (CUP 2006).

[481] As to when a criminal charge exists, see paras 6.123–6.132. For the application of this principle in the domestic context, see *Attorney-General's Reference No 2 of 2001* [2003] UKHL 68, [2011] 1 WLR 2435, paras 26–28; *Ambrose v Harris* [2011] UKSC 2435, para 62; and *O'Neill v HM Advocate (No 2)* [2013] UKSC 36, [2013] 1 WLR 1992, para 34.

[482] Often in a criminal case this will be when the sentence is passed (absent any appeal).

[483] See eg *Somjee v UK* (2003) 36 EHRR 16; *Darnell v UK* (1993) 18 EHRR 205; *Darnell v UK* (1993) 18 EHRR 205.

[484] *Triggiani v Italy* [1991] ECHR 20.

[485] *Gast and Popp v Germany* (2001) 33 EHRR 37; *Pélissier and Sassi v France* (2000) 30 EHRR 715; *Georgiev v Bulgaria* App No 4551/05, 24 February 2011; *Tanase v Romania* App No 41720/13, 25 June 2019 [GC], para 209f. For endorsement in the domestic context see *Dyer v Watson* [2004] 1 AC 379, [2004] 1 AC 379, paras 53–56.

[486] *GOC v Poland* App No 48001/99, 23 October 2001.

[487] *Korbely v Hungary* (2008) 25 BHRC 382. cf *McFarlane v Ireland* [2010] ECHR 1272.

[488] *Eckle v Federal Republic of Germany* (1983) 5 EHRR 1.

[489] *Zimmerman and Steiner v Switzerland* (1984) 6 EHRR 17; *Boddaert v Belgium* (1993) 16 EHRR 242; *Ewing v UK* (1988) 10 EHRR 141.

accused is in custody, and a delay in proceedings may cause pre-trial detention to be unlawful under Article 5(3).[490] Certain types of civil case will need to be dealt with more expeditiously than others, such as those concerning children or a life-threatening illness.[491]

The House of Lords took a robust approach to the right to a hearing within a 'reasonable time' in *Magill v Porter*. It held that this right is an independent element of Article 6(1), which should not be subsumed by general considerations of the right to a fair trial and which does not require the complainant to show himself prejudiced by the delay.[492]   6.173

A breach of the 'reasonable time' requirement in the criminal context does not require a criminal trial to be discontinued or a conviction quashed unless the fairness of the trial itself has been compromised.[493] An appropriate remedy for delay falling short of this is a public acknowledgement of the breach and an order for expedition to cure it.[494]   6.174

(v) *The opportunity to present one's case* This is often expressed as deriving from the principle of 'equality of arms'.[495] The precise content of the right is necessarily context-dependent: what is required is 'a reasonable opportunity' to present one's case and evidence 'under conditions that do not place [one] at a substantial disadvantage vis-à-vis [one's] opponent'.[496] The requirement can be breached merely by procedural inequality, without the need for quantifiable unfairness.[497]   6.175

The extent to which Article 6(1) requires disclosure is fact-sensitive. The ECtHR has held that generally all evidence must be produced in the presence of the applicant at a public hearing with a view to adversarial argument.[498] However, there is no 'absolute or unqualified right to see every document'.[499] There may be competing interests, such as protecting witnesses or keeping secret police methods of investigating crime.[500] Measures that restrict defence rights must be strictly necessary to be   6.176

---

[490] *Jablonski v Poland* (2003) 36 EHRR 27.

[491] *Hokkanen v Finland* [1996] 1 FLR 289; *Damnjanovic v Serbia* [2009] 1 FLR 339; *H v France* (1990) 12 EHRR 74.

[492] *Magill v Porter* [2001] UKHL 67, [2002] 2 AC 357. See also *Attorney General's Reference (No 2 of 2001)* [2001] EWCA Crim 1568, [2001] 1 WLR 1869; *R v HM Advocate* [2002] UKPC D3, [2004] 1 AC 462.

[493] Examples might include where the delay was the result of 'bad faith, unlawfulness and executive manipulation', or where the delay is inordinate and inexcusable: see *Attorney General's Reference (No 2 of 2001)* [2003] UKHL 68, [2004] 2 AC 72, para 25. Another likely example is where the passage of time has caused important evidence to become unavailable or unreliable.

[494] See eg *Spiers v Ruddy and HM Advocate General* [2007] UKPC D2, [2008] AC 873. See also *Attorney General's Reference (No 2 of 2001)* [2003] UKHL 68, [2004] 2 AC 72; *R v HM Advocate* [2002] UKPC D3, [2004] 1 AC 462; *R v Dunlop* [2019] NICA 72 (noting that courts also factor delay into their sentencing decisions).

[495] See eg *Vegotex International SA v Belgium* (2023) 76 EHRR 15 [GC], para 139.

[496] ibid.

[497] *Bulut v Austria* (1997) 24 EHRR 84; *Fischer v Austria* App No 33382/96, 20 May 2001.

[498] See eg *Vegotex International SA v Belgium* (2023) 76 EHRR 15 [GC], para 134; *Edwards v UK* (1992) 15 EHRR 417; *Lamy v Belgium* (1989) 11 EHRR 529.

[499] *Roberts v Nottinghamshire Healthcare NHS Trust* [2008] EWHC 1934 (QB), para 25.

[500] See eg *Regner v Czech Republic* (2018) 66 EHRR 9 [GC], para 148.

permissible under Article 6, and must leave the essence of the right unimpaired.[501] In *A and others v UK* the Grand Chamber held that the UK's closed material procedure (as used in the Special Immigration Appeals Commission)—which involved withholding material from a party on national security grounds, with their interests protected by the use of the 'special advocate' procedure—was compatible with Article 6 in light of the important interests at stake and the countervailing protections afforded.[502] In *AF (No 3)* the House of Lords applied the decision in *A and others v UK*[503] and held that non-disclosure to a person subject to a control order on grounds of national security could not go so far as to deny a party knowledge of the essence of the case against him.[504] If the open material used against a controlee consisted purely of general assertions, and the case against him was based solely or to a decisive degree on closed materials, the requirements of a fair trial would not be satisfied, regardless of how cogent the case based on the closed materials might be. Where the interests of national security were concerned in the context of combating terrorism, however, it might be acceptable not to disclose the source of evidence that founded the grounds for suspecting that a person had been involved in terrorism-related activities.[505]

6.177   The impact of non-disclosure on the fairness of proceedings may be cured at the appellate level.[506] The Grand Chamber has on at least one occasion found this to be the case even where central evidence was held from the applicant and his lawyers, and where the reasons for refusing him security clearance were not provided.[507]

6.178   Another facet of the right to a reasonable opportunity to present one's case is that courts or tribunals may not, consistent with Article 6, decide a case or dismiss an appeal on the basis of a ground it has raised of its own motion without giving the parties the opportunity to comment. The 'decisive factor' is whether one of the parties was 'taken by surprise' by the ultimate basis of the decision.[508]

6.179   (vi) *A reasoned decision* Article 6(1) requires a court or tribunal to give reasons for its judgment. The extent of this duty varies according to the nature of the decision and the circumstances of the case.[509] 'Sparse' reasoning will not violate Article 6(1)

---

[501] *Rowe and Davis v UK* (2000) 30 EHRR 1. See also *Regner v Czech Republic* (2018) 66 EHRR 9 [GC], para 149, noting that where evidence has been withheld from a party on public interest grounds the court 'must scrutinize the decision-making procedure to ensure that, as far as possible, it complied with the requirements to provide adversarial proceedings and equality of arms and incorporated adequate safeguards to protect the interests of the person concerned'.

[502] For later cases on closed material procedure see *Kennedy v UK* (2010) 52 EHRR 4, applied in *Tariq v Home Office* [2011] UKSC 35, [2012] 1 AC 452.

[503] *A and others v UK* (2009) 26 BHRC 1.

[504] *Secretary of State for the Home Department v AF (No 3)* [2009] UKHL 28, [2010] 2 AC 269.

[505] For subsequent discussion of the scope of this principle, see eg *QX v Secretary of State for the Home Department* [2022] EWCA Civ 1541; *R (Reprieve) v Prime Minister* [2021] EWCA Civ 972, [2022] QB 447; *K v Secretary of State for Defence* [2017] EWHC 830 (Admin); *Bank Mellat v HM Treasury* [2015] EWCA Civ 1052, [2016] 1 WLR 1187.

[506] See eg *Macklin v HM Advocate* [2015] UKSC 77, [2017] All ER 32, paras 13–14 (discussing ECtHR and domestic authorities).

[507] *Regner v Czech Republic* (2018) 66 EHRR 9 [GC], paras 150–62.

[508] *Vegotex International SA v Belgium* (2023) 76 EHRR 15 [GC], paras 134–36.

[509] See eg *McGinley and Egan v UK* (1999) 27 EHRR 1; *Moreira Ferreira v Portugal* (2017) 43 BHRC 312 [GC], para 84.

per se, and a detailed answer is not required to every argument,[510] but the court must address the essential issues submitted to its jurisdiction.[511] In cases involving the determination of Convention rights, 'automatic or stereotypical' reasons will not suffice.[512] This right is particularly important in cases where the applicant wishes to exercise a right of appeal.[513] The common law duty to give reasons has been held to be sufficient to satisfy Article 6 requirements.[514]

In relation to juries, (which do not give reasons for a verdict) the ECtHR has upheld the validity of this practice, provided there are safeguards in the proceedings to avoid the risk of arbitrariness and enable the applicant to understand why he or she has been found guilty.[515] This case was applied domestically in *R v Lawless*.[516]   6.180

(vii) The implementation of final decisions Article 6(1) also encompasses the right to the implementation of final, binding decisions of a court or tribunal.[517] As the Grand Chamber has explained, the right of access to a court 'would be illusory if a Contracting State's domestic legal system allowed a final, binding judicial decision to remain inoperative to the detriment of one party'.[518] For the same reason, Article 6(1) requires that final judgments be implemented without unreasonable delay.[519] Relevant factors will include the complexity of enforcement, the behaviour of the applicant and of the authorities, and the amount and/or nature of the award.[520] Taken with the principle of legal certainty, these principles also place limits on the circumstances in which final judgments can lawfully be called into question.[521]   6.181

Finally, it is important to note that the specific rights identified and discussed above are not exhaustive of the scope and requirements of Article 6(1). Other issues—such as   6.182

---

[510] *Van de Hurk v Netherlands* (1994) 18 EHRR 481; *Moreira Ferreira v Portugal* (2017) 43 BHRC 312 [GC].

[511] *Helle v Finland* (1997) 26 EHRR 159, paras 55–60; *Hiro Balani v Spain* (1995) 19 EHRR 566. In *Moreira Ferreira v Portugal* (2017) 43 BHRC 312 the Grand Chamber suggested that 'parties to judicial proceedings can expect to receive a specific and explicit reply to the arguments which are decisive for the outcome of those proceedings'.

[512] See eg *Moreira Ferreira v Portugal* (2017) 43 BHRC 312 [GC], para 84.

[513] *Hadjianastassiou v Greece* (1993) 16 EHRR 219.

[514] *English v Emery Reimbold & Strick* [2002] EWCA Civ 605.

[515] *Taxquet v Belgium* App No 926/05, 16 November 2010; and see more recently *Moreira Ferreira v Portugal* (2017) 43 BHRC 312 [GC], para 84 and the (arguably surprising) decision of the majority of the Grand Chamber in *Lhermite v Belgium* App No 34238/09, 29 November 2016 [GC], paras 66–69 (finding against the applicant where there was no discernible reason for a jury having found them criminally responsible for her actions in the face of unanimous expert evidence to the contrary). In the domestic context, see also *N (A Child)* [2019] EWCA Civ 1997, [2019] 4 WLR 154 (relationship between art 6(1) and observance of the protections for vulnerable witnesses).

[516] *R v Lawless* [2011] EWCA Crim 59.

[517] See eg *Ouzounis v Greece* App No 49144/99, 18 April 2002; *Scordino v Italy* (2007) 45 EHRR 7.

[518] *Scordino v Italy* (2007) 45 EHRR 7, para 196.

[519] See eg *Raylyan v Russia* App No 22000/03, 15 February 2007; *Gerasimov v Russia* App No 29920/05 and others, 1 July 2014.

[520] *Raylyan v Russia* App No 22000/03, 15 February 2007, para 31.

[521] See eg *Brumarescu v Romania* (2001) 33 EHRR 35 [GC]; *Sovtransavto Holding v Ukraine* (2004) 38 EHRR 44; *Agrokompleks v Ukraine* App No 23465/03, 6 October 2011; *Grazuleviciute v Lithuania* App No 53176/17, 14 December 2001.

the use against an applicant of evidence obtained in breach of their Convention rights or in breach of domestic law[522]—will be assessed pursuant to the 'composite approach' discussed above, which focuses on the question of whether the proceedings as a whole were fair.[523]

(b) Specific safeguards in respect of determination of criminal charges

6.183 The overarching protection offered by Article 6(1) is further supplemented in respect of criminal proceedings by the specific guarantees in Article 6(2) and (3). The courts have, under Article 6(1) alone or in association with the specific protections of Article 6(2) (the presumption of innocence) and (3) (specific rights of the defence), considered matters as diverse as reliance on evidence from anonymous witnesses;[524] entrapment;[525] witnesses giving evidence behind screens;[526] accomplices;[527] undercover agents;[528] the use of evidence obtained in violation of Article 3;[529] and admissions of guilt from co-defendants.[530] Article 6(1) also affords criminal defendants specific protections which are implied into its text in addition to those in Article 6(2) and (3). They include:

(i) a limited right to silence;

(ii) the right to effective participation in their trials;

(iii) the right to equality of arms.

6.184   (i) *Right to silence* The right to silence and the privilege against self-incrimination are core, albeit implicit, elements of the right to a fair trial.[531] They are regarded by the ECtHR as 'generally recognised international standards which lie at the heart of the notion of a fair procedure under article 6'.[532] They support the presumption of innocence and protect against 'improper compulsion' by the police and judicial authorities.[533] They mean that an accused may not be compelled to answer

---

[522] See eg *Ribalda v Spain* (2020) 71 EHRR 7, paras 150–51; *Cwik v Poland* (2021) 72 EHRR 19, paras 73–93 (use of evidence obtained in breach of art 3 rendering trial unfair).

[523] See eg *VCL and AN v United Kingdom* (2021) 73 EHRR 9, paras 208–09 (applying the 'overall fairness' approach in the context of breaches of art 4 which affected the criminal process—discussed in *AAD & others v R* [2022] EWCA Crim 106); *Akbay v Germany* (2023) 76 EHRR 21, paras 109 and following (doing the same in the context of entrapment by police, in respect of which there is an established line of art 6 case law—for comparison of the common law position see *R v Haroon Ali Syed* [2018] EWCA Crim 2809, [2019] 1 WLR 2459).

[524] *Kostovski v Netherlands* (1989) 12 EHRR 434; *Windisch v Austria* (1990) 13 EHRR 281; *Doorson v Netherlands* (1996) 22 EHRR 330; *Van Mechelen v Netherlands* (1997) 25 EHRR 647.

[525] *Teixeira de Castro v Portugal* (1999) 28 EHRR 101.

[526] *X v UK* (1992) 15 EHRR CD 113.

[527] *X v UK* (1976) 74 DR 115.

[528] *X v Germany* (1989) 11 EHRR 84.

[529] The use of such evidence will always violate art 6 and render a criminal trial unfair: *Gafgen v Germany* App No 22978/05, 1 June 2010 [GC], para 167, *Ibrahim v UK* [GC] 2016, para 254.

[530] *MH v UK* [1997] EHRLR 279.

[531] *Murray v United Kingdom* (1996) 22 EHRR 29; *Funke v France* [1993] 1 CMLR 897.

[532] ibid.

[533] *Saunders v UK* (1997) 23 EHRR 313.

questions during the investigation or to testify in court.[534] Thus, the use of improperly obtained evidence would violate Article 6(1).[535]

However, these notions are not absolute.[536] The ECtHR has confirmed that it may be permissible for a trial judge to leave a jury with the option of drawing an adverse inference from an accused's silence as occurs under the Criminal Justice and Public Order Act 1994. The jury must be properly directed as to a defendant's silence.[537] However, in *Adetoro v UK* the ECtHR found that a judge's failure to direct a jury properly in relation to the defendant's silence in a police interview did not violate Article 6(1) because he had not been convicted on the strength of his silence alone and there had been no unfairness in the trial as a whole.[538] Thus, adverse inferences cannot be the primary ground for conviction and an alleged breach of Article 6 is to be determined in the light of all the circumstances of the case, having particular regard to the situations where inferences may be drawn, the weight to be attached to them, and the degree of compulsion inherent in the situation.[539]

6.185

The privilege against self-incrimination does not generally apply to the production of blood, hair, or other physical or objective specimens used in forensic analysis, or voice samples.[540] Car owners can be required to disclose the driver of a vehicle at the time of a speeding offence as this was part of a regulatory regime relating to the use of cars and did not limit the privilege against self-incrimination sufficiently to constitute a breach of Article 6(1).[541] However, the production of drugs, which a street drug dealer had swallowed, by the forcible administration of emetics, was found to violate the prohibition on self-incrimination due to the nature and degree of compulsion used.[542]

6.186

(ii) *Right to effective participation* One of the 'essential requirements' of Article 6(1) read with Article 6(3)(d) is that a person 'charged with a criminal offence' is entitled to take part in the hearing and to be present when tried,[543] subject only to very tightly defined exceptions.[544] This is because a defendant has to be given a proper opportunity to respond to evidence, and question witnesses giving evidence against them.[545] Thus, the entitlement is not only to be physically present, but to

6.187

---

[534] *R v Kearns* [2002] EWCA Crim 748, [2002] 1 WLR 2815.

[535] *Jalloh v Germany* (2007) 44 EHRR 32. See also *G v UK* (1983) 35 DR 75; *Gafgen v Germany* (2011) 52 EHRR 1; Steven Greer, 'Should Police Threats to Torture Suspects Always Be Severely Punished? Reflections on the Gafgen Case' (2011) 11(1) Human Rights Law Reports 67.

[536] *Condron and Condron v UK* (2001) 31 EHRR 1.

[537] ibid. See also *Beckles v UK* (2003) 36 EHRR 13; *Heaney and McGuinness v Ireland* (2001) 33 EHRR 12.

[538] [2010] All ER (D) 109 (Apr).

[539] *John Murray v UK* (1996) 22 EHRR 29. See also *Ibrahim v UK* [GC], App No 50541/08, 13 September 2016

[540] *PG and JH v UK* App No 44787/98, 25 September 2001.

[541] *O'Halloran and Francis v UK* (2008) 46 EHRR 21.

[542] *Jalloh v Germany* (2006) 20 BHRC 575.

[543] *Hulki Gunes v Turkey* (2006) 43 EHRR 15; *Murtazaliyeva v Russia* [GC] App No 36658/05, 8 December 2018, para 91.

[544] *Hermi v Italy* (2008) 46 EHRR 46. cf *Ekbatani v Sweden* (1991) 13 EHRR 504.

[545] *Hermi v Italy* (2008) 46 EHRR 46.

be present in a meaningful sense: to be able to hear, follow, and understand proceedings, to take notes to facilitate the conduct of the defence, and to effectively participate through giving evidence and through a lawyer.[546] If the defendant is a child, the proceedings should take account of his or her age, level of maturity, and intellectual and emotional capabilities. This may involve special treatment.[547] Effective participation requires that the defendant has a broad understanding of the nature of the trial process and of what is at stake, including the significance of any possible penalty.[548]

6.188   (iii) *Equality of arms* The comments made in the preceding section on equality of arms also relate to criminal cases. In criminal cases, equality of arms means that a defendant and prosecution should enjoy a relatively level playing field at trial. This protection under Article 6(1) overlaps with some of the specific guarantees of Article 6(3) and the requirement for adversarial proceedings.[549] In practice, the requirement of equality of arms includes each party being afforded the opportunity to cross-examine the other's evidence and findings.[550] Where expert evidence is relied on, that may require disclosure of the technical basis of it in order to allow effective challenge to be made of it.[551] Equality of arms under Article 6(1), when read with Article 6(3), may also include an obligation on the prosecution to disclose any material in their possession, or to which they could gain access, which may assist the accused in exonerating him or herself or in obtaining a reduction in sentence.[552] It also means that defence and prosecution witnesses should be examined under the same conditions.[553] Both parties should certainly have the right to be represented by counsel, as well as the right to appear in person. In some cases equality of arms will require one party to be provided with funding through legal aid.[554]

6.189   In *Secretary of State for the Home Department v MB* Lord Bingham said that the ability of an individual to meet the case against him or her is integral to the notion of equality of arms which in turn is inherent in the concept of a fair trial.[555] However, mechanisms such as special advocates[556] and public interest immunity (PII) certificates,[557] which prevent the defendant directly knowing the evidence against him or

---

[546] *Moiseyev v Russia* App No 62936/00, 9 October 2008
[547] *SC v UK* (2004) 40 EHRR 226; *Blokhin v Russia* [GC] App No 47152/06, 23 March 2016.
[548] ibid. Applied domestically in *R (C) v Sevenoaks Youth Court* [2009] EWHC 3088 (Admin).
[549] *Ruiz-Mateos v Spain* (1993) 16 EHRR 505; *Krcmar v Czech Republic* (2001) 31 EHRR 41.
[550] *X v Austria* (1972) 42 CD 145.
[551] *Kartoyev v Russia* App No 9418/13, Judgment of 28 February 2022
[552] *Jespers v Belgium* (1983) 5 EHRR CD305; *Foucher v France* (1998) 25 EHRR 234. cf *Mckeown v UK* App No 6684/05, 11 January 2011; *Allison v Her Majesty's Advocate* [2010] UKSC 6, 2010 SLT 26; *McInnes v Her Majesty's Advocate* [2010] UKSC 7, 2010 SLT 266.
[553] *Bönisch v Austria* (1987) 9 EHRR 191.
[554] *Steel and Morris v UK* (2005) 41 EHRR 22.
[555] *Secretary of State for the Home Department v MB; Secretary of State for the Home Department v AF* [2007] UKHL 46, [2008] 1 AC 440.
[556] *A and others v UK* (2009) 26 BHRC 1; *Al-Rawi v Security Service* [2011] UKSC 34; *Tariq v Home Office* [2011] UKSC 35; *Secretary of State for the Home Department v MB; Secretary of State for the Home Department v AF* [2007] UKHL 46, [2008] 1 AC 440. See also *Secretary of State for the Home Department v AF (No 3)* [2009] UKHL 28, [2010] 2 AC 269.
[557] *Rowe and Davis v UK* (2000) 30 EHRR 1.

her, will not necessarily violate Article 6(1) provided they do not undermine the very essence of the right (see above, para 6.176). The ECtHR jurisprudence illustrates that evidence may only be withheld from the defendant if strictly necessary, a standard substantially higher than ordinary proportionality, and that evidence *must* be disclosed where it is necessary for an accused person to meet the case against him or her.[558]

6.190 The equality of arms guarantee is frequently read with Article 5(4) of the Convention, which allows the defendant to see the case against him or her so that he or she may challenge detention.

6.191 (iv) *Overall fairness: a composite approach* The fairness of proceedings for the purposes of Article 6(1) is assessed by reference to the trial process as a whole, including any appeals.[559] If first-instance proceedings do not meet the standard required by Article 6(1), that may be cured by appeal or review proceedings which do satisfy Article 6(1).[560] However, there are some violations which are so significant that Article 6 will be breached irrespective of the availability of subsequent appeals. In *Salduz v Turkey* the ECtHR held that the absence of a lawyer while in police custody had irretrievably affected a defendant's rights and this could not be remedied by his opportunity to challenge the evidence against him at trial or subsequently on appeal.[561] This was a violation of Article 6(3)(c) in conjunction with Article 6(1).[562] This decision was applied by the Supreme Court in *Cadder v HM Advocate*.[563] 'Admirable' as they were, later safeguards to the right to a fair trial could not rectify the unfairness which arose from a detained person having answered questions in the absence of a lawyer in his first interview.[564]

3. Article 6(2): presumption of innocence

6.192 Article 6(2) provides that everyone charged with a criminal offence shall be presumed innocent until proven guilty according to law. The presumption requires, inter alia, that when carrying out their duties, a court should not start with the preconceived idea that the accused has committed the offence charged; the burden of proof is on the prosecution, and any doubt should be resolved in favour of the accused. For the presumption to be meaningful the prosecution will need to produce evidence of guilt in the trial[565] and the defendant has a right to be heard in his or her own defence.[566] He also has a right to be treated in a manner which respects his presumed innocence and which does not cause practical impediments

---

[558] See eg *Fitt v UK* (2000) 30 EHRR 480; *Garcia Alva v Germany* (2001) 37 EHRR 335; *R v H* [2004] UKHL 3, [2004] 2 AC 134; *Secretary of State for the Home Department v MB; Secretary of State for the Home Department v AF* [2007] UKHL 46, [2008] 1 AC 440.

[559] See paras 6.135 and 6.182.

[560] See eg *Edwards v UK* (1992) 15 EHRR 417, paras 51–54.

[561] *Salduz v Turkey* (2009) 49 EHRR 19, para 54.

[562] ibid.

[563] *Cadder v HM Advocate* [2010] UKSC 43, [2010] 1 WLR 2601, para 70 per Lord Rodger.

[564] ibid.

[565] *Barberà v Spain* (1988) 11 EHRR 360.

[566] *Minelli v Switzerland* (1983) 5 EHRR 554.

to his participation in the trial. Thus, confining a defendant to a glass box in the court room for the duration of the trial, which constituted degrading treatment and impaired his communication with counsel and ability to hear proceedings, was found to breach Article 6.[567]

6.193 Article 6(2) governs criminal proceedings 'irrespective of the outcome of the prosecution'—so an acquittal or the lack of any conviction will not remove the state's liability if it violated the presumption of innocence by prejudging the accused's guilt or, for example, by making statements in an acquittal judgment that express an opinion that the accused is guilty.[568]

6.194 The ECtHR has held that the presumption of innocence may be violated where, following an acquittal, a court or other authority expresses an opinion of continuing suspicion which casts doubt on the innocence of the person concerned.[569] Article 6(2) will be engaged in subsequent (and non-criminal) proceedings if there is a sufficient link to the criminal proceedings, sometimes described as being the 'direct sequel' of, or 'consequent and concomitant on', the criminal proceedings, for example proceedings claiming costs of the criminal trial, or for compensation for miscarriages of justice.[570] Civil damages claims based on the same facts as a criminal prosecution generally do not engage Article 6(2), unless statements are made imputing criminal liability to the defendant (which then create the necessary link to the criminal proceedings to engage the presumption of innocence).[571] Nor does the use of acquittal information in Enhanced Criminal Record Certificates violate the presumption of innocence in Article 6.[572]

6.195 There remains a question whether the UK's regime for compensation for miscarriages of justice complies with the presumption of innocence under Article 6(2) since, in order to qualify for compensation, section 133(1ZA) of the Criminal Justice Act 1988 (inserted by way of the Anti-Social Behaviour, Crime and Policing Act 2014) requires an applicant to demonstrate that the new or newly discovered fact which led to their conviction being overturned 'shows beyond reasonable doubt that the person did not commit the offence'. The Supreme Court held by a majority that the provision did not violate Article 6(2);[573] at the time of writing, judgment from the Grand Chamber in *Nealon and Hallam v UK* is awaited.[574]

---

[567] *Belousov v Russia* App No 2653/13 and another, 4 October 2016.

[568] See eg *Kazmierczak v Poland* App No 4317/04, 10 March 2009, para 55; *Cleve v Germany* App No 48144/09, 15 April 2015.

[569] See eg *Sekanina v Austria* (1994) 17 EHRR 221; *Orr v Norway* App No 31283/04, 15 May 2008, *Allen v UK* [GC], App No 25424/09, 12 January 2013.

[570] *Allen v UK* App No 25424/09 [GC], 12 January 2013, paras 92–109.

[571] *Serious Organised Crime Agency v Gale* [2011] UKSC 49, [2011] 1 WLR 2760.

[572] *R (AR) v Chief Constable of Greater Manchester Police* [2016] EWCA Civ 490, [2016] 1 WLR 4125. While *AR* was appealed to the Supreme Court, the appeal was on the basis of art 8 and not art 6 and so the Court of Appeal judgment determines this issue.

[573] *R (Hallam) v Secretary of State for Justice* [2019] UKSC 2, [2020] AC 279.

[574] The previous scheme, prior to the insertion of the requirement that an applicant prove they 'did not commit the offence', would award compensation where the evidence was such that no reasonable conviction could be based on it. That scheme was held to be compatible with art 6(2) in *Allen v UK* App No 25424/09 [GC], 12 January 2013.

(a) Reverse onus provisions

'Reverse onus' provisions that require the defendant to prove certain elements of his **6.196** or her defence do not violate the presumption of innocence per se as long as the overall burden of establishing guilt remains with the prosecution.[575] Equally, the provision does not necessarily prevent presumptions of law or fact in favour of the prosecution and against the defendant. These presumptions must be 'within reasonable limits'.[576]

In *Sheldrake v DPP*, the House of Lords confirmed that reverse onus provisions may on occasion breach Article 6(2).[577] There, the legal burdens imposed on defendants by section 5(2) of the Road Traffic Act 1988 (to prove on the balance of probabilities that, despite being in charge of a vehicle while over the prescribed drink drive limit, there was no likelihood of him driving the vehicle), and section 11(2) of the Terrorism Act 2000 (to prove on the balance of probabilities that an organization had not been proscribed when he joined it and that he had taken no part in its activities since it was proscribed) were said to breach Article 6(2). The House of Lords found that the reverse onus in the Road Traffic Act was compatible with Article 6(2), but the reverse onus in the Terrorism Act 2000 (if interpreted as imposing a legal rather than evidential burden[578]) would breach Article 6(2), holding that the justifiability and fairness of reverse onus provisions should be judged in the particular context of each case. **6.197**

(b) Right to silence

The right to silence and 'adverse inferences' have been considered by the ECtHR **6.198** under Article 6(1) in conjunction with Article 6(2).[579] The Court has held that 'there can be no doubt that the right to remain silent under police questioning and the privilege against self-incrimination are generally recognized international standards which lie at the heart of the notion of a fair procedure under Article 6'.[580] Cases in relation to the right to silence are set out at paragraphs 6.184–6.185.

4. Article 6(3): specific rights in criminal cases

In addition to the safeguards set out in Article 6(1), an individual facing a crimi- **6.199** nal charge benefits from the additional rights set out in Article 6(3). Article 6(3) is described as containing 'an enumeration of specific applications of the general principle stated in paragraph 1 of the Article'.[581] It enshrines five specific safeguards

---

[575] *Lingens v Austria* (1982) 4 EHRR 373.

[576] *Salabiaku v France* (1988) 13 EHRR 379; *R v G* [2008] UKHL 37, [2009] 1 AC 92.

[577] *Sheldrake v DPP* [2004] UKHL 43, [2005] 1 AC 264.

[578] An evidential burden is one which allows the defendant to raise on the evidence an issue in their defence which must then be disproved (to the criminal standard) by the prosecution.

[579] *Murray v UK* (1996) 22 EHRR 29; *Saunders v UK* (1997) 23 EHRR 313 (violation of art 6(1) by the use at the applicant's criminal trial of statements obtained from him by DTI Inspectors in exercise of their statutory powers under the Companies Act 1985 to compel him to answer questions and provide information). For domestic discussion of *Saunders*, see *R v Dimsey* [2001] UKHL 46, [2002] 1 AC 509.

[580] *Murray v UK* (1996) 22 EHRR 29; *Funke v France* [1993] 1 CMLR 897.

[581] *Artico v Italy* (1981) 3 EHRR 1, para 32; *Edwards v UK* (1992) 15 EHRR 417.

which constitute a non-exhaustive list of the minimum rights to be afforded a defendant.

(a) Article 6(3)(a)

6.200   Article 6(3)(a) guarantees the defendant the right 'to be informed promptly, in a language which he understands and in detail, of the nature and cause of the accusation against him'. It relates to the information required to be given to the accused at the time of the charge or the commencement of the proceedings, and requires the prompt, intelligible notification of charges in a language the defendant understands.[582] Vague and informal notification is insufficient.[583] Thus, it goes further than the requirement of notification of reasons for detention under Article 5(2) (see paras 6.65-6.59). The right of an accused person to know the case against them is essential to preparing an informed defence. It also ensures that the offence of which a person is convicted is the one with which he or she was charged.[584] The protection is context-specific, so where, for example, the charge is serious and the person charged has mental health problems or a learning disability giving rise to difficulties understanding the charge, states must do more than simply inform them of the bare charge.[585]

(b) Article 6(3)(b)

6.201   Article 6(3)(b) requires that the accused be given adequate time and facilities to mount a defence. This is linked to Article 6(3)(c) and the right to legal assistance. The principle is relative and will depend on all the circumstances of the case, including the complexity and the stage of the proceedings.[586] A balance has to be achieved between allowing adequate time for preparation and ensuring proceedings are conducted within a reasonable time.[587] However, the courts have held that sufficient time to allow proper preparation is essential.[588] The ECtHR's approach is pragmatic, but the Court has confirmed that Article 6(3)(b) recognizes 'the right of the accused to have at his disposal, for the purpose of exonerating himself or to obtain a reduction in his sentence, all relevant elements that have been or could be collected by the competent authorities'.[589] The requirement for adequate facilities may mean that the conditions of a defendant's detention (and the impact those have on their ability to focus on and prepare their defence) are relevant factors in an analysis of whether Article 6(3)(b) has been satisfied.[590] Complaints have been declared inadmissible because the defect has been cured on appeal, but this does

---

[582] *Brozicek v Italy* (1989) 12 EHRR 371.
[583] *T v Italy* App No 14104/88, 12 October 1992; *Mattoccia v Italy* (2003) 36 EHRR 47.
[584] *Pélissier and Sassi v France* (2000) 30 EHRR 715.
[585] *Vaudelle v France* (2003) 37 EHRR 16.
[586] *Albert and Le Compte v Belgium* (1983) 5 EHRR 533; *Gregačević v Croatia* App No 58331/09, 10 July 2012, para 51.
[587] *OAO Neftanaya Kompaniya Yukos v Russia* App No 14902/04, 20 September 2011, para 540.
[588] *Öcalan v Turkey* (2005) 41 EHRR 45.
[589] *Jespers v Belgium* (1983) 5 EHRR CD 305. See also *Can v Austria* (1985) 8 EHRR 121 and *Hadjinastassiou v Greece* (1992) 16 EHRR 219.
[590] *Razvozzhayev v Russia and Ukraine* App No 75734/12, 19 February 2020, para 252.

not discharge the judge of the duty to confirm that this right is being protected in proceedings. If it is not, the judge must also consider whether the trial can proceed.[591] Any restrictions on the right must be no more than strictly necessary and must be proportionate to identified risks.[592]

(c) Article 6(3)(c)

Article 6(3)(c) provides that everyone charged with a criminal offence has: 6.202

(a) the right to defend themselves;

(b) the right to legal assistance of their choosing; and

(c) the right to free legal assistance if the interests of justice so require and they lack sufficient means.

The provision aims to guarantee the right to an effective defence. Thus, it is not   6.203
necessary to prove that the absence of legal assistance caused actual prejudice in order to establish a violation. These principles apply to the pre-trial stages as well as to the trial itself.[593] In *Imbrioscia v Switzerland*, the ECtHR was asked to consider whether the defendant was entitled to have a lawyer present at pre-trial questioning. It held that Article 6(3) may be relevant to the pre-trial stages if and so far as the fairness of the trial is likely to be seriously prejudiced by an initial failure to comply with its provisions.[594] The ECtHR went further in *Salduz v Turkey*, where the failure to provide legal assistance in the police station was held to fundamentally undermine the fairness of the subsequent proceedings (irrespective of the safeguards provided by those proceedings):

[A]s a rule, access to a lawyer should be provided as from the first interrogation of a suspect by the police, unless it is demonstrated in the light of the particular circumstances of the case that there are compelling reasons to restrict this right. Even where compelling reasons may exceptionally justify denial of access to a lawyer, such restriction ... must not unduly prejudice the rights of the accused under Article 6. The rights of the defence will in principle be irretrievably prejudiced when incriminating statements made during police interrogation without access to a lawyer are used for a conviction.[595]

The provision also gives the right for a detained person charged with a crimi-   6.204
nal offence to communicate with his or her lawyer out of the hearing of other persons.[596] In *S v Switzerland* the ECtHR confirmed that '[f]ree communication between a lawyer and his detained client is a fundamental right which is essential in a democratic society, above all in the most serious of cases'.[597] Consequently, it rejected an argument that intrusive acts such as surveillance of a lawyer, the

---

[591] *UK Campbell and Fell v UK* (1985) 7 EHRR 165.
[592] *Kurup v Denmark* (1986) 8 EHRR CD 93; *Kröcher and Möller v Switzerland* (1984) 6 EHRR 345.
[593] *Imbrioscia v Switzerland* (1993) 17 EHRR 441.
[594] ibid; *Magee v UK* (2001) 31 EHRR 822.
[595] *Salduz v Turkey* (2008) 26 BHRC 223, para 55. cf *Doyle v Ireland* App No 51979/17, 23 May 2019, where a lawyer was provided but excluded from the police interview itself, and no breach of art 6(3)(c) found.
[596] *Beuze v Belgium* [GC] App No 71409/10, 9 November 2018, para 132.
[597] *S v Switzerland* (1991) 14 EHRR 670. See also *Brennan v UK* (2002) 34 EHRR 18.

presence of a police officer at consultation, or the interception of communications were justified on the basis of fears of collusion.

6.205   Article 6(3)(c) also covers the right to free legal assistance on the grounds of (a) insufficient means, and (b) the interests of justice. In *Benham v UK* the ECtHR considered whether the lack of availability of full legal aid for a committal hearing in respect of an individual's failure to pay the poll tax constituted a violation of Article 6. In answering this question, the ECtHR stated that regard must be had to the severity of the penalty at stake and the complexity of the case. In general, the ECtHR held that where 'deprivation of liberty is at stake, the interests of justice in principle call for legal representation'.[598] In that case the ECtHR found a violation of Article 6(1) and (3)(c) of the Convention taken together. Legal aid may also be required 'in the interests of justice' for an appeal against conviction or sentence.[599] This is particularly relevant when an appellant appears for him or herself against leading and junior counsel for the Crown, as occurred in *Granger v UK*. The ECtHR in that case found a violation of Article 6(3)(c), citing the defendant's obvious lack of understanding regarding the intricacies of the law in the face of the professional prosecution.[600] The Court of Appeal has also held that this right extends to committal proceedings for contempt of court as, in the absence of unreasonable behaviour (such as unreasonably failing to cooperate with whatever legal assistance is offered, or refusing it), a litigant in person who is liable to be sent to prison is entitled to legal representation.[601] (As to the conditions which may be imposed on the provision through legal aid of free legal representation, see paras 6.141 and 6.188).

6.206   The right to be provided with legal representation means the right to be provided with genuine and effective representation, not the mere presence of a lawyer.[602] Assigning a legal representative does not in itself ensure the effectiveness of assistance afforded to an accused.[603] Thus, failures on the part of the lawyer can effectively deprive the accused of his right to legal assistance.[604] However, the state cannot be held responsible for every shortcoming of the accused's lawyer.[605] The duty on the court is to 'intervene only if a failure by legal aid counsel to provide effective representation is manifest or sufficiently brought to their attention in some other way'.[606]

6.207   Although the right is formulated as a choice between acting in person or being legally represented, the ECtHR has confirmed that the right to represent oneself in person is not an absolute one.[607] In *Correia de Matos v Portugal*, the Grand Chamber

---

[598] *Benham v UK* (1996) 22 EHRR 293. See also *Perks and others v UK* (2000) 30 EHRR 33.
[599] *Granger v UK* (1990) 12 EHRR 469. See also *Hoang v France* (1993) 16 EHRR 53.
[600] ibid.
[601] *Hammerton v Hammerton* [2007] EWCA Civ 248.
[602] *Artico v Italy* (1980) 3 EHRR 1.
[603] *Imbrioscia v Switzerland* (1994) 17 EHRR 441.
[604] *Czekalla v Portugal* App No 38830/97, 10 October 2002.
[605] *Sannino v Italy* (2009) 48 EHRR 25.
[606] *Kamasinski v Austria* (1991) 13 EHRR 36, para 65.
[607] *Croissant v Germany* (1993) 16 EHRR 135.

found no violation of Article 6(3) where the applicant had a lawyer assigned to him, rather than being permitted to conduct his own defence.[608] The Grand Chamber observed that Article 6(3)(c) guarantees that proceedings against the accused will not take place without adequate representation for the defence, but does not necessarily give the accused the right to decide himself the manner in which his defence is conducted; it is for the courts to decide whether the interests of justice require counsel to be appointed. Further, as a general observation, the Grand Chamber noted that:

> The minimum rights listed in Article 6§3, which exemplify the requirements of a fair trial in respect of typical procedural situations which arise in criminal cases, are not aims in themselves: their intrinsic aim is always to contribute to ensuring the fairness of the criminal proceedings as a whole.[609]

(d) Article 6(3)(d)

Article 6(3)(d) ensures the accused's right 'to examine or have examined witnesses against him and to obtain the attendance and examination of witnesses on his behalf under the same conditions as witnesses against him'. This is in keeping with the 'equality of arms' principle outlined in Article 6(1). Although the article refers to 'witnesses', it has been held to cover physical evidence as well. For example, the ECtHR found that the right had been violated in *Papageorgiou v Greece* where the court in a fraud trial had failed, despite repeated requests, to produce originals of cheques.[610]   6.208

This provision does not guarantee an absolute right to call witnesses or a right to force the domestic courts to hear a particular witness. The requirement imposes an overall requirement of fairness, so an applicant will have to establish that the failure to hear a particular witness prejudiced his or her case.[611] The ECtHR has held that whether to hear from witnesses or not will generally fall within the wide margin of appreciation given to judicial authorities.[612] Limitations on the right protected by Article 6(3)(d) are possible, and the ECtHR has approved them on a variety of grounds, such as permitting vulnerable witnesses to give evidence anonymously, behind screens, or via pre-recorded video interviews.[613] The ECtHR has held that a genuine fear of reprisals may justify reliance on hearsay evidence but this should be counter-balanced with procedures which preserve the rights of the defence and that these procedures may vary from case to case.[614]   6.209

---

[608] *Correia de Matos v Portugal* App No 56402/12, 4 April 2018 [GC].
[609] ibid paras 120–22.
[610] *Papageorgiou v Greece* (2004) 38 EHRR 30.
[611] *X v Switzerland* (1982) 28 DR 127.
[612] ibid.
[613] See eg *SN v Sweden* (2004) 39 EHRR 13; *PS v Germany* (2003) 36 EHRR 61; see also *R v Camberwell Green Youth Court, ex p D* [2005] UKHL 4, [2005] 1 WLR 393. cf *PS v Germany* (2003) 36 EHRR 61.
[614] *Saïdi v France* (1994) 17 EHRR 251; *Van Mechelen and others v Netherlands* (1998) 25 EHRR 647; *R v Davis* [2008] UKHL 36; *Al-Rawi v Security Service* [2011] UKSC 34; *Doorson v Netherlands* (1996) 22 EHRR 330, para 67.

6.210   The House of Lords concluded in *R v Davis* that the domestic law in this area had intruded too far upon the right. They held that, while no single step towards trials with anonymous witnesses was obviously wrong, the cumulative effect of these individual steps had eroded the essence of the right under Article 6(3)(d).[615] The effect of the judgment was to prevent witnesses from giving evidence anonymously if concealing their identity from the defendant and their lawyers hindered cross-examination or other challenges to their credibility. In response, Parliament rushed to legislate to overturn the ruling, and the Criminal Evidence (Witness Anonymity) Act 2008 was passed within days. This abolished the existing common law rules on anonymity of witnesses and replaced them with a framework in which witness anonymity orders could be granted by the court on the application of the prosecutor or defendant. The Act has since been replaced by sections 86 to 97 of the Coroners and Justice Act 2009.[616]

6.211   The ECtHR has held that a conviction cannot be based either solely or to a decisive extent on evidence from anonymous witnesses.[617] In *Al-Khawaja v UK* the ECtHR propounded a rule whereby the introduction in evidence of a hearsay statement which constituted the sole or decisive evidence against the defendant would breach Article 6(3)(d) and the general right to a fair trial under Article 6, unless the defendant (a) had had an opportunity at some stage to cross-examine the maker of the statement, or (b) had induced fear in the witness, that being the cause of them not giving evidence.[618] This rule conflicted with the decision of the Court of Appeal in *R v Horncastle*.[619] The Court of Appeal held that, provided the provisions of the Criminal Justice Act 2003 were observed, there was no breach of Article 6 and in particular Article 6(3)(d), if the conviction was based solely or to a decisive degree on hearsay evidence. In a striking departure from normal practice, the Supreme Court declined to follow the ECtHR on the basis that it was a rare occasion 'where this court has concerns as to whether a decision of the Strasbourg Court sufficiently appreciates or accommodates particular aspects of our domestic process'.[620] Amongst the reasons given for this conclusion, the Court found that in almost all the ECtHR cases in which violations of Article 6(3)(d) had been found it was clear that, if the law of England and Wales had been applied, the relevant evidence would have been declared inadmissible, and the defendant would not have been convicted.

6.212   The Grand Chamber of the ECtHR subsequently revisited the sole or decisive rule following the Supreme Court's decision in *Horncastle*. Whilst not prepared to accept the Supreme Court's criticisms of the rule, the Grand Chamber was prepared to accept that the rule should not be applied inflexibly and that, where a

---

[615] *R v Davis* [2008] UKHL 36, [2008] 1 AC 1128.

[616] See David Ormerod, Andrew Choo, and Rachel Easter, 'The "Witness Anonymity" and "Investigative Anonymity" Provisions' [2010] Criminal Law Review 368. For a discussion of relevant case law, see David Ormerod, 'Evidence: Hearsay Evidence—Anonymous Witness' [2011] 6 Criminal Law Review 475–79.

[617] *Doorson v Netherlands* (1996) 22 EHRR 330; *Kostovski v Netherlands* (1990) 12 EHRR 434.

[618] *Al-Khawaja v UK* (2009) 49 EHRR 1.

[619] *R v Horncastle* [2009] EWCA Crim 964.

[620] *R v Horncastle (Michael Christopher)* [2009] UKSC 14, [2010] 2 AC 373, para 11.

hearsay statement is the sole or decisive evidence against a defendant, admission of this evidence would not automatically result in a breach of Article 6 (eg where the absence of the witness is attributable to fear induced by the defendant). Admission of such evidence must be subject to the most searching scrutiny, but the question was always whether there were sufficient counterbalancing factors to ensure the overall fairness of the trial.[621] In *R v Ibrahim*,[622] the Court of Appeal found the Grand Chamber's approach to be reconcilable, in substance, with that of the Court of Appeal and Supreme Court in *Horncastle*. The development of the law on the 'sole and decisive' rule has been cited as an example of 'constructive dialogue' between the domestic courts and the ECtHR.[623]

(e) Article 6(3)(e)

Article 6(3)(e) guarantees the right to the free assistance of an interpreter if the accused cannot understand or speak the language used in court. A suspect must be informed of this right when charged with a criminal offence,[624] and is entitled to the provision of an interpreter throughout the investigative stage as well as at trial.[625] The ECtHR has held, in *Luedicke and others v Germany*, that the provision absolutely prohibits a defendant being ordered to pay the costs of an interpreter.[626] This applies irrespective of the defendant's personal means. Further, the principle covers 'those documents or statements in the proceedings instituted against him which it is necessary for him to understand in order to have the benefit of a fair trial'.[627] However, in *Kamasinski v Austria* the Court held that this did not necessarily mean that written translations of all documentation had to be provided. Assistance is provided so that the defendant 'should be ... [able] to have knowledge of the case against him and to defend himself, notably by being able to put before the court his version of the events'.[628]

6.213

Once it has been established that interpretation is required, informal and unprofessional assistance is unlikely to be sufficient. In *Cuscani v UK* the ECtHR found a violation of Article 6(3)(e) after a judge had accepted defence counsel's suggestion that they 'make do and mend' in the absence of an interpreter and instead call on the accused's brother to assist when required. The ECtHR held that the trial judge should have guarded the defendant's interests 'with scrupulous care' and satisfied himself that the absence of an official interpreter did not prejudice the defendant's full involvement in his sentencing hearing.[629]

6.214

---

[621] *Al Khawaja and Tahery v UK* (2011) 32 BHRC 1, para 147.
[622] *R v Ibrahim (Dahir)* [2012] EWCA Crim 837, [2012] 4 All ER 225. See also *R v Riat and others* [2012] EWCA Crim 1509, [2013] 1 All ER 349, explaining the guidance in *R v Ibrahim*.
[623] *Pinnock v Manchester City Council* [2011] 2AC 104, para 48 per Lord Neuberger.
[624] *Wang v France* App No 83700/17, 28 April 2022, paras 73–78.
[625] *Baytar v Turkey* App No 45440/04, 14 October 2014, para 50.
[626] *Luedicke and others v Germany* (1979–80) 2 EHRR 149, paras 40, 42, 46.
[627] ibid para 48.
[628] *Kamasinski v Austria* (1991) 13 EHRR 36.
[629] *Cuscani v UK* (2003) 36 EHRR 2.

5. Protocol 7

6.215   Protocol 7 supplements and, in some cases, deals with gaps in Article 6 protection. For example, it supplements the protection afforded to criminal defendants by providing a right of appeal against conviction (Protocol 7, art 2); and it provides procedural protection for aliens whom the state seeks to expel (Protocol 7, art 1).

6.216   The United Kingdom has not yet signed or ratified Protocol 7.

D. ARTICLE 7: NO PUNISHMENT WITHOUT LAWFUL AUTHORITY

6.217   Article 7 guards against the retrospective application of criminal law. It provides 'effective safeguards against arbitrary prosecution, conviction and punishment'[630] and is thus a crucial element of the rule of law, the protection of which is one of the central purposes of the Convention.[631] Article 15 permits no derogation from Article 7 in time of war or other emergency.

6.218   Article 7(1) has two limbs: it forbids finding an individual guilty of a crime which was not a crime at the time it was committed (the prohibition on 'retrospective offences'), and it forbids a heavier penalty being imposed than that which was in effect at the time of the crime (the prohibition on 'heavier penalties').

6.219   The ECtHR has made clear that three interrelated principles underpin Article 7.[632] First, 'only the law can define a crime and prescribe a penalty'. Secondly, an offence must be clearly defined in law, enabling individuals to know what acts and omissions will attract criminal liability. Thirdly, 'the criminal law must not be extensively construed to an accused's detriment, for instance by analogy'.

6.220   What this means is that:[633]

[A]n offence must be clearly defined in the law, be it national or international. This requirement is satisfied where the individual can know from the wording of the relevant provision—and, if need be, with the assistance of the courts' interpretation of it and with informed legal advice—what acts and omissions will make him criminally liable. The Court has thus indicated that when speaking of 'law' Article 7 alludes to the very same concept as that to which the Convention refers elsewhere when using that term, a concept which comprises written as well as unwritten law and implies qualitative requirements, notably those of accessibility and foreseeability.

The Court reiterates that however clearly drafted a legal provision may be, in any system of law, including criminal law, there is an inevitable element of judicial interpretation. There will always be a need for elucidation of doubtful points and for adaptation to changing circumstances. Indeed, in the Convention States, the progressive development of the criminal law through judicial interpretation is a well-entrenched and necessary part of legal tradition. Article 7 of the

---

[630] *Korbely v Hungary* (2010) 50 EHRR 48 [GC], para 69.
[631] See eg *Jorgic v Germany* (2008) 47 EHRR 6.
[632] *Kokkinakis v Greece* (1994) 17 EHRR 397.
[633] *Vasiliauskas v Lithuania* App No 35343/05, 20 October 2015 [GC], paras 154–55 (internal citations removed).

Convention cannot be read as outlawing the gradual clarification of the rules of criminal liability through judicial interpretation from case to case, provided that the resultant development is consistent with the essence of the offence and could reasonably be foreseen.

The requirements of Article 7(1) cover both legislation and the actions of the courts, subject to the narrow exception detailed in Article 7(2).[634] 6.221

1. 'Criminal'

Article 7 is applicable only to criminal proceedings resulting in a conviction and/or the imposition of a criminal penalty. It does not bite if a prosecution is abandoned,[635] or if the proceedings would result in something other than conviction, for example extradition.[636] 6.222

Measures not covered by Article 7, since they do not result in a finding of guilt or the imposition of a criminal penalty, include changes to parole rules[637] and remission procedures,[638] extradition,[639] student disciplinary measures,[640] or proceedings for breaches of military discipline.[641] 6.223

Article 7 is not applicable to civil proceedings. However, as with Articles 5 and 6, 'criminal' is an autonomous concept and proceedings which are classified as civil domestically may nevertheless be considered criminal by Strasbourg.[642] The *Engel* criteria apply to determine whether a charge is criminal for the purposes of Article 7, just as they do for Article 6, namely (a) the classification in domestic law; (b) the nature of the offence; and (c) the degree of severity of the penalty that the person concerned risks incurring. 6.224

2. Article 7(1): retrospective offences

The first sentence of Article 7(1) prohibits convicting or punishing people for behaviour which was not criminal under national or international law at the time it was committed. It guards against both the development of the law to impose criminal liability on acts that were not previously considered criminal and the extension of existing offences to include acts which were not previously covered by the offence.[643] 6.225

---

[634] *Kafkaris v Cyprus* (2009) 49 EHRR 35 [GC], para 139.

[635] *X v UK* 3 Digest 211 (1973).

[636] *X v the Netherlands* (1976) 6 DR 184.

[637] *Hogben v UK* (1986) 46 DR 231.

[638] *Kafkaris v Cyprus* (2009) 49 EHRR 35 [GC].

[639] *X v Netherlands* (1976) 6 DR 184; *Marais v Governor of HMP Brixton* [2001] EWHC 1051 (Admin).

[640] *Monaco v Italy* App No 34376/13, 8 December 2015.

[641] *Çelikates v Turkey* App No 45824/99, 7 November 2000.

[642] 'Autonomous concepts' in the Convention are explained further in Chapter 2, paras 2.14–2.16. In the context of art 7, see eg *Welch v UK* (1995) 20 EHRR 247, para 27; *Uttley v UK* App No 36946/03, 29 November 2005, 7; *Del Río Prada v Spain* (2014) 58 EHRR 37, para 81; *GIEM SRL v Italy* App No 1828/06, 28 June 2018 [GC].

[643] *Kingston v UK* App No 27837/95, 9 April 1997.

6.226   When speaking of 'law', Article 7—as elsewhere in the Convention—is referring to a concept that incorporates qualitative requirements, notably those of accessibility and foreseeability.[644]

6.227   Most complaints made under the first sentence of Article 7(1) concern the uncertainty or lack of precision of laws already in place, rather than entirely new statutes or laws being made which apply retrospectively. The key issue is usually whether the development or application of the existing law in the case was 'reasonably foreseeable'.

6.228   A paradigmatic example was *R v R*, heard before the passing of the Human Rights Act 1998, in which the House of Lords abolished the common law immunity for husbands who raped their wives.[645] In finding that the immunity was anachronistic and offensive, their Lordships held that 'the common law is … capable of evolving in the light of changing social, economic and cultural developments'.[646]

6.229   The House of Lords' decision was upheld when the case reached Strasbourg.[647] The ECtHR held that with the benefit of legal advice, the applicant husband could have foreseen that his actions might attract criminal liability and therefore Article 7 was not violated. The Court of Appeal has subsequently held that, even where the marital rape occurred in 1970, a solicitor would have advised that exceptions to the 'irrevocable consent' rule were being developed and so the development in the law did not offend Article 7.[648]

6.230   The ECtHR will ask whether a judicial development of the law is not only reasonably foreseeable but also 'consistent with the essence of the offence'. Thus in *Khodorkovsky and Lebedev v Russia*, even though the ECtHR found that an interpretation of an offence of tax evasion adopted by the Russian courts was novel, it found no violation of Article 7 as it was a reasonable interpretation of the relevant provisions and consistent with the essence of the offence.[649]

6.231   *Cantoni v France*[650] and *Chauvy v France*[651] have reiterated that the reasonable foreseeability requirement may be satisfied if the individual could have regulated his or her behaviour following appropriate legal advice. The ECtHR considers the legal advice caveat to be particularly relevant to individuals engaged in professional or commercial activities which are risky, such as selling alternative medicines (*Cantoni*) or publishing (*Chauvy*).

6.232   Laws that confer a discretion are not inconsistent with the Convention provided the scope of the discretion and the manner of its exercise are indicated with sufficient clarity. In the case of *O'Carroll v UK* the applicant was convicted of knowingly evading the prohibition on the importation of indecent material, in connection

---

[644] *Cantoni v France* App No 17862/91, 15 November 1996 [GC], para 29; *O'Carroll v UK* (2005) 41 EHRR SE1, 6; *Del Río Prada v Spain* (2014) 58 EHRR 37, para 91.
[645] *R v R* [1991] UKHL 12, [1992] 1 AC 599.
[646] ibid 601.
[647] *SW v UK* (1995) 21 EHRR 363.
[648] *R v C* [2004] EWCA Crim 292, [2004] 1 WLR 2098.
[649] *Khodorkovskiy v Russia* (2014) 59 EHRR 7.
[650] *Cantoni v France* App No 17862/91, 15 November 1996 [GC].
[651] *Chauvy v France* (2005) 41 EHRR 29.

with his receipt of photographs of a young naked child engaging in normal outdoor activity, such as playing on a beach.[652] He unsuccessfully argued that the law was not sufficiently precise for him to know in advance whether his behaviour was criminal. The ECtHR held that the fact that it is for a jury to decide in indecency cases whether the matter in question is indecent does not breach the foreseeability requirement of Article 7, as long as the parameters of the discretion are clearly identifiable.[653]

In a series of cases, the ECtHR considered convictions based on international criminal law. In *Jorgic v Germany* it found that the conviction of a Bosnian Serb for genocide did not infringe Article 7.[654] That is because Article 7 does not prevent the gradual clarification of the criminal law by judicial determination from case to case. In *Kononov v Latvia* the Grand Chamber, disagreeing with the Chamber's judgment, found that (rather than being a development of the law, as in *Jorgic*) the applicant could have reasonably foreseen that acts committed during the Second World War amounted to a war crime under the *jus in bello* applicable at the time.[655] There was therefore no violation of Article 7. The Grand Chamber reached a different conclusion in respect of an applicant convicted for crimes against humanity committed during the Hungarian Revolution of 1956 on the basis that it was not established by the domestic courts that his crimes were part of state policy and therefore one of the constituent elements of the crime was absent.[656]

6.233

English law has long recognized a general prohibition on retrospectivity in the criminal law.[657] In *R v Rimmington* Lord Bingham set out two common law principles on retrospectivity that are 'entirely consistent with article 7(1) of the European Convention':[658]

6.234

[N]o one should be punished under a law unless it is sufficiently clear and certain to enable him to know what conduct is forbidden before he does it; and no one should be punished for any act which was not clearly and ascertainably punishable when the act was done.[659]

It is clear that in the domestic courts, as in Strasbourg, the requirement of legal certainty has been flexibly interpreted. The House of Lords has indicated that, even when dealing with a precisely drafted statute, Article 7 may allow for some interpretative leeway.[660] The Northern Ireland Court of Appeal found that defendants who belonged to the Real IRA belonged to a proscribed organization within the meaning of the Terrorism Act 2000, even though that Act proscribed only the IRA and not the Real IRA, a separate organization. The House of Lords stated that the Court of Appeal had been correct to reject the defendants' Article 7 submission

6.235

---

[652] *O'Carroll v UK* (2005) 41 EHRR SE1.
[653] ibid 5.
[654] *Jorgic v Germany* (2008) 47 EHRR 6.
[655] *Kononov v Latvia* (2010) 29 BHRC 137 [GC].
[656] *Korbely v Hungary* (2009) 25 BHRC 382 [GC].
[657] *R v Misra* [2004] EWCA Crim 2375, [2005] 1 Cr App R 328, paras 29–34.
[658] *R v Rimmington* [2005] UKHL 63, [2006] 1 AC 459, para 33.
[659] ibid para 32.
[660] *R v Z* [2005] UKHL 35, [2005] 2 AC 645.

(that the proscription of the IRA did not make it clear that the Real IRA was also proscribed): 'while acknowledging, on the authority of *Kokkinakis v Greece* that a criminal offence must be clearly defined in law, the court was of opinion that the offence charged against the acquitted person had been clearly defined'.[661]

6.236 Their Lordships reached the same conclusion in *R v Rimmington* in respect of the common law offence of public nuisance.[662] Lord Rodger stated:

> While a lack of coherence in defining the scope of an offence may offend modern eyes, it does not follow that there is any violation of article 7. If the individual elements of the crime are identified clearly enough and the law is applied according to its terms, potential offenders and their advisers know where they stand: they cannot complain because the law could perhaps have been formulated more elegantly.[663]

6.237 The Article 7 compliance of strict liability offences was considered in *R v Muhamad*.[664] The appellant argued that a strict liability offence was inconsistent with the general requirement for sufficiently clear criminal provisions. The Court of Appeal rejected this, holding that only legal uncertainty, rather than factual uncertainty, contravenes Article 7. In *R v Budimir and Rainbird* the Court of Appeal found that Article 7 had not been breached by convictions for an offence which failed to comply with a procedural requirement imposed by EU law and was therefore technically unenforceable against them.[665]

3. Article 7(1): heavier penalties

6.238 Article 7(1) also prohibits the imposition of a heavier penalty than that applicable at the time the offence was committed. Where the law changes between the time of the commission of an offence and final judgment in a defendant's case, the court must apply whichever law is more favourable to the defendant. The latter principle is not stated expressly in Article 7 and was elucidated for the first time by the Grand Chamber in *Scoppola v Italy*.[666] Where later domestic sentencing laws are not expressed to have retrospective effect, this can create difficulties for the application of the principle in domestic law.[667]

6.239 Changes to the manner of enforcement or execution of a sentence, even if they have the effect that a defendant is required to serve more of a sentence of imprisonment than was previously the case, do not violate Article 7. That is because

> in [the ECtHR's] established case-law a distinction is drawn between a measure that constitutes in substance a 'penalty' and a measure that concerns the 'execution' or 'enforcement' of a 'penalty'.[668]

---

[661] ibid para 15 per Lord Bingham; citing with approval *R v Z* [2004] NICA 23, [2005] NI 106, paras 51–52.

[662] *R v Rimmington* [2005] UKHL 63, [2006] 1 AC 459.

[663] ibid para 45.

[664] *R v Muhamad* [2002] EWCA Crim 1856, [2003] QB 1031.

[665] *R v Budimir and Rainbird* [2010] EWCA Crim 1486, [2011] QB 744.

[666] *Scoppola v Italy (No 2)* (2010) 51 EHRR 12, paras 106–09.

[667] See eg *R v Doherty* [2014] EWCA Crim 1197, [2014] 2 CrAppR (S.) 76.

[668] *Kupinskyy v Ukraine* (2023) 76 EHRR 38, para 47.

Reflective of this distinction, in *Morgan v Ministry of Justice*[669] the Supreme Court held that changes introduced by the Counter-Terrorism and Sentencing Act 2021, removing provision for those convicted of terrorism offences to be automatically released on licence at the half-way point of a determinate custodial sentence (and requiring them to remain in prison until two-thirds of their sentence is served, subject then to a direction for release by the Parole Board) did not breach Article 7. That decision was in respect of Northern Ireland, but a similar change had been introduced and challenged in England and Wales, in respect of which the Divisional Court held that: 6.240

> the changes wrought by the 2020 Act were changes in the arrangements for early release; they were not changes to the sentence imposed by the sentencing judge. In the absence of a fundamental change of the sort described in Del Río Prada ... , a redefinition of the penalty itself, the principle is clear; an amendment by the legislature to the arrangements for early release raises no issue under article 7. A change to those arrangements does not amount to the imposition of a heavier penalty than that applicable at the time the offence was committed.[670]

(a) *Penalty*

As with the term 'criminal', 'penalty' has an autonomous meaning and the classification of a measure in domestic law will not be decisive. Relevant factors include:[671]   6.241

(a) whether the measure was imposed following a conviction for a criminal offence (the ECtHR's 'starting point' in art 7 cases);[672]

(b) its classification in domestic law;

(c) its nature and purpose;

(d) the procedures involved in its making;

(e) the procedures involved in its implementation; and

(f) its severity.

In *Adamson v UK* the ECtHR found that the retrospective imposition on the applicant, a man who had been convicted of a sex offence but had served his sentence and been released, of an obligation to register with the police was not a 'penalty' and therefore did not violate Article 7.[673] In *M v Germany* the ECtHR found that a measure which turned a limited period of detention into an unlimited period constituted an additional penalty.[674] In subsequent cases the Court has made clear that the state cannot invoke its positive obligation to prevent Article 2 and 3 treatment in order to justify a retrospective increase in sentence contrary to Article 7.[675]   6.242

---

[669] *Morgan v Ministry of Justice* [2023] UKSC 14, [2023] 2 WLR 905.

[670] *R (Khan) v Secretary of State for Justice* [2020] EWHC 2084 (Admin), [2020] 1 WLR 3932.

[671] *Welch v UK* (1995) 20 EHRR 247, paras 27–28; *Adamson v UK* (1999) 28 EHRR CD209.

[672] *Jamil v France* (1995) 21 EHRR 65.

[673] *Adamson v UK* (1999) 28 EHRR CD209. See also *Gardel v France* App No 16428/05, 17 December 2009.

[674] *M v Germany* (2009) 28 BHRC 521. See also *K v Germany* App No 61827/09, 7 June 2012 and *G v Germany* App No 65210/09, 7 June 2012.

[675] *K v Germany* App No 61827/09, 7 June 2012 and *G v Germany* App No 65210/09, 7 June 2012.

6.243   In *Welch v UK* the applicant was arrested on drug charges in November 1986. In January 1987 a law concerning the seizure of any proceeds gained as a result of the drug trade came into effect. The applicant argued that if this new law were applied to him, it would constitute retrospective criminal legislation in breach of Article 7. The ECtHR ruled that the retrospective application of the confiscation order was a penalty and offended Article 7. It found that Mr Welch faced more 'far-reaching detriment' as a result of the government seizure than he would have at the time he perpetrated the crimes.[676]

6.244   In *Gurguchiani v Spain* the ECtHR held for the first time that deportation may constitute a penalty where it virtually automatically replaced a custodial sentence imposed on the accused.[677] However, the Grand Chamber has held that deportation for the purposes of public protection following a criminal conviction does not generally constitute a penalty where it is imposed primarily as a preventative rather than as a punitive measure.[678] Similarly, in *AT (Pakistan) v Secretary of State for the Home Department* the Court of Appeal held that automatic deportation could not be characterized as a penalty as one reason for such a measure was to prevent a person reoffending in the United Kingdom.[679]

6.245   The domestic courts have tended to adopt a narrow approach to the meaning of 'penalty' for the purposes of Article 7. In *Gough v Chief Constable of Derbyshire*, for example, the Court of Appeal found that orders banning attendance at, and travel to, football matches do not constitute penalties.[680] In *R v Field; R v Young* the Court of Appeal held that an order disqualifying the appellants from working with children was not a penalty, and so could be imposed in respect of offences committed before the implementation of the statutory provisions creating the order.[681] In *Morgan v Ministry of Justice (Northern Ireland)*, the Supreme Court held that changes to release dates for terrorism prisoners which had the effect that they would serve longer in prison did not amount to the imposition of a penalty but were merely a change to the execution or enforcement of a penalty, and therefore not within the protections of Article 7.[682]

(b) *Sentencing*

6.246   As above, following *Scoppola (No 2) v Italy*,[683] where there has been a change in sentencing law between the commission of an offence and the time of sentencing, Article 7 will generally require the more lenient law to be applied to the defendant.

6.247   In *Achour v France*, however, the Grand Chamber held as a broader point that the rule against the imposition of heavier penalties will not be violated by a new

---

[676] *Welch v UK* (1995) 20 EHRR 247, para 34.
[677] *Gurguchiani v Spain* App No 16012/06, 15 December 2009.
[678] *Üner v the Netherlands* App No 46410/99, 18 October 2006 [GC], para 56.
[679] *AT (Pakistan) v Secretary of State for the Home Department* [2010] EWCA Civ 567, [2010] NLJR 806.
[680] *Gough v Chief Constable of Derbyshire* [2002] EWCA Civ 351, [2002] QB 1213.
[681] *R v Field* [2002] EWCA Crim 2913, [2003] 1 WLR 882.
[682] *Morgan v Ministry of Justice (Northern Ireland)* [2023] UKSC 14, [2023] 2 WLR 905.
[683] *Scoppola v Italy* (2010) 51 EHRR 12 [GC].

statutory provision increasing an applicable penalty if the development is broadly foreseeable given previous criminal justice policies.[684] The applicant had a prior conviction for drug offences, following which new sentencing provisions for recidivists were introduced. He went on to be convicted for a later drug offence and the recidivism rules were applied to him, increasing the sentence imposed. As the French courts had taken 'a clear and consistent position since the late nineteenth century' on the application of new recidivism rules, the applicant was 'manifestly capable' of regulating his conduct in light of this case law.[685]

It is clear from *Achour v France* that the practice of taking past events into consideration should be distinguished from the notion of retrospective application of the criminal law. By the application of the new recidivism rules to increase the applicant's sentence, he was not being punished for the earlier offence; rather, the new rules had been applicable when he committed the second offence, and he had been a recidivist in legal terms at that time.[686] The Grand Chamber therefore found there to be no breach of Article 7.

6.248

In the case of *Kafkaris v Cyprus* the Grand Chamber considered Article 7 in relation to a prisoner sentenced to life imprisonment for pre-meditated murder.[687] At the time of his sentence, the provisions of the Cypriot Criminal Code provided for a mandatory full-life sentence but the executive and authorities worked on the assumption that the Prison Regulations, which provided for remission of life sentences, imposed a maximum sentence of 20 years. A change to the Prison Regulations then abolished remission of life sentences and the applicant was expected to serve a full-life term.

6.249

The Grand Chamber found that there was no question of the retrospective imposition of a heavier penalty because the change in the law was not a part of the 'penalty' imposed upon him but rather related solely to the 'execution of the sentence'. Nonetheless, a majority of the Grand Chamber held that there had been a breach of Article 7. Recognizing for the first time a free-standing notion of 'quality of law' in Article 7, akin to the 'prescribed by law' criterion in relation to the qualified rights, the majority concluded that Cypriot law was not sufficiently clear for the applicant to discern the scope of the penalty of life imprisonment and therefore Article 7 had been breached.

6.250

In *Del Rio Prada v Spain*,[688] the Grand Chamber held, by a majority, that a change in the way in which remission was calculated under Spanish law breached Article 7. There had been a prior consistent practice whereby remission accrued through employment was calculated by reference to a statutory 30-year maximum period of detention rather than the notional total period of individual sentences imposed. However, a judicial decision altered this approach so that the applicant would, contrary to her clear expectation based on prior practice, be released a

6.251

---

[684] *Achour v France* (2007) 45 EHRR 2 [GC]
[685] ibid para 52.
[686] ibid.
[687] *Kafkaris v Cyprus* (2008) 49 EHRR 877 [GC].
[688] *Del Rio Prada v Spain* (2014) 58 EHRR 37 [GC].

significant number of years later. The Court found this novel judicial interpretation not to be reasonably foreseeable and to go beyond 'mere prison policy' so as in effect to redefine the penalty imposed.

6.252 In line with the Strasbourg jurisprudence on sentencing, the domestic courts have held that an increase in recommended or prescribed sentences in sentencing guidelines is not inconsistent with Article 7, provided the sentence does not exceed the maximum applicable at the time of commission of the offence.[689]

6.253 In *R v Offen* the Court of Appeal rejected the argument that the imposition of an automatic life sentence after the commission of a second serious offence constituted a heavier penalty for the first offence.[690] This approach is consistent with the Grand Chamber's decision in *Achour v France*.[691]

6.254 A number of domestic cases were brought concerning the application of Article 7 to 'extended' sentences.[692] These sentences comprise both a custodial and a licence period (in the latter of which the individual is released from prison but subject to supervision by the probation service, with various conditions breach of which results in recall to prison). Extended sentences may be imposed upon individuals convicted of certain serious offences where the criminal court assesses them to be dangerous. In *R v Uttley* the House of Lords held that the imposition of the licence period for sentences prior to coming into effect of the relevant statute (where, before, release would have been absolute rather than on licence) did not breach Article 7 because the length of the imprisonment and licence periods combined did not exceed the maximum sentence that could have been applied under the prior regime.[693] The defendant in *Uttley* had his complaint against the UK declared inadmissible by the ECtHR, on the basis that the licence period permitted early release from the custodial part of the sentence, and so could not be considered a penalty for the purposes of Article 7.[694]

6.255 A violation of Article 7 was found in the case of *Togher v Revenue and Customs Prosecution Office*.[695] In that case, the Court of Appeal held that the enforcement of a confiscation order made against an individual under the Drug Trafficking Act 1994 would offend the prohibition on retrospective heavier penalties as the confiscation order would have been discharged under the statutory provisions in force at the time of the offence. Despite the breach, the Court did not in fact discharge the order since the amendment to the law was in primary legislation and, by virtue of section 6(2)(b) of the Human Rights Act 1998, it was not unlawful for the magistrates to give effect to the order.

---

[689] *R v A (Barrie Owen)* [2001] EWCA Crim 296, [2001] 2 CrAppR 18: *R v Bao* [2007] EWCA Crim 2871, [2008] 2 CrAppR (S.) 10.

[690] *R v Offen* [2001] 1 WLR 253, [2001] 2 All ER 154.

[691] *Achour v France* (2007) 45 EHRR 2 [GC].

[692] *R v Griffiths (James Worton)* [2003] EWCA Crim 111: *R v BR* [2003] EWCA Crim 2199, [2004] 1 WLR 490; *R (Uttley) v Secretary of State for the Home Department* [2004] UKHL 38, [2004] 1 WLR 2278.

[693] *R (Uttley) v Secretary of State for the Home Department* [2004] UKHL 38, [2004] 1 WLR 2278, paras 18–23.

[694] *Uttley v UK* App No 36946/03, 29 November 2005.

[695] *Togher v Revenue and Customs Prosecution Office* [2007] EWCA Civ 686, [2008] QB 476.

4. Article 7(2): general principles of law of civilized nations

Article 7(2) sets out a narrow exception to the general principles embodied in **6.256** Article 7(1). It permits retrospectivity in relation to behaviour which was 'criminal according to the general principles of law recognized by civilized nations'. The original purpose behind it was to ensure that the rule against retrospectivity did not affect the laws passed in the aftermath of the Second World War in order to punish war crimes, treason, and collaboration.[696]

As Article 7(1) already provides that it will not be violated if the conduct in **6.257** question was illegal under international law at the time of commission, Article 7(2) is rarely relied upon in ECtHR decisions. The Court has repeatedly held that where it makes a finding under Article 7(1) it will not consider Article 7(2).[697] Indeed, the Court's Guide to Article 7 makes the following observation in respect of Article 7(2):

It transpires from the travaux préparatoires to the Convention that Article 7 § 1 can be considered to contain the general rule of non-retroactivity and that Article 7 § 2 is only a contextual clarification of the liability limb of that rule, included so as to ensure that there was no doubt about the validity of prosecutions after the Second World War in respect of the crimes committed during that war (Kononov v. Latvia [GC], § 186; Maktouf and Damjanović v. Bosnia and Herzegovina [GC], § 72). This makes it clear that the authors of the Convention did not intend to allow for a general exception to the non-retroactivity rule.

Case law shows that the Court will rarely accede to arguments based on Article **6.258** 7(2). For example, in *Maktouf and Damjanovic v Bosnia and Herzegovina*, the Grand Chamber rejected an argument that if an act was criminal under 'the general principles of law recognised by civilised nations' within the meaning of Article 7(2) at the time when it was committed, then the rule of non-retroactivity of crimes and punishments did not apply.[698] Domestic courts, however, have relied not only on the ECtHR's flexibility principle under Article 7(1) but also on the Article 7(2) exception. In the marital rape cases, for example, the courts have noted that Article 7(2) provides ample justification for a man's trial for the rape of his wife, according to the general principles recognized by civilized nations.[699]

E. ARTICLE 8: RIGHT TO RESPECT FOR PRIVATE AND FAMILY LIFE

The overarching concern of Article 8 is to protect 'rights of central importance to the **6.259** individual's identity, self-determination, physical and moral integrity, maintenance of relationships with others and a settled and secure place in the community'.[700]

---

[696] *Papon v France* (2004) 39 EHRR 10.
[697] See eg *Streletz, Kessler and Krenz v Germany* (2001) 33 EHRR 751, para 108.
[698] *Maktouf v Bosnia and Herzegovina* (2014) 58 EHRR 11 [GC], para 72.
[699] See eg *R v C* [2004] EWCA Crim 292, [2004] 1 WLR 2098.
[700] *Connors v UK* (2005) 40 EHRR 9, para 82.

These rights apply to 'everyone', which includes legal persons in some circumstances.[701]

6.260 Article 8 formally comprises four elements—private life; family life; home; and correspondence—but it is a sprawling provision that encompasses a growing number of diverse elements, including the right to privacy. In some cases an interference will affect more than one of the elements of Article 8, and in rare cases all four elements will be violated.[702] Given its scope, Article 8 rights are often closely connected to other rights protected under various other Convention articles, in particular Articles 9, 10, 11, and Article 1 of Protocol 1.

6.261 Article 8 has provided extremely fertile ground for domestic litigation. It has been raised in a vast number of contexts and has proved influential in many areas. This is in part because of the absence of any established freestanding right to privacy in UK law prior to the Human Rights Act 1998.[703]

6.262 Like the ECtHR, the domestic courts' threshold for engaging Article 8(1) is generally low, as Lord Bingham acknowledged in *London Borough of Harrow v Qazi*.[704] However, there have been a number of cases in which domestic courts and Strasbourg have markedly diverged, particularly in the areas of surveillance, data gathering, and retention.

1. Procedural and positive obligations

6.263 The notion of 'respect' under Article 8 encompasses both a positive and a negative aspect. As the ECtHR explained in early cases:

> [It] does not merely compel the state to abstain from interference: in addition to this, there may be positive obligations inherent in an effective respect for private and family life even in the sphere of the relations of individuals between themselves.[705]

This dual aspect has given the article much of its breadth in both European and domestic law. Since the early decisions under Article 8, which recognized positive obligations only where there was a serious impact on core rights, the positive aspect of Article 8 now accounts for a very significant part of the ECtHR's jurisprudence.

6.264 The principles applicable to the positive and negative obligations are similar.[706] In both cases, regard must be had to the fair balance that has to be struck between the

---

[701] *Wieser and Bicos Beteiligungen v Austria* (2008) 46 EHRR 54.

[702] See eg *Ayder and others v Turkey* App No 23656/94, 8 January 2004, para 119; *Selçuk and Asker v Turkey* (1998) 26 EHRR 477, para 86; *Mentes and others v Turkey* App No 23186/94, 24 July 1998 [GC], para 73.

[703] See *Wainwright v Home Office* [2003] UKHL 53, [2004] 2 AC 406; *Wainwright v UK* (2006) 42 EHRR 41. See also *Malone v Commissioner of Police* [1979] Ch 344; *Kaye v Robertson* [1991] FSR 62.

[704] *London Borough of Harrow v Qazi* [2003] UKHL 43, [2004] 1 AC 983, paras 8–10. See also *R (Wood) v Commissioner of Police of the Metropolis* [2009] EWCA Civ 414, para 28; *AG (Eritrea) v Secretary of State for the Home Department* [2007] EWCA Civ 801, para 28.

[705] *Marckx v Belgium* (1979) 2 EHRR 330, para 31; *Airey v Ireland* (1979) 2 EHRR 305, para 32; *Secretary of State for Work and Pensions v M* [2006] UKHL 11, [2006] 2 AC 91, para 62; *Söderman v Sweden* [GC] App No 5786/08, 12 November 2013, para 78; *López Ribalda v Spain* (2020) 71 EHRR 7, para 110.

[706] See eg *Evans v UK* (2008) 46 EHRR 34, para 75; *López Ribalda v Spain* (2020) 71 EHRR 7, para 111.

competing interests of the individual and of the community as a whole.[707] As the ECtHR has held, the concept of 'respect' is 'not precisely defined' and therefore the state enjoys a certain margin of appreciation in how it discharges its positive or negative obligations.[708] Although it can sometimes be difficult to assess whether a particular obligation is positive or negative, the domestic courts have consistently suggested that this is unlikely to be decisive of whether Article 8 has been breached.[709]

Some positive obligations are procedural in character—though not all procedural obligations are easy to classify as positive or negative (and, again, ultimately the distinction is likely to be of little importance). The general requirement is that a decision-making process which engages Article 8 rights must be 'fair' and that 'having regard to the particular circumstances of the case and notably the nature of the decisions to be taken, an individual [must be] involved in the decision-making process, seen as a whole, to a degree sufficient to provide her or him with the requisite protection of their interests'.[710]

The ECtHR has applied these principles in a wide variety of contexts, including (eg) decisions taken by public authorities in relation to fostering and access arrangements and taking children into care;[711] applications for family reunion with relatives abroad (emphasizing in this context the need for flexibility, speed, and efficiency);[712] and claims by asylum-seekers to be minors (drawing on relevant regional and international instruments to derive specific requirements for the appointment of a legal guardian/representative and informed participation in an age assessment procedure).[713]

Article 8 procedural rights have also been consistently recognized by the domestic courts. In the context of court or tribunal proceedings, they have been held to cover much the same ground as the guarantees of Article 6's civil limb[714] and to require in essence that the right of appeal or review be 'effective.'[715] Their application in other contexts is necessarily more varied. For example, the House of Lords has held that barring individuals suspected of misconduct from work without the right to make

6.265

6.266

6.267

---

[707] See eg *Von Hannover v Germany* (2006) 43 EHRR 7, para 57; *Botta v Italy* (1998) 4 BHRC 81, para 33; *Keegan v Ireland* (1994) 18 EHRR 342, para 49; *López Ribalda v Spain* (2020) 71 EHRR 7, para 111.

[708] *Ucar v Turkey* App No 52392/99, 14 April 2006, para 135.

[709] See eg *Ali v SSHD* [2016] UKSC 60, [2016] WLR 4799, para 32; *R (T) v Chief Constable of Greater Manchester Police* [2014] UKSC 35, [2015] AC 49, paras 26–27, 125–27; *R (Agyarko) v Secretary of State for the Home Department* [2017] UKSC 11, [2017] 1 WLR 823, para 41.

[710] See eg *Tysiac v Poland* (2007) 45 EHRR 42, para 113; see also *Turek v Slovakia* (2006) 44 EHRR 43, para 111. For endorsement and discussion in the domestic context see *Re W (a child)* [2016] EWCA Civ 1140, [2017] 1 WLR 2415, paras 69, 72–74, 88, and 94–98.

[711] *W v UK* (1987) 10 EHRR 29; *R v UK* (1988) 10 EHRR 74; *T and KM v UK* (2002) 34 EHRR 2.

[712] See eg *MA v Denmark* App No 6697/18, 9 July 2021 [GC], paras 138–39.

[713] *Darboe and Camara v Italy* App No 5797/17, 21 July 2022.

[714] *R (Gudanaviciene) v Director of Legal Aid Casework* [2014] EWCA Civ 1622, [2015] 1 WLR 2247, para 70.

[715] *R (Kiarie and Byndloss) v Secretary of State for the Home Department* [2017] UKSC 42, [2017] 1 WLR 2380; see also *Ahsan v Secretary of State for the Home Department* [2017] EWCA Civ 2009, [2018] HRLR 5.

representations violates Article 8.[716] Including damaging allegations or information in an Enhanced Criminal Record Certificate without consulting the person concerned may do the same.[717] The Court of Appeal has held that making highly critical findings against witnesses without the relevant matters being put to them also breaches Article 8's procedural guarantees.[718] It is now well established that where a child's Article 8 rights are engaged, they must be involved in the decision-making process (seen as a whole) to a sufficient degree to protect their best interests.[719] The Northern Ireland Court of Appeal has gone further and held that breach of a statutory duty to have regard to formal guidance on taking account of the best interests of children 'engages and contravenes the procedural dimension of Article 8'.[720]

6.268   Article 8 may also impose substantive positive obligations on the state in accordance with the general principles at paras 2.33-2.39 and 4.106-4.109. These 'may involve the adoption of measures designed to secure respect for [Article 8 rights] ... including both the provision of a regulatory framework and enforcement machinery protecting individuals' rights and the implementation, where appropriate, of specific measures'.[721] Relevant factors in assessing the nature and scope of positive obligations include: (a) the importance of the interest at stake (including whether 'fundamental values' or 'essential aspects' of art 8 are in issue); and (b) the impact of the alleged obligation on the state concerned (having regard to whether it is narrow and precise or broad and indeterminate and the extent of any burden it would impose on the state).[722] At least in cases involving acts of violence by private individuals which interfere with physical and psychological integrity as protected by Article 8, the state has a duty to take reasonable steps to prevent or stop breaches of which it is or ought to be aware (see further paras 6.275-6.276).[723]

6.269   To take just a few of many possible examples:

(a) The ECtHR has accepted that in some circumstances it may be necessary to provide social housing in order to fulfil Article 8 obligations.[724]

---

[716] *R (Wright) v Secretary of State for Health and another* [2009] UKHL 3, [2009] 2 WLR 267; see also *R (Royal College of Nursing and others) v Secretary of State for the Home Department* [2010] EWHC 2761 (Admin).

[717] See *R (L) v Commissioner of Police for the Metropolis* [2009] UKSC 3, [2010] 1 AC 410; *R (AR) v Chief Constable of Greater Manchester Police* [2016] EWCA Civ 490, [2016] 1 WLR 4125.

[718] *Re W (a child)* [2016] EWCA Civ 1140, [2017] 1 WLR 2415.

[719] *In the matter of D (a child)* [2016] EWCA Civ 12, [2016] 1 WLR 2469, para 48 (and the sources there cited).

[720] *JG v Upper Tribunal* [2019] NICA 27, para 36.

[721] *Tysiac v Poland* (2007) 45 EHRR 42, para 110; see also *Hämäläinen v Finland* (2014) 37 BHRC 55, para 66.

[722] *Hämäläinen v Finland* (2014) 37 BHRC 55, para 66. The approach in this case was applied by the Supreme Court in *R (Elan-Cane) v Secretary of State for the Home Department* [2021] UKSC 56, [2022] 2 WLR 133.

[723] See eg *Eremia v Moldova* (2014) 58 EHRR 2; and in the context of environmental issues *Tolic v Croatia* (2019) 69 EHRR SE7, para 95.

[724] *Marzari v Italy* (1999) 28 EHRR CD 175; *O'Rourke v UK* App No 39022/97, 26 June 2001; cf *Chapman v UK* (2001) 10 BHRC 48. In *Anufrijeva v Southwark LBC* [2003] EWCA Civ 1406, [2004] QB 1124 the Court of Appeal held that art 8 was capable of imposing a positive obligation on the state to

(b) The Grand Chamber has held that, where the state imposes public care which restricts the enjoyment of family life between parents and children, it has a positive obligation to 'take measures to facilitate family reunion as soon as reasonably feasible'.[725]

(c) The Grand Chamber has held that, in certain circumstances, Article 8 requires the adoption (and implementation in practice[726]) of a legislative framework in a particular area[727]—for example, suitable laws criminalizing child pornography[728] or a legal framework for protecting children against violence or abuse in educational institutions.[729]

(d) The Grand Chamber has held that Article 8 requires states to ensure 'recognition and protection for same-sex couples' in their domestic law.[730]

(e) The Grand Chamber has recognized that in certain circumstances states will have a positive obligation to grant entry clearance for the purposes of family reunification[731] (see para 6.349).

(f) The ECtHR has recognized a positive obligation on states to legally recognize the gender reassignment of transgender persons.[732]

The imposition and scope of positive obligations is not, of course, unbounded. As noted above, the impact on the state of their implementation is an important factor in determining whether they are owed at all. In addition, certain factors bear on the breadth of the margin of appreciation which states enjoy in implementing a positive obligation, such as (a) (again) the importance of the interests at stake; (b) the existence or otherwise of a European consensus on either the importance of the interests or the best means of protecting them; and (c) whether there are competing public interests and/or Convention rights in play.[733] Controversially, the ECtHR has at times refrained from recognizing obligations in relation to provisions for disabled

6.270

---

provide an individual with welfare support in order to ensure respect for his or her private and family life, although it was unlikely to do so when his or her predicament was not sufficiently severe to engage art 3; see likewise *R (C and others) v London Borough of Southwark* [2016] EWCA Civ 707, [2016] HLR 36, para 32.

[725] *Strand Lobben v Norway* (2020) 70 EHRR 14, para 205.

[726] *Tănase v Romania* App No 41720/13, 25 June 2019 [GC], para 127.

[727] *López Ribalda v Spain* (2020) 71 EHRR 7, para 113. This was not considered to extend to the adoption of legislation governing the use of video surveillance in the workplace.

[728] *Söderman v Sweden* App No 5786/08, 12 July 2013, GC. The ECtHR has explained that 'where acts that constitute serious offences are directed against a person's physical or moral integrity, only efficient criminal-law mechanisms can ensure adequate protection and serve as a deterrent factor': *Beizaras and Levickas v Lithuania* App No 41288/15, 14 January 2020, para 111 (a case concerning art 8 taken with art 14). See likewise *Tănase v Romania* App No 41720/13, 25 June 2019 [GC], para 127.

[729] See eg *FO v Croatia* App No 29555/13, 22 April 2021, para 91 (though the case turned not on the framework itself but on the diligence with which the authorities acted in the particular case).

[730] See the cases discussed in *Fedotova v Russia* (2022) 74 EHRR 28, paras 161–64, and the affirmation at para 178.

[731] *MA v Denmark* App No 6697/18, 9 July 2021 [GC].

[732] See *AP and Bicot v France* App Nos 79885/12 and others, 6 April 2017, paras 97–99; and see the following passages for a discussion of the margin of appreciation regarding the conditions for such recognition.

[733] ibid para 67.

people. In *Botta v Italy*, for example, it was held that respect for private life did not extend to giving a disabled person a right of access to the beach.[734] The ECtHR and the domestic courts have repeatedly held that Article 8 does not guarantee a right to medical treatment or a particular level of social care.[735] It is notable, too, that both Strasbourg and the domestic courts often take a 'light touch' approach to justification in cases raising positive obligations, emphasizing the resource implications of imposing them.[736]

6.271   Examples of substantive positive obligations under Article 8 are less abundant in the domestic context; a notable one is the obligation on courts or tribunals to make orders for anonymity or other restrictions on open justice where Article 8, balanced against relevant rights under Articles 6 and 10, is found to require this.[737]

2. Private life

6.272   The ECtHR takes an expansive approach to the notion of 'private life'. The Grand Chamber has repeatedly stated that this 'broad term' is not susceptible to exhaustive definition.[738] This has proven to be a malleable concept which the courts have adapted to the times, including the evolution of societal norms and technology. While Article 8 protects the right to live 'privately', away from unwanted intrusion by the state or other individuals, under the Convention the notion of private life extends far beyond what happens in the home and other private spaces, and beyond what happens within the circle in which an individual lives their personal life.[739] There are many circumstances in which the right to private life is engaged in respect of activities or relationships which take place in public places—some of these are discussed below.

6.273   What follows is an overview of the main facets of private life that have been recognized by the ECtHR and the domestic courts; these are not mutually exclusive, and many cases will concern several aspects of the right to a private life.

---

[734] *Botta v Italy* (1998) 26 EHRR 241; *R (D) v Haringey LBC* [2005] EWHC 2235 (Admin).

[735] *Sentges v Netherlands* App No 27677/02, 8 July 2003; *Pentiacova v Moldova* (2005) 40 EHRR SE23; *R (T and others) v London Borough of Haringey* [2005] EWHC 2235 (Admin); *R (AC) v Berkshire West Primary Care Trust* [2011] EWCA Civ 247; *R (Condliff) v North Staffordshire PCT* [2011] EWHC 872 (Admin); *R (Macdonald) v Royal Borough of Kensington and Chelsea* [2010] EWCA Civ 1109.

[736] See eg *Abdulaziz, Cabales and Balkandali v UK* (1985) 7 EHRR 471, para 67; *Pentiacova v Moldova* App No 14462/03, 4 January 2005; *Hudorovič v Slovenia* App Nos 24816/14 and another, 10 March 2020, paras 143–44 (concerning the extent of the obligation to provide access to utilities and noting that 'the level of realization of access to water and sanitation will largely depend on a complex and country-specific assessment of various needs and priorities for which funds should be provided'). In the domestic context see eg *R (W) v Lambeth LBC* [2002] EWCA Civ 613, [2002] 2 FLR 327; *Ekinci v London Borough of Hackney* [2001] EWCA Civ 776, [2002] HLR 2; *R (McDonald) v Royal Kensington and Chelsea Royal LBC* [2011] UKSC 33, [2011] 4 All ER 881 (upheld by the ECtHR in *McDonald v UK* App No 4241/12, 20 May 2014); *R (Elan-Cane) v Secretary of State for the Home Department* [2021] UKSC 56, [2022] 2 WLR 133, considering this and other factors to conclude that art 8 did not require the Secretary of State to issue an 'X'-designated passport for non-binary individuals.

[737] See eg *In re Guardian News and Media* [2010] UKSC 1, [2010] 2 AC 697, para 29.

[738] See eg *López Ribalda v Spain* (2020) 71 EHRR 7 [GC], para 87.

[739] *Bărbulescu v Romania* [2017] IRLR 1032 [GC], paras 70–71; *López Ribalda v Spain*, paras 88–89.

(a) *Physical and psychological integrity*

A person's physical and mental or psychological integrity form part of their pri-   6.274
vate life.[740] Interferences with this aspect of private life arise from the state taking
actions which impinge on a person's body or physical space. A common example is
a search of a person, their clothing, and/or their belongings conducted by a police
officer; there will be an interference with Article 8 regardless of whether any private
items or documents are searched/read.[741] Conducting medical interventions without proper consent will also interfere with this aspect of the right to private life,[742] as
will the imposition of sanctions for failing to undergo medical treatment, including
through a compulsory vaccination programme.[743]

There are also many areas in which states have positive obligations to ensure prac-   6.275
tical and effective protection of a person's physical or psychological integrity. That
includes a duty to take steps to protect individuals from violations of their physical
or psychological integrity by others, including by maintaining and applying an
adequate legal framework (including both criminal and/or civil law), and affording
protection against and remedies for acts of violence by private individuals.[744] So
far as the legal framework is concerned, the question is whether the law affords 'an
acceptable level of protection ... in the circumstances', whereas in the context of
investigations into acts by private parties, the ECtHR will examine whether there
was a 'significant flaw' in the process.[745]

Examples of situations in which the ECtHR has held that states have breached   6.276
these positive obligations include failing to protect women from domestic violence,[746] failing to prosecute or to permit the private prosecution of the perpetrators
of acts of violence,[747] failing to prevent a person from being attacked by a mentally
ill person in circumstances in which the authorities ought to have known there was
a real and imminent risk of violence,[748] failing to provide adequate legal protection
against the covert filming of a child by her father,[749] and failing to take effective
steps to identify and prosecute a person who impersonated a child and placed an
advert soliciting an intimate relationship.[750]

(b) *Identity*

The right to private life incorporates a person's identity, which includes being to   6.277
develop their identity and identify as they choose.[751] Identity is multifaceted but

---

[740] See eg *Bensaid v UK* (2001) 33 EHRR 10, para 47.
[741] *Gillan & Quinton v UK* (2010) 50 EHRR 45, paras 60–63; *Beghal v UK* (2019) 69 EHRR 28, para 76.
[742] *MAK and RK v UK* App Nos 45901/05 and 40146/06, 23 March 2010.
[743] *Vavřička v Czech Republic* (2021) 51 BHRC 241, paras 263–64.
[744] *Söderman v Sweden* App No 5786/08, 12 November 2013, paras 80–85; *Janković v Croatia* (2009)
App No 38478/05, para 45.
[745] *Söderman v Sweden* App No 5786/08, 12 November 2013, paras 90–91.
[746] See eg *A v Croatia* App No 55164/08, 14 October 2010.
[747] *Janković v Croatia* App No 38478/05, 5 March 2009, paras 47–58.
[748] *Milićević v Montenegro* App No 27821/16, 6 November 2018, paras 58–63.
[749] *Söderman v Sweden* App No 5786/08, 12 November 2013, para 117.
[750] *KU v Finland* App No 2872/02, 2 December 2008, para 49.
[751] See eg *Parillo v Italy* (2016) 62 EHRR 8 [GC], paras 153, 159.

includes ethnic, social, sexual, religious, and gender identities, as well as a person's appearance/image.[752]

6.278   An important aspect of this facet of private life is a person's ethnic and/or social identity.[753] The Convention gives individuals a right to identify as they choose and for this to be respected by the state (although that does not prevent a state for requiring objective evidence before giving official effect to a person's claim to a particular ethnic or social identity).[754] That includes a right *not* be treated as a member of a particular ethnic or social group.[755]

6.279   The protection afforded by this dimension of the right to private life extends to collective identity. The ECtHR has recognized that attacks on a group may, when they reach a certain level, be capable of impacting on the group's 'sense of identity and the feelings of self-worth and self-confidence of members of the group' and may, therefore, affect the private life of members of the group.[756] This will depend on, among other things, the nature and context of statements made about a group and the characteristics of the group.[757] Examples of situations in which this aspect of the right to private life has been relied on (usually on the basis that domestic courts have failed to uphold claims/afford remedies) include: comments made in an academic book and a dictionary which debased and insulted Roma people;[758] antisemitic statements and holocaust denial published in two books;[759] and highly inflammatory remarks about Holocaust survivors who were liberated from a concentration camp.[760]

6.280   The ECtHR has long recognized sexual orientation and identity as forming an important part of a person's private life.[761] More recently, the courts have accepted that gender identity forms part of an individual's private life; that is because it is part of an individual's 'sense of self'.[762] Article 8 has been held to protect the right of a trans person to have their new gender respected by the state. This is an area which has also given rise to an increasing amount of litigation around states' positive obligations. More than 20 years ago the Grand Chamber held that the failure to give legal recognition to a trans woman's gender (after she had reassignment surgery) was a breach of the UK's positive obligations in respect of private life.[763] Failing to allow a person to change their gender on identity documents has also been held to

---

[752] *Ciubotaru v Moldova* App No 27138/04, 27 April 2010, para 53 (concerning national law not permitting a person to change their identity).

[753] *S v UK*, para 66; *Aksu v Turkey* (2013) 56 EHRR 4, para 58.

[754] *Ciubotaru v Moldova* App No 27138/04, 27 April 2010, para 57.

[755] *Tasev v North Macedonia* App No 9825/13, 18 May 2019, para 33 (concerning a refusal to change the applicant's ethnicity on the electoral roll).

[756] *Aksu v Turkey* (2013) 56 EHRR 4, para 58.

[757] See a detailed discussion of relevant factors in *Behar v Bulgaria* (2021) 73 EHRR 19, para 67.

[758] *Aksu v Turkey* (2013) 56 EHRR 4. These applications failed on the facts.

[759] *Behar v Bulgaria* (2021) 73 EHRR 19.

[760] *Lewit v Austria* (2020) 71 EHRR 5.

[761] See eg *Beizaras & Levickas v Lithuania* App No 41288/15, 14 January 2020, para 109.

[762] *R (Elan Cane) v Secretary of State for the Home Department* [2021] UKSC 56, [2022] 2 WLR 133, paras 30 and 36.

[763] *Goodwin v UK* (2002) 35 EHRR 18 [GC].

breach these obligations.[764] But the ECtHR has held that a state's positive obligations do not require it to (re)issue a birth certificate removing any reference to a person's gender assigned at birth (in circumstances in which the applicant's birth certificate also showed their chosen gender).[765] While requiring persons to declare (in formal documents) their natal gender rather than their current gender amounts to a significant interference with their right to private life, the Court of Appeal has held that the requirement for a transgender father to be registered as a mother on his child's birth certificate was justified.[766]

6.281 Being non-binary is an aspect of gender identity which is also protected. The parameters of positive obligations in this context are evolving. In *Elan-Cane* the Supreme Court held that the UK's positive obligations under Article 8 did not extend to issuing passports with an X category of gender for people who do not identify as male or female.

6.282 A person's image or appearance is another aspect of their identity.[767] As the Grand Chamber has emphasized, 'a person's image constitutes one of the chief attributes of his or her personality, as it reveals the person's unique characteristics and distinguishes the person from his or her peers'.[768] The right to private life therefore encompasses a right to protection of one's image, which has arisen primarily in the context of the taking and publication of photographs by private parties,[769] but it can also arise in the context of the state's taking and storing photographs (see further paras 6.297 and 6.303).

(c) *Personal autonomy/self-determination*

6.283 The ECtHR has recognized the importance of personal autonomy manifested in the ability to conduct one's life as one chooses,[770] and the Court sometimes refers to the similar concept of self-determination.[771] Like many aspects of the right to private life, the right to autonomy or self-determination arises in many contexts. One area which has given rise to significant case law is the making of decisions about how and when to die. Restrictions on this interfere with Article 8 but the domestic courts and the ECtHR have hitherto held that that blanket bans on assisted suicide were justified.[772] Personal autonomy also extends to making decisions about where and with whom to live.[773]

---

[764] *B v France* (1993) 16 EHRR 1.
[765] *Y v Poland* App No 74131/14, 17 February 2022, paras 74, 80–83.
[766] *R (McConnell) v Registrar General for England and Wales* [2020] EWCA Civ 559, [2021] Fam 77, para 55.
[767] *Couderc & Hachette Filipacchi Associés v France* [2016] EMLR 19 [GC], paras 83, 85.
[768] ibid para 85.
[769] See eg *Couderc & Hachette Filipacchi Associés v France* [2016] EMLR 19 [GC]; *Von Hannover v Germany (No 2)* (2012) 55 EHRR 15 [GC].
[770] *Pretty v UK* (1998) 26 EHRR 241, para 32.
[771] *AM v Finland* App No 53251/13, 23 March 2017, para 76; *Parillo v Italy* (2016) 62 EHRR 8 [GC], paras 153, 159.
[772] *Pretty v UK* (1998) 26 EHRR 241, paras 67, 74–78; *Haas v Switzerland* (2011) 53 EHRR 33, para 51; *Koch v Germany* [2013] 1 FCR 595, paras 46 and 51; and *Gross v Switzerland* (2013) 35 BHRC 187, para 60; *R (Purdy) v DPP* [2009] UKHL 45, [2010] 1 AC 345; *R (Nicklinson and another) v Ministry of Justice* [2014] UKSC 38, [2015] AC 657.
[773] *AM v Finland* App No 53251/13, 23 March 2017, paras 76–77.

6.284   A further aspect of personal autonomy is being able to obtain information from the state about one's own childhood and development as a person (which gives rise to positive obligations)[774] and an associated right to tell one's own story. In *Re Angela Roddy (a child)*, having referred to the importance of discovering one's own past, Munby J stated that 'amongst the rights protected by Article 8 … is the right, as a human being, to share with others—and, if one so chooses, with the world at large—one's own story'; he went on to say the following:

> The personal autonomy protected by Art.8 embraces the right to decide who is to be within the 'inner circle', the right to decide whether that which is private should remain private or whether it should be shared with others. Article 8 thus embraces both the right to maintain one's privacy and, if this is what one prefers, not merely the right to waive that privacy but also the right to share what would otherwise be private with others or, indeed, with the world at large. So the right to communicate one's story to one's fellow beings is protected not merely by Art.10 but also by Art.8.[775]

6.285   Autonomy or self-determination extends to making decisions about what information about a person's life should appear in the public domain. The ECtHR has held that the right to private life encompasses a qualified right 'to be forgotten' where a person wishes to have information about them removed from the internet by a publisher or search engine.[776] This right may carry greater weight when a person seeks to have a publication about them deindexed or dereferenced from a search engine, as distinguished from having it removed from the internet entirely.[777]

(d) *Right to establish and maintain relationships with others*

6.286   The Grand Chamber has observed that the protection afforded by Article 8 is 'intended to ensure the development, without outside interference, of the personality of each individual in his relations with other human beings'.[778] The right to private life therefore includes the right to 'establish and develop relationships with other human beings'.[779] The ECtHR has recognized a right to lead a 'private social life', which includes 'the possibility of establishing and developing relationships with others and the outside world' and the development of a 'social identity'.[780] The case law refers to a 'zone of interaction' with others falling within the scope of this right.[781]

---

[774] *Gaskin v UK* (1990) 12 EHRR 36, para 49; *MG v UK* (2003) 36 EHRR 3, paras 27–32.

[775] *Re Angela Roddy (a child)* [2003] EWHC 2927 (Fam), [2004] EMLR 8, paras 35–36. These observations were cited with approval by the Court of Appeal in *Griffiths v Tickle* [2021] EWCA Civ 1882, [2022] EMLR 11, para 27.

[776] *Hurbain v Belgium* App No 57292/16, 4 July 2023 [GC], paras 187–99; *ML & WW v Germany* App Nos 60798/10 and 65599/10, 28 June 2018; *Biancardi v Italy* App No 77419/16, 25 November 2021. That right is also enshrined in the UK GDPR, art 17.

[777] *Biancardi v Italy* App No 77419/16, 25 November 2021, paras 59–60; *ML & WW v Germany* App Nos 60798/10 and 65599/10, 28 June 2018, para 97. See the applicable criteria at *Hurbain v Belgium* App No 57292/16, 4 July 2023 [GC], paras 205–06.

[778] *Von Hannover v Germany (No 2)* (2012) 55 EHRR 15 [GC], para 95.

[779] *Niemetz v Germany* (1993) 16 EHRR 97, para 29.

[780] *López Ribalda v Spain* (2020) 71 EHRR 7, para 88; *Bărbulescu v Romania* [GC] (2017) 44 BHRC 17 [GC], para 70.

[781] *López Ribalda v Spain* (2020) 71 EHRR 7 [GC], para 88.

Interferences with this right arise in a variety of ways including through measures   6.287
which affect a person's professional life/ability to work (as this is recognized as a context in which people have a significant opportunity to develop relationships with the
outside world),[782] the publication of information which affects the willingness of others
to deal with a person (professionally or otherwise),[783] and restrictions on contact and
the ability to form a relationship with others. In respect of the last of these points, it
is now established that the segregation of prisoners engages their Article 8 rights.[784] In
some circumstances the state's positive obligations may extend to providing support
to disabled people to enable them to establish and maintain relations with others.[785]

(e) *Parenthood*
The ECtHR has consistently held that the right to respect for family life does not   6.288
entail a right to start a family, as the former is concerned with existing family
relations.[786] However, decisions about whether or not to become a parent may fall
within the scope of private life. In *Evans v UK*[787] the Grand Chamber held that a
legal obligation to obtain the male partner's consent to the storage and implanta-
tion of embryos created prior to the breakdown of his relationship with the applicant did not violate the applicant's Article 8 rights.[788] The Court accepted that
'private life' encompassed the right to respect for the decision to become a parent,
but that right had to be balanced with the male partner's right under Article 8 to
choose not to become a parent. The domestic law struck a fair balance between
the two rights.

In contrast to *Evans*, in *Dickson v UK* the ECtHR took the view that there had   6.289
been a violation of Article 8 on account of the refusal to allow a request for artificial
insemination treatment by a prisoner whose wife was at liberty, since a fair balance
had not been struck between the conflicting public and private interests.[789] In *H
v Austria*, the Grand Chamber held that a prohibition on the use of donor eggs or
sperm (rendering IVF available only to couples who could provide both, though *in
vivo* fertilization was not subject to the same restriction) did not violate Article 8
at the point in time the domestic decisions were taken (1999), but noted that this
was an area subject to particularly dynamic development in science and law, and
appeared to signal that it could well reach a different conclusion in the future.[790] In
subsequent decisions the ECtHR has found the 'private life' limb of Article 8 to be

---

[782] See eg *Denisov v Ukraine*, App. No.76639/11, 25 September 2018 [GC], paras 100–01.
[783] *SW v UK* (2021) 73 EHRR 18, para 46.
[784] *R (AB) (a child) v Secretary of State for Justice* [2019] EWCA Civ 9, [2019] 4 WLR 42, paras 158–61;
R (Syed) v Secretary of State for Justice [2019] EWCA Civ 367, paras 58–61; *Musldk v Slovakia (No 2)* (2022)
75 EHRR 13, paras 138–41.
[785] *Jivan v Romania* App No 62250/19, 8 February 2022, paras 31–32, 34–35, 41.
[786] See further paras 6.327 and 6.348–6.349.
[787] *Evans v UK* (2008) 46 EHRR 34.
[788] *Dickson v UK* (2007) 22 BHRC 19 [GC]. cf *L v Human Fertilisation and Embryology Authority* [2008]
EWHC 2149 (Fam), [2008] 2 FLR 1999.
[789] *Dickson v UK* (2007) 24 BHRC 19 [GC].
[790] *H v Austria* (2011) 31 BHRC 443.

engaged by restrictions on the transfer or use of an applicant's embryos.[791] In assessing justification in all these cases, the presence or absence of a consensus among European Member States has been an influential feature.

6.290 The engagement of Article 8 by decisions about the availability of medically assisted parenthood has been echoed in the domestic context: in a notable recent case, the High Court found that a requirement that consent to the use of embryos be given in writing had to be read down where—as in the case before it, where the mother had died but there was ample evidence that she would have consented if fully informed of her options—insistence on it would infringe the father's right to become a parent via surrogacy.[792]

6.291 The general principle in *Evans v UK* has had other important applications. In *P v Poland* the ECtHR held that the private life limb of Article 8 required states to create a procedural framework enabling a pregnant woman effectively to access an abortion where this was permitted by domestic law.[793] In *YP v Russia* it led to a conclusion that sterilization without informed consent engaged (and, absent urgent medical necessity, breached) Article 8.[794]

6.292 The ECtHR has also held that Article 8 protects the right to choose where to give birth. In *Ternovszky v Hungary* the Court found that the liability of midwives to prosecution for assisting at home births violated Article 8.[795]

(f) *Use of private information and personal data by the state*

6.293 The right to a private life covers information about a person's private life. This may be engaged where the state uses private information. On a domestic level, the test for the engagement of Article 8 on this basis is whether a person has a reasonable expectation of privacy[796] (which is synonymous with a legitimate expectation of protection).[797] This is an objective test which must be applied having regard to all the circumstances of the case, including the nature of activity to which it relates[798]

---

[791] *Knecht v Romania* [2013] 1 FLR 726; *Parillo v Italy* (2016) 62 EHRR 8 [GC] (in this case, despite the fact that the applicant wished to donate the embryos to science and therefore there was no direct link with parenthood: ibid para 174).

[792] *Jennings v Human Fertilisation and Embryology Authority* [2022] EWHC 1619 (Fam), [2022] HRLR 14.

[793] *P v Poland* App No 57375/08, 30 October 2012. The domestic courts have also recognized that a decision as to whether or not to have an abortion engages art 8: see eg *Dulgheriu v Ealing London Borough Council* [2019] EWCA Civ 1490, [2020] 1 WLR 609, paras 53–54.

[794] *YP v Russia* (2023) 76 EHRR 27.

[795] *Ternovszky v Hungary* App No 67545/09, 14 December 2010; see also *Dubská and Krejzová* (2015) 61 EHRR 22.

[796] In *R (Catt) v Association of Chief Police Officers* [2015] UKSC 9, [2015] AC 1065 Lord Sumption suggested that in this context 'privacy' means 'the broader right of personal autonomy recognised in the case law of the Strasbourg court' (para 4) but, in practice, this test tends only to be used with reference to informational limb of the right to a private life.

[797] *Re JR 38* [2015] UKSC 42, [2016] AC 1131, paras 87–88, 97, 105, 110–12; *Sutherland v HM Advocate for Scotland* [2020] UKSC 32, [2021] AC 427, para 52.

[798] Notably there will not normally be a reasonable expectation of privacy in information which concerns or reveals the subject's wrongdoing. For example, the courts have held that there is no reasonable expectation of privacy in images of someone engaged in a riot (*JR 38*), racist, sexist, and homophobic WhatsApp messages (*BC v Chief Constable of Police Service of Scotland* [2020] CSIH 61, 2020 SCLR 887),

and where that occurred.[799] Often it is sufficient to focus on whether there is a reasonable expectation of privacy in the information per se but in some cases the assessment must also consider whether there is a reasonable expectation that information will not be used in a particular way and/or by a particular person.[800] There is a minimum threshold of seriousness which must be crossed before Article 8 will be engaged; notably, there is unlikely to be a reasonable expectation of privacy in trivial or anodyne information.[801]

The 'reasonable' or 'legitimate' expectation test also forms a significant part of the ECtHR's assessment of whether Article 8(1) is engaged in cases concerning private information but the ECtHR has said that this will not necessarily be conclusive.[802] In many cases the ECtHR makes no reference to this test and simply considers whether Article 8(1) is engaged with reference to its case law. In practice, however, there are very few cases in which this subtle difference in emphasis between the ECtHR and domestic courts is likely to make any difference.   6.294

There is an important overlap between the protection of private information under Article 8 and the law of data protection, which has its origins in Article 8 and contributes to the protection of private life. The Grand Chamber has stated on several occasions that the 'protection of personal data is of fundamental importance to a person's enjoyment of his or her right to respect for private and family life, as guaranteed by art.8 of the Convention'[803] and it recently re-emphasized that 'the right to protection of personal data is guaranteed by the right to respect for private life under Article 8'.[804] This does not mean, however, that Article 8 will be engaged every time a public authority processes personal data (still less that there will be a breach of art 8 every time such processing does not comply with data protection law).[805] There is a still a need to show that the subject of the information has a reasonable expectation of privacy in the data and its use in a particular manner (see above). All will depend   6.295

---

or in information concerning persons engaging in criminal conduct (*Kinloch v HM Advocate* [2012] UKSC 62, [2013] 2 AC 93).

[799] *Re JR 38* [2015] UKSC 42, [2016] AC 1131, paras 98, 100, 109; *Sutherland v HM Advocate for Scotland* [2020] UKSC 32, [2021] AC 427, paras 46, 50, 55; *ZXC v Blomberg LP* [2022] UKSC 5, [2022] AC 1158, paras 49–50.

[800] *Sutherland v HM Advocate for Scotland* [2020] UKSC 32, [2021] AC 427, paras 58–59 (where the sender of intimate communications to someone they thought was a child may have had a reasonable expectation that the police would not surveil those communications and that the messages would not be made available to the wider public but had no such expectation concerning the recipient providing them to the police); *R (W) v Secretary of State for Health* [2015] EWCA Civ 1034, [2016] 1 WLR 698, paras 35, 39, 44–45 (where patients had a reasonable expectation of privacy that non-clinical information—which revealed they had received medical treatment—would not be shared with third parties generally but no such expectation in respect of the NHS sharing the information with the Home Office for the purposes of exercising a power to prevent people from entering the UK if they had unpaid debts to the NHS).

[801] *Re JR 38* [2015] UKSC 42, [2016] AC 1131, paras 86–87; *ZXC v Blomberg LP* [2022] UKSC 5, [2022] AC 1158, para 55.

[802] *Von Hannover v Germany (No 2)* (2012) 55 EHRR 15 [GC], para 97; *Bărbulescu v Romania* [2017] IRLR 1032 [GC], para 73.

[803] See eg *Satakunnan Markkinapörssi Oy and Satamedia Oy v Finland* (2018) 66 EHRR 8 [GC], para 137.

[804] *LB v Hungary* App No 36345/16, 9 March 2023 [GC], para 103.

[805] *Lloyd v Google LLC* [2021] UKSC 50, [2022] AC 1217, para 130.

on the nature of the personal data and the circumstances of its use (the considerations referred to in the next paragraph are likely to be relevant).[806]

6.296 The storage/retention of information about a person's private life is capable of engaging Article 8, regardless of any further use that may be made of it.[807] As Lord Sumption explained in *R (Catt) v Association of Chief Police Officers*: 'it is clear that the state's systematic collection and storage in retrievable form even of public information about an individual is an interference with private life'.[808] However, not all retention of information about a person will engage their right to private life. In *S v UK* the Grand Chamber explained that 'in determining whether the personal information retained by the authorities involves any ... private-life aspects ... the Court will have due regard to the specific context in which the information at issue has been recorded and retained, the nature of the records, the way in which these records are used and processed and the results that may be obtained'.[809] In *Butt* (a case concerning a government press release identifying the claimant as an extremist speaker), the Court of Appeal considered the Grand Chamber's observations and explained that the storage of information will only amount to an interference with Article 8(1) if the information falls within the notion of a person's private life (in respect of which they have reasonable expectation of privacy) *and* the state has systematically collected and stored it.[810] The Court indicated that storage of information about a person is unlikely to be regarded as systematic unless a public authority has created a record concerning them as an individual.[811]

6.297 Examples of categories of information whose retention has been held to fall into this category include: DNA profiles and fingerprints (of both convicted and unconvicted persons),[812] details of criminal convictions,[813] information concerning offences for which a person has been acquitted,[814] allegations about a person which have not led to criminal proceedings,[815] information about a person's participation in political demonstrations,[816] photographs in police databases,[817] information

---

[806] *Satakunnan Markkinapörssi Oy and Satamedia Oy v Finland* (2018) 66 EHRR 8 [GC], para 137, citing *S v UK* (2009) 48 EHRR 50 [GC].

[807] *Rotaru v Romania* [GC] (2000) 8 BHRC 449, paras 43 and 46.

[808] *R (Catt) v Association of Chief Police Officers* [2015] UKSC 9, [2015] AC 1065, para 6.

[809] *S v UK* (2009) 48 EHRR 50, para 67; see also *R (Catt) v Association of Chief Police Officers* [2015] UKSC 9, [2015] AC 1065, para 6.

[810] *R (Butt) v Secretary of State for the Home Department* [2019] EWCA Civ 256, [2019] 1 WLR 3873, paras 75–76.

[811] ibid paras 78–83.

[812] *S v United Kingdom* (2009) 48 EHRR 50; *Gaughran v UK* App No 45245/15, 13 February 2020.

[813] See eg *R (QSA) v National Police Chiefs Council* [2021] EWHC 272 (Admin), [2021] 1 WLR 2962. Compelling a person to disclose information about historic criminal convictions also interferes with the right to private life (*R (R) v National Council of Police Chiefs* [2020] EWCA Civ 1346, [2021] 1 WLR 262).

[814] *R (YZ) v Chief Constable of South Wales Police* [2021] EWHC 1060 (Admin), [2022] EWCA Civ 683.

[815] See eg *R (II) v Commissioner of Police for the Metropolis* [2020] EWHC 2528 (Admin), which concerned 'soft' intelligence concerning alleged radicalisation of a child; *R (CL) v Chief Constable of Greater Manchester Police* [2018] EWHC 3333 (Admin).

[816] *R (Catt) v Association of Chief Police Officers* [2015] UKSC 9, [2015] AC 1065.

[817] *R (Wood) v Commissioner of Police for the Metropolis* [2009] EWCA Civ 414, [2010] 1 WLR 123; *Gaughran v UK* App No 45245/15, 13 February 2020.

which reveals a person's sexuality,[818] and information revealing that a person is a human rights activist and about their movements.[819]

The disclosure or publication of information concerning a person's private life is also likely to engage Article 8. Examples include: the inclusion in a criminal records certificate of 'soft intelligence' and/or information about a person being acquitted of an offence;[820] the sharing of information about a person's HIV status;[821] the sharing between public authorities of information they have gathered relating to children to whom they provide services;[822] the making public of medical information disclosed in criminal proceedings;[823] the passing on of medical information from a hospital to authorities in the process of verifying a claim for social insurance and disability benefits;[824] the sharing with other agencies of information obtained through covert surveillance in a criminal investigation,[825] the making public of information about taxpayers' income and assets;[826] the publication by tax authorities of information (including names and addresses) about people with significant tax arrears;[827] and the publication by a prosecutor of a victim's home address, occupation, financial matters, and names of their associates.[828] The state's positive obligations extend to taking steps to prevent unauthorized disclosures of information and investigating them where they have occurred.[829]

6.298

(g) Surveillance

Surveillance by the state generally constitutes an interference with the right to private life and, in the case of the interceptions of communications, it is also likely to interfere with the right to respect for correspondence (see paras 6.357-6.364). This includes both overt and covert/secret surveillance measures.

6.299

The rapid evolution of surveillance technologies means that the capacity for states to interfere with the private lives of large numbers of people has increased exponentially. In *Szabo & Vissy v Hungary*, a case concerning covert surveillance, the ECtHR made the following observations about new technologies:

6.300

The techniques applied in … monitoring operations have demonstrated a remarkable progress in recent years and reached a level of sophistication which is hardly conceivable for the average citizen, especially when automated and systemic data collection is technically possible and becomes widespread. In the face of this progress the Court must scrutinise the question as to whether the development of surveillance methods resulting in masses of data collected has been

---

[818] *Drelon v France* App Nos 3153/16 & others, 8 September 2022, para 86 (available in French only).

[819] *Shimovolos v Russia* (2014) 58 EHRR 26.

[820] *R (AR) v Chief Constable of Manchester Police* [2018] UKSC 47, [2018] 1 WLR 4079; *R (L) v Commissioner of Police for the Metropolis* [2009] UKSC 3, [2010] 1 AC 410.

[821] *Z v Finland* (1998) 25 EHRR 371, para 96.

[822] *Christian Institute v Lord Advocate* [2016] UKSC 51, 2017 SC (UKSC) 29, para 78.

[823] *Z v Finland* (1998) 25 EHRR 371.

[824] *MS v Sweden* (1999) 28 EHRR 313.

[825] *Ships Waste Oil Collector v the Netherlands* App No 2799/16, 16 May 2023, paras 40–41, 43.

[826] *Satakunnan Markkinapörssi Oy and Satamedia Oy v Finland* (2018) 66 EHRR 8 [GC].

[827] *LB v Hungary* App No 36345/16, 9 March 2023 [GC].

[828] *Ismayilova v Azerbaijan* App Nos 65286/13 and 57270/14, 10 January 2019.

[829] *Craxi v Italy* (2004) 38 EHRR 47, paras 73–75.

accompanied by a simultaneous development of legal safeguards securing respect for citizens' Convention rights.[830]

6.301 Challenges to surveillance measures have given rise to an extensive body of case law, covering both the collection of information, its retention, and any subsequent use (each of which constitutes a separate interference with the right to private life).[831] Examples of surveillance measures which have been held to constitute an interference with a person's private life include: the targeted interception of a person's communications (which the ECtHR regards as a very serious interference with a person's rights);[832] the GPS tracking of a vehicle;[833] the use of live facial recognition cameras in a public place to scan the facial biometrics of passers-by;[834] requiring communication service providers (CSPs) to retain information about users (in that case, the purchasers of sim cards) which can then be accessed[835] and subsequent secret state access to databases compiled by CSPs;[836] obtaining from a CSP (by way of a judicial order) information about a subscriber including their name and address;[837] obtaining information about phone numbers dialled from a particular phone;[838] accessing communications data held by CSPs (eg information about the source and destination of a communication, its time, and location);[839] installation of a listening device in a home;[840] and the use of computer network exploitation or hacking.[841]

6.302 The Grand Chamber has considered cases concerning the existence and operation of bulk, untargeted surveillance systems.[842] Put simply, these systems involve the interception of the internet-based communications of very large numbers of people (the overwhelming majority of whom are not suspected of wrongdoing or thought to pose any threat to national security), the subsequent application of selectors or key words to identify communications of interest, and the examination by analysts of communications identified through this process.[843]

---

[830] (2016) 63 EHRR 3, para 68; in *Catt v UK* (2019) 69 EHRR 7, the ECtHR held that these considerations apply equally to non-covert collection and retention of data, para 114.

[831] See eg *Catt v UK* (2019) 69 EHRR 7, para 95.

[832] See eg *Kennedy v UK* (2011) 52 EHRR 4; *Dragojević v Croatia* App No 68955/11, 15 January 2015; *Adomaitis v Lithuania* (2022) 75 EHRR 18.

[833] *Ben Faiza v France* App No 31446/12 (2018) (available only in French); *Uzun v Germany* (2011) 53 EHRR 24.

[834] *R (Bridges) v Chief Constable of South Wales Police* [2019] EWHC 2341 (Admin), [2020] 1 WLR 672.

[835] *Breyer v Germany* (2020) 21 EHRR 17.

[836] *Zakharov v Russia* (2016) 63 EHRR 17 [GC].

[837] *Benedik v Slovenia* App No 62357/14, 24 April 2018.

[838] *Malone v UK* (1984) 7 EHRR 14; *Ben Faiza v France* App No 31446/12, 8 February 2018 (available only in French).

[839] *Ekimdzhiev v Bulgaria* (2022) 75 EHRR 8.

[840] *Khan v UK* (2001) 31 EHRR 45; *PG & JH v UK* (2008) 46 EHRR 51.

[841] *Privacy International & others v Secretary of State for Foreign and Commonwealth Affairs & GCHQ* [2016] UKIPTrib 14_85-CH.

[842] For example, *Big Brother Watch & others v UK* (2022) 74 EHRR 17 [GC]; *Centrum för Rättvisa v Sweden* (2021) 52 BHRC 482 [GC].

[843] See the Grand Chamber's summary in *Big Brother Watch & others v UK* (2022) 74 EHRR 17 [GC], paras 325–30.

The Grand Chamber held that surveillance of this kind entails discrete interferences at each stage, which become progressively more significant at each stage.[844] However, the Court rejected the argument that bulk or mass surveillance for the purposes of protecting national security is inherently incompatible with the right to private life;[845] it must however be accompanied by minimum safeguards, which are considered as part of justification under Article 8(2) (see para 6.373–6.374).

Without more, CCTV recording and/or the taking of photographs of a person in a public place is unlikely to engage Article 8.[846] The right to private life is, however, likely to be engaged if public authorities retain imagery from CCTV (see para 6.296–6.297) and/or if the cameras are equipped with or accompanied by technologies which enable the extraction and/or exploitation of biometric information.[847] Collecting information about a person's movements and/or location is an interference with Article 8, even if this is done on the basis of information they have supplied. By way of example, the ECtHR held that the French system for drug testing in sport, which required athletes to provide detailed information about their daily movements and locations for the following three months, gave rise to a significant interference with their private lives.[848]   6.303

In respect of covert surveillance, the ECtHR does not require an applicant to demonstrate that a measure has been applied to them; it is possible to bring challenges (before the ECtHR) on the basis of the mere existence of secret surveillance measures or legislation permitting them, provided that the applicant is a member of a group of persons targeted by the legislation—including on the basis that it affects all users of a communications system.[849]   6.304

The state's positive obligations are also important in this area. The obligation to adopt measures to secure the respect for private life in relations between individuals extends to regulating surveillance by private actors and ensuring that remedies are available for unlawful surveillance.[850] The Grand Chamber has held that this is particularly important in the employment context, in respect of which states 'should ensure that the introduction by an employer of measures to monitor correspondence and other communications, irrespective of the extent and duration of such measures, is accompanied by adequate and sufficient safeguards against abuse'.[851] The Court has enumerated factors which are relevant to assessing whether surveillance   6.305

---

[844] *Big Brother Watch & others v UK* (2022) 74 EHRR 17 [GC], paras 325, 330–31, 346.
[845] ibid paras 346 and 424.
[846] *Peck v UK* (2003) 36 EHRR 41; *R (Wood) v Commissioner of Police for the Metropolis* [2009] EWCA Civ 414, [2010] 1 WLR 123.
[847] *R (Bridges) v Chief Constable of South Wales Police* [2019] EWHC 2341 (Admin), [2020] 1 WLR 672; *López Ribalda v Spain* (2020) 71 EHRR 7 [GC], para 93.
[848] *National Federation of Sportspersons' Associations and Unions v France* App Nos 48151/11 and another, 18 January 2018 [GC], paras 155–59, 169.
[849] *Zakharov v Russia* (2016) 63 EHRR 17 [GC], paras 165–72. See further Chapter 4, paras 4.20–4.22.
[850] *López Ribalda v Spain* (2020) 71 EHRR 7 [GC], paras 110–14.
[851] *Bărbulescu v Romania* [2017] IRLR 1032 [GC], para 120.

(including video surveillance and reading communications) by employers is lawful; there must also be an effective judicial remedy available.[852]

(h) Environmental issues

6.306 The ECtHR has accepted that—although the Convention does not explicitly guarantee the right to a clean and quiet environment—environmental issues, such as the amount of air traffic over an applicant's home[853] or exposure to water contamination[854] or industrial pollution[855]—may interfere with an individual's private life even if the intrusions are 'unavoidable consequences of measures not directed against private individuals'.[856] In *Lopez Ostra v Spain* the ECtHR held that permitting a waste treatment plant to operate in breach of a licence condition may affect the right to enjoyment of people's homes and so affect their right to private and family life even if it did not adversely affect their health.[857] The Court has also consistently held that the failure of the authorities to deal with noise pollution by private individuals may violate Article 8.[858] The interference complained of must attain a minimum level of severity for Article 8 to be engaged.[859] Exposure to an environmental hazard (which may or may not eventuate) can also engage Article 8 where there is a sufficient link to the enjoyment of a person's private life or their home.[860]

6.307 While the state enjoys a margin of appreciation in relation to environmental decisions, the ECtHR will intervene in cases where it finds a 'manifest error of appreciation' in the proportionality assessment[861] and in cases where there has been a clear failure to take reasonable steps to discharge positive obligations.[862] It will also carefully scrutinize the decision-making process undertaken by the state in imposing particular environmental burdens on groups of its citizens.[863] In *Fadeyeva v Russia* the ECtHR held:

---

[852] *Bărbulescu v Romania* [2017] IRLR 1032 [GC], paras 121–22; *López Ribalda v Spain* (2020) 71 EHRR 7 [GC], paras 115–16.

[853] *Rayner v UK* (1986) 47 DR 5; *Hatton v UK* (2002) 34 EHRR 1.

[854] *Tolić v Croatia* (2019) 69 EHRR SE7; *Hudorović v Slovenia* App Nos 24816/14 & another, 10 March 2020.

[855] *Dubetska v Ukraine* (2015) 61 EHRR 11.

[856] *Rayner v UK* (1986) 47 DR 5. See also *Hatton v UK* (2002) 34 EHRR 1. In both cases it was held that the intrusions were justified under art 8(2).

[857] *Lopez Ostra v Spain* (1995) 20 EHRR 27. See also *Taskin v Turkey* (2006) 42 EHRR 50 and *Dubetska v Ukraine* (2015) 61 EHRR 11. Many of these cases are also found to engage the right to respect for one's home, as to which see paras 6.350–6.356 ; see eg the reasoning in *Kapa v Poland* (2022) 74 EHRR 18, paras 148–49.

[858] See eg *DEES v Hungary* App No 2345/06, 9 November 2010.

[859] See eg *Cicek v Turkey* App No 44837/07, 4 February 2020, para 22 (and see paras 23–29 for a series of examples falling on both sides of the line).

[860] See eg *Hardy and Maile v UK* (2012) 55 EHRR 28; *Dzemyuk v Ukraine* App No 42488/02, 4 September 2014, paras 81–84.

[861] See eg *Fadeyeva v Russia* App No 55723/00, 9 June 2005, para 105; *Dubetska v Ukraine* (2015) 61 EHRR 11, para 142.

[862] See eg *Kapa v Poland* (2022) 74 EHRR 18; *Fadayeva v Russia* App No 55723/00, 9 June 2005.

[863] *Hatton v UK* (2002) 34 EHRR 1.

[I]t is certainly within the Court's jurisdiction to assess whether the Government approached the problem with due diligence and gave consideration to all competing interests. In this respect, the Court reiterates that the onus is on the State to justify, using detailed and rigorous data, a situation in which certain individuals bear a heavy burden on behalf of the rest of the community.[864]

6.308
Where the state fails to show how its analysis led to a particular policy decision, the ECtHR will draw an adverse inference that insufficient weight has been given to the interests of communities that are particularly badly affected. In certain circumstances, therefore, failure to conduct an environmental impact assessment (EIA) will violate the right to respect for private life, family life, and home under Article 8.[865] Conversely, where the state can demonstrate it has an appropriate regulatory system in place and has, in a particular case, appropriately weighed the relevant interests, the ECtHR will not find a breach of Article 8.[866] The domestic courts have applied this line of Strasbourg jurisprudence in a number of cases.[867]

(i) Private life and the media

6.309
As explained above, Article 8 places states under a positive obligation to secure respect for private life in the context of relations between private persons. That includes adopting measures to protect individuals from unjustified intrusion into their private lives by the media and ensuring that there are legal remedies available where intrusion has occurred or may occur.[868] In the UK this is done primarily through the law of tort, although some forms of intrusion and publication may engage the criminal law. Of particular relevance are the tort of misuse of private information (which evolved from the equitable action for breach of confidence under the influence of arts 8 and 10, after they were incorporated into British law through the Human Rights Act to the extent that those rights became 'the very content of the domestic tort');[869] the statutory tort under the Protection from Harassment Act 1997; the UK General Data Protection Regulation, and the defamation torts of libel and slander. The courts must, of course, apply these areas of law in a way that is consistent with Article 8 and other Convention rights.

6.310
In the context of media investigations and publications, the right to private life and the right to freedom of expression under Article 10 of the Convention (which states are also under a positive obligation to protect) are often in tension. In *Re S (a child) (identification: restrictions on publication)*, a case concerning the identification of children in legal proceedings, the House of Lords gave guidance on striking the balance between these qualified rights where they are in conflict:

---

[864] *Fadeyeva v Russia* App No 55723/00, 9 June 2005, para 128.

[865] *Piera Giacomelli v Italy* App No 59909/00, 2 November 2006.

[866] See eg *Hardy and Maile v United Kingdom* App No 31965/07, 14 February 2012.

[867] See eg *Dennis v Ministry of Defence* [2003] EWHC 793 (QB), [2003] Env LR 34; *Andrews v Reading Borough Council* [2005] EWHC 256 (QB); *R (Granger-Taylor) v High Speed Two Limited* [2020] EWHC 1442 (Admin). cf *Marcic v Thames Water Utilities* [2003] UKHL 66, [2004] 2 AC 42.

[868] See eg *Von Hannover v Germany (No 2)* (2012) 55 EHRR 15 [GC], para 98.

[869] *McKennitt v Ash* [2006] EWCA Civ 1714, [2008] QB 73, para 11; *Campbell v MGN Ltd* [2004] UKHL 22, [2004] 2 AC 457, paras 17–18, 132–33; *ZXC v Bloomberg LP* [2022] UKSC 5, [2022] AC 1158, paras 43–62.

First, neither article [8 or 10] has *as such* precedence over the other. Secondly, where the values under the two articles are in conflict, an intense focus on the comparative importance of the specific rights being claimed in the individual case is necessary. Thirdly, the justifications for interfering with or restricting each right must be taken into account. Finally, the proportionality test must be applied to each.[870]

6.311   This balancing exercise is carried out in the context of claims in the tort of misuse of private information, as well as, for example, in cases where the courts are considering whether to make orders restricting open justice on Article 8 grounds.

6.312   Applications concerning publications or intrusions by the media generally come before the ECtHR as Article 8 cases, where a person complains that the domestic law/courts have failed properly to protect privacy rights, or as Article 10 cases, where a publisher complains that domestic law/courts have wrongly prohibited or sanctioned publications on the basis of privacy rights. Strictly speaking, therefore, where Article 8 is relied on this concerns a state's positive obligations (unless it is the state that has published or otherwise misused private information). By contrast, Article 10 cases of this kind generally concern a state's negative obligations because a national a court has blocked, restricted, or sanctioned speech. In practice, however, the ECtHR's approach to these applications (and the margin of appreciation afforded to national courts) is substantially the same regardless of whether they are come before the Court as Article 8 or Article 10 cases.[871]

6.313   The ECtHR balances these competing rights with reference to what are commonly known as the 'Axel Springer' criteria.[872] Consideration needs to be given to (a) the contribution of the publication to a debate of general interest; (b) how well known the person who is the subject of the report is (including any role or function in public life); (c) the prior conduct of the person concerned; (d) the method of obtaining the information and the veracity of its content; and (e) the content, form, and consequences of publication. Balancing the rights of private parties falls within the state's margin of appreciation and, provided that the national courts undertake this exercise in accordance with the ECtHR's case law, the ECtHR will be very slow to interfere with their decisions.[873]

(j) Reputation

6.314   It is now well established that the right to a private life includes the right to protection of reputation,[874] which extends to what the ECtHR has called 'social' and 'professional' reputations.[875] This is primarily on the basis that attacks on a

---

[870] [2004] UKHL 47, [2005] 1 AC 593, para 17. See also *A v B* [2002] EWCA Civ 237, [2003] QB 195; *In re BBC* [2009] UKHL 34, [2009] 3 WLR 142.

[871] See the observations of the Grand Chamber in *Couderc & Hachette Filipacchi Associés v France* [2016] EMLR 19, paras 90–91.

[872] These take their name from the Grand Chamber's judgment in *Axel Springer AG v Germany* [2012] EMLR 15, paras 89–94.

[873] *Von Hannover v Germany (No 2)* (2012) 55 EHRR 15, para 107.

[874] See eg *SW v UK* (2021) 73 EHRR 18, para 45.

[875] *Denisov v Ukraine* App No 76639/11, 25 September 2018 [GC], para 112; *Re Guardian News & Media* [2010] UKSC 1, [2010] 2 AC 697, paras 37–42.

person's reputation may impinge on their psychological integrity and/or personal identity (see paras 6.274 and 6.277).[876] In order to engage Article 8 'an attack on a person's reputation must attain a certain level of seriousness and [be made] in a manner causing prejudice to personal enjoyment of the right to respect for private life'.[877] Domestically, it is rare for a reputational claim to be brought against a public authority under Article 8. That is because there are bespoke causes of action (including for defamation, malicious falsehood, and breaches of the UK GDPR) through which reputational rights can be asserted.[878]

(k) Private life in expulsion cases

Article 8 prohibits the expulsion of a person from the jurisdiction where this would violate the right to respect for private life. This can occur in two main ways: by exposing an applicant to breaches of Article 8 in the destination country (a so-called 'foreign case'); or by interfering with their continued enjoyment of private life in the 'host' state (a so-called 'domestic' case). In the former context, expulsion is only prohibited where the resulting breach of Article 8 would be 'flagrant' in character.[879] Most cases involve elements of both, and no flagrancy threshold is applied.[880]   6.315

Unlike in the context of Articles 2 and 3, there is no requirement that a claim that a person's expulsion would breach Article 8 automatically suspend their removal until it has been determined.[881]   6.316

As immigration control will always constitute a legitimate aim under Article 8(2),[882] the focus in expulsion cases is usually on proportionality. The ECtHR has developed specific principles applicable to particular types of case: for example, in *Maslov v Austria* the Court identified the specific criteria to be applied in assessing the proportionality of expelling, on the basis of offending behaviour, a young adult who has not yet founded a family of their own.[883] The Court also held (and the Grand Chamber has subsequently affirmed) that for 'a settled migrant who has   6.317

---

[876] *Pfeifer v Austria* (2009) 48 EHRR 8, para 35; *Denisov v Ukraine* App No 76639/11, 25 September 2018 [GC], para 97.

[877] *Axel Springer AG v Germany* [2012] EMLR 15, para 83; *Delfi AS v Estonia* [2015] EMLR 26 [GC], para 137; *Karakó v Hungary* (2011) 52 EHRR 36, para 23.

[878] See eg *Clift v Slough Borough Council* [2010] EWCA Civ 1171, [2011] 1 WLR 1774; *Butt v Secretary of State for the Home Department* [2019] EWCA Civ 933, [2019] EMLR 23.

[879] See the discussion in *SB (India) v Secretary of State for the Home Department* [2016] EWCA Civ 451, [2016] 1 WLR 103, paras 32–45 (citing key authorities).

[880] See eg ibid para 33.

[881] *De Souza Ribiero v France* (2014) 59 EHRR 10, paras 82–83; and in the domestic context see *R (FB (Afghanistan)) v Secretary of State for the Home Department* [2020] EWCA Civ 1338, [2022] QB 185, para 114.

[882] See eg *MA v Denmark* App No 6697/18, 9 July 2021 [GC], paras 142–43; *LR (Serbia) v Secretary of State for the Home Department* [2007] EWCA Civ 1554, para 8; and the Nationality, Immigration and Asylum Act 2002, s 117B(1). The weight it is afforded in the balancing exercise will, of course, depend on context.

[883] [2009] INLR 47. These are: (a) the nature and seriousness of the offence committed; (b) the length of the applicant's stay; (c) the time elapsed since the offence and the applicant's conduct during that period; and (d) the solidity of the social, cultural, and family ties with the host country and with the destination country. The Grand Chamber affirmed these criteria in *Savran v Denmark* (2021) 53 BHRC 201 and added that the duration of the exclusion order (and any possibility of its being revoked in future) will also be

lawfully spent all or the major part of his or her childhood and youth in the host country, very serious reasons are required to justify expulsion'.[884]

6.318 Ultimately it tends to make little difference whether an expulsion case is considered under the private or family life element of Article 8 (or both): for example, the principles in *Üner v the Netherlands*[885] (discussed in para 6.346), relating to the expulsion of an immigrant who has been convicted of criminal offences but enjoys family life in the 'host state', have been identified as relevant (with appropriate modifications) in private life cases.[886]

6.319 Where the domestic courts have engaged in reasoned consideration of all the factors identified by the ECtHR as relevant in an expulsion case, the ECtHR often defers to their conclusions; it is much more likely to intervene where they have failed to do so.[887]

6.320 In the UK, the operation of Article 8 in the expulsion context has been codified to a significant extent. In particular, where a person is liable to deportation their ability to resist expulsion on Article 8 grounds (whether under the private or family life limb) is governed by primary legislation,[888] which sets out specific criteria for different categories of offenders. These criteria, and their component parts, have generated a significant volume of domestic authority the full scope of which cannot be done justice here.[889] Of particular significance is the courts' affirmation that in interpreting and applying these criteria they must ultimately conduct a fact-sensitive balancing exercise in accordance with ECtHR authority.[890] This was crucial to the ECtHR's conclusion that the version of the regime for the deportation of foreign offenders in force prior to 2020 was compatible with Article 8.[891] For those liable to administrative removal rather than deportation the framework is slightly less prescriptive. Certain aspects of the Article 8 balancing exercise have

---

relevant: paras 183, 199–200. It also noted that these criteria are not exhaustive—eg on the facts of the case before it the applicant's mental health also fell to be taken into account: para 191.

[884] *Savran v Denmark* (2021) 53 BHRC 201, para 186. For discussion in the domestic context see *Sanambar v Secretary of State for the Home Department* [2021] UKSC 30, [2021] 1 WLR 3847. It is notable that the rejection of this as a freestanding requirement of the ECtHR jurisprudence pre-dated the latest restatements of it, including by the Grand Chamber.

[885] (2007) 45 EHRR 14.

[886] *Savran v Denmark* (2021) 53 BHRC 201, para 183; indeed the principles in *Maslov v Austria* [2009] INLR 47 are adapted from the *Üner* criteria.

[887] See eg ibid paras 188–89; *MA v Denmark* App No 6697/18, 9 July 2021 [GC], para 149.

[888] Part 5A of the Nationality, Immigration and Asylum Act 2002, in particular s 117C. For discussion of its purpose, effect, and limits see *KO (Nigeria) v Secretary of State for the Home Department* [2018] UKSC 53, [2018] 1 WLR 5273, paras 12–15; *Gosturani v Secretary of State for the Home Department* [2022] EWCA Civ 779, [2022] 1 WLR 4345, para 35.

[889] Recent significant cases in the context of private life include *CI (Nigeria) v Secretary of State for the Home Department* [2019] EWCA Civ 2027, [2020] Imm AR 503; *R Sanambar v Secretary of State for the Home Department* [2021] UKSC 30, [2021] 1 WLR 3847; *SC (Jamaica) v Secretary of State for the Home Department* [2022] UKSC 15, [2022] 1 WLR 3190.

[890] See eg *MF (Nigeria) v Secretary of State for the Home Department* [2014] 1 WLR 544, para 44; *Ali v Secretary of State for the Home Department* [2016] 1 WLR 4799, paras 38 and 50; *NA (Pakistan) v Secretary of State for the Home Department* [2017] 1 WLR 207, para 38; *HA (Iraq) v Secretary of State for the Home Department* [2020] EWCA Civ 1176, para 29.

[891] See *Unuane v UK* (2021) 72 EHRR 24, paras 81–83.

been enshrined in primary legislation,[892] and courts and tribunals will give weight to the now-longstanding government policy that an Article 8 claim based on life in the UK should only be allowed in 'exceptional circumstances' where the requirements of the Immigration Rules[893] have not been met.[894] Particularly where an applicant also relies on prospective interferences with Article 8 in the destination country, these considerations will inform—but not exhaust—the proportionality assessment.

Where an applicant relies on the absence of medical care for a naturally occurring condition in the destination country, the courts have held that an Article 8 claim is unlikely to succeed if an Article 3 claim fails (though it may not if there are additional factors relevant to the art 8 case).[895]   6.321

Importantly, the domestic courts have held that the right to respect for private life cannot be relied on in cases involving entry rather than expulsion.[896] This is in contrast to the right to family life, as to which see para 6.349. That said, the Court of Appeal has recognized—albeit not expressly in the language of positive obligations—that Article 8 may require a grant of leave to remain to an applicant already in the UK who has been kept in a sufficiently lengthy state of immigration 'limbo' due to legal and practical barriers to their removal.[897]   6.322

(l) Citizenship and nationality

The ECtHR has confirmed on a number of occasions that, although the Convention does not guarantee a right to citizenship as such, the denial or deprivation of citizenship may engage the private life limb of Article 8.[898] The Court has generally limited this to cases where the decision in question is 'arbitrary',[899] considering both this and the extent of the impact on the applicant's private life in order to   6.323

---

[892] Nationality, Immigration and Asylum Act 2002, s 117B. This provides, eg, that it is in the public interest that persons seeking leave to enter or remain in the UK are financially independent; and that little weight should be given to private life or a relationship formed with a qualifying partner that is established while a person is in the UK unlawfully.

[893] Presently contained in the Appendix: Private Life.

[894] This is because the Immigration Rules are now intended to reflect and comply with the requirements of Article 8 in the generality of cases: see *R (Agyarko) v Secretary of State for the Home Department* [2017] UKSC 11, [2017] 1 WLR 823, paras 46–48, 59–60; *NA (Pakistan) v Secretary of State for the Home Department* [2017] 1 WLR 207, para 38. The policy is most clearly reflected in the context of family life (see para 6.348), but is reflected in various places in the Home Office guidance *Family life (as a partner or parent) and exceptional circumstance* (v 18.0, 12 August 2022).

[895] See eg *SL (St Lucia) v Secretary of State for the Home Department* [2018] EWCA Civ 1894, paras 22–28.

[896] See *Secretary of State for the Home Department v Abbas* [2017] EWCA Civ 1393, [2018] 1 WLR 533.

[897] *RA (Iraq) v Secretary of State for the Home Department* [2019] EWCA Civ 850, [2019] 4 WLR 132; see also *Secretary of State for the Home Department v R (AM)* [2022] EWCA Civ 780.

[898] See eg *Genovese v Malta* (2011) 58 EHRR 25, paras 30, 33; *Ramadan v Malta* App No 76136/12, 12 June 2016, paras 62 and 84–85; *Ghoumid v France* App Nos 52273/16 and others, 25 June 2020, para 43.

[899] See eg *Genovese v Malta* (2011) 58 EHRR 25, para 30; *Ghoumid v France* App Nos 52273/16 and others, 25 June 2020, para 43. This requires consideration of whether the measures were lawful; whether they were accompanied by procedural safeguards; and whether the authorities acted diligently and promptly: para 44. It is strongly arguable that the better and more principled approach is that adopted in *Usmanov v Russia* App No 43936/18, 22 December 2020, where the consequences for the applicant were assessed to establish interference and arbitrariness was treated as relevant to justification: see paras 53–71.

determine whether there has been a breach.[900] Relevant factors on the latter front have included the extent of the applicant's personal connection with the relevant state, and the extent to which the decision was based on reasons of the applicant's own making.[901] This approach has now been affirmed by the domestic courts.[902]

3. Family life

6.324   Article 8 jurisprudence has undergone an evolution, and the definition of 'family life' now firmly encompasses more non-traditional relationships. As Lord Bingham explained in *EM (Lebanon) v Secretary of State for the Home Department*, 'there is no pre-determined model of family or family life to which article 8 must be applied'.[903]

6.325   In assessing whether or not family life exists, it is the substance, not the form of the individual's circumstances that matters. In recent cases the Grand Chamber has characterized the issue as 'essentially a question of fact depending upon the existence of close personal ties'.[904] The domestic courts have likewise held that the key question is whether there is 'the real existence in practice of close family ties' or 'effective, real or committed support',[905] which is essentially a question of fact.[906]

6.326   The 'family life' limb of Article 8 primarily concerns 'relationships between living human beings' but may, in some cases, extend to certain situations after the death of the relevant family member.[907] For example, it has been held to be engaged where a post mortem had been conducted on the body of the applicant's son against her will and declared religious convictions[908] and where a prisoner was prevented from attending her father's funeral.[909]

6.327   The boundaries between Article 8 and Article 12 (see paras 6.556–6.557), which protects the right to marry and found a family, are not always distinct. It is clear,

---

[900] See eg *Genovese v Malta*, paras 49–51.

[901] See *Genovese v Malta* (2011) 58 EHRR 25; *Ramadan v Malta* App No 76136/12, 12 June 2016.

[902] See *R (Begum) v Special Immigration Appeals Commission* [2021] UKSC 7, [2021] AC 765, para 64; *R (Vanriel) v Secretary of State for the Home Department* [2021] EWHC 3415 (Admin), [2022] QB 737; *R (Williams) v SSHD* [2017] EWCA Civ 98, [2017] 1 WLR 3283. See also the novel arguments explored in *In the matter of an application by Caoimhe Ni Chuinneagain for judicial review* [2022] NICA 56.

[903] *EM (Lebanon) v Secretary of State for the Home Department* [2008] UKHL 64, [2009] 1 All ER 559, para 37.

[904] See eg *Fedotova v Russia* (2022) 74 EHRR 28, para 145; *Paradiso and Campanelli v Italy* App No 25358/12, 24 January 2017 [GC], para 140.

[905] *K v UK* (1986) 50 DR 199; *Lebbink v the Netherlands* [2004] 3 FCR 59.

[906] *Singh v Entry Clearance Officer* [2004] EWCA Civ 1075, [2005] QB 608, para 20; *EM (Lebanon) v Secretary of State for the Home Department* [2008] UKHL 64, [2009] 1 All ER 559, para 37; *Uddin v Secretary of State for the Home Department* [2020] EWCA Civ 338, [2020] 1 WLR 1562, paras 35–40; *Mobeen v Secretary of State for the Home Department* [2021] EWCA Civ, paras 46–47.

[907] *Solska and Rybicka v Poland* App Nos 30491/17 and another, 20 September 2018, para 104.

[908] *Polat v Austria* App No 12886/16, 20 July 2021.

[909] *Guimon v France* App No 48798/14, 11 April 2019. For further examples see *Solska and Rybicka v Poland* App Nos 30491/17 and another, 20 September 2018, paras 105–06 (noting that they have tended to relate to 'the way in which the body of a deceased relative was treated, as well as issues regarding the ability to attend the burial and pay respects at the grave of a relative').

however, that Article 8 does not itself guarantee the right to found a family; it is only applicable once family life is established.[910]

Where family life is found to exist, the result is that (a) interferences must be justified under Article 8(2), and (b) procedural and positive obligations will arise in appropriate cases. The examples are near-endless. In *Mizzi v Malta*, for example, the ECtHR accepted that a legal presumption of the husband's paternity of a child born during the period of the marriage, combined with the absence of any domestic remedy by which he could have challenged it, violated his right to respect for both private and family life.[911] In *Kaya v Turkey*, the ECtHR held that requiring prisoners who wished to speak to family members in Kurdish on permitted phone calls to go through a 'preliminary procedure' designed to ascertain whether their relatives were 'genuinely unable to express themselves in Turkish' interfered with the right to respect for family life and was not 'necessary in a democratic society'.[912]   6.328

(a) Formal marital and similar relationships

Formal unions, such as a valid marriage, clearly fall within the scope of family life.[913] Engagements may also give rise to family life, if supported by evidence of the parties' intention to marry.[914]   6.329

The ECtHR has accepted that 'de facto family ties' may exist in the absence of such a formalized relationship.[915] In *Kroon v Netherlands* the ECtHR determined that factors such as cohabitation and the stability of the relationship may serve to demonstrate that a relationship has sufficient constancy to amount to family life[916] (though cohabitation is not a necessary criterion[917]). Polygamous unions may also constitute family life.[918]   6.330

(b) Same-sex relationships and relationships involving transgender people

In early ECtHR case law same-sex relationships were not protected as family life, although they were protected under the right to private life.[919] The ECtHR belatedly recognized that a stable relationship between cohabiting same-sex individuals   6.331

---

[910] See eg *EB v France* (2008) 47 EHRR 21; *Paradiso and Campanelli v Italy* App No 25358/12, 24 January 2017 [GC], para 141 (though note the potential exceptions for a child born out of wedlock and their natural father, or a couple in a genuine marriage where family life has yet to be fully established). See also *L v the Netherlands* App No 45582/99, 1 June 2004 (potential further exception for the relationship between a child and their biological father).

[911] *Mizzi v Malta* [2006] 1 FCR 256, para 113. See also *Kroon v the Netherlands* (1994) 19 EHRR 263, para 40.

[912] *Kaya v Turkey* App Nos 43750/06 & others, 22 April 2014.

[913] See eg *Benes v Austria* (1992) 72 DR 271.

[914] *Wakefield v UK* (1990) 66 DR 251; *Fedotova v Russia* (2022) 74 EHRR 28.

[915] See eg *Fedotova v Russia* (2022) 74 EHRR 28, para 145.

[916] *Kroon v Netherlands* (1994) 19 EHRR 263.

[917] *Fedotova v Russia* (2022) 74 EHRR 28, para 147.

[918] *A and A v the Netherlands* (1992) 72 DR 118.

[919] *Secretary of State for Work and Pensions v M* [2006] UKHL 11, [2006] 2 AC 91, para 30, though the ECtHR indicated in *JM v UK* (2010) 30 BHRC 60 that a same-sex couple would nowadays be regarded as a family.

was rightly classified as family life in *Schalk and Kopf v Austria*[920] and has since consistently affirmed this.[921] However, the ECtHR held that Article 8 read with Article 14 did not guarantee same-sex couples the right to marry and that there was no breach of Article 14 where they were able to 'obtain a legal status equal or similar to marriage in many [though not all] respects'.[922] In *Valliantos and others v Greece*, the Grand Chamber held that the exclusion of same-sex couples from the scope of a new form of civil partnership in Greece breached Article 8 (both private and family life aspects) in conjunction with Article 14.[923] Since then it has gone further, holding in several cases that Article 8 alone requires states to ensure 'recognition and protection for same-sex couples' in some form.[924] In *Fedotova v Russia* the Grand Chamber concluded that, in light of the 'ongoing trend' in this regard, states' margin of appreciation in this area has been 'significantly reduced'—though it is wider on the question of what form this recognition should take.[925] On the facts of the case it held that, by offering only de facto recognition—which did not permit couples to 'regulate fundamental aspects of life as a couple such as those concerning property, maintenance and inheritance' or to 'rely on the existence of their relationship in dealings with the judicial or administrative authorities'—Russia had overstepped this margin.[926]

6.332   A similar evolution has occurred in relation to relationships involving trans people. In *X, Y and Z v UK* the ECtHR found de facto family ties between X, a trans man, Y, his female partner, and Z, Y's child by artificial insemination.[927] In *Hämäläinen v Finland* the Grand Chamber confirmed that a trans woman's relationship with her partner and child fell to be protected under the family life aspect of Article 8, as well as the private life aspect.[928]

6.333   In this area, the domestic approach has proved more flexible than that of the ECtHR. The narrow approach to 'family life' taken by the ECtHR in *S v UK*[929] was not followed in *Ghaidan v Godin-Mendoza*[930] or *Fitzpatrick v Sterling Housing Association Ltd*,[931] the House of Lords holding that the terms 'spouse' and 'family' respectively under the Rent Act 1977 could apply to a same-sex partner. However, in *Secretary of State for Work and Pensions v M* the House of Lords adopted a narrow

---

[920] *Schalk and Kopf v Austria* (2011) 53 EHRR 20. See also *Valliantos v Greece* App Nos 29381/09 and 32684/09, 7 November 2013.
[921] See eg *Fedotova v Russia* (2022) 74 EHRR 28, paras 146–48.
[922] *Schalk and Kopf v Austria* (2011) 53 EHRR 20, para 109.
[923] *Valliantos and others v Greece* App Nos 29381/09 and 32684/09, 7 November 2013.
[924] See the cases discussed in *Fedotova v Russia* (2022) 74 EHRR 28, paras 161–64, and the affirmation at para 178.
[925] ibid paras 187–88.
[926] ibid paras 203–25.
[927] *X, Y and Z v UK* (1997) 24 EHRR 143.
[928] *Hämäläinen v Finland* (2014) 37 BHRC 55 [GC]. See also *AM v Russia* (2022) 74 EHRR 23. In the domestic context the Court of Appeal has recognized that the question of how a transgender parent is identified on a child's birth certificate engages both the private and the family life limbs of art 8: *R (McConnell) v Secretary of State for Health and Social Care* [2020] EWCA Civ 559, [2021] Fam 77, paras 55–56.
[929] *S v UK* (1986) 47 DR 274.
[930] *Ghaidan v Godin-Mendoza* [2004] UKHL 30, [2004] 2 AC 557.
[931] *Fitzpatrick v Sterling Housing Association Ltd* [2001] 1 AC 27.

view, holding that on the then-current state of Strasbourg jurisprudence same-sex relationships did not fall within the scope of the right to respect for family life. While their Lordships anticipated the shift in the ECtHR's case law that has now occurred, it 'was not for the courts of this country to pre-empt that decision'.[932] In *Re G (a child)* Baker J recognized that, following *Schalk and Kopf v Austria*,[933] it is 'now established beyond doubt that the relationship between a same-sex couple constitutes "family life" for the purposes of article 8'.[934]

(c) *Parents and children*

The biological parent/child relationship—at least between parents and minor children—is well-recognized in Article 8 case law.[935] The ECtHR has held that 'the mutual enjoyment by parent and child of each other's company constitutes a fundamental element of family life'.[936] In *Boughanemi v France* the Court held that the tie between parent and child, regardless of whether the child is legitimate, could only be broken in 'exceptional circumstances'.[937]   6.334

Biological ties give rise to a strong presumption of family life,[938] but are not con-clusive. In *X v UK* the ECmHR held that no sufficient nexus existed between the biological father and an unborn foetus,[939] and a similar result was reached in *G v Netherlands* concerning a sperm donor.[940] (Non-biological ties, such as in the case of adoptive parents and children, may also give rise to family life: see para 6.339.)   6.335

In *Ahrens v Germany*[941] and *Kautzor v Germany*,[942] fathers sought to rely on their family life rights to establish an entitlement to test for their paternity of children. The ECtHR was not convinced that the right to family life was engaged in either case. In the former case, the father had not demonstrated any interest or commit-ment to the child before or after birth; and in the latter, he had not spent any time or established a close relationship with the child. In both cases the Court found the private life aspect of Article 8, rather than the family life aspect, to be engaged.   6.336

---

[932] *Secretary of State for Work and Pensions v M* [2006] UKHL 11, [2006] 2 AC 91, para 30 per Lord Nicholls. The EctHR found a violation of art 14 taken with art 1 of Protocol 1: *JM v UK* (2010) 30 BHRC 60.

[933] *Schalk and Kopf v Austria* App No 30141/04, 24 June 2010.

[934] *Re G (a child)* [2013] EWHC 134 (Fam), para 113.

[935] *Ahmut v the Netherlands* (1996) 24 EHRR 62.

[936] *B v UK* (1988) 10 EHRR 87; *Strand Lobben v Norway* (2020) 70 EHRR 14, para 202. See also *EM (Lebanon) v Secretary of State for the Home Department* [2008] UKHL 64, [2009] 1 All ER 559, para 6.

[937] *Boughanemi v France* (1996) 22 EHRR 228, para 35.

[938] *Keegan v Ireland* (1994) 18 EHRR 342. See also *Mennesson v France* App No 65192/11, 26 June 2014, paras 48 and 87 (noting that there was no dispute that the 'family life' limb of art 8 was engaged by the applicants' inability to obtain recognition in France of a legal parent-child relationship lawfully established abroad in the context of a surrogacy agreement where there was a biological relationship with one parent). It is notable that in this case the Court found no violation of the applicants' right to respect for family life, but a breach of the children's right to respect for private life.

[939] *X v UK* (1980) 19 DR 244.

[940] *G v Netherlands* (1993) 16 EHRR CD 38.

[941] *Ahrens v Germany* App No 45071/09, 22 March 2012.

[942] *Kautzor v Germany* App No 23338/09, 22 March 2012.

6.337　The ECtHR has accepted that the fact that a child no longer lives with one of their parents—for example due to the parents' divorce—does not necessarily break the ties of family life, which will subsist where (eg) the parent and child continue to meet frequently and regularly.[943]

6.338　The right of a child to identify his or her parents is encompassed by family life.[944] However, such cases may raise others' Article 8 rights that conflict with the applicant's right to family life. In *Odievre v France*, for example, the Grand Chamber held that there was no violation of Article 8 in circumstances where the applicant was unable to obtain information about her natural family owing to French rules governing 'anonymous births' that protected the mother's interest in anonymity.[945]

6.339　Non-biological parental or equivalent relationships—for example in the context of adoption[946] and foster relationships[947]—may also engage the right to family life. Relevant factors include the closeness of the personal ties established, the role played by the adults vis-à-vis the child, and the time spent together (particularly the time cohabiting).[948] Any legal uncertainty created by the adults' conduct may also be taken into account.[949] The ECtHR has held on a number of occasions that the right to family life does not encompass a right to adoption.[950] Refusal to permit adoption may, however, fall within the ambit of private life for the purposes of Article 14.[951]

6.340　The ECtHR has confirmed that, in any cases involving the care of children or contact restrictions, the child's interests 'must come before all other considerations'.[952] Similarly, where the interests of a child and their parents conflict, a fair balance must be struck in which 'particular importance should be attached to the best interests of the child'.[953] In general it is taken to be in a child's best interests to maintain family ties 'except in cases where the family has proved particularly unfit'.[954] Further, measures such as adoption without the biological parents' consent are permissible only in 'exceptional circumstances' where 'motivated by an overriding requirement pertaining to the child's best interests'.[955] The state enjoys a wide margin of appreciation in assessing where the relevant interests lie, provided the

---

[943] *Berrehab v the Netherlands* (1988) 11 EHRR 322.

[944] *Mikuli v Croatia* [2002] 1 FCR 720; *Jevremović v Serbia* [2007] 2 FCR 671; *S v London Borough of Lambeth* [2006] EWHC 326 (Fam), [2007] 1 FLR 152.

[945] *Odievre v France* (2003) 14 BHRC 526 [GC].

[946] *Pini and others v Romania* App Nos 78028/01 and 78030/01, 22 June 2004.

[947] *Gaskin v UK* (1989) 12 EHRR 36. See likewise, in the domestic context, *Uddin v Secretary of State for the Home Department* [2020] EWCA Civ 338, [2020] 1 WLR 1562.

[948] See *Paradiso and Campanelli v Italy* App No 25358/12, 24 January 2017 [GC], paras 149–57. See also *Nazarenko Russia* App No 39438/13, 16 July 2015.

[949] *Paradiso and Campanelli v Italy*, paras 156–57. As usual, even where family life is found not to exist the situation is likely to engage the private life limb of art 8, such that there may be little difference to the ultimate outcome: see paras 161–64 and the analysis of proportionality which followed.

[950] See eg *Fretté v France* [2003] 2 FCR 39.

[951] *EB v France* (2008) 47 EHRR 21.

[952] *Ibrahim v Norway* (2022) 74 EHRR 25 [GC], para 145 (citing *Strand Lobben v Norway* (2020) 70 EHRR 14).

[953] ibid.

[954] ibid.

[955] ibid paras 149 and 162.

procedural requirements of Article 8 have been met and less drastic measures have been carefully considered.[956] Procedural rights, as discussed at para 6.265–6.267, are often particularly important in cases concerning interferences with family life between parents and children. In the particular context of custody and contact proceedings, the ECtHR has held that the procedural requirements of Article 8 include a duty of 'exceptional diligence' and that ineffectiveness or delay may therefore result in a breach.[957]

Where a case raises issues relating to the faith in which a child will be brought up, it will be considered under Article 8 as interpreted in light of Article 9.[958] This means that due account must be taken of the parents' interest in allowing the child to retain at least some ties to their religious 'origins'.[959]   6.341

As noted above, where the state places a child in state care which restricts the enjoyment of family life between parents and children, it has a positive obligation to 'take measures to facilitate family reunion as soon as reasonable feasible'.[960] In the domestic context, the courts have identified the provision of 'such support as will enable a child to remain with [their] parents' as an aspect of the state's positive obligations under Article 8.[961]   6.342

As to the relationship between parents and their adult children, the ECtHR has held that this is unlikely to amount to family life without 'additional elements of dependence', though this may not be necessary in cases involving young adults who are still living with their parents and have not yet started a family of their own.[962] The domestic courts have taken a similar approach, identifying the 'ultimate question' as being whether there is 'effective, real or committed support' or 'the real existence in practice of close personal ties'.[963] Cases where family life is not engaged are examined under the private life limb of Article 8.   6.343

(d) Other familial relationships

Other familial relationships, such as those between grandparents and grandchildren[964] and between siblings,[965] may also constitute family life, depending always on the facts. The courts will examine factors such as contact, length of the relationship,   6.344

---

[956] ibid para 151. For an example of the interaction of substantive and procedural factors in the assessment of proportionality, see *Strand Lobben v Norway* (2020) 70 EHRR 14, paras 214–26.

[957] See eg *Ribić v Croatia* App No 27148/12, 2 April 2015, para 92.

[958] *Ibrahim v Norway* (2022) 74 EHRR 25, paras 141–42.

[959] ibid para 161.

[960] *Strand Lobben v Norway* (2020) 70 EHRR 14, paras 205, 208.

[961] *H (Parents with learning difficulties: Risk of harm)* [2023] EWCA Civ 59, para 42 (citing *Re D (A Child) (No 3)* [2016] EWHC 1, [2017] 1 FLR 237).

[962] See eg *Savran v Denmark* (2021) 53 BHRC 201, paras 174, 178.

[963] See eg *Uddin v Secretary of State for the Home Department* [2020] EWCA Civ 338, [2020] 1 WLR 1562, paras 35–40 (note the endorsement of the same approach where the parent-child relationship arose from a fostering arrangement); *Mobeen v Secretary of State for the Home Department* [2021] EWCA Civ, paras 46–47.

[964] *GHB v UK* [2000] EHRLR 545; and see in the domestic context *Cases A, B and C (Adoption: Notification of Fathers and Relatives)* [2020] EWCA Civ 41, [2020] Fam 325, para 43.

[965] *Mustafa and Armag an Akın v Turkey* App No 4694/03, 6 April 2010; *Senthuran v Secretary of State for the Home Department* [2004] EWCA Civ 950, [2004] 4 All ER 365.

dependency, and emotional ties. The ECtHR has held that, in general, the relationship between children and (eg) their grandparents is 'different in nature and degree' from that between children and their parents and therefore 'generally calls for a lesser degree of protection'; as a result, the right to 'respect' for this kind of family life 'primarily entails the right to maintain a normal grandparent-child relationship through contacts between them'.[966]

(e) Expulsion and entry of migrants

6.345 The right for an 'alien' to enter or to reside in a particular country is not guaranteed by respect for family life,[967] but the ECtHR has held that the refusal of entry or the removal of a person from a country where close members of his family are living may amount to an interference with the right to respect for family life[968] and the result is that the state will be required to justify its interference under Article 8(2).[969] As noted above (para 6.315) in the context of private life, 'foreign' cases—that is, cases where the only interference with Article 8 rights flowing from expulsion would occur in the destination country—attract the 'flagrancy' threshold.[970]

6.346 In *Üner v the Netherlands*, the leading case on immigration and the right to family life in a domestic case, the ECtHR considered the withdrawal of a residence permit and deportation of a Turkish immigrant who was lawfully present and settled in the Netherlands, had founded a family there, and then committed a series of criminal offences.[971] The Court accepted that the state was pursuing the legitimate aims under Article 8(2) of protecting public safety and preventing crime, and set out a variety of factors that had to be taken into account in the proportionality analysis, including the seriousness and nature of the offence, the length of the applicant's stay in the country from which he or she was to be expelled, the nationalities of the various persons concerned, whether there were children of the marriage, and the seriousness of the difficulties the spouse was likely to encounter in the applicant's country of origin. The Court also made it explicit that the best interests of the children were a relevant consideration. The *Üner* criteria are consistently cited in both Strasbourg and domestic cases.

6.347 Also significant in this context is the case of *Jeunesse v the Netherlands*, where the Grand Chamber distinguished *Üner* on the basis that the family member in question had been unlawfully present in the Netherlands for some years. It affirmed that, where family life in the host state was created at a time where 'the persons involved were aware that the immigration status of one of them was such that the persistence of that family life within the host state would from the outset be

---

[966] *Mitovi v Macedonia* App No 53565/13, 16 April 2015, para 58; cf *Terna v Italy* App No 21052/18, 14 January 2021.

[967] *Abdulaziz, Cabales and Balkandali v UK* (1985) 7 EHRR 471.

[968] *Moustaquim v Belgium* (1991) 13 EHRR 802.

[969] See eg *Omoregie v Norway* App No 265/07, 31 July 2008.

[970] *R (Ullah) v Special Adjudicator* [2004] UKHL 26, [2004] 2 AC 323, approving *Devaseelan v Secretary of State for the Home Department* [2002] UKIAT 702; *EM (Lebanon) v Secretary of State for the Home Department* [2008] UKHL 64, [2008] 2 FLR 2067, para 37.

[971] *Üner v the Netherlands* (2007) 45 EHRR 14.

precarious', it was likely to be only in 'exceptional circumstances' that removal of the non-national family member would constitute a disproportionate interference with the right to family life.[972] In making this assessment, the best interests of any relevant children must also be taken into account[973] and indeed 'it is necessary to take due account of the situation of all members of the family, as [Article 8] guarantees protection to the whole family'.[974]

A significant proportion of domestic decisions on family life under Article 8 concern the removal of immigrants. In general, it is accepted that Article 8(1) will be engaged by interference with family ties existing in the UK but (as noted above) immigration control will always constitute a legitimate aim for removal under Article 8(2). The critical issue will therefore be the proportionality of the interference. As mentioned earlier, there have been increasing moves to codify the assessment of proportionality through a combination of Immigration Rules and primary legislation, rather than leaving it to the judgement of courts and tribunals. Today, the circumstances in which the expulsion of persons liable to deportation will constitute a disproportionate interference with the right to family life are circumscribed by statute and accompanying Immigration Rules (though these will be interpreted and applied in light of the ECtHR's jurisprudence).[975] In the context of administrative removal, the circumstances in which leave will be granted on the basis of family life in the UK—including (eg) to partners, children, and adult dependent relatives—are presently set out in Appendix FM to the Immigration Rules. Where these requirements are not met, the Rules themselves specify that leave on the basis of family life will be granted only in 'exceptional circumstances'.[976] Courts and tribunals will give weight to this policy position when assessing the proportionality of removal[977] and will also be required to apply the provisions of primary legislation which bear on the balancing exercise.[978]

6.348

---

[972] *Jeunesse v the Netherlands* (2015) 60 EHRR 17, paras 104, 108, 114. This has been consistently applied by the domestic courts (see eg *Mobeen v Secretary of State for the Home Department* [2021] EWCA Civ, paras 49–50), and indeed is now reflected in the Nationality, Immigration and Asylum Act 2002, s 117B.

[973] *Jeunesse v the Netherlands*, para 109.

[974] ibid para 117.

[975] In particular the Nationality, Immigration and Asylum Act 2022, Part 5A: see para 6.320. Again, a full treatment of the authorities on Part 5A is beyond the scope of this text. Recent significant cases in the context of family life include *KO (Nigeria) v Secretary of State for the Home Department* [2018] UKSC 53, [2018] 1 WLR 5273; *HA (Iraq) v Secretary of State for the Home Department* [2022] UKSC 22, [2022] 1 WLR 3784; *Gosturani v Secretary of State for the Home Department* [2022] EWCA Civ 779, [2022] 1 WLR 4345; *Alam v Secretary of State for the Home Department* [2023] EWCA Civ 30, [2023] 4 WLR 17.

[976] Guidance sets out what the Secretary of State considers will meet this threshold in more detail: the current version is *Family life (as a partner or parent) and exceptional circumstance* (v 18.0, 12 August 2022). The courts have also discussed the meaning of 'exceptional circumstances' in some detail: see eg *R (Agyarko) v Secretary of State for the Home Department* [2017] UKSC 11, [2017] 1 WLR.

[977] See eg *Gosturani v Secretary of State for the Home Department* [2022] EWCA Civ 779, [2022] 1 WLR 4345, para 39; *Mobeen v Secretary of State for the Home Department* [2021] EWCA Civ, para 52; *SC (Jamaica) v Secretary of State for the Home Department* [2022] UKSC 15, [2022] 1 WLR 3190, para 38.

[978] In particular the Nationality, Immigration and Asylum Act 2002, s 117B: see nn 882, 892. Section 117B also provides that the public interest does *not* require removal where 'the person has a genuine and subsisting parental relationship with a qualifying child' and 'it would not be reasonable to expect the child to leave the United Kingdom'. For discussion see eg *Runa v Secretary of State for the Home Department* [2020] EWCA Civ 514, [2020] 1 WLR 3760.

6.349   The right to respect for family life may also be invoked in the context of entry clearance, such that Article 8 may necessitate a grant of leave, if to refuse it would be disproportionate. The Grand Chamber has identified relevant factors as including 'the extent to which family life would be effectively ruptured [by a refusal], the extent of the ties in the [relevant] state, whether there are insurmountable obstacles in the way of the family living in the country of origin of the alien concerned, and whether there are factors of immigration control'.[979] The best interests of children must be afforded 'significant weight'.[980] The Court will also consider the proportionality of any waiting period imposed on the grant of entry clearance to family members of those with refugee status or similar forms of leave, though states have a wide margin of appreciation in this regard.[981] Like the ECtHR, the domestic courts have recognized the applicability of this limb of Article 8 to entry clearance cases while specifying that family life must be existing (a grant is not required to facilitate its future development).[982]

4. Home

6.350   In *Buckley v UK* the ECtHR highlighted that the identification of a 'home' is highly fact-specific, and depends on 'the existence of sufficient and continuous links'.[983] A 'home' will usually be 'the place, the physically defined area, where private and family life develops'.[984] The House of Lords has suggested that 'home' constitutes the place where a person 'lives and to which he returns and which forms the centre of his existence'[985] (though the Grand Chamber has held, arguably inconsistently, that the concept may apply to a holiday home[986]). 'Home' can also include premises which are unlawfully occupied.[987] A home has also been held to include a long-term

---

[979] *MA v Denmark* App No 6697/18, 9 July 2021 [GC], para 132, citing the seminar case of *Jeunesse v the Netherlands* (2015) 60 EHRR 17. For examples of cases where entry clearance has and has not found to have been required, see further paras 134–35.

[980] *MA v Denmark* App No 6697/18, 9 July 2021 [GC].

[981] ibid.

[982] See eg *Entry Clearance Officer, Sierra Leone v Kopoi* [2017] EWCA Civ 1511, para 30. For the application of family life considerations to the compatibility of policies about entry clearance with the family life limb of art 8, see eg *R (Quila) v Secretary of State for the Home Department* [2011] UKSC 45, [2012] 1 AC 26 and *R (MM (Lebanon)) v Secretary of State for the Home Department* [2017] UKSC 10, [2017] 1 WLR 771.

[983] *Buckley v UK* (1996) 23 EHRR 101; and see more recently *National Federation of Sportspersons' Associations and Unions v France* App Nos 48151/11 and another, 18 January 2018 [GC], para 154.

[984] *National Federation of Sportspersons' Associations and Unions v France* App Nos 48151/11 and another, 18 January 2018 [GC], para 154. Note also that a place does not cease to be a person's home simply because the state has denied them access to it and forced them to live in displacement: see *Chiragov v Armenia* (2016) 63 EHRR 9.

[985] *London Borough of Harrow v Qazi* [2003] UKHL 43, [2004] 1 AC 983, para 8 per Lord Bingham.

[986] See eg *National Federation of Sportspersons' Associations and Unions v France* App Nos 48151/11 and another, 18 January 2018 [GC], para 154.

[987] *McCann v UK* (2008) 47 EHRR 40; *Faulkner v Ireland* (2022) 75 EHRR SE8, para 91. However, the lawfulness of establishment or occupancy will be relevant to the assessment of justification: see eg *Chapman v UK* (2001) 10 BHRC 48; *Faulkner v Ireland* (2022) 75 EHRR SE8, para 96. In the domestic context, see *Malik v Fassenfelt* [2013] EWCA Civ 798, [2013] EGILR 22, para 43.

hospital stay,[988] second homes,[989] and offices (of a person or a company)[990] in certain circumstances.

Gillow v UK makes clear that the notion of 'home' may extend to the place where one intends to live.[991] The applicants were absent from their house in Guernsey for 18 years because the husband's job caused him to travel. The government refused the couple a new residence permit when they finally returned, arguing that this was not their home. The ECmHR and ECtHR held that, in this case, there was a right to re-establish home life.   6.351

So far, however, the Court has never found a violation of the notion of respect for home by a failure to provide a particular home.[992] This right may also be covered by the developing jurisprudence on legitimate expectations under Article 1 of Protocol 1 (see paras 7.11–7.12 and 7.18–7.23).   6.352

The right to respect for the 'home' includes the right 'to the quiet enjoyment of that area'.[993] This means searches of the home are capable of interfering with the right,[994] even where the applicant has adopted a cooperative approach.[995] Interference can also arise from noise and nuisance of sufficient seriousness and duration to impact the enjoyment of one's home,[996] and from the presence of uninvited strangers.[997] The ECtHR has held that a system for drug testing in sport which required athletes to provide detailed information about their daily movements interfered with the right to respect for the home, on the basis that it could require them to stay home at particular times to be tested and therefore to give up the peaceful enjoyment of their homes on pain of sanctions.[998]   6.353

Cases involving possession orders for people's homes have frequently been considered by the ECtHR and the domestic courts. The ECtHR has found that possession and eviction proceedings must be attended by procedural safeguards.[999] In *McCann v UK* the Court held that, whenever a person risked losing his or her home (the most serious kind of interference with this limb of art 8), there must be   6.354

---

[988] *Collins v UK* App No 11909/02, 15 October 2002; *R v North and East Devon District Health Authority, ex p Coughlan* [2001] QB 213.

[989] *Demades v Turkey* App No 16219/90, 31 July 2003.

[990] See eg *Niemietz v Germany* (1993) 16 EHRR 97; *Peev v Bulgaria* App No 64209/01, 26 July 2007; *Saint-Paul Luxembourg SA v Luxembourg* App No 26419/10, 18 April 2013, para 37; *National Federation of Sportspersons' Associations and Unions v France* App Nos 48151/11 & another, 18 January 2018 [GC], para 154.

[991] *Gillow v UK* (1986) 11 EHRR 335.

[992] See eg *Hudorovic v Slovenia* (2020) 71 EHRR 16 [GC], para 114.

[993] *National Federation of Sportspersons' Associations and Unions v France* App Nos 48151/11 and another, 18 January 2018 [GC], para 154.

[994] See eg *Sher v UK* (2016) 63 EHRR 24, para 171; and see para 172 for relevant factors in the assessment of proportionality.

[995] *Saint-Paul Luxembourg SA v Luxembourg* App No 26419/10, 18 April 2013, para 38.

[996] See eg *Dmitriyev v Russia* App No 17840/06, 1 December 2020, paras 33–34; *Kapa v Poland* (2022) 74 EHRR 18. For a case where this threshold was not reached see *Cherkun v Ukraine* App No 59184/09, 12 March 2019.

[997] *Smirnova v Ukraine* App No 1870/05, 13 October 2016, para 94.

[998] *National Federation of Sportspersons' Associations and Unions v France* App Nos 48151/11 and another, 18 January 2018 [GC], para 158.

[999] *Connors v UK* (2005) 40 EHRR 9.

a possibility of having the proportionality of the eviction measure determined by an independent tribunal.[1000] This requirement does not necessarily apply in cases where possession is sought by a private person or company rather than the state.[1001]

6.355 The House of Lords considered the applicability of Article 8 to repossession proceedings in a series of cases. In *Kay v Lambeth London Borough Council* the Appellate Committee held that a possession order would engage Article 8(1), but that the county courts could work on the assumption that domestic law satisfied the requirements of Article 8(2) and would not generally need to apply a case-specific proportionality test.[1002] Article 8(2) would be relevant only in cases where the legislation itself could be impugned. A majority of the Lords reached the same conclusion in *Doherty v Birmingham City Council*.[1003]

6.356 In *Kay v UK* the ECtHR favoured the minority approach in *Doherty*, finding that an individual resisting possession should in principle be able to have the proportionality of the measure determined by an independent tribunal in the light of the relevant principles under Article 8, notwithstanding that, under domestic law, the right of occupation had come to an end.[1004] The Supreme Court very swiftly adopted the approach of the ECtHR in three housing cases heard soon after the ECtHR decision. The Court emphasized that it would be rare for proportionality to be seriously arguable where a person otherwise has no domestic legal right to remain in the property.[1005] Both the domestic courts[1006] and (subsequently) the ECtHR[1007] (as noted in para 6.354) have held that this requirement does not automatically apply in cases involving private landlords.

5. Correspondence

6.357 The right to respect for correspondence is concerned with protecting the confidentiality of communications. This limb of Article 8 protects the 'confidentiality of 'private communications,' whatever the content of the correspondence concerned, and whatever form it may take,' and the ECtHR has explained that Article 8 'protects … the confidentiality of all the exchanges in which individuals may engage for the purposes of communication'.[1008] Correspondence is defined broadly and covers any mode of communication, including letters, phone calls, emails, instant messaging, and other forms of electronic communications.[1009] The protection of this right also extends to

---

[1000] (2008) 47 EHRR 40. Judicial review with parameters falling short of this will not suffice: see *Ivanova and Cherkezov v Bulgaria* (2017) 65 EHRR 20.

[1001] See eg *FJM v UK* App No 7602/16, 6 November 2018.

[1002] *Kay v Lambeth London Borough Council* (2006) 20 BHRC 33.

[1003] *Doherty v Birmingham City Council* [2008] UKHL 57, [2009] 1 AC 367.

[1004] *Kay v UK* App No 37341/06, 21 September 2010.

[1005] *Manchester City Council v Pinnock* [2010] UKSC 45, [2011] 2 AC 104; *London Borough of Hounslow v Powell* [2011] UKSC 8, [2011] 2 AC 186; *Leeds City Council and Hall* [2011] UKSC 8, [2011] 2 AC 186. For recent applications see *Davies v Hertfordshire County Council* [2018] EWCA Civ 379, [2019] 1 WLR 4609; *Dudley Metropolitan Borough Council v Mailley* [2022] EWHC 2328 (QB).

[1006] *McDonald v McDonald* [2014] EWCA Civ 1049, [2015] Ch 357.

[1007] See eg *FJM v UK* App No 7602/16, 6 November 2018.

[1008] *Michaud v France* (2014) 59 EHRR 9, paras 90, 118.

[1009] *Bărbulescu v Romania* [2017] IRLR 1032 [GC], paras 72, 74.

communications data; that is information concerning matters such as the time, place, and numbers/accounts used for correspondence, rather than its content.[1010]

This right extends to both personal and professional communications.[1011] It provides enhanced protection to communications[1012] between lawyers and their clients, and specifically covers legal professional privilege,[1013] albeit in more limited terms than the common law.[1014]   6.358

Any kind of opening, monitoring, screening, censoring, blocking, or seizure of correspondence constitutes an interference with this right. That is likely to be the case even if the correspondence is encrypted and so cannot actually be read.[1015] Interferences with this right often arise when correspondence is intercepted/examined while it is en route from one person to another but there will also be an interference if a public authority accesses correspondence which is stored in hard copy or electronic form. Where a public authority conducts a search of a person or premises and seizes, for example, communications devices or devices containing correspondence, or extracts/copies data from electronic systems, that will constitute an interference with the right to respect for correspondence.[1016] There is an interference in these circumstances regardless of whether a public authority gains access directly to a system holding correspondence or requires a person to provide access, and/or produce copies of documents on pain of criminal or civil sanctions.[1017]   6.359

The retention of correspondence obtained in these ways constitutes an interference in and of itself.[1018] Further, measures requiring the retention of communications or communications data, including by CSPs, also constitute an interference with this right.[1019]   6.360

Surveillance measures involving the interception of communications or gaining access to communications systems/devices are likely to interfere with both the right to respect for correspondence and the right to private life. In this context, the ECtHR tends to deal with these aspects of Article 8 interchangeably.   6.361

Communications of legal persons, such as companies, are protected by this right.[1020] They can therefore rely on this limb of Article 8 even though non-natural persons do not ordinarily have a right to a private life.   6.362

[1010] *PG & JH v UK* (2008) 46 EHRR 51, para 42; *Ekimdzhiev v Bulgaria* (2022) 75 EHRR 8, para 373.

[1011] *Bărbulescu v Romania* [2017] IRLR 1032 [GC], para 72.

[1012] This covers oral communications (*Altay v Turkey (No 2)* App No 11236/09, 9 April 2019, para 51).

[1013] See eg *Campbell v UK* (1993) 15 EHRR 137, paras 46–47; *Michaud v France* (2014) 59 EHRR 9, paras 117–19.

[1014] Although exceptional circumstances are still required to justify interference with legally privileged correspondence and this is a context in which the margin of appreciation afforded to states is narrow (*Altay v Turkey (No 2)* App No 11236/09, 9 April 2019, para 52).

[1015] *Kirdök & others v Turkey* App No 14704/12, 3 December 2019, para 36 (available only in French).

[1016] *Bernh Larsen Holding AS v Norway* (2014) 58 EHRR 8, para 105 (concerning access to a server), and *Saber v Norway* App No 459/18, 17 December 2020, para 48 (concerning the seizure and search of a smart phone); *Wieser and Bicos Beteiligungen GmbH v Austria* (2008) 46 EHRR 54, paras 44–45.

[1017] *Bernh Larsen Holding AS v Norway* (2014) 58 EHRR 8, para 105; *Michaud v France* (2014) 59 EHRR 9, paras 91–92.

[1018] See eg *Kirdök & others v Turkey* App No 14704/12, 3 December 2019, para 36 (available only in French).

[1019] *Ekimdzhiev v Bulgaria* (2022) 75 EHRR 8, paras 373, 375.

[1020] *Ships Waste Oil Collector v the Netherlands* App No 2799/16, 16 May 2023, para 41; *Ekimdzhiev v Bulgaria* (2022) 75 EHRR 8, para 374; *Bernh Larsen Holding AS v Norway* (2014) 58 EHRR 8.

6.363   The interception of prisoners' correspondence (particularly letters) with lawyers, medical professionals, families, and friends has generated voluminous case law before the ECtHR and domestic courts.[1021] A full discussion of this is beyond the scope of this book. The ECtHR has long accepted that a measure of control over prisoners' correspondence is compatible with the Convention.[1022] However, there must be sufficient protections in place to prevent arbitrary interferences with the right to respect for correspondence and the ECtHR has held that the monitoring of the entirety of a prisoner's correspondence is unlikely to be proportionate.[1023]

6.364   As with the other limbs of Article 8, the right to protection of correspondence requires states to take positive steps to ensure there is an adequate legal framework in place to prevent private parties from interfering with correspondence, and to ensure such conduct is properly investigated and/or that remedies are available where other people interfere with a person's correspondence. By way of example, the ECtHR held that this obligation had been breached where national authorities had failed properly to investigate allegations that an abusive partner had accessed and retained private electronic messages of the victim.[1024]

6. Article 8(2)

6.365   Article 8 is a qualified right. In order to be justified, an interference by the state with a person's Article 8 rights must (a) be in accordance with the law, (b) in pursuit of one of the legitimate aims identified in Article 8(2), and (c) necessary in a democratic society, which means that the interference must correspond to a pressing social need and be proportionate. Generally, the courts approach justification by considering each of these steps. Where the ECtHR concludes that an interference is not in accordance with the law, it does not normally go on to consider whether the interference was necessary in a democratic society. However, in some cases, particularly in the contexts of the use data and secret surveillance, the ECtHR considers these elements of Article 8(2) in the round.[1025]

(a) *In accordance with the law*

6.366   The ECtHR has summarized the accordance with the law requirement as follows:

The expression 'in accordance with the law', within the meaning of article 8(2), requires firstly [1] that the impugned measure should have some basis in domestic law; it also refers to the quality of the law in question, requiring that [2] it should be accessible to the person concerned, who

---

[1021] Heather Williams J's judgment in *R (Xavier) v Governor of HMP Whitemoor* [2021] EWHC 3060 (Admin) contains a helpful summary of the law.

[1022] See eg *Campbell v UK* (1993) 15 EHRR 137, para 45.

[1023] See eg *Doerga v the Netherlands* App No 50210/99, 7 April 2004, paras 45, 53; *Petrov v Bulgaria* App No 15197/02, 22 May 2008, para 44.

[1024] *Buturugă v Romania* App No 56867/15, 11 February 2020, paras 74–78 (available only in French).

[1025] See eg *Big Brother Watch & others v UK* [GC] (2022) 74 EHRR 17; *Zakharov v Russia* (2016) 63 EHRR 17; *Catt v UK* (2019) 69 EHRR 7; *S v United Kingdom* (2009) 48 EHRR 50.

[3] must moreover be able to foresee its consequences for him, and compatible with the rule of law.[1026]

For these purposes, 'law' is broadly defined, with the focus being on substance rather than form.[1027] Law includes both statutory and judge-made law. In the UK, a decision-maker's published policy can constitute law (or part of the legal framework).[1028] It does not matter that a policy is not legally binding because domestic public law requires that a decision-maker follow their own published policy unless there is a good reason to depart from it,[1029] and any such departure is challengeable by way of judicial review. If a policy is not published, it will *not* constitute 'law' for the purposes of Article 8(2).[1030] Regulatory standards also constitute law in this context.[1031] **6.367**

For an interference to have a basis in domestic law it must also comply with that law. A breach of domestic law arising in the context of a decision or the application of a measure that interferes with Article 8 rights will generally result in that interference *not being* in accordance with the law for the purposes of Article 8(2).[1032] There remains some uncertainty as to how far this goes and, in particular whether a breach of, for example, any procedural duty in domestic law would necessarily mean that an interference is not in accordance with the law. **6.368**

In *re Gallagher* Lord Sumption considered the ECtHR's case on the twin quality of law requirements of accessibility and foreseeability.[1033] Accessibility is generally straightforward: it must be possible to discover, if necessary with the aid of professional advice, what the law is in relation to the application of a measure which interferes with a qualified right; that means that the law must be 'published and comprehensible'.[1034] **6.369**

[1026] *Kruslin v France* (1990) 12 EHRR 547, para 27; *Huvig v France* (1990) 12 EHRR 528, para 26.

[1027] *Sanoma Uitgevers BV v the Netherlands* [2011] EMLR 4 [GC], para 83.

[1028] *Munjaz v UK* [2012] MHLR 351, *R (Bridges) v Chief Constable of South Wales Police* [2020] EWCA Civ 1058, [2020] 1 WLR 5037, para 121; *R (Catt) v Association of Chief Police Officers* [2015] UKSC 9, [2015] AC 1065, para 11.

[1029] *R (Lumba) v Secretary of State for the Home Department* [2011] UKSC 12, [2012] 1 AC 245, para 26.

[1030] *R (Bridges) v Chief Constable of South Wales Police* [2020] EWCA Civ 1058, [2020] 1 WLR 5037, para 121.

[1031] See by analogy *R (Ngole) v University of Sheffield* [2019] ELR 443, [2019] EWCA Civ 1127, paras 63 and 103.

[1032] See *Malcolm v Ministry of Justice* [2011] EWCA Civ 1538, paras 31–32; examples include *Shahid v Scottish Ministers* [2015] UKSC 58, [2016] AC 429, paras 41 and 73 (failure to follow rules in secondary legislation); *R (Syed) v Secretary of State for Justice* [2017] EWHC 727 (Admin), [2017] 4 WLR 101, paras 34, 74, and 78 (failure to follow published policy without good reason); *R (HM) v Secretary of State for the Home Department* [2022] EWHC 695 (Admin), [2022] 1 WLR 5030, para 135 (unlawful application of blanket and secret policies). Where private information is concerned, if it is used/processed in breach of data protection principles, that will mean that an interference with art 8 is not in accordance with the law (see *AB v Chief Constable of British Transport Police* [2022] EWHC 2749 (KB), para 43).

[1033] *In re Gallagher & others v Secretary of State for Justice* [2019] UKSC 3, [2020] AC 185, paras 17–24. See also the summary of the principles in *R (Bridges) v Chief Constable of South Wales Police* [2020] EWCA Civ 1058, [2020] 1 WLR 5037, para 55.

[1034] *In re Gallagher & others v Secretary of State for Justice* [2019] UKSC 3, [2020] AC 185, para 17.

6.370   In the context of discretionary measures/powers, foreseeability is essentially concerned with the breadth of and constraints upon the exercise of a power. If a power is not properly circumscribed, and not subject to appropriate safeguards, its exercise will not be foreseeable to those affected by it (and they may not be able to adjust their conduct accordingly). As Lord Hughes explained in *Beghal v DPP*, 'safeguards should be present in order to guard against overbroad discretion resulting in arbitrary, and thus disproportionate, interference with Convention rights'.[1035] The ECtHR has emphasized the importance of the law indicating 'with sufficient clarity the scope of discretion conferred on the competent authorities' and the 'circumstances in which and the conditions on which' a power may be exercised.[1036]

6.371   What is required in order for a measure to satisfy the foreseeability requirement is context specific; as the Grand Chamber explained in *S v UK*: '[t]he level of precision required of domestic legislation—which cannot in any case provide for every eventuality—depends to a considerable degree on the content of the instrument in question, the field it is designed to cover and the number and status of those to whom it is addressed'.[1037] When considering whether safeguards or constraints on the exercise of a discretionary power are sufficient, the courts can have regard to evidence of what has happened in practice.[1038]

6.372   The foreseeability requirement is of less relevance where an interference arises not from a discretionary power but the application general, non-discretionary measure to a particular class or category persons/cases. In this kind of case, the focus is on whether the rule/measure is necessary in a democratic society (see further below).[1039]

6.373   What is required for an interference to be in accordance with the law is modified in the context of covert/secret surveillance and other secret measures such as intelligence sharing.[1040] As the Grand Chamber explained in *Big Brother Watch v UK*:

> The meaning of 'foreseeability' in the context of secret surveillance is not the same as in many other fields. In the special context of secret measures of surveillance, such as the interception of communications, 'foreseeability' cannot mean that individuals should be able to foresee when the authorities are likely to resort to such measures so that they can adapt their conduct accordingly. However, especially where a power vested in the executive is exercised in secret, the risks of arbitrariness are evident. It is therefore essential to have clear, detailed rules on secret surveillance measures, especially as the technology available for use is continually becoming more sophisticated. The domestic law must be sufficiently clear to give citizens an adequate indication as to the circumstances in which and the conditions on which public authorities are empowered to resort to any such measures.[1041]

[1035] *Beghal v Director of Public Prosecutions* [2015] UKSC 49, [2016] AC 88, para 32.
[1036] See eg *S v United Kingdom* (2009) 48 EHRR 50, para 95; *Fernandez Martinez v Spain* (2015) 60 EHRR 3, para 117. *RE v UK* (2016) 63 EHRR 2, para 122.
[1037] *S v United Kingdom* (2009) 48 EHRR 50, para 96.
[1038] See eg *Gillan & Quinton v UK* (2010) 50 EHRR 45, paras 79, 84–85; *Iordachi v Moldova* (2012) 54 EHRR 5, paras 51–52.
[1039] See the discussion in *In re Gallagher & others v Secretary of State for Justice* [2019] UKSC 3, [2020] AC 185.
[1040] *Ships Waste Oil Collector v the Netherlands* App No 2799/16, 16 May 2023, paras 44–46.
[1041] *Big Brother Watch v UK* (2022) 74 EHRR 17, para 333.

In this context, the ECtHR has developed a set of bespoke safeguards which must form part of the applicable legal framework in order for interferences arising from surveillance (or the mere existence of such measures) to be in accordance with the law. The 'overarching requirement', the Grand Chamber has stated, is that 'a secret surveillance system must contain effective guarantees—especially review and oversight arrangements—which protect against the inherent risk of abuse and which keep the interference which such a system entails with the rights protected by art.8 of the Convention to what is "necessary in a democratic society"'.[1042] The safeguards required differ depending on whether the measure concerns targeted or bulk surveillance.[1043] But in both contexts a key requirement is that surveillance be authorized by an independent body.[1044]

6.374

(b) *In pursuit of a legitimate aim*

The legitimate aims are set out in Article 8(2): in the interests of national security, public safety, or the economic well-being of the country, for the prevention of disorder or crime, for the protection of health or morals, or for the protection of the rights and freedoms of others. The Grand Chamber has made it clear that this list of aims (or grounds for restricting the right to a private and family life) is exhaustive.[1045] Any restriction or limitation on the rights protected by Article 8(1) must be 'linked to' one of these aims.[1046] However, as the Grand Chamber has noted, the legitimate aims are 'broadly defined and have been interpreted with a degree of flexibility'.[1047] The ECtHR ordinarily deals with this issue summarily (focusing instead on whether the interference is a necessary in a democratic society, with reference to the aim); accordingly, states 'normally have a relatively easy task in persuading the Court that the interference pursued a legitimate aim'.[1048] As such, cases in which the ECtHR has rejected one of the aims relied on (less still held there to be a breach on that basis alone) are rare.[1049] The domestic courts adopt a very similar approach.

6.375

(c) *Necessary in a democratic society*

The ECtHR and domestic courts take different approaches to proportionality, which reflect their different roles. On a domestic level, a court considering a challenge based on Article 8 (or any other qualified right) must determine for itself whether an interference is proportionate.[1050] In doing so, it must give appropriate

6.376

[1042] *Ekimdzhiev v Bulgaria*, para 292.
[1043] In respect of targeted surveillance, see eg *Zakharov v Russia* (2016) 63 EHRR 17, paras 231 and 233–234 (in the national security context) and *Association for European Integration and Human Rights v Bulgaria* App No 62540/00, (2007) paras 75–76 (in the law enforcement context), and for bulk surveillance see *Big Brother Watch & others v UK* (2022) 74 EHRR 17 [GC], paras 361 (in particular) and 348–60.
[1044] *Big Brother Watch & others v UK* (2022) 74 EHRR 17 [GC], paras 336 and 351.
[1045] See eg *Parillo v Italy* (2016) 62 EHRR 8 [GC], para 163.
[1046] ibid.
[1047] *Merabishvili v Georgia* (2017) 45 BHRC 1 [GC], para 302.
[1048] ibid para 295.
[1049] ibid paras 297–302.
[1050] *R (Begum) v Governors of Denbigh High School* [2006] UKHL 15, [2007] 1 AC 100, para 30.

weight to the judgements of the public authority; how much weight will depend on, among other things: the nature of the measure giving rise to an interference (including whether the legislature has struck the balance or an executive body exercising its discretion in an individual case), the context in which the interference arises, and whether or not the public authority gave contemporaneous consideration to the competing rights/interests which are relevant to the proportionality of the interference (if they did not, any *ex post facto* justification offered is likely to attract greater scrutiny from the Court and may be afforded little weight).[1051] Domestically, there is no doctrine of margin of appreciation (see below in respect of the role of the ECtHR) but the domestic courts take a similar approach when assessing the proportionality of an interference; depending on the nature of the measure under challenge, the courts may allow public authorities a 'wide margin' or 'discretionary area of judgment'.[1052]

6.377   The British courts generally assess proportionality with reference to the four-stage test set out by the Supreme Court in *Bank Mellat v Her Majesty's Treasury (No 2)*:

(1) whether the objective of the measure is sufficiently important to justify the limitation of a protected right, (2) whether the measure is rationally connected to the objective, (3) whether a less intrusive measure could have been used without unacceptably compromising the achievement of the objective, and (4) whether, balancing the severity of the measure's effects on the rights of the persons to whom it applies against the importance of the objective, to the extent that the measure will contribute to its achievement, the former outweighs the latter [ie 'whether the impact of the rights infringement is disproportionate to the likely benefit of the impugned measure'].[1053]

6.378   This test applies regardless of whether a challenge is brought to the application of a measure/exercise of a power in an individual case or to a legislative provision itself. But where a claimant challenges a legislative provision, the threshold for establishing that it is not necessary in a democratic society/disproportionate is very high; a court needs to be satisfied that it will give rise to a disproportionate interference with Article 8 rights in 'all or almost all' cases.[1054]

6.379   For its part, the ECtHR examines whether or not an interference is necessary in a democratic society by applying well-established principles. In summary: (a) it is primarily for national authorities to strike the balance between competing interests; (b) but the Court will review their assessment and it makes the final evaluation of whether an interference is necessary and proportionate; (c) in doing so, the Court will afford national authorities a margin of appreciation, the breadth of which (and thus the intensity of the ECtHR's evaluation) depends on, among other things, the particular right(s)/seriousness of interests at stake and the context; and (d) as an important part of its evaluation, the ECtHR will

---

[1051] *Belfast Council v Miss Behavin' Ltd* [2007] UKHL 19, [2007] 1 WLR 1420, paras 37, 46–47; see also *Re Brewster* [2017] UKSC 8, [2017] 1 WLR 519, paras 51–52.
[1052] *R (SC) v Secretary of State for Work and Pensions* [2021] UKSC 26, [2022] AC 223, para 143.
[1053] *Bank Mellat v Her Majesty's Treasury (No 2)* [2013] UKSC 38, [2014] AC 700, paras 20 and 74.
[1054] *Re Abortion Services (Safe Access Zones) (Northern Ireland) Bill* [2022] UKSC 32, [2023] AC 505, paras 13, 19.

examine whether the reasons given by national authorities are 'relevant and suffi-cient'.[1055] The margin of appreciation afforded to states is narrower where the issue is 'crucial to the individual's effective enjoyment of intimate or key rights' and/or where 'a particularly important facet of an individual's existence or identity is at stake'.[1056]

Where the ECtHR is considering a challenge to what it calls a general measure,   6.380
that is, a legislative provision or rule (as opposed to the application of a measure on particular facts), the overarching question is 'whether in adopting the general measure and striking the balance it did, the legislature acted within the margin of appreciation afforded to it'.[1057] The Court addresses that question in accordance with the principles set out in *Animal Defenders v UK*, which focus on the quality of parliamentary and judicial review at the national level.[1058]

Both the ECtHR and domestic courts have accepted that, in principle, it is   6.381
legitimate to adopt general rules/measures which apply to pre-defined situations regardless of the individual facts of each case even if this might result in individ-ual hard cases, these are sometimes referred to as 'bright line rules'.[1059] Where an interference arises from the existence/application of this kind of rule, the Court will focus on whether the rule itself is proportionate, rather than its impact in an individual case.[1060]

F. ARTICLE 9: FREEDOM OF THOUGHT, CONSCIENCE, AND RELIGION

Article 9 protects the rights to hold religious and non-religious beliefs, to change   6.382
those beliefs, and to manifest them in 'worship, teaching, practice and observance', whether alone or with others, in public or in private. In emphasizing the impor-tance of freedom of thought, conscience, and religion, the ECtHR has stated that:

Freedom of thought, conscience and religion is one of the foundations of a 'democratic soci-ety' within the meaning of the Convention. It is, in its religious dimension, one of the most vital elements that go to make up the identity of believers and their conception of life, but

---

[1055] *Vavřička v Czech Republic* (2021) 51 BHRC 241 [GC], para 273.
[1056] *LB v Hungary* App No 36345/16, 9 March 2023 [GC], para 118.
[1057] See eg ibid para 126.
[1058] *Animal Defenders v UK* [2013] EMLR 28 [GC], paras 108–12. See also *MA v Denmark* App No 6697/18, 9 July 2021, paras 140–63.
[1059] See eg *Animal Defenders v UK* [2013] EMLR 28 [GC], para 106 (concerning a ban on paid political advertising on television and radio); *LB v Hungary* App No 36345/16, 9 March 2023 [GC] (concerning the publication of information about people who have not paid their taxes); *In re Gallagher & others v Secretary of State for Justice* [2019] UKSC 3, [2020] AC 185, paras 46–50 (concerning convictions to be disclosed on criminal records certificates); and *A v Criminal Injuries Compensation Authority* [2021] UKSC 27, [2021] 1 WLR 3746, paras 88–89 (exclusion of certain categories of person from a criminal injuries compensation scheme).
[1060] *In re Gallagher & others v Secretary of State for Justice* [2019] UKSC 3, [2020] AC 185, para 50; *R (R) v National Council of Police Chiefs* [2020] EWCA Civ 1346, [2021] 1 WLR 262, para 86.

it is also a precious asset for atheists, agnostics, sceptics and the unconcerned. The pluralism indissociable from a democratic society, which has been dearly won over the centuries, depends on it.[1061]

6.383   The right to hold and change beliefs is often said to be absolute, while the right to manifest one's religion or beliefs can be limited under Article 9(2).[1062] However, there is often no clear distinction between 'holding' and 'manifesting' beliefs, as many religions have an inherent requirement that their followers proselytize. The need to 'bear witness in word and deed' is bound up with the very existence of the conviction itself.[1063] Indeed, without a right to proselytize the 'freedom to change one's religion or belief, enshrined in Article 9, would be likely to remain a dead letter'.[1064] Nonetheless, the distinction between holding and manifesting a belief remains critical to the application of Article 9.

6.384   It is apparent that Article 9 will often overlap with other Convention protections, most notably Articles 10, 11, and 14, and Protocol 1, Article 2. In cases raising issues under both Articles 9 and 10 an applicant's complaints are often considered solely under Article 10 if possible (perhaps because the reach of art 10(1) is clearer than that of 9(1)).[1065]

6.385   Article 9 has not had equivalent impact to some of the other qualified rights, notably Article 10, in Strasbourg or the domestic courts. Claims have often failed either on the grounds that there has been no interference with a 'manifestation' of belief,[1066] or, increasingly, on the basis that such an interference is justified.[1067]

6.386   In domestic law, religious rights are commonly protected by recourse to the Equality Act 2010, which makes discrimination on the grounds of religion or belief unlawful.[1068] The courts have considered the impact of Article 9 on the 2010 Act on a number of occasions. The cases are discussed below.

1. 'Everyone'

6.387   The rights protected by Article 9 are guaranteed to 'everyone' (including 'aliens', regardless of whether they are yet resident in the state concerned, subject of course to the question of jurisdiction).[1069]

6.388   While this primarily refers to individuals, it also encompasses churches and associations with religious or philosophical aims, both in their own capacity and as

---

[1061] *Kokkinakis v Greece* (1994) 17 EHRR 397, para 31. See also *Bayatyan v Armenia* (2011) 54 EHRR 467, para 118.

[1062] See eg *Darby v Sweden* Series App No 11581/85, 9 May 1989, para 44.

[1063] *Kokkinakis v Greece* (1994) 17 EHRR 397, para 31.

[1064] ibid.

[1065] See eg *Paturel v France* App No 54968/00, 22 December 2005; *R (Singh) v Chief Constable of West Midlands Police* [2006] EWCA Civ 1118, [2006] 1 WLR 3374.

[1066] See eg *Ahmad v UK* (1981) 4 EHRR 126; *Copsey v Devon Clays Ltd* [2005] EWCA Civ 932, [2005] IRLR. 811; *R (SB) v Governors of Denbigh High School* [2006] UKHL 15, [2007] 1 AC 100.

[1067] *Leyla Sahin v Turkey* (2007) 44 EHRR 5; *Surayanda v Welsh Ministers* [2007] EWCA Civ 893.

[1068] Section 10 makes religion or belief a protected characteristic for the purposes of the Act.

[1069] *Darby v Sweden* Series App No 11581/85, 9 May 1989.

representative of their members.[1070] The Grand Chamber has held that Article 9 must be interpreted in light of Article 11, and that, consequently, the organization of religious communities must be protected by Article 9, as 'the believers' right to freedom of religion encompasses the expectation that the community will be allowed to function peacefully, free from arbitrary state intervention'.[1071]

2. Freedom of thought, conscience, and religion

(a) Scope of the freedom

Article 9 protects a very broad range of beliefs, both religious and non-religious. 6.389
Belief systems based on personal morality, such as pacifism[1072] and veganism,[1073] are protected by the Convention. The ECtHR has not yet considered whether political convictions, such as republicanism, fall within the scope of Article 9, but the Supreme Court has stated that there is no reason for treating political beliefs any differently.[1074] However, the courts will be more likely to consider political belief as engaging the right to freedom of expression under Article 10.[1075]

In order to attract the protection of Article 9, the thoughts or beliefs must attain a 6.390
'certain level of cogency, seriousness, cohesion and importance'.[1076] In *Campbell and Cosans v UK* the ECtHR distinguished between 'beliefs' (protected by art 9) and 'convictions' (protected by Protocol 1, art 2) on the one hand, and 'opinions' and 'ideas' (protected by art 10) on the other, though in particular cases these categories may overlap.[1077] Whether the applicant can show that he or she holds a belief rather than a lesser conviction, opinion, or idea is sometimes difficult to predict and will turn on the facts of the particular case.

Lord Nicholls in *R (Williamson) v Secretary of State for Education and Employment* 6.391
stated that to obtain the protection of Article 9 a belief must satisfy very modest threshold requirements.[1078] The threshold requirements should not be set a level which would deprive minority beliefs of the protection they are intended to have under the Convention.[1079]

[1070] See eg *X and Church of Scientology v Sweden* App No 7805/77, 5 May 1979. Such churches or associations may be considered 'victims' within the meaning of art 34 if they are non-governmental organizations (NGOs): *Holy Monasteries v Greece* (1995) 20 EHRR 1, para 49.

[1071] *Hasan and Chaush v Bulgaria* (2002) 34 EHRR 55. See also *Kimlya and others v Russia* [2009] ECHR 76836/01.

[1072] *Arrowsmith v UK* (1981) 3 EHRR 218.

[1073] *H v UK* (1993) 16 EHRR CD44, 45; *Jakóbski v Poland* (2010) 30 BHRC 417.

[1074] *RT (Zimbabwe) v Secretary of State for the Home Department* [2012] UKSC 38, [2013] 1 AC 152, para 36. The Supreme Court held that art 9 protects the right to political indifference: see ibid para 42.

[1075] See eg *Redfearn v UK* (2012) 33 BHRC 713.

[1076] *Campbell and Cosans v UK* (1982) 4 EHRR 293, para 36. See more recently *Doğan v Turkey* (2017) 64 EHRR 5, para 68.

[1077] *Campbell and Cosans v UK* (1982) 4 EHRR 293, para 36.

[1078] *R (Williamson) v Secretary of State for Education and Employment* [2005] UKHL 15, [2005] 2 AC 246, para 24 per Lord Nicholls. See also *R (Hodkin and another) v Registrar General of Births, Deaths and Marriages* [2013] UKSC 77, [2014] AC 610, para 57, discussing the meaning of religion in domestic law.

[1079] *R (Williamson) v Secretary of State for Education* [2005] UKHL 15, [2005] 2 AC 246, para 23. See also *Doğan v Turkey* (2017) 64 EHRR 5, para 114.

6.392   The House of Lords emphasized that the court has a limited role in judging the validity of a religion or belief: '[w]hen the genuineness of a claimant's professed belief is an issue in the proceedings the court will inquire into and decide this issue as a question of fact. This is a limited inquiry. The court is concerned to ensure an assertion of religious belief is made in good faith … But, emphatically, it is not for the court to embark on an inquiry into the asserted belief and judge its "validity" by some objective standard'.[1080] It is not, however, oppressive or contrary to Article 9 to require some level of substantiation of genuine belief and, if that substantiation is not forthcoming, to reach a negative conclusion.[1081]

6.393   However, both the ECtHR and the domestic courts have taken the view that not all religions or convictions, however sincerely or deeply held, constitute beliefs in the sense protected by Article 9. The ECtHR found that 'Pastafarianism', or being a follower of the 'Church of the Flying Spaghetti Monster' (which required the applicant to wear a colander on her head at all times and everywhere except at home), did not constitute a religion or belief.[1082] Similarly, Article 9 does not protect pro-hunting views, despite the hunters' view that 'hunting is at the very core of mankind's psyche'.[1083] It does not protect the wish to walk naked in public on the basis of a belief in the inoffensive nature of the human body.[1084] Neither does it protect a critical stance towards vaccination of children, at least where there is no evidence that such a view is religiously inspired.[1085]

6.394   Obliging a person to manifest a belief which they do not hold is an interference with Article 9.[1086] In *Lee v Ashers Baking Company* the Supreme Court held that requiring a bakery to produce a cake iced with a message with which the owners profoundly disagreed would breach their rights under Articles 9 and 10 of the Convention.[1087]

6.395   A belief will not be protected if it falls within Article 17 of the Convention.[1088] In *Forstater v CGD Europe* the Employment Appeal Tribunal held that the level at which Article 17 becomes relevant is 'clearly (and necessarily) a high one. The fundamental freedoms and rights conferred by the Convention would be seriously

---

[1080] *R (Williamson) v Secretary of State for Education* [2005] UKHL 15, [2005] 2 AC 246, para 22 per Lord Nicholls. See also *Khaira v Shergill* [2014] UKSC 33, [2015] AC 359, paras 43–46.

[1081] *Dyagilev v Russia* (2020) 71 EHRR 18, paras 62–63.

[1082] *De Wilde v Netherlands* (2023) 76 EHRR SE4, paras 54–55 (the ECtHR describes the tenets of the faith at paras 20–28).

[1083] *R (Countryside Alliance) v Attorney General* [2006] EWCA Civ 817, [2007] QB 305, para 177, citing *Chassagnou and others v France* (1999) 29 EHRR 615. Confirmed by the House of Lords: *R (Countryside Alliance) v Attorney General* [2007] UKHL 52, [2008] 1 AC 719.

[1084] *Gough v UK* (2015) 61 EHRR 8, para 188.

[1085] *Vavřička v The Czech Republic* [2021] 51 BHRC 241, paras 330–37.

[1086] *Buscarini v San Marino* [1999] 30 EHRR 208.

[1087] *Lee v Ashers Baking Co Ltd* [2018] UKSC 49, [2020] AC 413, paras 49–58. See also the decision of the Privy Council in *Commodore of the Royal Bahamas Defence Force v Laramore* [2017] UKPC 13, [2017] 1 WLR 2752.

[1088] This provides: 'Nothing in this Convention may be interpreted as implying for any State, group or person any right to engage in any activity or perform any act aimed at the destruction of any of the rights and freedoms set forth herein or at their limitation to a greater extent than is provided for in the Convention.' See *Campbell and Cosans v UK* (1982) 4 EHRR 293.

diminished if Article 17, and the effective denial of a Convention right, could be too readily invoked.'[1089] As such Article 17 only covers beliefs 'that would be an affront to Convention principles in a manner akin to that of pursuing totalitarianism, or advocating Nazism, or espousing violence and hatred in the gravest of forms, that should be capable of being not worthy of respect in a democratic society. Beliefs that are offensive, shocking or even disturbing to others, and which fall into the less grave forms of hate speech would not be excluded from the protection. However, the manifestation of such beliefs may, depending on circumstances, justifiably be restricted under Article 9(2) or Article 10(2) as the case may be.'[1090] For further discussion see paragraphs 6.686–6.691 below.

Finally, freedom of religion has been held to include the right not to be required   6.396
to disclose one's religion. In the case of *Sinan Isik v Turkey*, the Strasbourg Court ruled that it violated Article 9 to require a citizen to indicate his or her religion in an application for an ID card or formally ask for the religion box to be left empty.[1091]

(b) *State activities*

The existence of a state church does not, in itself, infringe Article 9, provided the   6.397
system includes specific safeguards for the individual's freedom of religion. States enjoy a margin of appreciation in choosing the forms of cooperation with the various religious communities.[1092] An individual may not be forced to be directly involved in religious activities against his will (unless he has voluntarily joined as a minister of that religion),[1093] nor can the state compel an individual to pay taxes to a church.[1094] However, in *C v UK* the ECmHR found no violation of Article 9 where there is a duty to pay general taxes that are not earmarked for a specific religious purpose, even if the state uses some of the money to support religious communities or religious activities.[1095]

The ECtHR shifted its position on the applicability of Article 9 to conscientious   6.398
objectors in *Bayatyan v Armenia*.[1096] Historically, the Commission had held that Article 9 did not guarantee a right to refuse to perform military service on the grounds of belief because Article 4(3)(b) excluded military service from the scope of forced labour (see further Chapter 4).[1097] In *Bayatyan*, the Grand Chamber argued that 'a failure by the Court to maintain a dynamic and evolutive approach would risk rendering it a bar to reform or improvement'[1098] and held that a new approach was justified by developments in domestic legal systems that permitted alternative forms of national service for conscientious objectors. The Court concluded that

---

[1089] *Forstater v CGD Europe* [2022] ICR 1, para 59.
[1090] ibid para 79.
[1091] *Sinan Isik v Turkey* App No 21924/05, 2 February 2010.
[1092] *Doğan v Turkey* (2017) 64 EHRR 5, para 183.
[1093] *X v Denmark* (1976) 5 DR 157.
[1094] *Darby v Sweden* (1990) 13 EHRR 774.
[1095] *C v UK* (1983) 37 DR 142.
[1096] *Bayatyan v Armenia* (2012) 54 EHRR 15. See also *Savda v Turkey* App No 42730/05, 12 June 2012.
[1097] *Grandrath v the Federal Republic of Germany* 10 (1967) YB 625.
[1098] ibid para 98.

the applicant's two-year prison sentence for failure to perform military service was disproportionate and violated Article 9.

6.399   The House of Lords considered the taxation of religious establishments in *Church of Jesus Christ of Latter Day Saints v Gallagher*.[1099] In a narrow interpretation of the ambit of Article 9, it found no interference with freedom of religion taken with Article 14 where the Mormon church was unable to claim an exemption on local government rates because the church was not open to the public. Lord Scott dissented, arguing that levying taxation on a place of religious worship would be capable of breaching Article 9, and therefore withholding relief from the rates fell within its ambit for the purposes of Article 14. The ECtHR agreed with Lord Scott that Article 14 was engaged but found that the measures were justified.[1100] It did not consider Article 9 in depth, but suggested there had not been an interference with the Church's Article 9 rights because the taxation had only a minor financial impact on the Church.

6.400   The ECtHR has frequently emphasized the state's role as 'the neutral and impartial organizer of the exercise of various religions, faiths and beliefs', and held that this duty of neutrality and impartiality is incompatible with any power on the state's part to assess the legitimacy of religious beliefs or the way in which those beliefs are expressed.[1101] Accordingly, the state's role is to ensure mutual tolerance between opposing groups and, in case of conflict, 'not to remove the cause of the tension by eliminating pluralism, but to ensure that the competing groups tolerate each other'.[1102] Any regulatory functions carried out by the state in relation to religious organizations must therefore be undertaken with complete neutrality.[1103]

6.401   Both the ECtHR and the domestic courts have similarly emphasized that the role of the state and the courts is a neutral one. That there is a debate among religious scholars concerning the historical foundations (or lack thereof) for the applicant association's beliefs, does not suffice to deny the religious nature of those beliefs.[1104] It is not for the Court to express an opinion on sensitive and controversial issues within theology.[1105] In the domestic courts, in a dispute between a local authority and prospective Christian foster parents who opposed same-sex relationships on religious grounds, Munby LJ set out the position of the common law, which mirrors the Convention approach:

[1099] *Church of Jesus Christ of Latter Day Saints v Gallagher* [2008] UKHL 56, [2008] 1 WLR 1852.

[1100] *Church of Jesus Christ of Latter-Day Saints v UK* (2014) 59 EHRR 18.

[1101] *Manoussakis and others v Greece* App No 18748/91, 26 September 1996, para 1365; *Hasan and Chaush v Bulgaria* (2002) 34 EHRR 55, para 78; *Moscow Branch of the Salvation Army v Russia* (2006) 44 EHRR 912, para 58; *Doğan v Turkey* (2017) 64 EHRR 5, para 107. See also *R (Fox) v Secretary of State for Education* [2015] EWHC 3404 (Admin), [2016] PTSR 405, para 30.

[1102] *Serif v Greece* App No 38178/97, 14 December 1999, para 53; *Supreme Holy Council of the Muslim Community v Bulgaria* App No 39023/97, 16 December 2004. cf *Miroļubovs and others v Latvia* App No 798/05, 15 September 2009.

[1103] *Metropolitan Church of Bessarabia v Moldova* App No 45701/99, 13 December 2001. cf the ECtHR's approach to manifestation of belief in *Leyla Sahin v Turkey* (2007) 44 EHRR 5, discussed at para 6.415.

[1104] *Doğan v Turkey* (2017) 64 EHRR 5, para 134; *Case of Ancient Baltic Religious Organisation 'Romuva' v Lithuania* App No 48329/19, 8 September 2021, para 118.

[1105] *Doğan v Turkey* (2017) 64 EHRR 5, para 69.

The starting point of the common law is thus respect for an individual's religious principles coupled with an essentially neutral view of religious beliefs and benevolent tolerance of cultural and religious diversity. A secular judge must be wary of straying across the well-recognized divide between church and state. It is not for a judge to weigh one religion against another. The court recognises no religious distinctions and generally speaking passes no judgment on religious beliefs or on the tenets, doctrines or rules of any particular section of society. All are entitled to equal respect.[1106]

3. Manifestation of one's religion or beliefs

The right to manifest one's religion or beliefs complements the primary right of freedom of thought, conscience, and religion. In deciding whether an applicant's conduct constitutes a manifestation, the ECtHR first identifies the nature and scope of the belief. The ECtHR will ask whether the act is 'intimately linked' to the belief.[1107] If, for example, the belief takes the form of a perceived obligation to act in a specific way, then, in principle, doing that act pursuant to that belief is itself a manifestation of that belief in practice. 6.402

The Strasbourg organs traditionally took a narrow approach to manifestation and afforded close legal protection only where it was in the private sphere of the practice of a religion, and not where the manifestation of faith had an effect on the practices and behaviour of others in the secular world. For example, where a pacifist distributed leaflets to soldiers urging them to decline service in Northern Ireland, this was not an expression of her 'pacifist ideas' as it had a broader aim—to contest British policy in Northern Ireland.[1108] 6.403

The Court has since softened its approach to manifestation and taken a broader view.[1109] The leading judgment on manifestation of religious belief is now *Eweida and others v UK*.[1110] The Court considered four applications by Christian employees in the UK who claimed that their employers had breached their right to manifestation of their beliefs. They had each claimed religious discrimination contrary to the Employment Equality (Religion or Belief) Regulations 2003 in the Employment Tribunal. Ms Eweida was employed by British Airways and wished to wear a cross in contravention of the company's uniform policy. Ms Chaplin worked as a nurse and had been asked by her employer to remove her cross on health and safety grounds. 6.404

[1106] *R (Johns) v Derby City Council* [2011] EWHC 375 (Admin), [2011] FLR 2094, para 41. See also *Ladele v London Borough of Islington* [2009] EWCA Civ 1357, [2010] IRLR 211; *Catholic Care v Charity Commission* [2010] EWHC 520 (Ch), [2010] 4 All ER 1041; *R (E) v The Governing Body of JFS and others* [2009] UKSC 15, [2010] 2 AC 728, para 157; *Macfarlane v Relate Avon Ltd* [2010] EWCA Civ 771, [2010] IRLR 872, paras 23–25; *R (National Secular Society) v Bideford Town Council* [2012] EWHC 175 (Admin), [2012] 2 All ER 1175, para 29.

[1107] *Application 10295/82 v UK* (1983) 6 EHRR 558; *R (Williamson) v Secretary of State for Education and Employment* [2005] UKHL 15, [2005] 2 AC 246; *R (Watkins-Singh) v Governing Body of Aberdare Girls' School* [2008] EWHC 1865 (Admin), [2008] ELR 561.

[1108] *Application 10295/82 v UK* (1983) 6 EHRR 558.

[1109] *R (Williamson) v Secretary of State for Education and Employment* [2005] UKHL 15, [2005] 2 AC 246.

[1110] *Eweida and others v UK* (2013) 57 EHRR 8.

Ms Ladele was a local authority registrar who refused to perform same-sex civil partnership ceremonies. Mr McFarlane was sacked as a counsellor at Relate for refusing to counsel same-sex couples. The domestic courts dismissed their claims under the Regulations on the basis that if indirect discrimination could be established by the actions of the employers, it was a proportionate means of achieving a legitimate aim. Article 9 did not play a significant part in the domestic courts' reasoning.

6.405 The ECtHR applied the established test for a manifestation of a belief, namely whether the act in question was intimately linked to the religion or belief, and found that all four of the applicants had been seeking to manifest their beliefs. The Court did not exclude their manifestations from the protection of Article 9(1) on the basis that they had an effect on others, but took that into account in the proportionality enquiry. The case suggests that the correct approach to manifestation is now a broad one which accepts that a person's sincerely held view about what they must do to manifest their belief will be sufficient to engage Article 9. Indeed the ECtHR has accepted that Article 9 protects the manifestation of religious beliefs which do not amount to 'core' principles of a religion, where the manifestation is a perceived religious duty. In *Hamidović v Bosnia and Herzegovina* the ECtHR accepted that although the wearing of a skullcap for a Muslim man does not represent a strong traditional duty, it has 'such strong traditional roots that it is considered by many people to constitute a religious duty', and was therefore protected by Article 9.[1111] In *SAS v France* the ECtHR accepted that the applicants were not required to 'establish that they acted in fulfilment of a duty mandated by the religion in question'.[1112]

6.406 The domestic courts have considered what constitutes a manifestation of a religion or belief on a number of occasions. In an example of a broad interpretation of manifestation, the House of Lords in *R (Williamson) v Secretary of State for Education and Employment* found that parents of children in a private Christian school who wished teachers to impose corporal punishment upon the pupils were manifesting a religion or belief.[1113] Their Lordships held that the statutory ban on corporal punishment in schools interfered with the parents' rights under Article 9(1) (although the ban was justified under art 9(2)), because the essence of the parents' belief was that it was part of proper upbringing that children should, where necessary, be disciplined in a particular way at home and at school, and so, when they placed their children in a school that practised corporal punishment, the parents were manifesting that belief.

6.407 Like the ECtHR, the domestic courts require a causal link between the belief and the manifestation. For example, in *Campbell v South Northamptonshire District Council*, an appeal against the refusal of housing benefit, the Court of Appeal found no violation of Article 9 or 14 as there was no link between the refusal of housing benefit for members of a religious housing cooperative living on church property and the manifestation of their beliefs.[1114] They could have elected to enter into a

---

[1111] *Hamidović v Bosnia and Herzegovina* App No 57792/15, 5 March 2018, para 30.
[1112] *SAS v France* App No 43835/11, 1 July 2014, para 55.
[1113] *R (Williamson) v Secretary of State for Education and Employment* [2005] UKHL 15, [2005] 2 AC 246.
[1114] *Campbell v South Northamptonshire District Council* [2004] EWCA Civ 409, [2004] 3 All ER 387.

commercial relationship with the church, or have lived communally in property let from a housing association—neither would have required any alteration or diminution of their communal living practices.

In *R (Ghai) v Newcastle City Council* the High Court found that a desire to be cremated on an open-air funeral pyre was a manifestation of Hindu belief because it was 'sufficiently close to the core of one strand of orthodox Hinduism'.[1115] The Court distinguished the position of Sikhs, for whom open-air cremation was simply a matter of tradition rather than of belief. Similarly in *R (Haq) v Walsall MBC* the Divisional Court accepted that the desire to have a raised edge around a Muslim grave to prevent it being stepped on was sufficiently linked to the underlying belief to constitute a manifestation of the belief.[1116]   6.408

Finally, both the ECtHR and domestic courts have drawn a distinction between the manifestation of a religious belief protected by Article 9 and improper proselytism which is not so protected.[1117]   6.409

4. Interference with manifestation of religion or beliefs

The threshold for establishing an interference with a manifestation of belief was historically set very high. In cases pre-dating *Eweida*,[1118] Strasbourg found that no interference will arise when an individual is left with a choice whether or not to comply with his or her religious obligations. Thus, in *Karaduman v Turkey*, in which a Muslim woman challenged a refusal to let her graduate from university unless she was photographed without her headscarf, the Commission found that the fact that the applicant had chosen to pursue higher education in a secular university meant that she had submitted to its rules and no interference was established.[1119]   6.410

The ECtHR made the same point in the context of restrictions on kosher slaughterhouses in *Jewish Liturgical Association Cha'are Shalom Ve Tesedek v France* stating: 6.411

[T]here would be interference with the freedom to manifest one's religion only if the illegality of performing ritual slaughter made it impossible for ultra-orthodox Jews to eat meat from animals slaughtered in accordance with the religious prescriptions they considered applicable.[1120]

Where an individual is subject to the coercive powers of the state, the Court has more readily found an interference with Article 9. Prisoners, for example, are subject to the coercive power of the state and have no choice but to abide by its rules.   6.412

[1115] *R (Ghai) v Newcastle City Council* [2009] EWHC 978 (Admin), [2009] NLJR 713, para 101. The Court of Appeal ([2010] EWCA Civ 59, [2010] 3 All ER 380) allowed the appeal on a different point.

[1116] The claimant's religious belief was that the grave is sacrosanct and stepping on the grave is an offensive religiously prescribed act that must be prevented: *R (Haq) v Walsall MBC* [2019] EWHC 70 (Admin), [2019] PTSR 1192, paras 61–64.

[1117] See *Kokkinakis v Greece* (1994) 17 EHRR 397; and *Kuteh v Dartford and Gravesham NHS Trust* [2019] EWCA Civ 818, [2019] IRLR 716, paras 63–64.

[1118] *Eweida and others v UK* (2013) 57 EHRR 8.

[1119] *Karaduman v Turkey* App No 16278/90, 3 May 1993.

[1120] *Jewish Liturgical Association Cha'are Shalom Ve Tesedek v France* (2000) 9 BHRC 27, para 80.

Failure to permit them to take part in weekly worship,[1121] restricting their access to a priest,[1122] or failing to provide appropriate food[1123] violates their Article 9 rights.

6.413   In the employment field the ECmHR traditionally took a particularly restrictive view of religious rights. In *Ahmad v UK*, it dismissed a complaint in which a teacher demanded that his employers accommodate his obligation to attend religious worship on a Friday. The Commission, finding that he remained free to resign if and when he found that his teaching obligations conflicted with his religious duties, dismissed his claim as manifestly ill-founded.[1124] Similarly, in *Stedman v UK* the ECmHR rejected the complaint of a Christian applicant who had been dismissed for refusing to work on Sundays on the basis that the employee could resign.[1125] In an admissibility decision, *Dahlab v Switzerland*, the ECtHR found that a prohibition on a female teacher wearing a headscarf while teaching in a primary school interfered with the manifestation of her religious beliefs despite the fact that she could in theory have taught at a private school where she could have worn the headscarf.[1126] However, the Court found that the wearing of a headscarf might have a proselytizing effect on young children that outweighed the teacher's right to manifest her beliefs. Therefore, the interference was justified under Article 9(2) and the application was manifestly ill-founded.

6.414   In *Eweida v UK* the ECtHR explicitly disavowed this jurisprudence.[1127] It abandoned its previous stance that there was no interference with an employee's right to manifest her religion if the employee could find alternative employment. Instead, the Court will take that into account in the overall proportionality assessment. The possibility of reasonable accommodation by the employer is therefore an essential part of the proportionality assessment.

6.415   Difficulties around the manifestation of religious belief have also arisen in the education context. In the controversial decision in *Leyla Sahin v Turkey* (the '*Sahin*' case), the Grand Chamber found that a ban on students wearing headscarves at the University of Istanbul interfered with the applicant's right to manifest her beliefs.[1128] This was so despite the fact that the applicant had been able to wear the headscarf at her former university and chose to continue her studies abroad. However, the Grand Chamber held that the ban was a proportionate response to the need to promote secularism in Turkey. The Court took a different approach in *Ahmet Arslan and others v Turkey* in which members of a religious group toured the streets of Ankara in distinctive religious dress.[1129] The Court found that their criminal convictions for wearing religious garb in public were unjustified on the basis

---

[1121] *Kuznetsov v Ukraine* App No 39042/97, 29 April 2003.
[1122] *Poltoratskiy v Ukraine* App No 38812/97, 29 April 2003.
[1123] *Jakóbski v Poland* App No 18429/06, 7 December 2010.
[1124] *Stedman v UK* (1981) 4 EHRR 126.
[1125] *Stedman v UK* (1997) 23 EHRR 168.
[1126] *Dahlab v Switzerland* App No 42393/98, 15 February 2001 [2001] ECHR 42393/98.
[1127] See n 828.
[1128] *Leyla Sahin v Turkey* (2005) 41 EHRR 8.
[1129] *Ahmet Arslan and others v Turkey* App No 41135/98, 23 February 2010. Judgment available in French only.

that dressing as they did in a public place did not pose the same threat to secularism as it did in public institutions.

The leading domestic decision on manifestation under Article 9 remains *R (SB) v* **6.416** *Governors of Denbigh High School* (the '*Shabina Begum*' case).[1130] Contrary to school policy, the claimant wished to wear a 'jilbab', a long coat-like garment that was considered to represent stricter adherence to the tenets of the Muslim faith. She argued that the uniform policy interfered with her right to manifest her religion under Article 9(1).

A majority of their Lordships accepted that Article 9(1) was 'engaged', as wear- **6.417** ing the jilbab was a sincere manifestation of her religious belief, but found that the refusal to allow the claimant to attend school wearing a jilbab did not amount to an interference with her right to manifest her religious beliefs. The case was determined shortly after the decision of the Grand Chamber in the *Sahin* case, in which a ban on wearing a headscarf at university was deemed to constitute an interference. Lord Hoffmann distinguished *Sahin* on the basis that there were other schools that Shabina Begum might have attended where she could wear the jilbab, while all the universities in Turkey imposed a similar ban on headscarves. Notably, this choice-based rationale did not feature as part of the ECtHR's reasoning in *Sahin*, despite the fact that the applicant had been able to wear her headscarf at another university in Turkey and had chosen to continue her studies abroad. The dissenting judges did not eschew this choice-based analysis.[1131] Following *Eweida*, it is now clear that this approach is inappropriate and the Supreme Court will need to reconsider its jurisprudence when it next hears an appeal that raises the issue.

5. Limitations under Article 9(2)

Article 9 is a qualified right, and the right to manifest one's beliefs and convictions **6.418** may therefore be subject to the limitations set out in Article 9(2). It is notable that Article 9 is the only qualified right in the Convention that does not permit the state to interfere with it on the basis of 'national security'.

Any such limitation must meet the threefold test set out in *Sunday Times v UK* **6.419** *(No 1)*:[1132] it must be (a) prescribed by law; (b) in pursuit of a 'legitimate aim' set out in Article 9(2); and (c) 'necessary in a democratic society', which includes a requirement of proportionality.

As under the other qualified rights, the first two limbs of the test are generally **6.420** easily satisfied.[1133] However, in *SAS v France*, a case concerning the ban on wearing face veils in public, the Grand Chamber examined the question of legitimate aim

---

[1130] *R (SB) v Governors of Denbigh High School* [2006] UKHL 15, [2007] 1 AC 100.

[1131] The High Court has applied the approach in *Shabina Begum* to challenges to school uniform policy based on art 9. See eg *R (Playfoot) v Governing Body of Millais School* [2007] EWHC 1698 (Admin), [2007] ELR 484; *R (X) v The Headteacher of Y School* [2007] EWHC 298 (Admin), [2007] ELR 278.

[1132] *Sunday Times v UK (No 1)* (1979) 2 EHRR 245.

[1133] For an example of cases in which the ECtHR found an interference not 'in accordance with law', see *Poltoratskiy v Ukraine* App No 38812/97, 29 April 2003; *Perry v Latvia* App No 30273/03, 8 November 2007.

in some detail.[1134] The French government claimed that the ban served multiple purposes, including public safety, gender equality, and 'respect for the minimum requirements of life in society'. The Court rejected all the government's contended aims with the exception of the notion of 'living together'. It stated:

> The Court takes into account the respondent State's point that the face plays an important role in social interaction. It can understand the view that individuals who are present in places open to all may not wish to see practices or attitudes developing there which would fundamentally call into question the possibility of open interpersonal relationships, which, by virtue of an established consensus, forms an indispensable element of community life within the society in question. The Court is therefore able to accept that the barrier raised against others by a veil concealing the face is perceived by the respondent State as breaching the right of others to live in a space of socialisation which makes living together easier.

The Court concluded that the ban was a proportionate response to the government's aim. The decision strains the boundaries of the concept of the rights of others and sits uneasily with the Court's previous decisions, such as *Eweida v UK*,[1135] in which it supported a tolerant attitude towards an individual's choices.

6.421   The central dispute under Article 9(2) usually concerns the application of the proportionality standard. Certain measures will attract particularly strict scrutiny from the Court. For example, when an applicant complains of a criminal or civil penalty arising as a result of the manifestation of his or her beliefs, the Court will give careful consideration to the government's justification. In *Kokkinakis v Greece*, a criminal conviction of two Jehovah's Witnesses who engaged in door-to-door evangelism was held to have a legitimate aim, but to be a disproportionate response, because no consideration had been given to whether the couple had used improper means to evangelize; hence, there was a violation of Article 9.[1136] Similarly, in *Thlimmenos v Greece* the Grand Chamber recognized that the exclusion of the applicant from the profession of chartered accountancy on account of a criminal conviction for religious objection to military service was disproportionate and in breach of Article 14 taken in conjunction with Article 9.[1137]

6.422   A less-exacting approach is taken to complaints concerning failure to accommodate beliefs.[1138] The ECtHR has consistently emphasized that in societies where several religions co-exist it may be necessary to limit manifestation rights under Article 9(1) in order to reconcile the interests of the various groups and to ensure that all beliefs are respected.[1139] For example, in *Dahlab v Switzerland*, the prohibition on a teacher wearing a headscarf at work was held not to have violated her right to freedom of religion, because it was designed to ensure the religious neutrality of the public education service in a society with diverse religious views and was therefore considered within the state's margin of appreciation.[1140]

[1134] *SAS v France* (2015) 60 EHRR 11.
[1135] *Eweida and others v UK* (2013) 57 EHRR 8.
[1136] *Kokkinakis v Greece* (1994) 17 EHRR 397.
[1137] *Thlimmenos v Greece* (2000) 31 EHRR 411. See also discussion at para 6.577.
[1138] See eg *McGuinness v UK* App No 39511/98, 8 June 1999.
[1139] *Kokkinakis v Greece* (1994) 17 EHRR 397, para 33.
[1140] *Dahlab v Switzerland* App No 42393/98, 15 February 2001.

A majority of the Grand Chamber adopted the same approach in the *Sahin* case, **6.423** upholding the prohibition on wearing headscarves in university on the basis that the principles of secularism and equality were fundamental to Turkish society.[1141] Citing the words of the ECtHR in *Dahlab*, the majority found that the ban pursued a legitimate aim because the headscarf constituted a 'powerful external symbol ... imposed on women by a religious precept' that infringed gender equality and posed a danger to the secular foundation of the Turkish state.[1142] In a judgment notable for its deference to the arguments of the national authorities and courts, the Grand Chamber conducted only the briefest proportionality analysis, finding that the ban was within the margin of appreciation. In a strong dissent, Judge Tulkens stated: 'In a democratic society, I believe that it is necessary to seek to harmonise the principles of secularism, equality and liberty, not to weigh one against the other.'[1143]

The Grand Chamber invoked the margin of appreciation to reach a different **6.424** result in a highly controversial decision concerning the display of the crucifix in Italian public schools.[1144] The Court found that the crucifix was a 'passive symbol' that did not have an influence on pupils and held that the decision whether to display the crucifix was one which fell within the state's margin of appreciation. The case was determined under the right to education in Article 2 of Protocol 1 and Article 9 was not considered in any detail. The Grand Chamber received more state party interventions in this case than in any other before and the decision may have been informed in part by a desire by the Court to avoid inflaming tensions about its role.

In *Eweida v UK*, the Court concluded that the domestic courts' approach to pro- **6.425** portionality in relation to Ms Eweida had been wrong.[1145] The Court of Appeal had accorded too much weight to British Airways' desire to project a certain corporate image. Ms Eweida's cross was discreet, the airline had previously authorized other items of religious dress, such as turbans and hijabs, and since Ms Eweida's case had been heard, it had amended its policy to allow staff to wear the cross. However, the Court found that there had not been a violation of the rights of the other applicants in the case. Revealing the factual sensitivity of the proportionality enquiry, the Court reached a different conclusion in Ms Chaplin's case. The health and safety concerns relating to Ms Chaplin's cross were of a greater magnitude than those in Ms Eweida's case and hospital managers were better placed to assess the legitimacy of the concerns than the courts. In relation to Ms Ladele and Mr McFarlane, the Court held that the state had a strong interest in prohibiting discrimination on the grounds of sexual orientation, and the state benefited from a wide margin of appreciation in determining how to strike the balance between the right to manifest religious belief and the employer's interest in securing the rights of others. Neither Ms Ladele's nor Mr McFarlane's Article 9 rights had been violated by their employers.

[1141] *Sahin v Turkey* (2007) 44 EHRR 5 [GC].
[1142] ibid para 111.
[1143] ibid para 4.
[1144] *Lautsi v Italy* (2012) 54 EHRR 3 [GC].
[1145] *Eweida v UK* (2013) 57 EHRR 8.

6.426   The House of Lords in the *Shabina Begum* case found no interference with the claimant's rights under Article 9(1), but nevertheless went on to hold that, had there been an interference, it would have been justified under Article 9(2).[1146] The refusal to permit the claimant to wear the jilbab was a proportionate response to the legitimate aim of protecting the rights and freedoms of others. The critical factor that appears to have influenced this conclusion was the care with which the school had designed a uniform policy that responded to the range of religious identities in the school community and permitted a wide variety of dress.[1147]

6.427   Other examples of the domestic courts considering Article 9(2) include the following:

- The statutory ban on corporal punishment of children in schools was held to be proportionate given the importance of protecting children.[1148]
- Limiting Article 9(1) rights through nuisance and harassment prohibitions was justified in the interests of public order.[1149]
- The criminalization of cannabis interfered with a Rastafarian's right to manifest his religion, but it was a justifiable limitation under Article 9(2).[1150]
- A ban in Northern Irish prisons on Catholic prisoners wearing Easter lilies to commemorate the Irish 1916 Rising was held to be proportionate and the 'minimum interference' possible in the circumstances.[1151]
- The slaughter of a sacred bullock belonging to a Hindu temple and suffering from bovine tuberculosis was proportionate to meet the needs of public health.[1152]
- The enforced closure of all places in worship in Scotland by regulations made in response to the Covid-19 pandemic was a disproportionate interference with Article 9.[1153]
- An order prohibiting campaigning within a prescribed area around a health clinic that offered abortion was a proportionate interference with Article 9.[1154]
- A finding by Ofsted that it was contrary to the Equality Act 2010 for an evangelical foster agency to adopt a recruitment policy confining applicants to be foster carers to married heterosexual couples was a proportionate interference with Article 9.[1155]

[1146] *R (SB) v Governors of Denbigh High School* [2006] UKHL 15, [2007] 1 AC 100.
[1147] ibid para 33 per Lord Bingham, and para 98 per Baroness Hale.
[1148] *R (Williamson) v Secretary of State for Education and Employment* [2005] UKHL 15, [2005] 2 AC 246.
[1149] *Church of Jesus Christ of Latter Day Saints v Price* [2004] EWHC 3245 (QB).
[1150] *R v Taylor* [2001] EWCA Crim 2263, [2002] 1 Cr App R 519.
[1151] *R v Byers* [2004] NIQB 23.
[1152] *Surayanda v Welsh Ministers* [2007] EWCA Civ 893. See also *Ghai v Newcastle City Council* [2009] EWHC 978 (Admin).
[1153] *Philip v Scottish Ministers* [2021] CSOH 32, [2021] SLT 559, paras 115–17. See, however, *R (Hussain) v Secretary of State for Health and Social Care* [2020] EWHC 1392 (Admin).
[1154] *R (Dulgheriu) v Ealing London Borough Council* [2019] EWCA Civ 1490, [2020] PTSR 79.
[1155] *R (Cornerstone (North East) Adoption and Fostering Services Ltd) v Chief Inspector of Education, Children's Services and Skills* [2021] EWCA Civ 1390, [2022] PTSR 595.

- The policy adopted by a coroner that no death would be prioritized for religious reasons was a disproportionate interference with the rights under Article 9 of Jewish and Muslim people whose religion required the funeral of a deceased person to take place as soon as possible.[1156]

6. Section 13 of the Human Rights Act

During the parliamentary debates on the Human Rights Bill, members of certain churches became concerned that the effect of Article 9 would be to prevent them from selecting employees in a manner consistent with the ethos and beliefs of their organization.[1157]   6.428

The solution adopted by the government is contained in section 13 of the Act. It provides that: 6.429

If the court's determination of any question under the Act might affect the exercise by a religious organization (itself or its members collectively) of the Convention right to freedom of thought, conscience, and religion, it must have particular regard to the importance of that right.[1158]

Lord Nicholls in *R (Williamson) v Secretary of State for Education and Employment* noted that section 13 emphasizes the importance of the Article 9 right, as 'it is one of two Convention rights singled out for special mention, the other being freedom of expression'.[1159]   6.430

Section 13 is really no more than an exhortation to apply the balance inherent in Article 9 properly.[1160] It does not place Article 9 on a 'pedestal, affording it presumptive priority over [other] Convention rights'.[1161] The provision has not featured prominently in the domestic cases concerning Article 9.   6.431

7. Article 9 and the Equality Act 2010

Domestic cases claiming infringement of religious rights are often brought under the Equality Act 2010.[1162] Article 9 informs the interpretation of the 2010 Act.[1163]   6.432

[1156] *R (Adath Yisroal Burial Society) v Inner North London Senior Coroner* [2018] EWHC 969 (Admin), [2019] QB 251, paras 103–12.

[1157] For details see *Hansard*, HL, cols 747–801 (5 February 1998).

[1158] For further discussion of s 13, see Chapter 3, para 3.83.

[1159] *R (Williamson) v Secretary of State for Education and Employment* [2005] UKHL 15, [2005] 2 AC 246, para 19.

[1160] *R (Core Issues Trust) v Transport for London* [2014] EWCA Civ 34, [2014] PTSR 785, para 94.

[1161] *Birmingham City Council v Afsar* [2019] EWHC 3217 (QB), [2020] 4 WLR 68, para 104.

[1162] Claims have also been made for race discrimination, see eg *R (Watkins-Singh) v Governing Body of Aberdare Girls' High School* [2008] EWHC 1865 (Admin), [2008] ELR 561.

[1163] See eg *MBA v Mayor and Burgesses of the London Borough of Merton* [2013] EWCA Civ 1562, [2014] 1 WLR 1501. The Court of Appeal held that the Employment Tribunal was required to read the 2003 Regulations compatibly with art 9 and found that art 9 rendered 'irrelevant' the question whether refusal to work on Sundays was a core component of a person's faith.

6.433   For example, in a series of cases domestic courts have considered Article 9 when deciding whether a philosophical belief is a protected characteristic for the purposes of section 10 of the 2010 Act.[1164]

6.434   Similarly, the domestic courts have considered whether the requirement not to discriminate in the 2010 Act or its predecessor legislation amounts to a breach of Article 9. This issue has arisen in particular in considering the prohibition on discrimination on the grounds of sexual orientation.

6.435   In *Bull v Hall* the Supreme Court considered the role of Article 9 in a claim brought by a gay couple against the Christian proprietors of a bed and breakfast who refused them a double room on the grounds that it offended their beliefs.[1165] The Court set out the potential conflict between the statutory prohibition on discrimination on the grounds of sexual orientation in the Equality Act (Sexual Orientation) Regulations 2007 (the predecessor legislation to the 2010 Act) and the protection for manifestation of religious belief in Article 9. The proprietors complained that the Regulations interfered with their Article 9 right to manifest their religion, but the Court found that the interference was justified by the aim of preventing discrimination. As Lady Hale noted, lesbians and gay men have long suffered an 'affront to their dignity as human beings'[1166] and the ECtHR has emphasized that 'very weighty reasons' are required to justify discrimination on the grounds of sexual orientation.

6.436   That conclusion reflects a line of cases in which the courts have protected the right to be free of discrimination on the grounds of sexual orientation over the manifestation of religious views.[1167]

6.437   In *Lee v Ashers Baking Co Ltd* the Supreme Court considered the tension between the prohibition on discrimination on political opinion in Northern Ireland and the rights protected by Article 9.[1168] The Court held that defendants' refusal to ice a cake with the claimant's message in support of same-sex marriage, with which they profoundly disagreed, was protected by Article 9 (and art 10). As such, pursuant to section 3(1) of the Human Rights Act the Fair Employment and Treatment (Northern Ireland) Order 1998 should not be read or given effect to in such a way as to compel providers of goods, facilities, or services to express a message which with they disagree, unless justification is shown for doing so.[1169]

[1164] See eg *Grainger plc and others v Nicholson* [2010] 2 All ER 253, [2010] ICR 360 (EAT), para 24; *Forstater v CGD Europe* [2022] ICR 1; and *Mackereth v Department for Work and Pensions* [2022] EAT 99, [2022] ICR 721.

[1165] *Bull v Hall* [2013] UKSC 73, [2013] 1 WLR 3741.

[1166] ibid para 53.

[1167] As the decisions of the ECtHR in *Ladele* and *McFarlane* illustrate. See also *R (Cornerstone (North East) Adoption and Fostering Services Ltd) v Chief Inspector of Education, Children's Services and Skills* [2021] EWCA Civ 1390, [2022] PTSR 595.

[1168] *Lee v Ashers Baking Co Ltd* [2018] UKSC 49, [2020] AC 413.

[1169] ibid paras 49–56.

G. ARTICLE 10: RIGHT TO FREEDOM OF EXPRESSION

Freedom of expression has been described as 'the lifeblood of democracy' and it **6.438** enables democracy to 'thrive'.[1170] In *Handyside v UK* the ECtHR described this right as 'one of the essential foundations of ... a [democratic] society, one of the basic conditions for its progress and for the development of every [person]'.[1171] The acknowledged purposes and benefits of this right include promoting: the autonomy and self-fulfillment of individuals across the political, literary, artistic, and scientific spheres; discovery of truth through a 'market place of ideas'; and the proper functioning of democracy by ensuring access to different ideas and opinions.[1172]

Article 10 often overlaps with other rights including the rights to a private and **6.439** family life (art 8),[1173] freedom of religion and belief (art 9),[1174] freedom of assembly and association (art 11),[1175] and the right to vote and stand for office (Protocol 1, art 3).[1176] In many cases these rights are mutually complementary and reinforcing. For example, the protection of private communications and correspondence (under art 8) may be important for the effective exercise of Article 10 rights, and the right to personal autonomy under Article 8 may dovetail with freedom of expression in the context of telling one's own story.[1177] In the context of restrictions on protests and demonstrations, Article 10 is often engaged alongside the right to freedom of association, and may enhance those Article 11 rights. Press reporting on court proceedings can support fair trial rights and expose potential concerns about trial processes and convictions.

Article 10 is, however, often in tension with other Convention rights, including **6.440** the right to a private and family life (speech may, eg, reveal information about the private lives of others or damage their reputations), the right to respect for freedom of thought, conscience, and religion (speech may, eg, attack religious beliefs or practices), the right to property (people may wish to engage in expressive acts on others' property), and the right to a fair trial (the press may reveal information which is prejudicial to proceedings).

[1170] *R v Secretary of State for the Home Department, ex p Simms* [2000] 2 AC 115, para 126 per Lord Steyn. See also *Handyside v UK* (1976) 1 EHRR 737, para 49; *NIT SRL v Republic of Moldova* App No 28470/12, 5 April 2022 [GC], para 185.

[1171] *Handyside v UK* (1976) 1 EHRR 737, para 49.

[1172] *Ziegler v DPP* [2019] EWHC 71 (Admin), [2020] QB 253, para 49.

[1173] This is particularly true of cases concerning surveillance. While the ECtHR has often declined to consider art 10 where it has found a breach of art 8, this is not invariably the case and there is nothing to preclude the domestic courts from considering art 10 in such cases (eg *Wilson v Commissioner of Police for the Metropolis* [2021] UKIPTrib IPT_11_167_H, para 318).

[1174] *Leyla Sahin v Turkey* (2005) 41 EHRR 8.

[1175] See eg *Hashman and Harrup v UK* (2000) 30 EHRR 241; *Rekvenyi v Hungary* (2000) 30 EHRR 519; *R (Laporte) v Chief Constable of Gloucestershire Constabulary* [2006] UKHL 55, [2007] 2 AC 105.

[1176] See eg *Hirst v UK (No 2)* (2006) 42 EHRR 41; *Kudeshkina v Russia* App No 29492/05, 26 February 2009.

[1177] See eg *Abbasi and another v Newcastle upon Tyne Hospitals NHS Foundation Trust* [2021] EWHC 1699 (Fam), [2022] Fam 180.

1. 'Everyone'

6.441 Article 10 states that 'everyone has the right to freedom of expression'. This includes both natural and legal persons, such as the media and non-governmental organizations (NGOs),[1178] as well as entities which trade for profit.[1179] The ECtHR has long recognized the special importance of the exercise of freedom of expression by the press; in an oft-cited passage, the Grand Chamber stated that:

> The duty of the press is to impart—in a manner consistent with its obligations and responsibilities—information and ideas on all matters of public interest. Not only does it have the task of imparting such information and ideas: the public also has a right to receive them. Were it otherwise, the press would be unable to play its vital role of 'public watchdog'.[1180]

6.442 The ECtHR has held that NGOs, academics, bloggers, election observers, and even social media users exercise a similar function when they draw attention to matters of public interest; in doing so these 'social' or 'public' watchdogs are afforded similar protection to the traditional press.[1181] Social media platforms and other providers of forums for expression by third parties are also recognized as making an important contribution to the exercise of Article 10 rights (as they facilitate access to information and debate) and their activities are also protected.[1182]

6.443 Freedom of expression is also enjoyed by state employees, including civil servants,[1183] doctors,[1184] army officers,[1185] police,[1186] and the judiciary.[1187] Restrictions on the exercise of Article 10 rights in or in connection with such roles may be easier to justify because, inter alia, state employees may be bound by obligations secrecy and/or confidentiality, and/or may owe what the ECtHR refers to as a duty of loyalty,[1188] and there may be good reasons for preventing certain categories of public servant from expressing themselves on some issues.[1189] However, the Article 10 case law affords protection to whistleblowers (including state employees) who disclose wrongdoing, and there will sometimes be very strong public grounds for protecting speech even where it involves the disclosure of state secrets or confidential

---

[1178] *Társaság a Szabadsagjogokért v Hungary* [2011] 53 EHRR 3.

[1179] See eg *Autotronic AG v Switzerland* (1990) 12 EHRR 485; *Sunday Times v UK (No 1)* (1979) 2 EHRR 245; *Groppera Radio AG v Switzerland* (1990) 12 EHRR 321.

[1180] *Bladet Tromsø and Stensaas v Norway* (2000) 29 EHRR 125 [GC], para 62.

[1181] *Magyar Helsinki Bizottság v Hungary* (2020) 71 EHRR 2 [GC], para 166; *Sharipov v Russia* (2023) 76 EHRR 25, para 25; *Társaság A Szabadságjogokért v Hungary* (2011) 53 EHRR 3, para 27.

[1182] See eg *Tamiz v UK* [2018] EMLR 6, para 90; *Magyar Kétfarkú Kutya Párt v Hungary* (2020) 49 BHRC 411 [GC].

[1183] *Vogt v Germany* (1995) 21 EHRR 205; *Ahmed v UK* (2000) 29 EHRR 1; *Guja v Moldova* (2011) 53 EHRR 16 [GC].

[1184] *Frankowicz v Poland* App No 53025/99, 16 December 2008.

[1185] *Grigoriades v Greece* (1997) 27 EHRR 464.

[1186] *Rekvenyi v Hungary* (2000) 30 EHRR 519.

[1187] *Wille v Lichtenstein* (1999) 30 EHRR 558.

[1188] *Guja v Moldova* (2011) 53 EHRR 16 [GC], paras 70–71. See also *Hadjianastassiou v Greece* App No 12945/87, 16 December 1992, paras 43 and 45.

[1189] See eg *Rekvenyi v Hungary* (2000) 30 EHRR 519 (concerning restrictions on political activities by police officers).

state information.[1190] The Grand Chamber has formulated criteria for assessing the necessity and proportionality of restrictions on their freedom of expression.[1191]

2. Scope of the right

At the core of Article 10 is the right to express or impart information, but Article 10 also protects the freedom to hold ideas and the right to receive opinions and information.[1192] The right extends beyond the content of expression and also protects the 'means' of dissemination/publication/communication.[1193] Article 10 does not, however, encompass a right to exercise freedom of expression wherever a person wishes; there is no 'freedom of forum.'[1194] That is particularly relevant in respect of private property: a person does not have a right to enter or trespass on private property to express themselves nor is there a right to be invited to speak in any particular place or platform.[1195] Similar reasoning is likely to apply to online spaces or forums.

6.444

(a) Forms of expression which are protected

Article 10(1) encompasses the right to communicate or to express oneself in any medium.[1196] Words, pictures, images, emblems, and actions intended to express an idea or to convey information constitute expression. By way of example, expressive or performative acts as diverse as the use of a 'like' (or similar) button to express (dis) approval for the views of others on social media,[1197] spraying graffiti,[1198] dressing in particular ways,[1199] hanging dirty laundry,[1200] displaying banners,[1201] erecting sculptures of genitalia with photos of high ranking-politicians and prosecutors hanging from them,[1202] pouring paint on statues of historical figures,[1203] plays,[1204] street

6.445

[1190] See eg *Bucur & Toma v Romania* App No 40238/02, 8 January 2013 (available only in French) (concerning the military intelligence service's improper tapping of the phones of journalists, politicians, and businesspeople).

[1191] *Guja v Moldova* (2011) 53 EHRR 16 [GC], paras 74–78.

[1192] *Sunday Times v UK (No 1)* (1979) 2 EHRR 245; *Groppera Radio AG v Switzerland* (1990) 12 EHRR 321; *Open Door Counselling & Dublin Well Woman v Ireland* (1992) 15 EHRR 244; *Delfi AS v Estonia* [2015] EMLR 26 [GC]; *Sanchez v France* App No 45581/15, 15 May 2023 [GC].

[1193] *Magyar Kétfarkú Kutya Párt v Hungary* (2020) 49 BHRC 411 [GC], para 36; *Ahmet Yildirim v Turkey* App No 3111/10, 18 December 2012, para 50; *Standard Verlagsgesellschaft MBH v Austria (No 3)* App No 39378/15, 7 December 2021, para 75.

[1194] *Appleby v UK* (2003) 37 EHRR 38, para 47. In that case there was no positive obligation requiring the state to ensure that a person could exercise their right to freedom of expression—concerning the proposed building of a school on parkland—in a private shopping centre. See also *DPP v Cuciurean* [2022] EWHC 736 (Admin), [2022] QB 888, paras 45–49, 77.

[1195] See eg *R (Butt) v Secretary of State for the Home Department* [2019] EWCA Civ 256, [2019] WLR 3873.

[1196] *Oberschlick v Austria* (1997) 25 EHRR 357, para 57.

[1197] *Melike v Turkey* App No 35786/19, 15 June 2022 (available only in French).

[1198] *N v Switzerland* (1983) 34 DR 208.

[1199] *Vajnai v Hungary* App No 33629/06, 8 July 2008.

[1200] *Tatár and Fáber v Hungary* App Nos 26005/08 and another, 12 June 2012

[1201] *Drozd v Poland* App No 15158/19, 6 April 2023.

[1202] *Mătăsaru v Moldova*, App Nos 69714/16 and another, 15 January 2019.

[1203] *Murat Vural v Turkey*, App No 9540/07, 21 October 2014.

[1204] *Ulusoy v Turkey*, App No 34797/03, 3 May 2007 (available only in French).

performance,[1205] a topless protest at a church altar which also involved miming an abortion using a piece of cow's liver,[1206] a rock band's impromptu performance of a protest song in an Orthodox cathedral,[1207] and even slicing and distributing a birthday cake[1208] have all been found to be forms of expression within the meaning of Article 10(1).

6.446　　The protection conferred by Article 10 is not limited to circumstances in which the person exercising the right is identified—it extends to anonymous expression. The Grand Chamber has recognized the importance of anonymity for protecting and promoting freedom of expression, particularly in the context of online speech.[1209] Anonymity helps to protect individuals against reprisals but there is no absolute right to anonymity. It must be balanced against other rights and interests which may be engaged by anonymous speech, including the protection of rights to private lives and reputation of the subjects of speech.[1210]

(b) Types of speech

6.447　Common categories of expression arising in Article 10 cases include political expression;[1211] artistic expression;[1212] commercial expression;[1213] expression in the academic sphere;[1214] and expression on religious matters.[1215] These categories are examples and there is no need for a claimant/applicant to establish that their speech falls within any of them in order for it to be protected by Article 10.

6.448　　There are two broad types of speech or expression which have long been regarded as being of preeminent importance: political speech and expression on matters of public interest.[1216] Baroness Hale described political speech or expression as being '[t]he free exchange of information and ideas on matters relevant to the organisation of the economic, social and political life of the country'.[1217] Noting that such speech is crucial to any democracy, Baroness Hale stated that this type of speech is 'top of

---

[1205] *H & K v UK* (1983) 34 DR 218.

[1206] *Bouton v France* App No 22636/19, 13 October 2022, paras 30–31 (available only in French).

[1207] *Maria Alekhina & others v Russia* App No 38004/12, 17 July 2018.

[1208] *Ete v Turkey* App No 28154/20, 6 September 2022 (available only in French).

[1209] *Delfi AS v Estonia* [2015] EMLR 26 [GC], paras 147 and 149.

[1210] ibid.

[1211] See para 6.448.

[1212] See eg *Patrício Monteiro Telo de Abreu v Portugal* App No 42713/15, 7 June 2022 (available in French only) (satire on a blog); *Maria Alekhina & others v Russia* App No 38004/12, 17 July 2018 (songs); *Lindon, Otchakovsky-Laurens and July v France* (2008) 46 EHRR 35 [GC] (a novel); *Vereinigung Bildender Künstler v Austria* (2008) 47 EHRR 5 (a painting).

[1213] *Casado Coca v Spain* (1994) 18 EHRR 1 (concerning commercial advertising of legal services); *Belfast City Council v Miss Behavin' Ltd* [2007] UKHL 19, [2007] 1 WLR 1420, para 16 (expression in form of the sale of pornography); *R (British American Tobacco Ltd) v Secretary of State for Health* [2004] EWHC 2493 (Admin) (on tobacco advertising).

[1214] *Kula v Turkey* App No 20233/06, 19 June 2018; *Sorguç v Turkey* App No 17089/03, 23 June 2009.

[1215] See eg *Religious Community of Jehovah's Witnesses v Azerbaijan* App No 52884/09, 20 February 2020; *Murphy v Ireland* (2004) 38 EHRR 13.

[1216] *Bédat v Switzerland* (2016) 63 EHRR 15 [GC], para 49.

[1217] *Campbell v MGN* [2004] UKHL 22, [2004] 2 WLR 1232, para 148. See also Beatson J's detailed review and application of the authorities in *R (Calver) v Adjudication Panel for Wales* [2012] EWHC 1172 (Admin), [2013] PTSR 378, paras 57–64, 80, and 82.

the list', when it comes to speech which is deserving of protection.[1218] For its part, the Grand Chamber has 'attached' the 'highest importance' to political speech.[1219] Public interest speech is a more nebulous concept. The ECtHR has explained that:

[W]hat might constitute a subject of public interest will depend on the circumstances of each case. The public interest relates to matters which affect the public to such an extent that it may legitimately take an interest in them, which attract its attention or which concern it to a significant degree, especially in that they affect the well-being of citizens or the life of the community. This is also the case with regard to matters which are capable of giving rise to considerable controversy, which concern an important social issue, or which involve a problem that the public would have an interest in being informed about.... In order to ascertain whether a publication relates to a subject of general importance, it is necessary to assess the publication as a whole, having regard to the context in which it appears.[1220]

It is clear, however, that 'what engages the interest of the public may not be material which engages the public interest'[1221] and, certainly, the public interest cannot be reduced to a thirst for information about the private lives of others.[1222]   6.449

Public interest speech includes legitimate, robust comment on public figures.[1223] While the ECtHR has never gone so far as the US Supreme Court in *New York Times v Sullivan*,[1224] which requires proof of malice in defamation cases brought by public figures, it affords considerable protection to those who criticize politicians and other public figures (see further para 6.478 and 6.483).   6.450

(c) *Protection of archives and historic speech*

While many Article 10 cases concern prior restraint or restrictions concerning recently published information, the ECtHR has stressed the importance of journalistic and news archives, with the Grand Chamber observing that: 6.451

in addition to its primary function as a 'public watchdog', the press has a secondary but nonetheless valuable role in maintaining archives containing news which has previously been reported and making them available to the public.... Internet archives make a substantial contribution to preserving and making available news and information. Digital archives constitute an important source for education and historical research, particularly as they are readily accessible to the public and are generally free [and] [f]or the press to be able properly to perform its task of creating archives, it must be able to establish and maintain comprehensive records. The Court considers ... that, since the role of archives is to ensure the continued availability of information that was published lawfully at a certain point in time, they must, as a general rule, remain authentic, reliable and complete.[1225]

[1218] *Campbell v MGN* [2004] UKHL 22, [2004] 2 WLR 1232, para 148.
[1219] *Sanchez v France* App No 45581/15, 15 May 2023 [GC], para 146.
[1220] *Magyar Helsinki Bizottság v Hungary* (2020) 71 EHRR 2 [GC], para 162. See also the detailed discussion in *Couderc & Hachette Filipacchi Associés v France* [2016] EMLR 19 [GC], paras 97–103.
[1221] *Jameel v Wall St Journal Europe* [2006] UKHL 44, [2007] 1 AC 359, para 31.
[1222] *Magyar Helsinki Bizottság v Hungary* (2020) 71 EHRR 2 [GC], para 162.
[1223] *Lingens v Austria* (1986) 8 EHRR 407; *Janowwskiv v Poland* (1999) 29 EHRR 705; *Yankov v Bulgaria* (2005) 41 EHRR 854.
[1224] *New York Times v Sullivan* (1964) 376 US 254.
[1225] *Hurbain v Belgium* App No 57292/16, 4 July 2023 [GC], paras 174, 180, 182, 184.

6.452 While there is a strong public interest in the maintenance of archives, there is no absolute right (or duty) to continue to publish/make available on a permanent basis, even if the publication was lawful at the time of it was published. In some circumstances, the rights and interests (particularly the right to a private and family life) of the subjects of articles may outweigh the Article 10 rights in the maintenance of archives.[1226] The rights of people with criminal convictions, who have served their sentences and are seeking to rebuild their lives, are especially relevant in this context and may give rise to a proper basis for the deletion/removal of information referring to their convictions.[1227]

(d) The limits of expression protected by Article 10

6.453 Expression does not generally fall outside the protection of Article 10(1) on the basis of its content. As Sedley LJ said in *Redmond-Bate v Director of Public Prosecutions*: '[f]ree speech includes not only the inoffensive but the irritating, the contentious, the eccentric, the heretical, the unwelcome and the provocative provided it does not tend to provoke violence. Freedom only to speak inoffensively is not worth having.'[1228] Speech which offends, shocks, or disturbs,[1229] is 'divisive'[1230] or 'vulgar'[1231] is still protected by Article 10—the 'pluralism, tolerance and broadmindedness', on which a democratic society depends, demand that speech of this kind be tolerated.[1232] There are, however, limits to the extent to which offensive or damaging expression must be tolerated. As the Grand Chamber has observed:

> Since tolerance and respect for the equal dignity of all human beings constitute the foundations of a democratic, pluralistic society, it follows that, in principle, it may be considered necessary in certain democratic societies to penalise or even prevent all forms of expression that propagate, encourage, promote or justify hatred based on intolerance ... [1233]

6.454 There is an important distinction between expression which is protected by Article 10 but which can be lawfully restricted or sanctioned (provided that is done in accordance with art 10(2)), and expression which falls outside of Article 10 entirely. Where this boundary lies is not always straightforward to discern and it is highly context-specific.

6.455 The ECtHR has identified two broad categories of what it refers to as 'hate speech'. The first concerns speech which is designed to stir up hatred or incite violence and

---

[1226] See eg *Hurbain v Belgium* App No 57292/16, 4 July 2023 [GC]; *NT1 & another v Google LLC* [2018] EWHC 799 (QB), [2019] QB 344.

[1227] See the reasoning in *Hurbain v Belgium* App No 57292/16, 4 July 2023 [GC], paras 194, 233–34; *Mediengruppe Österreich GMBH v Austria* App No 37713/18, 26 April 2022, paras 49, 59, 63; *ML & WW v Germany* App Nos 60798/10 & another, 28 June 2018, para 100; *NT1 & another v Google LLC* [2018] EWHC 799 (QB), [2019] QB 344, para 166.

[1228] *Redmond-Bate v Director of Public Prosecutions* (1999) 7 BHRC 375, para 20.

[1229] *Handyside v UK* (1976) 1 EHRR 737, para 49; *Jersild v Denmark* (1995) 19 EHRR 1; *R (ProLife Alliance) v BBC* [2003] UKHL 23, [2004] 1 AC 185.

[1230] The ECtHR has gone as far as to state that it is incumbent on the press to impart information on divisive public interest issues (*Dmitriyevskiy v Russia* App No 42168/06, 3 October 2017, para 90).

[1231] *Atmanchuk v Russia* App No 4493/11, 11 February 2020, para 47.

[1232] *Perinçek v Switzerland* (2016) 63 EHRR 6 [GC], para 196.

[1233] *Sanchez v France* App No 45581/15, 15 May 2023 [GC], para 149.

employs the right to freedom of expression for ends clearly contrary to the values of/which is aimed at destroying the rights and freedoms in the Convention.[1234] Expression of this kind falls outside the protection of Article 10 entirely and is likely to engage Article 17 (see paras 6.686–6.691), which applies only exceptionally and in extreme cases.[1235] Examples include a book which systematically denied the existence of the Holocaust;[1236] a book which justified war crimes and torture by the French military in Algeria;[1237] statements by members of Hizb ut-Tahrir calling for the violent destruction of Israel, the killing of Israelis, and suicide bombings;[1238] and broadcasts supporting PKK terrorism.[1239]

The second category concerns 'less grave' forms of hate speech; such speech may not include explicit calls for violence or criminal acts but nevertheless incites hatred including by attacking or ridiculing identified groups.[1240] Examples in this category have included comments on a radio show attacking gay people as being sexual deviants,[1241] a politician making racist public statements,[1242] the distribution of homophobic leaflets in schools,[1243] a newspaper article disparaging non-ethnic Russians and suggesting that they were responsible for various societal problems,[1244] and an academic making inflammatory comments about the Prophet at seminars.[1245] Speech in this category does not necessarily fall entirely outside Article 10 but restrictions on it are generally justified. 6.456

The Grand Chamber has given guidance on the factors relevant to the assessment of whether expression should be regarded as hate speech and whether it falls outside the protection of Article 10 altogether. These include: (a) whether a statement was made in what the Court has called a 'tense political or social background'; (b) whether a statement constitutes a direct or indirect call to violence and/or justifies violence, hatred, or intolerance; and (c) the manner in which a statement was made and its capacity to lead to harmful consequences.[1246] 6.457

(e) Protection of information gathering and journalistic sources

The protection of Article 10 extends to the gathering of information, which is regarded as an essential preparatory step in exercising the right to freedom of 6.458

[1234] *Perinçek v Switzerland* (2016) 63 EHRR 6 [GC], paras 114–15; *Lilliendahl v Iceland* App No 29297/18, 11 June 2020, paras 25–26, 34–35.

[1235] There is some case law which suggests that the threshold for speech to fall outside art 10 may be lower. Notably there is a line of authority which suggests that if expression amounts to 'wanton denigation' that will suffice (see eg *Atmanchuk v Russia* App No 4493/11, 11 February 2020, para 47).

[1236] *Garaudy v France* App No 65831/01, 24 June 2003 (available only in French).

[1237] *Orban v France* App No 20985/05, 15 January 2009 (available only in French).

[1238] *Kasymakhunov and Saybatalov v Russia* App Nos 26261/05 & another, 14 March 2013.

[1239] *Roj TV A/S v Denmark* App No 24683/14, 24 May 2018.

[1240] *Lilliendahl v Iceland* App No 29297/18, 11 June 2020, paras 35–37; *Atmanchuk v Russia* App No 4493/11, 11 February 2020, para 47.

[1241] *Lliliendahl v Iceland* App No 29297/18, 11 June 2020.

[1242] *Féret v Belgium* App No 15615/07, 16 July 2009.

[1243] *Vejdeland & others v Sweden* (2014) 58 EHRR 15.

[1244] *Atmanchuk v Russia* App No 4493/11, 11 February 2020.

[1245] *ES v Austria* (2019) 69 EHRR 4.

[1246] *Perinçek v Switzerland* (2016) 63 EHRR 6 [GC], paras 205–08.

expression.[1247] This is particularly relevant in the context of states obstructing journalists from gathering information,[1248] and taking steps to obtain information about journalists' sources or other confidential journalistic material. Journalistic sources (defined as anyone who provides information to a journalist)[1249] are afforded special protection under the Convention, as the Grand Chamber explained in *Big Brother Watch v UK*:

[T]he protection of journalistic sources is one of the cornerstones of freedom of the press. Without such protection, sources may be deterred from assisting the press in informing the public about matters of public interest. As a result the vital public-watchdog role of the press may be undermined, and the ability of the press to provide accurate and reliable information may be affected adversely.[1250]

(f) *Right to access information*

6.459 After a period of uncertainty in the ECtHR jurisprudence, the Grand Chamber has confirmed that Article 10 encompasses a limited right to access information held by the state. *In Magyar Helsinki Bizottság v Hungary* it said the following:

Article 10 does not confer on the individual a right of access to information held by a public authority nor oblige the Government to impart such information to the individual. However ... such a right or obligation may arise ... in circumstances where access to the information is instrumental for the individual's exercise of his or her right to freedom of expression, in particular 'the freedom to receive and impart information' and where its denial constitutes an interference with that right.[1251]

6.460 The ECtHR went on to set out criteria for assessing whether the denial of information by public authorities is likely to constitute an interference with Article 10,[1252] including (a) the purpose of the request for information,[1253] (b) the nature of the information, (c) the role of the person seeking it, and (d) whether the information is ready[1254] and available. The ECtHR has considered the scope and application of this right in a number of cases since *Magyar Helsinki*, reiterating that Article

---

[1247] *Satakunnan Markkinapörssi Oy and Satamedia Oy v Finland* (2018) 66 EHRR 8 [GC], para 128; *Társaság A Szabadságjogokért v Hungary* (2011) 53 EHRR 3, para 27.

[1248] *Szurovecz v Hungary* App No 15428/16, 8 October 2019, paras 52–53 (preventing a journalist from gaining access to a reception centre for asylum-seekers to conduct interviews about living conditions); *Schweizerische Radio- und Fernsehgesellschaft SRG v Switzerland* App No 34124/06, 21 June 2012, para 41 (preventing a broadcaster from filming inside a prison and interviewing a detainee).

[1249] *Telegraaf Media Nederland Landelijke Media BV v Netherlands* App No 39315/06, 22 November 2012, para 86.

[1250] *Big Brother Watch v UK* (2022) 74 EHRR 17 [GC], para 442.

[1251] *Magyar Helsinki Bizottság v Hungary* (2020) 71 EHRR 2 [GC], para 156.

[1252] ibid paras 158–70.

[1253] In subsequent case law this has emerged as the critical criterion, see *Studio Monitori v Georgia* App No 44920/09, 30 January 2020, paras 40 and 42; *Chumak v Ukraine* App No 23897/10, 18 March 2021, para 29; *Šeks v Croatia* App No 39325/20, 3 February 2022, paras 38–41.

[1254] Information will not be regarded as ready and available if the state has to undertake considerable work to collect or to create the information (see eg *Saure v Germany* App No 6106/16, 19 October 2021, para 37).

10 'does not confer, in general and absolute terms, on the individual a right of access to information held by a public authority'.[1255]

This element of Article 10 has not hitherto been recognized by the domestic courts. The leading domestic authority is the Supreme Court's decision in *Kennedy v Charity Commission*,[1256] which pre-dates the Grand Chamber decision in the *Magyar Helsinki* case. A majority of the Supreme Court held that Article 10 did not encompass a freestanding right of access to information as the ECtHR case law on this was not clear and consistent. Subsequent attempts to rely on *Magyar Helsinki* domestically have been unsuccessful, with courts and tribunals considering themselves to be bound by *Kennedy*,[1257] despite recognizing that *Magyar Helsinki* is a 'watershed' case in terms of the reach of Article 10.[1258] Accordingly, as a matter of domestic law, Article 10 does not encompass a right to access information from public authorities;[1259] that is likely to remain the case unless and until the Supreme Court revisits this issue. However, in most cases this is unlikely to make a practical difference because there are qualified rights to access to information under the Freedom of Information Act 2000 and, as recognized in *Kennedy*, at common law. 6.461

3. Interferences with the right to freedom of expression

Interferences with Article 10(1) can take many forms. As the Court of Appeal has observed, the 'Strasbourg court has made clear that there is wide protection for all expressive activities by virtue of a very broad understanding of what constitutes an interference with freedom of expression'.[1260] Broadly speaking, interferences can be grouped into the following categories, which are not mutually exclusive and often overlap: (a) measures which prevent, restrict, or discourage a person from exercising their right to freedom of expression before any such exercise; (b) measures which interfere with the gathering of information and/or the preparation of information for publication/communication to others; and (c) measures which restrict, sanction, or punish expression after it has occurred. 6.462

(a) Measures which prevent, restrict, or discourage the exercise of the right to freedom of expression before the right is exercised
Interferences with Article 10 rights often involve the state taking steps to prevent or restrict the exercise of the right to freedom of expression before it takes place. 6.463

[1255] *Saure v Germany* App No 8819/1, 8 November 2022, para 50.

[1256] *Kennedy v Charity Commission* [2014] UKSC 40, [2015] AC 455.

[1257] *Moss v Information Commissioner* [2020] UKUT 242 (AAC), paras 59, 75; *Dransfield v Information Commissioner* [2020] UKUT 346 (AAC), [2021] 1 WLR 4181, para 80.

[1258] *Moss v Information Commissioner* [2020] UKUT 242 (AAC), para 40.

[1259] *Foreign, Commonwealth and Development Office v Information Commissioner* [2021] UKUT 248 (AAC), [2022] 1 WLR 1132, para 82; *Dransfield v Information Commissioner* [2020] UKUT 346 (AAC), [2021] 1 WLR 4181, para 80.

[1260] *R (Miller) v Humberside Police and the College of Policing* [2021] EWCA Civ 1926, [2022] 1 WLR 4987, para 73.

Among the best known examples are pre-publication injunctions preventing the publication of certain information by the press. Other examples which fall into this category include bans on the publication of a particular newspaper or book,[1261] bans on using particular terminology,[1262] injunctions or orders to preventing the exercise of freedom of expression in a particular geographical area,[1263] preventing the broadcast of an advertisement,[1264] refusing to broadcast a party election broadcast on a publicly funded television channel,[1265] a public university withdrawing permission for academics to hold a conference,[1266] preventing an organization from putting up posters in public spaces,[1267] and preventing an organization from using advertising space operated by a public authority.[1268]

6.464　Measures which involve blocking access to information and publications (stopping it from being imparted) may interfere with the Article 10 rights of (a) the person whose expression cannot be accessed/viewed/heard by third parties, (b) would-be recipients of information, who have a right to receive information and ideas, and (c) a person that hosts or makes the expression available to others. For example, the ECtHR has held that orders blocking access to a website which made third parties' publications available to the world at large interfered with the Article 10 rights of the website operator as well as the public more broadly.[1269] The same was true of Turkey's ban on access to YouTube, in which case the ECtHR noted that blocking orders should be treated as forms of prior restraint.[1270] Measures of this kind constitute an interference with the rights of a website operator even if they are not targeted towards that particular website, as when Turkey blocked all Google Sites URLs and the applicant's site was essentially collateral damage.[1271]

6.465　Measures which do not directly block, prevent, or restrict expression may also interfere with Article 10 rights on the basis that they discourage a person from expressing themselves. Examples include threats of a criminal investigation or

---

[1261] *Fevzi Saygili v Turkey* App No 74243/01, 8 January 2008.

[1262] *ATV ZRT v Hungary* App No 61178/14, 28 July 2020 (concerning an injunction preventing a broadcaster from referring to a political party as 'far right').

[1263] *Annen v Germany* App No 3690/10, 26 November 2015 (concerning the distribution of anti-abortion leaflets in the vicinity of clinics); *Birmingham City Council v Afsar & others* [2019] EWHC 3217 (QB), [2020] 4 WLR 168 (imposing an exclusion zone to prevent, among other things, a person from exercising freedom of expression concerning teaching in the vicinity of a school).

[1264] *Murphy v Ireland* (2003) 38 EHRR 212 (concerning a proposed radio advertisement by a Christian group); *Animal Defenders International v UK* [2013] EMLR 28 [GC] (concerning proposed TV advertisements by an animal rights group).

[1265] *R (Prolife Alliance) v BBC* [2003] UKHL 23, [2004] 1 AC 185.

[1266] *R (Ben-Dor) v University of Southampton* [2016] EWHC 953 (Admin), [2016] ELR 279 (the conference on the challenge posed to international law by the State of Israel was cancelled due to a high risk of disorder).

[1267] *Mouvement Raëlien Suisse v Switzerland* App No 16354/06, 13 July 2012 [GC].

[1268] *R (Core Issues Trust) v Transport for London* [2014] EWCA Civ 34, [2014] PTSR 785 (concerning a refusal to accept an advertisement on buses from a Christian organization expressing views on homosexuality).

[1269] *Vladimir Kharitonov v Russia* App No 10795/14, 23 June 2020, paras 33–36.

[1270] *Cengiz & others v Turkey* App Nos 48226/10 & another, 1 December 2015, para 62.

[1271] *Ahmet Yildirim v Turkey* App No 3111/10, 18 December 2012, paras 51–55.

prosecution,[1272] or the police warning someone that speech would be unlawful (or ill-advised) if it goes ahead/continues.[1273]

(b) Measures which interfere with the gathering and preparation of information for publication

States sometimes take steps which, directly or indirectly, undermine or disrupt the process of gathering and preparing information for publication or broadcast to others. Common measures of this sort include production orders requiring journalists to reveal information about their sources and/or confidential journalistic material; searches of premises for such material;[1274] surveillance measures intended to uncover (or where this is a high probability of uncovering) information about journalistic sources or confidential journalistic material;[1275] seizures of journalistic material;[1276] orders compelling a media organization to hand over footage shot as part of the journalistic process;[1277] directions to cease information gathering/reporting on a particular event;[1278] and the arrest and/or detention of a journalist while they are performing journalistic activities.[1279] The seizure and/or destruction of manuscripts or journalistic material are particularly stark examples of a measure which interferes with steps preparatory to publication.[1280]

6.466

(c) Measures which restrict, sanction, or punish expression after the right to freedom of expression has been exercised

Interferences with freedom of expression which take place after information has been published or communicated take many forms. The ECtHR and domestic courts have stressed that retrospective measures not only impact on the subject of the measure but may have a chilling effect on freedom of speech that deters future public discussion of the subject in issue.[1281]

6.467

After-the-event restrictions, sanctions, or penalties relating to a person's exercise of the right to freedom of expression include arrest and detention;[1282]

6.468

[1272] *Altuğ Taner Akçam v Turkey* (2011) 62 EHRR 12.

[1273] *R (Leigh) v Chief Commissioner of Police for the Metropolis* [2022] EWHC 527 (Admin), [2022] 1 WLR 3141 (a warning about a planned vigil following the murder of Sarah Everard); *R (Miller) v College of Policing* [2021] EWCA Civ 1926, [2022] 1 WLR 4987 (a warning about expressing views online on transgender issues).

[1274] *Roemen and Schmit v Luxembourg* App No 51772/99, 25 February 2003.

[1275] *Big Brother Watch & others v UK* (2022) 74 EHRR 17 [GC], paras 448–49.

[1276] *R (Miranda) v Secretary of State for the Home Department* [2016] EWCA Civ 6, [2016] 1 WLR 1505 (concerning the seizure of journalistic material—which he had obtained from Edward Snowden—during a port stop).

[1277] *Nordisk Film & TV A/S v Denmark* App No 40485/02, 8 December 2005.

[1278] *Pentikäinen v Finland* (2017) 65 EHRR 21 [GC], para 83.

[1279] ibid.

[1280] See eg *Zayidov v Azerbaijan (No 2)* App No 5386/10, 24 March 2022.

[1281] See eg *Jersild v Denmark* (1995) 19 EHRR 1, para 44; *Jameel and others v Wall Street Journal Europe* [2006] UKHL 44, [2007] 1 AC 359, para 154.

[1282] See eg *Bryan & another v Russia* App No 22515/14, 27 June 2023 (concerning the arrest and detention of Greenpeace activists protesting against the extraction of oil in Arctic waters).

prosecution,[1283] the imposition of criminal liability,[1284] and sentences (including fines and terms of imprisonment); the imposition of civil liability (including for defamation, breaches of privacy, confidentiality and data protection law, and harassment) and associated damages awards[1285] and injunctive relief (preventing the re-publication/continuing publication of the information in issue); the imposition of costs orders in criminal or civil proceedings;[1286] the suspension or withdrawal of a publication from sale;[1287] orders to take down, block or alter (eg by anonymizing people) publications;[1288] and requirements that a book or other publication include warning labels relating to its content.[1289]

6.469   Other measures in this category include a person's removal from a particular place where they have exercised their freedom of expression;[1290] bans on future access to particular spaces or buildings;[1291] public authorities subjecting employees (such as judges, civil servants, and academics) to detriment or dismissing them in connection with speech;[1292] regulators suspending or striking off regulated professionals on the basis of views they have expressed;[1293] and public education institutions removing students from courses on fitness to practise grounds based on views they have expressed.[1294]

6.470   Interferences in this category also include surveillance and other information gathering, and the retention of information collected, where the information collected relates to a person's expression or views. As the Investigatory Powers Tribunal stated in *Wilson*: '[t]he right to hold opinions and exchange information and ideas must ... include the right to do so without attracting the attention of the police and being monitored and placed under surveillance'.[1295] For its part, the ECtHR has accepted that the storage in secret police files of personal data relating to, inter alia, political opinions constitutes an interference with the subject's Article 10 rights.[1296]

[1283] In the UK, art 10 rights in play may be relevant to a prosecutor's exercise of their discretion as to whether or not prosecution would be in the public interest which forms part of the Full Code Test applied when making such decisions.

[1284] See further paras 6.486-6.489.

[1285] *Tolstoy Miloslavsky v UK* (1995) 20 EHRR 442; see also *SIC—Sociedade Independente De Comunicação v Portugal* (2022) 74 EHRR 27.

[1286] *MGN v UK* [2011] 1 Costs LO 84; *Flood v Times Newspapers (No 2)* [2017] UKSC 33, [2017] 1 WLR 1415.

[1287] *Macatė v Lithuania* App No 61435/19, 23 January 2023 [GC], para 180.

[1288] *Hurbain v Belgium* App No 57292/16, 4 July 2023 [GC], para 167.

[1289] *Macatė v Lithuania* App No 61435/19, 23 January 2023 [GC], para 18 (this occurred in respect of a children's book which included references to same-sex relationships).

[1290] *Sharipov v Russia* (2023) 76 EHRR 25 (concerning the removal of an election monitor who was gathering information through filming).

[1291] *Drozd v Poland* App No 15158/19, 6 April 2023.

[1292] *Wille v Lichtenstein* (1999) 30 EHRR 558 [GC]; *Mahi v Belgium* App No 57462/19, 3 September 2020 (available only in French).

[1293] See eg *Adil v General Medical Council* [2023] EWHC 797 (Admin).

[1294] See eg *R (Ngole) v University of Sheffield* [2019] EWCA Civ 1127, [2019] ELR 443 (concerning the removal of a student studying social work owing to remarks made about homosexuality on social media).

[1295] *Wilson v Commissioner of Police for the Metropolis* [2021] UKIPTrib IPT_11_167_H, para 333. See also *R (Miller) v College of Policing* [2021] EWCA Civ 1926, [2022] 1 WLR 4987, paras 73, 76.

[1296] *Segerstedt-Wiberg & others v Sweden* (2007) EHRR 2, para 107.

The imposition of liability and/or penalties/sanctions on the host of other peo-   6.471
ple's speech constitutes an interference with the host's own Article 10 rights. This
issue has generated a significant body of case law in the context of web-based speech
including, for example: third party comments on an article published on a news
website;[1297] third party comments on a person's Facebook wall on which hate speech
was posted;[1298] and third party breaches of copyright using the file sharing platform
Pirate Bay.[1299] An order compelling a platform to reveal the details of people who
have posted comments anonymously may engage the platform provider's Article 10
rights, especially where the platform or host is a media organization. The ECtHR
has explained that this interference arises indirectly as orders of this kind could
'deter users/readers from contributing to debate and therefore lead to a chilling
effect among users posting in forums in general' and this, in turn, affects platform/
host's right to freedom of expression which extends to inviting users to comment
on their journalistic work.[1300] The Article 10 rights of a communications service
provider will also be engaged by the imposition of sanctions for providing a means
of communication which enables others to impart and receive information.[1301]

(d) Chilling effects
A thread which runs through all these categories of interference is the notion of   6.472
a chilling effect. As Dame Victoria Sharp P emphasized in *R (Miller) v College of
Policing*, '[t]he concept of a chilling effect in the context of freedom of expression
is an extremely important one'. Warby LJ has explained this concept and its role in
the engagement of Article 10 in the following terms:

> The notion of interference goes beyond conduct which directly prevents a person from exercis-
> ing their rights, such as censorship, confiscation of written material or the apparatus required
> to publish that material, or physically preventing people from meeting one another. It extends
> to the imposition of sanctions after the event and encompasses conduct which has a tendency to
> 'chill' the exercise of the right in question.[1302]

The ECtHR asks whether the measure is 'capable of discouraging the participa-   6.473
tion' in debates over matters of legitimate public concern or similar expression.[1303]
There is no need for an applicant to prove that, as a matter of fact, a particular
measure has had this effect.[1304] The engagement of Article 10 on this basis is not
limited to journalistic activity, it is 'equally important when considering the rights
of private citizens to express their views within the limits of the law'.[1305]

[1297] *Delfi AS v Estonia* [2015] EMLR 26 [GC].
[1298] *Sanchez v France* App No 45581/15, 15 May 2023 [GC].
[1299] *Neij and Sunde Kolmisoppi v Sweden (dec.)* App No 40397/12, 20 June 2012.
[1300] *Standard Verlagsgesellschaft MBH v Austria (No 3)* App No 39378/15, 7 December 2021, para 74.
[1301] *Magyar Kétfarkú Kutya Párt v Hungary* (2020) 49 BHRC 411 [GC], para 37.
[1302] *R (Leigh) v Chief Commissioner of Police for the Metropolis* [2022] EWHC 527 (Admin), [2022] 1
WLR 3141, para 9.
[1303] See eg *SIC—Sociedade Independente De Comunicação v Portugal* (2022) 74 EHRR 27, para 69; *Jersild
v Denmark* (1995) 19 EHRR 1, para 35.
[1304] See eg *MGN v United Kingdom* [2011] 1 Costs LO 84, para 201.
[1305] *R (Miller) v College of Policing* [2021] EWCA Civ 1926, [2022] 1 WLR 4987, para 68.

4. Justification for interferences with the right to freedom of expression

(a) *Exceptions under Article 10(2)*

6.474   Article 10 is a qualified right and its exercise may be restricted or limited in accordance with the requirements of Article 10(2). Article 10(2) contains a list of exceptions to the right to freedom of expression guaranteed by Article 10(1). The only legitimate aims for restrictions on freedom of expression are enumerated in Article 10(2), namely:

(a) national security, territorial integrity, or public safety;

(b) prevention of disorder or crime;

(c) protection of health or morals;

(d) protection of the reputation or rights of others;

(e) prevention of the disclosure of information received in confidence

(f) maintaining the authority and impartiality of the judiciary.

6.475   Save for restrictions which can be imposed through licensing of broadcasting, television, and cinema (see paras 6.491-6.496), these exceptions are exhaustive and should be interpreted narrowly.[1306] The Grand Chamber has stated consistently that they must be 'construed strictly, and the need for any restrictions must be established convincingly',[1307] and when cases reach the ECtHR, the reasons given by states for restricting the right to freedom of expression must be 'relevant and sufficient'.[1308] As with other qualified rights, an interference will not be compatible with Article 10 unless it is (a) prescribed by law; (b) in pursuit of a legitimate aim;[1309] and (c) necessary in a democratic society (which means that it must respond to a pressing need and be proportionate to the aim pursued). The applicable principles are considered in detail at paras 6.365-6.381.[1310]

6.476   Article 10(2) states that the exercise of the freedoms in Article 10(1) 'carries with it duties and responsibilities', which is a phrase that does not appear in the other qualified rights. This does not impose any additional test or stage in the Article 10(2) analysis. However, the ECtHR's case law has made reference to this language when considering the necessity and proportionality of interferences with freedom of expression on the basis of the rights of others. The Grand Chamber has stated that the 'duties and responsibilities' assume particular significance when expression bears on the rights of others, for example by attacking their reputation or revealing private information; the ECtHR has stressed that journalists should 'act in

---

[1306] *Magyar Kétfarkú Kutya Párt v Hungary* (2020) 49 BHRC 411 [GC], para 40.

[1307] *Von Hannover v Germany (No 2)* (2012) 55 EHRR 15 [GC], para 101.

[1308] See eg *Lingens v Austria* (1986) 8 EHRR 407, para 40.

[1309] It is rare for an interference to be held to be unlawful on the basis that it did not pursue a legitimate aim but in a high-profile case, the Grand Chamber held that restricting access to children's books referring to same-sex relationships based solely on considerations of sexual orientation did not pursue any legitimate aim (*Macatè v Lithuania* App No 61435/19, 23 January 2023 [GC], paras 215–16).

[1310] See in the specific context of art 10: *Magyar Kétfarkú Kutya Párt v Hungary* (2020) 49 BHRC 411 [GC], paras 93–98; *Pentikäinen v Finland* (2017) 65 EHRR 21 [GC], para 87; *Sanchez v France* App No 45581/15, 15 May 2023 [GC], paras 124–28.

good faith and on an accurate factual basis' and in 'accordance with the tenets of responsible journalism'.[1311] Similarly, in the context of speech concerning religion or belief, the ECtHR has stated that these duties and responsibilities include 'a duty to avoid as far as possible an expression that is, in regard to objects of veneration, gratuitously offensive to others and profane'.[1312]

A variety of considerations will be relevant to the assessment of whether an inter- **6.477** ference with freedom of expression is necessary in a democratic society, and the importance and weight attached to these will vary depending on the legitimate aim relied on to justify an interference. Considerations of general relevance include: the nature and content of the expression; whether the expression contributes to a debate of general interest; the impact or potential impact of the expression (including whether it justifies or incites violence or other criminality); the medium employed by the speaker/publisher to communicate the information in question; the conduct of the speaker/publisher (including in respect of the gathering of information);[1313] the nature and severity of any restriction, sanction, or penalty imposed;[1314] the importance of the legitimate aim relied on to restrict freedom of expression; and whether less restrictive means would achieve that aim.[1315]

The nature and content of the expression, and whether it contributes to a debate **6.478** of general interest, are particularly important factors when determining whether any restriction is necessary in a democratic society. An important theme in the Article 10 case law is that there is little scope for states to restrict political and public interest speech and they enjoy a narrow margin of appreciation when challenges to restrictions on such speech reach the ECtHR (see further para 6.483).[1316]

The ECtHR will often take into account the medium or format of the publication **6.479** when assessing whether an interference is proportionate because that has implications for its impact.[1317] The ECtHR has taken the view that audio-visual media has a more immediate and powerful impact than other forms of media.[1318] Information published on the internet is regarded by the ECtHR as posing a higher risk of harm to the rights of others than information published in the print media. That is primarily due to the ease with which information can be transmitted to very large numbers of people and will remain readily accessible, including through the use of search engines.[1319]

[1311] See eg *Lindon v France* (2008) 46 EHRR 35 [GC], para 67; *Couderc & Hachette Filipacchi Associés v France* [2016] EMLR 19 [GC], para 89; *Bédat v Switzerland* (2016) 63 EHRR 15 [GC], para 50; *Pentikäinen v Finland* (2017) 65 EHRR 21 [GC], paras 90–91.

[1312] *Rabczewska v Poland* App No 8257/13, 15 September 2022, para 47.

[1313] *Stoll v Switzerland* (2008) 47 EHRR 59 [GC], paras 112, 140–41; *Pentikäinen v Finland* (2017) 65 EHRR 21 [GC], paras 90–91; *Bédat v Switzerland* (2016) 63 EHRR 15 [GC], paras 56–57.

[1314] *Bédat v Switzerland* (2016) 63 EHRR 15 [GC], para 79.

[1315] *Perinçek v Switzerland* (2016) 63 EHRR 6 [GC], para 273.

[1316] *Bédat v Switzerland* (2016) 63 EHRR 15 [GC], para 49.

[1317] *NIT SRL v Republic of Moldova* App No 28470/12, 5 April 2022, para 182.

[1318] See eg *Delfi AS v Estonia* [2015] EMLR 26 [GC], para 134; *Gunduz v Turkey* App No 35071/97, 4 December 2003; *Murphy v Ireland* (2003) 38 EHRR 212; *R (Animal Defenders International) v Secretary of State for Culture, Media and Sport* [2008] UKHL 15, [2008] 1 AC 1312.

[1319] *Delfi AS v Estonia* [2015] EMLR 26 [GC], para 133; *Sanchez v France* App No 45581/15, 15 May 2023 [GC], paras 161–62; *ML & WW v Germany* App Nos 60798/10 & another, 28 June 2018, para 91.

(i) Prior restraint

6.480   In relation to the nature and severity of an interference, the ECtHR has long emphasized that prior restraints call for the 'most careful scrutiny' by the court.[1320] Such restrictions will only be justified in exceptional circumstances.[1321] News is regarded as a 'perishable commodity',[1322] and the courts have taken this into account in rejecting pre-publication delays or restrictions. Similar considerations apply to any speech dealing with 'topical' issues.[1323] In *Sunday Times v UK (No 1)* the ECtHR recognized that delaying the publication of news may amount in practice to it never being published, as news quickly becomes stale and delay would deprive it of its interest and value.[1324]

(ii) Protection of the rights of others and conflicts with other Convention rights

6.481   Among the most common aims for restricting freedom of expression is the protection of the rights of others. Domestically, this occurs primarily in the context of civil causes of action, such as the torts of libel and misuse of private information (and remedies therein), which can be brought in respect of exercises of expression. Causes of action designed to protect qualified rights in the face of exercises of freedom of expression either incorporate an assessment of the strength of the right to freedom of expression in respect of the speech in issue[1325] and/or have defences based on freedom of speech.[1326] In cases where Article 10 conflicts with another Convention right, the ECtHR will assess whether a 'fair balance' has been struck between the competing rights and interests at the national level.[1327] The rights of others are also protected through the criminal law including, for example, offences under the Communications Act 2003, the Malicious Communications Act 1988, the Public Order Act 1986, the Protection from Harassment Act 1997, and the law of contempt.

6.482   The most common conflict arises between the right to freedom of expression and the right to respect for private and family life (Article 8), which includes a right to reputation (see para 6.314). Where Articles 8 and 10 come into conflict, the approach which applied is that set out above (paras 6.310-6.313). The Grand

---

[1320] See eg *Ahmet Yildirim v Turkey* App No 3111/10, 18 December 2012, para 47.

[1321] *The Observer and The Guardian v UK* (1991) 14 EHRR 153; *Sunday Times v UK (No 2)* (1991) 14 EHRR 229; *Cumpana and Mazare v Romania* App No 33348/96, 17 December 2004.

[1322] *The Observer and The Guardian v UK* (1991) 14 EHRR 153, para 60.

[1323] *Ahmet Yildirim v Turkey* App No 3111/10, 18 December 2012, para 47.

[1324] *Sunday Times v UK (No 1)* (1979) 2 EHRR 245.

[1325] As is the case with the tort of misuse of private information, the second stage of which requires a balancing of privacy rights with, inter alia, the art 10 rights of the publisher/publishees.

[1326] For example, defamation law includes free speech protections by (a) requiring that claimants establish that the publication of a statement has caused or is likely to cause serious harm to their reputation as a condition of actionability (Defamation Act 2013, s 1), and (b) through statutory and common law defences including truth, honest opinion, and public interest defence (Defamation Act 2013, ss 2–4); the law of confidence incorporates a public interest and/or iniquity defence; and the statutory tort of harassment is accompanied by statutory defences applicable, inter alia, to courses of conduct pursued for the prevention and detection of crime, and those which were reasonable in all the circumstances (Protection from Harassment Act 1997, s 1(3)).

[1327] See eg *Couderc & Hachette Filipacchi Associés v France* [2016] EMLR 19 [GC].

Chamber has stated that the outcome before the ECtHR should not vary depending on whether an application is brought (under art 8) by the person whose rights were affected by the expression and who complains that the national authorities have not protected or upheld those rights, or is brought (under art 10) by the person who made the statement giving rise to civil (and in some cases criminal) liability. That is because these rights 'deserve equal respect'.[1328]

Where a restriction on Article 10 rights is based on the protection of the rights   6.483
of others, the status, role, and function of the person whose rights are affected by the expression are important.[1329] The ECtHR has consistently held that the limits of acceptable criticism are wider where the subject is a politician, or other public figure, as compared to a 'private citizen'. That is because they knowingly lay themselves 'open to close scrutiny of [their] every word and deed by both journalists and the public at large, and … must consequently display a greater degree of tolerance'.[1330] That is the case regardless of whether or not such comments are politely expressed, unless they are 'gratuitous personal attacks'[1331] and it may extend not only to value judgements/expression of opinion but also to statements of fact which turn out to be inaccurate.[1332] Those observations have frequently been made in respect of politicians but apply equally to others involved in public life.[1333] This principle extends to public servants (including the police and security forces) when acting in their official capacity, who are expected to 'display a particularly high degree of tolerance to offensive speech, unless such inflammatory speech is likely to provoke imminent unlawful actions'.[1334]

Conflicts also arise between freedom of expression and freedom of religion and   6.484
belief (art 9). In this context, the ECtHR has emphasized that those 'who choose to exercise the freedom to manifest their religion under Article 9 of the Convention, irrespective of whether they do so as members of a religious majority or a minority, therefore cannot expect to be exempt from criticism. They must tolerate and accept the denial by others of their religious beliefs and even the propagation by others of doctrines hostile to their faith'.[1335] But there are limits to this and '[w]here such expressions go beyond the limits of a critical denial of other people's religious beliefs and are likely to incite religious intolerance, for example in the event of an improper

---

[1328] *Perinçek v Switzerland* (2016) 63 EHRR 6 [GC], para 198. The ECtHR affords the domestic courts a margin of appreciation and will not readily interfere, particularly if those courts have undertaken any balancing exercise in accordance with ECtHR case law.

[1329] *Hurbain v Belgium* App No 57292/16, 4 July 2023 [GC], para 226.

[1330] *Lindon v France* (2008) 46 EHRR 35, para 46; *Lingens v Austria* (1986) 8 EHRR 407, para 42.

[1331] *Oberschlick v Austria* (1997) 25 EHRR 357; *De Haes v Belgium* (1997) 25 EHRR 1; *R (Calver) v Adjudication Panel for Wales* [2012] EWHC 1172 (Admin), [2013] PTSR 378, para 58.

[1332] *Banks v Cadwalladr* [2022] EWHC 1417 (QB), [2022] 1 WLR 5236, para 129.

[1333] Such figures can also include, eg, businesspeople (*Verlagsgruppe News GMBH v Austria (No 2)* App No 10520/02, 14 December 2006; religious leaders (*Mahi v Belgium* App No 57462/19, 3 September 2020); and prominent journalists/editors (*Zybertowicz v Poland* App No 59138/10, 17 January 2017).

[1334] *Savva Terentyev v Russia* App No 10692/09, 28 August 2018. See also *Chkhartishvili v Georgia* App No 31349/20, 11 May 2023, para 56.

[1335] *ES v Austria* (2019) 69 EHRR 4, para 42.

or even abusive attack on an object of religious veneration, a State may legitimately consider them to be incompatible with respect for the freedom of thought, conscience and religion and take proportionate restrictive measures'.[1336]

6.485   The rights of others are not confined to rights encompassed within the Convention and a state can in principle rely on other rights which may be recognized in national law. However, it is more difficult to justify an interference with Article 10 rights on this basis, requiring 'indisputable imperatives', than on the basis of a Convention right.[1337]

(iii) Criminal liability

6.486   The ECtHR requires particularly convincing justification for criminal convictions arising from acts of expression, which are among the most serious forms of interference with freedom of expression.[1338] A finding of criminal liability is considered to be a serious interference regardless of the penalty imposed as a result of that liability.[1339] When assessing the proportionality of criminal convictions and penalties, the ECtHR has often factored in the chilling effect that these interferences have on others wishing to exercise their freedom of expression in respect of similar issues.[1340] There have, however, been many cases in which criminal convictions (including for defamation) have been held to be necessary and proportionate.[1341]

6.487   When considering criminal liability (and sanctions on the basis of that liability) the courts must apply the criminal law in a manner that ensures compliance with Article 10 rights. That extends to the interpretation of constituent elements of offences.[1342] In the context of prosecutions arising from expression/speech, there is extensive case law concerning the circumstances in which the prosecution must prove, and the court be satisfied, that conviction would be a proportionate interference with the right to freedom expression. This is a complex area in which the law is evolving and a full discussion of this is beyond the scope of this book.

6.488   In summary, the Supreme Court has held that this is not required in respect of all offences,[1343] but when cases reach Strasbourg the ECtHR will generally assess the

---

[1336] ibid.

[1337] *Chassagnou v France* (1999) 29 EHRR 615 [GC], para 113.

[1338] *Kyprianou v Cyprus* (2007) 44 EHRR 27; *Perinçek v Switzerland* (2016) 63 EHRR 6 [GC], para 273.

[1339] See eg *Gaspari v Armenia (No 2)* App No 67783/13, 23 July 2023, para 31.

[1340] See eg *Mătăsaru v Moldova* App Nos 69714/16 and another, 15 January 2019, para 35.

[1341] See eg *Hoffer and Annen v Germany* (2011) 29 BHRC 654; *Sanchez v France* App No 45581/15, 15 May 2023 [GC]; *Monteiro da Costa Noqueira v Portugal* App No 4035/08, 11 January 2011 (available in French only).

[1342] See eg *Director of Public Prosecutions v Connolly* [2007] EWHC 237 (Admin), [2008] 1 WLR 276 (concerning sending a communication of an indecent or grossly offensive nature with the purpose of causing distress or anxiety, contrary to the Malicious Communications Act 1988, s 1); *Scottow v CPS* [2020] EWHC 3421 (Admin), [2021] 1 WLR 1828 (concerning making use of a public electronic network for the purpose of causing annoyance, inconvenience, or needless anxiety to another, contrary to the Communications Act 2003, s 127); and *Hicks v Director of Public Prosecutions* [2023] EWHC 1089 (Admin), [2023] 2 Cr App R 12 (concerning the offence of using threatening or abusive words or behaviour within sight or hearing of a person likely to be caused harassment, alarm, or distress, contrary to the Public Order Act 1986, s 5).

[1343] See *In re Abortion Services (Safe Access Zones) (Northern Ireland) Bill* [2022] UKSC 32, [2023] AC 505 and *Director of Public Prosecutions v Ziegler* [2021] UKSC 23, [2022] AC 408. *DPP v Eastburn* [2023] EWHC 1063 (Admin) contains a summary of the current state of the law.

proportionality of a conviction on the facts of the case.[1344] So far as domestic law is concerned, in many cases a conviction is taken to be a proportionate interference if the ingredients of the offence are made out; as the Divisional Court has put it: the 'necessary balance for proportionality is struck by the terms of the offence-creating provision'.[1345] In effect, convictions of this kind involve the application of a general rule (usually in legislation) and, subject to the rule itself being challenged as being incompatible with the Convention, there is no scope for disputing criminal liability on the basis that its imposition would constitute a disproportionate interference with Article 10 rights.[1346]

There are, however, some offences where satisfying the constituent elements does   6.489
not necessarily ensure the proportionality of the interference arising from a conviction; the elements of the offence are interpreted and applied in a manner which enables the proportionality of criminal liability to be assessed on the facts of the case.[1347] There is no definitive list of offences or type of case which this must be done but this approach generally applies to offences which are only made out if there is no reasonable/lawful excuse for the conduct in question. The inclusion of provisions of this kind does not necessarily mean that a proportionality assessment is required in all cases,[1348] not least because there is some speech in respect of which Article 10 is not engaged at all.[1349] Equally, the circumstances in which the proportionality of imposing criminal liability should be considered are not limited to offences in which a defendant is not liable if they have a reasonable lawful excuse. Notably, the Court of Appeal in Northern Ireland has held that proportionality must be considered where a person is prosecuted for a public order offence containing no such provision, arising from their exercise of expression.[1350]

(iv) Justifying inteferences concerning journalistic sources and confidential journalistic material
Where a measure is likely to identify or reveal a journalistic source or confiden-   6.490
tial journalistic material the interference arising from it 'cannot be compatible with Article 10 ... unless it is justified by an overriding requirement in the public

---

[1344] See the discussion in *Attorney General's Reference (No 1 of 2022)* [2022] EWCA Crim 1259, [2023] KB 37, paras 54–78.

[1345] *James v DPP* [2015] EWHC 3296 (Admin), [2016] 1 WLR 2118, para 35; see also *In re Abortion Services (Safe Access Zones) (Northern Ireland) Bill* [2022] UKSC 32, [2023] AC 505, para 55; *Bauer v DPP* [2013] EWHC 634 (Admin), [2013] 1 WLR 3617, para 40.

[1346] *In re Abortion Services (Safe Access Zones) (Northern Ireland) Bill* [2022] UKSC 32, [2023] AC 505, paras 54–55. See also *DPP v Cuciurean* [2022] EWHC 736 (Admin), [2022] QB 888, paras 58–63.

[1347] *In re Abortion Services (Safe Access Zones) (Northern Ireland) Bill* [2022] UKSC 32, [2023] AC 505, paras 56–58.

[1348] See eg *Hicks v Director of Public Prosecutions* [2023] EWHC 1089 (Admin), [2023] 2 Cr App R 12 concerning the offence under the Public Order Act 1986, s 5, which contains a defence on the basis that the conduct was reasonable (para 48).

[1349] *In re Abortion Services (Safe Access Zones) (Northern Ireland) Bill* [2022] UKSC 32, [2023] AC 505, paras 53–54, 58. See also paras 6.455-6.457.

[1350] *Brown v Public Prosecution Service of Northern Ireland* [2022] NICA 5. The prosecution was for an offence under Public Order (Northern Ireland) Order 1987 (the equivalent offence is contained in the Public Order Act 1986, s 19) of publishing/distributing threatening, abusive, or insulting written material intended or likely to stir up hatred/arouse fear.

interest'.[1351] This enhanced threshold is relevant when considering (a) whether a particular measure is prescribed by law because there must be sufficient safeguards to ensure that measures which may lead to the identification of a source are justified by an overriding requirement in the public interest (the procedural safeguards which are required include review by a judge or other independent and impartial decision-making body before accessing information capable of revealing sources),[1352] and (b) whether a particular interference is necessary in a democratic society.[1353]

(b) *The licensing exception under Article 10(1)*

6.491 Article 10(1) specifies that the right to freedom of expression does not prevent states from requiring the licensing of broadcasting, television, or cinema enterprises. The Grand Chamber has explained that states

> are permitted to regulate by means of a licensing system the way in which broadcasting is organised in their territories, particularly in its technical aspects. The latter are undeniably important, but the grant or refusal of a licence may also be made conditional on other considerations, including such matters as the nature and objectives of a proposed station, its potential audience at national, regional or local level, the rights and needs of a specific audience and the obligations deriving from international legal instruments. This may lead to interferences whose aims will be legitimate under the third sentence of paragraph 1 [of Article 10], even though they may not correspond to any of the aims set out in paragraph 2 [of Article 10].[1354]

6.492 When the right to freedom of expression is restricted pursuant to the licensing exception, this need not pursue one of the aims set out in Article 10(2). The interference must, however, comply with the other requirements of that paragraph; that is, it must be prescribed by law, pursue a legitimate aim, and be necessary in a democratic society.[1355]

6.493 As noted in the remarks of the Grand Chamber above, a legitimate aim in this context is not confined to those enumerated in Article 10(2). The ECtHR has accepted that using a licensing system to contribute to the quality and balance of programming will suffice. Further, and in any event, the preservation of impartiality in broadcasting on, and safeguarding the right to balance and unbiased coverage of, public interest matters pursues the legitimate aim of protecting the rights of others.[1356]

6.494 A critical issue in the context of the licensing of broadcasting and television is the importance of pluralism in audio-video media. The ECtHR has long expressed concerns about public monopolies on broadcasting and powerful economic or political groups obtaining a position of dominance over the audiovisual media, with the Grand Chamber stressing that:

[1351] *Sanoma Uitgevers BV v Netherlands* [2011] EMLR 4 [GC], para 51; *Goodwin v United Kingdom* (1996) 22 EHRR 123, para 39.
[1352] *Sanoma Uitgevers BV v Netherlands* [2011] EMLR 4 [GC], paras 90–92; *Big Brother Watch & others v UK* (2022) 74 EHRR 17 [GC], para 444.
[1353] *Becker v Norway* App No 21272/12, 5 October 2017, para 66.
[1354] *NIT SRL v Republic of Moldova* App No 28470/12, 5 April 2022 [GC], para 153.
[1355] ibid paras 151, 153.
[1356] ibid paras 175–76.

It is of the essence of democracy to allow diverse political programmes to be proposed and debated, even those that call into question the way a State is currently organised, provided that they do not harm democracy. In order to ensure true pluralism in the audiovisual sector in a democratic society, it is not sufficient to provide for the existence of several channels or the theoretical possibility for potential operators to access the audiovisual market. It is necessary in addition to allow effective access to the market so as to guarantee diversity of overall programme content, reflecting as far as possible the variety of opinions encountered in the society at which the programmes are aimed.[1357]

6.495 In this context there is sometimes a tension between the importance of ensuring pluralism and editorial freedom. Article 10 requires that states guarantee diversity of overall programme content, reflecting the diversity of views in society.[1358] Article 10 does not, however, prescribe a particular approach in terms of whether pluralism should be guaranteed with reference to broadcasting by all relevant operators in the round, as opposed to with reference to the coverage of any given operator.[1359]

6.496 A refusal to grant a broadcasting licence constitutes an interference with Article 10,[1360] as does the revocation of a licence.[1361] This extends to the de facto deprivation of a licence: in *Centro Europa 7 S.r.l. and Di Stefano v Italy* a private television company had been granted a licence for nationwide television broadcasting but was unable to broadcast because no frequencies had been allocated to it.[1362]

5. Positive obligations

6.497 As with other qualified rights, Article 10 imposes certain positive obligations[1363] upon states to facilitate and protect the exercise of freedom of expression. This can extend to taking positive steps to protect people against and/or provide redress for interferences with the exercise of free speech rights by other non-state actors. Actions taken by other private persons in response to exercises of freedom of expression include, for example, employers dismissing or taking disciplinary action on the basis of a worker's speech[1364] (which includes detriments against/dismissal of workers blowing the whistle on unlawful conduct),[1365] violence or threats of violence against a person due to the views they hold/have expressed,[1366] and (counter)

[1357] *NIT SRL v Republic of Moldova* App No 28470/12, 5 April 2022 [GC], paras 185–86.
[1358] *Centro Europa 7 S.r.l. and Di Stefano v Italy* App No 38433/09, 7 June 2012 [GC], para 138; *NIT SRL v Republic of Moldova* App No 28470/12, 5 April 2022 [GC], para 190.
[1359] *NIT SRL v Republic of Moldova* App No 28470/12, 5 April 2022 [GC], paras 188–90.
[1360] *Radio ABC v Austria* App No 19736/92, 20 October 1997.
[1361] *NIT SRL v Republic of Moldova* App No 28470/12, 5 April 2022 [GC].
[1362] *Centro Europa 7 S.r.l. and Di Stefano v Italy* App No 38433/09, 7 June 2012 [GC], para 138.
[1363] See paras 2.33–2.39 and 4.106–4.109.
[1364] *Palomo Sánchez v Spain* App Nos 28955/06 & others, 12 September 2011 [GC]; *Fuentes Bobo v Spain* (2001) 31 EHRR 50.
[1365] *Heinisch v Germany* (2014) 58 EHRR 31 (although the Court approached this as a negative obligations case, focusing on the interference arising from the domestic courts' dismissal of the applicant's claim challenging her dismissal by a private body).
[1366] *Özgür Gündem v Turkey* (2001) 31 EHRR 49.

protestors threatening violence against others exercising their right to freedom of expression at a protest.[1367]

6.498   The ECtHR has explained that a state's positive obligations under Article 10 'require States to create, while establishing an effective system of protection of journalists, a favourable environment for participation in public debate by all the persons concerned, enabling them to express their opinions and ideas without fear, even if they run counter to those defended by the official authorities or by a significant part of public opinion, or even irritating or shocking to the latter'.[1368] This involves putting in place an adequate legal framework and carrying out effective investigations in relation to (threatened) attacks against or harassment of people connected to their exercise of Article 10 rights.[1369] That includes protections in respect of freedom of expression-related conduct in the workplace and, in particular, whistleblowing in respect of unlawful/improper conduct.[1370] There are also positive obligations concerning putting in place a legislative and administrative framework to guarantee effective pluralism in the context of audio-visual media (see para 6.494-6.495).[1371] Importantly, however, the state's positive obligations do not extend to permitting or facilitating the exercise of freedom of expression on private property.[1372]

6. Margin of appreciation

6.499   As with other qualified rights,[1373] the ECtHR affords states a margin of appreciation when it considers whether an interference with the right to freedom of expression was necessary in a democratic society or whether a state was under a positive obligation to take particular steps. That is because the ECtHR's jurisdiction is supervisory and, as the Grand Chamber has explained, its task is to

> look at the interference complained of in the light of the case as a whole and determine whether it was 'proportionate to the legitimate aim pursued' and whether the reasons adduced by the national authorities to justify it are 'relevant and sufficient' ... In doing so, the Court has to satisfy itself that the national authorities applied standards which were in conformity with the principles embodied in Article 10 and, moreover, that they relied on an acceptable assessment of the relevant facts.[1374]

6.500   The width of the margin of appreciation varies considerably depending on, in particular, the type of expression in issue, the reason for which it has been restricted, and the nature of the restriction. It is long established that the margin

---

[1367] *Fáber v Hungary* App No 40721/08, 27 July 2012.

[1368] *Khadija Ismayilova v Azerbaijan* App No 65286/13, 10 January 2019, para 158.

[1369] See eg *Khadija Ismayilova v Azerbaijan* App No 65286/13, 10 January 2019, which concerned threats and intimidation (including the threatened use of intimate photographs of her private life) against an investigative journalist: see paras 160–66.

[1370] *Fuentes Bobo v Spain* (2001) 31 EHRR 50; *Heinisch v Germany* (2014) 58 EHRR 31.

[1371] *Centro Europa 7 S.r.l. and Di Stefano v Italy* App No 38433/09, 7 June 2012 [GC], para 134.

[1372] *Appleby v UK* (2003) 37 EHRR 38, para 47.

[1373] See paras 2.77–2.84 and 4.116–4.127.

[1374] *Stoll v Switzerland* (2008) 47 EHRR 59 [GC], para 101.

of appreciation is very narrow in the context of restrictions on political and public interest speech,[1375] whereas the ECtHR has long afforded states a wider margin of appreciation in the context of speech which concerns and/or is regulated on the basis of morals and/or religion.[1376] That is for a number of reasons: (a) there are no common European conceptions or standards in relation to issues of this kind; and (b) it recognizes that national authorities are better placed to assess the (potential) effects of statements and the necessity of particular restrictions or penalties, which depends on the situation in the country where the statements were made at the time and the context in which they were made.[1377] States also enjoy a wider margin of appreciation in the context of expression concerning commercial matters and advertising.[1378]

Where expression is restricted on the basis of other (qualified) rights of oth- 6.501
ers, this balancing exercise falls within the state's margin of appreciation but the ECtHR will consider whether national authorities have undertaken this exercise in accordance with Convention case law. The margin of appreciation applied to each of the competing rights should in principle be the same.[1379]

7. Section 12 of the Human Rights Act

Section 12 of the Human Rights Act applies where a court is considering whether 6.502
to grant relief that might affect the exercise of the right to freedom of expression. It imposes requirements concerning the grant of *ex parte* relief and interim relief which would affect the exercise of Article 10 rights. Section 12(2) enjoins courts not to grant *ex parte* orders without compelling reasons, whereas section 12(3) raises the bar for the prior restraint of publication. Section 12(4) requires courts to have 'particular regard' to the importance of the right to freedom of expression. This provision is a 'comfort clause'; it was introduced during the passage of the Human Rights Act to address the media's concerns about potential conflicts between privacy and freedom of expression, and in support of the principle that news is a time-sensitive commodity.

The House of Lords noted that section 12(3) was designed to buttress the pro- 6.503
tected afforded to the right to freedom of expression at the interlocutory stage by setting a higher threshold for the grant of interim relief preventing publication.[1380]

[1375] See eg *Satakunnan Markkinapörssi Oy and Satamedia Oy v Finland* (2018) 66 EHRR 8 [GC], para 167.
[1376] See eg *Mouvement Raëlien Suisse v Switzerland* App No 16354/06, 13 July 2012 [GC], para 61 (on a 'cult' seeking to place adverts in public spaces); *Otto-Preminger Institute v Austria* (1994) 19 EHRR 34 (on religious satire); *Murphy v Ireland* (2003) 38 EHRR 212 (on religious advertising); *Animal Defenders v UK* (2013) 34 BHRC 137 (on paid advertising concerning animal rights issues). cf *Akdas v Turkey* App No 41056/04, 16 February 2010 (available in French only) (on an erotic novel).
[1377] See eg *Rabczewska v Poland* App No 8257/13, 15 September 2022, para 52; *Handyside v UK* (1976) 1 EHRR 737; *Mouvement Raëlien Suisse v Switzerland* App No 16354/06, 13 July 2012 [GC], para 61.
[1378] *Mouvement Raëlien Suisse v Switzerland* App No 16354/06, 13 July 2012 [GC], para 63; *VGT Verein Gegen Tierfabriken v Switzerland* (2002) 34 EHRR 4.
[1379] *Couderc & Hachette Filipacchi Associés v France* [2016] EMLR 19 [GC], paras 90–91.
[1380] *Cream Holdings v Banerjee* [2004] UKHL 44, [2005] 1 AC 253, para 15.

A court must be satisfied that an applicant is likely to succeed at trial; this, held the House of Lords, is a flexible standard but it generally requires the person seeking interim relief to show that they are more likely than not to succeed at trial.[1381]

6.504   Section 12 has not had a significant impact on domestic jurisprudence. That is primarily because the Convention does not permit states to accord greater weight to Article 10 than other qualified rights and, in particular, Article 8; neither article has preference and they must be balanced, with an assessment of the proportionality of interfering with each article.[1382] As Warby J reiterated in *Afsar v Birmingham City Council*, it is 'clear that section 12(4) does not place freedom of expression on a pedestal, affording it presumptive priority over the Convention right to respect for private life'.

H. ARTICLE 11: FREEDOM OF ASSEMBLY AND ASSOCIATION

6.505   Article 11 protects the twin rights of freedom of peaceful assembly and freedom of association. Both rights are of a political nature and both have a collective dimension as they both protect 'people power'—individuals uniting and gathering to express or protect their common interests. Together with the right to freedom of expression, these rights are essential to the proper functioning of a democratic and pluralistic society.

1. Overlap between Article 11 and other rights

6.506   Article 11 rights often overlap with Articles 9 (freedom of thought, conscience, and religion)[1383] and 10 (freedom of expression).[1384] The protection of opinions and beliefs and the freedom to express them is one of the objectives of the freedom of assembly and association.[1385] Article 11 rights may also interlink with Article 8, for example where the authorities collate or retain information on an individual's political opinions or activities,[1386] or when police photograph or film protestors.[1387] But the ECtHR has generally considered those cases under Article 8. Article 5 may also be relevant in the context of protests, for example, where the police pre-emptively

---

[1381]   ibid para 22.

[1382]   *PJS v Newsgroup Newspapers* [2016] UKSC 26, [2016] AC 1081, paras 19–20.

[1383]   See eg *Chassagnou and others v France* (1999) 29 EHRR 615; *Sindicatul Păstorul cel Bun v Romania* (2014) 58 EHRR 10 [GC]; *R (Parminder Singh) v Chief Constable of West Midlands Police* [2006] EWCA Civ 1118, [2006] 1 WLR 3374.

[1384]   See eg *Hashman and Harrup v UK* (2000) 30 EHRR 241; *Rekvenyi v Hungary* (2000) 30 EHRR 519; *Christian Democratic People's Party v Moldova* App No 28793/02, 14 February 2006; *R (Laporte) v Chief Constable of Gloucestershire* [2006] UKHL 55, [2007] 2 AC 105.

[1385]   *Christian Democratic People's Party v Moldova* App No 28793/02, 14 February 2006, para 62.

[1386]   *Segerstedt-Wiberg and others v Sweden* (2007) 44 EHRR 2; *Catt v UK* (2019) 69 EHRR 7.

[1387]   *R (Wood) v Commissioner of Police for the Metropolis* [2008] EWHC 1105 (Admin), [2008] HRLR 34.

arrest would-be protestors[1388] or use 'crowd control' measures such as cordons or 'kettling' at protests.[1389]

In cases whose facts raise issues concerning the right to peaceful assembly and 6.507
another Convention right, the ECtHR will generally examine the interference under Article 11, as *lex specialis*, but it will do so 'in the light of' the other relevant article. This is most commonly the right to freedom of expression under Article 10.[1390] Freedom of expression is also closely connected to the freedom of association, particularly where associations exist to address or campaign on particular issues.[1391] In cases of this kind, the ECtHR ordinarily focuses exclusively on Article 11 but refers to other articles when assessing the proportionality of the interference.[1392] This is especially relevant where a peaceful assembly involves the expression of opinions on public interest matters; particularly strong reasons are required to justify restrictions on protests of this sort.[1393] In *R (Laporte) v Chief Constable of Gloucestershire* both Lord Rodger and Lord Carswell expressly approved the Strasbourg approach of treating Article 11 as the *lex specialis* and Article 10 as *lex generalis* in protest cases.[1394] However, the domestic courts increasingly consider Articles 11 and 10 in the round.[1395]

The ECtHR does not, however, take this approach in all cases where both articles 6.508
are engaged. For example, in recent years it has considered under Article 10 (and not art 11) cases concerning criminal convictions for staging an anti-corruption protests using sculptures of genitalia,[1396] and involving a protestor handcuffing himself to railings and holding signs challenging a bill.[1397] In those cases the court has interpreted Article 10 in light of Article 11.[1398] The ECtHR is more likely to focus on Article 10 where the impugned interference arises as a result of or focusses on the content of expression in the context of protests.[1399]

[1388] *R (Hicks) v Commissioner of Police for the Metropolis* [2017] UKSC 9, [2017] AC 256, which concerned the detention of would-be protestors prior to the royal wedding; *Alici v Turkey* App No 70098/12, 24 May 2022 (available only in French).

[1389] See eg *Austin v Commissioner of Police of the Metropolis* [2009] UKHL 5, [2009] 2 WLR 372.

[1390] *Ekrem Can v Turkey* App No 10613/10, 8 March 2022, para 68; *Navalnyy v Russia* (2018) 46 BHRC 452 [GC], para 102; see to the same effect in the context of the right to freedom of association: *Ecodefence & others v Russia* App Nos 9988/13 and others, 14 June 2022, para 72.

[1391] See eg *Ecodefence & others v Russia* App Nos 9988/13 & others, 14 June 2022, para 72.

[1392] *Ezelin v France* (1991) 14 EHRR 362; *Kudrevičius v Lithuania* (2016) 62 EHRR 34 [GC]; *Chkhartishvili v Georgia* App No 31349/20, 11 May 2023.

[1393] See eg *Chkhartishvili v Georgia* App No 31349/20, 11 May 2023, para 55 (a case concerning protests about a failure to reform the electoral system).

[1394] *R (Laporte) v Chief Constable of Gloucestershire* [2006] UKHL 55, [2007] 2 AC 105, paras 85 and 93.

[1395] See eg *Director of Public Prosecutions v Ziegler* [2021] UKSC 23, [2022] AC 408; *Shell UK Ltd v Persons Unknown* [2022] EWHC 1215 (QB); *Dulgheriu v Ealing London Borough Council* [2019] EWCA Civ 1490, [2020] 1 WLR 609.

[1396] *Mătăsaru v Moldova* App Nos 69714/16 & another, 15 January 2019.

[1397] *Bumbeş v Romania* App No 18079/15, 3 May 2022.

[1398] ibid paras 67–70.

[1399] An example of this *Annen v Germany* App No 3690/10, 26 November 2015 (concerning an injunction to prevent the distribution of leaflets in the vicinity of an abortion clinic).

2. Right to freedom of assembly

6.509 The right to protest has English origins, beginning with the ancient right to petition the English crown. Despite this 'long history', peaceful protests had little protection in English law prior to the Human Rights Act, which brought about a 'constitutional shift' in the protection of the right to freedom of assembly.[1400]

6.510 This right arises and is relied on in a wide range of contexts including challenges to restrictions on demonstrations or protests imposed by the police, in response to private bodies seeking injunctions to restrain protests (relying on trespass, harassment, conspiracy to injure, and nuisance, in particular),[1401] challenges to exclusion zones preventing protests in particular areas,[1402] challenges to arrests in connection with protests, when responding to criminal charges relating to protests,[1403] and in the context of sentencing following conviction for offences relating to protests.[1404] In recent years, this right has attained renewed significance with ongoing protests concerning the climate emergency and the response to these by both the state and private bodies. The UK has introduced a growing number of restrictions on protests in both criminal and civil law.[1405]

(a) *Scope of the right to freedom of assembly*

6.511 The right to freedom of peaceful assembly is one of the foundations of a democratic society. Given its importance, it must not be interpreted restrictively.[1406] Protests are the form of assembly which has given rise to most of the case law but 'assembly' is a far broader concept which encompasses, for example: large marches and processions,[1407] meetings of small groups on private premises,[1408] press conferences, static protests, 'sit-ins', or occupations of buildings or land,[1409] counter-demonstrations, and 'flash mobs'.[1410] The right can also extend to situations in which a person does

---

[1400] See eg *R (Laporte) v Chief Constable of Gloucestershire* [2006] UKHL 55, [2007] 2 AC 105, paras 34–37.

[1401] See eg *Ineos Upstream Ltd v Persons Unknown* [2019] EWCA Civ 515, [2019] 4 WLR 100 (concerning fracking protests); *Canada Goose UK Retail Ltd v Persons Unknown* [2020] EWCA Civ 303, [2020] 1 WLR 2802 (concerning protests against the use of fur and down outside a Canada Goose store); *Transport for London v Rodger & others* [2023] EWHC 1038 (KB) (concerning Insulate Britain's blocking of highways); and *Shell UK Ltd v Persons Unknown* [2022] EWHC 1215 (QB) (concerning Just Stop Oil and others blocking access to and damaging petrol stations).

[1402] See eg *Dulgheriu v Ealing London Borough Council* [2019] EWCA Civ 1490, [2020] 1 WLR 609.

[1403] See eg *Director of Public Prosecutions v Ziegler* [2021] UKSC 23, [2022] AC 408.

[1404] *R v Roberts (Richard)* [2018] EWCA Crim 2739, [2019] 1 WLR 2577; *R v Jones (Margaret)* [2006] UKHL 16, [2007] 1 AC 136; *Cuadrilla Bowland Ltd v Persons Unknown* [2020] EWCA Civ 9, [2020] 4 WLR 29.

[1405] See eg the Anti-social Behaviour Crime and Policing Act 2014; the Police, Crime, Sentencing and Courts Act 2022; and the Public Order Act 2023.

[1406] *Kudrevičius v Lithuania* (2016) 62 EHRR 34 [GC], para 91.

[1407] See eg *Christians Against Racism and Fascism v UK* (1983) 21 DR 138.

[1408] *Emin Huseynov v Azerbaijan* App No 59135/09, 7 May 2015.

[1409] See eg *G v Germany* (1989) 60 DR 256; *R (Tabernacle) v Secretary of State for Defence* [2009] EWCA Civ 23.

[1410] *Obote v Russia* App No 58954/09, 19 November 2019.

not intend to take part in an assembly but action is taken against them on the mistaken basis that they have done or will do so.[1411]

This right protects both organizers of assemblies and those who participate in them.[1412] It may be exercised by individuals, associations, and corporate groups.[1413] Because freedom of assembly protects 'the abstract possibility of holding an undisturbed peaceful assembly', its organizers may claim to be directly concerned by 'any negative decision of the authorities'.[1414] People who intend to, but are prevented from, participating in a protest will also have standing to challenge restrictions even if no protest took place. The courts may, however, require evidence that the applicant intended to take part before accepting that they are a 'victim'.[1415]   6.512

Freedom of assembly includes the right to choose the time, place, and conduct of an assembly, subject to restrictions being placed on this in accordance with the requirements of Article 11(2).[1416] By way of example, the Court of Appeal has held protestors' wish to express their views in Parliament Square was protected by Article 11.[1417]   6.513

Article 11 applies to all assemblies except those where the organizers and/or participants have violent intentions, incite violence, or otherwise 'reject the foundations of a democratic society'.[1418] Violent assemblies are completely excluded from its scope.[1419] The ECtHR will generally examine three issues when determining whether a protestor's actions fall within the scope of Article 11(1): '(i) whether the assembly was intended to be peaceful or whether the organisers had violent intentions; (ii) whether the applicant had demonstrated violent intentions when joining the assembly; and (iii) whether the applicant had inflicted bodily harm on anyone'.[1420] However, the Grand Chamber has emphasized that: 6.514

an individual does not cease to enjoy the right to freedom of peaceful assembly as a result of sporadic violence or other punishable acts committed by others in the course of the demonstration if the individual in question remains peaceful in his or her own intentions or behaviour ... The possibility of persons with violent intentions, not members of the organizing association, joining the demonstration cannot as such take away that right ... Even if there is a real risk that a public demonstration might result in disorder as a result of developments outside the control of those organising it, such a demonstration does not as such fall outside the scope of paragraph 1 of Article 11.[1421]

[1411] See eg *Navalnyy v Russia* (2018) 46 BHRC 452 [GC], para 109.
[1412] *Kudrevičius v Lithuania* (2016) 62 EHRR 34 [GC], para 91.
[1413] See eg *Hyde Park and others v Moldova (No 4)* App No 18491/07, 7 April 2009, paras 34–36.
[1414] *Bączkowski and others v Poland* App No 1543/06 and others, 3 May 2007.
[1415] *Patyi and others v Hungary* App No 5529/05, 7 October 2008, paras 26–28.
[1416] *Ekrem Can v Turkey* App No 10613/10, 8 March 2022, para 81.
[1417] *Mayor of London v Hall* [2010] EWCA Civ 817, [2011] 1 WLR 504, para 37.
[1418] *Navalnyy v Russia* (2018) 46 BHRC 452 [GC], para 98; *Kudrevičius v Lithuania* (2016) 62 EHRR 34 [GC], para 92; approved domestically in *In re Abortion Services (Safe Access Zones) (Northern Ireland) Bill* [2022] UKSC 32, [2023] AC 505, para 54.
[1419] See also paras 6.689-6.691 concerning art 17 of the Convention.
[1420] *Shmorgunov v Ukraine* App Nos 15367/14 and others, 21 January 2021, para 491.
[1421] *Kudrevičius v Lithuania* (2016) 62 EHRR 34 [GC], para 94. See also *Bauer v DPP* [2013] EWHC 634 (Admin), [2013] 1 WLR 3617, paras 37–38.

6.515   Where this happens, issues concerning the risk of violence fall to be determined under Article 11(2).[1422] Further, certain types of conduct in the course of and/or as a means of protest may fall outside the scope of Article 11. For example, the Court of Appeal has held recently that causing significant damage to property, which would amount to a criminal offence under the Criminal Damage Act 1971, falls outside the protection of Article 11.[1423]

6.516   Article 11 does not confer any right to trespass or protest on private property or publicly owned land from which the public is generally excluded.[1424] The ECtHR has considered whether the state's positive obligations may require it to permit access to privately owned property to exercise the right to freedom of assembly. In *Appleby v UK* the Court found no violation of Article 10 or 11 where the applicants had been prevented from campaigning (by setting up a stand and displaying posters) against a proposed green field development in a private shopping centre.[1425] There is, the Court held, no 'freedom of forum'[1426] inherent in Article 10 or 11 and no requirement of automatic access to private property in order to exercise these rights. The Court noted that the applicants had alternative ways of making their views known to the public, such as gathering elsewhere and canvassing door-to-door. Domestically the Lord Chief Justice has held that '[i]t would be fallacious to suggest that, unless a person is free to enter upon private land to stop or impede the carrying on of a lawful activity on that land by the landowner or occupier, the essence of the freedoms of expression and assembly would be destroyed' because legitimate protest can take many other forms.[1427]

6.517   The ECtHR has stated that a positive obligation could, in principle, arise in circumstances where a bar on access to property would effectively destroy the essence of the right to freedom of assembly; it gave the example of a corporate town controlled entirely by a private body.[1428] The Divisional Court has held that this could only arise in 'unusual' or 'extreme' circumstances and would involve establishing that 'the protection of a landowner's property rights has the effect of preventing any effective exercise of the freedoms of expression and assembly'.[1429]

(b) Interferences with the right to freedom of assembly

6.518   Interferences with the right to freedom of assembly arise in many different ways, including steps taken before, during, and after assemblies.[1430] What follows are some common examples.

[1422] See eg *R (Parminder Singh) v Chief Constable of West Midlands Police* [2006] EWCA Civ 1118, [2006] 1 WLR 3374.

[1423] *Attorney General's Reference (No 1 of 2022)* [2022] EWCA Crim 1259, [2023] KB 37.

[1424] *Ineos Upstream Ltd v Persons Unknown* [2019] EWCA Civ 515, [2019] 4 WLR 100, para 36; *Richardson v Director of Public Prosecutions* [2014] UKSC 8, [2014] AC 635, para 3; *DPP v Cuciurean* [2022] EWHC 736 (Admin), [2022] QB 888, para 45.

[1425] *Appleby v UK* (2003) 37 EHRR 38.

[1426] ibid para 47.

[1427] *DPP v Cuciurean* [2022] EWHC 736 (Admin), [2022] QB 888, para 46.

[1428] *Appleby v UK* (2003) 37 EHRR 38; *DPP v Cuciurean* [2022] EWHC 736 (Admin), [2022] QB 888, para 4.

[1429] *DPP v Cuciurean* [2022] EWHC 736 (Admin), [2022] QB 888, para 45.

[1430] *Kudrevičius v Lithuania* (2016) 62 EHRR 34 [GC], para 100.

Bans on/refusal to permit assemblies. Banning or refusing to permit protests consti- 6.519
tutes a particularly serious interference with the right to freedom of assembly. While
the ECtHR has sometimes ruled bans to be lawful (particularly where they were time
limited and/or limited to protests in particular locations),[1431] they are generally difficult
for states to justify.

A ban on protest can amount to an interference even if it did not in fact prevent the 6.520
protest from taking place. That is because, as the Grand Chamber has noted, 'a prior
ban can have a chilling effect on the persons who intend to participate in a rally and
thus amount to an interference, even if the rally subsequently proceeds without hin-
drance on the part of the authorities'.[1432] An interference may arise in this way even if
protestors ultimately decided to take part in a protest which had been banned because
they could have been discouraged from doing so.[1433] Civil injunctions preventing protests from taking place in particular areas may also constitute an interference.[1434]

Actions which prevent or discourage the exercise of the right to freedom of assembly. 6.521
Measures which prevent or dissuade people from participating in assemblies constitute an interference. A common example of this is the preventive arrest and detention of protestors prior to the start of a protest (which are often addressed under
art 5).[1435] Similarly, measures preventing people from travelling to take part in a
protest are likely to constitute an interference.[1436] A well-known example of this is
R (Laporte) v Chief Constable of Gloucestershire where police stopped coaches of protesters on their way to a protest demonstration at an airbase, unlawfully preventing
them from going on to exercise their right to freedom of assembly.[1437] An interference may also arise where the police wrongly (intentionally or unintentionally) tell
people wishing to protest that the would-be protest would be unlawful and would
expose to them the risk of criminal liability; this has a chilling effect on the exercise
of Article 11 rights, particularly where such a warning causes them to cancel/not
attend a protest.[1438]

Prior authorization and notification requirements. Requiring that notification 6.522
be given and/or authorization obtained for an assembly is an interference with
Article 11. This is an area that has given rise to extensive litigation. The ECtHR
has repeatedly emphasized that such requirements can be compatible with this
right, provided that their purpose is to allow the authorities to take reasonable and
appropriate measures to guarantee the smooth conduct of any assembly.[1439] Indeed,

---

[1431] *Christians Against Racism and Fascism v UK* App No 8440/78, 16 July 1980 (concerning a time-limited ban on demonstrations in London due to heightened tensions); *Pendragon v UK* App No 3146/96, 19 October 1998 (concerning a time-limited ban on assemblies of druids near Stonehenge).
[1432] *Kudrevičius v Lithuania* (2016) 62 EHRR 34 [GC], para 100.
[1433] *Baczkowski and others v Poland* App No 1543/06, 3 May 2007.
[1434] *Cuadrilla Bowland Ltd v Persons Unknown* [2020] EWCA Civ 9, [2020] 4 WLR 29, para 45.
[1435] See eg *Alici v Turkey* App No 70098/12, 24 May 2022 (available only in French).
[1436] *Kudrevičius v Lithuania* (2016) 62 EHRR 34 [GC], para 100.
[1437] *R (Laporte) v Chief Constable of Gloucestershire* [2006] UKHL 55, [2007] 2 AC 105.
[1438] *R (Leigh) v Commissioner of Police of the Metropolis* [2022] EWHC 527 (Admin), [2022] 1 WLR 3141, paras 75–76.
[1439] *Navalnyy v Russia* (2018) 46 BHRC 452, para 100; *Kudrevičius v Lithuania* (2016) 62 EHRR 34 [GC], para 147.

an authorization/prior notification procedure may even be required as part of the state's positive obligation under Article 11 to ensure that a protest is peaceful and that a fear of violence does not deter participants from expressing their views.[1440] However, regulation should not represent a hidden obstacle to freedom of assembly and the enforcement of compliance with pre-authorization measures cannot, the ECtHR has stressed, become an end itself.[1441] The ECtHR has emphasized that, even when there is a notification requirement and it has not been complied with, 'to disband the ensuing, peaceful assembly solely because of the absence of the requisite prior notice, without any illegal conduct by the participants, amounts to a disproportionate restriction on freedom of assembly'.[1442] Authorities are expected to show a degree of tolerance towards peaceful assemblies which have not complied with notification/authorization requirements.[1443] But the Grand Chamber has noted that this principle 'cannot be extended to the point where the absence of prior notification of a spontaneous demonstration can never be a legitimate basis for crowd dispersal'.[1444]

6.523   *Restrictions on the location and timing of assemblies.* Placing restrictions on where and when a protest takes place may amount to an interference with the right to freedom of assembly.[1445] But it is not the case that a protestor's choice of place and the form of a protest must be invariably respected.[1446] For example, in *Barda*, the High Court held that fencing off the Parliament Square Garden during Occupy Democracy protests was an interference with protestors' rights, albeit one that was limited (because they could continue their activities elsewhere) and justified on the facts.[1447]

6.524   *Breaking up protests and the use of force.* The forceful dispersal of a protest constitutes an interference with the right to freedom of assembly,[1448] as does the arrest and/or detention of people participating in assemblies.[1449]

6.525   *Ex-post facto penalties.* The imposition of criminal, civil, or administrative penalties for participation in assemblies constitutes an interference with the right to freedom of assembly. That includes sanctions flowing from being held in contempt of court for disobeying a civil injunction obtained by, for example, a landowner or council, which prevents or limit protests. Penalties include, at one end of this scale, the imposition of administrative fines, for example, for involvement in a protest or for refusing to follow police orders during a protest, even if the police did not take

---

[1440] *Rassemblement Jurassien and Unité Jurassienne v Switzerland* (1979) 17 DR 93, para 119 (ECmHR).
[1441] *Aldemir v Turkey* App No 32124/02, 18 December 2007, para 43; *Laguna Guzman v Spain*, App No 41462/17, 6 October 2020, para 50; *Kudrevičius v Lithuania* (2016) 62 EHRR 34 [GC], para 150.
[1442] *Bukta v Hungary* App No 25691/04, 17 July 2007, para 36; see also *Kudrevičius v Lithuania* (2016) 62 EHRR 34 [GC], para 152.
[1443] *Laguna Guzman v Spain* App No 41462/17, 6 October 2020, para 50.
[1444] *Kudrevičius v Lithuania* (2016) 62 EHRR 34 [GC], para 153.
[1445] *Lashmankin v Russia* App Nos 57818/09 and others, 7 February 2017, paras 405–06.
[1446] *R (Barda) v Mayor of London* [2015] EWHC 3584 (Admin), [2016] 4 WLR 20, para 90.
[1447] ibid paras 92, 101, 103.
[1448] See eg *Laguna Guzman v Spain* App No 41462/17, 6 October 2020.
[1449] See eg *Navalnyy v Russia*, para 103; *Ekrem Can v Turkey* App No 10613/10, 8 March 2022, para 86.

steps to stop the protest.[1450] At the other end of the scale is the imposition of custodial sentences for involvement in protests.

(c) *Justifications for interferences with the right to freedom of assembly*

6.526 The right to freedom of assembly is qualified. Restrictions can be placed on its exercise provided they are (i) prescribed by law, (ii) pursue a legitimate aim, and (iii) are necessary in a democratic society—the first and third of those requirements are addressed above (see paras 6.365-6.381) and apply in the same way.[1451] Article 11(2) provides that restrictions can be placed on the right to freedom of assembly 'in the interests of national security or public safety, for the prevention of disorder or crime, for the protection of health or morals or for the protection of the rights and freedoms of others'. The last of these often includes the freedoms of other members of the public to go about their daily lives. It also includes other qualified rights and, in particular, the Article 8 rights[1452] of other members of the public, which are of equal importance and have to be balanced with the right to freedom of assembly.[1453] Given that the right to freedom of assembly is one of the foundations of a democratic society, exceptions to or restrictions on the exercise of this right must be interpreted narrowly and convincingly established.[1454]

6.527 Most freedom of assembly cases turn on the question of the necessity and proportionality of interferences with this right. In making this assessment the courts are alert to the fact that Article 11 protects protest that annoys and causes offence,[1455] as the ECtHR has stated:

If every probability of tension and heated exchange between opposing groups during a demonstration was to warrant its prohibition, society would be faced with being deprived of the opportunity of hearing differing views.[1456]

6.528 Accordingly, the fact that a protest results in some disruption to ordinary life and inconvenience for other members of the public is not, of itself, a sufficient justification for restricting the exercise of the right.[1457] As Laws LJ said in *R (Tabernacle) v Secretary of State for Defence* (in a case concerning the compatibility of byelaws prohibiting camping in the vicinity of atomic weapons establishments with arts 10 and 11) '[r]ights worth having are unruly things. Demonstrations and protests are liable to be a nuisance. They are liable to be inconvenient and tiresome, or at least

---

[1450] See eg *Yilmaz Yildiz v Turkey* App No 4524/06, 14 October 2014.

[1451] In the art 11 context, see the summary in *Navalnyy v Russia* (2018) 46 BHRC 452 [GC], paras 114–15, 128.

[1452] See eg *Dulgheriu v Ealing London Borough Council* [2019] EWCA Civ 1490, [2020] 1 WLR 609 (which concerned the imposition of a public spaces protection order to prevent protests close to an abortion clinic, including on the basis that this was necessary to protect the private lives of service users).

[1453] See eg *Annen v Germany* App No 3690/10, 26 November 2015, paras 55–56.

[1454] *Kudrevičius v Lithuania* (2016) 62 EHRR 34 [GC], para 142.

[1455] ibid para 145.

[1456] *Öllinger v Austria* App No 76900/01, 29 June 2006, para 36; *Stankov and the United Macedonian Organisation Illinden v Bulgaria* App Nos 29221/95 and another, 2 October 2001, para 87.

[1457] *Cuadrilla Bowland Ltd v Persons Unknown* [2020] EWCA Civ 9, [2020] 4 WLR 29, para 42; *Kudrevičius v Lithuania* (2016) 62 EHRR 34 [GC], para 155.

perceived as such by others who are out of sympathy with them.'[1458] The Court of Appeal has reaffirmed this, noting that the 'side-effects of demonstrations and protests are a form of inconvenience which the state and other members of society are required to tolerate'.[1459] However, the ECtHR has stressed that, where the exercise of freedom of the right to freedom of assembly causes 'disruption to ordinary life and other activities to a degree exceeding that which is inevitable in the circumstances' and/or is combined with illegal conduct, states enjoy a wide margin of appreciation in their assessment of the necessity of measures taken in response.[1460]

6.529   The ECtHR and domestic courts have drawn a distinction between protests which cause disruption as an inevitable side-effect and those which are intended to cause disruption, for example by impeding lawful activities of which protestors disapprove.[1461] The former is not, the courts have held, 'at the core' of the freedom protected by Article 11 because 'the essence of the rights of peaceful assembly and freedom of expression is the opportunity to persuade others [which] is very different from attempting (through physical obstruction or similar conduct) to compel others to act in a way you desire'.[1462] It is therefore easier for the state to justify restrictions on forms of protest which are intended to disrupt the activities of others (examples have included the blocking of whaling boats and obstructing a hunt). That is particularly so where protestors' actions are not aimed at the activity about which they complain but at an unrelated activity—the deliberate slowing or blocking of traffic falls into this category.[1463]

6.530   When assessing whether an interference with the right to freedom of assembly is necessary in a democratic society, an important consideration is whether any restrictions prevent the exercise of the right entirely or only impose some restrictions on it.[1464] The former is, of course, more difficult to justify. The courts will pay particular attention to any possible 'less restrictive means' the state could have taken to protect the legitimate aim in question without unduly impairing the right to assemble. For example, in *Öllinger v Austria* the ECtHR accepted that an assembly to commemorate Salzburg Jews killed by the SS during the Second World War could interfere with other cemetery-goers' rights to manifest their religion and mourn their dead, yet nevertheless found that prohibiting the assembly violated Article 11. In the circumstances, having a police presence on hand in case of

---

[1458] *R (Tabernacle) v Secretary of State for Defence* [2009] EWCA Civ 23, para 43.

[1459] *Cuadrilla Bowland Ltd v Persons Unknown* [2020] EWCA Civ 9, [2020] 4 WLR 29, para 42; on the tolerance that authorities are expected to show, see *Kudrevičius v Lithuania* (2016) 62 EHRR 34 [GC], para 155.

[1460] *Ekrem Can v Turkey* App No 10613/10, 8 March 2022, para 91; *Kudrevičius v Lithuania* (2016) 62 EHRR 34 [GC], para 156.

[1461] *Cuadrilla Bowland Ltd v Persons Unknown* [2020] EWCA Civ 9, [2020] 4 WLR 29, para 43; *Kudrevičius v Lithuania* (2016) 62 EHRR 34 [GC], paras 97, 171.

[1462] *Cuadrilla Bowland Ltd v Persons Unknown* [2020] EWCA Civ 9, [2020] 4 WLR 29, para 94; *Director of Public Prosecutions v Ziegler* [2019] EWHC 71 (Admin), [2020] QB 253, para 53; *Kudrevičius v Lithuania* (2016) 62 EHRR 34 [GC], para 97.

[1463] See eg *Kudrevičius v Lithuania* (2016) 62 EHRR 34 [GC], paras 171–72.

[1464] *Shell UK Ltd v Persons Unknown* [2022] EWHC 1215 (QB), para 59.

disruption was a 'viable alternative' that would preserve the applicants' freedom of assembly while respecting mourners' sensitivities.[1465]

Content-based restrictions on the exercise of the right to freedom of assembly are difficult to justify and the courts subject them to particularly rigorous scrutiny.[1466] States cannot, consistently with Article 11, prohibit assemblies on the basis that they disagree with the views being expressed by participants.[1467] Further, as with Article 10 (see paras 6.483), the courts require particularly convincing reasons to justify an interference with an assembly involving political speech or debate on questions of public interest.[1468]   6.531

The ECtHR has long taken the view that the imposition of criminal liability for involvement in protest requires particularly strong justification, especially where that leads to a sentence of imprisonment.[1469] Accordingly, the Court will scrutinize any penal sanctions, and particularly those resulting in imprisonment, particularly carefully.[1470] However, the Court of Appeal has held that Article 11 does not preclude the imposition of a sentence of imprisonment for the commission of an offence arising from peaceful protest.[1471] Where, however, penalties are imposed on individuals without evidence that they *personally* behaved in a violent or disruptive manner, they are likely to be disproportionate.[1472] For example, in *Ezelin v France*, subjecting a lawyer to a disciplinary reprimand for taking part in a demonstration that had become violent, even though his personal actions were lawful, was held to be a disproportionate infringement of his Article 11 right to make his beliefs known in a peaceful way.[1473]   6.532

(d) Positive obligations and the right to freedom of assembly

States have positive obligations in respect of the right to freedom of assembly. As the ECtHR has explained: 6.533

The state must act as the ultimate guarantor of the principles of pluralism, tolerance and broad-mindedness. Genuine, effective freedom of peaceful assembly cannot, therefore, be reduced to a mere duty on the part of the state not to interfere: a purely negative conception would not be compatible with the object and purpose of art.11 of the Convention. This provision sometimes

---

[1465] *Öllinger v Austria* App No 76900/01, 29 June 2006.
[1466] *Navalnyy v Russia* (2018) 46 BHRC 452 [GC], para 136; *Centre for Societies of Krishna Consciousness v Russia* App No 37477/11, 23 November 2021, para 52.
[1467] *Centre for Societies of Krishna Consciousness v Russia* App No 37477/11, 23 November 2021, para 52.
[1468] *Öllinger v Austria* App No 76900/01, 29 June 2006, para 38; *R (Laporte) v Chief Constable of Gloucestershire* [2006] UKHL 55, [2007] 2 AC 105.
[1469] *Kudrevičius v Lithuania* (2016) 62 EHRR 34 [GC], para 146; *Chkhartishvili v Georgia* App No 31349/20, 11 May 2023, para 51.
[1470] *Ekrem Can v Turkey* App No 10613/10, 8 March 2022, para 92. The approach taken to the assessment of the proportionality of criminal convictions is addressed in more detail under art 10 (see paras 6.486-6.489) and substantially the same principles apply where criminal convictions interfere with art 11.
[1471] *R v Roberts* [2018] EWCA Crim 2739, [2019] 1 WLR 2577, paras 31–43.
[1472] See eg *Steel v UK* (1999) 28 EHRR 603 (an art 10 case but the reasoning is readily applicable in art 11 cases).
[1473] *Ezelin v France* (1991) 14 EHRR 362.

requires positive measures to be taken, even in the sphere of relations between individuals, if need be.[1474]

6.534 In that case the court went on to note that people exercising their right to freedom of assembly 'must ... be able, with the state's assistance, to hold the demonstration without having to fear that they will be subjected to physical violence by their opponents'.[1475] This means that states are under a duty to take reasonable steps to ensure protests proceed peacefully and to ensure the safety of those involved and/or affected.[1476] That may involve taking steps such as providing security and first aid at protests. This duty comes into sharp focus where protestors are members of or promoting the rights/interests of victimized or marginalized groups and/or where counterprotests are likely to occur.[1477]

3. Right to freedom of association

(a) Scope of the right

6.535 The right to freedom of association is the other core right protected by Article 11. Emphasizing the importance of this right to the functioning of a democratic society, the ECtHR has observed that 'the participation of citizens in the democratic process is to a large extent achieved through belonging to associations in which they may integrate with each other and pursue common objectives collectively'.[1478] The ECtHR has recognized the particular importance of certain types of associations in ensuring pluralism and democracy. While acknowledging the 'essential role' played by political parties in this regard, the Court has also noted that:

Associations formed for other purposes, including those protecting cultural or spiritual heritage, pursuing various socio-economic aims, proclaiming or teaching religion, seeking an ethnic identity or asserting a minority consciousness are also important to the proper functioning of democracy.[1479]

6.536 Both natural persons and organizations can raise complaints under this right. It is frequently relied on by, among many others, (would-be) political parties, trade unions, NGOs, and trade unionists.

(i) Right to form and join associations

6.537 The right to freedom of association protects the right to join or form associations. But Article 11 does not create a right to become or to continue to be a member of a particular association in all circumstances. The ECtHR recognizes the organizational autonomy of private associations; that is not absolute, however, and there may be circumstances in which it is necessary for the state to intervene in respect of

---

[1474] *Berkman v Russia* (2021) 73 EHRR 3, para 46.
[1475] ibid para 47.
[1476] See the summary in *Kudrevičius v Lithuania* (2016) 62 EHRR 34 [GC], paras 158–60.
[1477] See eg *Plattform 'Ärzte für das Leben' v Austria* (1988) 13 EHRR 204; *Bączkowski and others v Poland* App Nos 1543/06 & others, 3 May 2007; *Berkman v Russia* (2021) 73 EHRR 3.
[1478] *Ecodefence & others v Russia* App Nos 9988/13 and others, 14 June 2022, para 88.
[1479] *Gorzelik and others* (2005) 40 EHRR 4, para 92.

decisions made by associations.[1480] In *Cheall v UK* the ECmHR decided that generally an individual has no right to belong to a particular trade union. The decision to expel Mr Cheall was analysed as the decision of a private body exercising its rights under Article 11 not to associate with him. However, the ECmHR observed that:

> For the right to join a union to be effective the state must protect the individual against any abuse of a dominant position by trade unions ... Such abuse might occur, for example, where exclusion or expulsion was not in accordance with union rules or where the rules were wholly unreasonable or arbitrary or where the consequences of exclusion or expulsion resulted in exceptional hardship such as job loss because of a closed shop.[1481]

An example of an exclusionary policy being upheld by the courts can be found in *RSPCA v Attorney General*, where the RSPCA sought guidance on whether it could adopt a membership policy that excluded individuals who wished to change its policy on hunting. The Court found that the freedom of association of the RSPCA itself 'embraces the freedom to exclude from the association those whose membership it honestly believes to be damaging the interests of the Society. The exclusionary policy would not therefore violate Article 11.'[1482]   6.538

Refusals to register or give legal status to would-be associations have generated an extensive body of ECtHR case law.[1483] However, this does not always constitute a breach of the right to freedom of association. In *Gorzelik v Poland*, for example, the Grand Chamber upheld a refusal to register an association as a 'national minority' rather than an 'ethnic regional group'. It found that the disputed restriction was essentially concerned with 'the label which the association could use in law' rather than its ability to act collectively in a field of mutual interest. As such, it did not go to the core or essence of freedom of association, and the restriction was not disproportionate.[1484] In *Sindicatul 'Păstorul cel Bun' v Romania* the Grand Chamber held that the refusal to register a trade union for priests was justified under Article 11.[1485] It accepted that a trade union would imperil the autonomy of the church, protected by Article 9, to respond within its own rules to any dissident movement.   6.539

(ii) Right to non-association

Article 11 also protects the right to refuse to join (or to cease to be a member of) an association in most circumstances;[1486] this is sometimes called negative freedom of association. The ECtHR first recognized this in *Young, James and Webster v UK*, holding that 'the negative aspect of freedom of association is necessarily complementary to, and a correlative of and inseparable from its positive aspect'.[1487] The   6.540

[1480] *Lovrić v Croatia* App No 38458/15, 4 April 2017, paras 71–72.

[1481] *Cheall v UK* (1985) 42 DR 178.

[1482] *RSPCA v Attorney General and others* [2002] 1 WLR 448.

[1483] See eg *Yordanovi v Bulgaria* App No 11157/11, 3 December 2020 (available only in French); *Sidiropoulos Greece* App No 57/1997/841/1047, 10 July 1998; *Tsonev v Bulgaria* App No 45963/99, 13 July 2006; *United Macedonian Organization Ilinden and others v Bulgaria* (1998) 26 EHRR CD 103.

[1484] *Gorzelik v Poland* App No 44158/98, 17 February 2004, paras 105–06.

[1485] *Sindicatul 'Păstorul cel Bun' v Romania* (2014) 58 EHRR 10 [GC].

[1486] As to the limits of this, see *Chassagnou and others v France* (1999) 29 EHRR 615, para 114.

[1487] *Young, James and Webster v UK* (1982) 4 EHRR 38, para 59; *Vörður Ólafsson v Iceland* App No 20161/06, 27 April 2010.

Grand Chamber has confirmed the importance of non-association, which reflects the weight that the Court attaches to personal autonomy.[1488]

(iii) Public and professional bodies

6.541 Professional regulatory bodies set up by a state to regulate a profession, with compulsory membership within a profession, do not fall within the definition of an 'association'.[1489] For example, associations of lawyers, architects, and medical practitioners have been held to be outside the definition, whereas a taxi drivers' association has been held to fall within it.[1490]

(iv) Trade union freedoms

6.542 Article 11(1) states that freedom of association includes the right to form and join trade unions. The case law has established that the protection of trade union freedom also extends to the right of the union to address an employer on behalf of its members (and the concomitant right of union members to be represented by their union in negotiations), a general prohibition on closed-shop arrangements (ie agreements which made trade union membership a condition of employment), and the right to collective bargaining.[1491] These rights can be asserted by both individuals and trade unions.[1492]

6.543 The ECtHR has held that the state must 'both permit and make possible' freedom for individual trade unionists to protect their interests by trade union action.[1493] This extends to taking part in organized industrial action (although freedom of association does not extend to securing any particular outcome through strikes).[1494] But there is no absolute right to strike and the state can impose limitations upon this.[1495] Restrictions on strikes or actions taken in response to strikes constitute an interference with the right to freedom of association because they restrict a union's power to protect the interests of its members.[1496]

6.544 Article 11 protects the right of workers to join unions and engage in union activity without being subject to detriments.[1497] Where the state is the employer, subjecting an employee to a detriment for engaging in strike action will amount to an interference with Article 11.[1498] The position is more complex in respect of

---

[1488] *Sørensen and Rasmussen v Denmark* App No 52562/99 & another, 11 January 2006 [GC], para 54.
[1489] *Le Compte, Van Leuven and De Meyere v Belgium* (1981) 4 EHRR 1.
[1490] *Sigurdur A Sigurjónsson v Iceland* (1993) 16 EHRR 462.
[1491] *Demir v Turkey* (2009) 48 EHRR 54 [GC], para 145; *Sindicatul Păstorul cel Bun v Romania* (2014) 58 EHRR 10 [GC], para 135; *Association of Civil Servants and Union for Collective Bargaining v Germany* (2023) 76 EHRR 4, para 57; *Unite the Union v United Kingdom* (2016) 63 EHRR SE7, para 53.
[1492] *R (Independent Workers Union of Great Britain) v Central Arbitration Committee* [2021] EWCA Civ 952, [2022] ICR 84, para 10.
[1493] *National Union of Belgian Police v Belgium* (1975) 1 EHRR 578, para 39.
[1494] *Association of Academics v Iceland (dec)* App No 2451/16, 15 May 2018, para 24; *Mercer v Alternative Future Group Ltd* [2022] EWCA Civ 379, [2022] ICR 1034, para 62.
[1495] *Enerji Yapi-Yol Sen v Turkey* App No 68959/01, 21 April 2009 (available only in French), para 32.
[1496] *Hrvatski liječnički sindikat v Croatia* App No 36701/09, 27 November 2014, para 49.
[1497] See eg *Associated Society of Locomotive Engineers and Firemen (ASLEF) v UK* (2007) 45 EHRR 34, para 39; *Straume v Latvia*, App No 59402/14, 2 June 2022, paras 92–93.
[1498] *Mercer v Alternative Future Group Ltd* [2022] EWCA Civ 379, [2022] ICR 1034, para 62.

private sector employers but the state's positive obligations may require it to protect employees against detriments by such employers.[1499]

As noted above, the right to freedom of association encompasses a right to engage in collective bargaining.[1500] The ECtHR has held that it is 'one of the principal means—even the foremost of such means—for trade unionists to protect their interests'.[1501] There is, however, no requirement for states to establish a mandatory mechanism for collective bargaining.[1502] Where a trade union has been recognized for the purposes of collective bargaining, permitting employers to bypass a union and negotiate directly with employees may breach Article 11.[1503]   6.545

A 'closed shop' arrangement will generally, but not always, breach the right to freedom of association. In *Young*, it did so because the refusal to join a union led to 'a threat of dismissal involving loss of livelihood' which was 'a most serious form of compulsion' and, as such, struck 'at the very substance of the freedom guaranteed by Article 11'.[1504] In *Sørenson and Rasmussen v Denmark* the ECtHR emphasized that the Convention is a living instrument, and account must be taken of changing perceptions of the relevance of closed shop agreements for securing the effective enjoyment of trade union freedoms.[1505] The Grand Chamber rejected the distinction between pre-entry and post-entry closed shops, and held that the interference with the applicants' rights to be disproportionate as the government had failed to demonstrate that closed shops are 'an indispensable tool' for protecting trade union freedoms.   6.546

Domestic law has generally adopted a more conservative approach towards collective rights. Statutory limitations on the right to strike are unlikely to be deemed to be incompatible with Article 11.[1506] However, in the recent case of *Mercer* the Court of Appeal considered whether section 146 of the Trade Union and Labour Relations (Consolidation) Act 1992 (TULRCA), protects employees against detriments short of dismissal for taking part in or organizing industrial action. Concluding that it does not, the Court held that the TULRCA does not provide the range of protections required by the right to freedom of association under Article 11 and that failure to provide protection against sanctions short of dismissal (by private sector employers) for engaging in industrial action may place the UK in breach of Article 11. But the Court declined to make a declaration of incompatibility in respect of section 146.[1507]   6.547

[1499] See eg *Tek Gida iş Sendikasi v Turkey* App No 35009/05, 4 April 2017; *Mercer v Alternative Future Group Ltd* [2022] EWCA Civ 379, [2022] ICR 1034.

[1500] See eg *Association of Civil Servants and Union for Collective Bargaining v Germany* (2023) 76 EHRR 4, para 51.

[1501] *Demir v Turkey* (2009) 48 EHRR 54, para 129.

[1502] *Wilson and Palmer v UK* (2002) 35 EHRR 20, para 44.

[1503] *Kostal UK Ltd v Dunkley and another* [2021] UKSC 47, [2022] ICR 434, paras 60–62.

[1504] *Young v UK* (1982) 4 EHRR 38, 59.

[1505] *Sørenson and Rasmussen v Denmark* App No 52562/99, 11 January 2006, para 58.

[1506] See eg *British Airways Plc v Unite the Union* [2010] EWCA Civ 669, [2010] IRLR 423; *RMT v Serco Ltd* [2011] EWCA Civ 226, [2011] IRLR 399.

[1507] *Mercer v Alternative Future Group Ltd* [2022] EWCA Civ 379, [2022] ICR 1034, paras 54, 71, 85, 88.

(b) *Justifications for interferences with the right to freedom of association*

6.548　Any interference with the right to freedom of association must comply with the requirements of Article 11(2) as set out at para 6.526. A wide range of state actions may constitute an interference with this right (including preventing associations from forming, dissolving them, subjecting them to onerous registration, reporting and inspection requirements, and restricting their funding) and must therefore be justified.[1508]

6.549　Most cases turn on the question of whether an interference is necessary in a democratic society. The ECtHR has emphasized that the Article 11(2) exceptions are to be construed strictly: only 'convincing and compelling reasons'[1509] can justify restrictions on freedom of association, and 'all such restrictions are subject to a rigorous supervision by the Court'.[1510] This strict approach is due to the 'direct relationship between democracy, pluralism and the freedom of association', and the intensity of the ECtHR's scrutiny is particularly intense where the association is of a political nature.[1511] The ECtHR's jurisprudence on Article 11(2) attaches particular importance to pluralism, tolerance, and broadmindedness. In that context, the ECtHR has held that, although individual interests must on occasion be subordinated to those of a group, democracy does not simply mean that the views of the majority must always prevail: a balance must be achieved that ensures the fair and proper treatment of minorities and avoids any abuse of a dominant position.[1512]

6.550　The dissolution or banning of associations has given rise to a large body of case law before the ECtHR. This is, unsurprisingly, regarded as being a very serious interference which can only be justified in the most serious of cases. By way of example, in *Refah Partisi v Turkey* the Grand Chamber unanimously upheld the Chamber's majority finding that the ban was justified on the basis that a state is entitled to prevent the implementation of a political programme that is inconsistent with Convention norms and which, if given effect, might jeopardize civil peace and a country's democratic regime (in that case the party in question campaigned for a state based on Sharia law and had not ruled out the use of violence to achieve this).[1513] In *Herri Batasuna and Batasuna v Spain* a political party linked to the terrorist organization, ETA, was dissolved.[1514] The Court endorsed the position

---

[1508] See the examples given by the ECtHR in *Ecodefence & others v Russia* App Nos 9988/13 and others, 14 June 2022, paras 81, 83, and 85.

[1509] *Tüm Haber Sen and Çinar v Turkey* App No 28602/95, 21 February 2006, para 35.

[1510] See eg *United Communist Party of Turkey and others v Turkey* Reports of Judgments and Decisions 1998-I, 30 January 1998, para 42; *Socialist Party and others v Turkey* Reports of Judgments and Decisions 1998-III, 25 May 1998, para 41; *Refah Partisi (The Welfare Party) and others v Turkey* (2003) 14 BHRC 1, para 86.

[1511] *Gorzelik and others* (2005) 40 EHRR 4, para 88; *Les Authentiks and Supras Auteuil 91 v France*, App No 4696/11 & another, 27 October 2006, paras 74 and 84.

[1512] See eg *Young, James and Webster v UK* (1982) 4 EHRR 38, para 63; *Chassagnou and others v France* (1999) 29 EHRR 615, para 112.

[1513] *Refah Partisi v Turkey* (2003) 14 BHRC 1. In that case the ECtHR laid down guidance on determining whether the banning of party meets a pressing social need, see ibid para 104.

[1514] *Herri Batasuna and Batasuna v Spain* App Nos 25803/04 and 25817/04, 30 June 2009.

of the domestic courts in finding that a refusal to condemn violence amounted to tacit support for terrorism, in the context of the long-term threat from Basque terrorism. In *Ayoub v France* the ECtHR held that the dissolution of two neo-Nazi organizations (whose members were involved in acts of violence and formed a kind of militia, and who promulgated antisemitic propaganda) did not breach Article 11.[1515]

Powers to ban associations must nevertheless 'be used sparingly'.[1516] The ECtHR has held that bans on (or refusals to register) political parties which, in contrast to the applicants in the cases referred to above, did not reject democratic principles and/or advocate violence breached Article 11.[1517] In a series of cases against Turkey[1518] and Bulgaria[1519] the ECtHR found that the mere fact that an association expresses separatist views and demands territorial changes in speeches, demonstrations, or manifestos does not per se amount to a threat to a country's territorial integrity. Views or words which may appear 'shocking and unacceptable' to the authorities and the majority of the population should not be suppressed on this basis. The expression of views which challenge the existing order are unlikely to justify banning unless the association/party rejects the tenets of the democratic system and/or advocates violence.[1520] Further, in assessing whether an organization promotes violence, the ECtHR will take into account the fact that their statements or declarations may include 'an element of exaggeration' and harsh, acerbic language in order to attract attention.[1521] **6.551**

Article 11(2) permits states to place limitations on the exercise of the Article 11(1) rights by members of the armed forces, police, or members of the administration of the state/civil service. However, even where a person works for one of these entities a strict approach to the question of justification is nevertheless required.[1522] Restrictions placed on these groups should not impair the very essence of the right to organize and associate.[1523] **6.552**

(c) Freedom of association and positive obligations

Article 11 encompasses a positive obligation on states to secure the effective enjoyment of the right to freedom of association.[1524] The ECtHR has also held on a number of occasions that a state's failure to act to protect association **6.553**

[1515] *Ayoub v France* App Nos 77400/14 and others, 8 October 2020 (available only in French). See also *Vona v Hungary* App No 35943/10, 9 July 2013.

[1516] *Gorzelik and others* (2005) 40 EHRR 4, para 95.

[1517] See eg *Partidul Comunistilor (Nepeceristi) and Ungureanu v Romania* App No 46626/99, 3 February 2005; *Tsonev v Bulgaria* App No 45963/99, 13 April 2006.

[1518] *Freedom and Democracy Party (OZDEP) v Turkey* App No 23885/94 ECHR 1999-VIII, para 41; *Yazar and others v Turkey* App Nos 22723/93 and others, ECHR 2002-II, paras 57, 58.

[1519] *Stankov and United Macedonian Association Ilinden v Bulgaria* App Nos 29221/95 & others, 2 October 2001, para 97; *United Macedonian Association Ilinden v Bulgaria* (1998) 26 EHRR CD 103, para 76.

[1520] *United Macedonian Association Ilinden v Bulgaria* (1998) 26 EHRR CD 103, para 61.

[1521] ibid para 77.

[1522] *Tüm Haber Sen and Cinar v Turkey* App No 28602/95, 21 February 2006, para 35.

[1523] *Demir v Turkey* (2009) 48 EHRR 54 [GC], paras 97 and 119.

[1524] *Wilson and Palmer v UK* (2002) 35 EHRR 20.

violated Article 11. For example, this right was breached where domestic law did not prohibit employers imposing financial disincentives to trade union membership.[1525] In *Danilenkov and others v Russia*, the Court ruled that the state had a positive obligation to establish a judicial system that provided effective and clear protection against any discrimination based on membership of a trade union.[1526]

6.554 In *Redfearn v UK* the Court considered the dismissal of a bus driver on the grounds that he had been elected a councillor for the British National Party (BNP). He had been unable to bring a claim for unfair dismissal because he had not been working for the required qualifying period and he attempted instead to bring a claim for race discrimination. The Court of Appeal found that he had not been discriminated against because he was white and the Race Relations Act 1976 did not apply. The Court also held that the Convention did not assist him because his employer was a private company. The ECtHR disagreed, holding that 'there is a positive obligation on the authorities to provide protection against dismissal by private employers where the dismissal is motivated solely by the fact that an employee belongs to a particular political party'.[1527] If he had been able to bring an unfair dismissal claim, the Court held that he could have vindicated his Article 11 rights, but it was incumbent on the government to make comprehensive legislative provision to protect individuals discriminated against for their political beliefs.

I. ARTICLE 12: RIGHT TO MARRY AND FOUND A FAMILY

6.555 Article 12 has two constituent rights—the right to marry and the right to found a family.

6.556 While it has obvious links to the right to respect for family life in Article 8, Article 12 is a distinct provision (*lex specialis*). The ECtHR affirmed the distinction between Articles 8 and 12 in *P, C and S v UK*, holding that complaints regarding interference with family life between a parent and child engage Article 8, but cannot be raised under Article 12.[1528] In general, the ECtHR has taken a much narrower approach to the scope of Article 12 than that of Article 8.

6.557 In cases raising issues under both Article 8 and Article 12, the ECtHR has held that an interference with family life that is justified under Article 8(2) cannot constitute a violation of Article 12.[1529]

[1525] ibid. See also *Young, James and Webster v UK* (1981) 4 EHRR 38, para 49; *Gustaffson v Sweden* Reports of Judgments and Decisions 1996-II, 25 April 1996, para 45; *Sørensen and Rasmussen v Denmark* App Nos 52562/99 and another, 11 January 2006 [GC], para 57.
[1526] *Danilenkov and others v Russia* App No 67336/01, 30 July 2009.
[1527] *Redfearn v UK* (2012) 33 BHRC 713, para 43.
[1528] *P, C and S v UK* (2002) 35 EHRR 31.
[1529] *Boso v Italy* App No 50490/99, 5 September 2002.

1. Limitations on Article 12 rights

The text of Article 12, which refers to the right of 'men and women of marriageable age' to marry and found a family 'according to the national laws governing exercise of this right', appears to give the state considerable discretion. — 6.558

There has been some confusion over whether, in light of this, limitations on Article 12 rights must meet the same criteria as those generally applicable to other qualified rights—for example, that they serve a legitimate aim and are proportionate to that aim.[1530] The ECtHR has consistently held that (as with other qualified rights) limitations must not infringe 'the very essence of the right',[1531] but in earlier cases tended not to apply the same proportionality analysis adopted under Articles 8 to 11.[1532] More recently, the ECtHR has indicated that in light of the text of Article 12 it will not apply the tests of 'necessity' or 'pressing social need' but will consider 'whether, regard being had to the State's margin of appreciation, the impugned interference was arbitrary or disproportionate'.[1533] The Court has also indicated that measures which interfere with Article 12 rights must 'meet the standards of accessibility and clarity required by the Convention'—standards usually associated with the requirement that interferences with qualified rights be 'in accordance with the law' or 'prescribed by law' (see Chapter 2, paras 2.42–2.49 and this chapter, paras 6.366–6.374).[1534] — 6.559

In *Green v Commissioner of Police of the Metropolis* the Court of Appeal considered the test for justification under Article 12; while it reached no concluded view on whether a 'heightened level of justification is required' as compared with other qualified rights, it did affirm that the approach under (eg) Articles 8 and 14 could not simply be transposed.[1535] — 6.560

2. Positive obligations

Article 12 has not so far been interpreted as imposing extensive positive obligations on the state. For example, the ECtHR has held that there is no obligation to ensure that a married couple can cohabit or consummate their marriage.[1536] Nor is there a duty to provide living accommodation or subsistence to maintain a family.[1537] Positive obligations such as these are more likely to arise as a consequence of respect for private and family life under Article 8.[1538] — 6.561

[1530] See eg *R (Baiai and others) v Secretary of State for the Home Department* [2008] UKHL 53, [2008] 3 All ER 1094, para 46 per Baroness Hale.

[1531] See eg *Delecolle v France* (2020) 70 EHRR 1, para 50.

[1532] See eg *Goodwin v UK* (2002) 35 EHRR 18.

[1533] *Delecolle v France* (2020) 70 EHRR 1, para 53.

[1534] See eg *O'Donoghue v UK* (2010) 30 BHRC 85, para 83. cf *Jaremowicz v Poland* App No 24023/03, 5 October 2010, paras 63–64 (perhaps surprisingly, accepting that Polish law left relevant authorities 'a complete discretion in deciding on a detainee's request for leave to marry in prison' but holding that the 'decisive element' was the disproportionate exercise of the discretion in the particular case.

[1535] *Green v Commissioner of Police of the Metropolis* [2022] EWCA Civ 1686, [2023] ICR 429, paras 60–67, 79.

[1536] *Hamer v UK* (1979) 24 DR 5; *Draper v UK* (1980) 24 DR 72.

[1537] *Andersson and Kullman v Sweden* (1986) 46 DR 251.

[1538] See eg *Dickson v UK* (2007) 24 BHRC 19. See also the discussion under art 8 at paras 6.268–6.271.

6.562　　In line with this approach, the Northern Ireland Court of Appeal held in *Re Connor's Application for Judicial Review* that Article 12 does not confer an absolute right to cohabitation on spouses, and that such a right may be interfered with where this is proportionate.[1539]

3. The right to marry

(a) *Regulation and formalities*

6.563　　The right to marry is a right that can only be exercised in accordance with national law and it is therefore for the state in the first instance to decide how it wishes to regulate marriage. This can be done via both procedural rules (eg concerning matters such as notice, publicity, and witnesses) and substantive rules (such as requirements relating to consent, capacity,[1540] prohibited degrees of consanguinity, or the prevention of bigamy). The Convention also leaves it to states to determine marriageable age. National laws imposing a minimum age of consent for lawful marriage do not amount to a breach of the right to marry under Article 12, even if they conflict with differing religious laws.[1541]

6.564　　As noted above, regulations may not impair the 'very essence' of the right to marry. This may occur where, for example, the state imposes a substantial period of delay before permitting people to marry.[1542] However, a measure does not impair the 'very essence' of the right to marry (resulting in a violation) simply because its effect in all the circumstances is to prevent a particular marriage from occurring. For example, the domestic courts are able to make orders preventing a marriage where a vulnerable person lacks capacity to consent, or where to give effect to the wishes of a person with capacity would expose them to a real risk of Article 3 harm (eg in the context of a potentially coercive relationship).[1543] Similarly, a measure need not entirely prevent a marriage in order to engage Article 12. *Green v Commissioner of Police of the Metropolis* is an example of this: a rule disentitling the surviving partners of police officers to a pension if they entered into a new marriage, civil partnership or equivalent de facto relationship was held to engage Article 12 but to be justified.[1544]

6.565　　Arbitrary regulation is also prohibited. In *Hamer v UK*[1545] and *Draper v UK*[1546] the ECmHR ruled that prohibiting prisoners from marrying was an arbitrary interference with their Article 12 rights because it served no legitimate state objective.

[1539] *Re Connor's Application for Judicial Review* [2004] NICA 45.
[1540] See eg *Delecolle v France* (2020) 70 EHRR 1.
[1541] *Khan v UK* (1986) 48 DR 253. See also *ZH v Switzerland* (2017) 65 EHRR 30, paras 43–44.
[1542] *Hamer v UK* (1979) 24 DR 5; *F v Switzerland* (1987) 10 EHRR 411; cf *Shara and Rinia v Netherlands* (1985) 8 EHRR 307.
[1543] See eg *WU v BU (by her litigation friend the Official Solicitor)* [2021] EWCOP 54. See also the approach at first instance in *Green v Commissioner of Police of the Metrpolis* [2022] EWCA Civ 1686, [2023] ICR 429, endorsed by the Court of Appeal, whereby all factors going to justification may be examined in order to determine whether the 'very essence of the right' has been impaired: ibid para 69.
[1544] *Green v Commissioner of Police of the Metropolis* [2022] EWCA Civ 1686, [2023[ICR 429.
[1545] *Hamer v UK* (1979) 24 DR 5.
[1546] *Draper v UK* (1980) 24 DR 72.

In *B v UK* a father-in-law and daughter-in-law challenged the provisions of the Marriage Act 1949 which prevented them from marrying, subject to obtaining a waiver through a private act of Parliament.[1547] The ECtHR found that the inconsistency between the government's stated objectives and the waiver 'undermined the rationality and logic of the measure'.

Restrictions or regulations must also be compatible with the exercise of other 6.566 Convention rights, in particular Article 9, though this does not impose a positive obligation to match civil and religious marriage laws, nor preclude a requirement that a religious marriage ceremony may also need to be affirmed or registered under civil law.[1548]

(b) *Non-nationals*

The ECtHR has consistently held that conditions may be attached to the marriage of 6.567 non-nationals in Member States for the purposes of ascertaining whether the marriage is genuine or one of convenience.[1549] In *R (Baiai and others) v Secretary of State for the Home Department* the House of Lords considered measures put in place by the Home Office to prevent 'sham marriages' with persons subject to immigration control.[1550] With some limited exceptions, all such persons were required to seek a certificate from the Home Secretary regardless of the status of their partner. In practice, almost all these applications were refused without regard to the applicants' individual circumstances. The House of Lords held that while the government could legitimately take measures to prevent 'sham' marriages, the scheme disproportionately infringed the rights of non-nationals. Invoking Nazi race laws, Baroness Hale stated:

Denying to members of minority groups the right to establish formal, legal relationships with the partners of their choice is one way of setting them apart from society, denying that they are 'free and equal in dignity and rights'.[1551]

The government amended the scheme in response to the judgment in *Baiai*. The 6.568 amended scheme was challenged in *O'Donoghue and others v UK*.[1552] The ECtHR found that the scheme did not comply with Article 12 on the basis that the decision whether or not to grant a certificate of approval was not based solely on the genuineness of the proposed marriage; the scheme imposed a blanket prohibition on the exercise of the right to marry on all persons without sufficient immigration leave; and the system of refunding fees to needy applicants was not an effective means of

---

[1547] *B v UK* App No 36536/02, 13 September 2005.

[1548] *X v Germany* (1974) 1 DR 64; *Adams and Khan v UK* (1967) 10 YB 478. See, further, *Selim v Cyprus: Friendly Settlement* App No 47293/99, 16 July 2002; *ZH v Switzerland* (2017) 65 EHRR 30, paras 43–44.

[1549] *Sanders v France* (1996) 87 B-DR 160, para 163; *Klip and Krüger v Netherlands* (1997) 91 A-DR 66, para 71; *R (Baiai and others) v Secretary of State for the Home Department* [2008] UKHL 53, [2008] 3 All ER 1094, para 29.

[1550] *R (Baiai and others) v Secretary of State for the Home Department* [2008] UKHL 53, [2008] 3 All ER 1094.

[1551] ibid para 44.

[1552] *O'Donoghue and others v UK* (2010) 30 BHRC 85. Considered by the Court of Appeal in *MM (Lebanon) v Secretary of State for the Home Department* [2014] EWCA Civ 985 in relation to art 8.

removing any breach of Article 12 as the very requirement to pay a fee acted as a powerful disincentive to marriage.

(c) *Gender and the right to marry*

6.569 Initially Article 12 was interpreted as guaranteeing only a right to marry a person who was biologically of the opposite sex.[1553] According to the ECtHR, the adoption of biological criteria to determine sex for the purposes of marriage was 'a matter encompassed within the power of Contracting States to regulate by national law the exercise of the right to marry'.[1554]

6.570 However, in *Goodwin v UK* the ECtHR held that:

> While it is for the Contracting State to determine *inter alia* the conditions under which a person claiming legal recognition as a transsexual establishes that gender reassignment has been properly effected or under which past marriages cease to be valid and the formalities applicable to future marriages ... the Court finds no justification for barring the transsexual from enjoying the right to marry under any circumstances.[1555]

6.571 Domestic law is now in line with Strasbourg's position. In *Bellinger v Bellinger* the House of Lords issued a declaration of incompatibility, holding that section 11(c) of the Matrimonial Causes Act 1973 could not be construed so as to give effect to the decision of the ECtHR in *Goodwin*.[1556] Parliament then passed the Gender Recognition Act 2004, which provides that the marriage of a person who has obtained a 'full gender recognition certificate' to a person of the same biological sex as their original sex will not be rendered void on the basis that the parties are not respectively male and female. Coupled with developments in the availability of marriage to same-sex couples and of civil partnerships to opposite-sex couples, this has opened up a wider range of options.[1557]

(d) *Same-sex marriage*

6.572 The ECtHR has consistently held that Article 12 does not guarantee same-sex couples the right to marry.[1558] In *Schalk and Kopf v Austria* the Court held that the absence of European consensus on the issue meant that the Convention could not yet be interpreted as guaranteeing such a right in an absolute sense.[1559] However,

---

[1553] *Rees v UK* (1987) 9 EHRR 56; *Cossey v UK* (1990) 13 EHRR 622; *Sheffield and Horsham v UK* (1999) 27 EHRR 163.

[1554] *Cossey v UK* (1990) 13 EHRR 622.

[1555] *Goodwin v UK* (2002) 35 EHRR 18, para 103.

[1556] *Bellinger v Bellinger* [2003] UKHL 21, [2003] 2 AC 467.

[1557] For a discussion of the intermediate position, see *Parry v UK* App No 42971/05, 28 November 2006. The applicant was married with children and had undergone gender reassignment surgery; she could not obtain a full gender recognition certificate without dissolving her marriage, as the law at the time did not permit same-sex marriage. The complaint under arts 8 and 12 was held to be inadmissible, as the UK had not failed to give legal recognition to the applicant's gender reassignment and the applicants could continue their relationship through a civil partnership.

[1558] *Rees v UK* (1987) 9 EHRR 56; *Cossey v UK* (1990) 13 EHRR 622. See also the decision of the ECJ in *Grant v South-West Trains* [1998] ICR 449.

[1559] *Schalk and Kopf v Austria* App No 30141/04, 24 June 2010.

the Court considered the Charter of Fundamental Rights of the European Union, which includes in Article 9 a right to marry without a reference to men or women, thus leaving the decision to states whether or not to recognize same-sex marriages. On the basis of this, the ECtHR concluded that it

> would no longer consider that the right to marry enshrined in Article 12 must in all circumstances be limited to marriage between two persons of the opposite sex. Consequently, it cannot be said that Article 12 is inapplicable to the applicants' complaint. However, as matters stand, the question whether or not to allow same-sex marriage is left to regulation by the national law of the Contracting State.[1560]

Pending further developments in this area, a number of complaints have instead been brought under Article 14, taken with Articles 8 and 12. For example, in *Orlandi v Italy* the ECtHR held that, while Article 12 still did not guarantee a freestanding right for same-sex couples to marry, a complaint about Italy's failure either to recognize same-sex marriages contracted overseas or to offer a civil alternative engaged Article 14 with both Article 8 and Article 12.[1561] As it breached Article 14 taken with Article 8, there was no need to consider Article 12 further—but the same conclusion may well have been reached.

6.573

The domestic courts have taken a similar approach. In *Wilkinson v Kitzinger* the High Court was asked to declare that the recognition of a Canadian marriage between two women domiciled in England, valid as a matter of the law of British Columbia, was valid as a marriage in the UK;[1562] or alternatively that its recognition as a civil partnership under the Civil Partnership Act 2004, rather than a marriage, rendered English law incompatible with Articles 8, 12, and 14 of the Convention. The judge held that there was no such incompatibility: to afford legal recognition to same-sex relationships as civil partnerships rather than as 'marriages' met a legitimate aim of social policy and was proportionate. In *Re Close's Application for Judicial Review* the Northern Ireland Court of Appeal reviewed recent case law and confirmed that, notwithstanding the developments in the Article 8 case law, it was 'clear that Article 12 does not establish a right to same sex marriage'[1563]—but it did find that the ongoing exclusion of same-sex couples from the institution of civil marriage in Northern Ireland had become discriminatory under Article 14 prior to the introduction of legislative changes allowing for it.[1564]

6.574

For an illustration of the relationship between the developments in domestic law governing gender recognition (on the one hand) and same-sex marriage (on the other) in the context of the relevant Convention rights, including Article 12, see *AP v JP*.[1565]

6.575

[1560] ibid para 61.
[1561] *Orlandi v Italy* App Nos 26431/12 & others, 14 December 2017, paras 145–46.
[1562] *Wilkinson v Kitzinger* [2006] EWHC 2022 (Fam), [2007] 1 FLR 295.
[1563] *Re Close's Application for Judicial Review* [2020] NICA 20, para 41.
[1564] ibid paras 46–59.
[1565] *AP v JP* [2019] EWHC 3105 (Fam).

(e) Dissolution of marriage

6.576   The right to marry does not include its corollary—the right to dissolve or formally end a marriage.[1566] The *travaux préparatoires* to the Convention indicate that the omission of 'dissolution' from the text of Article 12 was a deliberate departure from the wording of Article 16 of the Universal Declaration on Human Rights.[1567] This has also been accepted by the domestic courts.[1568] However, in light of the 'living instrument' doctrine, the ECtHR has not ruled out the possibility that Article 12 could be breached 'where, despite an irretrievable breakdown of marital life, domestic law regarded the lack of consent of an innocent party as an insurmountable obstacle to granting a divorce to a guilty party'.[1569] The Court has also held that, if national legislation does allow for divorce, Article 12 'secures for divorced persons the right to remarry without unreasonable restrictions'.[1570] Accordingly, unreasonable delay in conducting divorce proceedings may raise an issue under Article 12.[1571]

4. Right to found a family

6.577   Article 12 also protects the right to 'found a family', again subject to 'national laws governing the exercise of this right'. This right has so far only been considered in the context of marriage; Article 12 does not create a free-standing right to found a family in the absence of a marital relationship.[1572]

(a) Adoption

6.578   A family can be founded by the adoption of children.[1573] However, the ECtHR has affirmed the early decision in *X and Y v UK*[1574] that Article 12 does not create a right to adopt.[1575] It might, however, form part of the right to personal development under Article 8.[1576] At least one domestic decision has adopted the same approach, interpreting the ECtHR authorities as 'saying that Contracting States are not currently required by the Convention to include within the right to found a family guaranteed by Article 12, the right to adopt a child'—a right which is 'left to the national law'.[1577]

[1566] *Johnston and others v Ireland* (1986) 9 EHRR 203.

[1567] Collected Edition of the Travaux Préparatoires, vol 1, 268.

[1568] See eg *Owens v Owens* [2017] EWCA Civ 182, [2017] 4 WLR 74, paras 76–81. See also *Akhter v Khan* [2020] EWCA Civ 122, [2021] Fam 277, para 81, reaching the same conclusion in respect of a religious marriage which had been void for civil purposes.

[1569] See eg *Babiarz v Poland* [2017] 2 FLR 613, paras 49–50.

[1570] *Chernetskiy v Ukraine* App No 44316/07, 8 December 2016, para 30.

[1571] ibid paras 30–33; see also *Babiarz v Poland* [2017] 2 FLR 613, paras 49–50.

[1572] *Marckx v Belgium* (1979) 2 EHRR 330; *R (SC) v Secretary of State for Work and Pensions* [2021] UKSC 25, [2022] AC 22, para 35.

[1573] *Van Oosterwijck v Belgium* (1979) 3 EHRR 581.

[1574] *X and Y v UK* (1977) 12 DR 32.

[1575] *Fretté v France* (2004) 38 EHRR 21, para 32; *EB v France* (2008) 47 EHRR 21, para 41.

[1576] *EB v France* (2008) 47 EHRR 21, paras 42–46.

[1577] *Mander and Mander v Royal Borough of Windsor and Maidenhead* [2019] 12 WLUK 79, Case No C01RG184, para 109.

The Court of Appeal in *Briody v St Helen's and Knowsley Health Authority* ruled that 6.579
Article 12 does not require that a woman rendered infertile by the negligence of an
NHS hospital be entitled to damages that would enable her to proceed with a surrogacy arrangement; nor does it include a right to be supplied with a child.[1578] *Briody* was
distinguished in *XX v Whittingon Hospital NHS Trust*, also a case about the availability
of damages for infertility, in part on the basis of societal developments bearing on the
public policy issues around surrogacy.[1579]

(b) Artificial insemination

The scope of Article 12 as a basis for challenges to restrictions on and regulation of arti- 6.580
ficial insemination or other reproductive technologies has yet to be fully tested before
the ECtHR. Cases raising these issues are more frequently brought under Article 8.[1580]

The ECmHR admitted complaints under Articles 8 and/or 12 about the refusal 6.581
by the state to allow artificial insemination by donor treatment of prisoners' wives
in 1987[1581] and 1991,[1582] and the Grand Chamber considered the issue in *Dickson v
UK*.[1583] In *Dickson* it considered that limiting prisoners' access to artificial insemination to 'exceptional circumstances' breached Article 8, but that no separate issue
arose under Article 12.[1584]

In *R (Rose) v Thanet Clinical Commissioning Group* the High Court rejected a 6.582
challenge to the refusal to grant a Crohn's sufferer access to assisted reproductive
technology without considering the Convention rights in any detail, on the basis
that there was no positive obligation on the state under Article 8 or 12 to fund
particular medical treatments.[1585]

Whether Article 12 includes a right to avail oneself of advances in reproductive 6.583
technology and, if so, whether a positive obligation arises upon the state to facilitate
access to such technology are future questions that are likely to arise either under
Article 12 or under Article 8.

J. ARTICLE 13: RIGHT TO AN EFFECTIVE REMEDY

The object of Article 13 is to provide a means whereby individuals can obtain relief 6.584
at national level for violations of their Convention rights without having to set in

---

[1578] *Briody v St Helen's and Knowsley Health Authority* [2001] EWCA Civ 1010, [2002] QB 856.
[1579] *XX v Whittingon Hospital NHS Trust* [2018] EWCA Civ 2832, [2021] AC 275; affirmed by the
Supreme Court [2020] UKSC 14, [2021] AC 275.
[1580] See eg the art 8 cases discussed at paras paras 6.288–6.292.
[1581] *PG and JH v UK* App No 10822/84, 7 June 1987.
[1582] *GS and RS v UK* App No 17142/90, 10 July 1991.
[1583] *Dickson v UK* (2007) 24 BHRC 19.
[1584] cf the earlier decision of the Court of Appeal in *R v Secretary of State for the Home Department, ex p
Mellor* [2001] EWCA Civ 472, [2002] QB 13.
[1585] *R (Rose) v Thanet Clinical Commissioning Group* [2014] EWHC 1182 (Admin).

motion the international machinery of complaint before the Court.[1586] Article 13 accordingly does not provide a free-standing right to an effective remedy. A claim under Article 13 must be brought in conjunction with an alleged breach of another Convention right. That breach need not be established in order for the ECtHR to find a violation of Article 13, but it must be 'arguable'.[1587] Equally, and despite the language of Article 13, a finding of a violation of another substantive right is not required.[1588] Article 13 will not apply where the applicant can obtain a remedy under another article that proscribes specific remedies, such as the right to review of detention under Article 5(4) or fair trial rights under Article 6(1).[1589]

6.585　　Article 13 is not incorporated into UK law under the Human Rights Act. This omission is discussed further in paragraph 6.600 and in Chapter 3.[1590]

1. Effective remedy

6.586　　The right to an effective remedy means that there must be both domestic procedures for dealing with the substance of an 'arguable complaint' and for granting appropriate relief in cases of actual breach of the Convention.[1591] Accordingly, as the ECtHR stated in *Klass v Germany*, the available remedy must 'involve the determination of the claim as well as the possibility of redress'.[1592] Thus the remedies must in aggregate be effective to prevent a violation or its continuation and to afford adequate redress where a violation has already occurred.[1593] Domestic incorporation of the Convention is not required to comply with Article 13 and states enjoy a margin of appreciation in conforming with their obligations.[1594]

6.587　　However, all state parties have in fact incorporated the Convention into their domestic legal systems.

6.588　　The scope of the Article 13 obligation varies depending on the nature of the complaint. For example, in situations where rights of fundamental importance such as Articles 2 and Article 3 are at stake, Article 13 will require, in addition to the payment of compensation where appropriate, a thorough and effective investigation capable of leading to the identification and punishment of those responsible, including effective access for the complainant to the investigation procedure.[1595]

[1586] European Court of Human Rights Registry Guide on Article 13 of the ECHR (version updated on 31 August 2022), para 2; Collected edition of the 'Travaux préparatoires' of the European Convention on Human Rights, vol II, 485 and 490, and vol III, 651; *Kudla v Poland* (2002) 35 EHRR 11 [GC], para 152.

[1587] *Boyle and Rice v UK* (1988) 10 EHRR 425.

[1588] *Klass v Germany* (1979–80) 2 EHRR 214, para 6; *Tamase v Romania* App No 41720/13, 25 June 2019 [GC], para 219.

[1589] *Håkansson and Sturesson v Sweden* (1991) 13 EHRR 1.

[1590] See Chapter 3, para 3.75.

[1591] *Aksoy v Turkey* (1996) 23 EHRR 553; *ND and NT v Spain* App Nos 8675/15 and 8697/15, 13 February 2020 [GC], paras 240–41.

[1592] *Klass v Germany* (1978) 2 EHRR 214.

[1593] *Kudla v Poland* (2002) 35 EHRR 11 [GC], paras 157–58.

[1594] ibid para 154.

[1595] *Keenan v UK* (2001) 33 EHRR 38; *Edwards v UK* (2002) 35 EHRR 19; *Centre for Legal Resources on Behalf of Valentin Campeanu v Romania* App No 47848/08, 17 July 2014 [GC], para 149; *O'Keeffe v Ireland* App No 35810/09, 28 January 2014 [GC], paras 178–79.

There is considerable overlap between this requirement and the procedural duty arising under Articles 2, 3, and 4 considered in Chapter 5. By contrast, compensation alone may be a sufficient remedy for breaches of other articles. In all cases the requisite remedy must be 'effective' in both law and practice.[1596] The requirement of practical efficacy means that exercise of the remedy must not be unjustifiably hindered by the acts or omissions of state authorities.[1597]

The question will often be whether all the procedures, in the lower tribunals and the courts, taken together, amount to an 'effective remedy'. For example, *Silver v UK* concerned a complaint by a prisoner that his correspondence had been interfered with contrary to Article 8 and that no effective remedy was available in respect of that breach. The ECtHR took the view that neither the prison board of visitors, the Parliamentary Commissioner for Administration, the Home Secretary, nor subsequent judicial review of the Home Secretary's decisions provided sufficiently effective remedies to comply with Article 13.[1598]   **6.589**

The Article 13 compliance of the United Kingdom's pre-Human Rights Act laws in relation to allegations of child abuse, triggering Article 3, came under scrutiny. In both *Z v UK*[1599] and *DP and JC v UK*[1600] the lack of any appropriate means of obtaining a determination of allegations that the local authority had failed to protect the applicants from ill treatment during childhood was found to breach Article 13.   **6.590**

In *Reynolds v UK*[1601] the Court considered an application by the mother of a man who killed himself while he was a voluntary mental health patient. She argued that there had been no mechanism by which she could obtain a civil remedy, that is, compensation, for an arguable breach of Article 2 arising from her son's death. The Court found a breach of Article 13 on the basis that domestic law did not, at that time, recognize the possibility of a breach of Article 2 in relation to those who were not formally detained by the state. Since the decision of the Supreme Court in *Rabone v Pennine Care NHS Trust*, it is now possible to bring a claim for compensation under the Human Rights Act in these circumstances and the UK ought no longer to be in breach of Article 13.[1602]   **6.591**

In *Beizaras and Levickas v Lithuania*,[1603] the Court held that, notwithstanding that there was no issue as to the adequacy of the criminal laws in force in Lithuania, discriminatory attitudes of the domestic courts in dealing with allegations of homophobic hate speech had resulted in a denial of an effective domestic remedy in respect of the applicants' complaints concerning a breach of their Article 8 right to respect for private life and had thereby violated Article 13.   **6.592**

[1596] *Aksoy v Turkey* (1996) 23 EHRR 553.
[1597] ibid.
[1598] *Silver v UK* (1983) 5 EHRR 347.
[1599] *Z v UK* (2002) 34 EHRR 3.
[1600] *DP and JC v UK* (2003) 36 EHRR 14.
[1601] *Reynolds v UK* (2012) 55 EHRR 35.
[1602] *Rabone v Pennine Care NHS Trust* [2012] UKSC 2, [2012] 2 AC 72.
[1603] *Beizaras and Levickas v Lithuania* App No 41288/15, 14 January 2020, paras 151–56.

6.593   In *Mugemangango v Belgium*[1604] the Grand Chamber held that the remedy available to the applicant to challenge election results and to seek a recount of certain ballot papers was not effective. The only remedy was a complaint to the Walloon Parliament, which had exclusive jurisdiction. While remedies need not necessarily be judicial to satisfy the requirements of Article 13, this procedure did not provide adequate and sufficient safeguards of impartiality, the relevant discretion of the Walloon Parliament was not circumscribed with sufficient precision by the provisions of domestic law, and the procedure did not afford effective guarantees of a fair, objective, and sufficiently reasoned decision.

6.594   The ECtHR has been critical of formal remedies that prevent examination of the merits of a claim. Thus, much of the Strasbourg case law concerning the United Kingdom's pre-Human Rights Act compliance with Article 13 addresses the extent to which *Wednesbury*-based judicial review, in which issues of fact can rarely be considered, could be treated as an effective remedy.[1605]

6.595   Whether the ECtHR regards judicial review as an adequate remedy appears to depend on the context, and, in particular, whether the ECtHR is satisfied that the domestic courts can afford a sufficient degree of review properly to examine the legality of the executive's actions in the particular circumstances. In the pre-Human Rights Act cases, the ECtHR's approach varied. In *Soering v UK* the applicant was threatened with extradition to the United States to face a charge of murder, to a state in which he risked being placed on death row (contrary to art 3). The fact that a UK court had jurisdiction to set aside a decision to extradite for this reason convinced the ECtHR that judicial review was an effective remedy for the purposes of Article 13.[1606] Thus, in *Vilvarajah v UK*, the ECtHR held that it had already decided that judicial review was an adequate remedy in the context of extradition, even though, in that case, the applicant had already left the United Kingdom.[1607]

6.596   However, in *Chahal v UK* the ECtHR held that there was no effective remedy for violation of Article 3, and hence a violation of Article 13, where a suspected terrorist was detained in custody for deportation purposes in response to the Home Secretary's determination that he was a threat to national security. The ECtHR found that Article 13 required independent scrutiny of the Article 3 claim, which did not take into consideration the national security threat. This was not provided by the advisory panel which at that time had responsibility for reviewing the deportation order of a terrorism suspect and whose view was anyway not binding on the Home Secretary. Neither was the required independent scrutiny provided by a court upon an application for judicial review.[1608] The Special Immigration Appeals Commission was set up in response to this judgment.

6.597   In *Smith and Grady v UK* the domestic courts could only review whether the policy of excluding homosexuals from the armed forces was irrational, not whether

---

[1604] *Mugemangango v Belgium* App No 310/15, 10 July 2020 [GC], paras 125–27 and 132–39.
[1605] See eg *Peck v UK* (2003) 36 EHRR 41; *Hatton v UK* (2003) 37 EHRR 28 [GC].
[1606] *Soering v UK* (1989) 11 EHRR 439. See also *Bensaid v UK* (2001) 33 EHRR 10.
[1607] *Vilvarajah v UK* (1991) 14 EHRR 248.
[1608] *Chahal v UK* (1997) 23 EHRR 413.

it met a pressing social need or was a proportionate infringement of Article 8. Even the heightened 'anxious scrutiny' standard applied by the domestic courts was held inadequate to comply with Article 13.[1609] In *Hatton v UK* the Grand Chamber of the ECtHR held that Article 13 had been violated because judicial review did not allow for consideration of whether an increase in night flights was a justifiable limitation on the right to respect for the private and family lives of those who lived near Heathrow airport.[1610] The issue of the standard of review is one which, theoretically at least, should have fallen into abeyance after the implementation of the Human Rights Act. However, it remains possible that it could yet form the ground of a complaint in an appropriate case. For example, excessive deference by domestic judges to the opinion of the primary decision-maker in reviewing Convention compatibility (such as in the assessment of the proportionality of an interference with a qualified Convention right) could in theory be held to deprive the judicial remedies under the Human Rights Act of effectiveness.

In a number of cases brought after the implementation of the Human Rights Act, the ECtHR has found that declarations of incompatibility issued under section 4 are not an effective remedy for a breach of a Convention right. The primary failing of the section 4 mechanism is that it places no binding legal obligation on the executive or legislature to amend the law following a declaration of incompatibility, nor can it form the basis of a monetary award of compensation.[1611] In *Burden and Burden v UK* the Grand Chamber held that as a result of these inadequacies a failure to seek a declaration did not mean that the applicant had not exhausted his domestic remedies.[1612] However, the Grand Chamber suggested that there might come a time when the ministerial practice of amending the law in response to a declaration was so certain that a declaration might in fact give rise to a binding obligation. If that point were reached it would be necessary to seek a declaration before making an application to the ECtHR.

6.598

2. National authority

The authority with the ability to provide the remedy must be independent of the body alleged to have breached the Convention obligation.[1613] In *Khan v United Kingdom*,[1614] the Court held that that the discretion of a Chief Constable whether or not to refer death or serious injury matters to the Police Complaints Authority for investigation deprived this remedy of the required standard of independence. If a body is sufficiently independent for Article 6 purposes it will also satisfy this

6.599

[1609] *Smith and Grady v UK* (2000) 29 EHRR 548. See also *Peck v UK* (2003) 36 EHRR 41. cf *D v UK* (1997) 24 EHRR 423.
[1610] *Hatton v UK* (2003) 37 EHRR 28 [GC].
[1611] See *Dodds v UK* App No 59314/00, 8 April 2003; *Walker v UK* App No 37212/02, 16 March 2004; *Pearson v UK* App No 8374/03, 27 April 2004; *B and L v UK* App No 36536/02, 29 June 2004.
[1612] *Burden and Burden v UK* (2008) 24 BHRC 709.
[1613] *Govell v UK* App No 27237/95, 14 January 1998; *Khan v UK* (2001) 31 EHRR 45; *Taylor-Sabori v UK* (2003) 36 EHRR 17.
[1614] *Khan v UK* (2001) 31 EHRR 45, paras 45–47.

requirement under Article 13. While a remedy from a non-judicial authority may suffice, the Court has found in certain contexts that an effective remedy before a judicial body is essential.[1615]

3. Human Rights Act implications

6.600   Article 13[1616] was omitted from the rights incorporated by the Human Rights Act because it was believed that the provisions of the Act itself provided an effective remedy as contemplated under Article 13.[1617] As the European case law on declarations of incompatibility shows, this has not proved to be the case.[1618]

6.601   Despite the fact that Article 13 is not incorporated, the English courts have had regard to the right since, by virtue of section 2 of the Act, Strasbourg case law must be taken into account when a UK court is considering a case 'in connection with' an incorporated right. In *R (Al-Skeini) v Secretary of State for Defence*, for example, Lord Brown held that Article 13 would be violated if the domestic courts were unable to consider extraterritorial complaints in line with the Strasbourg case law on the reach of Article 1.[1619] In *RB (Algeria) v Secretary of State for the Home Department* the House of Lords applied *Chahal v UK*[1620] in reaching its conclusion that the Special Immigration Appeals Commission procedure determined whether deportation would violate Article 3 to the extent required by Article 13.[1621]

6.602   In *Hammerton v United Kingdom*,[1622] the Court held that the scope of section 9(3) of the Human Rights Act, which (in the form in force at the time) relevantly restricted claims for damages in respect of judicial acts to situations of bad faith violated Article 13. The applicant had been detained as a result of an unfair (but good faith) committal order breaching Article 6, but was unable to seek compensation. Section 9(3) has since been amended to permit compensation in such circumstances.[1623] However, in *SW v United Kingdom*,[1624] the Court made a further finding of breach of Article 13 due to the continued restriction in section 9(3) on claims for damages for violations of, in that case, Article 8. Adverse findings had been made against the applicant social worker by a Family Court judge with damaging reputational consequences following a process which the Court of Appeal castigated as manifestly unfair. However, the applicant was advised that she could not seek

---

[1615] See eg *Ramirez Sanchez v France* (2007) 45 EHRR 49 [GC], paras 165–66 (serious repercussions of prolonged solitary confinement of a prisoner meant effective remedy before a judicial body was essential).
[1616] See also Chapter 3.
[1617] *Brown v Stott* [2003] 1 AC 681, [2001] 1 WLR 817, para 847; *In Re S (FC) and others* [2002] UKHL 10, [2002] 2 AC 29, para 61. See also Richard Clayton and Hugh Tomlinson, *The Law of Human Rights*, (2nd edn, OUP 2009) paras 21.02–21.03.
[1618] See para 6.598.
[1619] *R (Al-Skeini) v Secretary of State for Defence* [2007] UKHL 26, [2008] 1 AC 153, paras 147–49.
[1620] *Chahal v UK* (1997) 23 EHRR 413.
[1621] *RB (Algeria) v Secretary of State for the Home Department* [2009] UKHL 10, [2009] 2 WLR 512.
[1622] *Hammerton v United Kingdom* App No 6287/10, 17 March 2016.
[1623] The Human Rights Act 1998 (Remedial) Order 2020.
[1624] *SW v United Kingdom* App No 87/18, 22 June 2021, para 150.

compensation for the violation of her Article 8 rights due to the terms of section 9(3) of the Human Rights Act.

In *Al-Saadoon and Mufdhi v United Kingdom*[1625] the Court held that a violation   6.603
of Article 13 (read with art 34, the right of individual petition to the Court) arose from a failure of the national authorities to take all reasonable steps to comply with a rule 39 interim measures Order made by the Court. The proposals before Parliament in the Illegal Migration Bill at the time of writing which would authorize or even require the government to ignore rule 39 indications in certain circumstances raise an obvious problem of compatibility with the United Kingdom's obligations under inter alia Article 13.

K. ARTICLE 14: PROHIBITION ON DISCRIMINATION

1. The importance of Article 14

Affording equality of respect to all persons, treating like cases alike, and treating   6.604
unlike cases differently, are axioms of rational behaviour in a society which treats each individual as having fundamentally equal worth. Equality in this sense is 'one of the building blocks of democracy'.[1626] The non-discrimination guarantee contained in Article 14 is therefore a key provision of the Convention. As Lord Nicholls explained in *Ghaidan v Godin Mendoza*:

Discriminatory law undermines the rule of law because it is the antithesis of fairness. It brings the law into disrepute. It breeds resentment. It fosters an inequality of outlook which is demeaning alike to those unfairly benefited and those unfairly prejudiced.[1627]

Repeated decisions of the ECtHR have also explained the importance and value   6.605
of a realistic application of the equal treatment guarantee in protecting and preserving a democratic society.[1628]

From its earliest cases, the ECtHR has recognized that it constitutes discrimina-   6.606
tion both to fail to treat like cases alike but also to fail to treat unlike cases differently,[1629] but beyond those early statements, the case law of the ECtHR on Article 14 was until recently relatively undeveloped. However, there have now been a large number of important decisions defining the scope of Article 14, such as those of the Grand Chamber in *Stec v UK* and *DH v Czech Republic*,[1630] along with the clear extension of the positive obligations doctrine to the obligation to 'ensure equal enjoyment' of the underlying Convention rights in *Eremia v Moldova*.[1631]

[1625] *Al-Saadoon and Mufdhi v United Kingdom* App No 61498/08, 4 October 2010, paras 162–66.
[1626] Per Lord Hoffmann in *Matadeen v Pointu* [1999] AC 98, [1998] 3 WLR 18.
[1627] *Ghaidan v Godin-Mendoza* [2004] UKHL 30, [2004] 2 AC 557, para 9. See also other speeches in *Ghaidan*, and the decision of *the House of Lords in A v Secretary of State for the Home Department* [2004] UKHL 56, [2005] 2 AC 68.
[1628] See eg *DH v Czech Republic* (2008) 47 EHRR 3.
[1629] *Belgian Linguisitics Case (No 2)* (1968) 1 EHRR 252, para 10.
[1630] *Stec v UK* (2005) 41 EHRR SE18 [GC]; *DH v Czech Republic* (2007) 47 EHRR 59 [GC].
[1631] *Eremia v Moldova* (2014) 58 EHRR 2, paras 85–95.

2. Scope of Article 14

6.607 Article 14 requires states to secure 'equal enjoyment' by everyone of the Convention rights and freedoms without 'discrimination' on a broad variety of grounds. The listed grounds of prohibited discrimination are non-exhaustive examples only ('any grounds *such as* ... '), and 'other status' has been broadly defined. However, although Article 14 is 'deceptively simple',[1632] its application is not straightforward. It guarantees only *equal application* of the rights enshrined in the Convention, not a free-standing guarantee of equal treatment.

6.608 The protection afforded by Article 14 is therefore narrower than that found in other, more open-ended guarantees of equal treatment, such as that contained in Article 26 of the International Covenant on Civil and Political Rights 1966, or indeed Protocol 12 to the Convention itself (which the United Kingdom has declined to ratify). Article 14 requires only that the enjoyment of other Convention rights be secured without discrimination. This means that it can operate only within the 'ambit' or scope of another Convention right:

> Article 14 complements the other substantive provisions of the Convention and the Protocols. It has no independent existence since it has effect solely in relation to 'the enjoyment of the rights and freedoms' safeguarded by those provisions. Although the application of article 14 does not necessarily presuppose a breach of those provisions—and to this extent it is autonomous—there can be no room for its application unless the facts at issue fall within the ambit of one or more of the latter.[1633]

6.609 In *National Union of Belgian Police v Belgium* the ECtHR said, 'it is as though Article 14 formed an integral part of each of the articles laying down rights and freedoms whatever their nature'.[1634]

6.610 There can be a breach of Article 14 in connection with another article of the Convention where it is established that there has not been equal enjoyment of the underlying protected right, even if the departure from the underlying right in the case of the adversely affected party would not, taken on its own, violate the underlying right. Thus, breach of Article 14 does not require a *breach* of another article but merely that the facts of the case come within the ambit of another article.[1635] However, whether alleged discrimination 'falls within the ambit' of another Convention right is not always a straightforward issue.[1636] In broad terms, Article 14 will come into play whenever the subject matter of the disadvantage 'constitutes one of the modalities' of the exercise of a right.[1637]

[1632] *AL (Serbia) v Secretary of State for the Home Department* [2008] UKHL 42, [2008] 1 WLR 1434, para 20 per Baroness Hale.

[1633] *Abudulaziz, Cabales and Balakandi v UK* (1985) 7 EHRR 471, para 71.

[1634] *National Union of Belgian Police v Belgium* (1979–80) 1 EHRR 578.

[1635] *Abudulaziz, Cabales and Balkandali v UK* (1985) 7 EHRR 471; *Botta v Italy* (1998) 26 EHRR 241, para 39.

[1636] See the different views reached by the House of Lords and the ECtHR on whether criteria for assessing child support obligations which differentiated between those with same-sex and opposite partners fell within the ambit of 'family life': *Secretary of State for Work and Pensions v M* [2006] UKHL 11, [2006] 2 AC 91 paras 13–16 per Lord Nicholls; but held to breach art 14 by the ECtHR in *JM v UK* (2011) 53 EHRR 6.

[1637] *Petrovic v Austria* (2001) 33 EHRR 14, paras 22, 28.

This means that it is enough for a claimant to establish that the disadvantage   6.611
relates to the subject matter of another substantive Convention right, even if the
state has chosen to make provision which is not itself required by the Convention.[1638]
For example, in *Schmidt v Germany*, where only men were obliged to serve in a voluntary fire brigade or to pay a financial contribution in lieu, the ECtHR found that
the requirements for work did not breach the prohibition on 'forced or compulsory
labour' in Article 4 but nevertheless came within the ambit of Article 4 and thus
engaged Article 14.[1639]

This approach was confirmed by the Grand Chamber in *Stec v UK*, which held   6.612
that the prohibition of discrimination extends to 'those additional rights, falling
within the scope of any Convention article, for which the State has voluntarily
decided to provide'. Therefore, although Article 1 of Protocol 1 does not create a
right to acquire property, and places no restriction on a state's freedom to decide
whether or not to have in place a social security scheme, 'if a State does decide to
create a benefits scheme it must do so in a manner compatible with Article 14'.[1640]

In general, the ECtHR has been generous in its approach to ambit. Lord Justice   6.613
Hickinbottom, in the Court of Appeal judgment in *R (JCWI) v Secretary of State
for the Home Department*,[1641] observed that:

It is difficult to disagree with Baroness Hale's observation in *In re McLaughlin* [2018] UKSC 48;
[2018] 1 WLR 4250 at [20]:

'It is fair to say that the English courts have made rather heavy weather of the ambit point, particularly in connection with article 8, because of its broad and ill-defined scope'.

In my respectful view, our courts have laboured over European authorities in an attempt to identify a set of rules for the definition of 'ambit' of substantive rights in this context which can be
applied in the case before them and, indeed, generally; whilst, as on other issues, the ECtHR has
taken a relaxed and loose approach to the concept which makes such close and comprehensive
analysis difficult if not impossible.

In *Smith v Lancashire Teaching Hospitals NHS Foundation Trust*,[1642] the Court of   6.614
Appeal overturned the High Court's finding that the circumstances of the case (the
exclusion of cohabitees from bereavement damages under the Fatal Accidents Act
1976) were not within the ambit of Article 8, finding that the test was that 'the connection or link between the facts and the provisions of the Convention conferring
substantive rights must be more than merely tenuous'. Strasbourg has since clarified

---

[1638] *Ghaidan v Godin-Mendoza* [2004] UKHL 30, [2004] 2 AC 557, para 6 per Lord Nicholls.

[1639] *Schmidt v Germany* (1994) 18 EHRR 513. See eg *Van der Mussele v Belgium* (1983) 6 EHRR 162;
Adami v Malta (2007) 44 EHRR 33, para 46; *Belgian Linguistic Case* (1979-80) 1 EHRR 252, para 9;
Petrovic v Austria (2001) 33 EHRR 14; *Inze v Austria* (1988) 10 EHRR 394; *Abdulaziz, Cabales and
Balkandali v UK* (1985) 7 EHRR 471, paras 65, 71, 72.

[1640] *Stec v UK* (2006) 43 EHRR 1017 [GC], paras 40, 55. Affirmed as a matter of domestic law in *R
(RJM) (FC) v Secretary of State for Work and Pensions* [2008] UKHL 63, [2009] 1 AC 311; and by the Grand
Chamber in *Carson v UK* (2010) 51 EHRR 13 [GC], paras 64–65.

[1641] *R (on the application of Joint Council for the Welfare of Immigrants) v Secretary of State for the Home
Department* [2020] EWCA Civ 542, [2021] 1 WLR 1151.

[1642] *Smith v Lancashire Teaching Hospitals NHS Foundation Trust* [2017] EWCA Civ 1916, [2018] QB
804, paras 48, 55.

that, in respect of the ambit of Article 8, measures which 'necessarily affect the way in which family life is organised' fall within the ambit of Article 8;[1643] other tests suggested by earlier case law (eg that a measure is 'liable to affect' the way in which family life is organized or is a 'way in which the State shows its respect for family life') are no longer sufficient to establish ambit. A range of factors are relevant for determining whether a measure 'necessarily affects' the organization of family life. These include: the aim of the measure; the criteria for awarding, calculating, and terminating the benefit as set forth in the relevant statutory provisions; the effects on the way in which family life was organized, as envisaged by the legislation; and the practical repercussions of the benefit, given the applicant's individual circumstances and family life throughout the period during which the benefit was paid.

(a) 'Protected grounds' or 'status'

6.615 The grounds upon which discrimination is prohibited by Article 14 are very wide. The particular grounds of prohibited discrimination specified are only examples ('without discrimination on any ground *such as ...* '). The non-exhaustive examples given in Article 14 conclude with the open-ended phrase 'or other status' ('*toute autre distinction*' in the French text).

6.616 In *Kjeldsen, Busk Madsen and Pedersen v Denmark* the ECtHR equated 'other status' with 'personal characteristic'.[1644] The domestic courts have agreed that the focus for 'other status' must be 'on what somebody is, rather than what he is doing or what is being done to him'.[1645] 'Other status' has been broadly interpreted by the Strasbourg bodies, which have held that marital status,[1646] ownership of a particular breed of dog,[1647] trade union membership, military status,[1648] conscientious objection,[1649] residence,[1650] immigration status,[1651] and imprisonment are prohibited grounds of discrimination. In *S and Marper v UK*[1652] the ECtHR held that a rule that those who had been charged or investigated by the police could have fingerprints or DNA samples held indefinitely amounted to discrimination on the basis of that status (ie having been charged or investigated, though not convicted). This reflected the Court's previous finding in *Sidabras v Lithuania* that historic facts that affect status (in that case, former membership of the KGB) are included within the protection of Article 14.[1653] In *R (Mathieson) v Secretary of State for Work and Pensions*,[1654] the Supreme Court accepted that being a severely disabled child in

---

[1643] *Beeler v Switzerland* (2023) 76 EHRR 33 [GC].
[1644] *Kjeldsen v Denmark* (1979–80) 1 EHRR 711.
[1645] *R (RJM) v Secretary of State for Work and Pensions* [2008] UKHL 63, [2009] 1 AC 311, para 45.
[1646] *Sahin v Germany* (2003) 36 EHRR 43.
[1647] *Bullock v UK* (1996) 21 EHRR CD85.
[1648] *Engel v Netherlands* (1976) 1 EHRR 647.
[1649] *Thlimmenos v Greece* (2000) 31 EHRR 411.
[1650] *Darby v Sweden* (1990) 13 EHRR 774; *Carson v UK* (2010) 51 EHRR 13 [GC], paras 70–71.
[1651] *Bah v UK* (2012) 54 EHRR 21; *Hode & Abdi v UK* (2013) 56 EHRR 27, para 46.
[1652] *S and Marper v UK* App Nos 30562/04 & 40566/04; *TV Vest AS v Norway* (2009) 48 EHRR 51.
[1653] *Sidabras v Lithuania* (2006) 42 EHRR 6.
[1654] *Mathieson v Secretary of State for Work and Pensions* [2015] UKSC 47, [2015] 1 WLR 3250

need of lengthy in-patient hospital treatment (as compared to a severely disabled child who did not need such treatment) amounted to an 'other status'. As with ambit, the domestic courts have observed that, when considering whether a characteristic is sufficient to amount to 'other status' for the purposes of Article 14, a 'wide and generous approach to the question must be adopted'.[1655]

3. Discrimination

(a) *The concept*

Not all forms of differentiation amount to discrimination in Convention terms. Otherwise, Article 14 would have 'absurd results'.[1656] Indeed, in some cases Article 14 requires differentiation.[1657] However, discrimination will occur when: **6.617**

(i)   there is differential treatment of individuals in 'relevantly similar'[1658] or analogous[1659] situations; and

(ii) there is no 'objective or reasonable justification' for the distinction in treatment;[1660]

or where:

(iii) a measure has a disproportionate detrimental effect on a particular group, and

(iv) the measure is not objectively or reasonably justified.[1661]

Accordingly, the ECtHR has recognized that, as well as protecting against certain differences in treatment, the 'right not to be discriminated against in the enjoyment of the rights guaranteed under the Convention is also violated when states without an objective and reasonable justification fail to treat differently persons whose situations are significantly different',[1662] and where a measure which is neutral on its face has disproportionate adverse effects on a particular group.[1663] **6.618**

(b) *Persons in an analogous situation*

Article 14 only affords the right to equal treatment to those who can show that their situation is genuinely 'analogous' or comparable with that of the other with whom equality is sought. The burden lies on the applicant to establish that they are in a similar or analogous situation to a relevant comparator. Without evidence of differential treatment on a prohibited ground (or differential impact, if the claim relates to indirect discrimination) the claim will fail.[1664] **6.619**

[1655] R (*Stevenson*) v *Secretary of State for Work and Pensions* [2017] EWCA Civ 2123, paras 36–41.
[1656] *Belgian Linguistics (No 2)* (1968) 1 EHRR 252, para 10.
[1657] *Thlimmenos v Greece* (2000) 31 EHRR 411.
[1658] *National and Provincial Building Society v UK* (1998) 25 EHRR 127, para 88.
[1659] *Lithgow v UK* (1986) 8 EHRR 329.
[1660] *Fredin v Sweden* (1991) 13 EHRR 784.
[1661] *DH v Czech Republic* (2008) 47 EHRR 3 [GC].
[1662] *Thlimmenos v Greece* (2000) 31 EHRR 411, para 44.
[1663] *DH v Czech Republic* (2008) 47 EHRR 3 [GC].
[1664] See eg *Kaya v Turkey* (1999) 28 EHRR 1, para 113.

6.620　　The ECtHR has decided certain cases alleging discriminatory treatment by determining that no Article 14 question is raised because the comparison is not truly with a person in an analogous situation. For example, in *Van der Mussele v Belgium* the ECtHR held that trainee barristers could not legitimately be compared with trainees in other professions because the differences between their situations were too great.[1665] In *Stubbings v UK* the ECtHR rejected as 'artificial' the applicants' submission that, as victims of child sexual abuse, they were in an analogous position to victims of injuries inflicted negligently, as opposed to intentionally.[1666] In *Carson v UK*[1667] the Grand Chamber held that pensioners who retired abroad to countries with which the United Kingdom had not entered bilateral agreements were not in an analogous or comparable situation to those who had retired within the United Kingdom or to countries with which the United Kingdom did have such an agreement. Differences in entitlement to pension uprating therefore did not even require justification.

6.621　　However, in other cases the ECtHR 'elides ... the comparability of the situations—and focuses on the question whether differential treatment is justified. This reflects the fact that an assessment of whether situations are "relevantly" similar is generally linked to the aims of the measure in question.'[1668] In recognition of this, domestic courts have stressed that the selection of a comparator is only part of a 'framework' of useful analysis. It is not a barrier to asking the overarching question, namely whether two cases are sufficiently similar to require a court to ask itself whether a difference in treatment is nonetheless justified.[1669]

(c) *Failure to treat unlike cases differently*

6.622　　It is important to understand that Article 14 does not prohibit, and may indeed require, different treatment of groups in order to address 'factual inequalities' between them.[1670] In the leading case of *Thlimmenos v Greece*, the ECtHR considered the ban imposed by a professional regulatory body on anyone with a criminal record. The applicant had such a record because he had objected, on religious and conscientious grounds, to performing military service. Though the blanket ban on those with any criminal record was not intended to discriminate against those who had refused military service for reasons of conscience, it nonetheless had a particular adverse effect on persons with the applicant's belief, which was disproportionate and could not be justified, and was therefore held to be discriminatory on grounds of religion, contrary to Articles 9 and 14.[1671]

[1665] *Van der Mussele v Belgium* (1984) 6 EHRR 163.
[1666] *Stubbings v UK* (1997) 23 EHRR 213, para 71.
[1667] *Carson v UK* (2010) 51 EHRR 13 [GC].
[1668] *R (SG) v Secretary of State for Work and Pensions* [2015] UKSC 16, [2015] 1 WLR 1449, para 9.
[1669] See eg *R (Carson) v Secretary of State for Work and Pensions* [2005] UKHL 37, [2006] AC 173, para 3 per Lord Nicholls; *AL (Serbia) v Secretary of State for the Home Department* [2008] UKHL 42, [2008] 1 WLR 1434, paras 24–28 per Baroness Hale.
[1670] *Stec v UK* (2006) 43 EHRR 1017 [GC], para 51; *Belgian Linguistics Case (No 2)* (1968) 1 EHRR 252, para 10; *Thlimmenos v Greece* (2000) 31 EHRR 411 [GC], para 44.
[1671] *Thlimmenos v Greece* (2000) 31 EHRR 411 [GC].

(d) Indirect discrimination

The idea that unlike cases may, in some circumstances, require different treat- 6.623
ment overlaps with, but is not identical to, the developing concept of indirect
discrimination.[1672]

Indirect discrimination, also known as 'disparate effect' or 'adverse effect' discrim- 6.624
ination, may arise when apparently neutral policies or laws have a disproportionate
impact upon a particular individual or group. The *Belgian Linguistics* decision[1673]
implied that the Convention is capable of covering both direct and indirect discrimination since the ECtHR suggested that justification of a measure would be
required where the 'aims *and effects*' were prima facie discriminatory. For a long
time, the Strasbourg case law on this topic remained relatively undeveloped. For
example, in *Abdulaziz v UK*[1674] the ECtHR declined to treat as indirectly discriminatory Immigration Rules that disqualified those who had not met their partners
from entering the country for marriage, even though the 'practical effect' of the rule
was race discrimination against South Asian groups with a tradition of arranged
marriage. The ECtHR did not analyse the issue of indirect discrimination as an
independent question, preferring to run it together with the question of justification.

The *Thlimennos* case[1675] (see para 6.622) addressed the question of whether it was 6.625
justified to apply a generally acceptable rule without exceptions. The concept of
indirect discrimination is closely related, but involves a challenge to the justifiability of the very existence of such a rule, at least in its undifferentiated form.

A landmark decision on indirect discrimination under Article 14 was given by 6.626
the Grand Chamber in *DH v Czech Republic*.[1676] In that case, overturning an earlier Chamber judgment, the Grand Chamber took the major step of recognizing
that de facto discrimination could be proved by analysis of the effects of a policy
on a particular group, which therefore fell to be justified. The case concerned the
significantly disproportionate placing of Roma children in 'special schools' with a
reduced curriculum. The statistics for the over-representation of Roma children in
such schools were such that the Court was prepared to find indirect discrimination
that fell to be justified without analysing the precise facts of the individual cases
before it. This represents a substantial broadening of the Court's protection against
discriminatory policies or practices that have a disparate adverse effect on particular
groups without any overt discriminatory intention.

This decision brought the law of the Convention closely in line with discrimina- 6.627
tion law in other jurisdictions, such as Canada, Australia, and South Africa, which
have long recognized the objectionable nature of indirect discrimination. They
have noted that not only does indirect discrimination lead to the social exclusion,
political marginalization, and personal humiliation of minorities, but may lead

---

[1672] The conceptual distinction was analysed by Elias LJ (with whom Maurice Kay LJ and Mummery LJ
agreed) in *AM (Somalia) v Entry Clearance Officer* [2009] EWCA Civ 634, [2009] UKHRR 1073.
[1673] *Belgian Linguistics (No 2)* (1968) 1 EHRR 252.
[1674] *Abdulaziz v UK* (1985) 7 EHRR 471.
[1675] *Thlimmenos v Greece* (2000) 31 EHRR 411 [GC].
[1676] *DH v Czech Republic* (2008) 47 EHRR 3 [GC].

to systemic discrimination. For example, factors (such as discrimination against part-time working) may have the effect of causing the marginalized group more profoundly affected by them to 'internalize' the barriers as being in some way natural and necessary, and fail to see them as discriminatory. The Canadian Supreme Court has said that:

Discrimination is then reinforced by the very exclusion of the disadvantaged group because the exclusion fosters the belief ... that the exclusion is the result of 'natural' forces, for example, that women 'just can't do the job'.[1677]

6.628   Domestic courts have not had the same difficulty as the Strasbourg Court in recognizing that Article 14 encompasses both direct and indirect discrimination.[1678] In *R (SG) v Secretary of State for Work and Pensions*,[1679] the Supreme Court analysed the benefit cap (a general limit imposed on the total value of social welfare payment to which an individual is entitled) as being prima facie indirectly discriminatory against women, but held by a majority that the measure was justified despite its disproportionate adverse effect on women. In *R (SC) v Secretary of State for Work and Pensions*,[1680] the Supreme Court considered whether the two-child limit for entitlement to certain benefits violated Article 14 both by way of a direct discrimination and an indirect discrimination analysis. On direct discrimination, the Supreme Court did not consider that the appellants were in a relevantly similar position to their claimed comparator, and so direct discrimination was rejected for that reason. On indirect discrimination, the Supreme Court accepted there was an adverse differential impact on children living in larger families, but found that impact to be justified.

4. Justification

6.629   Where it is established that people in factually similar or analogous circumstances are treated dissimilarly, or people in relevantly different situations are treated similarly, or a disproportionate adverse impact accrues on a particular group, a case of prima facie discrimination arises. This will breach Article 14 unless the difference in treatment (or failure to differentiate; or, in the case of indirect discrimination, the measure itself taking full account of the disproportionate adverse impact) has an objective and reasonable justification. This means more than a rational explanation. In *Belgian Linguistics* the ECtHR said:

The existence of such a justification must be assessed in relation to the aims and effects of the measure under consideration, regard being had to the principles which normally prevail in democratic societies. A difference of treatment in the exercise of a right laid down in the Convention must not only pursue a legitimate aim: Article 14 is likewise violated when it is

---

[1677] *CNR v Canada (Human Rights Commission)* [1987] 1 SCR 1114, para 34. See also *Waters v Public Transport Corporation* (1991) 173 CLR 349, para 36.
[1678] *R (L and others) v Manchester City Council* [2001] EWHC 707 (Admin), [2002] 1 FLR 43, para 91.
[1679] *R (SG) v Secretary of State for Work and Pensions* [2015] UKSC 16, [2015] 1 WLR 1449.
[1680] *R (SC) v Secretary of State for Work and Pensions* [2021] UKSC 26, [2022] AC 223.

clearly established that there is no reasonable relationship of proportionality between the means employed and the aim sought to be realised.[1681]

The burden of proof is on the respondent state to justify the differential treat- **6.630** ment by reference to these twin criteria (legitimate aim and proportionality). The domestic courts approach justification under Article 14 through the lens of the four-stage proportionality analysis discussed in Chapter 4 and below, namely: (a) whether the measure pursues a legitimate aim; (b) whether it is rationally connected to the legitimate aim; (c) whether less intrusive measures are available to achieve the legitimate aim; and (d) whether a fair balance is struck.

(a) Legitimate aim

It is for the respondent state to advance a 'legitimate aim' in order to justify a prima **6.631** facie discriminatory measure, and states' defences have occasionally fallen at the first hurdle.[1682]

However, this is a relatively easy condition for states to fulfil. Article 14, unlike **6.632** Articles 8 to 11, has no inbuilt list of legitimate aims. The ECtHR has accepted, for example, that supporting and encouraging the traditional family unit[1683] and 'promoting linguistic unity'[1684] constitute legitimate aims for Article 14 purposes. Savings in public expenditure may also constitute a legitimate aim,[1685] but cost alone cannot justify discrimination. As the Court of Appeal explained in R (TP, AR and SXC) v Secretary of State for Work and Pensions:[1686]

If cost alone could justify discrimination, then any discrimination could be justified by reason of the fact that to pay people equally will entail greater cost, for example where women are paid 75% of what men are paid.

(b) Proportionality

If the respondent state establishes that its differential treatment pursues a legitimate **6.633** aim, it must also establish that there is a 'reasonable relationship of proportionality' between the aim and the means chosen to pursue it. The domestic courts consider the question of proportionality by reference to the staged analysis identified above, at para 6.630, while Strasbourg takes a less structured approach to determining whether a fair balance has been struck.

The ECtHR has rejected purported justifications by respondent states based on **6.634** generalizations rather than objective evidence. For example, in Marckx v Belgium the ECtHR rejected the state's unsubstantiated assertion that mothers of illegitimate children were more likely to abandon them.[1687] However, where a difference

---

[1681] Belgian Lingusitics (No 2) (1968) 1 EHRR 252.
[1682] See eg Canea Catholic Church v Greece (1999) 27 EHRR 521, para 47.
[1683] Marckx v Belgium (1979–1980) 2 EHRR 330, para 32.
[1684] Belgian Lingusitics (No 2) (1968) 1 EHRR 252, para 9.
[1685] R (JS) v Secretary of State for Work and Pensions [2015] UKSC 16, [2015] 1 WLR 1449, para 64.
[1686] R (TP, AR and SXC) v Secretary of State for Work and Pensions [2020] EWCA Civ 37; [2020] PTSR 1785.
[1687] Marckx v Belgium (1979–1980) 2 EHRR 330.

in treatment is based on evidence of real differences in situation or need, then differences of treatment may be justified.[1688]

(c) Margin of appreciation

6.635   In assessing justification under Article 14, the ECtHR affords states 'a certain margin of appreciation in assessing whether or not and to what extent differences in otherwise similar situations justify a different treatment'.[1689] The margin's breadth depends on 'the circumstances, the subject matter and its background',[1690] but the final decision as to observance of the Convention's requirements rests with the Court.[1691]

6.636   Greater leeway is afforded in cases involving an absence of a common standard among the contracting states.[1692] However, the ECtHR is increasingly willing to operate the 'living instrument' doctrine to develop protection—for example in relation to discrimination against trans people. It has explicitly stated that it will have regard to the changing conditions in contracting states and respond, for example, to any emerging consensus as to the standards to be achieved.[1693]

6.637   Discrimination based exclusively on certain 'suspect' grounds, such as sex, will not usually be accepted by the ECtHR. 'Very weighty reasons' or 'particularly serious reasons' would have to be put forward before the ECtHR could regard a difference of treatment based on such a ground as compatible with the Convention.[1694]

6.638   Over the years the ECtHR has gradually expanded the grounds that will require particularly weighty or serious reasons if discrimination is to be justified,[1695] using the 'living instrument' doctrine, and these now include nationality, religion, sexual orientation,[1696] race,[1697] disability,[1698] marital status, and birth.[1699]

6.639   This approach of applying heightened scrutiny to certain categories of discrimination ('suspect classes') is well developed in US Supreme Court jurisprudence. It

---

[1688] R (Hooper) v SSWP [2005] UKHL 29.

[1689] Barrow v UK [2006] ECHR 42735/02, para 34. See also Gillow v UK (1986) 11 EHRR 335; Inze v Austria (1987) 10 EHRR 394.

[1690] Rasmussen v Denmark (1984) 7 EHRR 371, para 40; Zarb Adami v Malta (2007) 44 EHRR 3, para 74.

[1691] Zarb Adami v Malta (2007) 44 EHRR 3, para 74.

[1692] Petrovic v Austria (2001) 33 EHRR 14, paras 36–43.

[1693] Zarb Adami v Malta (2007) 44 EHRR 33, para 74; citing Unal Tekeli (2006) 42 EHRR 53, para 54; and Stafford v UK (2002) 35 EHRR 32, para 68. See also the development of the concept of suspect grounds of discrimination, to include sexual orientation: EB v France (2008) 47 EHRR 21 [GC]; and the recent development of the concept of 'family life' to include same-sex relationships: JM v UK (2011) 53 EHRR 6.

[1694] Van Raalte v Netherlands (1997) 24 EHRR 503, para 39; Schuler-Zgraggen v Switzerland (1993) 16 EHRR 405, para 67; Schmidt v Germany (1994) 18 EHRR 513, para 24; Karner v Austria (2004) 38 EHRR 24; BB v UK (2004) 39 EHRR 30; Abdulaziz, Cabales and Blakandali v UK (1985) 7 EHRR 471, para 78; DH v Czech Republic (2008) 47 EHRR 3, para 196.

[1695] For a discussion of the development of the concept, see Pieter Van Dijk and Godefridus Van Hoof, Theory and Practice of the European Convention on Human Rights (Kluwer 1998) 728.

[1696] L and V v Austria (2003) 36 EHRR 55; EB v France (2008) 47 EHRR 21 [GC], para 91.

[1697] East Africans Asians v UK (1981) 3 EHRR 76, para 207.

[1698] Guberina v Croatia (2018) 66 EHRR 11, para 73.

[1699] Inze v Austria (1987) 10 EHRR 394, para 41; Pla v Andorra (2004) 42 EHRR 25, para 61.

received a subtle analysis by the House of Lords in *R (RJM) v Secretary of State for Work and Pensions*, where Lord Walker explained that

personal characteristics are more like a series of concentric circles. The most personal characteristics are those which are innate, largely immutable, and closely connected with an individual's personality ... Other acquired characteristics are further out in the concentric circles; they are more concerned with what people do, or with what happens to them, than with who they are; ... The more peripheral or debateable any suggested personal characteristic is, the less likely it is to come within the most sensitive area where discrimination is particularly difficult to justify.[1700]

In *R (SC) v SSWP*, Lord Reed observed that: 6.640

[I]t is doubtful whether the nuanced nature of the approach ... can be comprehensively described by any general rule. It is more useful to think of there being a range of factors which tend to heighten, or lower, the intensity of review. In any given case, a number of these factors may be present, possibly pulling in different directions, and the court has to take them all into account in order to make an overall assessment.[1701]

He identified the ground of difference in treatment (ie whether it is one of the   6.641
'suspect' grounds) as being important in this regard.

(d) *The intensity of proportionality review*

Some debate arose in the Article 14 case law about whether a different justification   6.642
test—'manifestly without reasonable foundation'—applied in certain categories of case, specifically those involving measures of social and economic policy, in which less intensive scrutiny of the proportionality of prima facie discrimination was appropriate. The ECtHR has now confirmed that in respect of discrimination on suspect grounds the 'manifestly without reasonable foundation' formulation—which involves a lower level of scrutiny than the ordinary proportionality assessment—applies only in cases involving the correction of an historic inequality.[1702]

In *R (SC) v Secretary of State for Work and Pensions*,[1703] the Supreme Court con-   6.643
firmed that 'manifestly without reasonable foundation' did not 'express a test' but 'indicates the width of the margin of appreciation, and hence the intensity of review, which is in principle appropriate in the field of welfare benefits, other things being equal'. However, 'it is more useful to think of there being a range of factors which tend to heighten, or lower, the intensity of review. In any given case, a number of these factors may be present, possibly pulling in different directions, and the court has to take them all into account to make an overall assessment'. Thus, where the ground of difference in treatment under Article 14 is one of the 'suspect' grounds of discrimination (such as sex or gender, race, disability or sexual orientation), a strict standard of proportionality review will ordinarily be adopted

---

[1700] *R (RJM) v Secretary of State for Work and Pensions* [2008] UKHL 63, [2009] 1 AC 311, para 5. See also *AL (Serbia) v SSHD* [2008] UKHL 42, [2008] 1 WLR 1434, paras 20–35 per Baroness Hale.
[1701] *R (SC) v SSWP* [2021] UKSC 26, [2022] AC 223, para 99.
[1702] *JD & A v UK*, 48 BHRC 36, para 88.
[1703] *R (SC) v SSWP* [2021] UKSC 26, [2022] AC 223.

and 'very weighty reasons' will be required to justify the interference. On the other hand, a wide margin is usually allowed to a state when it comes to general measures of social or economic strategy, and so a less intensive proportionality review may be appropriate in such cases. In this way, the justification stage under Article 14 (as with other qualified rights, such as arts 8 and 10) adapts to the circumstances in which the issue arises.

(e) Positive obligations

6.644 Some case law has suggested that the state has a positive obligation to ensure that systems of legal protection—such as the criminal justice system—operate in such a way as to guarantee equal protection of the law to specific groups, such as women or racial minorities. Where the evidence suggests inadequate domestic remedies, and a system which betrays an overall unresponsiveness to gender or racially based aggression, failure to investigate in a specific case may amount to violation of Article 14, read with Article 2 or 3.[1704] In *Eremia v Moldova*[1705] the state's inadequate approach to domestic violence amounted to condoning discrimination against women and was held to breach Article 14. A similar finding was reached in *Tunikova v Russia*.[1706] This approach to positive obligations may mean more focus on the obligation upon signatory states to 'secure' equal enjoyment of the other Convention rights.

L. ARTICLE 15: EXCEPTIONS IN TIME OF WAR

6.645 Article 15 allows a state to derogate from certain of its Convention obligations during 'war or other public emergency threatening the life of the nation'. Such derogation is only permitted to the extent strictly required by the exigencies of the situation. Further, a state cannot under any circumstances use Article 15 to derogate from certain fundamental Convention provisions.

6.646 The central object of Article 15 is to enable the derogating state to return to normality and respect all human rights as soon as possible. It is premised on the notion that it is sometimes necessary to limit human rights in order to protect them—a rationale not, of course, without its controversy.

6.647 There are five requirements for a valid derogation under Article 15:

(a) it must relate to a right that is derogable;

(b) there must be a 'war or public emergency threatening the life of the nation';

(c) the measures taken must be 'strictly required by the exigencies of the situation';

(d) the measures must comply with the state's international law obligations; and

(e) the procedural requirements must be satisfied.

[1704] See eg *Petropoulou-Tsakisi v Greece*| (2009) 48 EHRR 47; *Opuz v Turkey* (2010) 50 EHRR 28, paras 199–202.
[1705] *Eremia v Moldova* [2014] 58 EHRR 2, paras 85–95.
[1706] *Tunikova v Russia* (2022) 75 EHRR 1.

1. Non-derogable rights

Article 15(2) specifies the Convention provisions from which no derogation is per- 6.648
mitted: Article 2 (right to life—other than deaths resulting from lawful acts of
war); Article 3 (prohibition on torture and inhuman or degrading treatment or
punishment); Article 4(1) (prohibition on slavery and servitude); and Article 7 (prohibition on retrospective application of the criminal law).

2. Time of war or public emergency threatening the life of the nation

The precondition to any derogation under Article 15 is the existence of war or a 6.649
'public emergency threatening the life of the nation'. No derogation concerning
the former has yet been made. The ECtHR has defined the latter as 'an exceptional
situation of crisis or emergency that affects the whole population and constitutes a
threat to the organised life of the community of which the state is composed'.[1707] It
has also held that the emergency 'should be actual or imminent'; 'should affect the
whole nation to the extent that the continuance of the organized life of the community [is] threatened'; and should involve a crisis or danger which is 'exceptional'
in that 'the normal measures or restrictions permitted by the Convention ... are
plainly inadequate'.[1708]

The strict nature of this threshold requirement is arguably considerably qual- 6.650
ified by the fact that the ECtHR affords states 'a wide margin of appreciation'
in determining whether or not it is satisfied. The ECtHR considers that national
authorities are in a better position than national judges to assess the situation.[1709]
Unsurprisingly, given this margin, the claimed existence of a public emergency has
seldom been rejected. Contrasting examples are provided below.

In the *Greek Case*, the Greek government failed to persuade the ECmHR that 6.651
there had been a public emergency threatening the life of the nation.[1710] The
government—which had taken power in a military coup in 1967 and enacted a
series of repressive measures thereafter (for the lawfulness of which it relied on
art 15)—relied on three 'heads' of danger: the threat of a communist takeover or
government by force; a state of 'public disorder' which had manifested in violent
demonstrations and political strikes; and a 'constitutional crisis' (arising from a run
of short-lived governments and the threat of communism) which was said to have
virtually paralysed the machinery of state and threatened its continued existence.
The Commission considered the available evidence carefully and determined that
none of these factors, individually or cumulatively, resulted in a public emergency
of the requisite character.

[1707] *Lawless v Ireland (No 3)* (1979–1980) 1 EHRR 15; *Dareskizb v Armania* App No 61737/08, 21
September 2021, para 59.

[1708] *Dareskizb v Armania* App No 61737/08, 21 September 2021, para 59.

[1709] *Lawless v Ireland (No 3)* (1979–1980) 1 EHRR 15, para 28; *A and others v UK* (2009) 26 BHRC 1;
Dareskizb v Armania App No 61737/08, 21 September 2021, para 57.

[1710] *The Greek Case* (1969) 12 YB 1, para 153. See also Kathleen Cavanaugh, 'Policing the Margins'
(2006) 4 European Human Rights Law Review 422, 436–37.

6.652   In *A and others v UK* the Grand Chamber considered the UK's derogation from Article 5(1) under the Anti-Terrorism, Crime and Security Act 2001 on the grounds that the terrorist threat posed by Al-Qaeda was a 'public emergency threatening the life of the nation'.[1711] The Grand Chamber noted that the Court's case law had never required that the emergency be temporary, and thus the derogation could not be invalidated on the ground that the threat posed by Al-Qaeda and the consequent derogation were likely to be ongoing. Nor did the Grand Chamber accept the reasoning of Lord Hoffmann who, in a minority in the House of Lords, had rejected the existence of a relevant public emergency on the basis that the threat had to imperil 'our institutions of government or our existence as a civil community'.[1712] In the Grand Chamber's view that was too high a standard and a 'much broader' range of factors could legitimately be taken into account.[1713] The Grand Chamber applied a wide margin of appreciation to the government's assessment and held that it was entitled to conclude that a public emergency of the relevant kind existed.

6.653   In a number of cases concerning Turkey the ECtHR accepted—endorsing an assessment made by the domestic Constitutional Court—that an attempted military coup had posed a 'severe threat to the life and existence of the nation' sufficient to justify derogation from the Convention.[1714]

6.654   By contrast, in *Dareskizb v Armenia* the ECtHR held that Armenia's derogation under Article 15 was invalid as there had been no 'public emergency threatening the life of the nation'. The derogation concerned the city of Yerevan, where, after 10 days of peaceful protests following a presidential election, there had been violence and loss of life. Although the applicant had not specifically disputed the existence of a public emergency,[1715] the Court considered the evidence of its own motion and placed weight on (a) the fact that the existence of a public emergency had never been considered by the domestic judiciary;[1716] (b) the absence of evidence that violence had been planned or instigated by the protesters, and the fact that it was committed only by a minority; (c) the absence of evidence that those who were violent were armed with anything more than 'improvised objects'; and (d) the evidence that police had used unjustified force against protesters.[1717] The Court concluded that, while there was 'a serious public order situation', the government had 'failed to demonstrate convincingly and to support with evidence their assertion that the opposition demonstrations' were properly characterized as a public emergency 'threatening the life of the nation'.[1718]

[1711] *A and others v UK* (2009) 26 BHRC 1 [GC].

[1712] *A v Secretary of State for the Home Department* [2004] UKHL 56, [2005] 2 AC 68, para 96.

[1713] *A and others v UK* ((2009) 26 BHRC 1 [GC], para 179.

[1714] See eg *Alpay v Turkey* (2018) 45 BHRC 591, para 77; *Altan v Turkey* App No 13237/17, 20 March 2018, para 93.

[1715] *Dareskizb v Armenia* App No 61737/08, 21 September 2021, para 58.

[1716] ibid.

[1717] ibid paras 60–61 (see also para 7).

[1718] ibid para 62.

Although a number of states lodged derogations in the context of the Covid-19   6.655
pandemic,[1719] the ECtHR has not yet considered any cases arising out of them.

In *Al-Jedda v United Kingdom*, Lord Bingham opined that it was hard to think   6.656
of a situation in which the dual requirements of (a) a public emergency threatening the life of the nation, and (b) a derogation strictly required by the exigencies
of the situation could ever be met when a state had chosen to conduct an overseas
peacekeeping operation from which it could withdraw, however dangerous the conditions.[1720] In *Al-Waheed v Ministry of Defence* several members of the Supreme
Court agreed[1721] that the 'public emergency' criterion was unlikely to be capable
of fulfilment in an extra-territorial non-international armed conflict; in their view,
the resulting tensions between the Convention and international humanitarian law
could be resolved by the application of the Grand Chamber's approach in *Hassan v
United Kingdom*[1722] (discussed at paras 6.07–6.09 and 6.666–6.667).[1723]

3. Strictly required by the exigencies of the situation

As noted above, derogation is permitted only 'to the extent strictly required by the   6.657
exigencies of the situation'. The ECmHR in *Ireland v UK* stated:

There must be a link between the facts of the emergency on the one hand and the measures chosen to deal with it on the other. Moreover, the obligations under the Convention do not entirely
disappear. They can only be suspended or modified 'to the extent that is strictly required' as
provided in Article 15.[1724]

In practice, where an applicant claims that their rights under a particular article   6.658
have been violated during the period of a derogation, the ECtHR will begin by
considering whether there has been a breach of that provision on application of
the usual principles; if so, it will then consider whether the impugned measure was
nonetheless 'strictly required by the exigencies of the situation' underpinning the
derogation and therefore lawful.

Again, the ECtHR will afford states a wide margin of appreciation in relation   6.659
to this condition. This is particularly so where the domestic courts have given the
matter careful consideration.[1725] However, the ECtHR still retains a supervisory
role.[1726] Factors it will consider include the nature of the rights affected by the

---

[1719] Albania, Armenia, Estonia, Georgia, Latvia, North Macedonia, the Republic of Moldova, Romania, San Marino and Serbia. See <https://www.coe.int/en/web/conventions/derogations-covid-19>.

[1720] *R (Al-Jedda) v Secretary of State for Defence* [2008] 1 AC 332, [2007] UKHL 58, para 38.

[1721] Rejecting the earlier suggestion, made in *Mohammed v Ministry of Defence* [2014] EWHC 1369 (QB), paras 153–57, that the reference to 'the nation' might instead be read as referring to the nation on whose territory the conflict or operation was taking place.

[1722] *Hassan v UK* (2014) 38 BHRC 358.

[1723] *Ireland v UK* [2017] AC 821, [2017] UKSC 2, para 45 per Lord Sumption, para 163 per Lord Mance.

[1724] *Ireland v UK* (1978) 2 EHRR 25, para 588.

[1725] See eg *A and others v UK* (2009) 26 BHRC 1, para 174; *Alpay v Turkey* (2018) 45 BHRC 591, para 77; *Altan v Turkey* App No 13237/17, 20 March 2018, para 93; cf *Dareskizb v Armenia* App No 61737/08, 21 September 2021, para 58.

[1726] *Ireland v UK* (1978) 2 EHRR 25, para 588.

derogation, the nature and duration of the emergency, and any safeguards against arbitrary state behaviour;[1727] as well as whether the impugned measures are a genuine response to the relevant emergency,[1728] and whether ordinary laws would have been sufficient to meet the resulting threat or danger.[1729] The Court has insisted that general references to terrorism will not be sufficient evidence that a derogation is strictly required.[1730]

6.660   In *A and others v UK* the Grand Chamber agreed with the decision of the majority of the House of Lords (discussed at paras 6.673–6.679) and held that the UK's derogation from Article 5(1) did not satisfy the requirement of strict necessity.[1731] The derogating measures were disproportionate in that they drew a distinction between nationals and non-nationals contrary to Article 14 of the Convention.

6.661   In a string of cases concerning Turkey the Court held that pre-trial detention where there was no 'reasonable suspicion' that the applicant had committed an offence violated Article 5, notwithstanding Turkey's valid generic notice of derogation (see para 6.668), because it was not 'strictly required by the exigencies of the situation'.[1732] In several of these cases the Court also held that pre-trial detention (in circumstances which otherwise violated art 5(1)) under a law which pre-dated Turkey's domestic 'state of emergency', and had not been amended in response to it, was not sufficiently connected to the public emergency to be justified by it.[1733]

6.662   By contrast, where an applicant's right to be heard during reviews of his detention had been expressly restricted in response to the 'state of emergency', the ECtHR accepted that the resulting interferences with Article 5 rights were justified as strictly necessary for an initial period—having regard, in particular, to the difficulties the justice system was facing in dealing with investigations, prosecutions, and detentions associated with the attempted coup. However, the Court went on to observe that the force of these considerations necessarily diminished with the passage of time; that the restrictions on oral hearings had not been eased in the two-year period of the 'state of emergency'; and that the applicant had not been able to appear before a court at all for over a year. It concluded that this could not be regarded as 'strictly required by the exigencies of the situation', and found a violation of Article 5(4).[1734]

6.663   In a similarly nuanced judgment, the ECtHR recognized that Turkey's generic derogation may well be capable of justifying a streamlined procedure for dismissing civil servants considered to have been involved in the attempted coup—despite the Article 6 and 8 issues raised by the lack of procedural safeguards—if their access

---

[1727] *Brannigan and McBride v UK* (1993) 17 EHRR 297; *Dareskizb v Armenia* App No 61737/08, 21 September 2021, para 57.

[1728] See eg *Altan v Turkey* App No 12778/17, 16 April 2019, para 118.

[1729] See eg *Ireland v UK* (1978) 2 EHRR 25, para 212.

[1730] *Demir v Turkey* (2001) 33 EHRR 43.

[1731] *A and others v UK* (2009) 26 BHRC 1.

[1732] See eg *Alpay v Turkey* (2018) 45 BHRC 591, para 119; *Altan v Turkey* App No 13237/17, 20 March 2018, paras 140–41; *Altan v Turkey* App No 12778/17, 16 April 2019, paras 146–49; *Bas v Turkey* App No 66448/17, 3 March 2020, paras 197–201.

[1733] See eg *Altan v Turkey* App No 12778/17, 16 April 2019, paras 117–19; *Bas v Turkey* App No 66448/17, 3 March 2020, paras 159–61; *Sabuncu v Turkey* App No 23199/17, 10 November 2020, para 183.

[1734] *Bas v Turkey* App No 66448/17, 3 March 2020, paras 218–31.

to the courts to challenge the dismissal remained unrestricted.[1735] The emergency decree establishing the streamlined procedure did not provide expressly for any such restriction. However, in practice the Turkish courts had failed to conduct an effective review of the decision in the applicant's case—or indeed to engage in any meaningful way with the factual and legal issues he had raised. In these circumstances, the Court concluded that there had been a violation of Article 6(1) which was not covered by the derogation.[1736] The Court emphasized that 'even in the framework of a state of emergency, the fundamental principle of the rule of law must prevail'; and that it would be inconsistent with the rule of law for a state, without 'restraint or control by the Convention enforcement bodies', to be permitted to remove from the jurisdiction of the courts 'a whole range of civil claims'.[1737] For similar reasons it found that the applicant had not benefited from 'the minimum degree of protection against arbitrary interference required by Article 8', and that the measures which led to this were not 'strictly required by the special circumstances of the state of emergency'.[1738]

6.664 The ECtHR is particularly strict in assessing the territorial scope of a derogation. In *Yaman v Turkey* it held that it would undermine the 'object and purpose of Article 15' if, when assessing the scope of the derogation, it extended its effects to parts of Turkey not explicitly named in the derogation notice (the need for which is discussed at para 6.668).[1739] A similarly strict approach was adopted in *Sakik v Turkey*[1740] *and Barseghyan v Armenia*[1741]—in the former case, despite the fact that the applicants had been arrested outside the relevant region but in connection with the fight against terrorism within it.

4. International law obligations

6.665 Any derogation must be consistent with the state's 'other obligations under international law' (art 15(1)). This includes both treaty obligations and obligations arising under customary international law.

6.666 In *Hassan v United Kingdom*,[1742] the Grand Chamber 'read down' Article 5 of the Convention so as to avoid a potential conflict between Article 5(1) (which has been consistently interpreted as not permitting preventative detention) and the provision for preventative detention under international humanitarian law during international armed conflicts.[1743] The decision was based in part on the absence of any practice of states derogating from Article 5 during such conflicts.

[1735] *Piskin v Turkey* App No 33399/18, 15 December 2020, paras 121–29, 152, 222.
[1736] ibid paras 137–53.
[1737] ibid para 153.
[1738] ibid paras 223–229.
[1739] *Yaman v Turkey* App No 32446/96, 2 November 2004.
[1740] Reports of Judgments and Decisions 1997-VII, 26 November 1997.
[1741] *Barseghyan v Armenia* App No 17804/09, 21 September 2021.
[1742] *Hassan v UK* (2014) 38 BHRR 358.
[1743] International humanitarian law distinguishes between 'international armed conflicts' (generally conflicts between states, to which the Geneva Conventions apply) and 'non-international armed conflicts'

6.667   In *Al-Waheed v Ministry of Defence* a majority of the UK Supreme Court extended this approach, holding that in the context of a non-international armed conflict—and even in the absence of a derogation (which was in any event unlikely to be legally possible where the conflict was extra-territorial—see para 6.656)—Article 5(1) could and should be read in a manner consistent with powers of detention arising under a resolution of the UN Security Council.[1744]

5. Procedural requirements

6.668   Article 15(3) sets out the procedural requirements of a valid derogation: namely, to 'keep the Secretary General of the Council of Europe fully informed of the measures which it has taken and the reasons therefor'. Although this is not expressly stated, both the ECmHR and the ECtHR have held that notification must be made without delay.[1745] In a number of cases concerning Turkey, the ECtHR has been prepared to accept (in the absence of any objection from the applicant) that the procedural requirements were satisfied even though Turkey's notice of derogation did not specify which Convention rights would be derogated from.[1746] The Court has also found that Article 15(3) implicitly requires ongoing review of the need for emergency measures.[1747]

6. Derogations and the Human Rights Act

6.669   Section 1(2) of the Human Rights Act provides that the articles encompassed by the term 'Convention rights', as it appears throughout the Act, 'are to have effect for the purposes of this Act subject to any designated derogation' as defined in section 14. This means that, by making a 'designated derogation', the government can modify the scope of the obligations imposed on public authorities (and associated remedies) at the domestic level.

6.670   Section 14 of the Act defines a 'designated derogation' as any derogation from the ECHR which is made by UK and designated in an order made by the Secretary of State.[1748] The order must be approved by resolution of both Houses of Parliament within 40 days.[1749] Designated derogations cease to have effect when the underlying derogation is withdrawn, or otherwise after five years.[1750] The Secretary of State

---

(between non-state groups or between a state and a non-state group, to which a more limited and less formalized set of legal rules apply).

[1744] *Al-Waheed v Ministry of Defence* [2017] AC 821, [2017] UKSC 2, paras 59–68 per Lord Sumption, paras 158–67 per Lord Mance; cf paras 235, 295–301 and 307–15 per Lord Reed. See also *Alseran v Ministry of Defence* [2019] QB 1251.

[1745] *Greek Case* (1969) 12 YB 1, para 81; *Lawless v Ireland (No 3)* (1979–1980) 1 EHRR 15, para 47.

[1746] *Alpay v Turkey* (2018) 45 BHRC 591, para 73; *Altan v Turkey* App No 13237/17, 20 March 2018, para 89.

[1747] *Brannigan and McBride v UK* (1993) 17 EHRR 297, para 54.

[1748] Section 14(1).

[1749] Section 16(3)–(6).

[1750] Section 16(1).

has the power to extend their operation for another five years by making a further order.[1751] An up-to-date list of designated derogations is set out in Schedule 3.[1752]

The UK currently has no derogations lodged. It has, in the past, invoked Article 15 in relation to Northern Ireland and, following the attacks of 11 September 2001, the entirety of the United Kingdom.   6.671

(a) *Northern Ireland*

Until February 2001 a derogation was in force that allowed the police to detain peo-   6.672
ple in Northern Ireland under the Prevention of Terrorism (Temporary Provisions) Act 1989 for up to seven days. The derogation was made following *Brogan v UK*, where the ECtHR had decided that periods of longer than four days' detention for interrogation without access to a judge violated the Article 5(3) requirement to bring the suspect before a judge 'promptly'.[1753] The lawfulness of the derogation was subject to an unsuccessful challenge in *Brannigan and McBride v UK*.[1754] The introduction of judicial authorization for extended detentions in the Terrorism Act 2000 allowed the derogation to be withdrawn.

(b) *United Kingdom*

After the terrorist attacks in the United States on 11 September 2001, the UK   6.673
government concluded that certain non-nationals present in the United Kingdom were affiliated with Al-Qaeda and posed a national security threat. While the Immigration Act 1971 allowed for the deportation of non-UK citizens whose presence was 'not conducive to the public good' (including on grounds of national security), the Convention prevented the return of such individuals to countries where they faced a real risk of ill-treatment contrary to Article 3.

In order to address this problem, the government introduced provisions in Part IV   6.674
of the Anti-Terrorism, Crime and Security Act 2001 that gave the Home Secretary the power to detain non-nationals indefinitely based solely on his or her reasonable belief that the person's presence in the UK was a risk to national security and suspicion that the person was a terrorist. The provisions were plainly contrary to Article 5(1), which permits the detention of a non-national with a view to deportation only where 'action is being taken with a view to deportation'.[1755] The government therefore made (and designated[1756]) a derogation from Article 5(1)(f) on the grounds that the Al-Qaeda threat constituted a public emergency threatening the life of the nation.

The lawfulness of this derogation was successfully challenged before the House   6.675
of Lords in the first of the twin *A and others v Secretary of State for the Home Department* cases.[1757] The case was brought by nine foreign nationals who had

---

[1751] Section 16(2).
[1752] See s 14(2) and (5), and s 16(7).
[1753] *Brogan v UK* (1988) 11 EHRR 117.
[1754] *Brannigan and McBride v UK* (1993) 17 EHRR 539.
[1755] Article 5(1)(f): see *Chahal v UK* (1997) 23 EHRR 413, para 112.
[1756] Human Rights Act 1998 (Designated Derogation) Order 2001, SI 2001/3644.
[1757] *A and others v Secretary of State for the Home Department* [2004] UKHL 56, [2005] 2 AC 68.

been detained under the 2001 Act. In what was then perhaps the most important judgment since the Human Rights Act came into force, an enlarged House of Lords allowed the appeal by a majority of eight to one, quashing the derogation order and declaring that the statutory provisions were incompatible with Articles 5 and 14.

6.676   A majority did, however, accept that the threshold requirement that there be a 'public emergency threatening the life of the nation' was satisfied, despite the absence of a specific threat of an immediate attack. In so finding, they noted that 'great weight' was to be accorded to the judgement of the Home Secretary, the executive, and Parliament, and considered it would have been 'irresponsible not to err, if at all, on the side of safety'.[1758] Lord Hoffman dissented on this point on the basis that '[t]errorist violence, serious as it is, does not threaten our institutions of government or our existence as a civil community'.[1759] As noted above, the ECtHR considered this approach too demanding.

6.677   Despite the non-intrusive approach adopted by the majority as to the existence of a public emergency, the measures themselves were subjected to strict scrutiny. The House of Lords held that the 'exigencies of the situation' test is 'a test of strict necessity, or, in Convention terminology, proportionality',[1760] and it must be particularly carefully applied if the right infringed is personal liberty—among the most fundamental of Convention rights.[1761] The measures adopted were not strictly required, as they did not rationally address any threat to security, nor were they proportionate. They applied only to non-nationals, and not to British nationals who might pose the same threat. They were also capable of applying 'the severe penalty of indefinite detention' to individuals without any hostile intentions towards the UK, simply on the basis of their links to other individuals who may, in turn, be linked to Al-Qaeda. They amounted to unjustifiable discrimination on the basis of nationality or immigration status, which violated Article 14; and were inconsistent with the UK's international obligations to afford equality before the law and to protect the human rights of all individuals within its territory.

6.678   *A and others* suggests that the domestic courts are likely to afford significant leeway to the government in determining whether the 'public emergency' criterion is met. However, any measures implemented in response will be subjected to close scrutiny, particularly if they impact upon rights considered fundamental under the common law, the Convention, or international law.

6.679   As noted above, the Grand Chamber affirmed the House of Lords' reasoning in *A and others v UK*.[1762]

[1758] ibid para 29.
[1759] ibid para 96.
[1760] ibid para 30 per Lord Bingham.
[1761] See eg the judgment of Lady Hale at para 222.
[1762] *A and others v UK* (2009) 26 BHRC 1.

M. ARTICLE 16: RESTRICTIONS ON POLITICAL ACTIVITY OF ALIENS

On its face, Article 16 allows states considerable latitude to interfere with the political rights of aliens. Whether because, or despite, of this, the provision has barely featured in the Strasbourg jurisprudence. Only two cases concerning Article 16 have has ever reached the ECtHR: *Piermont v France*[1763] and *Perincek v Switzerland*.[1764] In January 1977, the Parliamentary Assembly of the Council of Europe recommended the removal of Article 16. Although Article 16 remains in force, the Strasbourg authorities have emphasized the extremely limited scope of its operation. **6.680**

In *Piermont* the ECmHR expressly recognized that the original intended scope of the provision is outdated. It observed that: **6.681**

Those who drafted it were subscribing to a concept that was then prevalent in international law, under which a general, unlimited restriction of the political activities of aliens was thought legitimate ... The Commission reiterates, however, that the Convention is a living instrument, which must be interpreted in the light of present day conditions, and the evolution of modern society.[1765]

Consonant with this interpretative direction, the expression 'political activities' might apply only narrowly to the setting-up and operation of political parties, expressions of opinion in connection with these parties, and voting in elections. **6.682**

The ECmHR and ECtHR in *Piermont* also indicated that members of the European Parliament cannot be regarded as aliens within any jurisdiction in the European Union.[1766] **6.683**

In *Perincek*, the applicant claimed that his Article 10 rights had been breached because he had been convicted and punished for publicly denying the Armenian genocide. Switzerland argued that any interference with these rights could be justified under Article 16 on the basis that the applicant was an 'alien' in Switzerland. The ECtHR referred to the background summarized above and noted that 'the unbridled reliance on [Article 16] to restrain the possibility for aliens to exercise their right to freedom of expression would run against the Court's rulings in cases in which aliens have been found entitled to exercise this right without any suggestion that it should be curtailed by reference to Article 16'.[1767] It continued that, '[b]earing in mind that clauses that permit interference with Convention rights must be interpreted restrictively ... Article 16 should be construed as only capable of authorizing restrictions on "activities" that directly affect the political process'.[1768] **6.684**

[1763] *Piermont v France* (1995) 20 EHRR 301.
[1764] *Perincek v Switzerland* (2016) 63 EHRR 6.
[1765] ibid; Commission Report, paras 59–69.
[1766] *Piermont v France* (1995) 20 EHRR 301, para 64. cf the jointly dissenting opinion of Judges Ryssdal, Matscher, and Jungwiert, and Sir John Freedland, para 4.
[1767] *Perincek v Switzerland* (2016) 63 EHRR 6, para 121.
[1768] ibid para 122.

6.685   The restrictive Strasbourg approach to Article 16 has been followed by the domestic courts. In *R (Farrakhan) v Secretary of State for the Home Department* the Court of Appeal described the provision as 'something of an anachronism',[1769] indicating that it was unlikely to feature prominently, if at all, in domestic decisions—and indeed it has not done so since.

N. ARTICLE 17: PROHIBITION OF ABUSE OF RIGHTS

6.686   The aim of Article 17 is to safeguard the provisions of the Convention from abuse at the hands of those who wish to use the Convention's provisions to undermine the rights of others,[1770] and to make it impossible for such individuals or groups 'to derive from the Convention a right to engage in any activity or perform any act aimed at destroying any of the rights and freedoms set forth in the Convention'.[1771] The ECtHR has described its 'general purpose' as being 'to prevent individuals or groups with totalitarian aims from exploiting in their own interests the principles enunciated by the Convention'.[1772] It may be invoked by persons against a government,[1773] or be used by a government to defend its actions against persons who wish to undermine the protections and values of the Convention. It is 'only applicable on an exceptional basis and in extreme cases'.[1774]

6.687   While Article 17 may be invoked by a state to restrict an individual's reliance on rights where they aim to destroy the rights of others, it may only be applied in relation to the rights that are being abused with this aim in mind. For instance, in *Lawless v Ireland* the ECtHR held that Article 17 could not be used to deny IRA members the right to liberty or a fair trial (neither of which they could be said to have abused).[1775]

6.688   Much of the case law under Article 17 concerns freedom of expression and racial hatred.[1776] In the admissibility decision in *Norwood v UK*, for example, the ECtHR upheld the domestic decision applying Article 17.[1777] The applicant, who worked for the British National Party (BNP), claimed that his rights under Articles 10 and 14 had been violated by police removal of a BNP poster from the window of his flat

---

[1769] *R (Farrakhan) v Secretary of State for the Home Department* [2002] EWCA Civ 606.

[1770] *Zdanoka v Latvia* (2007) 45 EHRR 17, para 99.

[1771] *Paksas v Lithuania* App No 34932/04, 6 January 2011 [GC], para 83.

[1772] *Norwood v UK* (2005) 40 EHRR SE 11.

[1773] No case alleging this has been successful so far, as it is often difficult to see how the allegation goes beyond one that the state has breached other provisions of the Convention: see eg the admissibility decision in *Maggio v Italy* App Nos 46286/09 and others, 8 June 2010, para 6.

[1774] See eg *Can v Turkey* App No 10613/10, 8 March 2022, para 72; *Mukhin v Russia* App No 3642/10, 14 December 2021, para 82; *Perincek v Switzerland* (2016) 63 EHRR 6, para 114.

[1775] *Lawless v Ireland* (1979–1980) 1 EHRR 15, para 7.

[1776] See eg *WP and others v Poland* App No 42264/98, 2 September 2004; *Garaudy v France* App No 65831/01, 24 June 2003; *Schimanek v Austria* App No 32307/96, 1 February 2000; *Glimmerveen and Hagenbeek v Netherlands* App Nos 8348/78 & others, 11 October 1979.

[1777] *Norwood v UK* [2003] Crim LR 888.

and his subsequent prosecution for a public order offence. The poster consisted of a photograph of the Twin Towers of the World Trade Center in flames, the words 'Islam out of Britain—Protect the British People', and a symbol of a crescent and star in a prohibition sign. The ECtHR held that the poster constituted such a vehement attack against Muslims that Article 17 applied and the applicant could not rely on Article 10. This decision has been criticized:[1778] Article 17 is a powerful but blunt tool that should be used sparingly. In subsequent cases involving Article 10 the ECtHR has held that Article 17 'should only be resorted to if it is immediately clear that the impugned statements sought to deflect this Article from its real purpose by employing the right to freedom of expression for ends clearly contrary to the values of the Convention'.[1779] This will be the case, for example, where the remark in issue is 'directed against the Convention's underlying values';[1780] examples have included 'statements denying the Holocaust, justifying a pro-Nazi policy, linking all Muslims with a grave act of terrorism, or portraying the Jews as a source of evil in Russia'.[1781] The result is that many attempts by states to invoke Article 17 have failed.[1782] In some cases where it was not prepared to find Article 17 applicable, the ECtHR has instead relied on it as an aid to the interpretation and application of Article 10(2), such that the interference in question was more likely to be considered necessary in a democratic society.[1783]

In *Vona v Hungary*, applying a restrictive interpretation, the ECtHR found 6.689 Article 17 not to be engaged in a case where a political group, which had been banned by the Hungarian government because of its expressions of racial hatred against Jewish and Roma citizens, complained of a breach of Article 11. The ECtHR found that the engagement of Article 11, as opposed to Article 10, was a distinguishing factor from earlier cases. Moreover, the evidence did not prima facie reveal any act specifically aimed at the destruction of the rights and freedoms set forth in the Convention or an intention publicly to defend or disseminate propaganda in support of totalitarian views. The ECtHR went on to find the banning of the group to be justified under Article 11(2).[1784] Subsequent cases have not suggested any difference in approach between cases concerning Articles 10 and 11.[1785]

[1778] Richard Clayton and Hugh Tomlinson, *The Law of Human Rights* (2nd edn, OUP 2009) para 15.245.

[1779] *Can v Turkey* App No 10613/10, 8 March 2022, para 72; *Mukhin v Russia* App No 3642/10, 14 December 2021, para 82; *Lilliendahl v Iceland* App No 29297/18, 12 May 2020, para 25; *Perincek v Switzerland* (2016) 63 EHRR 6, para 114.

[1780] See eg *Wojczuk v Poland* (2022) 75 EHRR 9, para 43. The applicant's purpose or intent may be an important consideration: See eg *Kilin v Russia* App No 1027/12, 11 May 2021, para 72.

[1781] *Delfi AS v Estonia* (2016) 62 EHRR 6 [GC], para 136 (citing the underlying cases). See also the examples in *Roj TV A/S v Denmark* App No 24683/14, 17 April 2018, paras 32–38.

[1782] See eg *Can v Turkey* App No 10613/10, 8 March 2022; *Mukhin v Russia* App No 3642/10, 14 December 2021; *Wojczuk v Poland* (2022) 75 EHRR 9; *Lilliendahl v Iceland* App No 29297/18, 12 May 2020. cf *Roj TV A/S v Denmark* App No 24683/14, 17 April 2018.

[1783] See eg *Pastors v Germany* App No 55225/14, 3 October 2019, paras 36–37 and 46; *Perincek v Switzerland* (2016) 63 EHRR 6, paras 115, 280–82.

[1784] *Vona v Hungary* App No 35943/10, 9 July 2013.

[1785] See eg *Can v Turkey* App No 10613/10, 8 March 2022, para 74.

There is now a fairly extensive body of case law on the application of Article 17 to different rights and in different context, ranging from incitement to violence to the promotion or justification of terrorism to Holocaust denial.

6.690   In 'exceptional circumstances' the ECtHR has also drawn on Article 17 to find that an applicant has abused their right of individual petition under Article 35, declaring their claim inadmissible as a result.[1786]

6.691   Article 17 has been raised in the domestic courts on a number of occasions. In *Douglas v Hello! Ltd* Sedley LJ noted that it would be inconsistent with Article 17 and section 3 of the Human Rights Act to read section 12 of the Act as giving the right to freedom of expression presumptive priority over other rights.[1787] In *DPP v Collins*, the respondent had been convicted of an offence under the Communications Act 2003 following repeated calls and messages to his MP in which he referred to 'Wogs', 'Pakis', 'black bastards', and 'Niggers'. He did not argue before the House of Lords that his conviction was inconsistent with Article 10, and Lord Bingham stated that he was 'right not to do so' as 'effect must be given ... to Article 17 of the Convention'.[1788] In *Ladele v London Borough of Islington* the Employment Appeal Tribunal (EAT) found 'considerable force' in the argument advanced by an intervener, Liberty, that Article 17 applied where a registrar and committed Christian invoked Article 9 to protect her refusal to perform civil partnerships on the grounds that same-sex unions were a sin.[1789] When the case reached the ECtHR the Court was invited by Liberty to invoke Article 17 if necessary, but it did not do so.[1790] The EAT again considered Article 17 in *Forstater v CDG Europe*, holding that a philosophical belief would only be excluded from the protection of Articles 9 and 10 (or the equivalent protections of the Equality Act 2010) if it fell within the scope of Article 17 (and that 'gender-critical' views did not meet this threshold).[1791] Like other recent cases, it stressed the high threshold for the application of Article 17.[1792] In *Sutherland v HM Advocate (Scotland)* the Supreme Court commented on the potential applicability of Article 17 to conduct said to be protected by Article 8.[1793]

[1786] See eg *Koch v Poland* App No 15005/11, 7 March 2017, para 32. The applicant had taken hair samples from his former partner and daughter by force with a view to proving he was not the father, then sought to claim a breach of his rights under arts 6 and 8 because he was unable to bring domestic legal proceedings disavowing paternity.

[1787] *Douglas v Hello! Ltd* [2001] QB 967.

[1788] *DPP v Collins* [2006] UKHL 40, [2006] 1 WLR 2223, para 14.

[1789] *Ladele v London Borough of Islingto* [2009] IRLR 154, para 126. The EAT's decision was upheld on appeal: [2009] EWCA Civ 1357, [2010] IRLR 211 without comment on this issue.

[1790] *Eweida and others v United Kingdom* App Nos 48420/10 and others, 15 January 2013.

[1791] *Forstater v CDG Europe* [2022] ICR 1.

[1792] ibid paras 59, 66–67. See also *R (Miller) v College of Policing* [2021] EWCA Civ 1926, [2022] 1 WLR 4987, para 102.

[1793] *Sutherland v HM Advocate (Scotland)* [2020] UKSC 32, [2021] AC 427, para 43. The case concerned the exchanging of inappropriately sexualized messages with a member of a 'paedophile hunter' group posing online as a 13-year-old boy.

O. ARTICLE 18: LIMITATION ON USE
OF RESTRICTIONS ON RIGHTS

Article 18 is a parasitic provision. An allegation that the state has acted for rea-   6.692
sons other than those permitted under the qualified rights in Article 18(2) must be
brought in conjunction with an allegation that another article has been breached.
There may be a violation of Article 18 even if there is no violation of that article
taken alone.[1794] In these respects Article 18 resembles Article 14.

Article 18 is inapplicable to absolute rights, such as Article 3. It follows from   6.693
the terms of Article 18 that 'a violation may only arise where the right or freedom
concerned is subject to restrictions permitted under the Convention'.[1795] It is not yet
clear whether this includes Articles 6 and 7.[1796]

A number of earlier authorities took the view that Article 18 effectively required a   6.694
finding of 'bad faith' on the part of a state. It was, unsurprisingly, extremely difficult to
make out a violation, and the Strasbourg organs very rarely found a breach.[1797] In the
majority of cases they either found that it was unnecessary to examine the Article 18
complaint in light of their adverse findings against the state under substantive articles,[1798]
or they held that the Article 18 complaint was unsubstantiated on the evidence.[1799]

In *Merabishvili v Georgia*, however, the Grand Chamber undertook a considered   6.695
review of the case law and concluded that Article 18 went beyond cases of proven
'bad faith', allowing for 'a more objective assessment of the presence or absence
of an ulterior purpose'.[1800] It also clarified that, for Article 18 to be engaged, the
ulterior purpose needs to be 'predominant'—an assessment which depends on all
the circumstances.[1801] Finally it stressed that there is no stricter standard of proof
for claims under Article 18 and that direct proof of intention is not necessarily
required, as inferences may be drawn where appropriate.[1802] However, it also reaffirmed that separate consideration of Article 18 will only be required where the
allegation of ulterior purpose 'appears to be a fundamental aspect of the case'.[1803]

[1794] *Kamma v Netherlands* (1974) 1 DR 4; *Merabishvili v Georgia* (2017) 45 BHRC 1 [GC], paras 287–88.
[1795] *Gusinskiy v Russia* (2004) 16 BHRC 427, para 73; *Oates v Poland* App No 35036/97, 11 May 2000;
Merabishvili v Georgia (2017) 45 BHRC 1 [GC], para 290.
[1796] See eg *Navalnye v Russia* App No 101/15, 17 October 2017, para 88; cf *Saakashvili v Georgia* App Nos
6232/20 & another, 1 March 2022, paras 60–61.
[1797] See eg *De Becker v Belgium* (1958) 2 YB 214; *Bozano v France* (1984) 39 DR 119; *Gusinskiy v Russia*
(2004) 16 BHRC 427.
[1798] See eg *Kaya and others v Turkey* App No 33420/96, 21 November 2005.
[1799] *Nesihe Haran v Turkey* App No 28299/95, 6 October 2005.
[1800] *Merabishvili v Georgia* (2017) 45 BHRC 1 [GC], paras 282–86.
[1801] ibid paras 305–07.
[1802] ibid paras 309–16. This approach, of course, has its limits: eg the mere fact that a politician is criminally prosecuted, even during an electoral campaign, does not show that the prosecution or any associated
detention was for an ulterior purpose: ibid para 323 (affirmed in *Demirtas v Turkiye* App No 14305/17, 22
December 2020 [GC], para 424). The ECtHR continues to describe itself as applying a standard of proof
'beyond a reasonable doubt', while stressing that its meaning is not the same as in the domestic criminal
context: see eg ibid para 314.
[1803] ibid para 291.

6.696   In *Gusinskiy v Russia*—a case pre-dating *Merabishvili*—the ECtHR found that the applicant's liberty had been restricted for a legitimate purpose under the Convention ('for the purpose of bringing him before a competent legal authority on reasonable suspicion of having committed an offence') but also for a purpose outside Article 5, namely to force him to sell his media business to the state on unfavourable terms.[1804] The detention was thus applied for a purpose other than that provided in the Convention, and the state had violated Article 18.

6.697   In three other pre-*Merabishvili* cases concerning the detention of high-profile opposition politicians, the ECtHR has found a breach of Article 18 in conjunction with Article 5 due to evidence of improper ulterior motives for the detentions. In *Lutsenko v Ukraine*[1805] the reasons for the detention of a former Minister of the Interior explicitly indicated that his communication with the media about criminal charges against him was a basis for his arrest. In *Tymoshenko v Ukraine*,[1806] one of the reasons for the arrest of the leader of the main opposition party was to punish her for a perceived lack of respect towards the Court considering criminal charges against her. In *Mammadov v Azerbaijan*,[1807] the ECtHR concluded that the actual purpose behind the arrest of the chairman of an opposition political party was to silence or punish him for criticizing the government and attempting to disseminate information that the government were trying to hide.

6.698   In *Merabishvili* itself, the applicant was unable to establish that his pre-trial detention had been for the predominant purpose of removing him from Georgia's political scene; the Grand Chamber was, however, persuaded to infer that from a certain point the predominant purpose *became* leveraging the applicant for information, resulting in a breach of Article 18. In *Demirtas v Turkey* the Grand Chamber, applying the same approach, found it possible to infer that the applicant's pre-trial detention during two crucial political campaigns was effected for an 'ulterior political purpose', namely 'stifling pluralism and limiting freedom of political debate'.[1808] Similarly, in *Navalny v Russia* the Grand Chamber concluded that—in circumstances where the applicant, an opposition political leader, had been arrested seven times in a relatively short period while exercising his right to freedom of assembly—two of these could in context be attributed to the ulterior purpose of suppressing political pluralism.[1809] In both the latter cases, the pattern of conduct by the state was a significant factor. In other cases the ECtHR has taken account of a pattern of conduct across cases in the state in question.[1810]

[1804] *Gusinskiy v Russia* (2004) 16 BHRC 427.
[1805] *Lutsenko v Ukraine* App No 6492/11, 3 July 2012.
[1806] *Tymoshenko v Ukraine* App No 49872/11, 30 April 2012.
[1807] *Mammadov v Azerbaijan* App No 15172/13, 22 May 2014.
[1808] *Demirtas v Turkey* App No 14305/17, 22 December 2020 [GC].
[1809] *Navalny v Russia* App Nos 29580/12 & others, 15 November 2018 [GC].
[1810] See eg *Democracy and Human Rights Resource Centre v Azerbaijan* App No 74288/14, 14 October 2021, para 109. Recent years have seen a number of cases involving Azerbaijan in which a breach of art 18 has been found.

Article 18 has been raised before the domestic courts on a number of occasions, but only as an aid to interpretation of other Convention articles. The courts have referred to Article 18 in passing, finding that phrases such as 'necessary ... in the interests of national security' and 'lawfulness' must be read in light of the strict requirements of Article 18.[1811] We are not aware of any domestic case in which a violation of Article 18 itself has been alleged. **6.699**

[1811] See eg *R v Shayler* [2002] UKHL 11, [2003] 1 AC 247, para 57; *S v Airedale NHS Trust* [2002] EWHC 1780 (Admin), para 91; *R (Middleton) v Secretary of State for the Home Department* [2003] EWHC 315 (Admin), para 64; *A v Scottish Ministers* 2002 SC (PC) 63, para 28.

7

THE CONVENTION PROTOCOLS

A. INTRODUCTION

This chapter summarizes the content of the significant Protocols of the European Convention. As in Chapters 5 and 6, an overview is given of the jurisprudence of the European Court of Human Rights (ECtHR) and any remaining important cases from the European Commission on Human Rights (ECmHR). Where the Protocol has been incorporated under the Human Rights Act the approach of domestic courts is discussed alongside the European case law, and any divergences are noted. 7.01

Blackstone's Guide to The Human Rights Act 1998. Eighth Edition. John Wadham, Helen Mountfield KC, Raj Desai, Sarah Hannett KC, Jessica Jones, Eleanor Mitchell, and Aidan Wills, Oxford University Press. © John Wadham, Helen Mountfield KC, Raj Desai, Sarah Hannett KC, Jessica Jones, Eleanor Mitchell, and Aidan Wills 2024. DOI: 10.1093/oso/9780192885050.003.0007

B. PROTOCOL 1, ARTICLE 1: PROTECTION OF PROPERTY

7.02   The extent to which, and the way in which, property interests should be protected by human rights instruments have always been controversial questions. The right to property is recognized in the Convention and the Universal Declaration of Human Rights, but it was omitted in both the International Covenant of Civil and Political Rights (ICCPR) and the International Covenant of Economic, Social and Cultural Rights (ICESCR). The subject was debated at length when these two documents were being drafted, and all accepted that individuals had a right to own property, but it proved impossible to reach agreement on a suitable text.[1]

7.03   Attempts to draft a Convention right to property were bedevilled by similar difficulties. Some argued that property was an economic interest rather than a civil/political right, and should not be protected in a human rights Convention. Others (including the UK) were sensitive to the possibility of a court interfering with important political choices, such as the state's power to nationalize industries, to create redistributive socio-economic programmes, to tax, and to fine.

7.04   These controversies explain why the initial Convention did not contain an article protecting property interests; why the right protected is to 'peaceful enjoyment of possessions' rather than a right actually to possess;[2] and why the ECtHR continues to afford a very wide margin of appreciation to states in reaching essentially political judgements about whether it is in the public interest for property rights to be curtailed. We note that the term 'right to property' is used as short-hand throughout this chapter, but that the precise terminology of Article 1, Protocol 1 (A1P1) is important and is discussed as relevant below.

7.05   This picture has gradually changed, both quantitatively and qualitatively. There has been a steady increase in the number of applications raising A1P1 issues. There has also been an increase in the proportion of successful applications under this article, either taken alone or with Article 14 across a wide range of property interests. Finally, the ECtHR has expanded the meaning of 'possessions' to incorporate 'legitimate expectations' and non-contributory statutory benefit entitlements, thus extending the scope of the right.

7.06   There has been fairly active domestic litigation involving A1P1. The approach adopted is in line with the Strasbourg jurisprudence with the domestic courts adopting the generally 'hands-off' approach of the ECtHR.[3]

---

[1] See, further, Nihal Jayawickrama, *The Judicial Application of Human Rights Law: National, Regional and International Jurisprudence* (CUP 2002) 909–10.

[2] See, generally, James Kingston, 'Rich People Have Rights Too? The Status of Property as a Fundamental Right' in Liz Heffernan (ed), *Human Rights: A European Perspective* (Round Hall Press 1994); David Anderson, 'Compensation for Interference with Property' (1999) 6 European Human Rights Law Review 543; S Whale, 'Pawnbrokers and Parishes: The Protection of Property under the Human Rights Act' (2002) European Human Rights Law Review 67.

[3] See eg *R (Countryside Alliance) v Attorney General* [2007] UKHL 52, [2008] 1 AC 719, paras 126–27 per Baroness Hale; *Belfast City Council v Miss Behavin'* [2007] UKHL 19, [2007] NI 89, para 16 per Lord Hoffmann.

1. The three rules

In *Sporrong and Lönnroth v Sweden* the ECtHR analysed A1P1, and interpreted it as containing 'three distinct rules'.[4] This interpretation of A1P1 was followed in subsequent cases.[5] In order to establish that there is a prima facie interference with the right to property it must be shown that: 7.07

(a) the peaceful enjoyment of the applicant's possessions has been interfered with by the state (rule 1); or

(b) the applicant has been deprived of possessions by the state (rule 2); or

(c) the applicant's possessions have been subjected to control by the state (rule 3).

But interference, deprivation, or control will not violate A1P1 if done 'in the public interest' or 'to enforce such laws [as the state] deems necessary to control the use of property in the public interest'.

Much of the earlier case law on the three rules is confusing, with the ECmHR and ECtHR often dealing with rules 2 and 3 before considering rule 1.[6] In recent cases, the ECtHR has adopted a more general approach, preferring to focus on the general principles in A1P1 rather than finding it necessary to decide which of the three rules is applicable,[7] and on occasion expressly stating that a particular infringement cannot be classified as falling within a precise category.[8] First, the ECtHR examines whether there has been an interference with the applicant's possessions. This interference may be direct or indirect, and may involve an actual deprivation of control which prevents peaceful enjoyment of the property, or any other form of interference. Secondly, the ECtHR examines whether that interference is justified. 7.08

2. Possessions

The ECtHR has interpreted the concept of 'possessions' broadly. The term has an autonomous meaning and the definition in domestic law is not determinative.[9] 7.09

In addition to physical items and land, 'possessions' have been held to include contractual rights,[10] bank account deposits,[11] leases,[12] company shares,[13] crystallized 7.10

---

[4] *Sporrong and Lönnroth v Sweden* (1983) 5 EHRR 35, para 61. Note that the ECtHR made clear in later judgments that the three rules are not 'distinct' in the sense of being unconnected: *James and others v UK* (1986) 8 EHRR 123; *Evans v UK* (2008) 46 EHRR 34 [GC] CHECK.

[5] See eg *Lithgow v UK* (1986) 8 EHRR 329, para 106.

[6] See eg *James and others v UK* (1986) 8 EHRR 123.

[7] See eg *Katsaros v Greece* (2003) 36 EHRR 58; *Jokela v Finland* (2003) 37 EHRR 26; *Bulves AD v Bulgaria* App No 3991/03, 22 January 2009. cf eg *Evans v UK* (2008) 46 EHRR 34, in which the ECtHR returned to the three-rule analysis.

[8] *Alisic and others v Bosnia and Herzegovina and others* App No 60642/08, 16 July 2014 [GC], para 99.

[9] See eg *Holy Monasteries v Greece* (1995) 20 EHRR 1; *Öneryildiz v Turkey* (2005) 41 EHRR 20 [GC].

[10] *Association of General Practitioners v Denmark* (1989) 62 DR 226. For a recent detailed discussion of when a contractual right amounts to a possession and in particular the qualified relevance of the assignability of the contract see *Solaria Energy UK Ltd v Department for Business and Industrial Strategy* [2020] EWCA Civ 1625, [2021] 1 WLR 2349, paras 33–41.

[11] *Alicsic and others v Bosnia and others* App No 60642/2008, 16 July 2014 [GC], para 99.

[12] *Mellacher v Austria* (1990) 12 EHRR 391.

[13] *Bramelid and Malmstrom v Sweden* ((1983) 5 EHRR 249.

debts,[14] the goodwill of a business,[15] liquor licences,[16] interests associated with a broadcasting licence,[17] and the benefit of such statutory pecuniary entitlements as from time to time exist.[18] Intangible claims to items of pecuniary value are also 'possessions' even before the claims have been realized: a claim for compensation in tort,[19] a right to compensation for lost land,[20] inheritance rights under a will,[21] and a retired judge's claim to a social tenancy have all been held to constitute possessions.[22] However, by way of example, neither a hereditary peerage[23] nor a human embryo[24] constituted possessions.

7.11   Future potential possessions will only come within the scope of A1P1 if they have already been earned or an enforceable, or at least arguably enforceable, claim to them exists.[25] This encompasses claims in respect of which an applicant can argue that he has at least a legitimate expectation based on settled domestic law.[26]

7.12   Domestic cases on the scope of 'possessions' in A1P1 have at times been inconsistent, reflecting the uncertainties and developing nature of the ECtHR case law. On the one hand, the domestic courts applied a broad definition of 'possessions' in certain cases, accepting that legitimate expectations (even those arising from ultra vires acts of public authorities)[27] and non-contributory benefits[28] may be covered. On the other hand, a narrow approach was evident in cases concerning a range of interests. For example, housing benefit was held to fall outside the right to property,[29] and in cases of benefit overpayments the overpaid money does not constitute a 'possession'.[30] However, the House of Lords has since affirmed the decision of the

---

[14] *Agneesens v Belgium* (1998) 58 DR 63.

[15] *Van Marle and others v Netherlands* (1986) 8 EHRR 483. Lord Bingham considered this area of Strasbourg jurisprudence unclear in *R (Countryside Alliance) v Attorney General* [2007] UKHL 52, [2008] 1 AC 719, para 21. See also *R (New London College) v Secretary of State for the Home Department* [2012] EWCA Civ 51, [2012] Imm AR 563 in which the Court of Appeal held that a student sponsor licence was not a possession in itself, but that evidence presented in a particular case may establish an interference with accrued goodwill in a business so as to give rise to an interference on this basis.

[16] *Tre Traktörer AB v Sweden* (1991) 13 EHRR 309.

[17] *Centro Europa 7 SRL and Di Stefano v Italy* App No 38433/09, 7 June 2012 [GC], para 178.

[18] *Stec v UK* (2005) 41 EHRR SE 295, para 43; affirmed by the Grand Chamber at *Stec v UK* (2006) 43 EHRR 1017 [GC].

[19] *Pressos Compañía Naviera SA v Belgium* (1996) 21 EHRR 301.

[20] *Broniowski v Poland* (2004) 15 BHRC 573.

[21] However, see below regarding the evolution in the interpretation of arts 2 and 3.

[22] *Teteriny v Russia* [2005] ECHR 11931/03.

[23] *De la Cierva Osorio de Moscoso and ors v Spain* App No 41127/98, 28 October 1999.

[24] *Parillo v Italy* (2016) 62 EHRR 8 [GC].

[25] *Wendenburg v Germany* (2003) 36 EHRR CD 154.

[26] *Gratzinger and others v Czech Republic* (2002) 35 EHRR CD202 [GC], para 69; *NKM v Hungary* (2016) 62 EHRR 33, para 35.

[27] *Rowland v Environment Agency* [2003] EWCA Civ 1885, [2005] Ch 1.

[28] *R (Carson) v Secretary of State for Work and Pensions* [2005] UKHL 37, [2006] 1 AC 173.

[29] *Campbell v South Northamptonshire DC* [2004] EWCA Civ 409, [2004] 3 All ER 387, though this decision was founded on the pre-*Stec v UK* (2005) 41 EHRR SE 295 distinction between contributory and non-contributory benefits, which is no longer good law: see *R (RJM) v Secretary of State for Work and Pensions* [2008] UKHL 63, [2009] 1 AC 311, para 59.

[30] *B v Secretary of State for Work and Pensions* [2005] EWCA Civ 929, [2005] 1 WLR 3796. In *B v United Kingdom* App No 3657/06, 14 February 2012, the ECtHR agreed that the overpaid benefits did not amount

Grand Chamber in *Stec v UK*,[31] finding that a disability premium is a possession for the purposes of A1P1.[32]

The narrow scope of the domestic approach to possessions was criticized by the ECtHR in *JM v UK*.[33] The House of Lords had held in *Secretary of State for Work and Pensions v M* that the payment of child support did not fall within the ambit of Article 1 of Protocol 1 for the purposes of Article 14 because it was primarily concerned with the expropriation of assets for a public purpose and not with the enforcement of a personal obligation.[34] Drawing a parallel with its jurisprudence on social security benefits, the ECtHR rejected this distinction and held that the domestic rules on payment of child support by same-sex partners were discriminatory. 　7.13

(a) Intellectual property rights

A1P1 encompasses intellectual property rights, such as patents,[35] trademarks,[36] and copyright.[37] 　7.14

In *Anheuser-Busch v Portugal* (the '*Budweiser*' case), the ECtHR Grand Chamber ruled that a pending application for registration of a trademark gave rise to interests of a proprietary nature so as to constitute a 'possession' within the meaning of A1P1.[38] 　7.15

(b) Public law rights

(i) *State pensions and benefits* Early ECtHR cases suggested that non-contributory benefits gained by virtue of public law were not protected by A1P1.[39] It is now clear from the decision of the Grand Chamber in *Stec v UK*[40] that, at least as regards entitlements to statutory benefits from time to time existing, such rights are protected. In *Stec* it was held that there was no longer any valid analytical distinction between those social security entitlements derived from contributions and those non-contributory benefits funded through general taxation. While A1P1 provided no right to the continuing provision of any particular social security benefit (ie the state could remove it if it regarded it as being in the general public interest to do 　7.16

---

to a possession, but considered that the assertable right to future benefits, which was reduced by the overpayment, brought the subject matter of the application within the scope of Protocol 1, art 1: at paras 40–41.

[31] *Stec v UK* (2006) 43 EHRR 47 [GC].

[32] *R (RJM) v Secretary of State for Work and Pensions* [2008] UKHL 63, [2008] 3 WLR 1023.

[33] *JM v UK* (2011) 53 EHRR 6.

[34] *Secretary of State for Work and Pensions v M* [2006] UKHL 11, [2006] 2 AC 91.

[35] *Smith Kline and French Laboratories Ltd v Netherlands* App No 12633/87, 4 October 1990; *Lenzing AG v UK* (1999) 27 EHRR CD323.

[36] *Anheuser-Busch v Portugal* (2007) 23 BHRC 307 [GC].

[37] *Societe Nationale de Programmes France 2 v France* App No 30262/96, 15 January 1997 (recognized through the 'rights of others' clause in art 10(2)).

[38] *Anheuser-Busch Inc v Portugal* (2007) 45 EHRR 36 [GC], (2007) 45 EHRR 36, para 78.

[39] The evolution can be traced through the cases of *X v Netherlands* App No 4130/69, 20 July 1971; *Muller v Austria* App no 5849/72, 1 October 1975; *Carlin v UK* (1998) 25 EHRR CD75; *Gaygusuz v Austria* (1996) 23 EHRR 364, para 41; *Poirrez v France* (2005) 40 EHRR 2, para 817; *Willis v UK* (2002) 35 EHRR 21; *Wessels-Bergevoert v Netherlands* (2004) 38 EHRR 37.

[40] *Sirverne v Chief Constable of Dorset* [1994] CL 1765 [GC].

so), there was a defined statutory right to be paid a particular benefit in accordance with the rules of a statutory scheme for so long as it continued to exist, irrespective of whether the scheme was contributory or non-contributory. Consequently, such entitlements unequivocally constitute possessions for the purposes of A1P1.[41]

7.17   However, economic and social policy remains a matter for Member States. The fact that a social security benefit constituted a 'possession' does not compel the Member State to continue to provide that benefit,[42] and even in cases where the Convention guarantees benefits to persons on the basis of what they have contributed into the social insurance system, the ECtHR has held that this cannot be interpreted as conferring an entitlement to a pension of a particular amount.[43]

7.18   (ii) *Legitimate expectations* The ECtHR has recognized that an individual may have a property right in the event of a sufficient 'legitimate expectation' of a benefit which is economic or property-like in nature. The Grand Chamber in *Malhous v Czech Republic* defined 'possessions' so as to include legitimate expectations—existing possessions or assets, including claims, in respect of which an applicant can argue that he or she has a legitimate expectation of obtaining the effective enjoyment of a property right.[44]

7.19   In *Pine Valley Developments Ltd and others v Ireland*, for example, a grant of planning permission created a legitimate expectation of benefits sufficient for it to qualify as a 'possession',[45] and a promise to provide land to displaced refugees sufficed in *Broniowski v Poland*.[46]

7.20   *Stretch v UK* demonstrates the ECtHR's expansive approach to this concept. The Court held that Mr Stretch had a legitimate expectation that a lease granted to him by the local authority would be renewed and that the failure to renew breached his rights under A1P1. This was despite the fact that the original grant had been ultra vires.[47]

7.21   The ECtHR has made clear that there are limits to the expectations it will recognize: if the claim is insufficiently concrete it will not constitute a 'possession'. In *Nerva v UK*, for example, the ECtHR found that waiters had no legitimate expectation that their tips would not be taken into account as part of their remuneration when calculating whether they were receiving the statutory minimum wage.[48] The distinction—repeatedly drawn by the ECtHR—is between a 'mere hope' and a 'legitimate expectation'.[49]

---

[41] The ECtHR reiterated its approach in *Stec* in *Carson v UK* (2010) 51 EHRR 13. See also *JM v UK* (2011) 53 EHRR 6; *R (British Gurkha Welfare Society and others) v Ministry of Defence* [2010] EWCA Civ 1098; and *Belane Nagy v Hungary* App No 53080/2013, 13 December 2016 [GC], paras 80–89.

[42] *Stec v UK* (2006) 43 EHRR 1017.

[43] *Muller v Austria* App no 5849/72, 1 October 1975; *Carson v UK* (2010) 51 EHRR 13.

[44] *Malhous v Czech Republic* App No 33071/96, 12 July 2001 [GC].

[45] *Pine Valley Developments Ltd and others v Ireland* (1992) 14 EHRR 319.

[46] *Broniowski v Poland* (2005) 40 EHRR 21 [GC].

[47] *Stretch v UK* (2004) 38 EHRR 12. See also *Beyeler v Italy* (2001) 33 EHRR 52.

[48] *Nerva v UK* (2003) 36 EHRR 4.

[49] See eg *MA v Finland* (2003) 37 EHRR CD 210; *Caisse Régionale de Crédit Agricole Mutuel v France* App No 58867/00, 19 October 2004; *Von Maltzan v Germany* (2006) 42 EHRR SE 11.

Claims that have no grounding in the domestic legal order are considered to be   7.22
outside the scope of A1P1.[50] The criterion is not whether there is a 'genuine dispute'
or an 'arguable claim', but an actual basis for claiming the possession in national law.
Thus if the applicant's contention regarding the existence of a claim in domestic law
is finally rejected by the national courts, there can be no 'legitimate expectation'.[51]

However, the fact that a benefit can be reduced or discontinued does not mean   7.23
that it will not be a 'possession' within the meaning of Protocol 1 of Article 1, at least
until it is revoked.[52] Difficult borderline cases arise. In *Belane Nagy v Hungary*,[53] the
applicant's contributory statutory disability pension was suspended on the strength
of an updated occupational assessment finding her not to meet the minimum statutory impairment level. That decision was later reversed, but by then the relevant
impairment criteria had been retrospectively altered so as to render her ineligible
in any event. The domestic authorities moreover did not act on a recommendation
made to grant the applicant a rehabilitation allowance. The Grand Chamber held
by a bare majority that these facts gave rise to an interference with A1P1 on the
basis that the applicant had a legitimate expectation of eventual receipt of a pension
benefit under domestic law.[54]

3. Positive obligations

The right to peaceful enjoyment of possessions entails a positive obligation on the   7.24
state to take necessary and reasonable steps to protect it. In *Öneryildiz v Turkey*
a landslide and explosion at a municipal refuse tip had destroyed the applicant's
home and killed nine members of his family.[55] The Grand Chamber held that the
state's failure to take steps to protect the applicant's property against the dangerous
man-made activities in question violated A1P1. The ECtHR has adopted a similar
approach to the state's obligation to protect property in the event of a natural dis-
aster, but distinguished what is required by way of protection of property in respect
of natural disasters from man-made dangerous activities such as those considered
in *Öneryildiz*. Less is required from the state pursuant to the positive obligation in
respect of the former as opposed to the latter.[56]

The domestic courts have also recognized that A1P1 includes a positive obliga-   7.25
tion. In *Marcic v Thames Water Utilities Ltd* the House of Lords accepted that the
failure by Thames Water to prevent regular flooding of Mr Marcic's house with
sewage was a prima facie breach of his right to property.[57]

---

[50] *Kopecky v Slovakia* (2005) 41 EHRR 43, para 52; *Wilson v First County Trust* [2003] UKHL 40, [2004]
1 AC 84 (contract improperly executed, hence unenforceable consumer credit agreement not a possession)

[51] *Centro Europa 7 SRL and Di Stefano v Italy* App No 38433/09, 7 June 2012 [GC], para 173.

[52] *Moskal v Poland* App No 10373/05, 15 September 2009, para 40.

[53] *Belane Nagy v Hungary* App No 53080/2013, 13 December 2016 [GC].

[54] ibid paras 90–127.

[55] *Öneryildiz v Turkey* App No 48939/99, 30 November 2004 [GC].

[56] *Budayeva and others v Russia* App Nos 15339/02, 21166/02, 20058/02, 11673/02, and 15343/02, 20
March 2008, paras 173–77.

[57] *Marcic v Thames Water Utilities Ltd* [2003] UKHL 66, [2004] 2 AC 42.

7.26   A1P1 also incorporates an implicit procedural obligation.[58] The state must afford a reasonable opportunity to individuals to put their case in order to challenge measures which interfere with their possessions. In *Paulet v United Kingdom*, the UK procedure for imposing confiscation orders under the Proceeds of Crime Act 2002 (POCA), which did not allow for any individual review of the proportionality of the confiscation order, was found to breach the procedural obligation under Protocol 1 Article 1.[59] In *R v Waya*, the Supreme Court held that the relevant provisions of POCA had to be read down so as to allow consideration of the proportionality of confiscation orders made.[60]

7.27   In *Grainger v United Kingdom*, the ECtHR held that the positive obligation did not extend to protecting private investors' investments in the distressed building society Northern Rock during the global financial crisis.[61] Similarly, in *Kotov v Russia*, the Grand Chamber rejected an application founded on alleged positive obligations owed by the state under A1P1 in circumstances where a liquidator's deliberate and unlawful actions had caused loss to investors, holding Russia's general system of regulation to be adequate to discharge its positive obligations.[62]

7.28   However, in contrast, in *Zolotas v Greece (No 2)*,[63] where an applicant had been prevented from claiming funds in his bank accounts due to his not having made a transaction for a period of 20 years, the Court found a violation of the state's positive obligations due to the absence in domestic law of any requirement to notify holders of dormant accounts of the expiry of such a time limit. In the absence of such a notification, an excessive and disproportionate burden was placed on the applicant.[64] And in *Dabic v Croatia* the ECtHR found a violation of the positive duty where the authorities had sequestered the applicant's property, and the property had been damaged and looted by the private occupant prior to its return to the applicant with no provision or procedure under domestic law to seek compensation for this damage and loss.[65]

7.29   Inadequate or ineffective procedures for enforcing court orders and debts have frequently been found to give rise to a breach of the positive obligation, although the extent of this obligation varies depending on whether the order or debt is against the state or a private party.[66] In particular, lengthy delays in court proceedings have been held to violate the positive requirement of Protocol 1, Article,1 in addition to violating Article 6 (fair trial).[67]

---

[58] See eg *AGOSI v the United Kingdom* App No 9118/80, 24 October 1986, paras 55 and 58–60; *Jokelala v Finland* (2003) 37 EHRR 26; *Megadat.com Srl v Moldova* App No 21151/04, 8 April 2008; and *GIEM SRL and others v Italy* App No 1828/06, 28 June 2018 [GC], para 302.

[59] *Paulet v United Kingdom* App No 6219/08, 13 May 2014, para 67.

[60] *R v Waya* [2012] UKSC 51, [2013] 1 AC 294.

[61] *Grainger v United Kingdom* App No 34940/10, 10 July 2012 [GC], para 42.

[62] *Kotov v Russia* App No 54522/00, 3 April 2012 [GC].

[63] *Zolotas v Greece (No 2)* App No 66610/09, 29 January 2013.

[64] ibid para 55.

[65] *Dabic v Croatia* App No 49001/14, 18 March 2021.

[66] See eg *Fuklev v Ukraine* App No 71186/01, 30 November 2005, paras 90–93; *Liseytseva and Maslov v Russian* App No 39483/05, 9 January 2015, para 183; and ECtHR Guide on A1P1 (31 August 2022), paras 216–31.

[67] *Immobiliare Saffi v Italy* (2000) 30 EHRR 756, [GC].

4. Interference with the right to property

Possessions may be interfered with in many ways by the state. The most straight-forward example is when there has been a deprivation of possessions. However, the state may also interfere with the right through excessive or arbitrary controls, or any other acts or omissions that have the effect of interfering with the use or enjoyment of the property. As explained below, interferences can be justified by the state where they are proportionate to a legitimate aim.

7.30

(a) *Deprivation of possessions*

In assessing whether an individual has been deprived of property the ECtHR will look at the realities of the situation, not the label.[68] In some circumstances the formal legal title may remain with the owner of the property, but if his or her rights are rendered useless in practice this may amount to a de facto deprivation.

7.31

The House of Lords in *Aston Cantlow v Wallbank* held that when individuals were obliged to fulfil an obligation which they had voluntarily taken on, they were not being deprived of their possessions for the purposes of A1P1.[69]

7.32

(b) *Controls on the use of property*

The second paragraph of A1P1 provides that the state is entitled to 'control' the use of property 'in accordance with the general interest or to secure the payment of taxes or other contributions or penalties'. The ECtHR has held that this is to be construed in light of the general principle enunciated in the opening sentence of A1P1. Controls on use of property are therefore subject to the fair balance test in the same way as deprivations of possessions.[70]

7.33

Applicants will often argue that a measure constitutes a de facto deprivation, but the ECtHR will instead find that it amounts only to a 'control'. In *Air Canada v UK*, for example, the applicants argued that the seizure of their aeroplane following a drugs find on board, and the requirement that they pay £50,000 to have it returned, amounted to a deprivation; the ECtHR instead held that it was 'a control on the use of property'.[71]

7.34

The ECtHR has held that planning controls,[72] inheritance laws, and taxes[73] constitute systems of controls. In *Pye v UK* the Grand Chamber, disagreeing with the Chamber, found that the UK's statutory provisions, which transferred ownership from registered landowners to squatters after 12 years of adverse possession, constituted a control on the use of land rather than a deprivation of possessions.[74]

7.35

---

[68] *Sporrong and Lönnroth v Sweden* (1982) 5 EHRR 35, para 63.
[69] [2003] UKHL 37, [2004] 1 AC 546.
[70] *Pye v UK* (2008) 46 EHRR 34 [GC]; *R (Countryside Alliance) v Attorney General* [2007] UKHL 52, [2008] 1 AC 719.
[71] *Air Canada v UK* (1995) 20 EHRR 150.
[72] *Pine Valley Developments and others v Ireland* (1992) 14 EHRR 319.
[73] *Gasus-Dosier and Fördertechnik v Netherlands* (1995) 20 EHRR 403.
[74] *Pye v UK* (2008) 46 EHRR 34 [GC].

7.36   Controls on the use of property have also included laws requiring positive action by property owners, as in *Denev v Sweden*, where environmental laws obliged a landowner to plant trees.[75]

7.37   In a number of cases the ECtHR has held that housing laws suspending or staggering the enforcement of eviction orders by residential property owners against their tenants constitute 'controls on the use of property'. The ECtHR stated in *Mellacher v Austria* that the housing field is 'a central concern of social and economic policies',[76] warranting a wide margin of appreciation both with regard to its assessment of the existence of a problem of public concern warranting measures of control, and as to the choice of the detailed rules for the implementation of such policies.

7.38   The domestic approach has largely been in line with the tendency of the ECtHR to find an interference with possessions to amount to a control rather than a deprivation. In *R (Countryside Alliance) v Attorney General* the House of Lords characterized a ban on fox hunting with dogs under the Hunting Act 2004 as a control on the use of property rather than a deprivation of possessions.[77] The courts have held that the ban on cigarette vending machines in the Health Act 2009 was a control on, rather than a deprivation of, the rights of cigarette vendors.[78] In *Cusack v Harrow LBC* the Supreme Court rejected the contention that a restriction on access to a property pursuant to a local authority's power to erect barriers between carriageways and footways amounted to a deprivation of property rather than a control.[79]

7.39   In *R (British American Tobacco UK Ltd and others) v Secretary of State for Health*[80] the Court of Appeal held that regulations requiring standardization of tobacco packaging constituted a control and not a deprivation of rights conferred by trademark registrations. The controls struck a fair and proportionate balance such that there was no violation of A1P1.

(c) *Interference with peaceful enjoyment*

7.40   An interference with the right to property may occur where there is no deprivation or control, provided it impinges upon the applicant's ability peacefully to enjoy or use the possessions in question. In *Stran Greek Refineries v Greece*, for example, an arbitral award in favour of the applicant company was a possession, and there was an interference when the state passed legislation rendering the award unenforceable.[81]

---

[75] *Denev v Sweden* (1989) 59 DR 127.
[76] *Mellacher v Austria* (1989) 12 EHRR 391.
[77] *R (Countryside Alliance) v Attorney General* [2007] UKHL 52, [2008] 1 AC 719.
[78] *Sinclair Collis Ltd v Secretary of State for Health* [2010] EWHC 3112 (Admin). Upheld in [2011] EWCA Civ 437, [2012] QB 394.
[79] *Cusack v Harrow LBC* [2013] UKSC 40, [2013] 4 All ER 97.
[80] *R (British American Tobacco UK Ltd and others) v Secretary of State for Health* [2016] EWCA Civ 1182, [2018] QB 149.
[81] *Stran Greek Refineries v Greece* (1994) 19 EHRR 293.

In *Breyer Group plc and another v Department of Energy and Climate Change*,[82]   7.41
the Court of Appeal considered the impact on various businesses of government
proposals to alter rates for a feed-in tariff for producers and installers of low-carbon
electricity generating schemes, which were never implemented due to a domestic
court ruling finding the proposals to be unlawful. Applying the line of Strasbourg
case law holding that the marketable goodwill of a company (as opposed to a stream
of future income) can count as a possession, it held that the proposals gave rise to an
interference with A1P1 due to their impact on secured and enforceable contracts,
but not due to the loss of possible future contracts, in circumstances where many
projects were abandoned in response to the unlawful proposals.

5. Limitations

In determining the level of permissible interference with the right to property the   7.42
ECtHR distinguishes between the types of interference. It will, in general, apply
closer scrutiny to interferences involving deprivations or expropriation than to
those involving control alone.

However, the test applied is one of proportionality: the interference must be   7.43
subject to conditions provided by domestic law and must achieve a 'fair balance'
between the legitimate public interest aim relied on and the infringement of A1P1.
The availability of an effective remedy and compensation is relevant in assessing
whether a fair balance has been struck.

Under domestic law, the question whether an interference with A1P1 is pro-   7.44
portionate is determined by reference to a four-stage test, namely: (1) whether the
objective of the measure is sufficiently important to justify the limitation of the
right; (2) whether the measure is rationally connected to the objective; (3) whether
a less intrusive measure could have been used; and (4) whether, having regard to
these matters and to the severity of the consequences, a fair balance has been struck
between the rights of the individual and the interests of the community.[83]

(a) Conditions provided by law

The interference must be 'subject to the conditions provided for by law'. This encom-   7.45
passes the substantive notion of 'quality of law' common to other qualified rights,
which requires that applicable provisions of domestic law are sufficiently accessible, precise, and foreseeable in their application and provide a sufficient measure
of protection against arbitrary interference.[84] This requirement was not satisfied
in *Hentrich v France*. A law creating a right of pre-emption over land to enable
the Commissioner of Revenue to collect tax was held to violate A1P1 because it

---

[82] *Breyer Group plc and another v Department of Energy and Climate Change* [2015] EWCA CIV 408,
[2015] 1 WLR 4559.
[83] *Bank Mellat v Her Majesty's Treasury No 2* [2013] UKSC 39, [2014] AC 700, paras 20 and 68–76.
[84] *Sud Fondi Srl and others v Italy* App No 75909/01, 20 January 2009; *Lekic v Slovenia* (2018) 67 EHRR
10 [GC], paras 86–87.

'operated arbitrarily and selectively and was scarcely foreseeable, and it was not attended by basic procedural safeguards'.[85]

(b) *The public interest*

7.46 In deciding whether an interference is in the public interest (ie whether it pursues a legitimate aim) the ECtHR also affords the state a wide margin of appreciation in deciding what public interest demands. The characterization of whether an objective constitutes a legitimate aim is a question left almost exclusively to the determination of the state. A wide range of aims have been accepted as legitimate and cases where the Court has found no such aim to exist are rare.[86] The domestic courts have followed the ECtHR's light touch in this area and applied a similarly gentle standard of review.

7.47 The ECtHR's approach to the public interest is evident from cases such as *James and others v UK*[87] and *Pye v UK*.[88] In *James* the ECtHR considered the compulsory transfer of ownership of residential properties in central London to the tenants of those properties pursuant to the Leasehold Reform Act 1967, which was designed to protect long-term tenants' moral entitlement to their properties at the end of their leases. The property owners complained that the compulsory nature, and the calculation of the price, of the transfers violated A1P1.

7.48 The ECtHR was unanimous in holding that compulsory transfer from one individual to another may be a legitimate means of promoting the public interest and that the objective of eliminating social injustice by leasehold reform is within the state's margin of appreciation. It also emphasized that the public interest need not be equated with the general interest, or the interests of the majority. A deprivation of property effected in pursuance of legitimate social, economic, or other policies may be 'in the public interest' even if the community at large derives no direct benefit from that deprivation.[89] The compulsory transfer at issue was not disproportionate, nor was it unreasonable to restrict the right of enfranchisement to less valuable houses since they were perceived as cases of greatest hardship.

7.49 Similarly, in *Pye v UK*[90] the UK's adverse possession laws, which gave squatters ownership of registered land after 12 years, were found to fall within the state's margin of appreciation 'unless they give rise to results which are so anomalous as to render the legislation unacceptable'. In dissent, Judge Loucaides disputed the existence of a public interest in the measures, noting that in fact they encouraged the illegal use of land.

7.50 The domestic courts now follow the ECtHR's lead on adverse possession. In *Beaulane Properties v Palmer*[91] the High Court had restricted the meaning of 'adverse possession' in order not to infringe the appellant's rights under A1P1,

---

[85] *Hentrich v France* (1994) 18 EHRR 440.
[86] See eg ECtHR Case Law Guide to A1P1, paras 130–41.
[87] *James and others v UK* (1986) 8 EHRR 123.
[88] *Pye v UK* (2008) 46 EHRR 34 [GC].
[89] ibid para 45. See also *Allard v Sweden* (2004) 39 EHRR 14, para 52.
[90] *Pye v UK* (2008) 46 EHRR 45 [GC].
[91] *Beaulane Properties v Palmer* [2005] EWHC 817 (Ch), [2006] Ch 79.

but this approach was reversed by the Court of Appeal in *Ofulue v Bossert*.[92] The Court simply applied *Pye v UK*, finding that a margin of appreciation applied to the domestic legislation.

The notion of the 'public interest' was addressed by the House of Lords in *R*   7.51 *(Countryside Alliance) v Attorney General*.[93] Under the Hunting Act 2004, Parliament banned fox hunting with dogs. The appellants, some of whom relied on fox hunting for their livelihood, complained that the ban interfered with their rights under A1P1. The House of Lords was reluctant to scrutinize the precise nature of the public interest at stake. Lord Hope held simply that it was 'open to [the legislature] to form their own judgment as to whether [the hunting activities] caused a sufficient degree of suffering ... for legislative action to be taken to deal with them'.[94]

(c) 'Fair balance'

The need to strike a fair balance between the public interest and the rights of indi-   7.52 vidual property owners pervades the whole of A1P1, including its second paragraph. Thus, in *Spadea v Italy* it was held that the applicants had been treated fairly by the laws suspending a tenant eviction order,[95] whereas the applicant in *Scollo v Italy* had not.[96] In both cases the suspensions of the eviction orders had the reasonable aim of preventing a large number of people all becoming homeless at the same time. The facts of each case meant that the application of the fair balance test produced different results.

Sporrong v Sweden related to town planning in Stockholm.[97] The applicants   7.53 owned properties that were subject to lengthy expropriation permits and prohibitions on construction. The ECtHR held that there had been an interference with the applicants' property rights by rendering the substance of ownership 'precarious and defeasible', which subjected them to an individual and excessive burden and did not achieve a fair balance between the protection of the individual right to property and the wider public interest.

Again, in *Chassagnou v France* the ECtHR found that to compel small land-   7.54 owners who were opposed to hunting to transfer hunting rights over their land, enabling others to hunt on it, did not strike a fair balance.[98] The compensation provided for, which involved a right to hunt on others' property, did not assist in achieving a fair balance since the compensation was not valuable to the landowners who were ethically opposed to hunting such that the compulsion constituted an individual and excessive burden. This decision was affirmed and applied by the Grand Chamber in *Hermann v Germany*, a closely analogous case concerning hunting rights in Germany.[99] However, *Chassagnou* and *Hermann* were distinguished

---

[92] *Ofulue v Bossert* [2008] EWCA Civ 7, [2008] 3 WLR 1253.
[93] *R (Countryside Alliance) v Attorney General* [2007] UKHL 52, [2008] 1 AC 719.
[94] ibid para 78.
[95] *Spadea v Italy* (1995) 21 EHRR 482.
[96] *Scollo v Italy* (1995) 22 EHRR 514.
[97] *Sporrong v Sweden* (1982) 5 EHRR 35.
[98] *Chassagnou v France* (2000) 29 EHRR 615.
[99] *Hermann v Germany* App No 9300/07, 26 June 2012 [GC].

in *Chabauty v France*, where no violation was found in circumstances where the landowner in question was not ethically opposed to hunting.[100]

7.55　In a series of cases the ECtHR has accepted that bankruptcy systems pursue a legitimate aim (protection of the rights of others) but that in order for interferences with A1P1 to be proportionate they must be limited to what is strictly necessary. This stringent test is in keeping with the severe impact of bankruptcy on the individual.[101]

7.56　The Grand Chamber has emphasized the importance of striking a fair balance in awarding compensation for expropriation of property. In *Perdigão v Portugal* the expropriation compensation awarded to the applicant had been completely absorbed by court costs.[102] In such circumstances, the Court found that the difference in legal character between the obligation on the state to pay compensation for expropriation and the obligation on a litigant to pay court costs did not prevent an overall examination of the proportionality of the interference complained of under A1P1.

7.57　The fair balance test will be more loosely applied in relation to the state's decisions concerning conferment of welfare benefits, as this involves a question of allocation of scarce resources.[103] However, as considered above, Article 14 operates as a check on discriminatory schemes[104] and in such cases the approach of the ECtHR is to ask whether, 'but for' the discriminatory ground about which the applicant complains, they would have had a right enforceable under domestic law.[105] Moreover, even under A1P1 taken alone, the ECtHR may also closely examine the circumstances of any group whose existing benefits are to be removed. For example, in *Ásmundsson v Iceland* the ECtHR found a breach of A1P1 when a disability pension was removed from a small class of disabled persons, but not others. This imposed an excessive and disproportionate burden on the applicant which was not justified by community interests.[106]

7.58　Taxation schemes are subjected to little scrutiny by the ECtHR, as the ability of the state to levy tax is specifically preserved in the second paragraph of A1P1. The fair balance test generally applies to tax cases only insofar as it requires that the establishment of the applicant's liability to make payments be subject to procedural guarantees—the state can decide for itself as to levels of tax, and the means of assessment and collection. As the ECtHR stated in one case, it 'will respect the legislature's assessment in [enforcing tax obligations] unless it is devoid of reasonable

---

[100] *Chabauty v France* App No 57412/08, 4 October 2012, para 57 [GC].

[101] See eg *Luordo v Italy* (2005) 41 EHRR 26; *Stockholms Försäkrings- och Skadeståndsjuridik AB v Sweden* (2004) 39 EHRR 23.

[102] *Perdigão v Portugal* App No 24768/06, 16 November 2010 [GC].

[103] See eg *Carson v UK* (2010) 51 EHRR 13.

[104] For example, *Stec v UK* (2006) 43 EHRR 1017 [GC]; *Barrow v UK* App No 42735/02, 22 August 2006; *Burden and Burden v UK* (2008) 47 EHRR 38; *JD and others v United UK* App Nos 32949/17 and 34614/17, 24 October 2019 (challenge to failure to exclude disabled persons and victims of domestic violence from the so-called 'Bedroom Tax').

[105] For example, *Fabris v France* (2013) 57 EHRR 19, para 52.

[106] *Ásmundsson v Iceland* (2005) 41 EHRR 42.

foundation'.[107] This permissive approach has even applied to retrospective taxation schemes.[108]

Forfeiture laws have been regularly upheld as proportionate by the ECtHR.[109] 7.59
The ECtHR has also upheld the proportionality of confiscation orders under the Drug Trafficking Act 1994. In *Phillips v UK* the ECtHR rejected the complaint that such confiscation orders were unreasonably extensive, given the important role such penalties play in efforts to combat drug trafficking.[110]

The domestic courts have frequently applied a light touch standard of review 7.60
to the justification of interferences with A1P1, although this approach has been expressed in various ways and it is evident that the intensity of review will be determined by a range of factors. In *Marcic v Thames Water Utilities Ltd* the House of Lords adopted a hands-off approach to the fair balance test, stating that it considered the pertinent question to be whether the scheme set up by Thames Water to control the sewage system which had flooded Mr Marcic's house had 'an unreasonable impact' on Mr Marcic. As it did not, the Court found the interference with his property rights to be justified.[111]

In *R (Countryside Alliance) v Attorney General* the House of Lords explained that 7.61
there was no test of strict necessity under A1P1, and that property rights could be 'more readily overridden' than the core rights such as Articles 8 and 9.[112]

In *Sinclair Collis v Secretary of State for Health*[113] the High Court held that it 7.62
could not interfere with a legislative measure banning cigarette vending machines unless it was found to be 'manifestly without foundation'. A similarly light touch standard of review was applied by the Court of Appeal, which affirmed the decision of the High Court on this point and confirmed that the Secretary of State had been entitled to conclude that the less rights-restricting option of a purely voluntary, non-statutory code to regulate the use of vending machines was not an equally suitable means of achieving the legitimate aim of enhancing human health.[114]

In *Axa General Insurance Ltd and others v HM Advocate and others*[115] the Supreme 7.63
Court rejected a challenge to the Damages (Asbestos-related Conditions) Scotland Act 2009, which had been enacted by the Scottish Parliament following extensive consideration and consultation in order to retrospectively reverse the effect of a recent case law development on compensation for asbestos-related disease. The Court found that the measure struck a fair balance between the rights of insurers and the general interest, emphasizing the broad margin of discretion that the Court

---

[107] *Gasus Dosier- und Fördertechnik GmbH v Netherlands* (1995) 20 EHRR 403.

[108] *National and Provincial Building Society v UK* (1997) 25 EHRR 127.

[109] See eg *Handyside v UK* (1976) 1 EHRR 737, *Allgemeine Gold und Silberscheideanstalt v UK* (1986) 9 EHRR 1; *Air Canada v UK* (1995) 20 EHRR 150.

[110] *Phillips v UK* App No 41087/98, 5 July 2001.

[111] *Marcic v Thames Water Utilities Ltd* [2003] UKHL 66, [2004] 2 AC 42.

[112] *R (Countryside Alliance) v Attorney General* [2007] UKHL 52, [2008] 1 AC 719, para 163 per Lord Brown.

[113] *Sinclair Collis v Secretary of State for Health* [2010] EWHC 3112 (Admin).

[114] By a majority: *R (on the application of Sinclair Collis Ltd) v Secretary of State for Health* [2011] EWCA Civ 437, [2012] QB 394.

[115] *Axa General Insurance Ltd and others v HM Advocate and others* [2011] UKSC 46, [2012] 1 AC 868.

would afford to the judgment of a democratically elected legislature in this context. In contrast, in *Re Recovery of Medical Costs for Asbestos Diseases (Wales) Bill*,[116] a majority of the Supreme Court held that more far-reaching retrospective legislation had not been demonstrated to be proportionate. Significant to the majority's conclusion in this case was an apparent misunderstanding during the passage of the Bill regarding how far and in what ways the proposed legislation went beyond legislation adopted by the UK Parliament.[117]

7.64　In *Bank Mellat v Her Majesty's Treasury No 2*,[118] a majority of the Supreme Court held that an Order made under Schedule 7 of the Counter-Terrorism Act 2008 against Bank Mellat, in effect shutting it out of the UK financial sector, constituted a disproportionate interference with its A1P1 rights. Despite the pressing public interest behind the measure (namely addressing the risk of funding for the Iranian nuclear programme) and the wide margin of discretion properly afforded to the government due to the subject matter, the majority of the Supreme Court found that the measure irrationally singling out Bank Mellat in circumstances in which the identified problem applied to all Iranian banks operating in the UK. This rendered the measure as a whole disproportionate.[119]

(d) Compensation

7.65　The basic approach to compensation was set out by the ECtHR in *Holy Monasteries v Greece*:

> In this connection, the taking of property without payment of an amount reasonably related to its value will normally constitute a disproportionate interference and a total lack of compensation can be considered justifiable under A1P1 only in exceptional circumstances. Article 1 does not, however, guarantee a right to full compensation in all circumstances, since legitimate objectives of 'public interest' may call for reimbursement of less than the full market value.[120]

7.66　A similar approach was taken in *Gaganus v Turkey* where the Court held that, in general, the amount of compensation in cases of expropriation in the public interest should bear a reasonable relationship to the value of the property.[121] However, the ECtHR emphasized in *Lithgow v UK* that where a state considers that objectives of public interest justify reimbursement at less than the full market value, the ECtHR will respect the national legislature's judgement unless manifestly without reasonable foundation.[122] The Court has also reiterated the indication in *Holy Monasteries v Greece* that exceptionally the payment of no compensation for a deprivation can be justified.[123]

---

[116] *Re Recovery of Medical Costs for Asbestos Diseases (Wales) Bill* [2015] UKSC 3, [2015] AC 1016.
[117] ibid paras 67–69 per Lord Mance.
[118] *Bank Mellat v Her Majesty's Treasury No 2* [2013] UKSC 39, [2014] AC 700.
[119] ibid paras 25–27 per Lord Sumption.
[120] *Holy Monasteries v Greece* (1995) 20 EHRR 1, para 71.
[121] *Gaganus v Turkey* App No 39335/98, 5 June 2001.
[122] *Lithgow v UK* (1986) 8 EHRR 329. See the House of Lords' decisions in *R v Rezvi; R v Benjafield* [2002] UKHL 2, [2003] 1 AC 1099 for consistent domestic findings on the issue of confiscation orders.
[123] *Holy Monasteries v Greece* (1995) 20 EHRR 1.

In *Vistins and Perepjolkins v Latvia*, notwithstanding the margin of appreciation   7.67
enjoyed in this context, the Grand Chamber found a violation of A1P1 in respect of
the level of compensation for the expropriation of property by the Latvian authorities as part of the expansion of the Port of Riga. A number of factors led the Grand
Chamber to the conclusion that a 'fair balance' had not been struck between the
interests of the community and the applicants' fundamental rights, including
the disproportion between the current value of the property and the compensation awarded and the fact that the disparity was a result, in part, of retrospective
legislation.[124]

C. PROTOCOL 1, ARTICLE 2: RIGHT TO EDUCATION

The existence and scope of 'a right to education' is one of the more controversial   7.68
Convention questions. During the drafting of Protocol 1, many states expressed
concern that the existence of such a right would impose onerous positive obligations upon governments. In an attempt to assuage these concerns, the opening
sentence of Protocol 1, Article 2 was changed from its original positive form ('Every
person has the right to education') to the current negative expression ('No person
shall be denied the right to education').

Several states, including the United Kingdom, have entered reservations to   7.69
Article 2 of Protocol 1. The UK reservation relates to the second sentence of the
article (the requirement that education be provided in conformity with parents'
religious and philosophical convictions). The United Kingdom has accepted this
provision only so far as it is compatible with the provision of efficient instruction
and training and the avoidance of unreasonable public expenditure. The reservation
is set out in Part II of Schedule 3 to the Human Rights Act.

Strasbourg and domestic jurisprudence concerning Protocol 1, Article 2 is   7.70
limited. This is often said to be due to the weak, negative phrasing of the article
itself. However, Convention rights with even weaker phrasing—notably Protocol
1, Article 3, the implied right to vote—have developed despite this constraint.[125]
The underdevelopment of Protocol 1, Article 2 is primarily due to the small number of cases that go to Strasbourg. The leading ECtHR decision remains *Belgian
Linguistics (No 2)*,[126] decided in 1968, and only a handful of cases are heard each
year. Similarly there are only a relatively small number of cases brought in the
domestic courts.

Other rights that involve personal development, such as Article 8 and the 'audi-   7.71
ence right' (the right to receive information) under Article 10, have developed more
rapidly in recent years. The principles developed in these cases are relevant in the
context of the right to education.[127] Indeed, in a number of the cases discussed

---

[124] *Vistins and Perepjolkins v Latvi* App No 71243/01, 25 March 2014 [GC].
[125] See eg *Hirst v UK (No 2)* (2006) 42 EHRR 41.
[126] *Belgian Linguistics (No 2)* (1979–80) 1 EHRR 252.
[127] *Ibrahim v Norway* (2022) 74 EHRR 25, para 142.

below, the ECtHR has found a breach of Protocol 1, Article 2 when read in the light of another Convention right.

7.72 In contrast, both the ECtHR and the domestic courts have seen an increase in cases claiming a breach of Article 14 taken with Protocol 1, Article 2. This case law is addressed in paragraphs 7.105–7.117.

1. Scope of the right

7.73 In *Belgian Linguistics (No 2)* the ECtHR held that despite the negative formulation, the first sentence of Protocol 1, Article 2 clearly enshrines a positive right.[128] The content of that right was identified as follows: (a) a right to an effective education; (b) a right of access to existing educational institutions; (c) a right to be educated in the national language or in one of the national languages; and (d) a right to obtain official recognition of completed studies.

7.74 The significance of the negative formulation was held to be that the article does not require states to establish at their own expense, or to subsidize, education of any particular type or at any particular level. Since all Member States at the time of signing the Protocol possessed, and continued to possess, a general and official educational system, there was no question of requiring each state to establish such a system. Rather, the article obliged states to guarantee that individuals could take advantage of the existing means of instruction.[129]

7.75 The right is that of the student, which can be exercised by the parents on his or her behalf when he or she is young and by the student personally when he or she grows older.

7.76 The state may require parents to send their children to school or to educate them adequately at home.[130] It may allow private education and schools, but is under no obligation to fund or subsidize these arrangements.

7.77 Until 2005 the extent of the article's applicability to higher education was unclear. Although the ECmHR as far back as 1965 stated that Protocol 1, Article 2 included 'entry to nursery, primary, secondary and higher education',[131] in a series of decisions over the next 30 years it observed that 'the right to education envisaged in Article 2 is concerned primarily with elementary education and not necessarily advanced studies such as technology'.[132]

7.78 In 2007 the Grand Chamber in *Leyla Sahin v Turkey* finally clarified that Protocol 1, Article 2 undoubtedly does extend to higher education. Any existing institutions of higher education clearly come within its scope, 'since the right of access to such institutions is an inherent part of the right set out in that provision'.[133] The Court applied *Leyla Sahin* in *Eren v Turkey*, in which it found a violation of the right

---

[128] *Belgian Linguistics (No 2)* (1979–80) 1 EHRR 252.
[129] *Simpson v UK* App No 14688/89, 4 December 1989.
[130] *Family H v UK* App No 10233/83, 6 March 1984.
[131] *Belgian Linguistics (No 2)* (1979–80) 1 EHRR 252, para 22.
[132] *X v UK* (1975) DR 2, para 50; *Kramelius v Sweden* App No 21062/92, 17 January 1996.
[133] *Leyla Sahin v Turkey* (2007) 44 EHRR 5, paras 134, 141.

where a university student's exam results had been arbitrarily annulled, thereby excluding the student from the whole university system.[134]

The ECtHR has applied Protocol 1, Article 2 to the provision of education in prisons. Whilst it does not provide a positive obligation to provide education in prison in all circumstances, where such a possibility is available it should not be subject to arbitrary and unreasonable restrictions.[135]   7.79

Despite the range of educational activities that Protocol 1, Article 2 touches, it has not proved a particularly potent right for domestic litigants. The leading domestic case on the scope of the right is *Ali v Head Teacher and Governors of Lord Grey School*, in which the House of Lords considered the right in the context of a child temporarily excluded from school for alleged arson.[136] Lord Bingham, with whom the majority of their Lordships concurred, stated: 7.80

[T]he guarantee is, in comparison with most other Convention guarantees, a weak one, and deliberately so. There is no right to education of a particular kind or quality, other than that prevailing in the state. There is no Convention guarantee of compliance with domestic law. There is no Convention guarantee of education at or by a particular institution. There is no Convention objection to the expulsion of a pupil from an educational institution on disciplinary grounds, unless (in the ordinary way) there is no alternative source of state education open to the pupil ... The test, as always under the Convention, is a highly pragmatic one, to be applied to the specific facts of the case: have the authorities of the state acted so as to deny to a pupil effective access to such educational facilities as the state provides for such pupils?[137]

Their Lordships held that the student had not been denied effective access to education on the basis that he had been offered a place at a pupil referral unit, which his parents had refused.

In *Re JR17's Application for Judicial Review* the Supreme Court applied *Ali* and found that a child's suspension from school for three months in the run-up to public examinations did not constitute a denial of the Convention right to education when very limited home tutoring had been provided.[138] The Court noted that the Convention guarantees access only to that education provided by the state and not to education of a particular quality or degree.   7.81

In the context of the provision of special education, the Supreme Court in *A v Essex County Council* considered the case of an autistic child who was not provided with schooling for 19 months.[139] The Court rejected the approach of the Court of Appeal,[140] which had held that the state's failings needed to have been systemic to engage the Convention. However, the fact that there had been a breach of domestic legal provisions obliging the local authority to provide education did not lead to a breach of Protocol 1, Article 2. The Court found that a triable issue arose only   7.82

---

[134] *Eren v Turkey* [2006] ELR 155. See also *Timishev v Russia* [2005] ECHR 55762/00.
[135] *Velyo Velev v Bulgaria* (2014) 37 BHRC 406, para 34.
[136] *Ali v Head Teacher and Governors of Lord Grey School* [2006] UKHL 14, [2006] 2 AC 363.
[137] ibid para 24 .
[138] *Re JR17's Application for Judicial Review* [2010] UKSC 27, [2010] HRLR 27.
[139] *A v Essex County Council* [2010] UKSC 33, [2011] AC 280.
[140] *A v Essex CC* [2008] EWCA Civ 364, [2008] ELR 321.

in very narrow circumstances, namely where it could have been shown that the defendant had either failed to make inquiries during any period that it knew the child was not receiving effective education or that such investigations as it conducted were wholly inadequate. Overall, the potential for domestic claims founded on the right to education is very limited.[141]

7.83   In *Ali v UK*,[142] handed down after the Supreme Court's decisions in *JR17* and *A v Essex*, whilst the ECtHR accepted that the student's temporary exclusion had been proportionate as adequate alternative provision had been offered to him, it observed that the situation 'might well be different if a pupil of compulsory school age were to be permanently excluded from one school and were not able to subsequently secure full-time education in line with the national curriculum at another school'.[143] The ECtHR therefore appeared to accept that the requirement imposed by domestic law that a child access the national curriculum is a relevant standard by which to judge compliance with Protocol 1, Article 2.

7.84   Subsequent decided claims for a breach of Protocol 1, Article 2 remain relatively infrequent and turn on their particular facts. In *R (E) v London Borough of Islington* the judge found that the failure to provide the claimant with access to mainstream education for 50 per cent of a school year 'amounted in her particular case to a denial of the essence of her right to education for that year', but the judge placed great weight on the grave personal circumstances of the claimant and emphasized that this finding 'is not to be taken as any kind of rule of thumb'.[144]

7.85   In *R (Q) v Staffordshire County Council* the judge found no breach of Protocol 1, Article 2 where the child had been out of mainstream education for 15 months but had received 'education' at a temporary facility from which he had obtained benefit, and had his needs assessed 'diligently and professionally' to the point that he was subsequently able to attend a special school.[145]

7.86   In *R (ZB and DB) v London Borough of Croydon* the judge found a breach of Protocol 1, Article 2 where the children did not attend school for 16 months. There had been a dispute between the local authority and the parent as to which school the children should attend, but the substantial delays in the local authority putting in place suitable transport to enable the children to attend the local authority's preferred school at which they were enrolled meant that the children were 'housebound' during this period.[146]

2. Parental right to educate children in conformity with convictions

7.87   The second sentence of Protocol 1, Article 2 seeks to prevent the state from indoctrinating children through the education system, by providing to parents the right

---

[141] See also *R (Holub) v Secretary of State for the Home Department* [2001] 1 WLR 1359. See also *R (Mdlovu) v Secretary of State for the Home Department* [2008] EWHC 2089 (Admin).

[142] *Ali v UK* (2011) 30 BHRC 44.

[143] ibid para 60.

[144] *R (E) v London Borough of Islington* [2017] EWHC 1440 (Admin), [2018] PTSR 349, para 86.

[145] *R (Q) v Staffordshire County Council* [2021] EWHC 3486 (Admin), [2022] ELR 660, paras 77, 79.

[146] *R (ZB and DB) v London Borough of Croydon* [2023] EWHC 489 (Admin), paras 28–31.

to have their religious and philosophical convictions respected. This applies to all educational systems, public or private, and to all functions the state exercises with respect to education, be they academic or administrative.

The provision naturally overlaps very significantly with Article 9, and complaints brought under the second sentence of Protocol 1, Article 2 will generally be coupled with a complaint under Article 9. While such cases will be influenced by Article 9, the ECtHR has emphasized that they will be determined under Protocol 1, Article 2 as it is the *lex specialis* in the area of education.[147]   7.88

In *Campbell and Cosans v UK* two parents challenged the existence of corporal punishment in state schools, on the basis that it was contrary to their philosophical beliefs.[148] The ECtHR upheld their complaint, finding that the obligation to respect religious and philosophical convictions is not confined to the content of educational instruction but includes the organization and financing of public education, the supervision of the educational system in general, and questions of discipline.   7.89

The House of Lords considered the converse situation in *R (Williamson) v Secretary of State for Education and Employment*.[149] The claimant parents argued that the statutory ban on corporal punishment in schools was contrary to their belief in the necessity of physical punishment and thus in violation of Protocol 1, Article 2. The House of Lords accepted that a belief in corporal punishment constituted a conviction for the purposes of Article 9 and by implication for Protocol 1, Article 2, and further held that the notion of education under the second sentence was wide enough to include the manner in which discipline was maintained in school. However, the legislation pursued the legitimate aim of protecting children, and the total prohibition on corporal punishment was proportionate in the circumstances.   7.90

The extent to which the religious and philosophical convictions of parents can influence the provision of education is limited in a number of ways. First, the conviction itself must come within the limited definition set out in *Campbell v UK*.[150] The parents must also show, secondly, that the holding of the belief is the reason for their objection to what the state is doing, and that they have brought the reason for their objection to the attention of the authorities. Lastly, the state will not violate Protocol 1, Article 2 if the education system conveys religious or philosophical knowledge in an objective, critical, and pluralistic manner.   7.91

In *Kjeldsen, Busk Madsen and Pedersen v Denmark*, parents challenged a law which made sex education a compulsory component of the curriculum of state primary schools.[151] The ECtHR held that while the state was forbidden from pursuing indoctrination, the instruction subject to challenge was a way of objectively   7.92

---

[147] *Folgerø v Norway* (2007) 23 BHRC 227, para 54.
[148] *Campbell and Cosans v UK* (1982) 4 EHRR 293.
[149] *R (Williamson) v Secretary of State for Education and Employment* [2005] UKHL 15, [2005] 2 AC 246.
[150] *Campbell and Cosans v UK* (1982) 4 EHRR 293.
[151] *Kjeldsen, Busk Madsen and Pedersen v Denmark* (1979) 1 EHRR 711. See also *Valsamis v Greece* (1996) 24 EHRR 294.

conveying information and did not therefore offend the parents' religious and philosophical convictions to the extent forbidden by Protocol 1, Article 2.

7.93   The ECtHR adopted a tougher approach in *Folgerø v Norway*, which concerned the refusal to grant total exemption to pupils in primary and early secondary education from lessons in Christianity, religion, and philosophy.[152] Non-Christian parents alleged that the obligation on their children to follow these lessons had been in breach of the parents' right to ensure that their children received an education in conformity with their religious and philosophical convictions. The Grand Chamber held that the state had not taken sufficient care that information and knowledge included in the curriculum be conveyed in an objective, critical, and pluralistic manner, and the system for partially exempting students from the lessons was not an adequate mechanism to safeguard respect for the parents' convictions.

7.94   Similarly, in *Papageorgiou v Greece* the ECtHR held that a system of exemption from a religious education course, which required parents to submit a 'solemn declaration' that their children were not Orthodox Christian placed an undue burden on parents.[153] The parents were required in effect to disclose their religious convictions, and the correctness of the declaration was to be verified by the school principal. The ECtHR held that this amounted to a breach of Protocol 1, Article 2 (read with art 9).

7.95   By contrast, in *Lautsi v Italy* the Grand Chamber found that the display of crucifixes in Italian state school classrooms did not violate Protocol 1, Article 2.[154] Unlike the lessons in *Folgerø*, the crucifix was essentially a 'passive symbol'.[155] The Court held that in light of Italy's historical development, the decision to display a crucifix fell with the state's margin of appreciation.

7.96   The domestic courts have considered the application of these principles in *R (Fox) v Secretary of State for Education*[156] and in *R (Isherwood) v Welsh Minsters*.[157] In *Fox* the Court held that the GCSE subject content for religious studies breached Protocol 1, Article 2 as it failed to include the teaching of non-religious views. As such, information would not be conveyed in a pluralistic manner.[158] In *Isherwood* the Court dismissed a claim that mandatory relationships and sexuality education (RSE) introduced in Wales breached Protocol 1, Article 2 as the relevant guidance documents took care to ensure that RSE teaching was conveyed in an 'objective critical and pluralistic manner, and does not breach the prohibition on indoctrination'.[159]

---

[152] *Folgerø v Norway* (2007) 23 BHRC 227.

[153] *Papageorgiou v Greece* (2020) 70 EHRR 36, paras 81, 84, 86–100.

[154] *Lautsi v Italy* (2012) 54 EHRR 3.

[155] ibid para 29.

[156] *R (Fox) v Secretary of State for Education* [2015] EWHC 3404 (Admin), [2016] PTSR 405.

[157] *R (Isherwood) v Welsh Minsters* [2022] EWHC 3331 (Admin), [2023] PTSR 901.

[158] *R (Fox) v Secretary of State for Education* [2015] EWHC 3404 (Admin), [2016] PTSR 405, paras 74–76.

[159] *R (Isherwood) v Welsh Minsters* [2022] EWHC 3331 (Admin), [2023] PTSR 901, paras 202–03. See also the useful summary of the ECtHR and domestic case law at para 198.

3. General limitations

Besides the limitation set out in the second sentence of the article, there are no other specific qualifications to the right to education. The state may supply any explanation for an interference with the right, but in order to be lawful the measures must be foreseeable and bear a reasonable relationship of proportionality between the means adopted and the alleged aim.[160] **7.97**

Further, and also unlike the qualified rights in Articles 8 to 11 of the Convention which require restrictions on the right to be 'in accordance with the law' or 'prescribed by law', Protocol 1, Article 2 does not contain such words and the ECtHR has not implied them in. Thus the ECtHR has considered as a matter of substance whether there is a breach of Protocol 1, Article 2, finding an infringement even when a measure was contrary to domestic law.[161] **7.98**

In *Leyla Sahin v Turkey* the Grand Chamber considered the prohibition on the hijab at universities in Turkey.[162] The applicant was a medical student who had been subjected to disciplinary proceedings after refusing to remove her hijab in classes. By a majority of 16 to 1, the ECtHR held that the purpose of the ban was to protect the secular character of educational institutions. The action taken against the applicant did not impair 'the very essence of her right to education'[163] and any restriction was a proportionate means of pursuing the legitimate aim of secularism. The case is notable for its very limited discussion of the educational consequences of the headscarf ban for students such as Ms Sahin. Like other cases involving Turkish secularism, the decision of the ECtHR can be explained in part by the extreme political sensitivity of the issues at stake.[164] **7.99**

The ECtHR has considered limitations placed on the right to education in the context of higher education on a number of other occasions. The ECtHR has concluded that a Member State is entitled to adopt a selection system for higher education courses, as long as the system is foreseeable to those concerned, pursued a legitimate aim, and there is a reasonable relationship of proportionality between the means employed and the aim sought to be achieved. In *Kiliç v Turkey* the ECtHR found that a new scoring system in the university entrance exam, which placed greater weight on a correspondence between subjects studied at high school and the chosen university course, did not breach Protocol 1, Article 2 as it was a proportionate means of achieving the legitimate aim of improving the standard of university studies. The ECtHR concluded that the application was manifestly ill-founded.[165] **7.100**

---

[160] *Leyla Sahin v Turkey* (2007) 44 EHRR 5; *Ali v UK* (2011) 30 BHRC 44.

[161] *Perovy v Russian* App No 47429/09, 20 October 2020. See also *Lautsi v Italy* (2012) 54 EHRR 3, para 57; *Ali v Head Teacher and Governors of Lord Grey School* [2006] UKHL 14, [2006] 2 AC 363, paras 24, 57–60; and *R (Isherwood) v Welsh Ministers* [2022] EWHC 3331 (Admin), para 164.

[162] *Leyla Sahin v Turkey* (2007) 44 EHRR 5.

[163] ibid para 161.

[164] See eg *Refah Partisi (the Welfare Party) and others v Turkey* (2003) 14 BHRC 1, discussed in Chapter 6, para 6.550.

[165] *Kiliç v Turkey* App No 29601/05 (5 March 2019), paras 20–34. See also *Tarantino v Italy* (2013) 27 EHRR 26 (rules limiting the number of students who could attend university courses in medicine and dentistry according to the resources of the university and the public health service demand for those professionals were proportionate and within the margin of appreciation, and did not breach Protocol 1, art 2).

7.101   In contrast, in *Çölgeçen v Turkey* the ECtHR found that a Turkish university had breached eight students' right to education under Protocol 1, Article 2 (read in the light of art 10) by expelling or suspending them after they submitted a petition requesting that Kurdish language classes be introduced as an optional module.[166] Neither the views expressed nor the form in which they were conveyed warranted disciplinary sanctions, and its imposition was neither reasonable nor proportionate.

7.102   The ECtHR has also considered the compatibility of restrictions placed in prisoners' studies with Protocol 1, Article 2. In *Mehmet Reşit Arslan and Orhan Bingöl v Turkey* the ECtHR found that a prohibition on the use of a computer or access to the internet by prisoners to study a higher education course breached Protocol 1, Article 2 as the state had failed to strike a fair balance between the applicants' right to education and the requirements of the maintenance of public order.[167] In particular, no detailed analysis of the security risks had been undertaken. In *Uzun v Turkey* the ECtHR held that preventing the applicant, who was in pre-trial detention, and suspected of membership of a terrorist organization, from sitting his university examinations during a state of emergency and during his imprisonment did not breach Protocol 1, Article 2.[168]

7.103   Domestic cases have tended to focus on the application of Protocol 1, Article 2 to schools. The House of Lords followed the *Leyla Sahin* case in *R (Begum) v Denbigh High School*, in which a girl was excluded from school for wearing the jilbab (a Muslim dress that covered her whole body).[169] Dealing only cursorily with the right to education, the House of Lords referred to their analysis in the *Ali* case (see para 7.76), finding that the pupil's exclusion from education was a result of her unwillingness to comply with a uniform rule that pursued a legitimate aim.

7.104   In *JR87's Application for Judicial Review*, however, the teaching arrangements for religious education and collective worship in controlled primary schools in Northern Ireland breached Protocol 1, Article 2 (read with art 9) as they were not conveyed in an objective, critical and pluralist manner. The syllabus prioritized the Christian faith, making no reference to any other faiths or non-religious beliefs until key stage 3, and Christians were the only people invited to collective worship assemblies.[170]

4. Discrimination

7.105   In common with all articles of the Convention, Protocol 1, Article 2 is subject to the prohibition on discrimination in Article 14 of the Convention. This issue was raised in the leading case on Protocol 1, Article 2, *Belgian Linguistics (No 2)*, which

---

[166] *Çölgeçen v Turkey* [2018] ELR 464, paras 52–57.
[167] *Mehmet Reşit Arslan and Orhan Bingöl v Turkey* App Nos 47121/06, 13988/07, and 34750/07 (7 October 2019), paras 60–72.
[168] *Uzun v Turkey* App No 37866/18 (10 November 2020), paras 31–38. The ECtHR declared the application inadmissible.
[169] *R (Begum) v Denbigh High School* [2006] UKHL 15, [2007] 1 AC 100.
[170] *JR87's Application for Judicial Review* [2022] NIQB 53.

concerned legislation that dictated the language of education in certain areas of Belgium.[171] A school that failed to comply with the language rules could suffer penalties, which included denial of public support and non-recognition. The ECtHR held that Article 14, read with Protocol 1, Article 2, could not be interpreted as guaranteeing children or parents a right to education in a language of their choice. The measures adopted by the Belgian government for the legitimate purpose of achieving linguistic unity were proportionate to meet that purpose.

In a series of cases, the Grand Chamber of the ECtHR has addressed educational discrimination in the context of placement of Roma children in special schools. In a thorough analysis of the Czech schooling system in *DH v Czech Republic*,[172] the Court held that as a specific type of disadvantaged and vulnerable minority, the Roma required special protection, including in the sphere of education. The placement of Roma in schools for children with mental disabilities meant that they received an education that compounded their difficulties and compromised their subsequent personal development. Although the state did not intend to discriminate, it could not justify the disproportionate adverse effect on the applicants' education. The ECtHR subsequently reached the same conclusion in relation to the Croatian,[173] Greek,[174] and Hungarian[175] systems, reiterating the principle that separate does not mean equal.

More recently the ECtHR has considered the position of disabled children in mainstream schools. The ECtHR has emphasized that inclusive education is the most appropriate means of guaranteeing universality and non-discrimination in the exercise of the right to education.[176] Article 14 taken with Protocol 1, Article 2 requires a duty of 'reasonable accommodation' to be made for disabled students, that is, the 'necessary and appropriate modification and adjustments not imposing a disproportionate or undue burden, where needed in a particular case' unless there is justification not to.[177] The duty of 'reasonable accommodation' derives from Article 2 of the Convention on the Rights of Disabled Persons (which along with other relevant international instruments is relevant to the interpretation of art 14).[178] The ECtHR's case law is not, however, consistent. In particular, it is not clear what test the ECtHR applies to determine when an unjustified failure to make a reasonable accommodation will amount to a breach of Article 14 taken with Protocol 1, Article 2.

In its most recent decision, *GL v Italy*, the ECtHR found that the failure to provide an autistic child with a specialized assistant whilst in school constituted a breach of Protocol 1, Article 2 taken with Article 14. The ECtHR noted that it

7.106

7.107

7.108

---

[171] *Belgian Linguistics (No 2)* (1979–80) 1 EHRR 252.
[172] *DH v Czech Republic* (2007) 23 BHRC 526.
[173] *Oršuš and others v Croatia* (2010) 28 BHRC 558.
[174] *Sampanis v Greece* App No 32526/05, 5 June 2008.
[175] *Horváth v Hungary* (2013) 57 EHRR 31.
[176] *Çam v Turkey* App No 51500/08, 23 June 2016, para 64.
[177] See eg *GL v Italy* App No 59751/15, 10 December 2020, para 62.
[178] *GL v Italy* App No 59751/15, 10 December 2020, paras 51, 53.

was not its task to define the 'reasonable accommodation' which could take different forms,[179] but authorities must pay particular attention to their choices in this sphere, in view of their impact on children with disabilities, whose high level of vulnerability must not be overlooked.[180] The ECtHR held that as the state had decided to provide the right of inclusive education to children with disabilities there was no justification for depriving the applicant of access to specialist assistance.[181]

7.109   In his concurring judgment in *GL v Italy*, Judge Wojtyczek found that the test applied by the majority to determine whether there had been a breach of the requirement to make 'reasonable accommodation' was unclear.[182] The majority noted the need to ensure that necessary and appropriate modifications are made where needed which do not impose a disproportionate or undue burden.[183] But the majority also referred to an apparently more exacting test for states, namely that an applicant should be able to 'attend primary school under conditions equivalent to those enjoyed by non-disabled pupils'.[184] The ECtHR had a further formulation, namely that an applicant should be able to 'attend primary schools under equivalent conditions, as far as possible, to those enjoyed by other children, without imposing a disproportionate or undue burden on the authorities'.[185]

7.110   Further, on the facts of *GL v Italy*, the ECtHR appeared to apply a more demanding standard than in *Stoian v Romania*,[186] also a case about a lack of a personal assistant for a child in a mainstream school. In *Stoian v Romania* the ECtHR relied on the efforts made by the state to find a personal assistant for the child and placed weight on the fact that the child was 'never completely deprived of education, as he continued to attend school, to be graded for his work, and to advance through the school curriculum' to find no breach of Article 14 taken with Protocol 1, Article 2.[187] But these features were also present in *GL v Italy*. This is clearly a developing aspect of the ECtHR's jurisprudence, and indeed the ECtHR has said that it is a topic on which it must have regard to any developments in international and European law and respond, for example, to any emerging consensus as to the standards to be achieved.[188]

---

[179] Citing *Çam v Turkey* App No 51500/08, 23 June 2016, para 66, the ECtHR stated that the national authorities were much better placed to reach this decision: *GL v Italy* App No 59751/15, 10 December 2020, para 63.

[180] *GL v Italy* App No 59751/15, 10 December 2020, para 63. See also *Enver Şahin v Turkey* App No 23065/12, 30 January 2018, para 67.

[181] *GL v Italy* App No 59751/15, 10 December 2020, paras 64–66. See also *Çam v Turkey* App No 51500/08, 23 June 2016 (refusal to enrol a blind student in the Music Academy despite her passing the relevant examination violated art 14 with Protocol 1, art 2), and *Enver Şahin v Turkey* App No 23065/12, 30 January 2018 (failure to make adaptation works to a university to make them wheelchair accessible because of insufficient funds amounted to a breach of Protocol 1, art 2).

[182] *GL v Italy* App No 59751/15, 10 December 2020, paras 1–5.

[183] ibid para 62.

[184] ibid para 66.

[185] ibid para 70.

[186] *Stoian v Romania* App No 289/14, 25 June 2019.

[187] ibid para 105. The ECtHR also found no breach of art 14 taken with Protocol 1, art 2 in *Sanlisoy v Turkey* App No 77023/12, 8 November 2016 and in *Dupin v France* App No 2282/17, 18 December 2018.

[188] *GL v Italy* App No 59751/15, 10 December 2020, para 53.

The ECtHR has also considered discrimination on the grounds of nationality   7.111
in the context of education. In *Ponomaryov v Bulgaria* the ECtHR found a breach
of Article 14 taken with Protocol 1, Article 2 where a state provided free primary
and secondary education, but charged non-national children to attend.[189] Although
states are usually given a wide margin of appreciation when it comes to general
measures of economic or social strategy, and ordinarily may, in the provision of welfare programmes, public benefits, and health care, justifiably differentiate between
different categories of non-nationals residing in its territory, such arguments cannot
be transposed to the field of education without qualification.[190] Education has a different status: it enjoys direct protection under the Convention, and it is also 'a very
particular type of public service, which not only directly benefits those using it but
also serves broader societal functions'.[191] The ECtHR emphasized, however, that at
university level higher fees for non-nationals can be 'considered fully justified' as
the margin of appreciation is considerably wider.[192]

The domestic courts have considered the issue of discrimination against disabled   7.112
children. In *C v Governing Body of a School* the Upper Tribunal held that in the
context of children excluded from school, the exclusion from the definition of disability those who had a 'tendency to physical abuse' contained in regulation 4(1)(c)
of the Equality Act 2010 (Disability) Regulations 2010 was contrary to Article 14
taken with Protocol 1, Article 2.[193]

There have been a number of domestic cases that have considered whether the   7.113
statutory rules on the provision of student support are discriminatory on various
grounds.

Immigration status. In *R (Tigere) v Secretary of State for Business, Innovation and*   7.114
Skills the Supreme Court held that the criterion that excluded from eligibility from
student loans those students who did not have indefinite leave to remain in the
United Kingdom were discriminatory on the grounds of immigration status contrary to Article 14, taken with Protocol 1, Article 2.[194]

Sex. In *R (OA) v Secretary of State for Education*[195] the requirement in the   7.115
Education (Student Support) Regulations 2021 that applicants for student loans
must be lawfully resident in the UK for three years prior to their course beginning,

---

[189] *Ponomaryov v Bulgaria* (2014) 59 EHRR 20, paras 53–55.
[190] ibid 52, 54, and 55.
[191] ibid para 55.
[192] ibid para 56. Indeed in *R (Hurley and Moore) v Secretary of State for Business, Innovation and Skills*
[2012] EWHC 201 (Admin), [2021] ELR 297 the Divisional Court held that the decision to allow higher
education institutions to increase fees to up to £9000 per year did not breach Protocol 1, art 2 (either alone
or taken with art 14): see paras 42–45, 46–65.
[193] *C v Governing Body of a School* [2018] UKUT 269 (AAC), [2019] PTSR 857. In *R (AA) v Secretary
of State for Education* [2022] EWHC 1613 (Admin), [2022] ELR 700 the Court held that the statutory
inability of the First-tier Tribunal to award damages in disability discrimination claims against schools was
not in the ambit of Protocol 1, art 2: see paras 59–60.
[194] *R (Tigere) v Secretary of State for Business, Innovation and Skills* [2015] UKSC 57, [2015] 1 WLR 3820.
The decision in *Tigere* was applied to the Scottish regulations in *Jasim v Scottish Ministers* [2022] CSOH 64,
(2022) SLT 1065, and the relevant regulations were found also to breach art 14 taken with Protocol 1, art 2.
[195] *R (OA) v Secretary of State for Education* [2020] EWHC 276 (Admin), [2020] ELR 290.

indirectly discriminated against women contrary to Article 14 read with Protocol 1, Article 2 as it made no provision for applicants who, because of domestic violence and abuse, had gaps in their lawful residence.

7.116   *Age.* In *Hunter v Student Awards Agency for Scotland*[196] the Education (Student Loans) (Scotland) Regulations 2007, which restricted eligibility for a loan to those under the age of 55, constituted discrimination on the grounds of age contrary to Article 14 taken with Protocol 1, Article 2.

7.117   Finally, in the context of schools the courts have also been asked to determine whether changes to home to school transport arrangements discriminate on the grounds of age or race. Thus in *R (Drexler) v Leicestershire County Council*[197] changes in the home to school transport policy which had the effect of treating pupils aged 5–16 more favourably than those aged 16–18 with special educational needs did not discriminate on the grounds of age contrary to Article 14 taken with Protocol 1, Article 2. In *R (Diocese of Menevia) v City and County of Swansea*[198] the local authority amended a home to school transport policy to that pupils attending voluntary aided faith schools would only be entitled to free transport if no suitable school, which would include a non-faith school, was located within three miles of a pupil's home. The policy continued to provide free home to school transport for pupils who wished to attend a Welsh medium school. The Court held that this was indirectly discriminatory on the grounds of race as the change to the home to school transport policy had a disproportionate impact on Black and minority ethnic children which could not be justified.

D. PROTOCOL 1, ARTICLE 3: RIGHT TO FREE ELECTIONS

7.118   By Article 3 of Protocol 1 (A3P1), states that have ratified the Protocol undertake to hold free elections. Although the provision appears to impose an obligation upon the state rather than conferring a right upon an individual, the ECtHR held in *Mathieu-Mohin v Belgium* that it does give rise to individual rights and can be the object of a complaint.[199]

7.119   *Mathieu-Mohin* established several general principles. First, the ECtHR held that A3P1 extends to subjective rights of participation—the right to vote and the right to stand for election to the legislature. However, it went on to state that these rights are not absolute. A state may impose conditions on them, provided that the conditions pursue a legitimate aim, are not disproportionate, and do not thwart the free expression of the opinion of the people in the choice of the legislature.

7.120   The Grand Chamber has reiterated these principles.[200] It explained in *Zdanoka v Latvia* that A3P1 is akin to Articles 10 and 11, as it guarantees respect for pluralism

---

[196] *Hunter v Student Awards Agency for Scotland* [2016] CSOH 71, [2016] SLT 653.

[197] *R (Drexler) v Leicestershire County Council* [2020] EWCA Civ 503, [2020] ELR 399.

[198] *R (Diocese of Menevia) v City and County of Swansea* [2015] EWHC 1436 (Admin), [2015] PTSR 1507.

[199] *Mathieu-Mohin v Belgium* (1988) 10 EHRR 1.

[200] See eg *Demirtas v Turkey (No 2)* App No 14305/17, 22 December 2020 [GC], paras 385–87.

of opinion in a democratic society.[201] However, unlike Articles 8 to 11, no limitations or qualifications are specified in the text of A3P1. In their absence the ECtHR has developed the concept of 'implied limitations', which it has held is of 'major importance for the determination of the relevance of the aims pursued by the restrictions on the rights guaranteed by the provision'.[202] States are 'always free to rely on any legitimate aim' in their justification of restrictions on the rights covered by A3P1.[203] As the provision is phrased in collective terms, the proportionality test will not be strictly applied and there is no test of 'necessity' or 'pressing social need'.[204] However, the ECtHR has emphasized that, as well as pursuing a legitimate aim by proportionate and non-arbitrary means, any limitation must not impair the 'very essence' of the rights guaranteed by A3P1.[205]

Historically, the ECtHR tended to afford states a very generous margin of appreciation in limiting these rights, but the decision in *Hirst v UK (No 2)* signalled something of a departure from its prior approach.[206] In that case, the ECtHR held that the absolute bar on prisoners voting violated A3P1. The ECtHR has subsequently indicated that the state retains a wide margin of appreciation in relation to the design of its electoral system[207] and the 'more technical' aspects of vote-counting,[208] while affirming that 'tighter scrutiny' will be given to 'departures from the principle of universal suffrage' and an intermediate 'broader margin of appreciation' to limits on candidates standing for election.[209]

7.121

The ECtHR has held that positive obligations also arise under A3P1. In *The Communist Party of Russia and others v Russia*[210] the applicants complained that unequal media coverage of the 2003 national elections detrimentally affected the outcome. The ECtHR found insufficient evidence of any overt manipulation of the media by the government, but made clear that the requirements of A3P1 went beyond the negative requirement to desist from such manipulation. First, the state needed to establish and maintain a domestic system to ensure effective examination

7.122

---

[201] *Zdanoka v Latvia* (2007) 45 EHRR 17 [GC], para 115. See also *Yumak and Sadak v Turkey* (2009) 48 EHRR 1.

[202] *Zdanoka v Latvia* (2007) 45 EHRR 17 [GC], para 115.

[203] *Georgian Labour Party v Georgia* App No 9103/04, 8 July 2008, para 124. As the text of the provision does not provide a list of permissible aims, an aim is 'legitimate' if it is 'compatible with the principle of the rule of law and the general objectives of the Convention': *Political party 'Patria' v Moldova* (2021) 73 EHRR 23, para 34.

[204] See eg *Zdanoka v Latvia* (2007) 45 EHRR 17 [GC].

[205] *Demirtas v Turkey (No 2)* App No 14305/17, 22 December 2020 [GC], para 387; *Davydov v Russia* (2018) 67 EHRR 25, paras 272–73.

[206] *Hirst v UK (No 2)* (2006) 42 EHRR 41 [GC].

[207] See eg *Scoppola v Italy No 3* App No 126/05, 22 May 2012 [GC]. See also *Allister v Prime Minister* [2022] NICA 15, [2022] 3 CMR 8, where the Northern Ireland Court of Appeal emphasized the breadth of the appropriate margin in adopting arrangements for the continued application of certain EU laws in Northern Ireland despite the inability of its citizens, post-Brexit, to vote in elections to the EU Parliament.

[208] *Davydov v Russia* (2018) 67 EHRR 25, para 287.

[209] ibid para 286. It has also held that the applicable margin will be 'substantially narrower' where a restriction on the right to vote applies to 'a particularly vulnerable group in society that has suffered considerable discrimination in the past, such as the mentally disabled': *Caamaño Valle v Spain* (2021) 73 EHRR 20, para 55.

[210] *The Communist Party of Russia and others v Russia* App No 29400/05, 19 June 2012.

of individual complaints and appeals in matters concerning electoral rights. Secondly, since there can be no democracy without pluralism, the adoption of certain positive measures to ensure pluralism were required; this entails an obligation to intervene in order to open up the media to different viewpoints. Finally the ECtHR contemplated, but did not explicitly lay down, a duty to ensure neutrality of the audio-visual media, noting the complex interrelationship with Article 10 freedom of expression rights.[211] The first of these positive obligations has been expressly confirmed by the Grand Chamber, which explained that the domestic system established to ensure effective examination of individual complaints must be accompanied by 'adequate and sufficient safeguards'; these include decisions being taken by a body 'which can provide sufficient guarantees of its impartiality' and which enjoys discretion which is 'circumscribed by the provisions of domestic law', and being taken via a procedure which is 'such as to guarantee a fair, objective and sufficiently reasoned decision'.[212]

7.123   The ECtHR has recognized that political parties, as well as individuals, have and can enforce rights under A1P3.[213]

1. 'Legislature'

7.124   A3P1 concerns only the choice of the 'legislature'. The term 'legislature' is not confined to the national parliament and its meaning will vary according to the constitutional structure of the state in question. For example, Belgian regional councils have been held to be constituent parts of the legislature,[214] yet a French regional council has been held not to come within the article.[215]

7.125   The flexibility of the term 'legislature' is demonstrated by the finding in *Matthews v UK* that the European Parliament had the requisite features of a 'legislature' for the residents of Gibraltar—meaning citizens' inability to vote in European elections while the UK was a member of the European Union (EU) breached A3P1.[216] However, the ECmHR decided that other elected bodies, such as the former metropolitan county councils in England, are not 'legislatures' for the purpose of A3P1.[217] Relevant factors include the extent of the competence and powers invested in the relevant body under the state's constitutional structure.[218]

---

[211] See ibid paras 123–28.

[212] *Mugemangango v Belgium* (2020) 71 EHRR 32 [GC], para 70. For a detailed discussion of these requirements on the facts of the case see paras 79–121.

[213] See eg *Yabloko Russian United Democratic Party v Russia* App No 18860/07, 8 November 2016, para 74; *Political party 'Patria' v Moldova* (2021) 73 EHRR 23, para 33.

[214] *Mathieu-Mohin v Belgium* (1988) 10 EHRR 1.

[215] *Malarde v France* App No 46813/99, 5 September 2000. See also the discussion in *Davydov v Russia* (2018) 67 EHRR 25, paras 278–79 (and the cases there cited).

[216] *Matthews v UK* (1999) 28 EHRR 361. cf *Allister v Prime Minister* [2022] NICA 15, [2022] 3 CMR 8, where two of the three members of the Northern Ireland Court of Appeal considered that A3P1 was not engaged at all where citizens of Northern Ireland would remain subject to certain EU legislation despite losing the right to vote in elections to the EU Parliament. An appeal to the Supreme Court, not concerning this point, was dismissed: *Re Allister's Application for Judicial Review* [2023] UKSC 5, [2023] 2 WLR 457.

[217] *Booth-Clibborn v UK* (1985) 43 DR 236.

[218] See *Davydov v Russia* (2018) 67 EHRR 25, paras 278–79.

2. 'Elections'

While the meaning of 'legislature' may have a degree of flexibility, a tighter approach is taken to the meaning of 'elections'. The ECtHR has held (as has the Supreme Court[219]) that A3P1 does not apply to referenda, even where these may result in significant changes to the parliamentary system.[220] It has also held that presidential elections are not generally included,[221] although this will depend on the precise political structures in any given state.

7.126

In *R (Barclay) v Secretary of State for Justice and another*[222] the Supreme Court considered the law governing elections in the Crown Dependency of Sark, one of the Channel Islands. The claimants challenged a new law designed to reform Sark's constitutional arrangements by which the Seigneur (head of state) and the Seneschal (President of the Sark Parliament and chief judge) remained unelected. The claimants contended that this breached their rights under A3P1. The Supreme Court held that there had been no breach of the claimants' rights on the grounds that the Strasbourg cases put 'no narrow focus on one particular element of democracy'.[223] The electoral rules needed to be examined in the round and in the light of historical and political factors. Applying those principles, there was no requirement that all members of a legislature be elected. Even if there were such an obligation under A3P1, the constitutional history of Sark would justify its limitation.

7.127

3. Right to vote

A3P1 contains an implied right to vote. The state may set conditions on this right, such as minimum age requirements and, in some circumstances, residency.[224] However, as 'any departure from the principle of universal suffrage risks undermining the democratic validity of the legislature thus elected and the laws which it promulgates', such conditions must not impair the 'very essence' of the right.[225] Exclusion of any groups or categories of the general population must be reconcilable with the article's underlying purposes and its democratic character.[226]

7.128

Procedural requirements for exercising the right to vote will not necessarily interfere with the rights protected by A3P1 (so as to require justification): for example, in *R (Andrews) v Minister for the Cabinet Office* the Administrative Court held

7.129

---

[219] *Moohan v Lord Advocate* [2014] UKSC 67, [2015] AC 901.

[220] See eg *Moohan and Gillon v UK* App Nos 22962 & another, 6 July 2017; *Partisi v Turkey* (2018) 66 EHRR SE4.

[221] *Guliyev v Azerbaijan* App No 35584/02, 27 May 2004; *Boškoski v the Former Yugoslav Republic of Macedonia* App No 11676/04, 2 September 2004.

[222] *R (Barclay) v Secretary of State for Justice and another* [2009] UKSC 9, [2010] 1 AC 464.

[223] ibid para 64.

[224] *Hilbe v Liechtenstein* App No 31981/96, 7 September 1999; *Melnychenko v Ukraine* App No 17707/02, 19 October 2004, para 56; *Schindler v UK* App No 19840/09, 7 May 2013 (upholding a restriction on voting to those who had not been resident in the UK for 15 years).

[225] *Hirst v UK (No 2)* (2006) 42 EHRR 41 [GC], para 62.

[226] *Labita v Italy* App No 26772/95, 6 April 2000. See also *Alajos Kiss v Hungary* App No 38832/06, 20 May 2010; *Sitaropoulos and another v Greece* App No 42202/07, 8 July 2010.

that the fact that visually impaired people could not vote unaided—but only with the assistance of another person, who was required on pain of criminal sanction not to disclose how they voted—did not interfere with the right to vote by 'secret ballot'.[227] By contrast, in *The 3Million Ltd v Minister for the Cabinet Office* the Divisional Court held that registration requirements for EU citizens wishing to vote in EU parliamentary elections from the UK did restrict the right to vote, but were justified as a means of 'regulating the electoral process, ensuring that only those who are eligible to vote may do so, preventing double-voting and ensuring the timely preparation and publication of electoral registers'.[228]

7.130　　In an illustration of the generous margin of appreciation that the ECtHR has afforded states in assessing the proportionality of a restriction on the right to vote, the Grand Chamber in *Sitapoulos v Greece* held that a complete absence of provision for expatriates to vote in Greek elections (other than by travelling to Greece to vote) was compatible with A3P1.[229]

7.131　　In *Moore v UK* the applicant argued that his right to vote was impaired as mental health patients were prevented from using a hospital as their residential address in order to register on the electoral roll. The government reached a friendly settlement with the applicant, agreeing to amend the Representation of the People Act 1983.[230] The ECtHR has subsequently held that restrictions on the rights of mentally disabled persons to vote will only be compatible with A3P1 if they entail an individualized judicial evaluation, and are not based solely on the individual's need for a guardianship arrangement in other aspects of their lives.[231] In *Hirst v UK (No 2)* the Grand Chamber found that the UK's automatic and indiscriminate statutory bar on convicted prisoners voting was an arbitrary and disproportionate restriction on a vitally important Convention right.[232] It fell outside any acceptable margin of appreciation, however wide.[233] The Court went further in the case of *Frodl v Austria*, holding that an automatic and general ban on all those serving a sentence of at least a year and whose crime was committed with intent also violated A3P1 because it lacked the crucial 'discernible and sufficient link between the sanction and the *conduct and circumstances* of the individual concerned' (emphasis added).[234]

7.132　　In *Scoppola v Italy (No 3)* the ECtHR reiterated that an automatic ban on voting by particular categories of prisoners without individual consideration was unacceptable: any decision on disenfranchisement should be taken by a court and be duly reasoned.[235] However, when the case came before the Grand Chamber it

---

[227] *R (Andrews) v Minister for the Cabinet Office* [2021] EWHC 2233 (Admin), paras 19–22.

[228] *The 3Million Ltd v Minister for the Cabinet Office* [2021] EWHC 245 (Admin), paras 99–105.

[229] *Sitapoulos v Greece* App No 42202/07, 13 March 2012 [GC].

[230] *Moore v UK* App No 37841/97, 30 May 2000.

[231] *Caamaño Valle v Spain* (2021) 73 EHRR 20, citing *Kiss v Hungary* (2013) 56 EHRR 19.

[232] *Hirst v UK (No 2)* (2006) 42 EHRR 41 [GC], para 82. The Registration Appeal Court of Scotland issued a declaration of incompatibility in relation to this point: *Smith v Scott* [2007] CSIH 9. See also *Frodl v Austria* App No 20201/04, 8 April 2010.

[233] The ECtHR reached the same conclusion in respect of a substantially identical blanket ban under Russian law in *Anchugov and Gladkov v Russia* App Nos 11157/04 and 15162/05, 14 July 2013.

[234] *Frodl v Austria* (2011) 52 EHRR 5.

[235] *Scoppola v Italy (No 3)* App No 126/05, 18 January 2011, para 43.

adopted a more flexible approach.[236] It held that individual judicial consideration of the proportionality of a ban was not essential and found the Italian system to be compatible with A3P1. Under the Italian system, prisoners were automatically disenfranchised if they were sentenced to three years' imprisonment or longer. The duration of the ban was five years for those sentenced to between three and five years, or permanently for those receiving longer sentences. There was also provision for earlier remission of the ban for good behaviour. As the lone dissenter, Judge Thór Björgvinsson, observed, the Grand Chamber's decision not only departed from *Frodl* and the Chamber's decision, but also from aspects of the Grand Chamber's own reasoning in *Hirst (No 2)*. He observed in particular that:

[J]ust like the United Kingdom legislation, Italy's legislation is a blunt instrument stripping of their Convention right to vote a significant number of persons and doing so in an indiscriminate manner and to a large extent regardless of the nature of their crimes, the length of their sentences and their individual circumstances.

The UK government prevaricated over the implementation of the *Hirst (No 2)* judgment (as understood in light of *Scoppola (No 3)*), leading to substantial further litigation both domestically and in Strasbourg. In *Smith v Scott*[237] the Court of Session made a declaration under section 4 of the Human Rights Act that section 3(1) of the Representation of the People Act 1983 was incompatible with A3P1. The government subsequently sought to persuade the Supreme Court not to follow the ECtHR's case law in *R (Chester and another) v Secretary of State for Justice*.[238] A seven-strong Supreme Court unanimously declined to accept the invitation. A majority expressed sympathy with the position and reasoning adopted by the ECtHR in response to the UK's blanket ban, remarking on its 'haphazard'[239] and 'arbitrary and discriminate'[240] effects.[241] However, the Court agreed with previous decisions of lower courts that there was no purpose to issuing a further declaration of incompatibility when the matter was already before Parliament and being overseen by the Committee of Ministers of the Council of Europe. 7.133

A Joint Parliamentary Select Committee was established to consider the issue and published a report on 18 December 2013 recommending that the government introduce legislation to allow all prisoners serving sentences of 12 months or less to vote in all UK parliamentary, local, and European elections. The Lord Chancellor and Justice Secretary, Chris Grayling, responded very briefly to the Committee's report on 25 February 2014 without committing the government to any timescale to introduce legislation,[242] and the proposals were never taken forward. 7.134

---

[236] ibid.
[237] *Smith v Scott* [2007] SLT 137.
[238] *R (Chester and another) v Secretary of State for Justice* [2013] UKSC 63, [2014] 1 All ER 683.
[239] See the leading judgment of Lord Mance, para 35.
[240] Lady Hale, para 98.
[241] See also Lord Clarke, para 110.
[242] http://www.parliament.uk/documents/joint-committees/Draft-Voting-Eligibility-Prisoners-Bill/Grayling-letter-to-Chair.pdf accessed January 2024.

7.135   At the Strasbourg level, in 2010 in the case of *Greens and MT* the ECtHR noted the ongoing violation of A3P1 and issued a pilot judgment.[243] It gave the UK six months to introduce legislative proposals to amend the blanket ban.[244] This period was subsequently extended, first pending the Chamber decision in *Scoppola v Italy (No 3)*, and then to six months after the Grand Chamber decision. As is clear from the chronology above, the deadline was never met. Around four years later, in *Firth and others v UK*,[245] the ECtHR declined to award any compensation by way of just satisfaction for breaches of A3P1 arising from the prisoner voting ban, and also declined to award legal costs, noting that, following an earlier decision in *McLean and Cole v UK*,[246] applicants need only submit a summary form of application to raise a petition with the ECtHR. In *McHugh and others v UK*[247] and *Millbank and others v UK*[248] the ECtHR again found a breach of the A3P1 rights of a large number of prisoners on the basis of its previous judgments—although, pursuant to *Firth*, the finding of a violation was held to constitute just satisfaction.

7.136   In late 2017 the government published proposals involving administrative amendments to prison service guidance which would allow prisoners released on temporary licence to vote. The Council of Europe considered that this addressed the issues in *Hirst (No 2)*,[249] and the amendments were made in late 2018. We are not aware of the ECtHR having yet considered whether these amendments avoid a breach of A3P1.

4. Right to stand for election

7.137   A1P3 also includes a right to stand for election to the legislature.[250] The right has been characterized as the 'passive' aspect of the provision, as opposed to the 'active' right to vote. However, the ECtHR has emphasized that 'it is essential to take a holistic approach to the impact which restrictions on either right may have on securing [the right to free elections]'.[251]

7.138   Legislation establishing domestic residence requirements for a parliamentary candidate is not, as such, incompatible with A1P3. However, the ECtHR has found that, while states have a margin of appreciation as to eligibility conditions of this kind in the abstract, the principle that rights must be effective requires that eligibility procedures themselves contain sufficient safeguards to prevent arbitrary decisions.[252] Thus, it found a violation when an individual was denied registration

---

[243] For information on the ECtHR's pilot judgment procedure, which is designed to deal with large groups of identical cases deriving from the same underlying problem, see Chapter 8, para 8.46.
[244] (2011) 53 EHRR 21. See also *Tovey and others v Ministry of Justice* [2011] EWHC 271 (QB).
[245] *Firth and others v UK* App Nos 47784/09 & others, 12 August 2014.
[246] *McLean and Cole v UK* App Nos 12626/13 & others, 11 June 2013.
[247] *McHugh and others v UK* App Nos 51987/08 & others, 10 February 2015.
[248] *Millbank and others v UK* App Nos 44473/14 & others, 30 June 2016.
[249] See eg *Miller and others v UK* App Nos 70571/14 & others, 11 April 2019, para 7.
[250] *Ganchev v Bulgaria* App No 28858/95, 25 November 1996, para 130; *Sadak and others v Turkey* (2003) 36 EHRR 23, para 33.
[251] *Tănase v Moldova* (2011) 53 EHRR 22, para 113.
[252] *Zdanoka v Latvia* (2007) 45 EHRR 17.

as a candidate on the basis of residence where the domestic law governing proof of residency lacked the necessary certainty and precision.[253] In *Podkolzina v Latvia* the disqualification of a candidate violated A3P1 because the body that determined the issue did not exhibit the necessary procedural safeguards against arbitrariness.[254]

Even where the legal framework is prima facie appropriate, a decision made under it may result in a violation of A3P1. For example, in *Abil v Azerbaijan (No 2)* the ECtHR considered the totality of the proceedings leading to the applicant's disqualification as a candidate (which had included proceedings before an appellate court) and found that in all the circumstances they did not afford him 'sufficient safeguards against arbitrariness'; the decisions also 'lacked sufficient reasoning and adequate assessment of the evidence'.[255] The ECtHR has adopted the same approach when examining decisions to disqualify political parties from fielding candidates in an election.[256]   **7.139**

In *R (Barclay) v Secretary of State for Justice and the Lord Chancellor* the Supreme Court considered that the prohibition on aliens standing for election in Sark was justifiable in light of its constitutional history.[257]   **7.140**

The right to stand for election includes the right to sit as a member of the legislature once elected. The ECmHR held, in a short admissibility decision, that the contingent right to take up one's seat is not violated by a requirement that elected MPs in the UK, including Northern Irish Republicans, take the oath of allegiance to the Queen.[258] The Grand Chamber found a violation of A3P1 where an elected member of Parliament had been subjected to pre-trial detention in a way which prevented him from being physically present to take part in the activities of the legislature.[259] Particularly important in its analysis was the fact that it had found the applicant's detention to violate Articles 5 and 10 of the Convention,[260] and that the national authorities had not conducted a proportionality exercise which took account of the interference with the applicant's A3P1 rights when making decisions about that detention.[261] A violation has also been found where a member of parliament's mandate was terminated in breach of applicable domestic law.[262]   **7.141**

---

[253] *Melnychenko v Ukraine* (2004) 19 BHRC 523.

[254] *Podkolzina v Latvia* App No 46726/99, 9 April 2002. See also *Tanase v Moldova* (2011) 53 EHRR 22.

[255] *Abil v Azerbaijan (No 2)* (2021) 72 EHRR 10, para 82. See also *Tahirov v Azerbaijan* (2016) 62 EHRR 23 (finding that, although the requirement for a minimum number of signatures to be nominated as a candidate was permissible, in practice the procedure for verifying the applicant's compliance with this requirement had not contained sufficient safeguards against arbitrariness).

[256] See eg *Political party 'Patria' v Moldova* (2021) 73 EHRR 23.

[257] *R (Barclay) v Secretary of State for Justice and the Lord Chancellor* [2009] UKSC 9, [2010] 1 AC 464.

[258] *McGuinness v UK* App No 39511/98, 8 June 1999.

[259] *Demirtas v Turkey (No 2)* App No 14305/17, 22 December 2020 [GC].

[260] ibid paras 392, 394.

[261] ibid paras 395–96.

[262] *Paunovic and Milivojevic v Serbia* App No 41683/06, 24 August 2016.

5. Electoral systems

7.142　There is no obligation to introduce a specific system of voting, such as proportional representation. The state has a wide margin of appreciation in this regard.[263] It does not have to introduce a system of voting which ensures that all votes have equal weight as regards the outcome of the election, or that all candidates have equal chances of victory.

7.143　In *Liberal Party v UK* a challenge was made to the system of 'first past the post' elections in the UK, which inevitably disadvantaged smaller political parties.[264] The ECmHR found the complaint inadmissible, stating that the UK system was a fair one overall and that it did not become unfair because of the results that flowed from it.[265]

7.144　The ECtHR in *Mathieu-Mohin v Belgium* observed that any electoral system must be assessed in the light of the political evolution of the country concerned. Features that would be unacceptable in the context of one system may be justified in another, as long as the chosen system provides for conditions that will ensure the 'free expression of the opinion of the people in the choice of the legislature'.[266]

7.145　In *Bowman v UK* the ECtHR examined the relationship of A3P1 to Article 10 of the Convention (freedom of expression) in the context of electoral laws. The impugned legislation limited the amount of money spent by unauthorized persons on publications during an election period. This limit was found to be a disproportionate infringement on the right of free speech, which was not outweighed by the need to hold free elections.[267]

7.146　The ECtHR has rarely been called upon to determine the validity of the result of an election. In one such case the ECtHR considered the invalidation of votes in a parliamentary election.[268] It held that the process had been arbitrarily conducted in violation of the right to free elections. In a subsequent case the Grand Chamber considered a claim that the state's refusal to recount ballot papers from a particular constituency which had been declared blank, spoiled, or disputed had violated A3P1. The Grand Chamber made it clear that 'a mere mistake or irregularity in the electoral process would not *per se* signify unfairness ... if the general principles of equality, transparency, impartiality and independence in the organization and management of elections were complied with', and that '[t]he concept of free elections would be put at risk only if there was evidence of procedural breaches that would be capable of thwarting the free expression of the opinion of the people, and where such complaints received no effective examination at the domestic level'.[269]

---

[263] See eg *Mugemangango v Belgium* (2020) 71 EHRR 32 [GC], para 73.

[264] *Liberal Party v UK* (1980) 4 EHRR 106.

[265] The same position was taken by the ECtHR in *Gitonas v Greece* (1980) 21 DR 211.

[266] *Mathieu-Mohin v Belgium* (1988) 10 EHRR 1. See also *Mugemangango v Belgium* (2020) 71 EHRR 32 [GC], para 73.

[267] *Bowman v UK* (1998) 26 EHRR 1.

[268] *Kovach v Ukraine* App No 39424/02, 7 February 2008. See also *Kerimova v Azerbaijan* App No 20799/06, 30 September 2010.

[269] *Mugemangango v Belgium* (2020) 71 EHRR 32 [GC], para 72. See also *Davydov v Russia* (2018) 67 EHRR 25, paras 287–88.

To determine whether the alleged breach of A3P1 was made out, it therefore considered first whether the allegations of irregularities requiring a recount were 'sufficiently serious and arguable', and second whether (if so) they had 'received an effective examination' having regard to the systemic requirements summarized at paragraph 7.122.[270]

E. PROTOCOL 6

Protocol 6 prohibits the death penalty in times of peace and thereby overrides the exception in the text of Article 2 permitting the death penalty.[271] The Protocol came into force on 1 March 1985 and all Member States have ratified it. 7.147

Protocol 6 was ratified by the UK in 1999. As originally drafted the Human Rights Act did not incorporate Protocol 6, but by the time it came into force the Protocol had been inserted into Schedule 1. Protocol 6 has now been superseded by Protocol 13, prohibiting the death penalty in all circumstances (see para 7.151). 7.148

As considered in Chapter 5, the ECtHR has held that the Convention has evolved as a result of state practice such that the administration of the death penalty violates Articles 2 and 3 in all circumstances.[272] 7.149

In *Al Nashiri v Poland*,[273] the ECtHR held that the transfer of the applicant from Polish territory into the custody of the US authorities with the knowledge and complicity of the Polish authorities violated Articles 2 and 3 taken with Protocol 6 due to the substantial and foreseeable risk that the applicant would be subjected to the death penalty following trial before a US military commission. Even once the applicant had been transferred, Poland remained subject to a duty to take steps to remove this risk as soon as possible, such as by making representations to seek assurances from the US authorities.[274] 7.150

F. PROTOCOL 13

Protocol 13 abolishes the death penalty in all circumstances. In so doing, it closes the gap left by Protocol 6, which did not exclude the death penalty in respect of acts committed in time of war or of imminent threat of war. Protocol 13 is non-derogable and no reservations may be made in respect of it.[275] 7.151

---

[270] ibid paras 79–123. See also *Davydov v Russia* (2018) 67 EHRR 25, paras 288–337.

[271] However, see para 7.140 regarding the evolution in the interpretation of art 2.

[272] *Al-Saadoon and Mufdhi v UK* App No 61498/08, 2 March 2010. See also *AL(XW) v Russia* App No 44095/2014, 29 October 2015, paras 62–64.

[273] *Al Nashiri v Poland* App No 28761/2011, 24 July 2014, para 578.

[274] ibid para 589.

[275] Protocol 13, arts 2, 3.

7.152   The UK ratified Protocol 13 on 10 October 2003 and in 2004, Protocol 13, Article 1 was incorporated into the Human Rights Act in place of Protocol 6.[276]

7.153   As considered in Chapter 5, the ECtHR has held that the Convention has evolved as a result of state practice such that administration of the death penalty violates Articles 2 and 3 in all circumstances.[277]

---

[276] Human Rights Act (Amendment) Order 2004, SI 2004/1574, art 2(3).

[277] *Al-Saadoon and Mufdhi v UK* App No 61498/08, 2 March 2010. See also *AL(XW) v Russia* App No 44095/2014, 29 October 2015, paras 62–64.

8

BEYOND THE DOMESTIC COURTS: TAKING A CASE TO STRASBOURG

Blackstone's Guide to The Human Rights Act 1998. Eighth Edition. John Wadham, Helen Mountfield KC, Raj Desai, Sarah Hannett KC, Jessica Jones, Eleanor Mitchell, and Aidan Wills, Oxford University Press. © John Wadham, Helen Mountfield KC, Raj Desai, Sarah Hannett KC, Jessica Jones, Eleanor Mitchell, and Aidan Wills 2024. DOI: 10.1093/oso/9780192885050.003.0008

A. INTRODUCTION

8.01   The Human Rights Act 1998 did not, and could not, end the practice of taking UK cases to the Strasbourg Court. There are a number of reasons a case may still be brought to Strasbourg. First, because the Human Rights Act 1998 respects parliamentary sovereignty, so that there will be cases in which breaches of Convention rights will still arise in primary legislation which cannot be rectified in domestic courts and where Parliament does not legislate to amend the law following a declaration of incompatibility. To date, however, the government has a good record in responding to declarations of incompatibility:

Since the HRA came into force on 2 October 2000 until the end of July 2022, 46 declarations of incompatibility have been made.

Of these, 40 have been fully addressed:

- 10 have been overturned on appeal (and there is no scope for further appeal);
- 5 related to provisions that had already been amended by primary legislation at the time of the declaration;
- 8 have been addressed by Remedial Order;
- 16 have been addressed by primary or secondary legislation (other than by Remedial Order);
- 1 has been addressed by various measures; and 6 are ongoing:
- 4 the Government has proposed to address by Remedial Order;
- 2 are currently subject to appeal.[1]

8.02   Secondly, and despite the independence of judges in the UK, domestic courts are more likely than an international body to succumb to local pressure from the media, politicians, and the state, and may not always be as robust in their protection of human rights as the Court in Strasbourg.[2] Thirdly, the Strasbourg Court may differ from the domestic courts in its interpretation of particular Convention rights. For example, in *S and Marper v UK*[3] the Grand Chamber took a very different view of the collection and retention of DNA samples and data and Article 8. The Administrative Court,[4] the Court of

---

[1] Responding to human rights judgments: Report to the Joint Committee on Human Rights on the Government's response to human rights judgments 2021–2022, Ministry of Justice, December 2022.

[2] See for instance Brice Dickson, *The European Convention on Human Rights and the Conflict in Northern Ireland* (OUP 2012).

[3] *S and Marper v UK* App Nos 30562/04 and 30566/04, 4 December 2008 [GC]. See an analysis of the different approaches in Brice Dickson, *Human Rights and the United Kingdom Supreme Court* (OUP 2013).

[4] *R (S) v Chief Constable of South Yorkshire Police and the Secretary of State for the Home Department* and *R (Marper) v Chief Constable of South Yorkshire Police and the Secretary of State for the Home Department*

Appeal,[5] and the House of Lords[6] all rejected the victims' cases and the House of Lords decided that Article 8 was barely engaged, whereas the 17 judges in Strasbourg were unanimous in finding a violation.[7] Fourthly, it is sensible for individuals with the stamina and real issues to seek redress in Strasbourg, for example to clarify the law or to seek compensation where the domestic court has made a declaration of incompatibility and compensation is not available. Fifthly, since in practice, the definitive interpretation of the Convention is reserved to the Strasbourg Court, practitioners are likely to want to contribute to this definitive jurisprudence.[8] Sixthly, a UK government may wish to amend or abolish the Human Rights Act (see Chapter 1, para 1.57), Strasbourg may then be the only means of directly enforcing Convention rights.[9]

The European Court of Human Rights (ECtHR) is a court of last resort and not an appeal court: it has never been permissible to take a case there without exhausting domestic remedies first. This requirement has been imposed more strictly since the Convention became part of UK domestic law, and this is likely to increase as a result of the implementation of Protocol 15 (see para 8.07). However, to note, a declaration of incompatibility is not regarded as an effective remedy for the purposes of Article 13, although the Court has not closed the possibility of this being the case in future.[10]   8.03

Although the number of cases against the United Kingdom lodged with the ECtHR before and after the Human Rights Act came into force originally remained roughly the same, the latest figures show that, per capita, the UK has the lowest number of cases heard in ECtHR in 2022 with only four judgments, and violations found in only two of those. At the end of 2022, there were 74,647 applications pending before the ECtHR and only 99 of those (0.12%) were from the UK.[11]   8.04

This chapter outlines the procedure for making applications to the European Court in Strasbourg. It is included to ensure that those who have exhausted their domestic remedies in the United Kingdom have information on how to proceed further.   8.05

Over the life of the Court there has been a huge increase in the number of cases that have been dealt with and this increase shows no sign of tailing off. In 2022 the Court ruled on some 39,570 applications and there were 4,168 judgments. At the end of 2021 there were 70,150 applications were pending and 74,650 at the end of 2022. However, nearly 75 per cent of those pending cases concerned five countries: Turkey, the Russian Federation, Ukraine, Romania, and Italy.[12]   8.06

[2002] EWHC 478 (Admin), [2002] EWCA Civ 1275, [2002] 1 WLR 3223; and *R (LS) v Chief Constable of South Yorkshire and R (Marper) v Chief Constable of South Yorkshire* [2004] UKHL 39, [2004] 1 WLR 2196.

[5] *R (on the application of S) v Chief Constable of South Yorkshire* [2002] EWCA Civ 1275, [2002] 1 WLR 3223.

[6] *R (LS) v Chief Constable of South Yorkshire and R (Marper) v Chief Constable of South Yorkshire* [2004] UKHL 39, [2004] 1 WLR 2196.

[7] See also *Hirst v UK (No 2)* (2005) 19 BHRC 546 [GC] where, on the right of prisoners to vote, the Court also took a much stronger pro-rights line.

[8] See Lord Bingham in *R (Anderson) v Secretary of State for the Home Department* [2002] UKHL 46, [2003] 1 AC 837, para 18.

[9] See Preface.

[10] See para 8.31.

[11] Annual report of ECtHR for 2022, 26 January 2023 <https://echr.coe.int/pages/home.aspx?p=home>.

[12] Annual report of ECtHR for 2022, 26 January 2023 <https://echr.coe.int/pages/home.aspx?p=home>.

8.07   Protocols 14 and 15 made a number of changes to the system to try to solve the Court's problems caused by its 'success'. Protocol 14 and the other internal changes made by the Court itself originally enabled the Court to start to clear its backlog. The stricter process for filing applications themselves, which was implemented by the Court itself at the beginning of 2014 (see para 8.12), also had an effect on the Court's workload. The changes set out in Protocol 15 were, however, only implemented in August 2021. Protocol 15:

- added a new recital to the Preamble to the Convention stressing the margin of appreciation enjoyed by states;
- reduced the maximum age of judges on selection from 70 to 65;
- removed the right of a party to object to a case being dealt with by the Grand Chamber;
- reduced the time for making applications from six months to four months;
- made it easier for certain specified cases to be declared inadmissible (see paras 8.32 and 8.39).

8.08   For more information on the procedure in the Court, see the amended Convention itself, the Rules of Court of the European Court of Human Rights, October 2021, and the Practice Directions.[13] References to 'rules' in this chapter are to the Rules of the Court unless otherwise stated.[14] The ECtHR's very helpful website (<http://www.echr.coe.int>) gives access to the Convention, the Rules, practice directions, application forms, and much other useful information for applicants and their lawyers.

B. THE STRUCTURE AND JURISDICTION OF THE COURT

8.09   The Court consists of one judge nominated by each of the countries belonging to the Council of Europe. These persons act in an individual capacity and cannot be government officials (though they can be ex-government lawyers). The vast majority of decisions in cases will be made by single judges or committees of three. In cases that lead on to substantive judgments the Court will sit in Chambers of seven judges. Reserve judges may also sit, so that the case does not need to be reheard if one judge falls ill, or cannot for some other reason deliberate. Where the Chamber considers that a case raises a serious question affecting the interpretation of the Convention, or where the resolution of a question before it might result in an inconsistency in the Court's case law, it may relinquish the jurisdiction to a Grand Chamber of 17 judges, under Article 30 of the Convention. Alternatively, within three months of a decision of a Chamber, any of the parties may request that the

---

[13] The Practice Directions are annexed to the Rules and set out at the end of that document.

[14] For more information, see Philip Leach, *Taking a Case to the European Court of Human Rights* (4th edn, OUP 2017) and *The European Court of Human Rights, Questions & Answers for Lawyers, Council of Bars and Law Societies of Europe, 2020.*

case be referred to the Grand Chamber under Article 43. This is an exceptional procedure, and the request will be accepted only if the case raises a serious question affecting the interpretation or application of the Convention or a serious issue of general importance. The first case referred to the Grand Chamber from the United Kingdom under Article 43, *Hatton v UK*,[15] concerning the Article 8 rights of those in the vicinity of Heathrow Airport, was decided in 2003.

The Court can also hear applications of alleged violations of the Convention brought by Member States themselves—as occurred, for example, when the Republic of Ireland complained to the Court about the UK's interrogation practices used in Northern Ireland.[16] This is very rare[17] but such cases are important.[18]   8.10

C. MAKING AN APPLICATION

Applications should be directed to: 8.11

The Registrar of the European Court of Human Rights

Council of Europe

F-67075 Strasbourg-Cedex

France

The application must be made on the form provided by the Court (available on its website) and as a hard copy. It is necessary to ensure that all the questions on the form are answered correctly and all of the documentation required is sent with the form before the end of four-month time limit for applications. The following information is required by the Court: 8.12

(a) the applicant's name, date of birth, nationality, sex, occupation, and address;

(b) the name, address, and occupation of anyone acting as the representative;

(c) the respondent country;

(d) a clear and concise statement of the facts, including, of course, the exact dates;

(e) a succinct statement of each and every alleged violation of the Convention and the relevant arguments (this should include the relevant domestic law and any relevant Convention case law);

(f) a succinct statement of compliance with the admissibility criteria, including the four-month rule and the details of all remedies (including any appeal) which have been pursued within the country concerned and, where appropriate, an explanation of why any available remedies have not been pursued (see para 8.30);

---

[15] *Hatton v UK* (2003) 37 EHRR 28 [GC].
[16] *Ireland v UK* (1978) 2 EHRR 25.
[17] There are 16 inter-state cases pending as of January 2023, Court website.
[18] See *Georgia v Russian Federation (II)* App No 38263/08, 21 January 2021.

(g) the object of the application (eg the repeal or amendment of certain legislation, or the reversal of a decision and compensation); and

(h) copies of the judgments, decisions, and any other documents relating to the application.

8.13   It used to be possible to write a short initial letter to the Court setting out the details of the application, but that is not sufficient to interrupt the four-month time limit. Only a fully completed application along with all the relevant documents will have the effect of instigating a case. The four-month time limit runs from 'the final decision in the process of exhausting domestic remedies',[19] and the application must be submitted by that date in order to be admissible.

1. Urgent cases, interim measures, and the Court's priorities

8.14   The Court's full procedures take some time (five years or more in many cases), but it will give priority to very urgent cases (eg where a person's life or well-being is immediately threatened, as in the case of a motor neurone disease sufferer in *Pretty v United Kingdom*[20]). The Court prioritizes urgent and important cases so they can be dealt with more quickly (see para 8.18). The Court can also be asked to implement its interim measures procedure.[21] In rule 39 the Chamber or its President may indicate to the parties interim measures which it considers should be adopted.[22] This will often be a request to refrain from taking action that will prejudice the case, with the test being whether there is an 'imminent risk of irreparable damage'—for instance the deportation of an applicant where the case concerns arguments about the possibility of Article 3 breaches if that person is sent out of the jurisdiction.[23] In such cases, the Court should be contacted directly to ask it to request the government to refrain from acting until the application has been considered. Telephone

---

[19] *Lekić v Slovenia* App No 36480/07, 11 December 2018 [GC], para 65.

[20] *Pretty v United Kingdom* (2002) 35 EHRR 1.

[21] See the Practice Direction, Requests for Interim Measures, and the ECtHR Fact Sheet, Interim Measures for more details.

[22] In November 2023, the Court proposed amendments to Rule 39, making it clear that requests can be adjourned if not extremely urgent, that the parties can be asked to submit information about the application, disclosing the identity of the judges that make decisions on interim measures requests, giving reasons for the decisions, and providing those decisions to the parties. Once the amendment to the Rule has been agreed, an updated Practice Direction will be published.

[23] In June 2022, the Court decided to grant an interim measure in the case of *K.N. v the United Kingdom* App No 28774/22, an Iraqi asylum-seeker facing imminent removal to Rwanda. In this case, the Court has indicated to the UK government that the applicant should not be removed to Rwanda until three weeks after the delivery of the final domestic decision in his ongoing judicial review proceedings. It is unusual for rule 39 applications to succeed: in 2019, Strasbourg received 82 requests for interim measures against the UK, with none granted; while in 2020, it received 47 requests, of which 2 were granted; and in 2021, it received 51 requests of which 5 were granted. This means that during the last three years, the Court has granted just 7 of 180 requests for interim measures (a success rate of just 3%): see <https://ohrh.law.ox.ac.uk/interim-relief-under-the-echr-getting-the-facts-right/>.

contact can be useful to alert the Registry of a request about to be made, which of course then has to be in writing (a telephone call on its own would not be enough). The Court has a dedicated fax line for such requests and all requests should initially be sent using this line.[24]

The United Kingdom has, generally, respected requests from the ECtHR for interim measures. However, in one case the government decided not to comply with a request from the ECtHR to refrain from handing over two people in Iraq to the Iraqi High Tribunal pending their trial for killing two British servicemen.[25] The Secretary of State for Defence stated that:

8.15

This follows the unanimous court of appeal ruling that Mr Al-Saadoon and Mr Mufdhi do not fall within the jurisdiction of the European Convention on Human Rights. After 31 December 2008, the UK had no legal power to detain any individuals in Iraq and continued detention would be a breach of the UK's international law obligations.[26]

The Court in Strasbourg however found that:

8.16

In conclusion, the Court does not consider that the authorities of the Contracting State took all steps which could reasonably have been taken in order to comply with the interim measure taken by the Court. The failure to comply with the interim measure and the transfer of the applicants out of the United Kingdom's jurisdiction exposed them to a serious risk of grave and irreparable harm.[27]

The Court now considers interim measures to be binding.[28] However, the Illegal Immigration Act 2023, provides that in the context of the issues dealt with by that Act that:

8.17

Any power of the court or tribunal to grant an interim remedy (whether on an application of the person or otherwise) is restricted as follows.

The court or tribunal may not grant an interim remedy that prevents or delays, or that has the effect of preventing or delaying, the removal of the person from the United Kingdom in pursuance of the decision …

A Minister of the Crown may (but need not) determine that the duty in section 2(1) (duty to make arrangements for removal) is not to apply in relation to the person.

A decision as to whether or not to make a determination under subsection (2) is to be taken personally by the Minister of the Crown.[29]

---

[24] The Court has a dedicated fax number for requests for interim measures: +33 (0)3 88 41 39 00, open from Monday to Friday, from 08.00 to 16.00. Requests sent after 16.00 will not usually be dealt with until the following working day. Lawyers requesting interim measures must respond to any letters and information requests sent by the Registry of the Court as a matter of urgency. Requests for interim measures are usually decided within 24 to 48 hours.
[25] See the judgment of the Court of Appeal, *R (Al-Saadoon and another) v Secretary of State for Defence* [2009] EWCA Civ 7, [2010] QB 486.
[26] Reported in the *Guardian*, 1 January 2009.
[27] *Al-Saadoon and Mufdhi v UK* App No 61498/08, 2 March 2010, para 165.
[28] *Mamatkulov v Turkey* (2005) 41 EHRR 25 [GC].
[29] Section 55.

2. The Court's priority policy

8.18 The Court approaches its workload on the basis of the following priorities:

I. urgent applications—threats to life or health;

II. applications raising questions about the effectiveness of the Convention system: structural or endemic situations or raising questions of general interest (including ones with possible major implications for domestic legal systems or the European system);

III. applications which raise as their main complaint Articles 2, 3, 4, or 5(1) and which have given rise to direct threats to the physical integrity and dignity of human beings;

IV. potentially well-founded applications based on other articles;

V. applications raising issues already dealt with by pilot or leading judgments;

VI. applications identified as giving rise to a problem of admissibility; and

VII. applications which are manifestly inadmissible.[30]

8.19 Obviously, the Court will decide which category any particular case fits into, but applicants may wish to ensure that arguments that might push their case up the list are set out in the application and any subsequent correspondence. The Court in 2021 decided to consider 'impact' issues in deciding on priorities:

Among these category IV cases, a small percentage may raise very important issues of relevance for the State in question and/or the Convention system as a whole and justify more expeditious case-processing. These cases will be identified and marked as 'impact' cases under a new category IV-High. To date, approximately 650 cases have been so identified.

'Impact' cases are identified on the basis of flexible guiding criteria as well as a list of examples. The criteria have been defined as follows: the conclusion of the case might lead to a change or clarification of international or domestic legislation or practice; the case touches upon moral or social issues; the case deals with an emerging or otherwise significant human rights issue. If any of these criteria are met, the Court may take into account whether the case has had significant media coverage domestically and/or is politically sensitive.[31]

3. Court's response to an application

8.20 The Court will register the application and give it a case number and may also request further information or documents.

4. Representation

8.21 Legal representation must be by a lawyer authorized to practise in any Convention country and resident in one of them, unless the President of the Chamber decides otherwise.[32] Although, in general, applicants may represent themselves at hearings, the Court has the power to direct that an applicant be represented by a lawyer, and

---

[30] <https://www.echr.coe.int/documents/d/echr/priority_policy_ENG> dated June 2009.

[31] *A strategy for more targeted and effective case-processing*, March 2021, <https://www.echr.coe.int/documents/d/echr/Court_that_matters_ENG>.

[32] Rule 36.

at any hearing representation by a lawyer is mandatory unless the President of the Court decides otherwise.[33]

D. ADMISSIBILITY AND MERITS

The Court's jurisdiction is limited and applications can be considered only if they meet the admissibility criteria set out in Article 35 of the Convention, which are rigorously applied and which are set out below.[34] More than 90 per cent of cases are dismissed as being 'inadmissible', and it is therefore critically important to ensure that an application complies with the admissibility requirements, and contains all the facts and arguments of law.[35] To have a real chance of success, it is necessary for the application to set out the facts, the relevant domestic law, and detailed submissions on the law of the Convention. One of the best ways of setting out the application is to model it on a judgment of the Court.[36]   8.22

Article 34 provides that an application under the Convention can be brought by 'any person, non-governmental organization or group of individuals claiming to be the victim of a violation'. Neither individuals nor legal persons have to be citizens of the state concerned, nor of any Member State. They do not have to be resident or physically present in the territory. Applications may not be brought by governmental organizations or other 'emanations of the state'.   8.23

Although applications may be brought by groups of individuals and non-governmental organizations (NGOs), the organization or group must itself be a victim of a violation. Thus, trade unions and NGOs can make applications about an action by the state but only if it was directed towards them. Finally, groups, trade unions, and NGOs can, of course, provide their members with representation, but cannot make applications on behalf of their members. However, in an exceptional case the Grand Chamber of the Court decided in a case concerning Article 2 and the respondent's responsibility for the death, where no one else could represent the deceased's interests an NGO was entitled to do so.[37] It is also possible for organizations to intervene in cases: see paragraph 8.50.   8.24

1. Who is a 'victim'?

An applicant must be one of three types of victim: actual, potential, or indirect. An *actual victim* is someone who is personally affected by the alleged violation. It   8.25

---

[33] Rule 36(2).

[34] See the Court's Admissibility Guide, August 2022.

[35] Rule 47 requires the prescribed form to be used and to give the prescribed details.

[36] See Philip Leach, *Taking a Case to the European Court of Human Rights* (4th edn, OUP 2017) for model applications.

[37] *Centre for Legal Resources on behalf of Valentin Campeanu v Romania*, 17 July 2014. The Court has not set out any criteria for how this exception will operate but the facts of the case suggest that the Court's discretion will be exercised in this way very rarely.

is not necessary to show that any detriment has been suffered, although this will be relevant to the remedy (see para 8.56). A *potential victim* is one who is at risk of being directly affected by a law or administrative act.[38] An *indirect victim* is one who is immediately affected by a violation which directly affects another, such as a family member of someone imprisoned or killed. Family members of those killed or imprisoned can also successfully include in their cases applications about *direct violations* of their rights—for example Article 3 in disappearance cases. Another example of an indirect victim is a family member of someone deported or facing deportation.

2. Against whom can an application be brought?

8.26 Only states are parties to the Convention, and therefore only those states can be liable for violations. Where there are several state organs involved, it will not be necessary for this purpose to identify which level of the state organization is responsible. Applications cannot be brought against private persons or institutions. However, the application may be based on the state's failure to fulfil positive obligations to ensure that human rights are respected by private persons within the state's jurisdiction.[39]

3. Extent of jurisdiction

8.27 Under Article 1, signatory states are required to 'secure to everyone *within their jurisdiction*' (emphasis added) the rights and freedoms protected by the Convention. This means that states are liable for all events that take place in the territory for which they are responsible, not just those affecting their own nationals, and even if the effects of the events might be felt outside the Council of Europe area. For example, cases have been brought concerning deportation to places where torture might occur, such as in *Chahal v UK*.[40] But the jurisdiction of a state may also extend to the acts of state servants that take place beyond the physical territory of the state.[41] The crucial test for extra-territorial jurisdiction is whether or not the state was exercising de facto control over the events in question. For a general discussion of the principles, see *Bankovic v Belgium and others*[42] and *Al-Skeini v UK*.[43]

---

[38] See eg *Dudgeon v UK* (1981) 3 EHRR 40 or *Burden and Burden v UK* (2008) 47 EHRR 38 [GC].

[39] See Chapter 2.

[40] *Chahal v UK* (1997) 23 EHRR 413.

[41] See eg *Loizidou v Turkey* (1997) 23 EHRR 513 concerning the effects of Turkish-sponsored troops in Cyprus.

[42] *Bankovic v Belgium and others* (2007) 44 EHRR SE5. See Chapter 2, para 2.23.

[43] *Al-Skeini v UK* (2011) 53 EHRR 18 [GC]. See also the 'special circumstances jurisdiction' issues, *Hanan v Germany* App No 4871/16, 16 February 2021 [GC] and *Güzelyurtlu and others v Cyprus and Turkey* App No 36925/07, 29 January 2019.

4. The application must concern a Convention issue

The Court's jurisdiction extends only to applications relating to the rights and free- 8.28
doms contained in the Convention and the Protocols that the Member State in
question has ratified.[44]

5. Exhaustion of domestic remedies

The ECtHR has consistently held that it 'may only deal with the matter after all 8.29
domestic remedies have been exhausted'.

This rule is applied strictly in practice. However, it applies only to the remedies 8.30
that are available, sufficient, and which relate to the breaches alleged. In considering the nature of the remedy, the Court takes into account 'the principles of
flexibility and avoidance of undue formalism developed in its case-law on Article
35, in particular that it is sufficient if the applicant has raised the substance of his
Convention application before the domestic authorities',[45] If a potential applicant
to the Court is in doubt as to whether alternative remedies have been exhausted, it
is usually sensible for the remedy to be pursued, though a 'protective' application to
the ECtHR could be lodged simultaneously to avoid falling foul of the four-month
time limit should the Court subsequently decide that the remedy was not effective
and did not need to be pursued.

It is most unlikely that a declaration of incompatibility will be regarded as 8.31
an effective remedy for the purposes of Article 13. This means that, at present,
the ECtHR is unlikely to exclude a case at the admissibility stage for failure to
exhaust domestic remedies if the only domestic remedy realistically available
was a declaration of incompatibility. This was confirmed in *Burden and Burden
v UK* where, in a lengthy discussion, the ECtHR held itself not to be satisfied
that a declaration of incompatibility could be considered to be an effective judicial remedy.[46] However, the ECtHR did accept that, should evidence emerge at
a 'future date' of a 'long-standing and established practice' of the government
giving effect to courts' declarations of incompatibility, this might support a different conclusion.[47] The best advice therefore for the purposes of an application
to the Court would be to seek a declaration of incompatibility before applying
to the Court.[48]

---

[44] The UK has not ratified Protocol 4, 7, or 12 so claimants against the UK cannot found applications on
breaches of the rights contained in those protocols.

[45] See eg *John Shelley v UK* (2008) 46 EHRR SE16, quoting *Cardot v France* (1991) 13 EHRR 853,
para 34.

[46] *Burden and Burden v UK* (2007) 44 EHRR 51, paras 30–40; confirmed by the Grand Chamber at
(2008) 47 EHRR 38.

[47] *Burden and Burden v UK* (2007) 44 EHRR 51, paras 30–40.

[48] See eg *Carson v UK* App No 42184/05, 16 March 2010 [GC], where the art 8 complaint was dismissed
as inadmissible on the grounds of non-exhaustion.

6. Four-month time limit

8.32　Applications to the ECtHR must be made within four months of the final decision of the domestic proceedings (or the date that the victim was informed about the final decision) or, where there are no effective domestic remedies, of the violation of the Convention. There is very little flexibility for cases to be brought outside this time limit, though lack of knowledge of the violation may make a later application possible. For example, in *Hilton v UK*[49] a journalist was refused a job within the BBC, but only discovered that this was as a result of a secret vetting process nine years later.

7. Other inadmissibility grounds

8.33　Under Article 35(2) and (3), the Court may declare an application inadmissible on further grounds, which are dealt with in turn below.

(a) *Anonymity*

8.34　Anonymous applications are inadmissible, although the complainant may request on the application form that he or she wishes his or her identity to be kept confidential (apart from the disclosure to the Court and the Member State itself).[50]

(b) *Petition is 'substantially the same as' previous applications*

8.35　This restriction prevents successive applications by the same applicant in respect of the same facts, and is not interpreted by the Court to restrict applications in respect of different instances even if the issues are substantially the same. Similarly, the provision does not act to bar a second application where new facts have arisen since the first application.

(c) *Examination by another international body*

8.36　If the matter has already been submitted to, and dealt with by, some other international procedure and contains no new information, it will be inadmissible. This is very unlikely to be an issue in the United Kingdom, because the United Kingdom has only ratified the individual complaints procedures created by the optional protocols of the United Nations' Convention for the Elimination of All Forms of Discrimination Against Women and the Convention on the Rights of People with Disabilities.

(d) *Incompatible with the provisions of the Convention*

8.37　This ground covers applications which do not concern the rights and freedoms protected by the Convention, situations in which the applicant is not within the

---

[49] *Hilton v UK* (1998) 57 DR 108.
[50] Rule 32. See Practice Direction: Requests for Anonymity, 14 January 2010.

jurisdiction of a Member State, or where the application is not directed against the state.

(e) Manifestly ill-founded

This is the most difficult criterion to assess. Ostensibly, this term is applied to applications that, on a preliminary examination, do not disclose any possible ground on which a violation could be established. Although the test is used to screen out clearly unmeritorious applications, it is applied very strictly. In effect, the Court's assessment of whether an application is 'ill-founded' is a strict merits test. The Court's assertion that a case is 'manifestly ill-founded' is not the same as saying that it is unarguable. Cases that are plainly arguable are nevertheless excluded on this ground.

8.38

(f) No significant disadvantage

The Court can declare the case inadmissible if 'the applicant has not suffered a significant disadvantage'.[51] If the Court makes this initial assessment it needs to go on to consider whether or not the application should be examined 'to ensure respect for human rights' before it can declare the case inadmissible. Both of these criteria have to be met before a case can be declared inadmissible:

8.39

- the applicant must not have suffered a significant disadvantage; and
- respect for human rights does not require an examination of the application on the merits.

The Court has helpfully set out the principles that can be derived from the cases decided under this provision in its 'Practical Guide to on Admissibility Criteria.'.[52]

(g) Abuse of the right of petition

The fact that an applicant does not come to the Court with 'clean hands' or for a proper motive will not itself be a reason to reject the application. An inadmissibility ruling on this ground may occur if the applicant is dishonest, has manufactured evidence, or is vexatious.

8.40

8. Decision on admissibility

A decision on admissibility can take several months and usually takes much longer.[53] The ECtHR will give its decision on admissibility in writing. Clearly inadmissible cases will go to the Single Judge within a few weeks, but where the issue is less clear the decision will be made by a Committee or the Chamber. This question

8.41

---

[51] Article 35(3)(b).
[52] https://www.echr.coe.int/documents/d/echr/admissibility_guide_eng August 2023.
[53] A recent small sample of cases against the UK examined by the authors took between 9 and 27 months to be 'communicated' to the UK government.

is likely to be decided without any further contact with the applicant and without 'communicating' the case to the government concerned, however, the Court may seek the government's observations, and even seek a hearing before deciding the issue of admissibility (although this is very rare). In the vast majority of cases the inadmissibility decision will be made solely on the basis of the application and the material provided by the applicant.[54] The Court is not required to seek any further submissions or alert the applicant that this approach is being taken, and is unlikely to do so. Over 90 per cent of the cases declared inadmissible exit the system at this early stage. No specific reasons will be given for the decision and there is no appeal against decisions on admissibility.

9. Consideration by a Chamber and communication to the government

8.42 If the case is not declared inadmissible at the initial stage it will be referred to a Chamber of the Court, which will decide on what further action needs to be taken in respect of the application. Often applications are also declared inadmissible by the Chamber at this early stage without the opportunity for any further evidence or submissions. Alternatively, the Chamber may decide that further information is required from the applicant and/or state concerned. If this occurs, the application will be formally 'communicated' to the state, which is then invited to make any observations it thinks fit.

8.43 In such cases, both parties are sent a statement of the facts of the case, prepared by the Court, together with a series of questions. Both the applicant and the Court then have an opportunity to comment on the account that the Court has produced and respond to the questions. For those interested in monitoring pending cases, and for NGOs or others interested in intervening, the communication decision is the first point at which the Court discloses any details of cases pending in the system.

8.44 Once the government has responded to the case, the applicant is given a chance to respond to that in writing.[55] In most cases the Court will decide any outstanding issues of admissibility as part of the judgment on the merits.

10. Friendly settlements

8.45 Article 38(1)(b) provides that once the Court has declared an application admissible, it shall place itself at the disposal of the parties concerned with a view to securing a friendly settlement. Thus, after an admissibility decision, the Court will write to the parties, asking whether or not they wish to explore the possibility of a settlement and, if so, inviting proposals on the subject. The Court acts as a go-between if the parties enter into negotiations.

---

[54] Article 35 and r 49.

[55] For the form of pleadings, see the Court's Written pleadings, September 2014 and Guidelines on submitting pleadings following simplified communication, September 2014.

11. Pilot judgments

The Court has developed a procedure for dealing with large groups of identical 8.46 cases that derive from the same underlying problem.[56] In such circumstances the Court will select one or more of the cases for priority treatment and will use that case or cases to try to achieve a solution that will resolve the issues in all of those other identical cases. The Court will, in such cases, freeze all the other applications pending the resolution of the lead case.

12. Assessing the merits

Once the Court has made a positive admissibility decision and any friendly settle- 8.47 ment negotiations have failed, it undertakes an investigation into the merits of the application.

The Convention and rules allow a committee of three judges to decide on issues 8.48 of admissibility and merits of an application where the issues in the case are already the subject of well-established case law from the Court. This provision is designed to deal with repetitive cases and cases that stem from the same fault in a domestic system (eg primary legislation which has already been held to violate the Convention).

13. Court's investigative powers

The Court is empowered to obtain any evidence that it considers capable of provid- 8.49 ing clarification of the facts of the case, either of its own motion or at the request of any party to the application (or a third party—see para 8.50).[57] This can even include its judges (usually three or four judges) holding fact-finding hearings, conducting an inquiry or taking evidence in some other way. In practice, however, this occurs only very rarely.[58]

14. Third-party interventions

According to Article 36 and rule 44, the President of the Court may permit any 8.50 state, or any natural or legal person, to submit written observations about the application. Such applications can arise because a possible lacuna exists in areas of the argument, which neither the state nor the applicant is willing to fill. The United Kingdom has used the intervention process itself in the case of *Saadi v Italy*.[59] This

---

[56] For examples of how this procedure has been used, see the Court's Fact Sheet: 'Pilot Judgments', note also Rule 61 and 'The Pilot-Judgment Procedure: Information note issued by the Registrar', https://www. echr.coe.int/documents/d/echr/pilot_judgment_procedure_eng.

[57] Rule 49, see also *Annex to the Rules (concerning investigations)*, October 2022.

[58] See eg the use of this power the *in camera* evidence session held in the rendition cases against Poland, *Al Nashiri v Poland* and *Husayn (Abu Zubaydah)* App No 28761/11, 24 July 2014 (evidence sessions held on 2 December 2013).

[59] *Saadi v Italy* (2008) 24 BHRC 123. The UK also intervened more recently in *Hanan v Germany* App No 4871/16 and in the request for an advisory opinion from France concerning the recognition in domestic law of a legal parent-child relationship between a child born through a gestational surrogacy arrangement abroad and the intended mother.

case concerned deportation and the absolute nature of the prohibition of treatment contrary to Article 3 of the Convention. The United Kingdom was concerned that the Court's jurisprudence meant that the risk of such treatment in the country to which the applicant was to be sent could not be weighed against the reasons (including the protection of national security) put forward by the respondent state to justify expulsion.

8.51   NGOs often intervene to set out their view of human rights, or because the case raises an issue of particular interest to them. A third party has 12 weeks from the date the notification has been 'communicated' to the state party (see para 8.39).[60] The details of selected cases communicated to state parties are now published on the Court's website. Liberty, for instance, has frequently intervened in cases, as, for example, in *S and Marper v UK*.[61] The Equality and Human Rights Commission can also seek to intervene in cases in the Court, and did so for the first time in February 2009 in the case of *RP v United Kingdom*.[62] Businesses also intervene on occasion: for example, in the case of *Hatton v UK*[63] (concerning night flights from Heathrow airport and the effect on the private lives of those living under the flight path), both British Airways and an environmental pressure group, Friends of the Earth, submitted written interventions. The joint Grand Chamber cases of *Big Brother Watch and others v UK* is a recent example of a case with a very significant number of interventions.[64]

15. Oral hearing

8.52   Hearings are now extremely rare and the vast majority of cases are decided on the papers alone. However, there are still a few hearings held in the Strasbourg building each year. If a hearing is to take place (whether for an admissibility decision and/or the merits), the applicant will be notified and contacted by the Registry with a date for the hearing (it is difficult to alter the date once it has been fixed). The parties will also be invited to send their final proposed oral arguments in advance to the Court to aid the work of the interpreters. The official languages of the Court are English and French.

---

[60] See r 44(1)(b).
[61] *S and Marper v UK* App Nos 30562/04 and 30566/04, 4 December 2008.
[62] *RP v United Kingdom* App No 38245/07, 9 October 2012.
[63] *Hatton v UK* (2003) 37 EHRR 28.
[64] *Big Brother Watch and others v UK* App Nos 58170/13 & others, 25 May 2021 [GC], interveners in the first case: Human Rights Watch, Access Now, Dutch Against Plasterk, Center For Democracy & Technology, European Network of National Human Rights Institutions and the Equality and Human Rights Commission, the Helsinki Foundation For Human Rights, the International Commission of Jurists, Open Society Justice Initiative, The Law Society of England and Wales, and Project Moore. In the second case, the Center For Democracy & Technology, the Helsinki Foundation For Human Rights, the International Commission of Jurists, the National union of Journalists, and the Media Lawyers' Association. In the third case, art 19, the Electronic Privacy Information Center and the Equality and Human Rights Commission.

Hearings are held in the Human Rights Building in Strasbourg. In practice, 8.53
hearings take approximately two hours, with the parties each being allowed only
30 minutes in all to present their case (followed by a brief period each in which to
respond to the other party and answer any questions posed by the judges). Hearings
are now webcast (via the Court's website) and can provide a real insight on the procedure and how advocates might best promote their client's case.

16. Judgment

Chamber judgments are not read in open court, although the judgment of a Grand 8.54
Chamber will be read out in summary. In both cases printed copies are made avail-
able, and electronic copies are sent to the parties and are published on the website.
The judgment of a Chamber does not become final until:

- the parties declare that they will not be requesting a referral of the case to the
  Grand Chamber;
- three months after the date of the judgment; or
- when a panel of five judges of the Court rejects the request for referral to the
  Grand Chamber.

17. Applications to the Grand Chamber

Under Article 43, either party can seek permission for a referral to the Grand 8.55
Chamber.[65] In order to gain permission, either party must satisfy a panel of five
judges that there exists either a serious question affecting the interpretation of the
Convention or the Protocols thereto, or a serious issue of general importance. The
request must be made in writing within three months of the Chamber judgment.
The process involves a re-examination of the case rather than an appeal as such. It
is rare for a case to be referred to the Grand Chamber after an oral hearing by a
Chamber.

18. Remedies

Where the Court finds that a violation of the Convention has occurred, it is 8.56
required under Article 41 to consider whether the applicant is entitled to any
compensation and/or costs in 'just satisfaction'. Any award is at the discretion
of the Court and a specific claim for compensation must have been made by the
applicant in advance. A claim can include pecuniary loss and non-pecuniary
loss.[66] The Court has declined to award aggravated, exemplary, or punitive
damages:

---

[65] Rule 73.
[66] See Practice Direction: Just Satisfaction Claims, June 2022.

The purpose of the Court's award under Article 41 of the Convention in respect of damage is to compensate the applicant for the actual harmful consequences of a violation ...

It is also not intended to punish the Contracting Party responsible. The Court has therefore, until now, considered it inappropriate to accept claims for damages with labels such as 'punitive', 'aggravated' or 'exemplary'; nor does the Court make symbolic awards.[67]

8.57   The Court can order a state to take or refrain from taking specific action and will occasionally include specific proposals for change as part of its declaration of the law. In property cases the Court has ordered the return of property, and in unlawful detention cases the release of the detained person. In the case of *Greens and MT v UK*,[68] which concerned the right of prisoners to vote and the failure of the government to amend the law following the Court's finding of violation in *Hirst v UK*,[69] the Court, in the first pilot judgment decision involving the United Kingdom, decided that the United Kingdom must:

(a) bring forward, within six months of the date upon which the present judgment becomes final, legislative proposals intended to amend the 1983 Act and, if appropriate, the 2002 Act in a manner which is Convention-compliant; and

(b) enact the required legislation within any such period as may be determined by the Committee of Ministers.[70]

8.58   The government sought a reference to the Grand Chamber but the Court rejected the application for a referral.

8.59   It has also been suggested that in the future the Court may be willing to order that a criminal conviction obtained in breach of Article 6 should be quashed or subject to a re-trial.[71]

8.60   Costs cannot be awarded against an applicant.

E. ADVISORY OPINIONS FROM THE EUROPEAN COURT OF HUMAN RIGHTS

1. Requests for advisory opinions by the Committee of Ministers

8.61   The Court may provide advisory opinions if requested to do so by the Committee of Ministers.[72] However the opinions may not deal with the content or scope of the Convention so this procedure has rarely been used.[73]

---

[67] ibid para 2.
[68] *Greens and MT v UK* (2011) 53 EHRR 21.
[69] *Hirst v UK (No 2)* (2005) 19 BHRC 546.
[70] *Greens and MT v UK* (2011) 53 EHRR 21.
[71] See Philip Leach, *Taking a Case to the European Court of Human Rights* (4th edn, OUP 2017) para 3.69 onwards.
[72] Article 47.
[73] The Court's website suggests only twice—both concerning the list of candidates submitted with a view to the election of candidates to the ECtHR.

2. Requests for advisory opinions by a national court

Protocol 16 of the Convention allows the highest court or tribunal of a Member State to request an opinion from the ECtHR 'on questions of principle relating to the interpretation or application of the rights and freedoms defined in the Convention or the protocols thereto'.[74] The UK has not ratified this protocol. If it were implemented, it would allow the UK's Supreme Court to seek an opinion from the Strasbourg Court on a particular issue before giving judgment itself.   8.62

F. FUNDING FOR CASES IN STRASBOURG

Funding for cases to Strasbourg is very meagre. However, it is important for potential applicants to be aware that they will not be liable to pay the government's costs, and that, in the statistically rare case of their application being successful, at least some of their legal costs will be met by the government.   8.63

1. Domestic legal aid funding

The structure of the Human Rights Act does not make the Convention or its procedures part of the law of England and Wales directly and therefore: 8.64

Legal help may be used to advise a client of their position under England and Wales law and the options available but may not be used to make an application to ECtHR or for legal aid from that court. This is because the law of ECtHR is not formally part of the law of England and Wales as required by section 32of the Act.[75]

It might be possible to argue that Convention law could be 'relevant for determining any issue relating to the law of England and Wales', but an applicant will generally have had to exhaust domestic remedies first such that the position under domestic law will have been resolved, and the ECtHR, unlike the European Court of Justice (ECJ), does not allow interim references to resolve the interpretation of a Convention issue (see, however, Protocol 16 8.62 above).   8.65

2. Other sources of funding

Trade unions or pressure groups may fund litigation or provide legal representation themselves, or lawyers may act *pro bono* or on a conditional fee basis in important cases.   8.66

---

[74] The Court gave opinions requested by: Armenia, the Court of Cassation of Armenia, 26 April 2022 and the Armenian Constitutional Court, 29 May 2020; France, the *Conseil d'État*, 13 July 2022 and the French Court of Cassation, 10 April 2019; and Lithuania, the Supreme Administrative Court of Lithuania, 8 April 2022. The Court declined to give an opinion to the Slovak Supreme Court, 14 December 2020.

[75] *Guidance on authorities and legal aid for cases in courts outside England and Wales*, Legal Aid Agency, August 2013, Section 2.2. The Act referred to is the Legal Aid, Sentencing and Punishment of Offenders Act 2012.

3. Strasbourg legal aid

8.67 The Court itself will provide legal aid (subject to means), but only for those cases which have already been communicated to the government. As most cases fail before this stage this is a real disincentive for lawyers to take on cases. However, legal costs are recoverable where an application is successful.[76] No fees are payable to the Court and there is no liability to meet the costs of the government in any event.

8.68 Once the case has been communicated, legal aid will be available for those who would qualify on income and capital grounds for civil legal aid in the United Kingdom (even if, in an assessment for UK legal aid, a contribution would have been required no contribution will need to be made). Legal aid is available from the Court, although the means test for legal aid is carried out by the civil legal aid authorities in the United Kingdom.[77] Legal aid, once granted, will pay a lump sum to cover all the fees in preparation of a case (€850); appearance at a hearing (€300), travel costs and a subsistence allowance in connection with representation at an oral hearing (per diem (per day), €175).[78] If the case is never communicated, no legal aid is available.

8.69 Further payments are available to assist in friendly settlement negotiations and to cover representation by one lawyer at any hearing (€300), and the travel and accommodation costs of the lawyer and the applicant. In certain circumstances Strasbourg legal aid will stretch to two lawyers.

G. IMPLEMENTATION OF JUDGMENTS

8.70 The Committee of Ministers of the Council of Europe is responsible for ensuring that judgments are implemented by the state concerned.[79] When supervising the implementation of judgments the Committee is concerned to ensure that any just satisfaction awarded has been paid and:

Rule 6(2)(b) (i) individual measures have been taken to ensure that the violation has ceased and that the injured party is put, as far as possible, in the same situation as the party enjoyed prior to the violation of the Convention;

(ii) general measures have been adopted, preventing new violations similar to that or those found or putting an end to continuing violations.[80]

---

[76] Rule 100.

[77] Information on the process is summarized in *Guidance on authorities and legal aid for cases in courts outside England and Wales*, Legal Aid Agency, August 2013, Section 2.2.

[78] Legal aid rates applicable since 2013.

[79] Article 46 of the Convention; and the Rules of the Committee of Ministers for the Supervision of the Execution of Judgments and of the Terms of Friendly Settlements, January 2017.

[80] Rules of the Committee of Ministers for the Supervision of the Execution of Judgments and of the Terms of Friendly Settlements, January 2017, (as amended July 2022) r 6. For more details see the website of the Committee of Ministers (part of the Council of Europe) <http://www.coe.int/>.

Lawyers, NGOs, and others can send submissions to the Committee of Ministers   8.71
requesting that it urges the state party to implement the judgment in a particular
way or they can comment on proposals made by a state for implementation.[81] The
staff working for the Committee are anxious to hear from those with experience or
expertise about the practicalities of implementation, particularly to ensure practical
compliance with the Convention in the light of the judgment.

The Parliamentary Joint Human Rights Committee (JCHR) has also taken a   8.72
keen interest in implementation and the execution of Court judgments.

---

[81] See for instance the submissions made by the human rights NGO, the Committee on the
Administration of Justice, in relation to the art 2 cases on the 'troubles' in Northern Ireland still being
supervised by the Committee of Ministers—'Submission to the Committee of Ministers in relation to the
supervision of the cases concerning the action of the security forces in Northern Ireland', January 2023.

APPENDIX

Supplemental

HUMAN RIGHTS ACT 1998

1998 CHAPTER 42

An Act to give further effect to rights and freedoms guaranteed under the European Convention on Human Rights; to make provision with respect to holders of certain judicial offices who become judges of the European Court of Human Rights; and for connected purposes.

Be it enacted by the Queen's most Excellent Majesty, by and with the advice and consent of the Lords Spiritual and Temporal, and Commons, in this present Parliament assembled, and by the authority of the same, as follows:

Introduction

1 The Convention Rights.

(1) In this Act "the Convention rights" means the rights and fundamental freedoms set out in—
   (a) Articles 2 to 12 and 14 of the Convention,
   (b) Articles 1 to 3 of the First Protocol, and
   (c) Article 1 of the Thirteenth Protocol, as read with Articles 16 to 18 of the Convention.

(2) Those Articles are to have effect for the purposes of this Act subject to any designated derogation or reservation (as to which see sections 14 and 15).

(3) The Articles are set out in Schedule 1.

(4) The Secretary of State may by order make such amendments to this Act as he considers appropriate to reflect the effect, in relation to the United Kingdom, of a protocol.

(5) In subsection (4) "protocol" means a protocol to the Convention—
   (a) which the United Kingdom has ratified; or
   (b) which the United Kingdom has signed with a view to ratification.

(6) No amendment may be made by an order under subsection (4) so as to come into force before the protocol concerned is in force in relation to the United Kingdom.

2 Interpretation of Convention rights.

(1) A court or tribunal determining a question which has arisen in connection with a Convention right must take into account any—
   (a) judgment, decision, declaration or advisory opinion of the European Court of Human Rights,
   (b) opinion of the Commission given in a report adopted under Article 31 of the Convention,
   (c) decision of the Commission in connection with Article 26 or 27(2) of the Convention, or
   (d) decision of the Committee of Ministers taken under Article 46 of the Convention, whenever made or given, so far as, in the opinion of the court or tribunal, it is relevant to the proceedings in which that question has arisen.

(2) Evidence of any judgment, decision, declaration or opinion of which account may have to be taken under this section is to be given in proceedings before any court or tribunal in such manner as may be provided by rules.

(3) In this section "rules" means rules of court or, in the case of proceedings before a tribunal, rules made for the purposes of this section—
   (a) by ... the Lord Chancellor or the Secretary of State, in relation to any proceedings outside Scotland;
   (b) by the Secretary of State, in relation to proceedings in Scotland; or
   (c) by a Northern Ireland department, in relation to proceedings before a tribunal in Northern Ireland—
     (i) which deals with transferred matters; and
     (ii) for which no rules made under paragraph (a) are in force.

Legislation

3 Interpretation of legislation.

(1) So far as it is possible to do so, primary legislation and subordinate legislation must be read and given effect in a way which is compatible with the Convention rights.

(2) This section—

    (a) applies to primary legislation and subordinate legislation whenever enacted;

    (b) does not affect the validity, continuing operation or enforcement of any incompatible primary legislation; and

    (c) does not affect the validity, continuing operation or enforcement of any incompatible subordinate legislation if (disregarding any possibility of revocation) primary legislation prevents removal of the incompatibility.

4 Declaration of incompatibility.

(1) Subsection (2) applies in any proceedings in which a court determines whether a provision of primary legislation is compatible with a Convention right.

(2) If the court is satisfied that the provision is incompatible with a Convention right, it may make a declaration of that incompatibility.

(3) Subsection (4) applies in any proceedings in which a court determines whether a provision of subordinate legislation, made in the exercise of a power conferred by primary legislation, is compatible with a Convention right.

(4) If the court is satisfied—

    (a) that the provision is incompatible with a Convention right, and

    (b) that (disregarding any possibility of revocation) the primary legislation concerned prevents removal of the incompatibility, it may make a declaration of that incompatibility.

(5) In this section "court" means—

    (a) the Supreme Court;

    (b) the Judicial Committee of the Privy Council;

    (c) the Court Martial Appeal Court;

    (d) in Scotland, the High Court of Justiciary sitting otherwise than as a trial court or the Court of Session;

    (e) in England and Wales or Northern Ireland, the High Court or the Court of Appeal.

    (f) the Court of Protection, in any matter being dealt with by the President of the Family Division, the Chancellor of the High Court or a puisne judge of the High Court.

(6) A declaration under this section ("a declaration of incompatibility")—

    (a) does not affect the validity, continuing operation or enforcement of the provision in respect of which it is given; and

    (b) is not binding on the parties to the proceedings in which it is made.

5 Right of Crown to intervene.

(1) Where a court is considering whether to make a declaration of incompatibility, the Crown is entitled to notice in accordance with rules of court.

(2) In any case to which subsection (1) applies—

    (a) a Minister of the Crown (or a person nominated by him),

    (b) a member of the Scottish Executive,

    (c) a Northern Ireland Minister,

    (d) a Northern Ireland department,

is entitled, on giving notice in accordance with rules of court, to be joined as a party to the proceedings.

(3) Notice under subsection (2) may be given at any time during the proceedings.

(4) A person who has been made a party to criminal proceedings (other than in Scotland) as the result of a notice under subsection (2) may, with leave, appeal to the Supreme Court against any declaration of incompatibility made in the proceedings.

(5) In subsection (4)—

"criminal proceedings" includes all proceedings before the Court Martial Appeal Court; and

"leave" means leave granted by the court making the declaration of incompatibility or by the Supreme Court

Public authorities

6 Acts of public authorities.

(1) It is unlawful for a public authority to act in a way which is incompatible with a Convention right.

(2) Subsection (1) does not apply to an act if—

   (a) as the result of one or more provisions of primary legislation, the authority could not have acted differently; or

   (b) in the case of one or more provisions of, or made under, primary legislation which cannot be read or given effect in a way which is compatible with the Convention rights, the authority was acting so as to give effect to or enforce those provisions.

(3) In this section "public authority" includes—

   (a) a court or tribunal, and

   (b) any person certain of whose functions are functions of a public nature,

but does not include either House of Parliament or a person exercising functions in connection with proceedings in Parliament.

(4) . . .

(5) In relation to a particular act, a person is not a public authority by virtue only of subsection (3)(b) if the nature of the act is private.

(6) "An act" includes a failure to act but does not include a failure to—

   (a) introduce in, or lay before, Parliament a proposal for legislation; or

   (b) make any primary legislation or remedial order.

7 Proceedings.

(1) A person who claims that a public authority has acted (or proposes to act) in a way which is made unlawful by section 6(1) may—

   (a) bring proceedings against the authority under this Act in the appropriate court or tribunal, or

   (b) rely on the Convention right or rights concerned in any legal proceedings, but only if he is (or would be) a victim of the unlawful act.

(2) In subsection (1)(a) "appropriate court or tribunal" means such court or tribunal as may be determined in accordance with rules; and proceedings against an authority include a counterclaim or similar proceeding.

(3) If the proceedings are brought on an application for judicial review, the applicant is to be taken to have a sufficient interest in relation to the unlawful act only if he is, or would be, a victim of that act.

(4) If the proceedings are made by way of a petition for judicial review in Scotland, the applicant shall be taken to have title and interest to sue in relation to the unlawful act only if he is, or would be, a victim of that act.

(5) Proceedings under subsection (1)(a) must be brought before the end of—

   (a) the period of one year beginning with the date on which the act complained of took place; or

(b) such longer period as the court or tribunal considers equitable having regard to all the circumstances,

but that is subject to any rule imposing a stricter time limit in relation to the procedure in question.

(6) In subsection (1)(b) "legal proceedings" includes—

    (a) proceedings brought by or at the instigation of a public authority; and

    (b) an appeal against the decision of a court or tribunal.

(7) For the purposes of this section, a person is a victim of an unlawful act only if he would be a victim for the purposes of Article 34 of the Convention if proceedings were brought in the European Court of Human Rights in respect of that act.

(8) Nothing in this Act creates a criminal offence.

(9) In this section "rules" means—

    (a) in relation to proceedings before a court or tribunal outside Scotland, rules made by ... the Lord Chancellor or the Secretary of State for the purposes of this section or rules of court,

    (b) in relation to proceedings before a court or tribunal in Scotland, rules made by the Secretary of State for those purposes,

    (c) in relation to proceedings before a tribunal in Northern Ireland—

        (i) which deals with transferred matters; and

        (ii) for which no rules made under paragraph (a) are in force, rules made by a Northern Ireland department for those purposes,

and includes provision made by order under section 1 of the Courts and Legal Services Act 1990.

(10) In making rules, regard must be had to section 9.

(11) The Minister who has power to make rules in relation to a particular tribunal may, to the extent he considers it necessary to ensure that the tribunal can provide an appropriate remedy in relation to an act (or proposed act) of a public authority which is (or would be) unlawful as a result of section 6(1), by order add to—

    (a) the relief or remedies which the tribunal may grant; or

    (b) the grounds on which it may grant any of them.

(12) An order made under subsection (11) may contain such incidental, supplemental, consequential or transitional provision as the Minister making it considers appropriate.

(13) "The Minister" includes the Northern Ireland department concerned.

7A Limitation: overseas armed forces proceedings

(1) A court or tribunal exercising its discretion under section 7(5)(b) in respect of overseas armed forces proceedings must do so—

    (a) in accordance with subsection (2), and

    (b) subject to the rule in subsection (4).

(2) The court or tribunal must have particular regard to—

    (a) the effect of the delay in bringing proceedings on the cogency of evidence adduced or likely to be adduced by the parties, with particular reference to—

        (i) the likely impact of the operational context on the ability of individuals who are (or, at the time of the events to which the proceedings relate, were) members of Her Majesty's forces to remember relevant events or actions fully or accurately, and

        (ii) the extent of dependence on the memories of such individuals, taking into account the effect of the operational context on the ability of such individuals to record, or to retain records of, relevant events or actions;

    (b) the likely impact of the proceedings on the mental health of any witness or potential witness who is (or, at the time of the events to which the proceedings relate, was) a member of Her Majesty's forces.

(3) In subsection (2) references to "the operational context" are to the fact that the events to which the proceedings relate took place in the context of overseas operations, and include references to the exceptional demands and stresses to which members of Her Majesty's forces are subject.

(4) The rule referred to in subsection (1)(b) is that overseas armed forces proceedings must be brought before the later of—

(a) the end of the period of 6 years beginning with the date on which the act complained of took place;

(b) the end of the period of 12 months beginning with the date of knowledge.

(5) In subsection (4), the "date of knowledge" means the date on which the person bringing the proceedings first knew, or first ought to have known, both—

(a) of the act complained of, and

(b) that it was an act of the Ministry of Defence or the Secretary of State for Defence.

(6) "Overseas armed forces proceedings" means proceedings—

(a) against the Ministry of Defence or the Secretary of State for Defence, and

(b) in connection with overseas operations.

(7) "Overseas operations" means any operations outside the British Islands, including peacekeeping operations and operations for dealing with terrorism, civil unrest or serious public disorder, in the course of which members of Her Majesty's forces come under attack or face the threat of attack or violent resistance.

(8) In this section the reference to the British Islands includes the territorial sea adjacent to the United Kingdom and the territorial sea adjacent to any of the Channel Islands or the Isle of Man.

(9) In this section "Her Majesty's forces" has the same meaning as in the Armed Forces Act 2006 (see section 374 of that Act).

8 Judicial remedies.

(1) In relation to any act (or proposed act) of a public authority which the court finds is (or would be) unlawful, it may grant such relief or remedy, or make such order, within its powers as it considers just and appropriate.

(2) But damages may be awarded only by a court which has power to award damages, or to order the payment of compensation, in civil proceedings.

(3) No award of damages is to be made unless, taking account of all the circumstances of the case, including—

(a) any other relief or remedy granted, or order made, in relation to the act in question (by that or any other court), and

(b) the consequences of any decision (of that or any other court) in respect of that act, the court is satisfied that the award is necessary to afford just satisfaction to the person in whose favour it is made.

(4) In determining—

(a) whether to award damages, or

(b) the amount of an award,

the court must take into account the principles applied by the European Court of Human Rights in relation to the award of compensation under Article 41 of the Convention.

(5) A public authority against which damages are awarded is to be treated—

(a) in Scotland, for the purposes of section 3 of the Law Reform (Miscellaneous Provisions) (Scotland) Act 1940 as if the award were made in an action of damages in which the authority has been found liable in respect of loss or damage to the person to whom the award is made;

(b) for the purposes of the Civil Liability (Contribution) Act 1978 as liable in respect of damage suffered by the person to whom the award is made.

(6) In this section—

"court" includes a tribunal;

"damages" means damages for an unlawful act of a public authority; and "unlawful" means unlawful under section 6(1).

9 Judicial acts.

(1) Proceedings under section 7(1)(a) in respect of a judicial act may be brought only—
   - (a) by exercising a right of appeal;
   - (b) on an application (in Scotland a petition) for judicial review; or
   - (c) in such other forum as may be prescribed by rules.

(2) That does not affect any rule of law which prevents a court from being the subject of judicial review.

(3) In proceedings under this Act in respect of a judicial act done in good faith, damages may not be awarded otherwise than—
   - (a) to compensate a person to the extent required by Article 5(5) of the Convention, or
   - (b) to compensate a person for a judicial act that is incompatible with Article 6 of the Convention in circumstances where the person is detained and, but for the incompatibility, the person would not have been detained or would not have been detained for so long.

(4) An award of damages permitted by subsection (3) is to be made against the Crown; but no award may be made unless the appropriate person, if not a party to the proceedings, is joined.

(5) In this section—

"appropriate person" means the Minister responsible for the court concerned, or a person or government department nominated by him;

"court" includes a tribunal;

"judge" includes a member of a tribunal, a justice of the peace (or, in Northern Ireland, a lay magistrate) and a clerk or other officer entitled to exercise the jurisdiction of a court;

"judicial act" means a judicial act of a court and includes an act done on the instructions, or on behalf, of a judge; and

"rules" has the same meaning as in section 7(9).

Remedial action

10 Power to take remedial action.

(1) This section applies if—
   - (a) a provision of legislation has been declared under section 4 to be incompatible with a Convention right and, if an appeal lies—
     - (i) all persons who may appeal have stated in writing that they do not intend to do so;
     - (ii) the time for bringing an appeal has expired and no appeal has been brought within that time; or
     - (iii) an appeal brought within that time has been determined or abandoned; or
   - (b) it appears to a Minister of the Crown or Her Majesty in Council that, having regard to a finding of the European Court of Human Rights made after the coming into force of this section in proceedings against the United Kingdom, a provision of legislation is incompatible with an obligation of the United Kingdom arising from the Convention.

(2) If a Minister of the Crown considers that there are compelling reasons for proceeding under this section, he may by order make such amendments to the legislation as he considers necessary to remove the incompatibility.

(3) If, in the case of subordinate legislation, a Minister of the Crown considers—
   (a) that it is necessary to amend the primary legislation under which the subordinate legislation in question was made, in order to enable the incompatibility to be removed, and
   (b) that there are compelling reasons for proceeding under this section,
he may by order make such amendments to the primary legislation as he considers necessary.

(4) This section also applies where the provision in question is in subordinate legislation and has been quashed, or declared invalid, by reason of incompatibility with a Convention right and the Minister proposes to proceed under paragraph 2(b) of Schedule 2.

(5) If the legislation is an Order in Council, the power conferred by subsection (2) or (3) is exercisable by Her Majesty in Council.

(6) In this section "legislation" does not include a Measure of the Church Assembly or of the General Synod of the Church of England.

(7) Schedule 2 makes further provision about remedial orders.

Other rights and proceedings

11 Safeguard for existing human rights.

A person's reliance on a Convention right does not restrict

(a) any other right or freedom conferred on him by or under any law having effect in any part of the United Kingdom; or

(b) his right to make any claim or bring any proceedings which he could make or bring apart from sections 7 to 9.

12 Freedom of expression.

(1) This section applies if a court is considering whether to grant any relief which, if granted, might affect the exercise of the Convention right to freedom of expression.

(2) If the person against whom the application for relief is made ("the respondent") is neither present nor represented, no such relief is to be granted unless the court is satisfied—
   (a) that the applicant has taken all practicable steps to notify the respondent; or
   (b) that there are compelling reasons why the respondent should not be notified.

(3) No such relief is to be granted so as to restrain publication before trial unless the court is satisfied that the applicant is likely to establish that publication should not be allowed.

(4) The court must have particular regard to the importance of the Convention right to freedom of expression and, where the proceedings relate to material which the respondent claims, or which appears to the court, to be journalistic, literary or artistic material (or to conduct connected with such material), to—
   (a) the extent to which—
      (i) the material has, or is about to, become available to the public; or
      (ii) it is, or would be, in the public interest for the material to be published;
   (b) any relevant privacy code.

(5) In this section—
"court" includes a tribunal; and
"relief" includes any remedy or order (other than in criminal proceedings).

13 Freedom of thought, conscience and religion.

(1) If a court's determination of any question arising under this Act might affect the exercise by a religious organisation (itself or its members collectively) of the Convention right to freedom of thought, conscience and religion, it must have particular regard to the importance of that right.

(2) In this section "court" includes a tribunal.

Derogations and reservations

14 Derogations.

(1) In this Act "designated derogation" means—
any derogation by the United Kingdom from an Article of the Convention, or of any protocol to the Convention, which is designated for the purposes of this Act in an order made by the Secretary of State

(3) If a designated derogation is amended or replaced it ceases to be a designated derogation.

(4) But subsection (3) does not prevent the Secretary of State from exercising his power under subsection (1) to make a fresh designation order in respect of the Article concerned.

(5) The Secretary of State must by order make such amendments to Schedule 3 as he considers appropriate to reflect—
    (a) any designation order; or
    (b) the effect of subsection (3).

(6) A designation order may be made in anticipation of the making by the United Kingdom of a proposed derogation.

15 Reservations.

(1) In this Act "designated reservation" means—
    (a) the United Kingdom's reservation to Article 2 of the First Protocol to the Convention; and
    (b) any other reservation by the United Kingdom to an Article of the Convention, or of any protocol to the Convention, which is designated for the purposes of this Act in an order made by the Secretary of State.

(2) The text of the reservation referred to in subsection (1)(a) is set out in Part II of Schedule 3.

(3) If a designated reservation is withdrawn wholly or in part it ceases to be a designated reservation.

(4) But subsection (3) does not prevent the Secretary of State from exercising his power under subsection (1)(b) to make a fresh designation order in respect of the Article concerned.

(5) Secretary of State must by order make such amendments to this Act as he considers appropriate to reflect—
    (a) any designation order; or
    (b) the effect of subsection (3).

16 Period for which designated derogations have effect.

(1) If it has not already been withdrawn by the United Kingdom, a designated derogation ceases to have effect for the purposes of this Act—
at the end of the period of five years beginning with the date on which the order designating it was made.

(2) At any time before the period—
    (a) fixed by subsection (1), or
    (b) extended by an order under this subsection,
comes to an end, the Secretary of State may by order extend it by a further period of five years.

(3) An order under section 14(1) ceases to have effect at the end of the period for consideration, unless a resolution has been passed by each House approving the order.

(4) Subsection (3) does not affect—
    (a) anything done in reliance on the order; or
    (b) the power to make a fresh order under section 14(1) ....

(5) In subsection (3) "period for consideration" means the period of forty days beginning with the day on which the order was made.

(6) In calculating the period for consideration, no account is to be taken of any time during which—

(a) Parliament is dissolved or prorogued; or

(b) both Houses are adjourned for more than four days.

(7) If a designated derogation is withdrawn by the United Kingdom, the Secretary of State must by order make such amendments to this Act as he considers are required to reflect that withdrawal.

17 Periodic review of designated reservations.

(1) The appropriate Minister must review the designated reservation referred to in section 15(1)(a)—

(a) before the end of the period of five years beginning with the date on which section 1(2) came into force; and

(b) if that designation is still in force, before the end of the period of five years beginning with the date on which the last report relating to it was laid under subsection (3).

(2) The appropriate Minister must review each of the other designated reservations (if any)—

(a) before the end of the period of five years beginning with the date on which the order designating the reservation first came into force; and

(b) if the designation is still in force, before the end of the period of five years beginning with the date on which the last report relating to it was laid under subsection (3).

(3) The Minister conducting a review under this section must prepare a report on the result of the review and lay a copy of it before each House of Parliament.

Judges of the European Court of Human Rights

18 Appointment to European Court of Human Rights.

(1) In this section "judicial office" means the office of—

(a) Lord Justice of Appeal, Justice of the High Court or Circuit judge, in England and Wales;

(b) judge of the Court of Session or sheriff, in Scotland;

(c) Lord Justice of Appeal, judge of the High Court or county court judge, in Northern Ireland.

(2) The holder of a judicial office may become a judge of the European Court of Human Rights ("the Court") without being required to relinquish his office.

(3) But he is not required to perform the duties of his judicial office while he is a judge of the Court.

(4) In respect of any period during which he is a judge of the Court—

(a) a Lord Justice of Appeal or Justice of the High Court is not to count as a judge of the relevant court for the purposes of section 2(1) or 4(1) of the Senior Courts Act 1981 (maximum number of judges) nor as a judge of the Senior Courts for the purposes of section 12(1) to (6) of that Act (salaries etc.);

(b) a judge of the Court of Session is not to count as a judge of that court for the purposes of section 1(1) of the Court of Session Act 1988 (maximum number of judges) or of section 9(1)(c) of the Administration of Justice Act 1973 ("the 1973 Act") (salaries etc.);

(c) a Lord Justice of Appeal or judge of the High Court in Northern Ireland is not to count as a judge of the relevant court for the purposes of section 2(1) or 3(1) of the M6Judicature (Northern Ireland) Act 1978 (maximum number of judges) nor as a judge of the Court of Judicature of Northern Ireland for the purposes of section 9(1)(d) of the 1973 Act (salaries etc.);

(d) a Circuit judge is not to count as such for the purposes of section 18 of the M7Courts Act 1971 (salaries etc.);

(e) a sheriff is not to count as such for the purposes of section 14 of the Sheriff Courts (Scotland) Act 1907 (salaries etc.);

    (f) a county court judge of Northern Ireland is not to count as such for the purposes of section 106 of the County Courts Act Northern Ireland) 1959 (salaries etc.).

(5) If a sheriff principal is appointed a judge of the Court, section 11(1) of the Sheriff Courts (Scotland) Act 1971 (temporary appointment of sheriff principal) applies, while he holds that appointment, as if his office is vacant.

(6) Schedule 4 makes provision about judicial pensions in relation to the holder of a judicial office who serves as a judge of the Court.

(7) The Lord Chancellor or the Secretary of State may by order make such transitional provision (including, in particular, provision for a temporary increase in the maximum number of judges) as he considers appropriate in relation to any holder of a judicial office who has completed his service as a judge of the Court.

(7A) The following paragraphs apply to the making of an order under subsection (7) in relation to any holder of a judicial office listed in subsection (1)(a)—

    (a) before deciding what transitional provision it is appropriate to make, the person making the order must consult the Lord Chief Justice of England and Wales;

    (b) before making the order, that person must consult the Lord Chief Justice of England and Wales.

(7B) The following paragraphs apply to the making of an order under subsection (7) in relation to any holder of a judicial office listed in subsection (1)(c)—

    (a) before deciding what transitional provision it is appropriate to make, the person making the order must consult the Lord Chief Justice of Northern Ireland;

    (b) before making the order, that person must consult the Lord Chief Justice of Northern Ireland.

(7C) The Lord Chief Justice of England and Wales may nominate a judicial office holder (within the meaning of section 109(4) of the Constitutional Reform Act 2005) to exercise his functions under this section.

(7D) The Lord Chief Justice of Northern Ireland may nominate any of the following to exercise his functions under this section—

    (a) the holder of one of the offices listed in Schedule 1 to the Justice (Northern Ireland) Act 2002;

    (b) a Lord Justice of Appeal (as defined in section 88 of that Act).

Parliamentary procedure

19 Statements of compatibility.

(1) A Minister of the Crown in charge of a Bill in either House of Parliament must, before Second Reading of the Bill—

    (a) make a statement to the effect that in his view the provisions of the Bill are compatible with the Convention rights ("a statement of compatibility"); or

    (b) make a statement to the effect that although he is unable to make a statement of compatibility the government nevertheless wishes the House to proceed with the Bill.

(2) The statement must be in writing and be published in such manner as the Minister making it considers appropriate.

Supplemental

20 Orders etc. under this Act.

(1) Any power of a Minister of the Crown to make an order under this Act is exercisable by statutory instrument.

(2) The power of the Lord Chancellor or the Secretary of State to make rules (other than rules of court) under section 2(3) or 7(9) is exercisable by statutory instrument.

(3) Any statutory instrument made under section 14, 15 or 16(7) must be laid before Parliament.

(4) No order may be made by the Lord Chancellor or the Secretary of State under section 1(4), 7(11) or 16(2) unless a draft of the order has been laid before, and approved by, each House of Parliament.

(5) Any statutory instrument made under section 18(7) or Schedule 4, or to which subsection (2) applies, shall be subject to annulment in pursuance of a resolution of either House of Parliament.

(6) The power of a Northern Ireland department to make—

(a) rules under section 2(3)(c) or 7(9)(c), or

(b) an order under section 7(11),

is exercisable by statutory rule for the purposes of the Statutory Rules (Northern Ireland) Order 1979.

(7) Any rules made under section 2(3)(c) or 7(9)(c) shall be subject to negative resolution; and section 41(6) of the Interpretation Act Northern Ireland) 1954 (meaning of "subject to negative resolution") shall apply as if the power to make the rules were conferred by an Act of the Northern Ireland Assembly.

(8) No order may be made by a Northern Ireland department under section 7(11) unless a draft of the order has been laid before, and approved by, the Northern Ireland Assembly.

21 Interpretation, etc.

(1) In this Act—

"amend" includes repeal and apply (with or without modifications);

"the appropriate Minister" means the Minister of the Crown having charge of the appropriate authorised government department (within the meaning of the [M13]Crown Proceedings Act 1947);

"the Commission" means the European Commission of Human Rights; "the Convention" means the Convention for the Protection of Human Rights and Fundamental Freedoms, agreed by the Council of Europe at Rome on 4th November 1950 as it has effect for the time being in relation to the United Kingdom;

"declaration of incompatibility" means a declaration under section 4; "Minister of the Crown" has the same meaning as in the Ministers of the Crown Act 1975;

"Northern Ireland Minister" includes the First Minister and the deputy First Minister in Northern Ireland;

"primary legislation" means any—

(a) public general Act;

(b) local and personal Act;

(c) private Act;

(d) Measure of the Church Assembly;

(e) Measure of the General Synod of the Church of England;

(f) Order in Council—

(i) made in exercise of Her Majesty's Royal Prerogative;

(ii) made under section 38(1)(a) of the [M15]Northern Ireland Constitution Act 1973 or the corresponding provision of the Northern Ireland Act 1998; or

(iii) amending an Act of a kind mentioned in paragraph (a), (b) or (c);

and includes an order or other instrument made under primary legislation (otherwise than by the Welsh Ministers, the First Minister for Wales, the Counsel General to the Welsh Assembly Government, a member of the Scottish Executive, a Northern Ireland Minister or a Northern Ireland department) to the extent to which it operates to bring one or more provisions of that legislation into force or amends any primary legislation;

"the First Protocol" means the protocol to the Convention agreed at Paris on 20th March 1952;

"the Eleventh Protocol" means the protocol to the Convention (restructuring the control machinery established by the Convention) agreed at Strasbourg on 11th May 1994;

"the Thirteenth Protocol" means the protocol to the Convention (concerning the abolition of the death penalty in all circumstances) agreed at Vilnius on 3rd May 2002;

"remedial order" means an order under section 10; "subordinate legislation" means any—

(a) Order in Council other than one—
   (i) made in exercise of Her Majesty's Royal Prerogative;
   (ii) made under section 38(1)(a) of the Northern Ireland Constitution Act 1973 or the corresponding provision of the Northern Ireland Act 1998; or
   (iii) amending an Act of a kind mentioned in the definition of primary legislation;

(b) Act of the Scottish Parliament;

(ba) Measure of the National Assembly for Wales; (bb) Act of the National Assembly for Wales;

(c) Act of the Parliament of Northern Ireland;

(d) Measure of the Assembly established under section 1 of the Northern Ireland Assembly Act 1973;

(e) Act of the Northern Ireland Assembly;

(f) order, rules, regulations, scheme, warrant, byelaw or other instrument made under primary legislation (except to the extent to which it operates to bring one or more provisions of that legislation into force or amends any primary legislation);

(g) order, rules, regulations, scheme, warrant, byelaw or other instrument made under legislation mentioned in paragraph (b), (c), (d) or (e) or made under an Order in Council applying only to Northern Ireland;

(h) order, rules, regulations, scheme, warrant, byelaw or other instrument made by a member of the Scottish Executive Welsh Ministers, the First Minister for Wales, the Counsel General to the Welsh Assembly Government a Northern Ireland Minister or a Northern Ireland department in exercise of prerogative or other executive functions of Her Majesty which are exercisable by such a person on behalf of Her Majesty;

"transferred matters" has the same meaning as in the Northern Ireland Act 1998; and

"tribunal" means any tribunal in which legal proceedings may be brought.

(2) The references in paragraphs (b) and (c) of section 2(1) to Articles are to Articles of the Convention as they had effect immediately before the coming into force of the Eleventh Protocol.

(3) The reference in paragraph (d) of section 2(1) to Article 46 includes a reference to Articles 32 and 54 of the Convention as they had effect immediately before the coming into force of the Eleventh Protocol.

(4) The references in section 2(1) to a report or decision of the Commission or a decision of the Committee of Ministers include references to a report or decision made as provided by paragraphs 3, 4 and 6 of Article 5 of the Eleventh Protocol (transitional provisions).

22 Short title, commencement, application and extent.

(1) This Act may be cited as the Human Rights Act 1998.

(2) Sections 18, 20 and 21(5) and this section come into force on the passing of this Act.

(3) The other provisions of this Act come into force on such day as the Secretary of State may by order appoint; and different days may be appointed for different purposes.

(4) Paragraph (b) of subsection (1) of section 7 applies to proceedings brought by or at the instigation of a public authority whenever the act in question took place; but otherwise that subsection does not apply to an act taking place before the coming into force of that section.

(4A) Section 7A (limitation: overseas armed forces proceedings) applies to proceedings brought under section 7(1)(a) on or after the date on which section 7A comes into force, whenever the act in question took place.

(5) This Act binds the Crown.

(6) This Act extends to Northern Ireland.

SCHEDULES

SCHEDULE 1   Section 1(3).

THE ARTICLES

PART I

THE CONVENTION RIGHTS AND FREEDOMS

ARTICLE 2
RIGHT TO LIFE

1. Everyone's right to life shall be protected by law. No one shall be deprived of his life inten-tionally save in the execution of a sentence of a court following his conviction of a crime for which this penalty is provided by law.
2. Deprivation of life shall not be regarded as inflicted in contravention of this Article when it results from the use of force which is no more than absolutely necessary:
   (a) in defence of any person from unlawful violence;
   (b) in order to effect a lawful arrest or to prevent the escape of a person lawfully detained;
   (c) in action lawfully taken for the purpose of quelling a riot or insurrection.

ARTICLE 3
PROHIBITION OF TORTURE

No one shall be subjected to torture or to inhuman or degrading treatment or punishment.

ARTICLE 4
PROHIBITION OF SLAVERY AND FORCED LABOUR

1. No one shall be held in slavery or servitude.
2. No one shall be required to perform forced or compulsory labour.
3. For the purpose of this Article the term "forced or compulsory labour" shall not include:
   (a) any work required to be done in the ordinary course of detention imposed according to the provisions of Article 5 of this Convention or during conditional release from such detention;
   (b) any service of a military character or, in case of conscientious objectors in countries where they are recognised, service exacted instead of compulsory military service;
   (c) any service exacted in case of an emergency or calamity threatening the life or well-being of the community;
   (d) any work or service which forms part of normal civic obligations.

ARTICLE 5
RIGHT TO LIBERTY AND SECURITY

1. Everyone has the right to liberty and security of person. No one shall be deprived of his liberty save in the following cases and in accordance with a procedure prescribed by law:
   (a) the lawful detention of a person after conviction by a competent court;

(b) the lawful arrest or detention of a person for non-compliance with the lawful order of a court or in order to secure the fulfilment of any obligation prescribed by law;

(c) the lawful arrest or detention of a person effected for the purpose of bringing him before the competent legal authority on reasonable suspicion of having committed an offence or when it is reasonably considered necessary to prevent his committing an offence or fleeing after having done so;

(d) the detention of a minor by lawful order for the purpose of educational supervision or his lawful detention for the purpose of bringing him before the competent legal authority;

(e) the lawful detention of persons for the prevention of the spreading of infectious diseases, of persons of unsound mind, alcoholics or drug addicts or vagrants;

(f) the lawful arrest or detention of a person to prevent his effecting an unauthorised entry into the country or of a person against whom action is being taken with a view to deportation or extradition.

2. Everyone who is arrested shall be informed promptly, in a language which he understands, of the reasons for his arrest and of any charge against him.

3. Everyone arrested or detained in accordance with the provisions of paragraph 1(c) of this Article shall be brought promptly before a judge or other officer authorised by law to exercise judicial power and shall be entitled to trial within a reasonable time or to release pending trial. Release may be conditioned by guarantees to appear for trial.

4. Everyone who is deprived of his liberty by arrest or detention shall be entitled to take proceedings by which the lawfulness of his detention shall be decided speedily by a court and his release ordered if the detention is not lawful.

5. Everyone who has been the victim of arrest or detention in contravention of the provisions of this Article shall have an enforceable right to compensation.

ARTICLE 6
RIGHT TO A FAIR TRIAL

1. In the determination of his civil rights and obligations or of any criminal charge against him, everyone is entitled to a fair and public hearing within a reasonable time by an independent and impartial tribunal established by law. Judgment shall be pronounced publicly but the press and public may be excluded from all or part of the trial in the interest of morals, public order or national security in a democratic society, where the interests of juveniles or the protection of the private life of the parties so require, or to the extent strictly necessary in the opinion of the court in special circumstances where publicity would prejudice the interests of justice.

2. Everyone charged with a criminal offence shall be presumed innocent until proved guilty according to law.

3. Everyone charged with a criminal offence has the following minimum rights:

(a) to be informed promptly, in a language which he understands and in detail, of the nature and cause of the accusation against him;

(b) to have adequate time and facilities for the preparation of his defence;

(c) to defend himself in person or through legal assistance of his own choosing or, if he has not sufficient means to pay for legal assistance, to be given it free when the interests of justice so require;

(d) to examine or have examined witnesses against him and to obtain the attendance and examination of witnesses on his behalf under the same conditions as witnesses against him;

(e) to have the free assistance of an interpreter if he cannot understand or speak the language used in court.

ARTICLE 7
NO PUNISHMENT WITHOUT LAW

1   No one shall be held guilty of any criminal offence on account of any act or omission which did not constitute a criminal offence under national or international law at the time when it was committed. Nor shall a heavier penalty be imposed than the one that was applicable at the time the criminal offence was committed.
2   This Article shall not prejudice the trial and punishment of any person for any act or omission which, at the time when it was committed, was criminal according to the general principles of law recognised by civilised nations.

ARTICLE 8
RIGHT TO RESPECT FOR PRIVATE AND FAMILY LIFE

1   Everyone has the right to respect for his private and family life, his home and his correspondence.
2   There shall be no interference by a public authority with the exercise of this right except such as is in accordance with the law and is necessary in a democratic society in the interests of national security, public safety or the economic well-being of the country, for the prevention of disorder or crime, for the protection of health or morals, or for the protection of the rights and freedoms of others.

ARTICLE 9
FREEDOM OF THOUGHT, CONSCIENCE AND RELIGION

1   Everyone has the right to freedom of thought, conscience and religion; this right includes freedom to change his religion or belief and freedom, either alone or in community with others and in public or private, to manifest his religion or belief, in worship, teaching, practice and observance.
2   Freedom to manifest one's religion or beliefs shall be subject only to such limitations as are prescribed by law and are necessary in a democratic society in the interests of public safety, for the protection of public order, health or morals, or for the protection of the rights and freedoms of others.

ARTICLE 10
FREEDOM OF EXPRESSION

1   Everyone has the right to freedom of expression. This right shall include freedom to hold opinions and to receive and impart information and ideas without interference by public authority and regardless of frontiers. This Article shall not prevent States from requiring the licensing of broadcasting, television or cinema enterprises.
2   The exercise of these freedoms, since it carries with it duties and responsibilities, may be subject to such formalities, conditions, restrictions or penalties as are prescribed by law and are necessary in a democratic society, in the interests of national security, territorial integrity or public safety, for the prevention of disorder or crime, for the protection of health or morals, for the protection of the reputation or rights of others, for preventing the disclosure of

information received in confidence, or for maintaining the authority and impartiality of the judiciary.

ARTICLE 11
FREEDOM OF ASSEMBLY AND ASSOCIATION

1 Everyone has the right to freedom of peaceful assembly and to freedom of association with others, including the right to form and to join trade unions for the protection of his interests.

2 No restrictions shall be placed on the exercise of these rights other than such as are prescribed by law and are necessary in a democratic society in the interests of national security or public safety, for the prevention of disorder or crime, for the protection of health or morals or for the protection of the rights and freedoms of others. This Article shall not prevent the imposition of lawful restrictions on the exercise of these rights by members of the armed forces, of the police or of the administration of the State.

ARTICLE 12
RIGHT TO MARRY

Men and women of marriageable age have the right to marry and to found a family, according to the national laws governing the exercise of this right.

ARTICLE 14
PROHIBITION OF DISCRIMINATION

The enjoyment of the rights and freedoms set forth in this Convention shall be secured without discrimination on any ground such as sex, race, colour, language, religion, political or other opinion, national or social origin, association with a national minority, property, birth or other status.

ARTICLE 16
RESTRICTIONS ON POLITICAL ACTIVITY OF ALIENS

Nothing in Articles 10, 11 and 14 shall be regarded as preventing the High Contracting Parties from imposing restrictions on the political activity of aliens.

ARTICLE 17
PROHIBITION OF ABUSE OF RIGHTS

Nothing in this Convention may be interpreted as implying for any State, group or person any right to engage in any activity or perform any act aimed at the destruction of any of the rights and freedoms set forth herein or at their limitation to a greater extent than is provided for in the Convention.

ARTICLE 18
LIMITATION ON USE OF RESTRICTIONS ON RIGHTS

The restrictions permitted under this Convention to the said rights and freedoms shall not be applied for any purpose other than those for which they have been prescribed.

PART II
THE FIRST PROTOCOL

ARTICLE 1
PROTECTION OF PROPERTY

Every natural or legal person is entitled to the peaceful enjoyment of his possessions. No one shall be deprived of his possessions except in the public interest and subject to the conditions provided for by law and by the general principles of international law.

The preceding provisions shall not, however, in any way impair the right of a State to enforce such laws as it deems necessary to control the use of property in accordance with the general interest or to secure the payment of taxes or other contributions or penalties.

ARTICLE 2
RIGHT TO EDUCATION

No person shall be denied the right to education. In the exercise of any functions which it assumes in relation to education and to teaching, the State shall respect the right of parents to ensure such education and teaching in conformity with their own religious and philosophical convictions.

ARTICLE 3
RIGHT TO FREE ELECTIONS

The High Contracting Parties undertake to hold free elections at reasonable intervals by secret ballot, under conditions which will ensure the free expression of the opinion of the people in the choice of the legislature.

PART 3
ARTICLE 1 OF THE THIRTEENTH PROTOCOL
ABOLITION OF THE DEATH PENALTY
The death penalty shall be abolished. No one shall be condemned to such penalty or executed.

PART III
THE SIXTH PROTOCOL

ARTICLE 1
ABOLITION OF THE DEATH PENALTY

ARTICLE 2
DEATH PENALTY IN TIME OF WAR

SCHEDULE 2   Section 10
REMEDIAL ORDERS

Orders

1   (1) A remedial order may—
    (a) contain such incidental, supplemental, consequential or transitional provision as the person making it considers appropriate;
    (b) be made so as to have effect from a date earlier than that on which it is made;

    (c) make provision for the delegation of specific functions;

    (d) make different provision for different cases.

(2) The power conferred by sub-paragraph (1)(a) includes—

    (a) power to amend primary legislation (including primary legislation other than that which contains the incompatible provision); and

    (b) power to amend or revoke subordinate legislation (including subordinate legislation other than that which contains the incompatible provision).

(3) A remedial order may be made so as to have the same extent as the legislation which it affects.

(4) No person is to be guilty of an offence solely as a result of the retrospective effect of a remedial order.

Procedure

2 No remedial order may be made unless—

    (a) a draft of the order has been approved by a resolution of each House of Parliament made after the end of the period of 60 days beginning with the day on which the draft was laid; or

    (b) it is declared in the order that it appears to the person making it that, because of the urgency of the matter, it is necessary to make the order without a draft being so approved.

Orders laid in draft

3 (1) No draft may be laid under paragraph 2(a) unless—

    (a) the person proposing to make the order has laid before Parliament a document which contains a draft of the proposed order and the required information; and

    (b) the period of 60 days, beginning with the day on which the document required by this sub-paragraph was laid, has ended.

(2) If representations have been made during that period, the draft laid under paragraph 2(a) must be accompanied by a statement containing—

    (a) a summary of the representations; and

    (b) if, as a result of the representations, the proposed order has been changed, details of the changes.

Urgent cases

4 (1) If a remedial order ("the original order") is made without being approved in draft, the person making it must lay it before Parliament, accompanied by the required information, after it is made.

(2) If representations have been made during the period of 60 days beginning with the day on which the original order was made, the person making it must (after the end of that period) lay before Parliament a statement containing—

    (a) a summary of the representations; and

    (b) if, as a result of the representations, he considers it appropriate to make changes to the original order, details of the changes.

(3) If sub-paragraph (2)(b) applies, the person making the statement must—

    (a) make a further remedial order replacing the original order; and

    (b) lay the replacement order before Parliament.

(4) If, at the end of the period of 120 days beginning with the day on which the original order was made, a resolution has not been passed by each House approving the original or replacement order, the order ceases to have effect (but without that affecting anything previously done under either order or the power to make a fresh remedial order).

Definitions

5   In this Schedule—

"representations" means representations about a remedial order (or proposed remedial order) made to the person making (or proposing to make) it and includes any relevant Parliamentary report or resolution; and

"required information" means—

   (a)   an explanation of the incompatibility which the order (or proposed order) seeks to remove, including particulars of the relevant declaration, finding or order; and

   (b)   a statement of the reasons for proceeding under section 10 and for making an order in those terms.

Calculating periods

6   In calculating any period for the purposes of this Schedule, no account is to be taken of any time during which—

(a)   Parliament is dissolved or prorogued; or

(b)   both Houses are adjourned for more than four days.

7   (1)   This paragraph applies in relation to–

   (a)   any remedial order made, and any draft of such an order proposed to be made,–

      (i)   by the Scottish Ministers; or

      (ii)   within devolved competence (within the meaning of the Scotland Act 1998) by Her Majesty in Council; and

   (b)   any document or statement to be laid in connection with such an order (or proposed order).

   (2)   This Schedule has effect in relation to any such order (or proposed order), document or statement subject to the following modifications.

   (3)   Any reference to Parliament, each House of Parliament or both Houses of Parliament shall be construed as a reference to the Scottish Parliament.

   (4)   Paragraph 6 does not apply and instead, in calculating any period for the purposes of this Schedule, no account is to be taken of any time during which the Scottish Parliament is dissolved or is in recess for more than four days.

SCHEDULE 3   Sections 14 and 15.

DEROGATION AND RESERVATION

PART I

DEROGATION

United Kingdom's derogation from Article 5(1)

. . . .

. . . .

. . . .

. . . .

. . . .

PART II
RESERVATION

At the time of signing the present (First) Protocol, I declare that, in view of certain provisions of the Education Acts in the United Kingdom, the principle affirmed in the second sentence of Article 2 is accepted by the United Kingdom only so far as it is compatible with the provision of efficient instruction and training, and the avoidance of unreasonable public expenditure.

Dated 20 March 1952

Made by the United Kingdom Permanent Representative to the Council of Europe.

SCHEDULE 4   Section 18(6).
JUDICIAL PENSIONS

Duty to make orders about pensions

1   (1) The appropriate Minister must by order make provision with respect to pensions payable to or in respect of any holder of a judicial office who serves as an ECHR judge.

(2) A pensions order must include such provision as the Minister making it considers is necessary to secure that—

    (a) an ECHR judge who was, immediately before his appointment as an ECHR judge, a member of a judicial pension scheme is entitled to remain as a member of that scheme;

    (b) the terms on which he remains a member of the scheme are those which would have been applicable had he not been appointed as an ECHR judge; and

    (c) entitlement to benefits payable in accordance with the scheme continues to be determined as if, while serving as an ECHR judge, his salary was that which would (but for section 18(4)) have been payable to him in respect of his continuing service as the holder of his judicial office.

Contributions

2   A pensions order may, in particular, make provision—

    (a) for any contributions which are payable by a person who remains a member of a scheme as a result of the order, and which would otherwise be payable by deduction from his salary, to be made otherwise than by deduction from his salary as an ECHR judge; and

    (b) for such contributions to be collected in such manner as may be determined by the administrators of the scheme.

Amendments of other enactments

3   A pensions order may amend any provision of, or made under, a pensions Act in such manner and to such extent as the Minister making the order considers necessary or expedient to ensure the proper administration of any scheme to which it relates.

Definitions

4   In this Schedule—

"appropriate Minister" means—

    (a) in relation to any judicial office whose jurisdiction is exercisable exclusively in relation to Scotland, the Secretary of State; and

    (b) otherwise, the Lord Chancellor;

"ECHR judge" means the holder of a judicial office who is serving as a judge of the Court;
"judicial pension scheme" means a scheme established by and in accordance with a pensions Act;
"pensions Act" means—

(a) the County Courts Act Northern Ireland) 1959;

(b) the Sheriffs' Pensions (Scotland) Act 1961;

(c) the Judicial Pensions Act 1981; or

(d) the Judicial Pensions and Retirement Act 1993;

(e) the Public Service Pensions Act 2013; and "pensions order" means an order made under paragraph 1.

Index